T4-AUF-688

All the Best in the Mediterranean

SYDNEY CLARK

ALL THE BEST IN THE
MEDITERRANEAN

WITH ILLUSTRATIONS AND MAPS

DODD, MEAD & COMPANY

NEW YORK

Acknowledgment is hereby made of the research and editorial services rendered by Margaret Zellers Lenci in the preparation of this edition.

LIBRARY OF CONGRESS CATALOG CARD NUMBER: 63-17076

PRINTED IN THE UNITED STATES OF AMERICA
BY VAIL-BALLOU PRESS, INC., BINGHAMTON, N.Y.

An awareness of tourism's potential and the need to keep ahead of expectations has kept government wheels turning in most of the Mediterranean countries, as well as throughout Europe. The inevitable political problems, particularly for newly independent nations, seldom seem to affect tourism very strongly, the impression suggesting a cartoon I recently saw in which leaders of two disputing countries agree "to hold off the war until after the tourist season."

Any changes and additions affecting official sources of information about the Mediterranean countries appear later in this supplement, in the sections pertaining to specific countries. Suffice it to say here that all such offices are invaluable sources of information. They do not charge for their freely given information and they do prepare you fully to go to a travel agent, or directly to the airline or steamship line and hotel, to make your reservations.

One essential word here about customs regulations that have changed from those given on page 39 and following. Since October, 1965, returning U.S. residents have been permitted to bring home duty-free only $100 worth (at *retail* value) of goods acquired abroad, and only those goods actually accompanying the returning traveler may be included in the exemption. Further, the liquor quota has been reduced to one quart per person, with no allotment for minors. However, you may send "unsolicited gifts" home to your relatives and friends each day as long as each gift is valued at less than $10, and no more than one gift is sent on any one day to any one person. (Alcohol, tobacco or perfume costing over $1 may not be sent as a gift.) If you plan big purchases abroad, a check with customs officials before you leave the States may be wise. You may find that many of the Mediterranean prices, even with the duty payable, are lower than you would pay at home for the same items. The Bureau of Customs has published an informative booklet called simply "Customs Hints," which may be obtained from the

Bureau of Customs, Treasury Department, Washington, D.C. 20226. The booklet spells out all dos and don'ts and is much safer to rely on than the advice of your "best friend," since customs regulations are often something that only customs officials fully understand!

CONTENTS

Illustrations follow page 208

THE FOREGROUND OF THE PICTURE

vii

YOURSELF IN THE PICTURE

THE FOREGROUND OF THE PICTURE

CHAPTER 1

A PREVIEW FROM WEST TO EAST

Portugal's Atlantic Islands

THIS chapter is intended to catalogue the chief units or entities—horrid word for things so nice—that will be covered by this book. Some are countries, some islands, some stretches of holiday shore line.

Portugal's Atlantic outpost islands, five in the Madeira group and nine in the Azores group, lie about five hundred miles and nine hundred miles respectively from the Pillars of Hercules, so it would require a special dispensation to sneak them into a volume on the Mediterranean were it not that they bulk so large in the transportation picture. Nearly all the Mediterranean cruise ships make Funchal, the lovely capital of Madeira, their first port of call and they give their passengers a day of glamor ashore as curtain-raiser for the whole extensive tour. Some regularly scheduled liners likewise halt at Funchal, others at Ponta Delgada, capital of the Azores, and in all cases the passengers are given ample opportunity to test their land legs and see the most glamorous sights.

Air travel to island Portugal is simple in the case of the Azores, which are visited regularly by planes of Pan American Airways and TWA, less simple but getting rapidly better in the case of Madeira. This latter has been something of an aviation orphan ever since Aquila Airways, operating seaplanes, folded up years ago, but now, I am happy to report, TAP, which stands for Transportes Aéreos Portugueses, is vigorously fathering the island. For some time air-and-steamer connections have existed, planes flying from Lisbon to Porto Santo only, a minor island of the Madeira group, with steamer from there to Funchal, but an airport laboriously carved out of the main island's mountainous terrain has now opened and TAP flies its planes, small DC-3's at present but very soon Caravelles and Comets, directly to its

3

goal, Funchal. This development is a major milestone in holiday travel.

Perhaps you're asking me just why it is so important and I'm bursting to tell you. Of the five islands of the Madeira group only the main one, Madeira itself, is of tourist interest, but that one is of overwhelming stature in the thought of all who know it. I am reluctant to unleash superlatives so early in this report, but for monumental scenery, enhanced by subtropical luxuriance of forests, flowers and flowering trees, nothing on earth, from Hawaii to Rio de Janeiro and from the Dolomites to scenic New Zealand, surpasses this Pride of Portugal. As a couple of special fillips, Madeira offers the visitor wines in abundance, some of them so rich as to be almost in the class of dessert wines, and quantities of hand-embroidered linens, the best work being scarcely equaled anywhere else for artistry and perfection of craftsmanship. The processes that go into the making of both fine wines and embroidery may be seen by even the brief stayer. Full information on Atlantic Portugal as well as the mainland lures may be had from *Casa de Portugal*, 447 Madison Avenue (corner of East 50th Street), New York City 20.

Portugal's Capital and Its Riviera

Lisbon is the mother of Rio de Janeiro and has named one of its garden squares for its stunning daughter. If you know Rio you will see the family resemblance in many features, notably in the sidewalk patterns of black and white flints, though in the present city these have largely succumbed, in recent decades, to more utilitarian pavements.

Lisbon is the perfect doorwoman of the Mediterranean, certainly not a door*man*. I believe it was H. V. Morton who asserted that all great cities of the world have a distinctive sex and if this is true Lisbon is certainly a woman, and what's more a lady. She is gracious and assured and very neat about her person. For all her age, her curves are perfect.

I'll escape from this entangling metaphor and mention that Lisbon has everything. The city itself is as bright as a winning dollar in Nevada. It has an immense past, attested by its monuments of architecture, when it centered the world's interest in new lands and seas unveiled by Portuguese explorers. It has a mode of life in its humble, fishy quarters that never fails to fascinate. Lisbon's location, on the vast estuary of the Tagus near the open sea, is unsurpassed. There is a River-and-Sea Riviera so alluring that Europe's royalty has chosen it as its special retreat from the world's woes. There are nearby Atlantic beaches too, where the surf thunders with a fury rarely matched even on the outside beaches of Rio. At night the city is gay and uninhibited. There are lively little cabarets and several hard-to-find restaurants of fado entertainment native to this capital and unique in the night world of tourism.

In wooded, hill-girt Sintra (formerly spelled Cintra), the old royal town a few miles distant, Lisbon has a special attraction that poets have come far to see and sense.

The Mediterranean traveler who visits Portugal as an opener to his journey has no need to wander more than thirty miles from the capital. There is enough right there to hold him spellbound for a week if he is fortunate enough to have a week for it.

Mediterranean Spain, with Gibraltar and Tangier

Spain's capital, great as it is, will be the barest incidental in most Mediterranean trips, if indeed it figures at all, for Madrid is rather far from any shore, on a plateau in the exact geographical center of the country. The cities on and near the coast are those that count chiefly in this picture and their very names are eloquent: Algeciras, Ronda, Málaga, Granada, Valencia, Barcelona etc. A preview has only to flash their names on the page to reveal the color of them. It takes a bit of zeal and stamina to see them all, for several are not linked up by air service, and Spanish rails and roads, though improving, are in need of much further development, but the reward, in every case of the six selections above, is far greater than the traveler's effort to attain it. The same is true of Cádiz and Seville even though these cities are less easy to "attain."

Gibraltar, the European Pillar of Hercules—the African Pillar is Cape Ceuta fifteen miles distant across the strait—has been a familiar landmark to generations of steamer travelers but this book will view it in terms of air travel, for Gibraltar Airways, linking the Rock with Seville, Málaga and Tangier, has made such a viewing possible and very practical. The airport, by the way, is in the lee of that stupendous rock face (on the north side, toward Spain) which the Prudential Life Insurance Company made famous in its advertising as long ago as the turn of the century. From the steamer's deck you don't see *that* Gibraltar at all. You see a crouching lion, of sorts.

Gibraltar has a life of its own, a life that still speaks Spanish after two hundred and fifty years of British occupation. For sightseeing purposes one day is ample, but that one day can be full of interest.

Tangier is now an outpost of Morocco. In 1956, Morocco became a completely independent state, a kingdom ruled now by King Moulay Hassan II, successor to the revered Mohammed V. In relinquishing what had long been Spanish Morocco Spain retained two very Spanish port cities on the Mediterranean coast, Ceuta and Melilla, but Free Tangier, that internationally governed hotbed of free-port goods, free currency and gold exchange, free everything, including vast smuggling operations, was fully and completely absorbed by the new Kingdom of Morocco. The changeover from colonial status to independence was remarkably free from upheavals, political or military, and as a young member of the society of independent nations Morocco has proved refreshingly stable. Tourism, to bring in you and me, may be pursued with full confidence. Americans now need no visa, but this should be checked at the time of your proposed visit. Information may be had from the Consulate General of Morocco, 342 Madison Avenue, New York 17. Tetuán, the former capital of Spanish Morocco, is only an easy taxi or bus trip distant from Tangier.

Everybody is saying, and I concur, that "Tangier isn't what it used to be," but that should *not* be taken to mean that it is lacking in interest. Far from it. The Grand Sokko and Petit Sokko are still colorfully explosive, the hillside warren of the Kasbah is still strange and exciting, and on the comfort front Hotel El Minzah is still its same delightful self, still run by the same experienced manager. Night life, both European and native, still carries on, though perhaps less abundantly than when this was a Free City.

The Balearic Isles

The Balearic Isles, Majorca, Minorca, and Ibiza, are very easily reached by air and by good steamer service both from Barcelona and

Valencia. Majorca is the all-important isle for every average traveler. You may sojourn there in luxury, swimming all year from your hotel's beach or float. You may revel in Palma, the island capital, and in Majorca's mighty scenery. You may visit the mountain retreat of Chopin and Sand. And for Chopin's music you may go underground, quite literally, but I am getting ahead of my story.

Mediterranean Spain will be a problem to you, there is so much of it that is so good—and everything you do there and buy there *now* (this may well change) will probably cost less than in any other land of Europe.

(Spain's more distant *Canary Islands*, rival in beauty of the Balearics, are presented in Chapter 5 in connection with Madeira.)

The French Riviera and Monaco

Mediterranean France, from Port Bou at the Spanish border to Menton at the Italian border, is a highway of holiday so famous, from Phoenician to tourist times, that "no comment" is needed in this preview. It includes, of course, that independent enclave, the Principality of Monaco, and *that* includes, in its 370 acres, not only the casino of Monte Carlo, but the romantic rock of Prince Rainier and Princess Grace and the Condamine of Sainte-Dévote.

Tangent to Corsica

From La Turbie, on French soil high above Monaco, I have seen, on clear days, the headlands of Corsica, and the first sight of them was enough to convince me that I had to go there. Now I have, in fact, gone twice, once by ship and once by plane. Corsica is known for its photogenic old port cities, for its rugged mountains and still more rugged red wines, and for Napoleon Bonaparte. We will have a look at these lures in Chapter 8.

Coastal Italy and Its Islands

The eight hundred miles and more of Italy's western coastline, fronting the Ligurian and Tyrrhenian Seas, from the French border to the tip of the toe of Calabria, are about as satisfying miles as are to be found in tourist Europe. I have covered almost the whole distance by train, much of it by car and much of it also in a chartered bus of an American-operated tour under the management of Boston's Metropolitan Travel Service, a high-grade specialist in European group travel. In beauty there is little to choose between the rail and road routes, but the roads have two obvious advantages, offsetting the slower pace. Your car or bus puts you in touch with innumerable lovely villages and the people in them, and when it comes to the many hills it climbs over them instead of plunging through them, as the trains do, in a frustrating chain of tunnels.

A pleasant and easy method that is available at any time, all through the year, is the regular and frequent service of the de luxe motor coaches of CIAT (Compagnia Italiana Autoservizi Turistici), which will be discussed in Chapter 9. They take off from Nice, put you through the Italian border formalities *en masse* and carry on to Genoa, where the traveler spends the night. Next day another coach of the same company continues to Pisa and, veering a little bit inland, to Florence, where a stopover is usually made. On another day, a long one, CIAT carries on through the hill towns (via Perugia and Assisi *or* via Siena and Orvieto) to Rome. A separate trip covers the stretch from Rome to Naples in half a day. Below Naples there is no CIAT service except around the perimeter of Sicily (see later section), but the train route hugs the shore the whole way to the Strait of Messina, then crosses that fabled barrier to Sicily in a big train-swallowing ferry.

The above information, hardly suitable to a preview shot, is inserted here to emphasize the simplicity of seeing much of Italy's magnificent western littoral, along with Florence, Rome and some famous hill towns, in a week or two that may be added to a general Mediterranean tour.

The islands of Italy's coast, aside from the Sicily Special and such local essentials as Capri and Ischia, sentinels of the Bay of Naples, include little Elba, big Sardinia and the tiny volcanoes of the Lipari, one of which is volcanic Strómboli and another of which is named Vulcano. Elba is a lovely place for visitors as well as for imperial exiles. It is reached by steamer from the midget port of Piombino, below Leghorn.

Sardinia's capital, Cagliari, is reached by air from Rome in just a hundred minutes by the frequent services of Alitalia. At the present time Sardinia is in process of being discovered by tourism and those who visit it will be on the crest of the wave. More on this color-saturated island in Chapter 9.

The Lipari, or Aeolian, Islands lie a bit north of Sicily, and more specifically they lie some thirty to fifty miles north of the small port of Milazzo, west of Messina. Frequent boats go from there to the capital island, named Lipari, and biweekly services connect Lipari with Vulcano, which, despite its name, erupts only at rare intervals, and with Strómboli, which erupts many times a day, pouring out great quantities of lava. I never did manage to see the controversial Rossellini film named for this island but if it was half as exciting as the island itself it must have been a thriller. I have not landed on Strómboli but I once circled it, close to shore, on a French steamer that was proceeding from the Piraeus to Marseille. The captain considered it the show piece of his whole voyage and so did all his passengers. Its dramatic cone rises more than three thousand feet into the Aeolian air.

The Sicily Special

Sicily, the Trinacria of the ancients, is definitely a three-sided island, and each side differs strongly from the other two in basic tourist appeal. The north side is, for tourist intent and purpose, Palermo, with its superb setting and its Arab-Norman background. The south side, from the Marsala angle to Selinunte, Agrigento, Gela and Ragusa, is steeped in Hellenic background and splendid temples. The east side, with Syracuse, has very much of Hellas too, but for most travelers Mount Etna is more important, and especially that ace of travel, Taormina, on the vast volcano's flank. I have met travelers who expressed disappointment in almost everything they had seen, including Paris, Zermatt and Venice, but I've never yet happened upon a traveler to Sicily who was disappointed in Taormina. There must be such a person somewhere.

The symbol of Sicily, and you see the design everywhere—it even *grows* in the Bellini Garden of Catania—is three running legs emerging as a sort of triangle from a central hub, but the symbol of island travel nowadays is the *Nastro d'Oro*, or Golden Ribbon tour of CIAT. The tour operates in five day-long stages and may be taken in whole or in any part. One of the stages is devoted to an ascent of Mt. Etna by bus and cableway, the summit observatory being 9650 feet above sea level.

This stage starts and ends at Taormina, thus providing two successive nights in the same spectacular town and the same hotel.

This tour is worth jotting down on the firmest tablet of your memory, for unless you travel by private car CIAT is the only way to do Sicily in comfort. I should know because I once did the whole thing by train—and what a thing! The trains are not bad, but the necessary connections and arrangements present many a problem. Details on the CIAT circuit will be presented in Chapter 9.

Malta of the Knights

Malta has been a British naval base for well over a century and a half, and in World War II it earned the gratitude of the free world, along with prized letters of tribute from King George and President Roosevelt, by its remarkable stand "alone but unafraid in the center of the sea," to quote our president's words. It was terribly bombed, but the best of its mellowed sights, dating from the era of the Knights of the Order of St. John of Jerusalem, still stand and are not much the worse for war.

The island is a greatly appealing one, and an easy one to see in a short visit, for it has less than a hundred square miles all told, and the best of the best is in or near Valletta, the seagirt capital. The people speak Maltese, a language that has been cooked up by time and and history from many ingredients, chiefly Italian, Saracenic and French, but almost everyone speaks also English, of a sort. Valletta has an excellent hotel, the Phoenicia, which is no small matter in so small a city.

Thoughts of independence are beginning to brew in the Maltese mind, for the leaders say to their compatriots and to the British authorities, "What's good for Cyprus is good also for us." This movement will be interesting to follow. Meanwhile, Malta already has self-government under a new constitution that went into effect in 1962.

Moslem North Africa (Morocco; Algeria; Tunisia; Libya)

Morocco's cities reveal sharp contrasts between French enterprise of the colonial era and the vivid colors of Moslem life. Don't be dainty when you explore the medinas and kasbahs and souks of these much-mixed races, where life goes on about as it always has. Wade right in. You'll have a wonderful time. And when you emerge the French quarters, with their bright cafés, smart shops and good hotels, will seem like the Elysian Fields, which is to say les Champs Elysées.

Casablanca, the chief metropolis of Morocco, is a living tribute to the wisdom and colonizing skill of one of the greatest colonial administrators France has ever had, Marshal Louis Hubert Gonzalve Lyautey. The capital of the country, however, with the king's palace and court, is not big Casablanca but Rabat, a gleaming white coastal city about a hundred miles to the northeast.

Algeria long shuddered under storm clouds of bitterness that rained violence and carnage on it, but with the coming of final independence, in July, 1962, the clouds began, at last to lift. One must believe that in time they will fully roll away. Exciting land of cruelly mixed legacy, Algeria will again be flooded with tourists, clicking cameras in hand.

Tunisia came through the holocaust of the changeover from colonialism to independence far faster and with far fewer scars than did Algeria. Its leaders, especially President Habib Bourguiba, have been statesmen deserving of the term. In August, 1962, the last issue between Tunisia and France, the dispute over Bizerte, was amicably settled and friendly relations between the two countries established.

Tunis, in my opinion, has the most exciting souks (bazaars) to be found in any North African city, not even excepting Cairo, and it has also, as close neighbor, the Carthage that was destroyed at Cato's insistence but didn't stay destroyed. You can walk into and through half a dozen of its civilizations. Your tax dollars have helped exhume it as a tourist attraction and you'll want to see it "to get your money's worth." Carthage is one of the Mediterranean's neglected spectacles.

Libya, whose capital, Tripoli, was once a Barbary State famous in history, legend and song, was born of World War II after the downfall of Mussolinian Italy. During Mussolini's heyday the Italians, goaded on by the driving colonial urges of Il Duce, developed the country substantially, but when world events weaned it from Italian nourishment it had a hard time to grow up. It has still scarcely reached the age of puberty though it struggles toward maturity, being aided in spectacular fashion by the relatively recent discovery of vast fields of oil beneath its sands, now in process of development by American and other foreign interests.

For the tourist, Libya has valid and important lures, among them being Tripoli itself, a port city of about 150,000 inhabitants, Benghazi, of war fame, the province of Cyrenaica and, fairly close to Tripoli, the ruins of Leptis Magna which are quite unknown to tourists but are rated by archeologists as among the most important and best preserved of the entire Roman world. Libya is now a monarchy, its first and present king being Idris I.

I will confess that although I booked air passage from Athens to Tripoli and return I was forced to cancel it, due solely to the fact that through a bungling that was largely my fault at the airport of Tel Aviv my passport was stamped with an Israeli visa. Had I spoken up quickly this need not have happened. Libya, like other Arab lands, including Egypt, Jordan and even half-Christian Lebanon, will not admit the bearer of a passport containing an Israeli visa. Israel is ready to help out by providing the traveler, upon request, with a *separate visa paper* (which can be destroyed after use) in lieu of a standard passport visa. In my case I must secure a new passport before I may visit Libya.

The Mainland and Islands of Greece

The Greek mainland is no brow-wrinkling problem, since "all the best," or nearly all, is easily reached in short trips from that city of cities, Athens, which was the classic capital and is the modern capital. Athens, in its own ineffable self, sums up "the glory that was Greece," and if one tires of those well-worn lines of Poe one does not tire of Greece itself. The Acropolis is still a hill of magic. The old Greek theater at its base still echoes to the clever lines of Aristophanes. The Areopagus, where Paul identified the Unknown God, still recalls the apostle, as the Pnyx recalls Socrates the philosopher. The modern stadium of marble, in another part of the city, reminds us that the Olympic Games were here revived at the turn of the century.

The places to be reached from Athens by coach or private car in an hour, or in half a day, include the Piraeus, whose curving waterfront is always alive with sea traffic, the pleasant beach resorts along the Saronic Gulf, the Phalerons, Old and New, the plain of Marathon, Cape Sounion. More distant places that can be seen between dawn and dusk include Eleusis, Delphi, Corinth, Nauplia, Mycenae, Epidaurus, whose names need no gilding here. And a boat trip in the Bay of Salamis brings the Greece of Themistocles right into the realm of water fun. The places to be reached by Olympic Airways in flights of an hour or so include nearly all of continental Greece and many of her fabled isles.

Island Greece is so infinitely extensive—there are more than five hundred isles and islets—that one can only pick and choose. The most likely choices are Crete, Rhodes and Corfu, all reached easily by air. All are wonderful goals. Rhodes is the most developed for travel, having good roads and two large, de luxe hotels, plus several others of first-class rating.

Those visitors to Greece who are not too pressed for time will consider Olympia, in the western part of the Peloponnesus, and for this Olympic Airways will give them a lift, in 55 minutes, to the port city of Kalamata. Another exciting goal, but for "men only," is the group of monasteries on Mount Athos.

Greece cries for a stay of a full month, but in a country so relatively small and compact (except for its islands, five of which are reached by air from Athens) the rugged traveler can see a lot in a well-managed fortnight or even a week. And if he sees even Athens alone, in half a week, he has not too sorely cheated himself.

Egypt-on-the-Nile

In Egypt this book will go much farther from the Mediterranean Sea than in any other land discussed. It will, in fact, go some six hundred miles up-Nile, for it would seem a crime against horse sense for any traveler who reaches Egypt at all not to reach the Luxor-Karnak-Thebes complex, which is more than four hundred miles south of Cairo; and having gone that far he should surely push on another 130 miles to Aswan, whence came all the granite used in Egypt's monuments, including the tombs within the pyramids near Cairo. Another 200 miles or so, if time permits, will bring him to and beyond the Nubian border for a look at Philae and the monumental sculptures of Abu Simbel. If a *flood* of money can be raised—the estimated amount is at least a hundred million dollars—these famous relics of a far-past civilization will be raised from the flood of waters which will result from the building of the colossal new dam.

Egypt is of such geographical length, as well as tourist importance, that any general itinerary covering the whole Mediterranean must groan at having to condense it into a few days or a week. It is quite impossible to speak of "Mediterranean Egypt," as we have in the case of Spain, France and Italy, for that would cut the heart clean out of it and leave little but Alexandria. Even Delta Egypt would add only Cairo, and greatly important as that metropolis is, and despite its proximity to the great pyramids, the Sphinx and the marvels of Memphis, it is not the heart of *ancient* Egypt—which travelers go so far to see. The Egypt of the Nile is supremely important and in Chapters 16 and 17 this book shall wander up there—without further apology. It hopes most heartily that the reader can do likewise.

Cyprus, an Eastern Hub

Cyprus, only a 90-minute leap from Athens, is an independent country, voluntarily associated with the British Commonwealth of Nations. It lies in the farthest eastern corner of the Mediterranean, and from the air traveler's point of view it is a key to many countries. Fortunately it is a shiny key and would be of the first importance even if it were less easy to reach. Because of the island's sheer necessity to travel, as well as its full kit of personal charms, it supports an attractive hotel, the Ledra Palace, in Nicosía, the capital, and a luxurious Hilton is under construction in the same city. In most of the port cities, Kyrenía, Lárnaca, Limassol and Famagusta, it now has good first-class hotels.

Cyprus has lofty mountain resorts where skiing is done every winter, and at less high altitudes it has an almost startling assortment of hilltop monasteries and castles, one of the former, Stavrovouni, being among the most dramatically located monasteries I have ever seen, and one of the latter, St. Hilarion, being claimed by Cypriots to be the fantastic original of the one made familiar by Walt Disney in "Snow-White." Cyprus has also *most* of the cedars of Lebanon, the western forests having far more of these regal trees than are now found in Lebanon itself. Cyprus has also some vivid memories of Paul and Venus, though they did not, be assured, come here together! As a matter of fact, Paul, along with Barnabas and John called Mark, set sail for Pamphylia from that very place, Paphos, on the island's western tip, where Venus, known in this Greek-speaking island as Aphrodite, rose from the foam a millennium or so earlier.

Cyprus speaks Greek, but because the island belonged to Britain from the time she took it over from Turkish suzerainty during World War I until the year 1961 there are still substantial Turkish elements in Nicosía and some few Armenians as well. Very many of the inhabitants speak fluent English. The street signs appear only in Greek, and occasionally Turkish as well, but all English street names have been rather crudely painted out. In cinemas that run American and British films, captions are often provided both in Greek and Turkish. The island is awash with relics of the Lusignan (Crusader) kings and also with relics of periods when Genoa, and then Venice, ruled it. Much of *Othello* was laid by Shakespeare in Famagusta. No visitor can complain of lack of variety here. For the tourist there is never a dull moment.

Israel Comes of Age

The speed with which Israel, a nation only since 1949, has grown to maturity is a source of pride to all Jewish visitors and of wonder to all gentiles. There is nothing else quite like it anywhere. Refugees from a score of lands have poured in by tens of thousands, even hundreds of thousands, and some are still coming, though the torrents have largely subsided. The absorption of these hordes, many from Yemen, one of the most primitive places on earth, has taxed young Israel almost to the breaking point, but not quite. The authorities have not refused them and it has been a point of pride to accept all and sundry. This drama of race is exciting to see.

Israel is a queerly shaped country, resulting from the effort to draw border lines between predominantly Jewish and predominantly Arab regions without causing an intolerable strain on nationalistic tempers. If you take a dish of succotash some day and try to draw a line between the corn and the beans you'll have some idea of the problem faced by the United Nations mediator, Count Bernadotte, and, following his assassination, Dr. Ralph Bunche. Israel has more than a hundred miles of coast line, from Lebanon's boundary on the north to the Gaza strip on the south, now administered by Egypt but guarded by United Nations forces. In the Plain of Sharon, north of Tel Aviv, the country is but ten miles wide. Up north it widens to some forty miles, taking in Nazareth and most of the shore of Lake Galilee. At Jerusalem, such delicate juggling was done that the Holy City is cut squarely in two, the spots most sacred in Christian tradition being on the Arab side, a part of Hashemite Jordan. Bethlehem, Jericho, Hebron and Schechem (Nablus) are likewise on Jordan's side.

But the most significant thing, in Israel's view, is her retention of the Negev, that big arrowhead of utter desert whose narrow tip touches the Gulf of Eilat (or Aqaba), offshoot of the Red Sea. The rapidly developing port of Eilat is a major source of pride. The Negev itself is called the Future of Israel, in capital letters, but it is rapidly becoming a part of the Present. It is the country's only hinterland, and vast irrigation plans are being pushed. Important oil resources have also been found.

The devoted efforts of Israel, plagued by a host of problems all at once, including the fanatical religiosity of its own side-curl element, the Orthodox Jews, to amalgamate and develop as a going nation have been a stirring sight since the birth of the nation. For the tourist, be assured, there is nothing grim or difficult about traveling in Israel. Excellent hotels, some of them de luxe, have sprung up in many parts of the country and the roads are steadily improving.

In conclusion I would say that Israel is something of a phenomenon. Where else in the world, where else in history, has any nation, however much helped by foreign aid, grown from infancy to young adulthood in anything like so brief a time, and this despite being ringed about by openly hostile neighbors? One reason for this growth is the obvious and unmistakable dedication of its people to their task. Another is Israel's recognition of the fully equal status of its women with its men, even to the extent of requiring almost the same period of military service (two years) from its girls as from its boys (two and a half years). The girls and women of this nation are a sight for tourist eyes.

Jordan of the Arabs

Transjordan has become Cisjordan as well, and is thus Ambijordan, for a great chunk of territory west of the river, extending to and beyond Jerusalem, is now under its administration. A long-winded but correct name for the country is the Hashemite Kingdom of the Jordan, based on the genealogical fact that the present king, like the previous King Abdullah, victim of an assassin, is of the proud Moslem house of Hashem, tracing its male line directly back to Fatima, the daughter of Mohammed.

One must discuss this country, including its portion of Jerusalem, with certain reservations, for any intending visitor may be prevented, as I was twice prevented by *temporarily* closed borders, from entering it. I have had to fall back on memories of a much earlier visit, which memories, concerned only with Jerusalem, Bethlehem and a few other places in "Cisjordan," are still vivid.

My own experiences can be put down to bad luck, for actually it is not normally difficult to enter Jordan. Through Jerusalem's famous Mandelbaum Gate the traveler may pass *one way*, but is not allowed to go and come back. Many make their way from Lebanon to Jordan and thence to Israel (securing their Israel visa on a separate paper, not on the passport) and later emerge from Israel to go anywhere they like. Others reverse the process. By a remarkable pretense Jordan will admit you from Israel (one way) if your *passport* does not reveal that you have been in that country. The fact that you come boldly *from* Israel, in broad daylight, is concealed by a self-imposed astigmatism that is one of the great curiosities of tourist travel.

Jordan Jerusalem includes within its tortuous confines many of the famous spots sacred to Christendom for their associations with the life and death and resurrection of Jesus; and Bethlehem, the place of His birth, lies but five or six miles to the south of the Holy City.

Middle East Airlines, a company which has greatly advanced of late years, maintains a regular daily service between Beirut (Lebanon) and Jordan Jerusalem and vice versa, some of the planes continuing to, or coming from, Nicosía, Cyprus. Air Liban, a subsidiary of Air France, has also an excellent daily service between Beirut and Jerusalem. Jordanian, called also Jordan Airways, has a service between Jerusalem and Amman, the Jordan capital, continuing to Beirut.

Lebanon of the West

The Mediterranean is a mighty mélange, contrast piled on contrast, but nowhere are the contrasts so striking as in those neighbor lands of Lebanon and Syria, both members of the Arab League. Lebanon is the most Westernized of the Moslem lands, more so in some ways than even free-wheeling Turkey, with the possible exceptions of İstanbul and Ankara. Syria clings firmly to the ancient traditions of Islam, accepting few incursions of Western life even in Damascus and Aleppo.

Lebanon is a holiday land, out and out, with everything that tourists love while on vacation—luxury hotels and fine clubs, sea bathing and pool bathing, mountain roads that lead to cool resorts in summer, to fields and hillsides of deep snow in winter, with an impressive ski lift to one very lofty mountain saddle. Beirut, substantially more Christian than Moslem in its population, has one of the Near East's finest hotels, Pan Am's new Phoenicia Intercontinental. It has shiny American cars by the thousand, and big American-style movie houses. It has, in the environs, a huge and spectacular gambling casino. It has night clubs almost by the dozen, some of them smart and international in style, others mere *boîtes* and dives. In Beirut almost everybody speaks at least a little English and this is due, in no small part, to the educational influence of the great American University there, which has put its stamp on the country of its adoption as no other institution anywhere in the world has done.

Syria of the East

Syria's capital, Damascus, is but two or three hours away from Beirut as the car rolls, thirty minutes as the plane flies, but it is "light years" away in its manner of life. It is as Eastern and Moslem as Beirut is Western and half Christian. Its charm—and the city is awash with it—is the charm of something *different*, utterly and amazingly different. Conceivably the traveler might be able to forget Beirut, since it is not too unlike certain cities of the modern West, but he could never forget the crowded motley of the Damascus bazaars, where business is done much as it was in the days of Mohammed, and for that matter in the days of Paul, who was on the road to this city when he saw "a great light" and fell to earth.

Damascus goes to bed with the sun. Damascus observes with rigor the fast of Ramadan. Many women of Damascus are at least lightly veiled and one ultra-Moslem quarter considers those who wear thin veils grossly indecent. European evening life—there is little night life—centers chiefly in the large hotels, but you won't mind that. It is not for dancing and floor shows that you come to this most-different city.

Turkey on Two Continents

A visit to Turkey on two continents is the ideal culmination of any traveler's west-to-east journeying in the Mediterranean. There is not a more thrilling city on any sea than is Istanbul on the Bosporus and the Golden Horn, and by plane or train one may easily reach Ankara, a brand-new capital that has become of prime importance in the racing currents of world affairs, as is attested by the notably large diplomatic colony there. In Asiatic Turkey, which is Asia Minor, which is Anatolia, there are other places than Ankara to visit, for instance Bursa, the ancient many-mosqued capital of Turkey, nowadays a famous resort of mineral springs, above which towers Mount Uludag, sought by skiers every winter, and on the Aegean Sea the ancient port of Izmir, or Smyrna, near which are the imposing ruins of Ephesus, City of Diana.

As for Istanbul, words quail and fail in trying to describe it. It is one of the supreme character cities that the tides of civilization have cast up. To present a few first-primer facts, it was known to the ancients as Byzantium. In 328 A.D., Constantine the Great rebuilt it and gave it his name, Constantinople, which clung to it (in foreigners' usage only) until 1929, when the new Turkish state firmly established the universal acceptance of the name Istanbul. From Constantine's day for more than eleven hundred years it was the capital of the Eastern Empire, heart and head of Greek culture. Then it was captured for the Ottoman Empire by Mohammed II, in 1453. The sultanate held sway until 1920, when the signing of the Treaty of Sèvres reduced it to political impotence. Two years later the last sultan, Mohammed VI, was compelled to abdicate. Mustafa Kemal Atatürk appeared on history's stage as the father of his country, modern Turkey. Since then it has become more and more a *Western* country in its way of life, at least in the cities, though still also a Moslem country. Its present tolerance, with full respect for the Four Freedoms, is notable in a country of the Near East, and this is of real significance to all who travel.

Istanbul catches and holds our interest, not only for its location, for its colossal mosques and lofty minarets, for its Seraglio and its incredibly lavish modern palace, and for its endless acres of bazaars, but also for the plain good times and good food to be had. The restaurants of this metropolis are a story in themselves, ranging from the half-hidden places of the knowing epicure in the old city to such gleaming and palatial establishments as the Casino Taksim and the Kervansaray (meaning Caravansary) in Beyoglu. Luxury hotels were lacking until the 300-room Istanbul Hilton was opened in 1953, though there are several others of first-class rating. The Hilton, a distinguished center of lodging and living, plays a considerable role in the social and diplomatic life of Turkey. Its site, on high ground directly overlooking the Bosporus, is superb.

REVISION SUPPLEMENT TO CHAPTER 2

ALTHOUGH all airlines charge standard fares on regular runs to Mediterranean cities, special tours are offered by most airlines and these *can* be different. It is well worth a visit to the airline offices or to a travel agent to find out which would be the best tour for you. There are 17-day excursion fares, 21-day excursion fares, off-season fares, group rates, family plans and a complete roster of equally confusing but economically wise offerings. Spain's *Iberia Air Lines*, to give one example, has offered a "Fiesta Iberia" trip to Spain and Portugal for 15 days of touring for $529, which is stated to include "jet air fare, hotel, most meals, land tours, sightseeing, parties, tips/taxes and *the works!*" *Pan American*, in conjunction with steamship lines and American Express, offers a luxury, first-class "Magic Mediterranean" tour including Portugal, Spain, Morocco, France, Italy and Greece from $1498 for 54 days. In addition, *Alitalia*, the airline of Italy; KLM–*Royal Dutch Airlines; El Al*, Israel's airline; and most other national airlines have tour offerings.

A thorough rundown of air services to the Mediterranean countries is given in Chapter 2 and much of that information is still correct, acknowledging the fact that more travelers have meant more flights on all of the major carriers, and therefore better service. There are a few welcome additions, however, to some of the lines formerly flying only local or limited routes for their countries but now in the big time, with routes to the European mainland and the United States.

Middle East Airlines Airliban, using the familiar MEA letters, is the result of a merger of Middle East Airlines and Air Liban, mentioned separately on page 420. MEA, with offices in Beirut, flies between Beirut and London, Paris, Frankfurt, Geneva, Vienna, Rome, Athens and Istanbul to the north and many southern points in Africa and India. The merger of the two lines has resulted in a wider network for the one, and MEA is now the national airline of Lebanon. New York offices are located at 680 Fifth Avenue, Room 1304, where you will find folders on many of MEA's destinations and can get information on some of the less-traveled countries, notably those that do not have other New York sources of information.

Olympic Airlines, the national air service of Greece, which is covered in Chapter 14, now flies from New York to Paris and Rome en route to Athens and on to Tel Aviv or Beirut or Cairo, all of which are Olympic's familiar territory. Service is by Boeing 707-320 Fan Jets. The company now has a street-floor office in quarters formerly occupied by American Express in midtown New York City at 647 Fifth Avenue.

TAP (Transportes Aéreos Portugueses), the Portuguese national airline, with offices in New York City at 601 Fifth Avenue, hopes to be flying transatlantic, although, as of this writing, they fly only around Portugal and from Portugal to their islands and to Continental capitals.

American Export-Isbrandtsen Lines is the result of a merger of American Export and the Isbrandtsen Lines. The company operates the *Independence* and the *Constitution,* plus the 20,000-ton *Atlantic,* on regular cruises to Mediterranean ports during the spring, summer and fall, as discussed on page 24.

The *Greek Line,* with offices now at 32 Pearl Street, New York City, operates the 26,000-ton flagship *Queen Anna Maria* (named for the young queen of Greece), which entered service in 1965, in addition to the *Olympia,* from New York and Boston to Lisbon, Naples, Messina, Piraeus, Limassol (Cyprus) and Haifa, adding occasional halts at Malta. The Royal Diadem Cruise, the Mediterranean cruise mentioned on page 267 for the *Olympia,* has now been taken over and expanded by the *Queen Anna Maria.*

The *Italian Line* retired its aging liners *Saturnia* and *Vulcania* in 1965 in favor of the magnificent new 43,000-ton liners *Michelangelo* and *Raffaello,* each of these twins accommodating 1700 passengers in three classes (see page 25). These ships, plus the *Leonardo da Vinci* and the *Cristoforo Colombo,* all stop at Gibraltar and vary their schedules from that port. Italian Line has its main New York office at 1 Whitehall Street, downtown, with an attractive midtown office at 696 Fifth Avenue.

In early 1966, *North German Lloyd's Europa* sailed into New York on her maiden voyage. The *Europa* is the Swedish American Line's veteran *Kungsholm* reincarnated and she joins her sister ship, the *Bremen*, in transatlantic and cruise service. North German Lloyd's New York office is at 666 Fifth Avenue.

Norwegian America Line, 29 Broadway, New York City, christened the new flagship *Sagafjord* late in 1965. Weighing 21,000 tons, she has a capacity of 820 passengers, mostly in tourist-class accommodations. On cruises she will carry only 450. The *Sagafjord* joins the *Oslofjord* and the *Bergensfjord* in NAL transatlantic and cruise service.

Swedish American Line has a new *Kungsholm* of 24,000 tons, equipped with all modern appointments, which started service in May 1966. This *Kungsholm* is the fourth ship to carry the name, a revered one by long-time ship travelers, and she joins the *Gripsholm* as the "White Viking Fleet." Swedish American Line's New York office is at 636 Fifth Avenue.

Zim Lines' Shalom (meaning Peace) made her maiden voyage to New York in 1964. In 1966 the line inaugurated a new policy, scheduling a regular monthly halt at Lisbon from May through September by the *Shalom*. The *Zion* and the *Israel* (page 26) were retired in the spring of 1966. Zim Lines' ships, the *Jerusalem* and the *Theodor Herzl* included, operate kitchens and dining rooms "in strict compliance with the dietary laws" (meaning kosher), except on certain cruises.

In addition to the many lines mentioned throughout this book as their services directly concern areas discussed, there are other lines that carry boatloads of eager tourists on short trips among Mediterranean ports.

The number of cruises through the Greek Islands, touching Turkey and sometimes other countries, is legion. Among the lines offering such service (with their New York addresses) are the *Hellenic Cruises* (consult the Cruise and Coach Corporation at 680 Fifth Avenue); the *Chandris Lines Cruises*, 666 Fifth Avenue; the *Typaldos Lines*, 500 Fifth Avenue (page 266); the *Sun Lines*, represented in New York by the Holland-America Line at Pier 40, North River; the *Nomikos Lines*, represented by the Greek Line at 32 Pearl Street; and the *Epirotiki Lines*, at 608 Fifth Avenue. This is just a start in the roster of Greek shipping lines, but the above-mentioned six offer a wide sampling of departure dates and ports of call.

The *Adriatic Lines*, whose United States agent is the Italian Line, has luxury Near-East cruises, touching at 15 or 18 fabulous ports of the eastern Mediterranean, including those of Egypt, Lebanon, Greece, Turkey, Cyprus, Syria, Rhodes and Crete. Cruises are aboard the *Bernia, Stelvio* and *Brennero* and usually last 19 or 20 days.

The *Compagnie Française de Navigation* (CFN) has the *Galilée* in service between Genoa, Messina, Haifa, Izmir, Piraeus and Naples, replacing the aging *Césarée*. The *Galilée* is a good, small ship built in 1952 and reconditioned in 1963. The newer *Renaissance* began service in mid-1966 and carries 416 passengers. Arrangements have been made to have CFN departures coincide with transatlantic crossings of American Export-Isbrandtsen Lines to make a complete cruise possible.

Ford's *Freighter Travel Guidebook* (page 26) is now $2.75 and can be obtained from Robert E. Clark, publisher, P.O. Box 505, Woodland Hills, California 91366.

Touring by car is popular and easy. Although it is discussed as it directly pertains to the countries mentioned below, let me say here that more and more countries are *not* requiring an international driver's license, but will accept your home-state license without question. Spain and Portugal, as of this writing, still *do* require the international driver's license, which may be obtained for $3 and two passport pictures from Auto-Europe at 25 West 58th Street, New York City, as well as at AAA offices and most car rental firms here and abroad.

CHAPTER 2

THE MEDITERRANEAN BY AIR, BY SEA—AND BY CAR

Jets to Everywhere

THE Jet Age was born, as a commercially feasible form of travel, only in the late 50's, yet it has taken such a firm grip on public consciousness that travel by piston engine propeller planes tends to seem slightly old-fashioned. The DC-3, though still proclaimed by air men as one of the best and most dependable aircraft ever built, takes on the overtones of a faithful winged jalopy, and even the big fellows of piston engine type such as DC-7s and "Connies" are looked upon merely as high-grade plodders. Jets rule the air, but the present craft, capable of only 600 to 650 mph speeds, would do well to reflect that in a few years, with the dawn of the Supersonic Age, involving speeds of 1200 to 2400 mph, they, in their turn, may be looked upon as faithful old plodders. One views such possibilities dimly and with a sort of resignation, for already, in the case of medium distance flights, the speed of planes makes the serving of a meal on board a touch-and-go scramble for stewards and hostesses, a stuff-it-down challenge for passengers, and even on transatlantic flights there seems to be barely time enough for a leisured luncheon or dinner and a cat nap.

On the other side of the picture, jets get you there *now*, or a few minutes after now, and getting there is your main purpose. Long-distance jets of Boeing and Douglas design leap the Atlantic in six to seven hours and the speed is "no respecter of classes," for budget travelers using Economy Class get there quite as soon as those who blow themelves to luxurious services such as first class on Air France's *Golden Parisian*, winging from New York daily at 10 A.M., or Pan Am's *President Special* or BOAC's *Monarch*. Caravelles and Comets leap from anywhere to anywhere within Europe and the Mediterranean in one to two hours. Practically all of your vacation is yours to enjoy in the place or places of your choice.

My own current "renewal trip" to and around the Mediterranean may be set forth in personal terms as a sample of what you may devise for yourself, subject to infinite permutations and combinations. Only the North Africa flights to the countries of former French Africa and a couple of the short hops (Gibraltar–Tangier; Rome–Malta) are from earlier travels made a few years ago and now carefully checked for current facts. There is a soothing simplicity in placing oneself, so far as is practicable, in the hands of some single world-girdling company. For extensive Mediterranean travels, both on this and earlier tours, I have chosen Air France for the basic reason that this company, together with its associated and subsidiary companies, reaches more Mediterranean points than any other of the world systems, but there were other reasons based on more personal judgments, which I will list.

First, I happen to like the French Caravelle rather better than any other middle-distance jet. Its smoothness of takeoff and landing are proverbial and have won it top honors all over the world. I have flown Caravelles operated by many *other* companies in many lands, including a dozen flights in South America, and have never heard anything but praise for their performance. Air men agree that the plane is a triumph of French engineering and design. From the two airports of Paris seventy-five Caravelles a week fan out in all directions, many of them heading for Mediterranean points. Caravelles, by the way, bear the old names of France's regions, for example *Quercy*, *Artois*, *Dauphiné* and *Comté de Nice*. The transatlantic Boeing Intercontinental jets bear the aristocratic names of French châteaux, as *Château de Versailles*, *Château de Chambord*, *Château de Chenonceaux* and *Château de Fontainebleau*.

Second, I like French food, whether aground or aloft. One could almost say the French invented fine food, an assertion that is borne out by the fact that nearly every major airline in the world prints its menus in the French language and strives, as best it can, to present its luncheons and dinners in the French manner. If imitation is the sincerest flattery then this is flattery indeed, but the original is rarely matched by the imitation. Air France meals, even the simplest ones on short flights, are served with a Gallic grace and flair that delights the gourmet and wins over the chronic grouch. Always they are enhanced by French wines, white and/or red or rosé, and in first class by champagne. Incidentally, the beverages that accompany fine meals all over the Western world often bear French place names. Champagne is an old province of France, centered by Reims. Cognac is a town of the Charente, in south-western France. Bénédictine's secret formula was worked out in a Bene-dictine monastery in Normandy.

Third, I like the French *Welcome Service*, so signed *in English*, which is in operation in key cities of the system's vast network all over the world. When you see that conspicuous blue and white sign in an Air France office in Lisbon, Barcelona, Athens, Beirut, Istanbul or any other center, you know you have an immediate friend in court. The functions of the Welcome Service are to help the visitor to get off to a good start in any or each locality. Do you want to know what's doing today, tonight, in the city of your sojourn? Do you need a baby sitter? Do you want some advice on shopping? Ask Welcome Service. Com-menced on a full scale only in 1961/1962 this service now operates in fifteen U.S. cities and dozens of foreign ones. Neat multilingual host-esses, natty in uniform and white gloves, staff some of the centers, and they are specially trained to answer the questions that travelers are most likely to ask. If they don't know the answers by heart they look them up in information files or phone to various authorities to find out.

*   *   *

There are, of course, innumerable air patterns for stitching together one's travels in the Mediterranean, and the means of access to that sea are numerous. Virtually all of the world's chief systems of international air transport make Rome a major knot in their networks and Italy has risen to the occasion by providing a new jet airport named for Leonardo da Vinci at Fiumicino, near Ostia. Its terminal building is one of Europe's largest and most magnificent, befitting its role as a takeoff point for almost everywhere in the central and eastern portions of the Mediterranean. Both of America's major overseas air systems, Pan Amer-ican and TWA, have southern routes to Rome, with halts at Lisbon and at Madrid or Barcelona. From northern Europe it seems that quite liter-ally all air roads lead to Rome. BEA (in association with world-girdling BOAC) flies there from London; KLM, small Holland's flying giant, from Amsterdam; SAS of Scandinavia from Copenhagen; Sabena from

Brussels; Lufthansa from many German cities; Swissair from Zurich and Geneva; and of course, Air France from Paris, including the new non-stop Caravelle flights to Naples. I should, however, supplement this European roster by adding that Greece's Olympic Airways maintains two major international routes to Athens, one from London and Paris by way of Rome, the other from Amsterdam by way of Frankfurt and Zurich. There is also a daily international service between Brindisi, Italy, and the Greek island of Corfu. From Athens Olympic flies on to all the Near East lands bordering the Mediterranean except Syria.

Among transatlantic lines from New York I should certainly include Alitalia, which has grown greatly since its absorption of other Italian air lines; Air India, whose justified claim is that it treats its customers like a maharajah or a maharani, according to the sex; El Al Israel Airlines, whose service from New York to London–Paris–Rome–Tel Aviv is of good repute; and Spain's Iberia to Lisbon and Madrid.

Seaways and Leisured Cruises

Ships are fun, always have been, always will be. If you are so amply provided with holiday time that you can devote, say, from sixteen to twenty-two days of it to the round-trip passage to and from Italy or six to eight weeks to a leisured cruise you will be rewarded by that many days or weeks of sheer delight, for the journey will be enlivened by exciting halts all along the route. Roll through your mind such names as Ponta Delgada, Madeira, Lisbon, Gibraltar, Palma, Cannes, Palermo, Athens, Lárnaca, Alexandria, Rhodes, Haifa, Beirut, Istanbul and let them wreck your resistance. Perhaps you will find those weeks that you thought did not exist.

Regularly scheduled passenger liners from New York to Mediterranean ports are operated chiefly by four companies and we may take them up in turn.

AMERICAN EXPORT LINE is rightly proud of its 30,500-ton twin sisters, the *Independence* and the *Constitution*, each carrying over 1000 passengers. Both were expensively modernized in 1959. The company's "Four Aces," popular cargo-passenger ships carrying 125 passengers each, are now reduced to two, the *Exeter* and the *Excalibur*, but a new acquisition is the *Atlantic*, purchased in 1960 from the now defunct Banner Line. This ship, converted in 1958 by its former owners from a mariner-class cargo ship, is one of very few transatlantic vessels catering almost exclusively to tourist class passengers. Its full complement is 860 in tourist class, only 40 in first. The big twins of this company ply only as far as Genoa and Naples, but they make interesting stops en route at Algeciras (across the bay from Gibraltar) and Cannes, with occasional "extra dividend" calls at Ponta Delgada (Azores) and Barcelona. The Ex ships circle almost the whole Mediterranean, including in their schedules Greece, Cyprus, Egypt, Lebanon and Syria.

CUNARD commenced a new southern route in 1963, the 35,600-ton *Mauretania* sailing ten times a year between New York and Naples, with halts at Gibraltar, Cannes and Genoa. A choice of return from Europe is offered by any other Cunard route.

ITALIAN LINE has been an eager builder of new and newer ships, of ever increasing size and luxury, the process being only temporarily set back by the tragic sinking of the *Andrea Doria* in 1956. To work backwards in presenting this fleet, the 32,000-ton *Leonardo da Vinci*, commissioned in 1959, is the super-luxurious flagship, carrying 1250 passengers in three classes. The 29,000-ton *Cristoforo Colombo*, almost as luxurious and carrying almost as many passengers, was commissioned in 1954. The *Augustus* and the *Giulio Cesare*, both of 27,000 tons, date from 1952 and 1951 but are being maintained in the same top condition that has made and kept them popular. The smaller and much older twins *Vulcania* and *Saturnia* are due to be retired from the New York–Italy service within a year or so, to be replaced by two splendid turbo-liners of 43,000 tons each, the *Michelangelo* and the *Raffaello*, now being built. The first four ships named above ply to Gibraltar, Naples, Cannes and Genoa, in that sequence, while the last two serve Lisbon, Gibraltar, Naples and Genoa, continuing thence around to the Adriatic and so to Venice and Trieste, this latter being their home port.

NATIONAL HELLENIC AMERICAN LINE operates the 21,000-ton *Queen Frederica* to Gibraltar, Málaga, Cannes, Palermo and Naples, continuing to Patras (Greece). Like the *Atlantic* it carries mostly tourist passengers, with space for over 1000 in that class as against 150 in first. It was commissioned in 1927, reconditioned in 1949.

GREEK LINE operates the 23,000-ton *Olympia* to Lisbon, Naples,

Messina and Piraeus, the port of Athens.

The COMPANHIA COLONIAL DE NAVEGAÇAO, a Portuguese shipping concern as its name reveals, has two modern ships of about 22,000 tons each, the *Santa Maria* and the *Vera Cruz*, the former being the vessel that was so spectacularly "shipnaped" by Galvão in February, 1961, and compelled to seek refuge, for a time, in Recife, Brazil. These sail on regular schedules between Miami (Port Everglades) and Lisbon, with halts both ways at Madeira and Tenerife, in the Canaries. Eastbound, they go direct from Miami to Tenerife and then to Funchal (in only 8 days from Florida to Madeira), continuing to Lisbon, sometimes with a preliminary halt at Vigo, Spain. Westbound, after leaving the island ports, they follow a circuitous route via La Guaira, Curaçao and Kingston before reaching Miami. For information on this interesting service consult James Elwell Co., 17 State Street, New York, or Shaw Brothers, P.O. Box 306, Miami.

ZIM ISRAEL LINE'S *Zion, Israel* and *Jerusalem* touch regularly—a good talking point—at Madeira en route to Gibraltar, Piraeus and Haifa. Occasional sailings touch also at Naples.

Canadians may give thought not only to their own huge CANADIAN PACIFIC, which operates some very comprehensive Mediterranean cruises, but to the GRIMALDI-SIOSA LINE's 20,000-ton *Irpinia*, which sails from Montreal and Quebec to Gibraltar, Palermo and Naples.

Ships on the North Atlantic run are far too numerous to list in connection with Mediterranean travels, the most spectacular newcomer being the FRENCH LINE's $75,000,000 *France*, which made her maiden voyage from Le Havre to New York in February, 1962. With a length of 1037 feet this is the world's longest passenger liner, though not quite the heaviest (66,000 tons) and certainly it is one of the most luxurious.

Turning from luxury to thrift, those wishing to consider freighter travel, and it can be marvelous, leisured fun, either on the North Atlantic or the Mediterranean route, should send for Kenneth Ford's *Freighter Travel Guidebook*, a $2.50 volume which is published in revised editions semiannually in March and September, the above price including both editions. The address is Kenneth Ford, 2031 Glendon Avenue, Los Angeles 25. A similar book, this an annual, called *Where to Travel by Freighter*, priced at only $1.00, is published by Harian Publications, Greenlawn, New York.

The passenger lists on low-fare ships that serve four meridional countries directly and many more indirectly, will be, of course, very diversified in nature. There will be fewer American vacationists, more people going back to their motherland for a visit, and in the case of westbound sailings, more that are coming to the New World for the first time. Some of the passengers, especially westbound, will speak no English at all, others will speak it haltingly, with a strong foreign accent. This can be highly interesting to the traveler whose spirit is open and exploratory. We can talk with our own kind, our own friends and neighbors, any time. A slow crossing of the ocean in the company of a widely mixed group may prove fascinating. One feels oneself to be at a floating seminar of the United Nations!

During the off season of tourist passenger traffic to the ports of northern Europe, that is from late fall to early spring, many of the world's famous liners devote themselves to cruises, the two most favored portions of the globe being the Caribbean and the Mediterranean. These cruises are so assiduously advertised by many media, that they need no mention in a book. Two good compendiums dealing with late winter and spring travel, are the International Travel Section of the *New York Times* and the World Travel Guide of the *New York Herald Tribune*, both customarily published on a Sunday in February. The *Chicago Tribune* and the *Christian Science Monitor* also publish excellent travel annuals, and various other large newspapers offer their readers a similar supplement yearly. These are packed with all that is latest, often including a listing of current visa requirements.

The New Role of Motor Travel

Not until relatively recent times has the traveler to Mediterranean lands as a whole been able to think seriously and sensibly of using his car or one rented overseas for the purpose of skirting the entire northern perimeter of the Inland Sea behind the wheel of an automobile, but this can now be logically considered. It is possible, and not too difficult, to drive from Lisbon clear to Istanbul and then even to cross the Bosporus by car-ferry to Anatolia. The intrepid motorist may push along even farther, perhaps to Damascus, Beirut, Jordan, Jerusalem and through the Mandelbaum Gate to Israel, returning to the States ultimately (or sending his car back) by a ship of Zim Israel Line. It is not, of course practicable to motor from Israel to Egypt, but that country can be made a separate side trip, as can Cyprus. Admittedly, it would take a good deal of doing to drive clear through vast Anatolia and Syria, but road travel from Damascus to Beirut to Jerusalem is common, every-day motoring.

The immense trip from Lisbon to Istanbul would present no serious obstacles except, perhaps, the setting in of road fatigue unless a couple of months could be devoted to it. I have talked with a young couple who recently made this whole trip and they pooh-poohed its hardships. They are blessed, however, with unlimited time and money, two blessings which are denied to most of us. From the sea's perimeter the lucky ones who have little concern for time or money may enjoy several side trips to islands, taking their car along by steamer or ferry. Majorca (from Barcelona or Valencia) is one obvious goal. Others are Corsica (from Marseilles or Nice); Sardinia (from Naples); and, of course, Sicily, which can be reached handily by car-ferry across the Strait of Messina or by Tirrenia's overnight car-ferry from Naples to Palermo.

A major link for motorists was opened in 1961 and 1962, when Greece's *Hellenic–Mediterranean Lines* and Italy's *Adriatica Line*, working together in harmony, inaugurated a splendid car-ferry service between Brindisi, a fast-growing port on the heel of Italy, and several ports in Greece, specifically the island port of Corfu, then Igoumenitsa in Epirus and finally Patras, the second port city of Greece, located at the entrance to the Gulf of Corinth, from which city a good coastal highway follows the southern shore of the gulf all the way to Corinth and then to Athens. The Greek ship is named *Egnatia*, the Italian ship *Appia*, this being, as it were, a native of Venice (built at nearby Marghera), evidenced by the winged Lion of St. Mark on its funnel. Each is a splendid motor vessel with accommodations for 750 passengers and 120 to 150 cars. Each has all the comforts and amenities any exigent passenger could ask, including swimming pool. Cabins are comfortable, and for those wishing to economize each has a vast observation lounge filled with reclining chairs where one may doze through the night. Between them the ships make six trips a week, leaving Brindisi every night except Tuesday at 10:30 and arriving at Corfu next morning at 7:30. Igoumenitsa is reached about two hours later, Patras in the early evening between 6 and 7 o'clock.

I have not actually made the trip by either vessel, but I have been all through the *Appia*, which is the newer (though both are newly built) and larger (8000 gross tons as against 6200) and have been immensely impressed. The Greek *Egnatia* is potentially faster (19 knots vs. 17), though speeds are kept the same, and can carry more cars, while the *Appia* is a shade more spacious. Each has Denny Brown stabilizers to minimize the roll of the ship, each has a duty-free shop and each has a travel information office. The *Appia* boasts a new gimmick, being a "telecinema" equipment that transmits to various parts of the ship normal TV programs, films, live entertainments and news reports.

All in all, the opening of this sea road from Italy to Greece, including the superlatively lovely island of Corfu, where, too, you may drive your car from ship to shore, has done more than any other recent development to open up eastern Mediterranean travel to the motorist. But before leaving the subject of transferring yourself and your car to Greece I should mention certain other important services. Hellenic Mediterranean Lines operates good car-taking ships such as the M.S. *Massalia* from Marseille, Genoa, Naples to Piraeus (Athens); and *Olympic Cruises S/A*, a Greek maritime concern associated with Olympic Airways, operates two fine ships, the *Agamemnon* and the *Achilleus*, from France and Italy to Piraeus. They follow two different routes, one from Venice and Brindisi, the other from Marseille and Genoa. Continuing beyond Greece, on varying courses, they touch at Alexandria, Port Said, Limassol (Cyprus) and Beirut. Their schedules and prices are set forth on the regular Olympic Airways timetables.

Finally, as regards Mediterranean motoring, or perhaps this should have been firstly, the intending traveler would do well, before getting too far with plans, to talk over the whole matter with the American Automobile Association, joining the AAA for this purpose if not already a member. The office of the International Travel Department is at 250 Park Avenue, New York 17, but any branch office can furnish full information. The AAA's own annual *Travel Guide to Europe*, distributed gratis to members only, gives detailed information on every phase of motoring and on buying, reselling, renting, etc. More recently an AAA *Travel Guide to the Middle East and the Orient* has appeared and although it lacks the Europe book's information on motoring procedure I have found it very good as a condensed handbook. A publication of comprehensive nature, *ABC's of European Auto Travel*, is offered free by Auto-Europe, a company with offices in several U.S. cities. The New York office is at 25 West 58th Street. A guide that stresses all possible angles of economy is Norman Ford's cheerfully optimistic paperback, *It's Cheaper to Travel*, sold for $1.50 by the firm previously mentioned in connection with freighter travel, Harian Publications, Greenlawn, New York.

Those primarily interested in renting a self-drive car in Italy—the Italian word for rental is *noleggio*—will find an embarrassment of firms to choose from. CIT can handle everything. So can any Fiat dealer and so can Hertz or Avis. There are dozens more. The Hertz rental station in Rome is at Via Sallustiana 28. Avis, with central Rome office at Via Urbana 176, advertises, "We rent other cars but feature Fiat."

CHAPTER 3

TWENTY QUESTIONS, MORE OR LESS—WITH ANSWERS

About Your Passport and Its Visas

To SECURE an American passport, a document that millions of people all over the world would all but sell their souls for, is a simple thing for those of us who were born in the United States, and it is not difficult for naturalized citizens. For citizens it involves merely going to the nearest large-city passport bureau or your local U.S. District Court with ten dollars, two passport-size photographs and, if you have it, proof of citizenship such as birth certificate or a previously granted passport. If you are a noncitizen it is necessary to secure a Treasury Permit, Form 1040D, certifying that you owe no Federal taxes. Your travel agent or transportation company can aid you in securing it. The passport now has a life of three years (formerly only two) and may be extended for two more years for five dollars additional. Processing has been greatly speeded up. One may now expect to get the passport back (accompanied by a booklet of counsels and sound advice) in three to five days maximum.

Passport photography has long been exploited in the large cities, notably including New York, by certain unprincipled shysters who are much more interested in wringing from timid first-timers all the traffic will bear than they are in making good pictures at a fair price, but there are also plenty of reputable persons and firms in the passport photo business. One in New York that I have found dependable, skillful and easy to visit is Columbia Photo Studio at 74 West 50th Street, close to Sixth Avenue (officially and heavily named Avenue of the Americas). It is one flight up in a tiny building that still maintains a toehold in the complex of skyscrapers of Rockefeller Center. The Mediterranean traveler should get at least a dozen or eighteen prints, for in spite of the welcome easing of visa regulations, several consular offices will demand two or three prints, or sometimes even five. They may melt away fast.

One more word, a glowing one, about your American passport. Having never been unable to get one at the drop of a ten-dollar bill you can perhaps have no idea of the incomparable treasure that this pale blue-covered document is today. Its value to travelers in any of the countries covered in this book has advanced to a new high and is beyond computing. Since America reluctantly climbed into a position of leadership in world affairs, and especially since it began distributing recovery dollars, the bearers of its passport have been as welcome as a bright sun after a week of cold rain. The Marshall Plan operations had a major part in putting the postwar tourist industry of Europe and the Mediterranean on its feet, and State Department encouragement to tourism in general strongly stimulated the outflow of dollars, too much so, in fact, as it has turned out, for this has played some part in the depletion of U.S. gold reserves. The rise of America to leadership of the free world has one important and beneficial result for us who travel abroad, namely that the mere casual display of an American passport often gives us a "favored person" rating with frontier functionaries. Time and time again customs men and other border officials whom I have encountered during recent entrances and exits have all but *escorted* me, in the manner of honor guards, through the barriers, as they have done to any other traveler lucky enough to have the distinctive passport, formerly green but now light blue. Quite frankly, I make it a practice to hold the passport very visibly in my hand until I am through with *all* the formalities. Douaniers, as often as not, quickly chalk my bags and wave me on without speaking a single word.

Still another thing, on the practical side. Guard your passport at least as sedulously as you do your money. A lost passport *can* be replaced with another, but this may prove to be a slow, awkward and nerve-racking business. A postwar racket of selling U.S. passports to wealthy refugees, sometimes for fabulous sums, increased the State Department's watchfulness. Fortunately, this racket has now largely died down, but even so hold on to the precious document and *never* leave it lying around carelessly. When frontier officials occasionally pick it up and promise that it shall be returned to you on the plane or train you have to grin and bear it, feeling uneasy till you get it back, but I can say that in a total of many such hazards I have never yet failed to recover mine at the promised place and time.

Visas are an infinitely less thorny matter now than they were a few short years ago. *Every* European non-Communist country has now abolished the visa requirement for Americans. America doesn't reciprocate by abolishing the visa for Europeans, but the authorities over there have decided, after swallowing hard, that it is good business to overlook this inequity, though they still, quite understandably, complain about it.

To get down to business, Mediterranean travelers need no visa for the following countries: Portugal, Spain, Morocco, Tunisia, France, Italy, Greece, Cyprus, Turkey (including the Anatolia portion in Asia). They *do* need a visa for Libya, Egypt, Israel, Lebanon and Syria. Exact regulations and fees (where demanded) are altered from time to time, so there is little point in setting down today's rules, which may be different tomorrow. I can say, however, that in no case of my own recent travels have I found any special or onerous demands such as are still made by a few Latin-American countries, meaning individual letters vouching for one's solvency, bank balance, general health, lack of police record. All you need is a cluster of passport photos, the smallpox vaccination certificate which your own government requires, a few ready dollars and a good-natured willingness to fill in long application forms in duplicate and then the patience to wait a day or two.

I have found Israel the most accommodating, granting your visa gratis *upon arrival* and with no delay whatever. Furthermore, if I may be forgiven for repeating this very important warning from earlier mentions of it, upon request *Israel will grant you a visa on a separate paper instead of stamping it in your passport.* This is of utmost importance in case you intend to visit any of the Arab countries *after* Israel, for if your passport proclaims that you have been to Israel you will almost certainly be denied entrance. The immigration authorities may suspect, or even well know, that you have been to Israel and this probably won't matter, but the passport must not give damning printed *proof* of it. The reason for this anomaly is, I suppose, that a *technical* state of war continues to exist year after year and acceptance by an Arab country of a passport with an Israel visa would be tantamount to recognition that Israel exists. No mail or telegrams from Israel are accepted by the Arab states, so if, while in Israel, the necessity arises to write to anyone in an Arab state you have to enclose your missive in a letter to some friend in a neutral country, say Greece or Turkey (which latter is Moslem but *not* Arab), and ask that your friend mail it for you from that country.

Let me counter the above by stating that an atmosphere of real friendliness to intending American tourists is evident in the consulates and embassies of the Arab countries. The forms to fill in are long and tedious, those of Libya being perhaps the most so, but the officials seem to be generally cordial and personally helpful so long as the applicant doesn't display a chip on his shoulder. I will long remember, for instance, the friendly manner of the UAR (Egypt) official when I applied for my visa in the New York passport office of that country. His smile was enough to melt away any feeling of apprehension, and the officials in the UAR State Tourist Offices both in New York and Cairo have proved as warmly welcoming as any I have encountered.

The addresses of the New York and Washington consulates and embassies from which Mediterranean visas are to be secured in advance of your visit are as follows: given in sequence from west to east:

Libya: The Libyan Embassy, Washington D.C.
United Arab Republic (Egypt): The New York Consulate General is at 902 Park Avenue.
Lebanon: The New York Consulate General is at 9 East 76th Street.
Syria: The *Syrian Arab Republic*, as it is now called, maintains a New York consulate at 307 East 44th Street. For other information address: The Embassy of the Syrian Arab Republic, Washington, D.C.

About Your Vaccination Certificate

This answer may be given in reassuring terms. You *must* be in possession of a smallpox vaccination certificate since your own U.S. government makes it a requirement for your re-entry into the States and the date of the certificate must be within three years of your re-entry. The yellow form approved by the World Health Organization must be used, but this is sent with the passport and it is also securable from the nearest office of the U.S. Public Health Service (or inquire at any passport office). Most probably you will be able to secure it also from the office of the air or steamship line you are using for your departure from home shores. Your own physician will do the vaccinating, but you have to allow a week or ten days to determine the success of it. Then the certificate must be stamped by your state's Department of Public Health or by the Public Health Service office of the area in which you were vaccinated.

I am happy to say that no special "shots" or immunization except the standard one against smallpox are now *required* by any of the Mediterranean countries, but cautious travelers planning to visit North African shores often take inoculations against typhoid and a few of the most cautious go the whole way, submitting to inoculations against cholera, typhus and influenza. To go that far when visiting merely the lands that fringe the Mediterranean seems to me as needless as it is boresome, expensive and time-consuming. I have never followed the "shot course" to its limits unless compelled to do so, but my example should not necessarily be followed. Maybe I've just been lucky.

About Health Hazards

Tourist talk, if my ears are to be trusted, tends to devote an inordinate proportion of its time to three burning subjects, in this order: costs; tipping (this in lowered tones); and health considerations. In unfamiliar lands of unfamiliar races and customs the third subject often moves up to the number one spot.

I am not a good person to give advice, since I have too often taken a chance and gotten away with it—so far. But even so I feel moved to state that countless tourists worry far too much about health hazards, especially when traveling for the first time. The world's health has improved greatly in the period since World War II and, so, to a lesser extent, has its sanitation, and so has its medical knowledge, especially with the development of antibiotics.

Public water supply is a conspicuous villain and thousands of U.S. tourists will have none of it in any country outside their own and, presumably, Canada and Britain. I have drunk it without ill effects almost everywhere, at least in leading hotels and restaurants, but there again I am not a good counselor. Perhaps I have built up a full set of immunities or perhaps, next time, I will drink it once too often. If you are of very cautious mold, a wise virgin or matron or man, be advised that bottled mineral water is available all over the civilized and semicivilized earth. If you stick to that, without openly doubting the reassurances of hôteliers and restaurateurs, you will endear yourself to them and to their balance sheets. If you are a middle-of-the-roader you will probably drink the water almost everywhere in Europe including the lands that border the Mediterranean, but will tend to shy away from it in Africa and Asian coastal areas, except when assured of its safety by people whom you trust. The commonest threat of impure water is what doctors call D.D. (diarrheic disturbance).

Food presents more varied threats than water, especially the threat of dysentery, so I will set down here, for the consideration of whom it may concern, some elemental counsels on food which I have included in a book on certain tropical or semitropical lands of Latin America. Here they are: Avoid lettuce, uncooked vegetables and fruit that cannot be peeled.

About Foreign Tourist Offices in New York

Many of the Mediterranean countries, like those of central and northern Europe, maintain in New York tourist offices that are entirely distinct from their consulates. In every case I have found them well-springs of helpful information, reinforced by tourist literature that makes one's forthcoming trip far easier to plan

Without elaboration I will list their official titles and addresses, following the west-to-east sequence of this book. In a number of cases these governments maintain offices also in several other cities of the U.S. and Canada.

1. *Casa de Portugal*, 447 Madison Avenue (corner of 50th Street).
2. *Spanish National Tourist Office*, 485 Madison Avenue (corner of 52nd Street).
3. *French Government Tourist Office*, 610 Fifth Avenue. (In this same building the office of the *French National Railroads* is also very co-operative in the giving of information and attractive literature. The building of *Air France* is near by, at 683 Fifth Avenue.)
4. *Italian National Tourist Office* (ENIT), 626 Fifth Avenue (Palazzo d'Italia). (The *Italian State Railways* and CIT have

offices at 11 West 42nd Street; *Alitalia* is at 666 Fifth Avenue.)

5. *National Tourist Organization of Greece*, 69 East 79th Street.
6. *Cyprus* has no New York tourist office but dispenses information from its embassy in Washington, or one may address the Ministry of Commerce and Industry, Tourist Section, Nicosía, Cyprus.
7. *Israel Government Tourist Office*, 574 Fifth Avenue.
8. *Lebanon* has no New York tourist office but dispenses information through the Consulate General at 9 East 76th Street.
9. The *Syrian Arab Republic* gives out tourist information from its consulate at 307 East 44th Street.
10. *Turkish Information Office*, 500 Fifth Avenue.

Note: For tourist information on *Morocco, Algeria, Tunisia* and *Libya*, one should address the respective embassies in Washington. In the case of Morocco one may also contact the Consulate General in New York (342 Madison Avenue).

About Mediterranean Moneys and Your Dollars

The day of one-world currency seems as remote as ever but at least the rigid frontier money controls that were in force during the first decade after the war have been very greatly relaxed or abandoned by most countries. On the Mediterranean trips that went into the making of this book I used sixteen different kinds of money and encountered some strange and amusing kinks in the jigsaw puzzle, but it is comforting —for Americans—to know that American dollars are quite as welcome everywhere as is the currency of the country concerned. In some cases bills, as for the purchase of domestic airplane tickets, are rendered in dollars and must be paid in dollars or their equivalent at the exchange rate prevailing on the particular day of the transaction.

As to the relative cost of all the things that make up tourism, I should say that Spain, Portugal, Egypt and Turkey are still very inexpensive, France and Italy very expensive. Greece used to be inexpensive but prices have soared. I think it is fair to say that it is now in the middle range.

Perhaps this book can perform a service to travelers by telling in brief, down-to-the-pocket language the present money situation in each of the countries to be covered, but rather than present the whole roster of the moneys here I shall present the currency of *each country in turn*, as this book, in the "Yourself" chapters (4 through 25), reaches it.

Some printed lists of exchange are so bankerish and legalistic that they tend to confuse rather than help the lay traveler, though one or two good ones are sold in bookstores and several air lines give currency converter cards gratis to their customers. Air France recently brought out a new one, well organized in columns, with eighty countries listed alphabetically and by continents. The converter may be had in advance by addressing Colette d'Orsay, Travel Consultant Air France, 683 Fifth Avenue, New York 22. The lady will also be ready to offer current hints on packing, on how to bone up for your tour and on Paris shopping. What we are concerned with is what the money looks like, what it is worth in dollars, what it will buy.

And speaking of dollars, *your* dollars, a few words of counsel may be order here. Most travelers nowadays take their money in the form of travelers checks rather than letters of credit and that is as it should be. In foreign countries letters of credit are ponderous affairs, convertible into cash only at certain banks and sometimes after many minutes of tedious red tape. Unless you are planning to stay a long time in one or two countries and spend a lot of money there it is well to travel with the world-wide American Express checks that are known everywhere and are cashed instantly, even, in very many cases, by hotels and shops. Take some of your funds in small checks, $10 and $20, so you will not be stuck in some country at the last minute for a little money and have to change a big check into escudos, drachmas or Near East pounds. This caution seems elementary but it is very often overlooked. I recently met a tourist who was forced to cash a $50 check on his last day in Greece to pay a laundry bill of 60 drachmas ($2.00).

In addition to travelers checks I think it is smart practice to take at least some money in ten-dollar and five-dollar bills, and for last-minute surprises, like the laundry bill above, a roll of ones is comforting.

There are some exchange brokers, especially in New York, whose sole business is the purchase and sale of foreign moneys. The reputable ones know the day-to-day rates and quote them honestly. They will tell you, also, how much of any given currency you may legally take into the country of its origin and how much you may take out when leaving. In all such matters they are valuable consultants. A New York concern that I personally have dealt with for years and found always courteous and reliable is *Lionel Perera, Manfra and Brookes*, whose convenient midtown office is on the street-floor corridor (north side) of the RCA Building, 40 Rockefeller Plaza, with an entrance also from West 50th Street (Number 48). The firm's downtown office is at 44 Whitehall. The firm sells, for $10 each, what it calls "tip packs" of the more important currencies, such as French francs, Italian lire and Spanish pesetas. This is ten dollars' worth of the foreign money concerned in small denominations, both paper and coins. The idea is to tide the traveler over the awkwardness of arrival in the said countries, providing actual tip and taxi money in handy form. Instead, for instance, of arriving in Spain with only 500-peseta or 1000-peseta notes when 50 pesetas would be ample for the taxi from the airport terminal to your hotel, and 25 pesetas for the luggage porter's tip, you have the bills or coins you need for first things. This tip pack is a smart idea, as I need hardly tell you, since taxi men in foreign cities that cater to tourists are rarely possessed of the proper amount of change, if, indeed, they admit having any at all.

If you wish to buy money of certain specific countries not on the beaten tracks of trade or tourism it is advisable to give advance notice to this concern or some other of your choice, since it may take a day or two to secure the needed currency, but the moneys of all the *European* countries bordering the Mediterranean seem always to be in good supply. The moneys of the African and Asiatic countries warrant special inquiry. Sometimes there is a substantial spread between the free rate and the government's pegged rate but in such cases there are likely to be sharp restrictions on currency importation. At the present time I think you will have no thorny problems in the case of Israel, Lebanon or Cyprus, but the situation as regards the UAR (Egypt) may call for a heart-to-heart talk with your broker. Turkey's requirements used to be thorny but have recently been greatly eased.

About Your U.S. Customs Exemption When Returning

A backlash of the storm of concern that developed in 1960 and 1961 over the continuing drain on the gold supply of the United States was the drastic reduction of the free customs allowance for returning

U.S. residents from $500 to $100, the figure that had prevailed until the inauguration of the Marshall Plan. The big raise in the figure at that time was intended, of course, to spur the flow of foreign currency to war-torn countries striving to rebuild their economies. The scheme worked well, too well as it turned out, and our Treasury Department became alarmed. It has been said by many a disgruntled tourist, foreign shopkeeper and lay economist that so sharp and sudden a reduction was intended not so much as a measure to save a few paltry millions in a fiscal matter involving many billions as it was to awaken the American public to the fact that the dollar is not, after all, almighty, but could actually be endangered.

Well—here's the story as of now: In September, 1961, the free allowance was reduced, as I've said, from $500 to $100 for the period ending June 30, 1963, presumably then to be extended. This was a sharp blow to tourist shopkeepers all over the world, and not least in the Mediterranean lands. Many tourists were and still are a bit sore about this turn of events, but there are some mitigating features. For one thing, allowances for returning families can still be lumped together, as formerly, even babes in arms being allowed the full $100. For another thing, the *wholesale prices* of goods bought abroad form the basis for figuring the totals and that is usually considered to make an average difference of about 20 to 25 per cent. In my own experience, U.S. customs officers are sometimely annoyingly vague in acknowledging that this is actually a part of the law, and the declaration itself specifically instructs us to list "the actual price paid or the fair value of items acquired otherwise than by purchase," but a bit of friendly pressure, *not* angry storming, generally seems to win acknowledgment in the end.

Another mitigating provision of utmost importance, though this *may* soon be rescinded, is this: You may send home by mail from abroad, or have shops send for you, as many gifts, each one not to exceed $10 in value, as you like, provided each parcel is an *Unsolicited Gift, Value Under $10*, and is so marked. The only restriction, as I understand the law, and that a very innocuous one, is that you may not mail more than one such gift to the same person on the same day. The "ten dollar privilege" has been grossly abused by some travelers and Congress is now debating the desirability of cutting the $10 figure to $1, which might as well be zero.

One gallon of alcoholic beverages may be included in the customs exemption, but "customs officials will not release liquors destined to any state for use in violation of its laws."

Perfume—this is the direct wording of a government folder—is admitted as follows: one bottle, of any size, of each fragrancy of those brands—there are now about twenty—sold under their registered trademarks in America. Other brands are subject to no special limitation. Shops selling perfumes are supposed to know which brands are under the protection of American trade-mark agreements and thus to be able to give the needed information to purchasers.

About Weather and Seasons

No all-inclusive statement about Mediterranean weather can be given, though some generalities may be ventured. There is certainly much more "meteorological harmony" in the lands of the Inland Sea than in Europe or America. As a personal report, I may mention that on my earlier journey for this book, lasting four months, from late September to late January, only *three* days were ruined by rain, and about half a dozen others more or less marred. On my recent three-months' journey for this edition I had equally good luck, a thing which I would not have thought possible. I am sure I had a far better than average break in this. Egypt, however, is as steady as a rock. In the latitudes from Cairo to Aswan inclusive, it virtually never rains, and the days from November to March are straight out of the Handbook of Perfections, neither too hot nor too cold. On both trips, totaling seven months, I carried no winter coat nor topcoat but only an all-weather raincoat, which proved quite enough.

French North Africa can be raw and cold in winter. It does, in fact, find it easy to be "that way." Portugal, southern Spain, the Balearics and the Alp-protected French Riviera are usually mild and balmy. The same is true of Italy's two Rivieras, the Ponente one, centering around San Remo, being especially pleasant. Florence and Rome can often be raw. Naples is generally well-behaved and Sicily delightful, as is Malta. Israel looks for the annual big, raw rains at, or right after, Christmas time. Athens can be temperamental in winter, but much oftener balmy than otherwise. Crete, Rhodes, Cyprus and the other islands thereabouts are, in general, winter havens. Istanbul has almost all weathers, including rare snows, and Ankara, on high, inland ground, can have a good deal of that winter commodity.

In summer it is undeniably hot in most parts of the Mediterranean but in coastal towns and resorts the heat is nicely tempered by sea breezes. In most of the countries except Egypt there are hill towns or cool mountain resorts not far from the big ports or capitals. An advantage of summer travel, except in Spain, Portugal, France and Italy, is that the tourist crowds aren't there. You have the Mediterranean more or less to yourself. In *The Pageant of theMediterranean*, by Sheridon H. Garth, there is a weather comment which seems to me fair and discerning. Says the author: "The Mediterranean climate is characterized by warm days with clear blue skies, exceptional luminosity and bright light; however the nights are cool even on the desert. . . . The typical Mediterranean climate covers those limits in which the olive tree grows, which include the entire perimeter of the great sea and from 10 to 200 miles inland, depending upon the altitude."

About Luggage and Clothing

Cruise passengers have no special worries about luggage weight. They may take virtually all they want, and with no transfers involved (except light bags on shore excursions) they are "all set." Those who cross by steamer have a very ample free allowance—now 275 pounds—but in traveling about with trunks after quitting the steamer they are faced with the universal problems of high charges for excess weight, difficulty in finding porters at the stations, and so on. Air travelers are so obviously concerned with the weight problem that they generally take due thought of it in advance. Transatlantic lines now permit 30 kilos (66 pounds) free of charge in first class, 20 kilos (44 pounds) in economy class (which replaced the former tourist class, lowering the tariff). Short local services in the Mediterranean, not taken in conjunction with a first-class overseas flight, generally allow 20 kilos free and occasionally only 15 (33 pounds). Excess weight charges are customarily 1 per cent per kilo of the normal first-class one-way fare. For a transatlantic crossing this means that you pay, at present, well over

$2.00 a pound, each way, for the extra weight, so it is no negligible matter.

One of the airlines acquainted me with the luggage of *Daisy Products* of New York and I stocked myself with two Daisy suitcases, along with a big leather briefcase that held my Hermes Rocket typewriter and a lot of guides and booklets, and used them as my total luggage on both of the long Mediterranean journeys that went into the making of this book. The suitcases are claimed to be the world's lightest and I should think they must be at least as light as any, unless one goes in for sheer cardboard, for the larger of my two, being 26 inches by 16 by 9, weighs just over six pounds. They are zipper bags, but the zippers are devised so that may be zipped from both sides to a padlock in the center, making them far more secure and resistant to porter roughage than if the padlock were at the bottom. Perhaps the padlock would not present too formidable a challenge to thieves, but, for that matter, half the bags carried by tourists could be opened, it seems, by a paper clip or a hairpin! I have been delighted with my featherweight bags. They may be tricked out, upon request, with inside pockets, front back and/or sides, held by flexible steel. I have figured that on each of the Mediterranean tours they saved me, in all, a good sixty dollars that I would have had to pay in excess weight charges had they been of a heavy material. For women's use the same company puts out a smart-looking, outsized overnight bag for toiletries, with room for an amazing number of additional items, such as I have not seen duplicated.

Clothing for air travel is a subject that is so often covered in airline literature—Air France, in its Practical Advice folder, outlines the exact suggested contents of your bags, whether masculine or feminine—that it need not be discussed in detail here, but the subject of nylon, and its younger textile cousins and indeed all the drip-dry race, is of perennial interest. More and more men are taking along only four or five shirts, instead of ten or twelve, and washing out one every night for its quick-drying, self-ironing performance. Nylon pajamas and shorts are too hot in warm weather but undershirts and socks, if of the ribbed type and absorbent, seem to work out all right. It takes only a quarter of an hour to whip through one's nightly laundry and it saves a *lot* on hotel laundry charges.

Women travelers are, of course, even more addicted to these quick-drying textiles than are men, and nowadays blouses and dresses of such materials have taken on a remarkable variety and charm. They are the answer to a light-traveler's prayer. Knitwear garments, in various materials and suitable for almost any occasion, have multiplied as the practicality of them has become more and more apparent.

About Electric Appliances

Most hotels in Europe and throughout the Mediterranean take a very dim view of guests who attempt to use portable electric irons in their rooms, but electric shavers are quite another matter. Not only is their use permitted but in many de luxe hotels it is facilitated by special plugs specially labeled, with the voltage given. I have found that such shavers as the Philips Norelco, with voltages adjustable to either 110 or 220 volts and with a plastic plug converter to fit foreign sockets, can be used practically anywhere and everywhere. Not once on this complicated Mediterranean trip did I have to revert to the lather-and-razor equipment that I had brought along in case of need.

About Mail, Coming and Going

The receiving and sending of home mail is a matter of such major importance to tourists, including those who are traveling "to get away from it all," that it can almost make or unmake a trip. Passengers on cruise steamers have the whole problem solved for them, all along the route, but others must take due thought of it.

There are various channels for receiving mail, when abroad, and I think I have tried them all. After such trial, and error, I have come to the conclusion that the most satisfactory channel is through a few key hotels at key points on one's journey. This is more direct and I have found it quite as safe as any. On an all-Mediterranean trip one might pick a large hotel in each of three centers, say one in Spain, one in Italy and one in Athens. If the traveler will take time, in each case, to cultivate the head porter, supplementing this personal effort with generous pourboires and some extra money for the forwarding of all letters *by air* —steamer mail, except to Europe, is useless, often taking a month or more—he will be pretty sure to receive all letters safely and in reasonably quick time. I have found the head porters of the leading hotels remarkably dependable, and if they are given the forwarding job as a personal and honorable commission they will generally take pride in doing it well.

A great many travelers use the American Express or Cook offices, which have a lot of knowledge and assurance in doing their mail duties, but such offices are often not open at the particular hour you wish to visit them, and with throngs of tourists always using their services a duplication or triplication of names is not uncommon, causing endless confusion.

Probably the worst of all mail channels is *Poste Restante*, which is Europe's phrase for General Delivery. Post office clerks are rushed and indifferent, and in many countries, including Italy, the surname is used first in addressing letters. Once, before I knew better, I haunted the Rome central post office for days on end, getting more and more disturbed as the clerk said each day, "*Niente, signor.*" Finally, in desperation, I begged, "Look under *S.* Maybe you have filed my letters under my first name." He did and he had. In a rather contemptuous manner he handed me fourteen accumulated letters.

In sending off letters—and one should use only air mail unless time matters not at all—I suppose the simplest way, in a complicated, many-country journey, is to do as most tourists do, use the services of the hotel mail clerks and depend on them. Ordinarily I rebel at this. I like to know what the postage is and put on the correct stamps myself. Furthermore, some clerks are not above putting on surface-mail postage when you have given them the money for air-mail postage, pocketing the very considerable difference. But in moving rapidly from country to country it may not be "worth the pain" to master all the different quirks of the varying rates. In Egypt, for instance, the system is extremely complex, with many different rates for different countries, and the same, to a lesser degree, is true of Greece. It is quite easy, on the other hand, to ascertain the 5-gram and 10-gram and post card tariff for air mail to your own country, presumably the U.S.A., and do your own stamping. Air France recently got out, and now distributes, a post card-sized international postal rate guide, giving the current minimum charge for air mail postage from almost every country in the world to the United States and, similarly, the charge for air mail post cards to the

States. I have found this invaluable as a time saver and hope the company will continue to distribute it, with such revisions from time to time as may be necessary. The guide, actually a single card, can be obtained from any AF office or by writing to P.O. Box 3577, New York 17.

Air-mail postage, by the way, is considerably more expensive *to* America than *from* it. Nearly all other countries except those following British traditions, use the gram system of weighing and charging, and five grams, the usual basic weight, will allow you only one thin sheet and envelope. Overweight letters come high. A half-ounce letter sent from Europe to America will often cost two or three times as much as a letter of the same weight sent from America to Europe. But whatever it costs, air mail is the only thing nowadays.

About Language and Languages

English has gone round the world. Even before either of the World Wars it was advancing like a strong tide, but with their coming and going it picked up a swift pace, replacing French in many lands. French is still, of course, the language of North Africa and it is of some importance in Egypt, Greece and Turkey. Syria and Lebanon, which were under French mandate between the wars, still use a good deal of French in the upper strata of business and society. In Israel alone, German is fairly important because of the influx to that country of Hitler-persecuted Jews. Travelers who speak enough Spanish and Italian to use these tongues in Spain and Italy are lucky. Their knowledge certainly enhances their travel pleasure. But Portuguese, spoken virtually nowhere except in Portugal and its empire and in Brazil, is hardly worth struggling to acquire. It is an ugly language in sound, as any candid Portuguese will admit, because of the very frequent recurrence of the *ão* sound (as in a cat's "meow") and the *sh* and *zh* sound for *s*. To give examples, San Sebastian becomes São Sebastião, and *dois escudos* (two escudos) evolves in speech as doizh eshcudozh. English has some ugly sounds, too, and it has a great many indefensible oddities, but over a quarter of a billion people speak it as their native tongue and it is today the nearest thing there is to a world language.

In a valiant effort, if I do say it, to be as useful as I can in this book,

I propose to indicate the pronunciation of certain difficult place names, and above all the *accented syllable* of such names. Pronunciations I shall indicate only once, usually when the name or word first occurs, but in stress of syllable I shall put on an accent, in a few important cases of presumable tourist doubt, whenever the name recurs, even though the language concerned may actually have no graphic accent on such syllables. It would have saved me some minor embarrassments, for instance, had I known upon arrival there that Nicosía, the capital of Cyprus, is accented that way rather than Nicósia. And, for a more obvious example—it hurts the sensitive ear to hear the fabulous island of Naples' bay called Caprí, as it is nowadays by nine Americans out of ten, simply because one of our popular songs of many years back required an accent on the last syllable in order to fit the rhythm of the music. The place is, of course, Cápri, as it has been since the days of Emperor Tiberius; and since I have disposed of this conspicuous name I shall *not* accent it later in the book. Another very common tourist mispronunciation is Monáco, instead of the correct Mónacó. (Strictly correct French would have no strong accent on any syllable, but would certainly avoid stressing the penult.)

Greek, Arabic, Hebrew and Turkish names, which must be set into approximate sounds in Latin letters, present dreadful problems. Assouan, to give one instance, is spelled Assuan, Asswan, Aswan and in several other ways. I may sometimes be guilty hereinafter of similar inconsistencies. I make no guarantees. But I will do my best to decide, in each case, and cling to my decision. Aswan shall be my choice for the above name.

About Tips—Air, Sea and Land

The giving of tips is no more an exact science than is theology or luck. The best I can do, in trying to cope with it, is to make a few "observations," with which the next traveler you meet will promptly disagree—and the next one will disagree with him.

In airplanes tips are forbidden and tipping actually isn't done. This raises aircraft personnel to the level of business associates.

In sea travel tipping is universal, but there is no rule or schedule for it. A traveler once told me that the total steamer tips should be 10 per cent of the fare, which I thought, and think, absurd. The fare has nothing to do with it, any more than it would on a train or bus. Sometimes 10 per cent would be too little, sometimes too much. All you can do is to figure approximately what the service is worth, in tips, and act accordingly. A steward or stewardess, or both, take care of your room, so you may figure what such service is worth per day and multiply it by the number of days of the trip. (This thing is more awkward if two of the ship's staff share the work. You can only divide up the sum as fairly as possible.) In the dining saloon you will want to tip not quite as if for each meal, but say a dollar and a half or two dollars a day to your table steward (this in first class; one dollar in tourist class) and, at the end of the voyage, five or ten to the head steward, depending upon what he has done for your comfort. The deck steward, the bar steward, the lounge steward and the library steward will all "rate," but not in any major way (unless, in the case of the bar steward, you have given him a lot of trade). The purser is, of course, an *officer*, and nothing could be more socially inept than to try to tip him, unless it were to tip the captain!

Nearly all Mediterannean countries, as well as all European countries —but never England—have adopted a service charge in hotels. Often it is 10 per cent, oftener 12 or 15 per cent, and sometimes, as in Rome, 18 per cent. That certainly is plenty, yet most travelers stopping at good hotels and eating at good restaurants add a small sweetener. You occasionally see signs that "tipping is abolished" in lieu of the service charge, but this notice is rarely to be taken at its full face value. Your servitor will show his disappointment if you do so take it. In hotels it is well to remember the head porter rather specially. He is a good cut above the room and table servants and often he makes the difference between a pleasant stay and a mere stay. In Turkey there is a 10 per cent service charge in hotels, but here, I should say, another 10 per cent in tips is certainly expected. The total percentage is hardly any more than you would pay in Italy or France or Spain.

Theater ushers often and taxi drivers almost always expect a small tip. Luggage porters often work theoretically on a tariff basis, but few travelers ever know what the tariff is. It is pretty safe, and frequently it is very lavish, to give, in the currency of the country, about what you would give in American money at home. To close with a little homily, overtipping is "immoral," but stinginess is worse. If, in all cases, you can hit upon the happy medium, certain that you have been fair to all, "you're a better man than I am, Gunga Din!"

About Shops and Souks in Many Countries

This is not going to be a halt-by-halt compendium on shopping, but a miscellaneous collection of remarks on a mighty subject that is more feminine than masculine.

Portugal tempts the shopper with charming items of costume jewelry, notably gold and silver filigree work, with pleasant novelties made of Portuguese cork, and with exquisite embroidered linens from Madeira, of which more will be said in Chapter 5.

Spain offers certain specialties to the eager shopper, but is not by any means another France or Italy. Its great charm, at present, is the cheapness, in dollars, of many of the offerings. Beautiful pottery and faience and damascened Toledo work are to be found, all except the last-named being difficult to get home, and there is still a fairly brisk trade in antiques, of interest to those who *know* antiques and are not easily fooled. Spanish mantillas are often very lovely and after all, who cares if they *may* have been manufactured in some Oriental country and imported to Spain? Linens, gloves and leather goods will prove tempting. Dresses, custom-made suits and handmade shoes are vastly cheaper than would be their counterparts in America.

North Africa has some wonderfully fascinating souks, which are native bazaars, and, as I have said, the one in Tunis that climbs the hill beyond the Place de France, is, to my mind *the* souk of souks in all of French North Africa. Innumerable open shops present a dazzling array of just about everything Oriental and Arabic that your imagination could dream up. Brass and copper ware, costume jewelry and hand-woven textiles and rugs seem to predominate, but these are only a few of the myriads of things for sale.

France has set up a special advance service to shoppers, available at AF ticket offices. There, through the Travel Consultant Service, one may secure up-to-date tips on current shopping opportunities in any French city. The French Riviera, to come to Mediterranean shores, is proud of Grasse, the perfume town, par excellence. It is easy, and fascinating, to visit the perfume factories (and sales rooms) of this town, whose floral fragrance you can smell for miles, and you will ultimately leave Grasse poorer in pocket but laden with exquisite items that you had no intention whatever of buying.

Italy's wealth of things to buy is proverbial. Florence is the shopper's special paradise, but Venice, Rome and Taormina are almost equally full of temptations. Silks, embroidered blouses and fancy lingerie, tooled leather items, Murano glassware, Naples coral and cameo works of craftsmanship, superb books of art, these are but the merest samples of what the visitor finds. Ties, Borsalino hats, handbags, tortoise shell and amber ware are other samples.

Malta's lace is deservedly famous. Homespun cotton cloths and wool rugs are also of interest. The *Malta Industries Association* is pleased to show how these various things are made in its factory in the village of Rabat, and it is more than pleased to have you buy things in its factory shop.

Egypt is the crossroads of East and West, but in its bazaars, especially those on and near the famous *Mousky* of Cairo, the East is in complete control of the situation. In the covered bazaars of *Khan Khalil*, just off the Mousky on the north side, wonderful works of craftsmanship in gold, silver, copper and brass stop you in your tracks time and again. There are items in amber and in ivory and in sandalwood; queer trinkets and curios and bibelots; Oriental carpets and rugs; strange spices and perfumes, such as attar of lotus; intricately wrought jewels; brooches and rings set with alexandrite stones, this being a strange stone of the chrysoberyl family looking pale blue or greenish by daylight, reddish-purple by electric light. Cairo is one of the world's great lures to the exploratory shopper and to the mere gazer at things of the East.

Greece is by no means a bargain country like Spain in prices of things to buy but it does offer many attractive, hand-wrought items, some of them novel and eye-catching, that are just right for gifts to take or send home. Several shops in Athens' hotel sector, on Stadion Street and Venizelos Avenue, are as bright and appealing as any gift shops (of inexpensive nature) in Europe. On the island of Rhodes similar articles are in evidence in great profusion and they are called tax-free. Tourists may take them back freely to mainland Greece, but native Greeks, as I was told, are not supposed to do so.

Cyprus, being ethnically Greek, offers the same sort of things one finds in Athens and Rhodes. Some of the silk and linen blouses in the Ledra Street shop windows of Nicosía are so beautifully embroidered that they hypnotized even a resister like myself. I went in—and succumbed.

Israel's shopping possibilities have developed considerably in the short span of the nation's life and one may now find fascinating shops, especially in the fast advancing cities of Tel Aviv and Haifa. Among the more interesting gift and souvenir shops are those operated by WIZO, meaning Women's International Zionist Organization. Attractive souvenirs in metal, olive wood and costume jewelry are available in many a shop.

Lebanon offers marvelous handmade brocades, procurable in various Beirut shops and in the widely known establishment called *Papa George's Shop* in Baalbek or in its smaller Beirut branch near the St. George Hotel. It also offers alluring souvenirs in inlaid woods and in brass and copper. European and American goods are procurable in wide variety.

Syria also offers brocades of the very finest quality, those of *S. G. Nassan & Company* of Damascus being probably the best known. This was the firm that made the brocade for the celebrated wedding dress of Princess (now Queen) Elizabeth, with the lovebird design in gold thread on white silk. The same design and scores of others are still being woven into elegant goods in the firm's various plants at prices that seem like excellent bargains. I was told that silver-thread brocade is priced as low as $5.00 a meter, and that even the de luxe brocade in the lovebird design selected by Elizabeth may be purchased for about $14.00 a meter. Two expert craftsmen, working together, can weave about two and a half yards of this cloth in a day. Nassan & Company, calling itself "the oldest factory in the oldest city of the world," also produces wonderful brassware, some pieces inlaid with gold, silver or copper, woolen and silk rugs, fancy tables and table nests inlaid with ivory or mother of pearl, Oriental tiles and bric-a-brac of all sorts. Another large firm making fine brocades and the other things named above, is *Asfar and Sarkis*, with a store in Damascus' main Souk Hamidieh and a branch in Beirut.

In the seething bazaars of Damascus fine rugs, inlaid woodwork and artistic cabinetry may be found in abundance and it is almost fair to say that in its multitude of shops and booths *anything* may be found. Silver filigree work is one thing, of many, that comes to my mind. The bazaars of Damascus, mile upon mile, are a sort of Caledonian Fair, raised to the nth power and touched by the authentic wand of the East.

Turkey has bazaars that must be seen to be believed, and this goes even for those who have been "initiated" in the ruder and noisier souks of Cairo and Damascus. The chief bazaar, in the old part of Istanbul, fairly "sears the senses" and I cannot dismiss it here in a sentence or two. It will be viewed later, in Chapter 25. It is enough to say here that when you enter it—the thing is all under cover—you'll do remarkably well to emerge within three hours. It is a prodigious labyrinth of wares, from pure gold, literally millions of dollars' worth of it in every form of jewelry—but alas, you may not legally export *any* gold except charms from Turkey—to rose-leaf liqueurs, to hand-painted ceramics, to meerschaum masterpieces, to Bursa silks and handmade embroideries, to rugs in their thousands, to acres of furniture that must have been brought in by magic since there is obviously no human means of getting such big stuff through the tortuous alleys of trade. Istanbul's Grand Bazaar can be a fitting climax to the explorations of the maddest Mediterranean shopper. There's nothing to surpass it anywhere.

And now two final shopping notes: (1) The AAA issues an 80-page *Shopping Guide*, available to members; (2) *Be My Guest, Inc.*, 10 West 43rd Street, New York City 36, has instituted a gift service whereby you may send to relatives and friends a bon voyage gift quite different from the standard flower-fruit-books routine. The service, like the corporation, is called Be My Guest and by means of it the person you wish to favor receives your invitation to have, on foreign soil, a fine dinner, a pair of theater tickets or concert or opera tickets, a delivered package of perfume, accessories or whatever you designate. The idea is an interesting one and it works. *Town and Country Magazine* has pushed the project.

About Mediterranean Evenings and Nights

I have never had a "night club tan" and am but a timid pilgrim in lush nocturnal fields, but in many parts of the Mediterranean I have "looked into the matter" and as this book rolls along from west to east I will submit some tentative notes and findings. Here I may report some generalities and a few specific attractions that may conceivably have some bearing on the course of your itinerary. In the case of cities that have after-dark importance, a closer look will be taken when this book reaches those cities in the chapters following.

Lisbon is a good night town, with some sophisticated, international nightspots and, far more distinctively, some *adegas* (literally cellars) of food and fado singing that captivate all comers. Fado is Lisbon's very own invention, a sad-sweet type of song that is like nothing else in the night world. It will be explained in Chapter 6.

Spain is fairly lavish in providing night fun. Madrid has numerous lively cabarets, with dancing, but the most distinctively Spanish places are the summer restaurants, for dining and dancing under the stars. Barcelona appeals rather more in this respect because of its milder climate, with a six-month summer. Some of its open-air restaurants-with-floor-show have wonderful verve and color. In this subtropical city it is pleasant, also, to sit and sip in its sidewalk *horchaterías*—but I am going to save that word for unveiling in Chapter 7.

Casablanca is *not*, at least now, the city of glamorous, intrigue-laden nights that Hollywood would have us think, though a few pleasant dives do exist. *Algiers'* storied Kasbah still, or again, climbs its motley slopes. *Tunis* is dead at night. By nine o'clock its streets and cafés are pretty well deserted.

The *French Riviera* has so much and such widely-known night life, especially in Cannes, Nice and Monte Carlo, that it needs no discussion here.

Rome is more newsworthy. It must be reported that the Eternal City is now striving rather earnestly to give tourists what they are supposed to want. Many of its night clubs, however, still come more under the head of "dancings," with beguiling hostesses boldly on the make, than of Paris-style cabarets. Rome, like Lisbon, has some cellars of song —bottles by the hundred in wall recesses, Greek-looking amphorae filled with nectar, guitars in skillful hands—and some of them have special character. Since this book will not be lingering much in Rome I may mention two or three names here. Ask your taxi man, or preferably your driver of a horse-drawn calèche, to take you to *La*

Biblioteca del Valle or to *Taverna Ulpi* or, above all, to *Hostaria dell'Orso*, a most elegant and distinctive night restaurant in a house where Dante is supposed to have lived. A newer and very lively four-part nightspot on famous Via Véneto is called *Angolo di Roma*. For terrace dining consider *Capriccio*'s, and for a terrace café high above central Rome the establishment called the *Casino*, on the Pincian Hill, or, in less central locations, the *Shaker*, in the Parioli section, and the *Palazzi* on Monte Mario, near the new Hilton Cavalieri Hotel. For sidewalk cafés, so much loved by Americans abroad, ride or walk to the upper section of winding Via Véneto and you will find the street lined with them on both sides. *Doney*'s is one of the most celebrated places of this type in all Europe.

For a gay summer evening of dancing and entertainment under the stars visit the *Casina delle Rose* in the Villa Borghese. For loftier summer entertainment there are the outdoor symphony concerts in the *Basilica di Massenzio*, and for summer opera, also in the open air, there are performances in the *Baths of Caracalla*. In all your wanderings, in all the world, you will never find stage settings to surpass in glamor the ancient Basilica and the imperial Baths.

To close my nocturnal comment on Rome on a newer and brighter note, be sure to inquire about two *Suoni e Luci* (Sound and Light) shows that are winning great popularity. One is presented in the *Roman Forum*, the other in *Hadrian's Villa*. Guests are seated in sections, according to their native languages, and the spectacles are presented with the spoken part in four languages, one of them, of course, English.

Cairo's celebrated belly-dancing shows are toned down in these days, since a wave of Moslem reform closed and sealed the lurid vice sectors that used to be the talk of tourism. The city has its quota of very smart international night clubs, a leader being the *Auberge des Pyramides*, and there are still several casinos and dives where Oriental muscle dancing is done for hours every night, but there is little of Minsky about these shows.

Egyptian winter nights are so uniformly perfect that merely sitting on a hotel terrace under the stars, glass at elbow, is a holiday occupation hardly to be surpassed, but there is one important night feature that should by no means be overlooked. Throughout most of the year a really superb *Sound and Light Show* is presented at Giza, the audience being seated in chairs on the sand in front of the Sphinx and the three pyramids. It is given on successive nights in four languages, one of which, as everywhere in these spectacles, is English. I found it one of the most effective such shows I have ever seen, and there are now many of them throughout Europe.

Athens has its grist of downtown dancings, as does also the Piraeus, patronized by such tourists as believe that the entertainment fare provided, and the eager-eyed bar girls, warrant the guest in paying 60 drachmas ($2.00) for each thimbleful of more-or-less whisky. It also has, on an infinitely more attractive level, some very lively high-class tavernas and cabarets. These are, in fact, of such importance in the tourist picture that they will be further discussed in Chapter 11, where also I shall tell about the glamorous *Sound and Light Show* whose central piece is the *Acropolis*.

Beirut maintains a galaxy of small night clubs, as shall be further discussed in Chapter 23, and to them it has more recently added a casino some twenty miles from the center, that is one of the largest and most sumptuous in Europe or the Near East. More later on this ambitious tourist lure. Beirut is about as wide open as any city in the whole Mediterranean, forming the sharpest possible contrast to Damascus, its neighbor-capital of Syria, which goes to bed with the sun.

Istanbul is a night surprise. It has several large and extremely smart restaurant-cabarets, among them the *Taksim Casino* and the *Kervan-saray*, each with its late-hours *boîte* on a lower floor. The Hilton has a smart night club called the *Şadirvan*. Istanbul has also an outdoor amphitheater, where spectacles of every sort, including ice shows, are staged; and for winter entertainment a huge new opera house is nearing completion. *Ankara* has the look of a brand-new boom city, but there is plenty of night life there too, as also in *Izmir* (Smyrna). The belly dance as done in some Turkish night clubs is a far bolder thing than is its counterpart in Egypt.

About Civilities and Different Customs

There are as many different hues to the social spectrum of the Mediterranean as there are races and religions, but the traveler with a sound social heart melts into the rainbow like a human chameleon and does a job for his country wherever he goes. The power of tourism, to permit myself a half-page sermon with nothing new in it, is beyond computing. It can further divide a divided world or it can heal a few crevices and brighten the name of America. Nothing tarnishes that name more directly and effectively abroad than the attitude of that type of traveler who sounds off incessantly and noisily in hotel lobbies, cafés and public conveyances about the backwardness and follies of the particular country whose guest he is at the moment—only he would never use the word "guest." The voice of one such banal bungler can pack more weight of the wrong kind than many carefully thought out radio talks on the international air can offset. He is the Ugly American. For each example of him, or her, there are, I am convinced, a score of Understanding Americans, but they make far less noise, so they are less noticed.

And now some specific thoughts, brief and more to the point, about certain customs of Mediterranean lands, particularly those in the Near East. In the view of the Moslem, common courtesy absolutely *demands* that when you visit his home or his office he give you something to drink, and since he is a Moslem, the drink will, almost certainly, be thick, black Turkish coffee or—Coca-Cola, which last has swept the Moslem world. (Alcohol is forbidden by the Koran and the current popularity of Coca-Cola is a phenomenon of the first magnitude. The Cairo concession is said to be one of the most profitable in the world.) You may not happen to like either of these drinks but it would be a gross affront to refuse it. You need do hardly more than moisten your lips. That constitutes acceptance of the hospitality.

In entering a mosque, it is required—and there can be no exceptions —that the visitor take off his shoes or else put huge, scuffy slippers on over them. An appropriate small fee is expected by the attendant who hands you the slippers.

Remember that in all Moslem lands—Turkey is an exception—*Friday* is the Holy Day, the day when all government offices and some banks are closed, though perhaps not the shops. European shops and offices treat it like any day of the week and remain open, but *they* close on Sundays.

In entering Catholic churches, but this need hardly be pointed out, women must wear a covering on the head, even if only a handkerchief (presumably because Paul entertained strong views on this subject; see I Corinthians 11). Perhaps this custom is not very strictly observed in all parts of all lands, but it certainly is in Italy.

In entering a Jewish synagogue in Israel and other lands the *man* must have his head covered. If you make it your custom to go hatless in balmy latitudes a handkerchief draped over your locks will suffice to indicate a courteous reverence.

In Greek Orthodox churches, it is a friendly gesture to buy (for a mere two drachmas or so, being six cents) a pencil-like taper, and then light it and place it before an ikon. Failing this, an offering should be dropped in the church box seen near the door.

No tourist would be so boorish as to cause offense by deliberately violating these customs or any others that may be strange to him, and the people of Meridional and Eastern lands are almost always tolerant if they see that a visitor has erred through ignorance. They are quick to recognize good intent.

Finally, I would offer a tribute to Pan American's *New Horizons World Guide* for a subject that is treated in nearly every one of the hundred-or-so countries. The title is *Common Courtesies and Local Customs* and in a few crisp sentences the text explains, in each case, exactly what the title says. This has saved me, more than once, from committing a social *faux pas* or even a downright "blooper."

YOURSELF IN THE PICTURE

REVISION SUPPLEMENT TO CHAPTER 4

IN Portugal's *Azores, Hotel São Pedro,* in Ponta Delgada, capital of São Miguel, is something "more than special." The hostelry *was* the home of America's first consul, Thomas Hickling, built by him in 1812. The place is a house builder's dream, in spacious colonial style, with the builder's name and the date, 1812, over the fireplace. In the Second World War it was the residence of Admirals Dunn and Jackson, but it has been extensively rebuilt as a tourist hotel, without sacrificing any of its old lines. It has 35 ultramodern rooms, most of them with private bath. Walls of polished cork and floors of Brazilian and island hardwoods (macacauba and acacia) lend gleaming dignity, and the first-rate plumbing lends comfort. The lounge is enriched by beautiful antiques. The dining room, overlooking the garden, shore boulevard and sea, is done in mahogany and the bar is made alluring by its arty ceiling beams. Even the kitchen has something to show with its charming blue tiles. The garden boasts a lovely blue bank of agapanthus, three curious dwarf cedars and the only two paradise trees on the island. In short, you'll love the new-old São Pedro and its setting.

CHAPTER 4

THE NEGLECTED AZORES, ROMANCE EN ROUTE

Some Notes on Terra Nostra

TERRA NOSTRA, "Our Land" of the Azoreans, consists of nine Portuguese islands, which are among the most charming and—so far as tourism is concerned—the most neglected portions of Portugal. I hope I shall be forgiven if I state that Terra Nostra is Terra Incognita even to many mainland Portuguese. Any tourist who has spent a few days on the islands can give them an Azorean travelogue almost as if he were reporting to friends back in America. He is sure to interest and even surprise them as he stresses various volcanic wonders, the stirring scenery, the unmatched hydrangea highways, some curiosities of the pineapple industry and a hotel of surprising nature, of which more later. It is *not* in Ponta Delgada, which still lacks hotels worthy of a capital city. Madeira is very well known everywhere, Spain's Balearics and even her distant Canaries are widely advertised, but this is not true of the Azores, steppingstones though they are between the New World and the Old. To see them—and the reward is great—you must *ask* about them and do a little personal pushing. Perhaps, if you are a rugged individualist, this will increase their appeal.

For the Azores, though not for any of the other island groups, the American traveler still needs a visa in his passport, but this is easily securable at any Portuguese consulate.

The nine islands are: Eastern Group—Santa Maria and São Miguel; Central Group—Terceira, Graciosa and São Jorge; Western Group—Pico, Faial, Flores and Corvo. It seems that in 1811, a tenth island, named Sabrina for a British man-of-war whose men saw it "happen," appeared above the surface and shortly sank again. And as recently in the islands' life as 1957 an eleventh island, this a belching volcano, arose near Faial but later subsided to or just below sea level.

Only the Eastern Group concerns the average traveler, for Santa

Maria contains the airport where transatlantic planes land, and São Miguel is the all-in-all of tourism, containing the only city, Ponta Delgada, and more than half the Azorean population of 350,000

Steamer service from New York is occasionally offered by American Export's *Constitution* and *Independence*, on their sailings to the Mediterranean, but for regular service it may be necessary to fall back on a Portuguese freighter-and-passenger line called *Carregadores Açoreanos*, represented by East Coast Overseas Corporation, 80 Broad Street, New York. The same line connects the Azores with Madeira; and in addition to its regular freighters it operates several small "pineapple ships" carrying eight passengers each. Between Lisbon and the Azores, with a halt at Madeira, a semimonthly service is maintained by a line called *Emprêza Insulana de Navegação*, with its new 9000-ton liner, *Funchal*.

Air service from New York is regularly maintained by two major American air systems, Pan American Airways and TWA, providing a halt at Santa Maria en route to Lisbon. Pan American, having originally built the airport for the U.S. government during World War II, has naturally a special proprietary interest.

I shall have more to say about small Santa Maria with the big airport, but here a word is needed about air connections to São Miguel and its very small airport. This service and other shuttlings among the islands are now handled by a local air line called SATA, for *Sociedade Açoreana de Transportes Aéreos*. It takes only about half an hour for the flight to São Miguel, but the planes are small and the field on the large island is not very adequate. Inquiry should be made at the time of your intended visit, and I should emphasize two things here. First, there can be no doubt that São Miguel will win recognition in the tourist world. Second, there can be no doubt that as it wins recognition the connecting air service with Santa Maria will enlarge and develop. Even now, however, São Miguel is promoted with zeal, efficiency and courtesy by the *Bureau de Turismo Terra Nostra, Ponta Delgada, São Miguel,* to which one may air-write for on-the-spot information, both printed and personal.

Santa Maria, Lost and Lovely

Terra Nostra, almost a second name for the Azores, is used as the name of *all* the best hotels, including the modern one, of bungalow type, at Santa Maria airport, and the leading, though inadequate, one of Ponta Delgada. Santa Maria's Hotel Terra Nostra caught me by surprise right in the middle of my nostalgia, for its bedspreads were worked with designs and names of Cape Cod! I am a permanent resident of the Cape and my eyes popped as I saw the designs of old schooners, slickered fishermen, lighthouses, spinning wheels, and such town names as Provincetown, Wellfleet, Truro, Dennis, Barnstable, Yarmouth and Chatham. What a welcome was this to Santa Maria dos Açores!

A circuit of the island by car, if SATA schedules permit time for it, can provide a pleasing initiation to Azorean life and scenes. In the tiny island capital, Vila do Porto, I happened to find as convoy a most erudite resident who earnestly recommended that I gain some knowledge of Santa Maria by a careful perusal of no less than seven tomes, in Portuguese, French, German and English. I'm afraid I haven't yet completed this homework, but at least one of the books is certainly recommendable, namely Samuel Eliot Morison's *Portuguese Voyages to America in the Fifteenth Century*, published in 1940 by the Harvard University Press. My island savant lightened the atmosphere of learning by taking me to the combined town hall and prison, where I saw a tax book eight feet in width, when opened, and where I met Santa Maria's only prisoner. I met the man through a peep-door in his cell and found him very nice. He was permitted, I learned, to stroll in the town garden at certain hours, on the understanding that he would return in due course to his cell—to which he had a key!

The circuit of the island took me to a lot of stunning belvederes, whence surf-and-mountain views left snapshots in my memory; to the seaside hamlet of *São Lourenço*, which has a good beach and good vineyards producing a red name-wine; to *Santa Barbara*, a lofty community soothed by the soft roar of surf far below; to the *Church of Nossa Senhora dos Anjos* (Our Lady of the Angels), where, on February 16, 1493, Columbus' sailors, but not the admiral, having come ashore from the good ship *Santa Maria*, homeward bound, knelt in prayers of Thanksgiving.

Santa Maria Island is as lovely, though not in its flat airport section, as it is unknown. Its neat-as-a-pin hamlets co-operate with its scenery to make it so. Most of them are sentineled by windmills churning their wings against the sky, and many individual houses are certain to attract the eye. They do not *huddle* with others, but keep their distance. Nearly all of them are as white as the woolly clouds above them, and a characteristic touch is the round white chimney. If you haven't thought that a chimney can be a thing of beauty and a joy forever, wait until you see those of Santa Barbara and São Lourenço.

Surprises and Special Sights of Ponta Delgada

The Theater of São Miguel, called *Teatro Micaelense*, gave me my first big surprise in Ponta Delgada. Completed in 1951 as a business venture by the Carregadores Açoreanos Line, it is rumored to have "saved the line money" because of its impact on the company's corporation income tax. Be that as it may, the theater is a marvel for a small island city of perhaps fifty thousand inhabitants. It cost 14,000,000 escudos, which is over half a million dollars. Its glittering foyers and café-bar, its handsome auditorium seating twelve hundred, its large stage, with ample dressing rooms, and the show windows in its lobby displaying various Portuguese and island goods make this a theater apart. In Lisbon itself there is hardly a finer one. In the Teatro Micaelense, jammed to its utmost capacity on four successive nights, I once saw the university students put on a show that was a riotous success in burlesquing faculty personages and student customs during intervals of more serious scenes and lovely dancing by the coeds. I, having come a long way by air, was forgiven, I hope, for being almost the only man present not wearing a tuxedo. The sophistication of that all-island audience was one of the surprises of my evening.

Sights of tourist interest seen in Ponta Delgada are varied and numerous but a few stand out. I think of the country women in their traditional old costume, a cape and an enormous black hood, collectively called *capote e capelo*. I think of the remarkable errand dogs called *cães de recados* seen running briskly to market or to a store, each with a basket in his mouth containing money and a written order so that he may complete some transaction for his mistress and then return with the purchase. I think of the arresting view from the hill called *Mãe de Deus* (Mother of God), reached by the lane called Passeio Publico Theodore Roosevelt! I think of several churches, especially *St. Joseph*,

rich in gold leaf, and the *Collegiate Church*, with its extremely lavish
baroque altar of fragrant brown cedar, carved by Jesuit padres two or
three centuries ago.

I think, too, of Ponta Delgada's *Museum*, occupying an old convent.
It has no artifacts of aboriginal island inhabitants for there were none,
but it has much to compensate for this lack. One sees a stuffed *açor*,
a hawklike bird that gave its name to the islands. One sees beautiful tilework, mostly the blue and white so typical of Portugal, a room of paintings sent here by an American artist named Howard Fremont Stratton,
who lived for some years on São Miguel, other paintings by an islander
named Domingos Rebelo, who became director of the National Art
Gallery in Lisbon. Perhaps the most interesting item of all is seen in a
cloister of the convent-museum, namely a history of the islands, from
Gonçalo Velho's time (1432) to 1650, chiseled on big stone "pages"
ranged on the wall. A local chronicler named João Arruda Botelho e
Câmara did the arduous job.

Pineapples in Smoke

Pineapple culture and marketing is big business in the Azores, as in
the distant Pacific islands of Hawaii, but I learned certain things about
the business here that I had never learned in Hawaii. In the Azores pines
are grown under glass and there are said to be well over a thousand hothouses on São Miguel alone. A well-known grower with thirty-eight of
them on his estate at the edge of the capital city gave me some pine lore
that was astonishing to me.

The pines may be forced, it seems, by *smoke*. They may be made to
blossom or to bear fruit at the grower's wish in *any month of the year*.
The forcing process involves shutting up the plants for four or five
consecutive days in an atmosphere of thick smoke, made from burning
straw or other material. Responding to this curious "diet" they develop
so that you can almost watch them grow. Each chunk of root can be
made to develop from two to five plants and the grower allows but two
years "from root to pine." This modern smoke method, seeming to the
uninitiated so bizarre and "agin natur'," was discovered by sheer chance
when a poor Azorean growing a few pines once built a fire for his own
warmth inside his hothouse. With an excitement that we can dimly im-

agine he presently saw the miracle that his chance act had wrought.

São Miguel now raises in its thousand-odd hothouses a million and a half pines annually in good years. The fruit is exported—whole pines, not canned as in Hawaii—chiefly to Europe, in the aforementioned fruit ships of Carregadores Açoreanos.

Hydrangea Highways

The highways of the Azores, and especially those of São Miguel, which is known in folders and in fact as *A Ilha Verde*, The Green Island, have a special beauty of a type I have never seen duplicated elsewhere. They are like green tunnels through luxuriant shade trees and are lined for mile after mile with thick hedges of blue hydrangeas, whose blossom clusters must be numbered in the tens of millions. These give a blue glory to the otherwise green island that must be seen to be believed. Even in winter the hedges are very evident on almost every road, but not until May are they in their flowering glory, and the display then lasts until September.

Azorean gardens, both public and private, are brilliant with camellias, azaleas and countless other varieties of plants and shrubs, not to mention a wealth of ferns, native to New Zealand, and palms, native to Africa. The cosmopolitanism of these gardens is a notable feature, plants and trees from all the continents finding here a congenial home.

Lake of the Seven Cities

A fairly short motor trip or a long and climbing hike from Ponta Delgada brings the traveler to one of the most thrilling scenic spectacles in any Iberian isle. The climax is reached at a high pass from which one looks down to the lake and village called *Sete Cidades*, or Seven Cities. Very far below this pass lies a double lake in an extinct crater. One part is a pellucid blue, the other an emerald green, and we are told that a legendary princess, dying in an earthquake that was inflicted upon the island to punish her wicked father for his sins, caused the beautiful coloring by tossing her blue parasol into one lake, her green slippers into the other. Whatever your reaction to fanciful legends, you will certainly react with genuine excitement to the wonder of the bicolored lakes of your heptapolitan goal.

Furnas, Luxury in a Caldron

The Valley of Las Furnas, about an hour's distance from Ponta Delgada, is a magnet that draws all who visit the island of São Miguel. It is one of the most curious volcanic regions anywhere in Europe or its islands, and seeing it is made easy by a delightful first-class hotel named, as you would expect, *Terra Nostra*. This is the surprise hotel referred to in the opening of this chapter and to be further mentioned below.

On or near the highway leading to Las Furnas, this Valley of Vulcan, are two special sights. *Gorreana* is the first. Here one may see a tea plantation and a factory where expert girl operatives sort the leaves, picking out the choice "pearls," young ball-like leaves of special value, and dividing the leaves destined to make green tea from those destined to make black.

Pico de Ferro (Iron Crest) is the other high point en route to Furnas and this is a literal high spot, with a *miradouro* (belvedere) commanding a magnificent view of the Furnas Valley, with its many caldrons sending up jets of steam, and of the lovely Lago das Furnas.

Eagerness for a close-up examination is whetted by this spectacle, so much like a scene from a Wagner opera, and the reality does not let the visitor down. There are many fumaroles, extending for a mile or more from the edge of the town to and through it. In several cases the roar of the boiling water is so strong that it can be heard for a hundred yards around. Many houses have the water piped directly into their kitchens. In other cases the housewives go to the nearest bubbling spring and scoop up a bucket of boiling water as needed. They make their coffee the easy way by this method and sometimes they cook their meat by wrapping it in heavy cloth and merely burying it in hot mud and leaving it for a couple of hours. They do the family wash in the nearest warm stream or pool, tempering the water, when necessary, with a cool spring, for there are twenty-two different types of water here, ranging in temperature from boiling to cold.

As curative waters, many of the springs have won international recognition, and a learned brochure has been written in French about their medicinal properties. The best-known of the mineral waters for table use are *Serra do Trigo* and *Agua da Helena*. The first development of Furnas as a medical spa was pioneered as early as 1770 by America's first consul to the Islands, Thomas Hickling, then a youth, whose name, with the above date, we see carved on a stone near one of the big fumaroles, so the remarkable valley should have an enhanced interest for his compatriots. Thoman Hickling was the grandfather of William H. (for Hickling) Prescott, the celebrated historian.

Hotel Terra Nostra is notable not only for its own sophistication, so far from the sophisticated world—it has a casino and a good nine-hole golf course built by a Scot—but for the handsome riverside park adjacent to it. The Furnas River flows through this park and tall, rib-barked cypresses add grandeur to it, but its chief attraction is the big swimming pool filled with warm (82 degrees) ferruginous water. This pool-in-a-park, surrounded by cabins where the bather may change, adds an extra touch of magnetism to a basically alluring valley.

Let Vulcan Be Your Cook

Furnas is a natural tripping center. One may drive to the nearby sea beach (ten minutes) of *Ribeira Quente* by a typical hydrangea highway, being one more of those finely fashioned tunnels of verdure lined with blue. One may visit *Povoação* for its seaside charm or *Lomba da Cavaleiro* for its belvedere, commanding a view of seven coastal villages. One may explore the coast to *Vila Franca do Campo*, known for its strange and tragic past. It was once the capital of the island, but in 1522 it was completely buried in a sudden volcanic upheaval that destroyed all of its five thousand inhabitants.

The trip of trips, however, is to *Lake Furnas* for an earth-cooked meal. I shall never forget my own experience of having Vulcan as ever-ready, unpaid chef. A group of a dozen Furnas folk whom I was invited to join took me to the lake and there we invoked nature's aid in preparing a vast outdoor meal. A large burlap bag was filled with several kinds of meat, plus blood sausages, plus chicken, potatoes, cabbages, onions, a superior local variety of elephant's ear called *inhame* and I know not what else. The whole bag was sunk in a hole in steaming mud, covered over, and left there for about two hours.

To while away this interval, we tried out all sorts of island dances, especially the weaving, finger-snapping *baile furado*, in which I was plenty clumsy, thank you. We drank cocktails, with *favas* (broad, flat beans) for canapés, and at last we *ate*. What a meal it was, comprising much of everything I've named and many things I haven't been able to name, all washed down with several wines, a red type called *vinho de cheiro*, a rosy local wine and a white Pico Island wine whose brand I did not catch. Joy was unconstrained, but I am pleased to report that inebriation did not set in. The Portuguese can "take it," and this alien was mighty cautious about all those cordially urged refills!

As a note of ethnic interest I may mention that the majority of Portuguese-speaking residents of the U.S. are of Azorean heritage, a fact that is due to the collapse of the whaling industry in the Islands about a century ago. Thousands emigrated to New England, especially to New Bedford, Massachusetts, to engage in their usual calling in the New World. Others got jobs as sailors and fishermen. Many went to Hawaii to work as cane cutters and many went to Monterey, California, where they played a large part in building up the industry of sardine fishing. In New Bedford I have noted that certain signs in the railway station and other public buildings are in English and Portuguese, which is to say Azorean, with overtones of Madeira and the Cape Verde Islands.

REVISION SUPPLEMENT TO CHAPTER 5

MADEIRA becomes more popular each year as a prime stop on Mediterranean cruises and as an outpost worth at least a week's stay by many who want peace, quiet and sun. The *Savoy* was slighted in the rundown on Funchal's hotels (page 74). It has been enlarged to 300 rooms, more than double the count of Reid's, some being in separate villas. Much money is being spent, too, on modernizing the entire hotel, including its public rooms, which now boast complete new decor. There's a gaiety and casual atmosphere in the Savoy that just fits the desires of some visitors, and the prices, so far, are not much over half those of Reid's, which have jumped one third to $32 double. Even so, Reid's is, and will undoubtedly remain, the choice of those to whom economy is not of paramount importance.

To the four trips outlined in the text, I should like to add a fifth and long trip involving a circuit of the western part of the island and taking a full day. You may either take a picnic lunch, or plan to stop over for lunch at *Porto Moniz*. This village is on the island's northwestern point, 61 miles from Funchal by the clockwise circuit, starting from Funchal along the southern coast, 42 miles by the cross-island and north-coast counterclockwise route, the two together totting up to a big 103 miles, much of it on corkscrew roads. The going is magnificent all the way and Porto Moniz may prove to be a delightful break in the long haul. It has a simple pension, *Pensão Lar da Baia,* and for a special feature it has *surf*, and a swimming pool fed by the surf. I saw it on a calm day, yet even then the combers were simply gigantic. All the bigger waves bounced over the retaining wall of the pool with a curtain of foaming water, yet there is, of course, no danger to the bather. What it might be, however, on a rough day I can only imagine. Porto Moniz is due for much more attention than it has yet had, and this is the way and how of it: The concessionaires of the casino at Funchal are under contract with the island government to achieve a threefold program, which must be started, if my information is correct, in 1967. This involves (1) a new and much more luxurious Funchal casino; (2) a first-class 200-room hotel in Funchal, and (3) a new, high-quality 30-room *pousada* (inn) at Porto Moniz. This last feature of the contract will, of course, make the big circuit much more attractive, enabling the traveler to spend a night en route in lodgings much better than those now existing.

The Canaries, proud possessions of Spain, are developing so rapidly that today's facts become yesterday's while one watches, but certain basic advances may be reported and certain dependable forecasts made. First, let's look at air transportation, starting with *Las Palmas,* the capital of *Gran Canaria*. In addition to Spain's *Iberia Air Lines,* which flies jets from Madrid to the islands in two and a half hours, TAP (Transportes Aéreos Portugueses), the Portuguese national airline, ties Madeira to Las Palmas in regular flights now operating twice a week. *British United Airways,* a relative newcomer to the Atlantic islands, joins KLM–*Royal Dutch Airlines, Sabena, Lufthansa* and SAS (*Scandinavian Airlines System*) in offering extensive service from European capitals. Airports on both islands can now receive and dispatch full jet planes.

Gran Canaria hotels are almost beyond counting in Las Palmas—almost, but not quite, for in the official list I have counted 121, including the pensions and hostels. Three thousand new rooms were added in a single recent period of 12 months and the pace keeps up. The *Las Palmas Palace,* which has a tie-in with the Ritz and the Palace in Madrid, is more than a decade newer than the 1953 *Santa Catalina,* which means it has new architectural ideas that were not available when the other was designed. It is a 10-story, 240-room hotel (6 elevators), deserving the name Palace. On the 7th floor is a gymnasium, on the 8th a swimming pool and on the 10th two restaurants: one the regular dining room for guests on a full-pension arrangement; the other, called the Starlight Grillroom, a deluxe restaurant with a grand view of the animated harbor. On the hotel's ground floor there is a folksy snackshop-café, partly on an open veranda, and just off the entrance lobby is the *Scottish Corner,* whose bartender used to serve only Scotch, but has broadened his contacts with alcohol to serve anything you name. On the same floor there are about a score of shops, smart ones of many sorts.

In addition to the port area with its Las Palmas Palace, hotels seem to spring from the ground along the city's two beaches, *Playa de las Alcaravaneras*, with its famous Hotel Santa Catalina, mentioned above and on page 82, and *Playa de las Canteras*, with its string of superior hotels led by the luxury 390-bed *Reina Isabel*, which was fully opened in 1966, complemented by such first-class, modern hotels as the *Gran Canaria* and *Las Caracolas* (the Snails). Many more good hotels, new or nearly new, compete with these I have named. Las Canteras Beach is vastly more attractive to me than the other. It is aglow with gay holiday spirit, including, in winter-spring, Swedish lasses in bikinis, and it has lots of international restaurants, as well as hotels, along its two-mile course.

The *Caldera de Bandama*, mentioned on page 83, has been bought by a group of British capitalists who propose to develop it as a tourist resort, perhaps with a fine restaurant and nightclub down in the caldron and, presumably, a funicular for the descent and ascent. The farmer family has had to go, soothed, no doubt, by the profit motive. An asset of major importance to the new owners is the existence of the *Campo de Bandama del Club de Golf de las Palmas*, whose 14 syllables mean a fine 18-hole golf course, located on high ground in the Bandama neighborhood above the caldron.

I should add a further word, too, about Teror, for *Nuestra Sēnora del Pino* (by which name Teror's church is also known, at least by local folk) is the patroness of the Diocese of the Canaries and the people's veneration for her is deep and sincere. She does not now wear the jeweled robe I have mentioned, lest it prove an irresistible temptation to thieves, but she looks distinguished in her substitute robe. Crowds of Canarians and tourists climb up to a loft where there is a dedicatory museum, with hundreds of votive offerings. Two that I noticed were a calling card of a gentleman from Worcester, Massachusetts, and a Kennedy half-dollar. I have to report with regret that the church is now considered unsafe and plans have been made to raze it and build a new one. We must hope that the new one will not be BIG and SHOWY, as is too often the custom in such cases.

Island tours in *Tenerife* are many and wonderful, and they can include a visit to, or perhaps a stay in, Spain's loftiest parador (government inn), the *Parador de las Cañadas del Teide*, being at an altitude of 7200 feet, almost a mile and a half above sea level. It is cool to cold

here much of the year, sometimes even in summer, but the air is bracing and the scenery "wild to the point of savagery." One can keep
warm by playing tennis, one can swim in a heated pool, and of course
the parador, with its pleasant public rooms and 21 bedrooms, all with
full shower or bath, is well heated.

The resort of *Puerto de la Cruz*, a favorite goal of Scandinavians, is
situated on the north coast, across the island from the capital. It is one of
today's major phenomena of holiday travel. How can it have "happened" in a decade or so? Where there was virtually nothing but nature
there are hotels galore, big, skyscraperish, Miamiesque ones, full of
bars, nightclubs, swimming pools, smart restaurants, smart people. There
are nearly 50 of them already, counting pensions, with more rising all
along the line wherever a few acres can possibly be secured by some
syndicate or chain. The leaders are the huge *Gran Hotel Tenerife
Playa;* the *Valle-Mar* (Valley-Sea); the *Las Vegas* (significant name);
the *Oro Negro* (Black Gold), 15 stories tall with a view-bar up top-
side; and, surely, the smart "newestcomer" (for the moment), the *San
Felipe*, a property built by British and Spanish capital. This is a large
hotel (465 beds) of top luxury, one of its features being a bar and grill,
turning into a nightclub in the late hours, overlooking an Olympic-
sized swimming pool.

And so the legend of the Canaries continues with burgeoning tourism
at every corner. There are still some areas left to be discovered, but
hurry!

CHAPTER 5

PORTUGAL'S MADEIRA AND SPAIN'S CANARIES

Geography and Means of Access

THE islands of Iberia that are far out in the Atlantic may seem like geographical interlopers, but since many a big cruise ship halts at one or more of them to give its guests extra glamor-days ashore it seems fitting to give these islands rather full coverage. Both groups—Madeira is also a group, though the main island is the only one of tourist interest—lie on approximately the same meridian of longitude, the Canaries being about four hundred miles south of Madeira. I shall tell of Madeira first, since Portugal precedes Spain in Mediterranean geography as the traveler enters the picture.

Air travelers to Portugal and the Mediterranean are finding it progressively easier to visit Madeira by plane from Lisbon, thanks to the steady efforts of TAP, Portugal's national air line, and to the current development of Madeira's airport. And as regards sea travel to the island I am happy to report that there is now a newly commissioned 9000-ton Portuguese luxury liner, the *Funchal*, briefly mentioned in Chapter 4, which offers regular service from Lisbon to Madeira and the Azores. Two round trips monthly are made to Madeira *and* the Azores (São Miguel, Faial and Terceira Islands) in a total time of 7 days, and one monthly round trip is made to Madeira alone, the transit taking only 28 hours each way. The *Funchal*, equipped with stabilizers for smooth sailing, carries 400 passengers and has a speed of 20 knots. I have not taken this trip but I have seen the *Funchal* and been impressed. Friends who have been passengers assure me that its modernity and comforts deserve high marks.

For air travel TAP (*Transportes Aéreos Portugueses*) is now the carrier, two other companies, Aquila Airways and a minor Portuguese line, both operating seaplanes, having long since folded. TAP is healthy,

70

and growing all the time. Its present service to Madeira is maintained by Comet Jets to Porto Santo, a small island of the Madeira group, whence a new steamer carries passengers to Funchal. The air portion of the journey takes 90 minutes, but the steamer portion from Porto Santo to Funchal takes 4½ hours, which can be rough ones if Neptune so decrees. At last, however, the Madeira airport is being energetically carved out of Madeira's hilly soil and can already be used by piston planes. If, for a short period of time, the airport is unable to receive planes larger than DC-3s there will be a service of Caravelles or Comets, as now, from Lisbon to Porto Santo, with transfer to smaller planes. The building of Madeira's airport has presented problems with which few communities on earth have had to cope, but it is safe to say that within a few weeks, middle-distance jets will be in use.

(The means of access to Spain's Canaries, chiefly by plane from Madrid or Seville, will be mentioned in a following section.)

Funchal Facts for "Cruiser" and Vacationist

The cruise-ship traveler's Madeira, which is almost always seen in but one fleeting day ashore (the *Funchal*, from Lisbon, provides two days) is a very different thing from the island of the airborne traveler who can allow himself perhaps a full week. The "shore-leave" passenger is virtually limited to Funchal, though sometimes a short, swift scenic tour is offered. If such a tour is taken it is but a teaser, for the splendor of the island is so varied and so stimulating to the senses that it cannot be grasped in one small sample.

I do not mean to disparage the Funchal Day of cruise passengers. It may be a great day, a red-letter one, in all cases where the Madeira Week is simply not to be had. Funchal, taking its name from the fennel (*funcho*) which the island's Portuguese discoverer, João Gonçalvez Zarco, found here in abundance, is a most satisfying little capital, and not so little either, its population now approaching the hundred thousand mark. Its shops are eagerly sought, local embroidery being the great magnet to all visitors. This ranges from the superbly artistic work being done by the embroideresses of such houses as *Emile Marghab Limitada* and *G. Farra & Co. Lda.* to inconsequential but pretty items turned out for tourists who merely want "some little thing" as a souvenir.

The doings of the Funchal Day are traditional and well publicized, but no less pleasant because of their hackneyed character. They include a delightful crawl about town in a gay sledge "with a fringe on top" drawn by plodding bullocks over the smoothly pebbled streets, and an ascent to one of the high spots back of the city for the swift toboggan ride in a man-guided "running car," as it is locally called, to the center. The chief high spots for this sport, unique to Funchal and its vicinity, are the hill resort called *Monte*, at about the 2000-foot level, and the restaurant called *Terreiro da Lucta*, a thousand feet above Monte. Men are always ready and eager, for fees that seem ridiculously small, about a dollar plus tip, to provide a car and their own legwork, racing down perhaps three-quarters of a mile as they guide the car with ropes, only to be faced with the grim task of hauling it up aloft again for the next customer.

Monte was formerly reached by a funicular railway, but this was torn up during the Second World War and its rails sold for scrap, so one must now ascend by prosaic taxi or on foot. The place is worth visiting, quite regardless of its importance as an upper station for running cars. Its little church of *Nossa Senhora do Monte* contains the tomb of Emperor Karl, last of the Habsburg rulers of Austria-Hungary, who lived and died in exile in a villa close at hand. The walks and climbs to be made from Monte are numerous and all provide glorious views. The best of the shorter strolls seems to me the one to the belvedere called *Babozas*, barely five minutes distant. From here one may continue in a much more rugged workout to the settlement called *Choupana* (Hat), descending thence to Funchal by running car.

Still another form of locomotion unique to Madeira needs mention here and that is *hammock riding*. At various points, including Monte, a hammock (*rêde*) and bearers may be hired for day or half-day excursions on the mountain paths. The hammock is slung on poles and as soon as the customer is ensconced in it two bearers start off at a steady, shuffling pace which they can maintain for hour after tireless hour. Their pay comes to no more than three dollars per day per man, which is a very good wage in the Madeiran's view. Hammock traffic has dwindled as motor roads have advanced to most parts of the island, but it will probably never be abandoned altogether. It is the sybarite's

dream of fair travel and as an experience it is something not to be re-
sisted, but those who are sound of heart and lung and limb will usually
prefer to propel themselves on their own feet, for walking in Madeira's
mountains, especially along its fabulous *levadas*, or water courses, is one
of the finest holiday sports on earth. More presently on this subject.

"What to do" in the Funchal Day of one-day visitors should include
much personal strolling, guided by a clear city map procurable at the
office of the *Delegação de Turismo da Madeira* (Madeira Tourist
Office). This office, with an energetic staff, some of whose members
speak English, is conspicuous on the main thoroughfare, Avenida
Arriaga, a distinguished street shaded by a magnificent double row of
jacarandas, whose lovely blue blossoms, in billions, form a cerulean
canopy over the street for half a mile during the late spring. The day
should include a visit to the market in the eastern part of town and of
course to one of the big wine lodges where Madeira's smooth specialties
such as *Sercial*, *Boal* and *Malmsey* may be sampled. It should include,
too, a swim in one of the splendid bathing establishments to the west,
the sea-pool of world-famous Reid's Hotel or perhaps the rooftop pool
of the new Hotel Santa Isabel or the suburban *Lido*, a mile or two
beyond Reid's. In the evening, your sailing hour permitting, though it
probably won't, it may include a look-in at the seaside Casino do
Funchal when that ambitious project, now hardly more than a business
dream, shall have been brought to completion.

The Madeira Week of the lucky unhurried is a many-chapter thriller
of scenery unsurpassed on any island or any continent in the world. It
is given very special character by the aforementioned levadas, or irrigation canals, which not only form a life-giving labyrinth, carrying water
from the wet north side around and even *through* the mountains to
reach every part of Madeira, but provide practical paths, on their sides
or on their concrete rims, for scores of miles of almost matchless hiking
that reveal new breathtakers of outlook at every turn.

Reid's Hotel and Others

Reid's Hotel, sometimes called Reid's Palace Hotel, is one of the best-
loved hostelries in the whole vast area of the Mediterranean and its approaches. Along with its modern comforts and modern bathroom

plumbing it has an enviable Old World serenity and character. Perched on a high cliff above the sea, with a stirring view of Funchal and its harbor, it has long been famous in England and has now come to be known by American travelers for the superlative place it is. With a beautiful flowered park of eleven acres on the cliff's edge and with every possible amenity, including tennis courts, it is in the front rank of the world's resort hotels. Its swimming pool and deep-sea bathing pier are reached by a cliffside elevator, and there are a hundred or more dressing cabins for the use of guests. For the inner man and inner woman there is a sumptuous dining room with excellent and lavish fare, plus a bar-lounge, concert music being provided in the former, dance music in the latter. Afternoon tea, served on the open terrace, is a daily event that few guests are willing to miss. The view from the terrace is one of Madeira's finest. In the summer months breakfast and lunch may be had in a gay pavilion a little above the bathing pier. An orchestra plays for lunch, and here, too, dancing and gala nights are frequently offered.

Reid's is a place of genuine social elegance. British tradition calls for evening dress at dinner but in these days of transoceanic plane travel when "going light" is the accepted custom very few American travelers, especially men, bother to bring evening gear. One is not conspicuous if wearing an ordinary business suit or afternoon dress. Reid's charges, on the very moderate Portuguese scale, are low, especially in summer, as compared with quality hotels of its high caliber in most tourist lands, the charge for mine, with a balcony overlooking the garden, being about $23 for two, with all meals and a high tea. All hotel charges in the island tend to be 20 per cent lower in summer than in winter. Reid's publishes a useful Madeira Bulletin with all prices, including local tours, given in dollar quotations.

Funchal has other good hotels, led by the *Santa Isabel*, which opened in 1961. A great charm of this place is its rooftop terrace, with swimming pool, where lunch may be had from May to September, and where starlight dances are held twice a week during the same months. The big sea front *Savoy* (with pool), the *New Avenue Hotel*, with brilliant gardens, and the somewhat lower-priced *Miramar* are all in the same edge-of-city section as Reid's and the Santa Isabel, while downtown there is the good *Golden Gate*, dating in its present form from 1958, with a roof terrace commanding a close-up view of city and harbor. Here, too, open-air lunch is served in summer, and likewise afternoon tea and dinner. Like any downtown hotel, the Golden Gate appeals more to businessmen than tourists but surprisingly enough it boasts the only respectable night club in Funchal. (There is a small new fado nightspot called *Sete Saias* in the nearby fishing village of Camara de Lobos.) Finally, there is a good and very inexpensive *pensão* (pension) in downtown Funchal called *Monte Rosa Residencia*. It opened its doors late in 1961.

Tripper's Glory, in Four Cantos

In the attempt to give the Madeira Week a form and substance useful to the reader, I will cull four triple-star excursions from my own week, which I confess has totaled nearer three in three cumulative visits. These point-by-point journeys, with some suggested extensions, are hardly more than samples from the island's wealth. The rugged walker with *months* at his disposal would still not cover everything of scenic importance.

For printed aid, be advised that the Madeira Tourist Office publishes an illustrated *Guide to Madeira*, with clear maps of the island and the city; another, with more exciting illustrations called *What to See in Madeira;* and, for easy pocket carrying, a separate *Tourist Map of Madeira*, with ample comment on the reverse side. In both maps the more important footpaths, mostly beside levadas, are shown by green lines, and the government and local rest houses are clearly indicated. One of the levadas is claimed to wind and twist and zigzag and back-track for a total of *sixty miles*, which sounds like a tall story, but "that's what the man said," and the man was one of the most trusted guides of the Tourist Office. For background about the island's history, people and customs, Cecil H. Miles' *A Glimpse of Madeira*, published some years ago, is readable and amply illustrated. So now for my own Big Four, the first three of which were planned in detail for me, as they may be for you, by the Madeira Tourist Office.

First Trip, East and North—to *Santana* and back, by car. On the outward trip I took a route of circuitous grandeur that provided the following various treats.

1. At a point short of Caniço my driver took me over a rough side road down to *Cape Garajau*, on whose bleak and lonely summit stands an impressive 34-foot statue of Christ, with arms outstretched, to bless passing mariners. It is marked simply *Sagrado Coração de Jesus*, meaning Sacred Heart of Jesus. In rather odd contrast to it is a small whale-oil refinery of former days at the base of the cliff. One can see great piles of the bones of cachalots, or sperm whales.

2. *Camacha* is an upland village devoted almost exclusively to the making of wicker furniture and basketry. You may see tall bundles of willow withes everywhere and may admire the verdant raw material growing luxuriantly in a deep ravine. Visitors are permitted to enter any of the establishments to watch the craftsmen at work. That of José de Sousa & Irmãos (the last word means Brothers) showed me its stock and offered me a set of two sturdily made armchairs, a table and a settee for $17.50; or I could have had a good plain chair alone for $2.40 or a table for $3.20.

(A levada path extends from Camacha to Choupana and another one leads to Santo da Serra.)

3. *Santo da Serra* is an important crossroads village that is the proud possessor of a golf course. From here a good paved road lured my motor on a sortie down to the fishing and boat-building port of *Machico*, next town in population to Funchal itself, though hardly one tenth the size of the capital. The new airport is on the outskirts of Machico and to achieve it the government had to erect a new, modern village for the country families that were displaced. The cost of the airport has been estimated at five million dollars but the final figure may be much higher. There is a pleasant teahouse called *Paraiso* (Paradise) at Machico. (It is possible, though some of the going is rough, to motor in safety, partly through a half-mile tunnel, from Machico to remote Caniçal, at Madeira's far-eastern tip.)

4. *Portela*, reached by an excellent new highway from Santo da Serra, offers a superb view of the striking *Penha d'Aguia*, or Eagle Rock, one of the wonders of the island. It also is the starting point of an equally superb levada path that winds along the cliff at an easy gradient—back to Santo da Serra.

5. *Porto da Cruz*, nestling in the lee of Eagle Rock, is a center of

vineyards that produce a good red table wine, whereas the famous Madeiras are largely dessert wines.

6. *São Roque do Faial* is one of the world's oddest-looking villages, straight out of a children's book of fantasies.

7. *Faial* is the established place for lunch on all trips to this part of the north coast, unless the tripper has brought his own picnic lunch from his hotel in Funchal. Faial's privately owned *Casa de Chá* (Tea-house) provides first-rate hot meals, but one should avoid delay by making advance arrangements through the tourist office or the hotel porter. It should not be assumed that one can "pick up" a good meal casually in any part of the island except at Funchal.

8. *Santana* is a remarkably photogenic village on the north coast, and it actually boasts a nice little pension, called *Pensão Figueira,* where those with time for north-shore explorations may secure lodging and meals.

9. *Queimadas,* at an altitude of 3000 feet, is at the dead end of a mountain road leading in from Santana. There is a small rest house here where hikers may put up for the night—and what hiking is to be had! The two-hour levada walk to *Caldeirão Verde* (Green Caldron) is unsurpassed on Madeira, which is to say unsurpassed anywhere. The walker may continue in a further hour to the source of this levada and to the *Caldeirão do Inferno* (Caldron of Hell). A more challenging path from Queimadas leads, in rather less than three hours, to *Pico Ruivo* (Purple Peak), which is the highest point of Madeira, 6050 feet above the sea. Here, too, there is a rest house where, by making advance arrangements at Queimadas, one may spend the night.

The return from Santana to Funchal is generally made, as it was in my own case, by the road through Ribeiro Frio and over the Poiso Pass.

10. *Ribeiro Frio* (2900 feet altitude) is an upland valley where trout fishing may be enjoyed. From here it is but a twenty-minute walk beside a babbling levada to a belvedere named *Balcões* (Balconies), sometimes singularized to Balcão, where the spellbound viewer feels himself "way in de middle ob de air," poised 2000 feet above the valley and with a spectacular background of Madeira's central mountain range in the middle distance. This goal of goals may be easily reached by the ordinary tripper. More ambitious hikers may continue, in two hours,

along a mountain path (glorious, of course) to *Fajã de Nogueira*. From the motor road several other levada paths, "each better than any other," lead to *Porto da Cruz*, to *Lamaceiros* and back to *Santo da Serra*.

11. *Poiso Pass*, traversed by the main highway nearly a mile above sea level, is a crossroads point of no special importance except for its height. And so back to Terreiro da Lucta, Monte and Funchal.

Second Trip, North by West—to Curral das Freiras.

1. *Santo Antonio* is a valley suburb of Funchal. Each year, in early June, it blows its top in a *festa* to honor its patron, St. Anthony of Padua, the holy man who tired of human coldness and preached to the fishes. In a painting in the village church you may see him doing it. Festas, by the way, are the very heartbeats of Madeira. It will be unusually bad luck if you do not run into such a celebration in some saint-named village. The general festa on New Year's Eve is just about the greatest show on earth. At night, the hills back of Funchal become a veritable holocaust of colored fireworks.

2. The *Miradouro do Pico dos Barcelos* is a hilltop developed and landscaped by the Tourist Office. It offers good close-up views of Funchal and its environs.

3. *The Serrado "Balcony"* and *Curral das Freiras* form a superb two-fold goal. This Balcão—I like that word for a belvedere—provides a sensational view, perhaps the island's most celebrated, of the serrated Curral Mountain Chain. A very short, easy climb leads to the Balcony, which was opened to tourism in 1962. From the point where the path takes off, a new road, said to have cost two million dollars, winds down in many a hairpin turn and through many a tunnel to the village of Curral das Freiras, which was formerly accessible only by a long and toilsome path. It nestles in a very deep extinct crater and its significant name means Corral of the Nuns, referring to the fact that in medieval times the island's nuns were "corraled" here to keep them from the clutches of lascivious corsairs.

Third Trip, West and North—to São Vicente and Seixal by car.

1. *Camara de Lobos* is a fishing village six miles west of Funchal. When Sir Winston Churchill vacationed at Funchal in 1950 (in a suite at Reid's Hotel) this village was the favorite theme of his paintbrush.

When you see it you will understand why.

2. *Cabo Girão* is one of the two or three highest sea cliffs in the world, shooting up a sheer 1930 feet from the waves. The view from the government balcony on its summit is unforgettable. The name of the cliff means Cape Turning, this being the point at which the Portuguese discoverer of the island turned back during his exploratory voyage in 1420.

3. *Ribeira Brava* is the port village from which the road to São Vicente heads inland.

4. *Pousada dos Vinháticos* (the last word is the name of a local tree), at 2200 feet altitude, is a pleasant rest house amid stupendous scenery, built and maintained by the Madeira Tourist Office. It has a telephone, so one may easily order a meal, as desired, for any given hour. If you have as good luck as I did you will eat very well.

5. *Encumeada* means Pass, and here it is the 3430-foot pass across the mountain range from south to north Madeira. The two-way outlook from this particular encumeada is another adjective-killer! From this point long and notable levada walks are to be made toward the west (*Bica de Cana, Rabaçal,* etc.) and toward the east (Pico Ruivo, etc.).

6. *São Vicente*, on the north coast, is notable for its very photogenic chapel built *inside* an isolated rock at the mouth of the São Vicente River.

7. *Seixal*, about five miles west of São Vicente along the north coast, is the take-off point for a relatively new stretch of the coastal highway that now continues from that point, running clear around the western tip of Madeira, to join the south-coast road at *Prazéres* and *Calheta*. (From Calheta a mountain road leads up to Rabaçal, mentioned just above, a gloryspot of the first importance, complete with waterfalls. This is not covered in the four trips here outlined.)

My *Fourth Trip*, on a meandering little public steamer from Funchal to many south coast ports, was strictly of my own contriving. The ship was ambitiously named *Tigre* (Tiger), though its modest horn, like the lion of Bottom the Weaver, roared "as gently as any sucking dove." A newer steamer called the *Milano* now supplements the *Tigre*. We halted at Camara de Lobos, where a swarm of naked boys swam all around the ship, submerging frequently to salvage coins, escudos and half escudos, tossed into the water by passengers. We continued under the towering cliff of Cabo Girão, to make successive halts at *Campanario, Ribeira Brava, Ponta do Sol, Madalena do Mar*. I had intended to stay aboard the *Tigre* clear to Paül do Mar, but at Madalena I was persuaded by a young Portuguese whom I met on board to disembark for a visit to his uncle's home in that village and a drink of wine.

We scrambled ashore from a small rowboat that served as tender, walked half a mile along a perilous cliff path and finally reached his uncle's villa, amid luxuriant vineyards. The visit was a memorable one for me, saturated as it was with Madeiran hospitality. This family, like nearly every family and individual I met on the island, had relatives living in the States, in this particular case at North Easton, Massachusetts, and many were the ardent messages sent overseas by the medium of myself as courier. If the lovely island of Madeira is not yet very widely known to Americans, be assured that America *is* widely known to Madeirans. As the acquaintanceship becomes gradually more mutual it will be to our own great gain.

The Canaries' Siren Song

Those who heed the Canaries' call may voyage by one of the steamers that sail weekly from two mainland ports of Spain, Barcelona and Cádiz, but most tourists go by air. One may fly by Caravelle from Madrid to Las Palmas, Gran Canaria, in two hours flat, continuing in 35 minutes more to Santa Cruz de Tenerife. Spain has two air lines, big Iberia and the smaller Aviación y Comercio, which appears confusingly on the Iberia timetable as AO. Between the two chief cities just named there are eight or ten flights a day and, shuttling among the group of islands, with service to five of them, the two friendly competitors maintain a considerable network.

The Canary Islands did not get their name from songbirds. They gave it to them, for wild warblers, still abundant there, were exported to Europe and domesticated as early as 1600. The siren lure that now draws overseas visitors in increasing numbers to these tropical islands of Spain is the islands' own song or, in more practical terms, their perfection-for-a-song. I do not use such an extravagant word as perfection in any careless, excited mood, for the Canaries seem to me, soberly, to have every quality that vacationists want most. These include glorious ever-spring climate, spectacular and varied beauty, creature comforts of high rank, and a special ingredient that enhances all the other virtues. This ingredient is a fantastic cheapness of living, emphatically including holiday living, that is hardly matched elsewhere in today's tourist world and is unsurpassed by anything that I personally have experienced. The Islands are substantially less expensive than even mainland Spain.

They lie at latitude 28 degrees north, well out in the Atlantic, off the African coast at a point between Dakar and Casablanca. They are nine islands, forming an integral part of Spain, divided into the Western Group, with *Tenerife* (so spelled in Spanish, with one *f*) the chief island, *Santa Cruz* its capital, and the Eastern Group, with *Gran Canaria* (Grand Canary) the chief island, *Las Palmas* its capital. Each capital city has about 100,000 inhabitants. Each city has also an energetic tourist office, aiding travelers to see all parts of their respective islands.

The climate is as near to year-round perfection—there's that word again—as climate can be. Official meteorological records for Santa Cruz give the average minimum for January and February as 60 degrees Fahrenheit, the average maximum for July and August as 83 degrees. Sea breezes, being northerly trade winds every summer day, temper the warmest noons; and for a coolness that verges on cold one may take a short taxi ride from this city to the flanks of the highest mountain in Spain or its possessions, the *Peak of Teide,* soaring to an altitude of 12,200 feet. I went well up its flanks by car in April and found the crest to be snow-covered. In winter, snow three feet deep often blocks even this motor road.

The beauty of these islands ranges from softest verdure, with areas of brilliance from flowering trees that give a patchwork-quilt effect, to beaches beaten by savage surf, to wild mountain scenery as awesome, though not as high, as anything in the Andes.

Among special arboreal wonders are two that the islanders are rightly proud of, the dragon-tree and the *Higuera Religiosa* (Religious Fig). The dragon-tree forms an extremely broad, almost leak-proof umbrella of branches, whose sword-shaped leaves are packed together so tightly that nothing short of a hard, prolonged rain can penetrate the shelter. The circumference of one such umbrella, near the Tenerife village of *Icod*, is nearly fifty feet. The Religious Fig produces leaves of an incredibly delicate lace-like texture, an inspiration surely, to the thousands of Canarian women who spend their lives doing fine drawn-thread work and embroidery.

There is a healthy rivalry between the two chief islands, and Solomon himself, had he been here on vacation after completing his temple, would have been hard pressed to decide which is the lovelier, which the more interesting. I, no sort of Solomon, reached earth first on Gran Canaria, arriving in an Iberia plane from Madrid, and easily convinced myself that no rival could equal it in beauty. Its capital, Las Palmas, is a city strung out chiefly in one street three or four miles long, backed by a steep hill, the street being traversed by almost continuous lines, in both directions, of güagüas, the local busses that demand hardly more than one cent as fare. To this macaroni-shaped city Camille Saint-Saëns came frequently, and Canarians say that here he wrote part of *Samson et Dalila*. There is a fine theater (with a Saint-Saëns foyer), capable of providing a proper setting for his works.

The thirty-million-peseta *Hotel Santa Catalina*, opened in 1953, was an important news item in the tourist world. Its wealth of architectural and decorative beauty in marble, hard woods, copper and brass work, frescoes, fountained patios and so on defies swift description and I will not try to cope with it, yet every bit of this hostelry was designed by islanders, the leading spirit being an architect named Don Miguel Martín Fernández de la Torre. Two swimming pools, and likewise two beaches, these on opposite sides of a narrow isthmus not far distant, provide facilities for all varieties of bathing, and a golf course, called the oldest one in Spain, is situated on a high plateau back of the hotel. The newer 220-room *Hotel Metropol*, overlooking the harbor, features its own swimming pool, private beach and a balcony with every room.

Features Strange and Beautiful of Grand Canary

A special feature of this island, as distinguished from its modern city, is its heritage, both anthropological and archeological, from the *white* aborigines, called *Guanches*. These fair-skinned people, of uncertain origin, were conquered by Spanish invaders in 1483, and within a few years were efficiently liquidated. In certain villages, notably one called *Galda*, they may have lingered a bit longer, for the blond hair and light complexion of many villagers is said to be directly traceable to the Guanches. Aboriginal relics include burial mounds, labyrinths and queer storage cliffs that look like honeycombs.

A Grand Canary specialty of rare loveliness is its multitude of small private reservoirs, looking from any of the heights like blue jewels. I have counted up to thirty visible from a single vantage point such as *Monte de Aruca*. Canarians, favoring a metaphor of a different color, call these treasuries of water "transparent gold," since they are life-savers, in the occasional dry summers, to the extensive crops of tomatoes and bananas. Dry summers are not a common plague, but they can, though rarely, be menacing.

There are countless other remarkable attractions on this island and from the multitude I will mention but two.

The *Caldera de Bandama* is a crater as round as any kettle, which is the meaning of caldera, but rather larger than most, being more than half a mile across, from brim to brim, and nearly seven hundred feet deep. To see it you may go by car to the *Pico de Bandama* (with a refreshment pavilion), at an altitude of 1900 feet, and look down into it. In the bottom of the kettle is one farm, exactly one, and it appears to be well kept up. What a hermit life must that one farmer family live!

Teror is the name of the island's most handsomely situated and al-together romantic inland town, lying thirteen miles west of Las Palmas. I could not learn the source of this name, which somehow just grew, but the significance of the town to all pious Canarians is evident enough, for Teror is a revered pilgrim goal. It seems that in 1481 the Virgin appeared here in the branches of a pine tree, so a church was accord-ingly erected. In it is a silver statue of *La Virgen del Pino* (The Virgin of the Pine) and the *wealth* of this image is almost beyond computing, for *every* finger of the Virgin is embellished with rubies, emeralds and diamonds. Other jewels are on the head, the arms and the robe. The *Treasure* of the church is also a veritable mint. For a single priestly robe of the seventeenth century, gorgeously embroidered in gold and silver thread, an American millionaire once offered—and this is fact, not fiction—forty thousand dollars. As part of the bargain he offered also to replace it with an exact modern replica. The Church of Nuestra Señora del Pino rejected the offer.

Rival Wonders of Tenerife

Tenerife, which I reached from Las Palmas by a good overnight steamer, though I could have flown in an hour, threw me into the doldrums of indecision. It was every whit as beautiful as Grand Canary and had certain features all its own. I have mentioned the lofty Pico de Teide, but that is only the exclamatory center of a ring of attractions. Near it, at a mile-high place called *Boca de Tauce*, nature has built a completely level cinder airport five miles long, surrounded by monumental teeth that gnash the sky, but this is rather too far from Santa Cruz for regular use, so a nearer airport has had to be built.

Other Tenerife attractions surrounding the sky-piercing peak include the belvederes of *Cruz del Carmen* and *Cruz de Tajur;* the lovely picnic region called *Llano de los Viejos* (Plain of the Old Men) and *Llano de los Loros* (Plain of the Parrots); the university town of *La Laguna*, with perhaps the best food in the island at the *Aguere Inn;* the lush *Orotava Valley*, with the big *Hotel Taoro;* the black beach at *Puerto de la Cruz;* the new beach hotel called Valle-Mar; the queer straw hats of the east-coast countrywomen; and the big shrine church to Mary, Mother of the Canaries, rising from the very surf at *Candelaria*. The image of the *Virgin of Candelaria*, patroness of the islands, is supposed to have appeared on the beach to astonish the Guanches in the days of a "mencey" (king) named Damarmo, but this miracle did not prevent their extermination by the pious Spaniards, who took over the statue as their own. It is the honored cynosure of the islanders in the "Surf Church," and in the heart of the capital there is a lofty statue of this Virgin by none other than the great Canova. It is called *El Triunfo de la Candelaria*.

Big, busy Santa Cruz, the capital of this island, is a considerable city, and although it lacks good beaches it has everything else that one expects in a big resort capital. Its *Hotel Mencey* is only a trifle less luxurious than its rival on Grand Canary. It has handsomely frescoed lounges and attractive bedrooms and baths. There is a good night club grill room, with dancing and entertainment, and for special attractions folk dances of the islands are sometimes offered, such as the somber *Folia* and the contrasting *Isa*, a gay and youthful dance. Of course the lively *Malagueña* is also done. There are several good lesser hotels in the city. One of them, inexpensive and of good homelike quality, with a lovely private garden, is *Hotel Pino de Oro* (Golden Pine).

Paradise for the Pocket

The Spanish government has built four of its handsome and artistic tourist inns at scenic spots on four of the islands, namely *Grand Canary* (*Parador de la Cruz de Tejeda*, at 5000 feet altitude, with stupendous view); *Tenerife* (*Parador de las Cañadas* [Ravines] *de Teide*, in the lee of snow-crested Mt. Teide); the small island of *La Palma*, not to be confused with the *city* of Las Palmas (*Parador de Santa Cruz de la Palma*); and *Lanzarote* (*Parador de Arrecife*, named for the capital of the island). In all of them the tariff is uniform, averaging just over 100 pesetas for room and three meals. Only a few of the rooms have private bath, but all have running water. Two persons can have a room with bath, if they are lucky enough to get one, for 220 pesetas, with all meals, and very good ones, included for both.

Those fortunate people who can settle for a substantial period on the Islands find that costs work out about as follows. A good villa with four or five rooms, a garden and a garage may *at present* be rented by the month for about $70, or an unfurnished apartment for $25 to $50 a month. For a skilled cook one must pay $8 to $12 a month, for a maid $6, for a topflight gardener as high as $12 or $15 a month.

And what about taxes? A Canarian government syllabus in English has this to say. I quote: "Are there any taxes which the visitor or foreign resident must pay, and what are they?" The syllabus answers laconically, "None."

I could go on stressing the cheapness of virtually everything, including American cigarettes, Scotch whiskies, French wines and champagne, but perhaps I've said enough to establish the Islands as today's paradise-for-the-pocket. If they were *only* low in costs this documentation would hardly be worth setting down, but relegating the budget to a back room of the mind, it is entirely fair to say that in all essential ways they are a traveler's paradise—period.

I must not conclude this reportage of the Canaries without adding a few words about Lanzarote, for as the Canaries gain in popularity this island, hitherto almost unknown to Americans, has become a weird and interesting discovery to increasing numbers. Most easterly of the Canaries and consequently in the group headed by Gran Canaria, Lanzarote is in great part a volcanic desert, blasted in its most fertile areas by a six-year eruption (1730–36) that covered many square miles with a deep layer of lava. I very rarely quote from a tourist folder but I find one passage from one such folder issued by Las Palmas' Junta Provincial del Turismo so eminently quotable that I cannot resist the urge to set it down here. "Lanzarote is one of the world's most fantastic islands, with very little resemblance to the other Canary Islands, a never-never land that will give you a year's worth of dinner-table conversation back home. The visitor experiences a fierce emotion of dizziness, a sense of the Almighty in action, creating the world. It is a living picture from the Bible; also it resembles those wastes seen by a telescope on the moon. Here you may observe the simple man in a land with hardly two inches of rain a year overcoming nature by placing his seeds and vines in lava holes and covering them with black volcanic cinders that act as a condenser, extracting moisture from the air."

If you have a yen for the unusual you will love seeing Lanzarote, where old customs and costumes have yielded very little to the demands of modernity. Despite the island's Biblical otherwordliness you may reach it easily six days a week by an hour's Iberia flight from Las Palmas, or twice a week by an overnight sea voyage on one of the ships of the *Compañía Transmediterránea;* and you may lodge and eat well in the government's parador.

REVISION SUPPLEMENT TO CHAPTER 6

THE official list of hotels available from the Portuguese Tourist Information Office, 570 Fifth Avenue, New York City, or the Lisbon
office in *Palácio Foz*, can be a valuable acquisition whether you limit
your stay to Lisbon and its area or roam the provinces. This Supplement will concern itself only with Lisbon's environs, especially the
"Royal Riviera" and its extension, referring you to another book in
this series, called *All the Best in Spain and Portugal*, for full information on all of Portugal.

The *Estoril Royal Riviera*, continuing to Cascais and then "around
the corner of Portugal" to Guincho, has a number of new developments
that space prevents me from little more than listing. *Hotel Estoril-Sol*,
a property of the owners of the new *Casino Estoril* that will replace the
former casino some time in 1967, is Portugal's largest hotel to date.
Located at a beach point between Monte Estoril and Cascais, it has 400
air-conditioned rooms and baths. It is a 16-story holiday palace with
two entrances (one from the shore road, another in the rear) to the
10th floor, which is the level of the hill at that point. It offers a garage
for 200 cars and a complete service station, bowling lanes and several
huge suites renting for around $70 per day. *Hotel Palácio do Estoril*, the
former *grande dame* of Estoril hotels, has had a complete face-lifting
and the 50-room *Hotel Cibra*, near by, makes up in holiday atmosphere
what it lacks in size.

Monte Estoril, an extension of the main resort, has its first-class
Hotel Atlântico and nearby Cascais is going strong touristwise, with
two or three new hotels. One of them, *Hotel Baia*, has 60 balconied
rooms, each with bath. The *Estalagem do Albatross* is an ingeniously
converted garden villa (16 rooms) of luxurious nature near the sea, its
kitchen featuring Portuguese and French cooking. These two are supplemented by the *Pensão Solar Dom Carlos* and the *Residência Vista
Alegre*, both pleasant and small.

At *Guincho*, three good seaside inns demand mention. They are the *Hotel do Guincho*, a government-owned 40-room inn created by the conversion of an old fort; the *Estalagem do Forte "Muxacho,"* a rustic inn with tiled patio and attractive restaurant; and the *Mestre-Zé* (Master Joseph), smaller, but located, like the other two, *directly* on the shore.

At Sintra (pages 104–5), the *Estalagem da Raposa* and *Pouso sa Urca* are closed, unfortunately, but the restaurant at the Queluz Palace is still open to the public and must be mentioned. Called the *Cozinha Velha* (Old Kitchen), the restaurant *is* the old kitchen, faithfully and royally restored for modern use. Here you may enjoy a good meal, high tea or merely a drink at the bar.

The trans-Tagus ferries have always been a strand of color in the river scenes of Lisbon and they will continue to play their role, but it will be a reduced one now that the Tagus River Bridge is completed. The United States Steel Export Company built the bridge across the two-mile estuary, although the Export-Import Bank got into the act with a big loan. This is now the largest expansion bridge in Europe, its central span being well over half a mile. Although the bridge is geared to carry four lanes of traffic, it is designed so that two more lanes can be added at a later date. The bridge approach on the Lisbon side is not far from Belém, and on the trans-Tagus side it emerges at a point close to the towering statue of *Christ the King*. It opens up, even to the one-day tourist, an interesting new beach area, the *Costa da Caparica*, on the open Atlantic, and the lovely hill area called *Serro da Arabida*, with the south-facing beaches of Sesimbra and Portinho, plus the port city of Setúbal. In case a substantial period of time is allotted to Portugal, the motorist may wish to tour Portugal's increasingly popular south. The development of the southern provinces, particularly Algarve, with its beach resorts and big new hotels, has brought these holiday sections to the attention of the tourist world, especially the motoring part of it, and I may state, more than incidentally, that Portugal's self-drive car rates are claimed to be the lowest in Europe.

CHAPTER 6

LISBON INTRODUCTION

To Earth Beside the Tagus

THE air traveler's arrival at Lisbon's Portela de Sacavém Airport is delightfully painless. You get through immigration and customs formalities "with all deliberate speed," to quote the Supreme Court's famous phrase, and as for your money, nobody cares how much you carry or in what form or currencies, for Portugal is a hard-money country and exchange is completely free.

The ride into town in the company bus, or by taxi at a fare of only about a dollar, including the special luggage charge, is a crescendo in little initiatory excitements, and in beauties too, for the route leads through some of the best and most modern residential quarters, not through dreary near-slums as is so often the case in one's approach to big cities. As you ride you presently become aware that *blue tilework* is the symbol of Portugal, for you see it everywhere, and you realize that flowers, including smothering masses of bougainvillea, are of the essence of this favored land and city. You make the approach by rolling into and around several circular park-plazas such as the Circle of Duke Saldanha and the Circle of the Marquis of Pombal, and are presently at the city terminal or at your hotel. The Pombal Circle, a real étoile, is at the head of the broad central avenue of Lisbon called Avenida da Liberdade, which is the city's Champs Elysées, really three parallel streets separated by two strips of parkway that are enlivened by open-air cafés. Lisbon does not let you down when you reach its center, though of course its ancient parts are congested and with narrow streets. It is a *clean* city even in the oldest and poorest parts such as the Alfama quarter, setting a mark for many an American city to shoot at.

The Pedigreed City of Ulysses

Lisbon claims that its name, originally Olisipo or Ulissipo, is from its alleged founder, Ulysses, the much-traveling king of Ithaca whose Greek name gave us the word Odyssey, but more ambitious chroniclers insist that the Ithacan was a relative newcomer and that Abraham's grandson founded the city! They even have a date for it, 3259 B.C., which you will see on travel folders, but in any case the first thousand years were *not* the hardest, for on November 1, 1755, shortly after completing its fifth millennium, Lisbon was rocked by one of the most terrific earthquakes that ever devastated a city. Forty thousand inhabitants, at least a third of its then population, died in the resulting fire and in the tidal wave that invaded the quays. The Marquis of Pombal, whose imposing statue rises in the center of the Circle named for him, guided the rebuilding of Lisbon with remarkable courage and energy.

If 1755 was the city's low point it has had plenty of high ones before and since. In the late fifteenth and early sixteenth centuries it was the chief implement used by fate to pry open the world and reveal it to ambitious men and nations. It missed two supreme opportunities, first by throwing away its chance to sponsor the voyages of Columbus and later by estranging Magellan, just before that pioneer undertook his greatest voyage, which led one of his ships around the world, but in spite of these bleak failures it frequently outshone its rival, Spain, in early voyages of discovery. On the wall of an unimpressive building of yellow stucco on the water front near Cais do Sodré you may read, in Portuguese, the following inscription: "In this place were built the ships that discovered new lands and seas and carried to the whole world the name of Portugal." Consider some of the men who commanded or sponsored these ships, for they, in essence, are the background of the picture of Portugal and the buildings associated with them are among the greatest sights of the city.

Prince Henry the Navigator was the father of modern navigation and it was his spirit that sparked Portugal's long pre-eminence in exploration. Half English and half Portuguese, he eagerly sought the kingdom of "Prester John," which then possessed men's minds. He didn't find this mythical region of wealth but he did initiate the opening of Africa's vast perimeter.

Diogo Cam followed Prince Henry and discovered the mouth of the Congo and other key points of the western coast of Africa.

Bartolomeu Dias, sailing a few years later, reached the Cape of Good Hope and even rounded the southern tip of Africa, but was forced by the discontent of his men to return to Lisbon.

Vasco da Gama completed the major discovery route that his predecessors had pioneered. Sailing around South Africa and between Mozambique and Madagascar, he finally reached India, the goal of many a spicy and golden dream. His journeys made him famous, but his fellow-countryman, *Camões,* made him immortal through *The Lusiads.* Luis Vaz de Camões was himself something of an explorer but his great achievements were, of course, in epic poetry and sonnets. *The Lusiads* is the classic that established the Portuguese language as Dante had already established the Italian language and Chaucer the English.

Pedro Alvarez Cabral set out from Lisbon to fix more firmly the Indies Route, but was driven by currents and storms to the unknown coasts of Brazil, which he promptly claimed for his king. That is why Brazil today speaks Portuguese. On the Beira Mar of Rio de Janeiro a conspicuous feature of that daughter city of Lisbon is an imposing statue of Cabral.

Ferdinand Magellan, in Portuguese Fernão de Magalhães, was perhaps Portugal's greatest discoverer but unhappily he fell into disfavor with his king, renounced his nationality and set out on his celebrated earth-girdling voyage under the patronage of the Spanish throne. He was killed in the Philippines but one of his ships did sail clear around the earth, Seville to Seville. Portugal naturally claims at least a half interest in him and deeply regrets the relatively minor squabble that led its king to dismiss from royal service so great a man.

King Manuel the Fortunate was the monarch who, in the year 1500, consolidated the various Portuguese discoveries mentioned above, and many more by minor explorers, into the Portuguese Empire, which was confirmed by the Pope two years later. His name, given to an ex-uberant style of architecture, Manueline, leads us straight to those buildings, and that quarter of Lisbon, most directly associated with the explorers. I refer to *Belém*, this being a shortened Portuguese form of Bethlehem, a Tagus-side suburb on the western edge of the capital. Belém is dramatized by the *Torre de Belém*, a magnificent tower at the water's edge once rising from a rocky island. It was completed under King Manuel and is a symbol of Lisbon. From it, on many an occasion, anxious kings and princes watched hopefully for the return of their intrepid mariners. A short distance from this is Manuel's greatest architectural monument, the Hieronymite church and convent and cloister of Belém, designed during his reign in the extravagant but still beautiful late Gothic (or Composite) style that bears the king-emperor's name. Over the portal of the church is a statue of Prince Henry the Navigator. Inside its dim recesses is the rich sarcophagus of Manuel, along with those of other royal personages, and also the coffins that contain the bones of Vasco da Gama and Camões. This church is important in many ways, and the convent and cloister are masterpieces. The ensemble seems somehow the soul of that Portugal which helped so greatly to tear away the shrouds of mystery and fear that hid half the world.

Portuguese Money; Tourist Counsel; Lodging; Dining

Portugal, as I've said, is one of Europe's dependably hard-currency countries, with the result that there are virtually no fluctuations in exchange and no restrictions on frontier money controls, a feature that has long been pleasingly evident to travelers. The unit of currency is the *escudo*, which means shield, or escutcheon. The present worth of this escutcheon is a trifle over $3\frac{1}{2}$ cents, which figures out at about 28 to the dollar. The folding money comes in denominations of 20 escudos and up. In nickel there are coins of 50 centavos ($\frac{1}{2}$ escudo) and 1 escudo, and in silver, or silverish metal, coins of $2\frac{1}{2}$, 5 and 10 escudos. The subsidiary copper coins are of 5, 10 and 20 *centavos*. It is easy for the newcomer to mistake the nickel coins for those that are worth ten times as much. If, for instance, the face of your shoeshine boy lights up with an incandescent glow when you tip him 50 centavos you may be pretty sure you have given him 5 escudos. In many countries such confusions exist, and in case you care, it is worth taking time out, whenever you meet a new form of money, to *make its acquaintance.* Few travelers actually do this and only by the time they leave a country have they really come to know, by trial and error, what they are handling. We are not amused, as a book, by those helpless persons who fill their hand with money and say to each creditor, "Here, take what I owe you. I never can get the hang of this crazy money."

Portugal's hotels are all regulated by the *Secretariado Nacional da Informação*, which includes the National Tourist Bureau, with its Information Office, and which we may call simply SNI. This several-armed organ of the government publishes an easy-to-use list of hotels, to be acquired at the Tourist Information Office, a goal which every visitor to Lisbon should seek. It is to be found on the rambling Praça dos Restauradores, at the base of the central Avenida in a lovely pink plaster building called the Palacio Foz. In three languages, one of which is English, the hotel list gives all essential information about cost of room, of meals included or taken separately and of service charges. It tells the facts, for each place, about private bath, running water, heating, elevator, garage and so on.

While in the Information Office seeking counsel be sure to ask also for two pamphlets that are of prime tourist interest, each serving to supplement the other. One is a 32-page *Selective Shopping Guide of Lisbon*, offered gratis by the monthly magazine *Portugal Today*. The other is called *The Tourist Guide of Lisboa*. This I find one of the most compact yet comprehensive city guides I have ever seen. In a dozen pages that fold into the shape of one fat business letter, it presents a plan of Lisbon, maps of Lisbon's choicest suburban areas, a tourist map of Portugal and any quantity of detail on hotels, restaurants, amusements, shops, cultural attractions, transportation, postal rates, special festivals and so on—and on. This portable gold mine should be acquired early by everyone. The two-legged selective shopper, by the way, should also be aware of two organizations that can greatly help him or her in dispatching gifts to home folks. One is the long-established *American Visitors Bureau*, located in the rear of the TWA Building on Avenida da Liberdade, near the Pombal Circle; the other is a newer place called *International Travel Service*, at Rua Castilho 61. Both of these concerns will take over, for modest fees, the wrapping and dispatching of any packages, whether "Unsolicited Gifts Valued Under $10" or more ambitious sendings. Both also have a great variety of gift items of their own for sale. The American Visitors Bureau is part of a three-link chain, the other links being in Madrid and Barcelona.

As regards those distressing extras that crop up in such abundance on the hotel bills of, for instance, France and Italy, I have a bit of very good news. In 1962, Portugal simplified and sharply reduced these extras by dropping completely the 15 per cent tax on meals in luxury and first-class hotels, a tax that applied also to breakfast served in one's room, even when the breakfast was included in the room's price. This left only the 10 per cent service charge, a very moderate one in present-day Europe, a 10 per cent tax on alcoholic drinks and a *local* tax of 3 per cent assessed by local authorities in many tourist centers, including Lisbon. Since the service charge is so moderate it is customary to leave a small sweetener here and there, at least to waiter, chambermaid and hall porter. This last functionary, as is usually the case in Europe, is a personage of real importance in the tourist picture, since he knows all and tells all, and sells postage stamps as well, or handles letters for the customer if requested. He should be rather "well remembered" by the guest upon departure.

Lisbon hotels have experienced an amazing upsurge in number and quality, this tide occurring about a decade later than the similar surge that made such tourist news in Madrid in the 50's. On the crest of the highest wave is a hotel whose opening made headlines all over the tourist world. It is still newsworthy and I will attempt to cope with it.

Hotel Ritz is its name. This is the newest link in the international chain of *Les Grands Hôtels Européens*, whose guiding genius, the late Georges Marquet, was one of the best-known and most respected hotel proprietors in Europe. His family now runs the chain with unabated zeal and success. Among other famous links are the *Palace* and the *Ritz* in Madrid, the *Ritz* in Barcelona, the *Alfonso XIII* in Seville and the *Continental Palace* in San Sebastián. In discussing Lisbon's Ritz I shall have to hitch a checkrein to my pen, for it is hard to avoid sounding like a Hollywood blurbster. To tell first how it came into being, the Ritz was conceived as a sort of showcase of Portuguese achievement, the investment coming largely from a group of about a dozen of the nation's wealthiest men. Its cost, and remember that

Portuguese labor costs are vastly less than those in the U.S., was about $8 million, but this doesn't tell the whole story.

First, the "Ritz Law" was devised and passed by the national government, setting a very low price on the 10,000 square meters of land on which the hotel is built and providing that the luxury materials for its construction and decoration, coming from a score of different countries, should enter Portugal duty-free. Then the "Tourist Law" was invoked. This provides that *any* new hotel all of whose rooms will have private bath shall be relieved, for a period of twenty years, of all State taxes. (The net result of this law is that virtually every Portuguese hotel recently built does indeed have a bath with every room, which is a situation *quite without parallel in Europe*.) So the Ritz was off to a flying start and no expense or effort was spared to secure the absolute best in materials, construction, design and décor. Built on a slope well above Edward VII Park, on the west side, it has a magnificent panoramic view of the city's "cradle" and the opposite heights. It has fourteen floors and a roof terrace, four of the floors being given over to services, the remaining ten to 300 air-conditioned, soundproofed bedrooms and baths, including a number of superlative suites. All the rooms that face the park are provided with broad private balconies. Its main portals open from an upper street named Rua Rodrigo da Fonseca. One of its underground floors is a 100-car garage with a complete service station.

The service areas through which I was guided seemed like those of a *Queen Mary* or a *France*. The great kitchen is "a long way out of this world." The main lounge is a deliberate paradox of décor, two outsized modernistic murals defying quiet, conservative furnishings and carpetings. The wall separating the entrance lobby from this lounge consists of ninety-six large panels of suede leather, beige with gold designs, and in front of the wall stand four seven-foot alabaster vases, illumined from within. The dining room and the grill are unsurpassed anywhere in quiet elegance. At the entrance to the dining room I noted, on a recent visit, a contrasting bit of bright decoration, namely a faithful replica of Notre Dame de Paris constructed in sugar by the head chef. This too was illumined from within. The ballroom symbolizes Versailles' Galerie des Glaces, and all its furniture is of period design, individually made to order. A *boîte* for dancing was recently opened. Ten thousand square meters of hand-made carpeting cover every inch of hallway and bedroom floors.

There is more, much more, to tell, but I'll spare you. What I *have* told is by way of explaining that this Ritz is a sight, an experience, a conversation piece. By Portuguese standards, but *not* by American, it is expensive. A large, double front room with bath and balcony *and Continental breakfast*, is currently priced at about $13.50 for one, $21 for two.

The small but famous luxury hotel named the Aviz must have become discouraged at the prospect of competing with the Ritz for it has closed and the building has been razed.

The *New Tivoli*, on Lisbon's central stem, Avenida da Liberdade, should by no means be confused with the old, mediocre Tivoli. The new hotel is officially rated in the first-class A category and from having stayed there on two occasions I would say that it borders on the luxury class. Its rooms, each with private bath and with radio, are modern and cheerful, its marble-floor lounge is large and comfortable and a terrace night club on the roof provides a close-up view of the heart of Lisbon, as well as of the city's environs. The adjacent "old Tivoli" has been torn down and replaced by another section of the New Tivoli, bringing the total number of rooms and baths to over 300. This excellent hotel is second only to the Ritz, yet its prices are very moderate. They may serve here as a gauge of the bargain rates that prevail in Lisbon and, to a much greater degree, in provincial Portugal. The rate for an excellent eighth-floor room I occupied not long ago was only $7 for single occupancy and $9.50 for double, without meals. With full meals it was about $10 for one person, $15 for two persons. Let's compare these figures with the charges in a first-class hotel in any American city!

Hotel Fenix, a 1-A hotel facing the beautiful Marqués de Pombal Circle, was opened in 1960, with 125 rooms and baths. Its convenience of location is in its favor, for it is at the upper end of Avenida da Liberdade and a subway station is directly opposite its doors, yet it is also on a corner of Rua de Aguias, at the edge of what may be called the "midtown" area of business, of quality shops and of good residential streets.

Hotel do Imperio, a 1-A hotel on Rua Rodrigues Sampaio, a street parallel to the main stem, is nearly a score of years old, but it is well kept up and very recommendable. This hotel and the Fenix are both members of the high-grade HUSA chain, whose links are found chiefly in Spain. Good radios are in every room of both Lisbon hotels.

Four other 1-A hotels in the city, all centrally located, call for mention.

Hotel Avenida Palace, recovering from a long period of decline, has at last undergone an extensive renewal worthy of its wonderful location on Praça dos Restauradores adjacent to the Rossío, heart square of the city.

Hotel Embaixador (Ambassador), on Avenida Duque de Loulé near the central Pombal Circle, was opened in 1956. Its main restaurant is on the 9th floor and there is a popular night club restaurant on the 10th and an open-air roof-garden above that, so this hotel capitalizes on *view*. Each of its 100 rooms has bath, radio and good music from records.

Hotel Condestável, a rather recently built hotel on Travessa do Salitre very close to the New Tivoli, started with a 1-B rating, but improvements have brought it up a notch to 1-A. It, too, has approximately 100 rooms and baths.

Hotel Mundial, on Rua Dom Duarte near the Rossío, is a veteran which is kept young by continual attentions and renewals. Its location in the very-old quarter called Mouraria just below the dramatic Castelo de São Jorge is decidedly "different." Its dining room, on the seventh floor, provides a fascinating close-up view of "early Lisbon." Fado is said to have originated in Mouraria, and Maria Severa, the most famous fadista of all, lived here.

Of 1-B hotels, all good, there are now four of fairly recent construction in addition to the aging *Victoria*.

Hotel Edward VII, near the Embaixador, a modern skyscraping (by European standards) hotel, is of about the same size and quality as its neighbor, though its entrance lobby is very small. The lounge is on the 4th floor, the dining room on the 10th, and it has, like its neighbor, an open-air garden-café on the roof. Service in the dining room is à la carte only.

Hotel Infante Santo (Holy Child), on a like-named avenida, is a small place whose chief advantage is that it closely overlooks the busy

Tagus River. Every room has a balcony to enhance the guest's pleasure in surveying the lively river scenes. There is a small, separate restaurant just below the hotel, connected with the lobby by an elevator. Here, too, service is à la carte only.

Hotel Flórida, on the lower perimeter of the Pombal Circle, and *Hotel Rex*, on Rua Castilho, this with à la carte service only, are the other 1-B hotels. The Flórida's new section of 72 rooms and baths is splendidly located, with entrances both on the circle and on Rua Castilho. With restaurant, snack bar and boîte, it is well equipped to cater to tourists, and from various parts of it there is a lovely view of King Edward VII Park. The older part of the hotel is to be torn down to make room for a new addition of 50 rooms and baths.

Hotel Flamingo, on Rua Castilho, is a thoroughly good place of second-class rating. It has 35 rooms and baths and a pleasant restaurant (à la carte). In this hotel two persons may lodge comfortably for $7.00 and may have all meals for an additional $5.25.

Hotel Miraparque (Parkview), pleasantly placed on Avenida Sidónia Pais flanking Edward VII Park, is another second-class hotel deserving thought.

Among Lisbon's *thrift hotels*, the *Alexandre d'Almeida* group is outstanding. Its properietors believe, with reason, that Lisbon has an abundance, if not an overabundance, of first-class accommodations and they cling to a policy of providing good second-class hotels in good locations at thrift tariffs. The *Metropole*, where I have twice stayed, has fascinated me because of its balcony rooms overlooking the Rossío. There are 16 of these large rooms, each with bath, and they may be occupied by two persons for $7.50 without meals or $11.50 with meals. The dining room, up one floor from the street, is not in the least pretentious, but restaurants are available in the neighborhood for those who wish to "eat around."

Among Lisbon's *pensions*, the *Mansão* (Mansion) *Nazaré* is very well rated, though it lacks rooms with private bath. The *Pensão Residência América* and the *Pensão Moderna*, each with 10 rooms, are well recommended. The former, high up in a business building, has its dining room on the top (12th) floor.

Lisbon restaurants, fado places and night clubs have not advanced to anything like the same extent as the city's hotels, but there are some places well worth knowing, perhaps the most important one being the *Locanda Aviz*, at Rua Serpa Pinto 12B, a restaurant opened in 1962 by the owners of "the late" Hotel Aviz. Its décor is in lively Gay Nineties style. Fortunately for gourmets the same chef who delighted guests of the hotel was secured for the new restaurant.

The *Vera Cruz*, on Avenida da Liberdade, is one of Lisbon's best. Its *Bife Especial*, a steak enhanced with sherry and Madeira wines and several mysterious condiments, is cooked in a pan in full view of the guest, whose taste buds wriggle as the ritual proceeds.

Restaurant Galeota, on Avenida Sidónio Pais, is a very good French place flourishing under the eye of its French owner.

Tágide, on Largo Biblioteca, is an attractive doubleton, being a high-class restaurant downstairs and a fashionable night club upstairs.

A Gondola, on Avenida de Berna, is a place of some luxury, with a small garden, known chiefly for its Italian dishes.

Montes Claros, on a crest called Monsanto west of the city, has a view to match its good food, but the prices are moderate.

Solmar, just east of Praça dos Restauradores, is a "multiple" restaurant, chiefly marine, with fancy features such as a central fountain, glass fish tank (pick your fish) and large seascape murals.

Cozinha Alentejana, on the avenue leading to the airport, is typical of Alentejo, an eastern province of Portugal, in its fare and in the costumes of the cute little waitresses, who need to be cute to wear with success the tight-fitting skirt-pants, polychrome stockings and broad-brimmed hat of their province.

Restaurant Folclore, making its bow in 1959, is primarily an evening restaurant of special quality, offering a big and very good folklore show, along with fado by top fadistas. All of Portugal's provinces are represented by songs and bright dances done in costume, and to conclude the show the guests themselves join the performers to march around the restaurant carrying lighted lanterns and flowered arches. The Folclore also features exhibits in glass wall cases of folklore handicrafts, supplementing these with a gift shop in the entrance hall. This restaurant is one *not to miss*. It is located on Rua Nova da Trindade in the Bairro Alto.

The Lisbon Cradle and Its Surroundings

Lisbon is shaped like a cradle. The bottom of the cradle is the *Cidade Baixa* (Lower City), and from it rack-and-pinion trams, outright elevators and streets of hairpin curves lead to the heights, which are always called seven in number. It seems that any self-respecting city with hills must claim seven of them, because that is the admitted number in Rome, but Lisbon is so utterly individual that it has no need to lean on any magic number.

The bottom of the cradle is easy to explore. At its riverside end a magnificent square bears the dull name Praça do Comércio but is popularly called Black Horse Square because of the equestrian statue of Joseph I that centers it. Ten parallel streets lead north from this, and one of them, Rua do Ouro, the Street of Gold, may be considered the main shopping stem, though it is rivaled by the newer Rua Nova do Almada, continuing as Rua Nova do Carmo, just to the west. As a tangent from the point where this street changes its name, the modern Rua Garrett, formerly "the Chiado," is a very animated center of fashionable shops and cafés.

Four of the south-to-north streets from Praça do Comércio lead into the Rossío, which has been mentioned in connection with the hotel list as the heart of the city. This big, fountained oblong is surrounded by cafés and small shops, and on the north side is the *Teatro Nacional Dona Maria II*, the home of drama and other assorted attractions. Around a little jog from this is the main (Rossío) railway station, which is surely one of Europe's oddest, for one must take an elevator to the third floor to reach the track gates.

For a long time the Rossío, like Milan's heart square, Piazza del Duomo, has been a *mess* because of subway construction. Lisbon's new subway runs from Praça dos Restauradores under Avenida da Liberdade to the Pombal Circle and from there far out to the suburbs, in two branches. Downtown, it is now being extended from the Praça-with-the-long-name to the Rossío and then all the way to Black Horse Square and the Tagus quays. Maybe the extension will be completed by the time you come and the Rossío mess cleared up, but subways move slowly, if their trains do not.

From the railway station entrance and the nearby Praça the main avenida, "low, wide and handsome," leads straight to the Pombal Circle and the *Edward VII Park*, at the northern end of the cradle. This park, which could do with a Portuguese name, is a Garden of Eden if I ever saw one. In one corner of it is the *Estufa Fria*, or "Cool Hothouse," so landscaped that Portugal's warm sun seeps through a heavily latticed roof, providing just that degree of cool warmth necessary for certain shrubs and plants. Little streams, crossed by rustic bridges, trickle through the Estufa Fria and there are many benches suitable for siesta. Good orchestral concerts are given here from time to time (admission about 5 cents!) and you sit where you like or merely stroll around if the seats are taken. The orchestra is concealed by shrubbery. At the top of the park is a curious new structure with a *miradouro* (tower) on either side. (In the residential part of Lisbon farther out, three special sights are the ultramodern *Church of Our Lady of Fátima*, the impressive park-like avenue known as the *Alameda* and a Zoo with a *miniature town* that delights children of all ages.)

The *Upper City*, the city of the hills, is reached by an amazing variety of means, including good climbing muscles. The funiculars are fun and two of the seven or more lead steeply up from opposite sides of the Avenida da Liberdade, not far from the Foz Palace. The one on the west side that ascends the Calçada da Gloria puts you promptly in touch with a lofty section of great interest, including a marvelous belvedere, the *Jardim de São Pedro de Alcântara*. The *Botanical Garden* and the adjacent *Praça do Rio de Janeiro*, a little park in its own right, are near by.

Unless you hire a guide, and even if you do, you will have great need of a good map, which, as I've said, the National Tourist Office will provide. With map in hand I shall try to list, in as simple a way as I can, and necessarily abridged, all the best, or at least "part of the best," of Lisbon's high spots.

West of the Cradle

1. The belevedere mentioned above and the beautiful Rio de Janeiro Square, at its west corner, offer grand prospects of many things, including the Tagus.

2. The *Carmo Church*, reached by elevator from the Street of Gold, near its Rossío end, is interesting, and so is its pleasant Largo do

Carmo. Another church, the late-Renaissance *São Roque*, is a near neighbor. From the lower levels of the city it can be seen looming up above and behind the Rossío Station.

3. The *Praça de Luiz de Camões*, reached from Rua Garrett, has a monument to Portugal's genius of poetry.

4. *Largo São Carlos*, a few steps from Rua Garrett, has the big *Teatro Nacional de São Carlos*, Lisbon's opera house, built in the style of La Scala.

5. On the *Largo da Biblioteca Pública*, as its name proclaims, is the *National Library of Lisbon*, containing many treasures, including a first edition of *The Lusiads*.

6. Some miles west of the cradle, reached by the splendid automobile highway leading to Estoril and Sintra, is the hill called *Monsanto*, and on its highest point the *Miradouro* (Belvedere) *dos Montes Claros*, with a comprehensive view of city, sea and mountain chain. And speaking of views, I should conclude this West Side Story by stating that the balconies of Hotel Ritz provide a prospect of the Lisbon ensemble that is hardly surpassed by that from any of the public heights.

East of the Cradle

1. The *Sé Patriarcal* is Lisbon's cathedral. It is at the beginning of a chain of scenic and romantic wonders culminating in the conspicuous summit where the Castle of St. George commands the central city. Much of this region can be reached by simple tramway (Number 11 from the Rossío) and it is worth hours of exploration.

2. Look for *Largo de Santa Luzia*, with an exciting "close-down" view over the Alfama quarter, the port and the river; then try to find, and I hope you succeed, *Largo de São Estevão*, very near Santa Luzia and below the church of that name.

3. The *Castle of St. George* is the classic, unmissable high spot of this section of the city. It is the old Moorish citadel and on this site also stood Roman Lisbon, then called *Felicitas Julia*.

4. The *Church of São Vicente de Fora* (St. Vincent Without the Walls) is conspicuous on a hilltop, one of Lisbon's seven—or seventeen.

5. *Nossa Senhora do Monte*, north of the Castle, is a hermitage chapel of no great account except that it contains "the stone chair of São Gens, the first bishop of Lisbon, which is held in much esteem by pregnant women." The quoted words are from an ancient Baedeker,

and I find them just a bit bold for so conservative a sage! Even if you are not a pregnant woman I urge you to visit Our Lady of the Hill for the best three-star view, in my opinion, to be had from any high point *east* of the cradle.

6. *Nossa Senhora da Penha de França* (Our Lady of the Rock of France) rises from its own hill considerably to the north of those just mentioned, but for its view of the Sintra Range and the ocean beyond it, it is worth finding.

Covering the Water Front

The water front of Lisbon is an unfolding panorama of color piled on color. No artist could ever do it justice. I think a logical way to cover it is to start with the humble Alfama quarter, east of Black Horse Square, and work westward to Belém. And a wonderful way to experience Alfama itself is to walk down tortuously through it, from the Largo de Santa Luzia to (see your map) the fishy square called *Largo do Chafariz de Dentro*, meaning Square of the Water Trough of the Center. In a restaurant of epicures here, by name *A Parreirinha* (The Little Vinestock), you may buy yourself a bowl of Portuguese bouillabaisse by asking for *caldeirada à fragateira*. Alfama is jampacked with interest. It is violently up and down, often resorting to steps. Its streets are as quaint and as narrow as those of old Naples and five times as clean. Its vendors and hucksters are a story in themselves and they include the water vendors who continually call out "Água," the voice rising a full octave on the second syllable. Try to find *Beco do Espirito Santo* (Holy Spirit Alley), the very narrowest lane of the narrow. It leads off from Rua de São Miguel.

There is much more to find and luck can be your guide. This quarter was once, if you can believe it, one of fashion and elegance. You *will* believe it when you chance upon stray touches of Manueline decoration in houses of the struggling poor. They reveal that the smart set of the sixteenth century considered Alfama *the* place to live.

From Alfama the coverer of the water front will hasten, perhaps by taxi, over a relatively dull section to the electric railway station called Cais do Sodré. Between this station and the river he will en-counter—it is much the best in the morning hours—an unending procession of *varinas*, or fish-women, hurrying, and often actually *running*, to sell their finny goods in all parts of the city. Speed is essential since this is a case of "first come first sold." Old and young, pretty and plain, fat and skinny, they pant along, each woman with a tray of fish, or sometimes some market vegetables or a sack of potatoes, on her head, each shuffling ahead at an amazingly swift pace but never losing the erect grace she has developed from being long accustomed to balancing her burdens in the traditional way of Mediterranean women.

In the wharf sheds you may see the mountains of produce, sea produce predominating, where these ambulant traders make their deals, fill their trays and rush out to sell. And moored to the wharves, or riding the river, are the colorful, crescent-prowed craft that have brought the produce. Some are said to be direct descendants of Phoenician fishing boats. Many display a pair of painted eyes, one on either side of the prow, "to see the fishes." Out in the river, whose tidal current on flow and ebb attains a ten-knot speed, are larger lateen-rigged sailing ships, their big triangular sails dyed orange or brown or red. The Portuguese Navy, such as it is, strives to add its touch of dignity, and through all the river traffic go the ferries. An easy one for tourists to take is that to *Cacilhas*, just across the river, and a 35-minute trip to *Barreiro*, on the Tagus' southern shore, may be made by the regular ferry that ties in with the trains for Setúbal and southern Portugal (and so to Seville). All in all, there is no water front in the whole Mediterranean more exciting than that of Lisbon, which is the Mediterranean's city of introduction.

A natural climax to these shore wanderings is Belém, not only for the Torre and the buildings of King Manuel the Fortunate but for the *Ajuda Palace*, Portugal's White House, which is pink, and for the very noteworthy *Museum of Royal Coaches*, the greatest of its kind in Europe. Perhaps you have visited many royal palaces and have crossed showy coaches off your list of musts, but to cross off this collection would be, I think, a serious error. Of the whole collection, including a charming baby coach built for Don Carlos of Portugal by his grandfather, Victor Emmanuel II of Italy, the ones that appealed to me most were three huge, lumbering vehicles built in Rome some 250 years ago for the return of the Portuguese ambassador and his en-

tourage to Lisbon. In 1716, the ambassador made the formidable journey
—in three months. In this air age we may cover the same distance in
fewer *hours*. I believe someone has mentioned that the world is growing smaller!

A recent embellishment of Belém is a magnificent monument honoring Prince Henry the Navigator. Standing on the very edge of the
broadening Tagus estuary, it represents the Prince at the crest of a
seaside cliff holding in his hands a model of a sailing ship. In two
parallel lines Portuguese discoverers and navigators are clambering up
the slope toward their leader.

Across the Tagus, more or less opposite Belém, stands a gigantic
statue of *Cristo Rei* (Christ the King), topping a 450-foot shaft.

Estoril is *the* retreat of exiled royalty, and of such Britons as still
manage to have the means for it, and also of the international playboy
and playgirl world. It is Portugal's Monte Carlo, but with a beach of
real sand, where one may hire a cabin, change, then sunbathe and
seabathe under top conditions. It has swank hotels, and many of
humbler category, shops, beach cafés, a well-manicured park, a million
flowers and blossoming shrubs *and* a sumptuous gambling casino with
all the attractions and accouterments customary in such establishments.
This, however, is still not sumptuous enough and a grandiose new one
is soon to be built.

The coastal highway of the Royal Riviera, blossoming with new and
newer hotels, becomes less royal, though no less interesting, as it
pushes westward to *Monte Estoril;* to *Cascais,* a fishing-and-art community of much color; to the *Boca do Inferno* (Mouth of Hell),
where waves rush through an arch into a caldron roaring like dragons
from Pluto's stable; to *Cabo Raso,* the "turning point," being the
absolute western ultimate of the European continent; and finally to
Hotel do Guincho, an old coastal fort that has been converted by the
Portuguese government into a delightful 40-room inn stretching out
over the surf.

Auto-Estrada *to Sintra*

A splendid automobile highway leads out of Lisbon's Pombal Circle
across a spectacular viaduct, past Montes Claros, then fairly near the

big, modern stadium, and so to *Queluz Palace*, just within the wide-spreading Municipality of Sintra.

Queluz is just what you have guessed it to be, Portugal's Versailles. Every royal land of Europe had to have a Versailles when Louis XIV had set the example and this one of Portugal is far better than most. It is, in fact, one of my personal favorites of the whole race. The palace itself is a very beautiful example of pink rococo, with unusual half-circling wings, and although it was badly damaged by fire in 1934 it has been restored with intelligence and artistic sympathy. The grounds manage to avoid the stiffness so common in the "Versailleses" of Europe. The topiary effects are interesting and not too bizarre, the fountain-pools are lovely, and the chief one, through which a natural brooklet flows, is given a desirable Portuguese touch by a lavish use of blue *azulejos*, which is to say tiles. Queluz is still used by the government for rare official functions and festas, but in general it is a gleaming goal of tourism, enhanced now by a character restaurant called the *Cozinha Velha*. This remarkable eating place is literally what its name proclaims, the Old Kitchen—of the Queluz Palace. It has been faithfully and royally restored for modern use without sacrificing its old charm, for it still retains, more or less in the center of the room, the original chimney, supported by 8 stone columns along its rim, soaring aloft over an open hearth that is 30 feet long and 8 feet wide; and it still keeps in a place of honor an original 15-foot table with a top consisting of a single 14-ton slab of stone. In this lovely old kitchen you may enjoy a good meal, a high tea or merely a drink at the bar.

Sintra, which used to be spelled Cintra, is a name whose drawing power must be worth millions to Portugal, yet the town has definitely not been spoiled, nor even damaged, by its long-lasting and wide-spread popularity. I have been acquainted with it for over thirty years and to me it is even more glamorous than it was on first sight. It is an outer suburb of Lisbon, some eighteen miles to the northwest, and now has about ten thousand permanent inhabitants, whose number is augmented in summer by vacationists. It is, of course, the pre-eminent royal suburb, in a much more classical sense that Estoril, and has been so since about 1390, when John I began constructing palaces here. Three are still to be seen, the old *Moorish Castle*, now hardly more than a ruined wall, the *Castle of Pena*, high on a hill, and the *Royal Palace of Sintra*, in the main square. From the two former the view is magnificent. The Castle of Pena was the royal summer residence to the very end of the monarchy, and Manuel's car raced madly up the steep curving road until just before that October day in 1910 when he was forced to flee for his life. Down in the Royal Palace lived the dowager queen, Maria Pia, grandmother of Manuel, until the debacle. Its interior is far more interesting than that of the garish Pena, which is nineteenth-century German. The whole atmosphere of the Royal Palace is more attractive and more imbued with the personality of those who dwelt in it.

Sintra is a very lovely and restful community for a "retreat vacation" in such dream places as *Hotel Palácio de Seteais*, which I'll attempt to describe presently, and such lesser but very pleasant country inns as *Estalagem da Raposa* and *Pouso da Urca*. The Palácio de Seteais—Seteais means "Seven Ahs" of rapture—rouses *my* enthusiasm more even than all else in this garden town, for it *was* the palace of the Marquis of Marialva and its present owners (who also own Lisbon's New Tivoli) have shown impeccable taste in retaining the noble elegance of the past while providing every imaginable luxury and modern comfort. Much of the furniture consists of valuable antiques and where two or more examples of the same item were needed these antiques were faithfully copied. The two-way view from the Seteais is not the least of its wonders, for toward the east you gaze over a peerless lawn and garden to the lofty Pena Castle, and toward the west, beyond rolling meadows, to the open Atlantic. This palace of holiday is reputed to be one of the most expensive hostelries in Portugal, yet couples sojourning here for their first or nth honeymoon need feel no alarm for their budgets, since $14 to $24 a day, according to the room or suite chosen, plus 10 per cent service and 3 per cent tax, will give them lodging and gourmet meals for two. It has, however, only 18 rooms, with 28 beds, so reservations should be made well in advance.

Afternoon Bullfun; Evening Fado

In the bull rings of Portugal neither bulls nor horses get killed, though on very rare occasions men have been killed. The bulls' horns are padded, and the horses used are strong young stallions rather than the broken-down nags so commonly seen in Spanish rings. At the end of an "act"—it really is an afternoon of comedy rather than tense drama—several placid oxen are sometimes led into the ring, and they easily decoy the bull and lead him back to his pen.

To illustrate the mild nature of Portuguese bullfighting, I may record a tale familiar to Portuguese fans. It seems that the nation's most famous bullfighter, one Manuel dos Santos, who really *fought* in Spain but had to play in Portuguese rings, once killed a bull by mistake in Portugal. This is against the national law and dos Santos was actually arrested and fined!

Campo Pequeno is Lisbon's ring, easily reachable by subway from Praça dos Restauradores. Spectacles are held here on Sunday afternoons from Easter to the end of October.

I once witnessed a hilarious comedy of bullfun that I have never forgotten. The main show was like a circus stunt. In the center of the ring an "equestrian statue" was set up, being a human rider on his horse with several mock-heroic figures ranged on the pediment, the whole statue surrounded by a flimsy railing. The bull was let into the ring, snorting with pent-up rage. He charged furiously at the motionless statue but drew up short just in front of it, the very picture of baffled anger and frustration. He charged a second time, and came near enough so that a part of the light railing, loosened by a kick from the horseman of the statue, came free and got draped over the beast's horns, a piece of ill luck that made him look grotesque. It also increased his rage, while diminishing his effectiveness.

The statue came to life and presently the fun grew fast and furious. Innocuous darts were planted in the bull's neck, hurting him, I suppose, no more than a hungry mosquito hurts a human being, but keeping his anger at white heat. There was magnificent horsemanship and fleet work on the part of the *banderilheiros,* and before the animal was finally led out of the ring there was humor enough to keep the crowd rocking with glee. The *moços de forcados* had the thankless task of furnishing much of this, as they were required to subdue the bull by force of numbers. Gathering around the animal they plunged at him simultaneously and clung on as best they could. The bull thrashed about, tossing some in air and wiping others in the dirt in a way that was highly comic to the beholder, but must have left the *moços* with many sore spots before they finally brought the monster under control. Other bulls were brought in and ingenious variants of the first performance were given. Altogether, it was a wonderfully amusing show rather than a sixfold slaughter. To any dyed-in-the-wool *aficionado* of Spain, however, it would have seemed a deplorably tame affair.

The *fado* is Lisbon's own child-of-the-evening, the object of unflagging devotion. Speaking generally, it is a sad, sweet song, often about unrequited love, jealousy, fruitless yearning, sometimes with a pious touch, nearly always with a deep and moving sentiment, usually melancholy, that does not cloy *if* you catch the spirit of it. Catching on is not too easy, even when the words are translated for you. The fado is an integral part of Lisbon's way of life. Fado restaurants and cafés abound in the capital's Bairro Alto (Upper Quarter), while others are near the water front at the base of the Alfama jungle. Fado singers have their passionate fans (or sharp detractors), almost as Spain's bullfighters have *their* fans and detractors.

Both men and women become *fadistas* (the noun is neuter), usually being accompanied in their singing by one or more guitars, and in general they seem almost equally popular, but one woman, by name Amalia Rodrigues, surged to the front some years ago and far outranked all competitors. Her fame in Portugal, enabling her to command up to a thousand dollars a night, grew to fabulous proportions. It spread to all Europe and, at one time, to America, where she was engaged by New York's night club *La Vie en Rose* and proved an instant success, though patrons could not understand any of the words. One reviewer tried to analyze her technique of alternating "a passionate, reedy wail with a tone of warm caress," but good fado really defies analysis. One thing, however, is certain. The singing must not be elegant, brilliant, nor even pretty. I have been told repeatedly in Portugal that nothing is so intolerably dull to a fado audience of Lisbon as "bel canto stuff." The voice must be a bit rough, earthy, "spoiled by too much wine," to move its hearers.

Among the typical fado goals in the Bairro Alto are *A Severa*—*o* and *a* in Portuguese are the masculine and feminine singulars for "the"—; *A Tipoia; Mesquita; Adega Machado* (perhaps too tourist-conscious); and a place called *A Toca* (The Cave), a property of the famous male fadista Carlos Ramos. In the Alfama quarter *A Parreirinha* (see earlier mention) and its neighbor *Nau Catrineta* are outstanding. Fadistas of both sexes dress in black clothes, the girls wearing dolorous black shawls as they sing their sad, sweet ballads. Often the Portuguese guests join heartily in the choruses, but if the fado is movingly melancholy they remain absolutely silent, drinking in great drafts of vicarious sorrow.

To give you an idea of fado, I will transcribe and translate three that I heard sung in A Tipoia.

> 1. *Tinha uma filha, morreu;*
> *Deus levou-ma, fez-me guerra.*
> *Pôs uma estrela no céu*
> *E uma saudade na terra.*

> I had a daughter, she died;
> God took her from me, He made war on me.
> He put a star in the sky
> And a sweet longing on the earth

> 2. *Vi minha mãe resando*
> *Aos pés da Virgem Maria.*
> *Era uma santa escutando*
> *O que outra santa dizia.*

> I saw my mother praying
> At the feet of the Virgin Mary.
> It was one saint listening
> To what another saint was saying.

> 3. *Fui ante o altar do Cristo*
> *As minhas magoas contar.*
> *Eram tantas e tão tristes*
> *Que o Cristo pôs-se a chorar.*

> I was before the altar of Christ
> To recount my pains.
> They were so many and so sad
> That Christ had to cry.

REVISION SUPPLEMENT TO CHAPTER 7

In New York City, the Spanish National Tourist Office, listed with other government offices on page 36, has moved to spacious ground-floor quarters at 589 Fifth Avenue. In addition, the SNTO, as it is called for short, has offices in Chicago, Dallas, Washington, D.C. and St. Augustine, Florida, plus offices in San Juan, Puerto Rico, and in capitals throughout Europe.

The Spanish government, ever conscious of the effect of tourism on its economy, is making great efforts to keep hotel rates from soaring and to improve accommodations and facilities throughout the country. Government-owned accommodations, as distinguished from the many that are privately owned, are divided into four main categories: *Paradores* are buildings which were formerly castles, palaces or monasteries but which have been modernized to provide every comfort in delightful settings; *Albergues* are wayside inns, usually on well-traveled routes, often in new buildings, providing lodging, meals and a service station at all hours; *Refugios* are shelters in mountain areas popular with campers and outdoorsmen planning to explore the remote regions of Spain; and, finally, the *Hosterías* are regional restaurants, usually decorated in the antique style of the district and providing regional foods.

Another aid for the visitor is a plan required by the government for all restaurants. In addition to being graded from 5 to 1, each restaurant is required to serve a fixed-price *menu touristique* in addition to its regular fare. The maximum prices for fixed-price meals range from $4, including wine and service, in a first-category restaurant to $1, all inclusive, in a fifth-category restaurant.

For touring around Spain, *Meliá Tours* provides transportation in luxury coaches. Their tours are carefully spelled out in a booklet available from their offices in New York City (580 Fifth Avenue), Chicago (244 South Michigan Boulevard) and Los Angeles (6363 Wilshire Boulevard). ATESA, discussed in detail throughout the Spain portion of the book, offers information on their tours from their own office in

New York at 680 Fifth Avenue or through the *Europabus* office at 630 Fifth Avenue. Information and arrangements for car rental can also be obtained through these offices.

Consideration of Mediterranean Spain brings us right off to *Gibraltar*, a rock that is not Spain at all but a possession of Britain. Reaching Gibraltar by ferry from Algeciras is a simple matter, but reaching it by motorcar from Spain's Costa del Sol and, more immediately, La Linea, on the Spanish frontier, is becoming somewhat sticky due to Spanish aspirations to regain the Rock. There is no danger, but there can be an interminable wait while customs officials, Spanish first, and, about ten feet away, British, search your belongings to be sure you are a bona fide tourist. The British have eased things for sea travelers to Gibraltar by opening a weekly ferry service from Southampton, England, available from July through October, cars being carried, inexpensively, as well as passengers. The line is *Kloster Sunward Ferries*.

On the Rock there is a 150-room hotel in the making that is quite a story, notable for its encounter with some of the problems of an English outpost bounded on three sides by water and on the fourth by the Spanish frontier. The new hotel, which is abuilding, is in the works in Portland, a seaport in Dorset, England! All the prefabricated concrete parts of this rather large hotel are being shipped to Gibraltar, a process which the owners say is $500 per room cheaper than building it on the Rock. The hotel is now nearing completion. Although the architect has been quoted as saying that it "would be reerected like a house of playing cards," all interested parties will be quickly reassured by the fact that the rigidity of the concrete construction, under stresses and strains, will withstand winds of 100 miles per hour. The bedrooms all have recessed balconies, not only to protect guests from the excessive summer heat, but to provide a view with each room. Plans for the main floor include a shopping mecca devoted to tax-free items; above that a three-story garage; and from the fourth story up to the roof garden on the tenth, the individually air-conditioned rooms.

The *Caleta Palace Hotel*, near the fishing village of that name, is only about two years old and therefore offers many conveniences that the older *Rock Hotel* (page 118) cannot.

Presumably you will include a visit to the somewhat tired, though world-famous Barbary apes of Gibraltar (p. 119). No one is sure how they *got* on the Rock, but local legend says that when they leave the British will also leave. The British feel so strongly about this that Sir Winston Churchill, despite his onerous duties and concerns during the war, arranged for a special shipment of apes from Morocco to replenish the dwindling family living on the Rock.

The development of Spain's *Costa del Sol* during the years since 1950 has been one of the major tourist happenings of Europe, a traveler's conversation piece for years past and no less so today. But first a word about Málaga, which is the takeoff point for the Sunny Coast. Málaga's most significant recent tourist advance is the coming, in 1966, of the big, luxurious *Hotel Málaga Palace*, perfectly located on Avenida Cortina del Muelle adjacent to the city's large central plaza. Rated by the government in the deluxe category, it has 180 rooms, including 24 suites, all rooms with private bath. Not quite so new, but very attractive, is the 75-room *Las Vegas*, well placed on the Paseo de Sancha, an eastern extension of the main in-town Pasea del Parque. It has a good pool and a good view of the sea.

Of special interest to sightseers, as well as to those in search of accommodations, is the development of a new and striking government inn on a spur of the Gibralfaro hill. It started as a small hostería, but 12 double rooms, each with bath, have been added to give it rebirth as the *Parador de Gibralfaro*. From it guests may look *straight down* into the city's bullring to watch the *corridas de Toros* without leaving their abode! In connection with the parador is a good restaurant, whose charges are moderate, as in other paradores.

The Costa del Sol is given deplorably meager mention in the text, an omission which shall now be offset, if only briefly, by the rundown that follows. Full details on this and other parts of Spain may be found in "*All the Best in Spain and Portugal*," another book in this series to which I have referred earlier.

Torremolinos, a lively community of 5000 inhabitants is 9 miles from Málaga, and now lists five deluxe hotels, followed by seven 1-A hotels, plus the delightful *Parador Nacional del Golf*, with pool and beach. There are at least 30 lesser hotels, pensions and hostels. The five deluxe hotels of Torremolinos, alphabetically listed, are: *Al-Andalus*, the Moorish name of Andalusia, a hotel opened rather recently, yet with a repeaters' roster already; *Carihuela Palace; Gran Hotel Nautilus; Pez Espada* (Swordfish); *Tres Carabelas* (Three Caravels). All five are excellent but to me there is something about the first-named, its atmosphere, its decor, its appealing garden-terrace, that sets it apart from its rivals.

In nearby *Benalmádena*, the *Riviera*, which has a striking two-level terrace close to and almost over the sea waves, with a salt-water pool on the lower level, and the *Tritón*, a double hotel with two huge and rather widely separated sections, lead the roster, followed by about eight less pretentious hotels and inns.

Fuengirola is a town of 8000 that splits like an amoeba into *Los Boliches* and *Carvajal*. Although there are no luxury hotels to be included in this quick rundown, one of the nine 1-A facilities is the *Mare Nostrum*, a big, white hotel, with two round towers like chess castles, the whole hotel and its surroundings constantly serenaded by the *roar* of the surf.

Marbella, the only real resort-town rival of Torremolinos, has two deluxe hotels, the *Don Pepe* and the 1966 *Hotel Elvira Hilton*. The latter, although not quite finished as of this writing, will follow the formidable lead of other Hilton properties in offering every comfort. Plans include villas, cottages, restaurants and nightclubs, shops and service establishments and a yacht harbor, the whole complex to be completed by 1968. The Don Pepe has tasteful Spanish decor and a big salt-water pool close to the sea on an extensive and beautifully kept lawn. It has a marvelous dining room and grillroom and, suitable to such a tourist place, a smart nightclub called *El Serallo*.

The Costa del Sol continues westward to *San Pedro de Alcántara*, 40 miles from Málaga, and on to *Estepona*, 13 miles farther on, this latter being virtually the last resort. La Linea and Gibraltar are at the end of the road another 30 miles or so distant. In San Pedro de Alcántara there is the *Hotel Golf Guadalmina* and in Estepona the 190-room *Atalaya Park*, plus three other 1-A hotels.

To the east of Málaga, the town of *Nerja* deserves special mention. Although the spectacular caverns have been there for hundreds of years, the past few years have seen them develop for visitors, complete with guides and tours. A government parador has recently opened at Nerja, the 41-room *Parador Nacional*.

In *Barcelona*, the *Hotel Presidente*, located at 574 Avenida del Generalísimo and wrongly referred to on page 127 as the Fénix (its first "intended name") has about 150 rooms, mostly doubles, but some in suites. Carrying on the good name of the HUSA hotels, of which it is a unit, the 17-story, air-conditioned Presidente has a full kit of luxuries, including a pool. Rooms on the higher floors offer incomparable views of the harbor and city.

All along the *Costa Brava*, running northeast from Barcelona to Port-Bou, a frontier town on the French side, resorts grow up overnight, little disturbing the white-cottage villages of the sardine and anchovy fishermen, whom we, like "beach superintendents," may watch pulling in their nets. Although still an area for offbeat pioneering, particularly inland, visitors pursuing sophisticated water sports are more and more in evidence. *Lloret de Mar*, to mention one conspicuous resort, has more tourist rooms than any other place on the coast. *Hostal Roger de Flor*, one of the resort's large hotels, under the same management as Barcelona's Avenida Palace, seems to grow each year in scope and luxury. *Hotel Monterrey*, large (200 rooms) and rather luxurious, is located back of the village rather than on the beach. Possessed of an outsized swimming pool and a ballroom it has considerable appeal to youthful guests. *Hotel Solterra Playa* and *Hotel Carabela* are first-class places overlooking the sea. Being central and a bit noisy, these too attract young bloods. The official booklet lists an overwhelming number of hotels and pensions in Lloret, but perhaps the above will serve as samples of the better ones.

At *San Feliú de Guixols*, the *Hotel Reina Elisenda* prides itself quite properly on its rather unique atmosphere of "family luxe," encouraging its guests to enjoy informal bathing-suit luncheons in the garden restaurant. *Hotel Alábriga* is a pleasant 1-A place a mile or so beyond the center. Other San Feliú hotels are the small *Montjoi*, on a height overlooking the sea, and the *Murla*, back in the village, both 1-A.

Calella, a beach near Palafrugell and not to be confused with another Calella near Barcelona, has *Hotel San Roc*, a charming place of 1-A rating and modest tariffs, perched on a gardened cliff very close to and above the surf. Another 1-A place is *Hotel Alga*, not so close to the sea but with a pool.

At *Playa de Aro, Hotel Mar Condal* is a 1-A place of 150 rooms, quiet and distinguished, with private park and beach. A modern 200-room hotel, the *Columbus*, also on the beach, is one of the best 1-A hotels, while the *Costa Brava*, *Mar Blau* and the *Xaloc*, all three with beachfront locations, are good 1-B hotels with consequent lower rates.

Bagur and nearby *Aiguablava* offer, as their newest and most prideful feature, *Hotel Cap Sa Sal*, a place of utmost comfort and distinguished quality, located on a majestic site on a rocky promontory. Advertising itself, quite fairly, I think, as "a land of dreams, strange to traffic, noise and crowds," this paradise hotel is among the most luxurious on any of the Spanish *costas*, well worth a visit if only as a sight to see. At Aigua-blava, a beach area along with Sa Tuna and Sa Riera located less than a mile from Bagur, is the *Hotel Aigua Blava* (Blue Water), in a sylvan setting above a rocky cove. One of the newer of the government-run paradores is also located in the area.

Rosas, far along the coast toward the French border, has an inn called the *Hostal del Port* offering more than 100 rooms.

Before leaving the Costa Brava one should head inland to visit *Gerona*, the provincial capital, which deserves far more attention than it gets from American tourists, its cathedral alone, with a lovely 12th-century cloister, being enough to warrant a visit. For stayers-over the *Residencia Ultonia* 1-A is the best hotel.

Most of the area comprising *Sitges* and *Tarragona*, on the opposite (southeast) side of Barcelona, has fallen under the *Costa*-naming spell and is now referred to as the *Costa Dorada* (Golden Coast). Two hotels at Tarragona make a visit to that town pleasant and easy. The *Hotel Imperial Tarraco* offers 170 double rooms, all air-conditioned, and has tennis courts, a swimming pool and nightclubs on the premises. It is on the sea, as is the smaller, neighboring *Carabela-Roc*. Tarragona is not a resort but a very ancient city, once a Roman town named Tarraco, said to have had more than a million inhabitants, its walls being 40 miles in circumference. That sounds like a tall story, but remnants of the wall may still be seen, and also a Roman aqueduct. Halve the figures, if you like, and Tarragona is still a great relic of antiquity.

CHAPTER 7

MEDITERRANEAN SPAIN

The Map Confronts the Planner

SPAIN's geography presents a full kit of problems to the planner who wants to see all the best, for the country's Mediterranean coast line is as long as the coast line of the whole remainder of the Iberian Peninsula, meaning the northern and western coasts of Spain plus the full coast of Portugal. Not only that, but the most exciting points of it are widely spaced and some stretches of the coastal highway leave much to be desired. If the planner turns to the air lines he discovers that Madrid serves as Iberia's chief hub for flights to everywhere, but despite this there *is* hope in the air. Málaga, key city to the greatly developing Costa del Sol, is only 85 miles by bus or car from Algeciras and Gibraltar. This may serve as a take-off point for air-touring to Valencia–Majorca–Barcelona.

Leaving such problems to you and your travel agent, this book shall take up in sequence the high points of Mediterranean Spain, offering first the essential practicalia.

Counsel; Lodging; Dining; Spanish hours; Shopping

The DGT, for *Dirección General del Turismo*, is the tourist's friend throughout Spain. The central office is, of course, in Madrid (39 Avenida Generalísimo, with Information Office on Calle Medinaceli beside the Palace Hotel), but in every provincial city and resort of any importance one may find a local branch of this government agency. The addresses of the chief ones in the coastal cities that now concern us are as follows: *Málaga*, Calle Larios 5; *Valencia*, Ayuntamiento (City Hall); *Barcelona*, Avenida de José Antonio 658; *Palma de Mallorca* [this is the Spanish spelling, Anglicized by us to Majorca], Paseo del Generalísimo

Franco. All of these offices cheerfully dispense maps, free literature, including hotel lists, and verbal counsels, the offices of Barcelona and Palma being, I think, of special importance to the tourist.

Lodging, despite some recent inflation, is still wonderfully inexpensive throughout all southern and Mediterranean Spain; and there is, by the way, a difference between those two words. The Mediterranean coast line "climbs" so steeply to the northeast that Barcelona is well north of Madrid and even the Balearic Isles are about on the same parallel of latitude. In all this long littoral of holiday hospitality, including metropolitan Barcelona with its constellation of luxury hotels, the tariffs are still very low by comparison with those almost anywhere else in Europe. A few months ago an experienced travel man living in Barcelona told me that he considered $10 a day, American Plan (with meals), per person to be the absolute ceiling in his city in de luxe hotels. Add, if you like, $2.50 for a margin of safety and the figure is still low enough to bring a delighted smile to any traveler's budget. In smaller cities and resorts the tariffs are, of course, substantially lower than in the big Catalan capital.

Spanish food does not need to be "learned," like the red-hot dishes of Mexico, for instance. It is liked by most American visitors "on acquaintance," and some of its specialties are well known to certain restaurants of large American cities.

Perhaps the one most famous and beloved Spanish dish is *paella*, often tagged with the name of Valencia, where it is superbly made. *Paella Valenciana* is a dish based on saffron-flavored rice, not, in this case, a chicken dish, but served with a variety of sea food items all mixed together in a grand potpourri, with tidbits of meat and chicken added. Over the top of it are spread ornamental and spicy scarlet strips of pimento and perhaps some green peas. In Valencia this "namesake dish" is often followed by *langostinos* (crayfish), prepared by a local formula and dipped by the diner in a tasty onion sauce.

Sea food is excellent in Spain, especially in the big coastal cities. Some items to know, along with langostinos are: their larger cousins *langostas* (lobsters); *gambas* (shrimps); *cangrejo* (crab); *calamares* (squid; and this food can be delicious); *anguilas* (eels); *lenguado* (sole); *bonito* (tuna); *bacalao* (codfish), which, if it is the popular *à la Vizcaína*, will be casserole-cooked in tomato sauce and olive oil. A Barcelona waterfront dish called *zarzuela* (literally "musical comedy") is a sort of shellfish bouillabaisse. (The word for fish is *pescado*.)

Gazpacho is a humble summer dish of Andalusian peasants that has become a Spanish "gentleman," more or less, in recent years. It's a cold soup (ugh!), with tomatoes, cucumbers, peppers and what not "developed" in oil and vinegar. At first I recoiled from gazpacho, but I learned to endure it and then to like it.

Cocido is the national dish, a boiled dinner of whatever the cook has on hand, to which *garbanzos* (chick peas) are added.

Among basic items of *carne* (meat) the traveler should have the following in his food vocabulary: *carne de vaca* (beef, but he will frequently find on menus the borrowed and garbled words *rosbif*, for roast beef, and *bistec*, for beef steak); *carne de ternera* (veal); *carne de cerdo* (pork); *jamón serrano* (mountain ham); *carne de cordero* (mutton).

Some vegetables to know by name are: *patatas* (potatoes); *arroz* (rice); *guisantes* (peas); *judías* (beans); *coliflor* (cauliflower); *espárragos* (asparagus); *fondos alcachofas* (hearts of artichoke); *ensalada* (salad).

Some fruits and berries: *naranja* (orange); *manzana* (apple); *melocotón* (peach); *melón* (melon); *fresas* (strawberries); *cerezas* (cherries).

Some assorted words: *sopa* (soup); *huevos* (eggs); *postre* (dessert); *queso* (cheese); *sal* (salt); *aceite* (oil); *vinagre* (vinegar); *leche* (milk); *té* (tea); *agua mineral* (mineral water); *vino* (wine); *cerveza* (beer); *coñac* (brandy).

Some "table" words to know: *comedor* (dining room); *parrilla* (grill); *servilleta* (napkin); *plato* (plate); *vaso* (glass); *cuchillo* (knife); *tenedor* (fork); *cuchara* (spoon). The word for waiter is *mozo*.

The wines of Spain are a delight to the palate and the purse. It is not in the least extravagant to order a good bottled wine (avoiding *vino corriente*, the *vin ordinaire* of Spain) to accompany each meal. A half bottle of a good brand may cost no more than 30 or 35 cents even in a luxury hotel.

Riojas and *Valdepeñas* are among the more familiar table wines, two popular brands being Marqués de Riscal and Paternina. Try the latter firm's *Chablis*, white, like its Burgundy prototype, or its good *tinto*, which is to say red, though the bottle is decorated with a proud *Banda Azul*, meaning Blue Ribbon. Among other brands I have liked—and I claim no connoisseur status—are: *Perellada*, both white and red, *Viña*

Pomal, a dry red, and *Viña Paceta*, a dry white type from Bilbao. Among mineral waters, two popular sparkling types are: *Vichy Catalan* and—less carbonated—*Mondariz*. Other favorites are *Solares* and *Insalus*.

Sherries, are, of course, the very symbol of Spain. All the sherries that have found their way to the remotest corners of the world took their name from *Jerez* de la Frontera, near Cádiz, and the distinguished *Amontillado*, which Edgar Allan Poe immortalized in a great story, is a dry wine, originally of Jerez, made to imitate the white *Montilla* of Córdoba. One sees in the wine shops, at temptingly low prices, assorted bottles of *Amontillado Fino, Tío Pepe*, a dry, pale wine, *Dry Sack*, which is a Spanish sherry in spite of its name, and various *olorosos*, which are more in the nature of dessert wines.

Some sherry facts are too irresistible to be crowded out of any Spanish wine discourse, however brief. Sherry is the most capricious wine on earth. When it is half a year old no one can tell what it will be like when grown up. It may turn dry or sweet. The same vineyard may produce an entirely different type one year from that which it produced the year before.

New sherry does not turn to vinegar when exposed to the air, as do other wines. Barrels are never quite filled and bungs are never driven in tight.

Sherry is dated, sometimes on the cork, from its *bottling*, not its vintage, since it deteriorates slowly *in the bottle*, and the date is supposed to protect the customer.

Strangest of all, in sherry making, is the *solera* system. Barrels are piled four deep in the solera and like a ship stepping down the locks of a canal the wine steps down from the top barrels to the bottom as it grows in grace. The lower tier of barrels is never emptied. The wise, "experienced" wine in the barrels at the lowest level trains the less experienced wine from tier two (i.e. next to the bottom), which in turn has trained tier three, which has taught the first essentials of winehood to tier four at the top. Some trace of wine in every good bottle of sherry should be sixty or seventy or eighty years old, fine old stuff, full of knowledge and poise, quite capable of conversing on even terms with seasoned philosophers. Sherry marked "Solera 1850" means that the barrels of the solera from which it was bottled have not been empty for well over a hundred years.

Spanish brandy (*coñac*) is somewhat sweeter than French and quite different in taste. Four much-advertised brands are *Veterano, Terry, Fundador* and *Soberano* (the last less sweet); and among more aristocratic brands *Carlos Primero* is specially esteemed. All Spanish brandies cost only a fraction of what their French cousins cost in France.

Other liqueurs favored in Spain include *Anise*, served with ice and tasting much like France's *Marie Brizard; Calisay,* a digestive; *Royal Kit,* resembling *Cointreau;* and *Palo,* a very sweet Majorcan liqueur made from figs.

And would you like a fine anticlimax to this alcoholic discussion? Very well. A popular *soft drink,* favored especially in the south and the Valencia-Barcelona area, is *horchata.* It is a delicious long drink that looks like milk but tastes only like its pleasant self. It is made from crushed chufa nuts, near relatives of almonds, and is served in many a café and outdoor *horchatería.* I think you will welcome to your palate so good and distinguished a "garden drink."

The hours of Spain's day and night are utterly different from those of others lands and they "take a lot of getting used to." Breakfast can usually be had at a normal hour. For lunch, the very earliest possible hour, even in tourist hotels, is one o'clock or one-thirty, and two-thirty or three o'clock is far more customary. Dinner can rarely be had before nine or nine-thirty, while ten or ten-thirty is the usual time. If you enter the dining room at nine you will probably be quite alone in your glory.

Matinées for the theaters and cinemas begin at six-thirty and evening performances at ten-thiry or eleven. If you go to a cinema at six o'clock or at ten you will usually find it dead and deserted. A quarter of an hour later it begins to come to life. At seven and eleven respectively it has finally received its audience.

Shopping and sightseeing must be carefully planned. The shops are generally closed between one and four in the afternoon, and museums, with some exceptions such as Madrid's Prado, are open only in the forenoon. In view of this it is well to "sightsee" in the traditional sense until about two, this being still "forenoon" in Spain, and devote the time after your late lunch to outdoor things and perhaps shopping. If darkness descends and the shops close and the final hours before ten o'clock dinner threaten to drag interminably, you may take refuge in a personal siesta or possibly in a cinema matinée, where you will probably find the attraction an American film speaking Spanish. Perhaps you can be philosophical about the Spanish dubbing and consider it a cheap language lesson.

To return to the subject of shopping, I would call your attention to the *American Visitors Bureau*, mentioned in Chapter 6 for its Lisbon office. Spanish offices are: *Madrid*, Avenida José Antonio 68, 3rd floor, and *Barcelona*, Avenida José Antonio 591, 2nd floor. This company is a major boon to shoppers in Spain and Portugal, for it takes over, as just one of its duties, the arduous business of wrapping and mailing your packages to the home folks. It can also arrange sightseeing tours, local and countrywide, and it offers current lists of shopping places granting a 5 per cent discount and of the most interesting restaurants. Don't miss the AVB.

Bulls and Men in Battle

Bullfights, in every part of Spain are of the essence. American visitors are often vaguely or volubly against this sport. They say they don't want to see it, but it is to be noticed that they do see it and that they go to some trouble to arrange their tour so that they shall be in some large city on a *corrida de toros* date. I take it that some elemental bits of information would be useful to those who "don't want to see" a bullfight.

The tickets, very inexpensive except for the big fights, are all marked either *Sol* (Sun) or *Sombra* (Shade), and the shady seats naturally cost more and are well worth the difference, for Old Sol stares down into the open arenas of Spain with a sizzling, white-hot gaze.

The corridas occur on Sunday afternoons from early spring to late autumn, generally at four o'clock, and on the occasion of popular fairs or great religious fiestas extra ones are generally advertised.

The bullfight season starts on Easter Sunday at Seville before a very fashionable crowd, which a few hours previously has been worked up to a pitch of religious emotion in the cathedral. From Easter onward the season is at its height in Andalusia and all southern Spain. In summer and early fall it is at its height in Madrid and northern Spain. The out-of-season corridas are called *novilladas* because "new," that is young, bulls and untried *toreros* are the participants.

Every Spanish city has its *plaza de toros* (bull ring), but in the small cities the corridas are sometimes clumsy slaughterings scarcely endurable to the gaze of any except the local *aficionado* (fan). Baedeker, ever chivalrous, used to advise us to sit near an exit "when ladies are of the party."

If it is true that nearly every American who visits Spain sees a bullfight it is equally true that many visitors see only one, which is not necessarily a matter of soft-heartedness but may be due to boredom. If the beholder has sat through one afternoon and seen six bulls killed by what seems *to him* exactly the same routine of *suertes* (freely, "acts") he has little interest in watching the game another six times. Of course these games, in the eyes of the true aficionado, are *anything but identical*. He is roused to the highest pitch of excitement by infinitesimal differences of technique that quite escape the uninitiated, but unless one intends to become an aficionado one will scarcely take time, on a short visit to Spain, to sit through a second corrida.

The traditions of toreros are, however, worth knowing by even the casual one-time looker-on. These fighters are, by axiom, *brave* men or they would get nowhere in so dangerous a profession. They are often pious men who would not dream of entering a bull ring without previously praying to the Virgin in the bullfighters' chapel. Their costume, an integral part of the tradition, is queer and archaic, including pink socks, pants so skin-tight that the garment must be dragged on and off, and a knot of false hair at the back of the neck. Their gait is a torero's gait, a charming, wimbling "dance step" quite their own. But their techniques vary, like those of expert musicians. Bravery often borders on recklessness, to the crowd's howling delight, for the fighters will even deliberately *look away* when the bull charges, estimating precisely where his horns will graze their flanks, and this bravado is maintained even when fighting the most dangerous types of bulls, the ones that charge with their eyes open instead of obtusely and angrily shut.

There is a vast "taurine literature," including Ibáñez' *Sangre y Arena*, not to mention our own great aficionado, Ernest Hemingway, and although I saw from start to finish a Barcelona corrida and have seen several others in other cities, something tells me that I should not add another detailed description to the countless ones already published. Furthermore, no book that aims to be pleasant reading can describe a bullfight with photographic exactitude. If I were to set down meticulously the appearance of the bull as he makes his last rush to meet the *estocada* (death blow) and were to spare you no detail of whence and in what volume the blood pours from him, you would be a bit sickened, whether or not "ladies are of the party" and whether or not you know all about it from having witnessed a corrida. If I were to describe with equal exactitude the appearance of a wretched over-age nag, overturned and then gored and disemboweled, it would be quite as emetic as any of the passages in Joyce's *Ulysses*.

Since 1928, Spanish laws have forbidden the use of *banderillas de fuego*, or darts tipped with explosives, which used to terrify or enrage the bull, and have also required that the "horses" (one cannot call the poor broken-down quadrupeds horses without using quotation marks) shall be padded on the exposed side. It is like humane regulations governing warfare. I suppose if I were a bull I would a little rather be stabbed by six plain darts before being killed than by six torpedo-pointed darts. If I were a horse I suppose I would rather be tipped on end and have my neck broken than be gored outright at the first rush by two stilettos of horn plunged into my flanks by a brute with the power of a steam locomotive.

If just *one* huge Andalusian bull out of six, in *one* corrida, should, by some miracle, be equipped with a spark of intelligence, what a world sensation he could make! How easily he could put himself on the front pages of the world's journals. He comes snorting into the ring, the very embodiment of glorious strength, on fire with furious animosity toward everything in sight. But instead of charging fifty times in succession at the pink cape of the *capeadores* and then the red *muleta* of the matador, he says to himself, "After all, red is not so bad. I don't like it, but there's no sense in going into a fury over any *color*. It's those spangled *men* that I really hate. Now that fool over there with the pink cape, I believe I'll kill *him* first.

The bull rushes, ignores the flapping cape, catches his man on both horns and tosses him thirty feet to a quick death.

"Too easy," says the bull, and then he charges at one of the mounted *picadores* who is preparing to torment him with a long pointed *pica* (pike). He tips over the horse, then tramples the picador to death while the capeadores flap their capes in vain.

He makes short work of the *banderilleros*, having only to swerve a foot or two from his course when charging. Not a dart is thrust home.

The *matador*, with his long curved sword, is an opponent worth more consideration, but the bull gets him too. A quick shrug of the massive shoulders deflects the sword from any vital part. He shakes it off and it describes a great parabola in the air, landing in the stands. [I saw this happen once.] The "ladies of the party" shriek. The bull, instead of allowing the matador to scamper for shelter, as naturally happens in case of a disarming, makes a quick rush, gores him, and for a bit of extra satisfaction tosses him over the ring's barrier.

At this point someone presumably brings a rifle and shoots the toro. He cannot outmaneuver bullets, but he dies a happy bull. He has shown what a bit of intelligence can do. If one fighting bull out of a thousand possessed this divine spark, the *corridas de toros* would quickly cease to exist and the bull rings of Spain would become as lifeless as Rome's Coliseum.

It must be said, however, in fairness to the whole idea of the corridas, that if the bulls in the arena are stupid beyond belief the men are keen, agile, absolutely fearless and brilliantly intelligent. They can calculate to the centimeter just where those rubbery hoofs will beat their futile tattoo on the hard-packed sand. It is wonderful, if one can harden one's heart and freeze all pity for the beasts, to watch the toreros at their graceful, clever, cruel, bloody game. They are all valiant men, no doubt of that, and occasionally they have to pay for their valor with their lives.

Coastal Trails to Catalonia
(GIBRALTAR-PLUS-TANGIER; RONDA; MÁLAGA; GRANADA; VALENCIA; BARCELONA)

Mediterranean Spain is so rich in successive travel thrills that it is hardly possible to do more than list them, with brief comments on the "highest lights," but perhaps this hurrying review may serve at least to whet the appetite for personal trailing.

Gibraltar, with a leap to Tangier, is our logical starting point for the trail to Catalonia and the French frontier, but I should preface this by stating that an Andalusian Tour comprising Cádiz, Seville, Granada and Málaga, starting from Algeciras (across the bay from Gibraltar), may be made by comfortable motor coach of ATESA, which is Spain's branch of the EUROPABUS system. This all-embracing company, organized jointly by the national railway administrations of Europe, has an office in New York at 630 Fifth Avenue, where full details about all ATESA offerings may be had.

Gibraltar and the somewhat similar Mons Abyla across the Strait on the African side, form, as every schoolboy knows, the Pillars of Hercules of the ancients. These two pillars, connected by a scroll, are supposed to have been the prototype of the American dollar sign.

I have thrice visited Gibraltar and on one memorable occasion I stayed nine days, which I think must constitute a world's record for an alien without specific business to attend to. I was swinging Spain's Gibraltar Gate eastward on that occasion and had to wait for a Japanese ship that was to take me to Marseille. In one day it is easy to see the sights of the Rock, from Europa Point to the strip of neutral sand on the north, and from the Alameda Gardens to the Spanish village on Catalan Bay. Without the privileges of the Garrison Library I suppose nine days would have brought on a critical case of ennui.

Gibraltar *town* (*Rock Hotel*) consists practically of one street, which deserves the name it bears, Main Street. It is not interesting but it is clean. The fishing village of Caletas on the other side of the Rock, now reached by a modern tunnel road called Williams Way, is not clean but it is interesting, and also a trifle "ghostly," since the sun sets on it shortly after noon.

To add to its spookiness, it is more exposed to danger than is any other settlement on Gibraltar. One is disconcerted, on approaching it, to read on signboards placed beside the road this warning: BEWARE OF FALLING STONES. THE PUBLIC ARE WARNED NOT TO LOITER BETWEEN THE THREE NOTICE BOARDS. The public will indeed be very unlikely to loiter "between" these three boards. One glance at the wicked, beetling cliffs overhead is enough to dispel any such tendency. Various tragedies have occurred here. In 1811, an immense stone broke loose and plunged down on the unfortunate village, killing eighteen and wounding as many more. In 1870, a large slip wiped out the road close by but did not touch the village. In 1875, a flood occurred which loosened such immense quantities of sand and stones that much of the village, including the little St. Mary's Chapel, was wiped out. In 1917, a great rock plunged down on the corrugated iron water catchments, tearing jagged holes and loosening such quantities of sand beneath them that a large part of the village was again wiped out. But these intermittent tragedies, emphasizing the obstinate loyalty of the human race, have only served to strengthen the hold of this little village of Catalan Bay upon its inhabitants, who are descended from rugged Genoese fishermen. The oftener they are endangered the more tenaciously they cling to their ancestral homes.

At the southern tip of Gibraltar lies Europa Point, to me the most fascinating spot on the Rock, not even excepting the village of Catalan Bay or the habitat of the famous Gibraltar apes, which trace their line to African ancestors of the prehistoric days before the two continents broke apart here to let in the Atlantic. It has proved a never-ending source of pleasure to search out some convenient ledge or stone wall at Europa Point and with a pair of glasses study the shipping that passes through the Strait. The variety of the traffic is infinite. It is generally possible to make out the nationality of the craft and occasionally the name, but to guess whence it comes and whither it is bound is another matter.

Sailing craft frequently have a hard time to make their way from the Mediterranean through the Pillars of Hercules unless the Levanter, an east wind, is blowing. A strong current, often setting at the rate of five miles an hour, flows *continuously* from the Atlantic into the Mediterranean along the coasts of Spain and Africa. The existence of this strong, unvarying Atlantic current, pouring a steady and mighty volume of water into the land-locked Mediterranean, was formerly a source of mystification and sharp controversy. What becomes of the water, was the unanswered question. Evaporation could hardly take care of it. It was finally established that because of the greater salinity, and therefore the greater heaviness, of the Mediterranean waters, a countercurrent from the Mediterranean flows out *underneath* the lighter current setting in. But this scientific explanation of the phenomenon does not help the skipper of the sailing ship who must deal only with the surface currents and must wait, perhaps for days together, for a favorable wind.

The bold 1400-foot face of the Rock rises at an angle of ninety degrees (or at the very least eighty-nine) straight from the sand. It looks not toward the sea but toward Spain, and in its shadow is the North Port Airfield, take-off point for the frequent planes of Gibraltar Airways making the less-than-half-hour leap across the Strait.

Tangier was founded rather a long time ago by Antheus, a son of the sea god Neptune, and bears the name, somewhat altered by time and history, of the founder's wife Tingis. The story has a sad ending, for Antheus was killed by Hercules and buried at a point near the beach.

The city was occupied successively by Phoenicians, Carthaginians, Romans, Moslems until the early part of the present century when it was made an international city, clumsily administered by a consortium of seven European nations *and* the United States. It was then that the heyday of smuggling and currency manipulations set in, but this finally came to an end in 1956 when Tangier was integrated with the Kingdom of Morocco.

If this change robbed the city of some of its color and excitement it had certain counteracting advantages for tourism. One may now travel freely, with no thought of the former free-city frontiers, to nearby points such as fascinating Tetuán and primitive Xauen, not to mention the more distant goals of Morocco such as Rabat, Casablanca and Marrakesh, easily reachable by Royal Air Maroc. There is a branch of the National Moroccan Office of Tourism in Tangier and for information one may address this office at Boulevard Pasteur 29.

Tangier is a double city, the European part centering around the Place de France and Avenue Pasteur, and the native quarter, Old Tangier, huddling on and below the Kasbah, or Citadel. In the European quarter you will lodge well and eat well, as in any modern European city, the traditional, and delightful, mecca of tourists being *Hotel El Minzah*. The view from the high ground of the Place de France over the harbor and the two-mile beach is marvelous; and at the beach itself, where there are several good hotels, especially the *Rif*, the swimming is good during more than half the year. But Old Tangier, beginning at that big, rackety square called the Grand Sokko, is *the* thing.

The *Grand Sokko* is explosive. All the colors of the Arab world burst into sights and sounds here, and if you are lucky enough to encounter a

Moslem fiesta, on one of the holy days, as I did, you will find very literal explosions going on. The bedlam of the fiesta I saw was unique in my experience. All evening long, rockets by the hundreds were set off and their aim mattered not a whit. I saw at least fifty rockets hurtle into open balconies of houses on the upper side of the square. Several charged horizontally into theater crowds queuing up in front of a cinema and many fiery duds simply sped along the ground. One of them slithered between my legs as I was attempting to dodge it. Apparently there were no casualties, though there must have been some minor burns.

The walk through the narrow, jampacked main street of Old Tangier, from the Grand Sokko to the *Petit Sokko*, is a pedestrian adventure from start to finish, and if you conclude it by seating yourself in a native café in the Petit Sokko you may watch, close-up, a kaleidoscope of "all the races of the earth," from sleek French blondes, in the latest fashions of Paris, to the most primitive of Arabs, African Berbers and African Jews. Throughout Tangier and neighboring Morocco the Moslem women, notably excepting the Berbers, are very often shrouded from head to toes. They are like walking bags—excuse the word—of thick cloth resembling canvas, which is usually gray in color. Only their eyes are allowed to peep through a narrow slit in the head shroud to let them see where they are going. If they are human they must greatly envy their free feminine-looking sisters from Europe, but after all, Arab women *of the old tradition* as against the emancipation that exists, for instance, in Egyptian town life and now, increasingly, in the North African countries, are not supposed to be human. They are simply useful chattels to their men, good for doing chores, carrying burdens and bearing babies so that there may be more men, and more women to work for them.

By the tortuous Rue de la Marine, to return rather suddenly to our Sokko walk, the stroller may continue to an open terrace with a magnificent outlook over the harbor.

Two sights from this teeming center of Old Tangier linger in my mind from the hundreds I saw. One was an Arab boy nonchalantly wheeling an American popcorn-machine through the throng. The other was a group of ten burly, sweating natives of assorted races attempting to move a *colossal* chunk of solid mahogany. They grunted, groaned and heaved but could not budge the thing. I cannot imagine how it ever got there and I wonder if it ever has left that spot.

The summit of Old Tangier and the summit of tourist interest is the hilltop Kasbah, the old palace of the sultanate, and, fairly hanging over the lower reaches of the Old City, the so-called *Moorish Café of the Riad Sultan*. You'll need a guide, and you may secure one through your hotel porter or the Moroccan Tourist Office. Failing this, guides of a sort will appear from nowhere and everywhere and you may follow almost any presentable character, preparing to give him, at the end of the tour, a reasonable amount of *baksheesh* for his services. I started the Kasbah tour quite on my own, inquiring the way from a policeman and then ascending the steep Rue d'Italie from the Grand Sokko and turning to the right, through an ancient gate, up Rue Blad Sultan. Not until this point, for a wonder, did two youths attach themselves to me as guides. They clung like leeches and I let them cling.

They took me into an ancient and royal Moorish garden, into a museum of antiquities, and finally, insistently, into a Moorish café, or *The Moorish Café*. I was a bit stubborn in resisting this last, thinking it a mere tourist trap, but yielded to their pleadings and presently found myself walking through an exceedingly colorful Arabic coffee house and out upon an open terrace very high above the warren of the Old Town. Such a place for coffee or tea I have rarely seen. I ordered tea and then sat there, toying with the beverage and *devouring* the view, for nearly an hour, while the bill for baksheesh mounted like the figures on a taxi's meter. It was a shining hour and I wouldn't have missed it for twenty times the amount it cost. The tea, of Arab brew, had green leaves floating in it and it was fearfully sweet to the taste but I would have downed medicine of any taste rather than miss that Moorish terrace.

Almost anticlimactic, though very good fun, at that, are Tangier's night clubs, which are of international character. They are perhaps "disappointingly unwicked," despite all one hears, but the best ones are cheerful and entertaining. The best one of all is the night club of *Hotel Rif*, but I also liked the *Emsallah Gardens*, very near Hotel El Minzah and another place called *Villa de France*, both being of open-air garden type. In cooler seasons plenty of indoor "dancings" are available.

Algeciras, Spain's port across the bay from "Gib," is famous chiefly for its well-loved *Hotel Reina Cristina*, with a lovely subtropical garden and a small bathing beach. From this point I took off for Málaga by rented car, as you may easily do, traversing the burgeoning *Costa del Sol* (Sun Coast), with its seemingly unbroken fringe of hotels and pensions, whose present popularity is a headline of tourism. I sidetracked, as you may not wish to do because of tortuous mountain roads, to the small upland town that has been dubbed "Preposterous Ronda."

The eagle's aerie named *Ronda*, one of the strangest works of nature and man, lies some sixty miles north of Algeciras, and those who tour by car may reach it by a thirty-mile branch road from *San Pedro de Alcántara* on the coastal highway between Gibraltar and Málaga. The road is full of serpentine twists but *this* branch is not too hard on your car. Some of the still-lesser roads are really tough. Ronda is a geological curiosity quite as dramatic as Gibraltar itself, and there is that about it which seems to command strong personal loyalty and affection from persons who make the effort to visit it. It straddles an astonishing gash in the earth, the enormously deep (350 to 550 feet) gorge of the River Guadalevin, which separates the old town from the new, and on the west it rims a cliff which falls away in one plunge more than six hundred feet. The gash is said to have been caused by a prehistoric earthquake, enabling the river to pierce a mass of solid rock which it could hardly have cut for itself. When you look down upon this cleft from the *Puente Nuevo* you won't quite believe it is real, for you'll be ready to swear that nothing on earth, or in earth, can be that deep!

Ronda is a historic rendezvous of smugglers and bandits who have become very picturesque since they have ceased to exist. It is also the original habitat of the institution of bullfighting, the basic rules of the bloody game having been here formulated by a torero named Pedro Romero. The medieval-looking bull ring, with two tiers of wooden seats covered by a roof in most unusual fashion for Spain, was owned in former times by the *Real Maestranza*, and therby hangs an explanation. The Real Maestranza was a tight organization of the local aristocracy and such organizations existed, I have been told, in six cities of Spain only, Seville, Madrid, Saragossa, Granada, Valencia and little Ronda. It was *so* tight, in Ronda's case at any rate, that even a marquis or a duke could not become a member unless he was the scion of an unimpeachable *local* family. The Real Maestranza existed for three purposes. One was to develop the finest possible breed of horses, another was to foster bullfighting and the third, the most important of all, was to build up and maintain its own social prestige.

There is a good modernized hotel in Ronda, the veteran *Victoria*, with a terrace and a cliff-edge garden that give you a stupendous view over the plain below and the extensive sierra. When I stayed there the garden in its foreground was brightened by thousands of bright blue nemophila blossoms, if I spell the word correctly.

Málaga (*Hotel Miramar*, large and inviting) is a soft and civilized city boasting a splendid, palm-shaded *Paseo* that rims the harbor and, straight above the city, a double hill called the *Alcazaba* and the *Gibralfaro* that provides striking views *down* upon the city and harbor, *out* upon the Mediterranean and its shores. The Alcazaba was the site of a Moorish citadel-palace, while the Gibralfaro was an outright fortress. A good motor road leads to the summit, with a pleasant, government-operated *Hostería de Gibralfaro* for snacks on a terrace-in-the-sky.

Granada is one of the most glamorous names on the map of Spain, made so chiefly by the *Alhambra*, which, together with the *Garden of the Generalife,* constitutes the heart of the city for travelers. One should see the grand Gothic-into-Renaissance *Cathedral,* enshrining the remains of Ferdinand and Isabella and other royalty, and possibly a few churches of lesser importance, but the Alhambra is the thing, and fortunately you may lodge *in it,* to use the word Alhambra in its broader sense as meaning the whole cliff-bordered hill on which rises the *Alhambra Palace of the Moorish Kings.*

The *Parador de San Francisco* is the inn to which I refer and it is one of the most glamorous of Spain's government inns, in artistic effect, in background, in decoration, in its gardens, and above all, in its setting. The building, originally the palace of an Arab prince, was reconstructed centuries later, in the 1300's, by another Arab, and when the Christian era reached Granada it was assigned by Ferdinand and Isabella to the Franciscans for use as a monastery. Upon the death of the joint monarchs their remains rested in the monastery chapel until their tombs were ready in the cathedral, in 1521. The monastery had several more uses in later centuries, including its conversion into a school of painting. Finally, the present government converted the building into this exquisite Parador. All of the rooms are both artistic and comfortable, and from some of them snow views are to be had of the *Sierra Nevada*

(Snowy Range).

Meals in the Parador's dining room are dreams of fair eating, and the room itself fascinates as much as the food. There are gleaming brass and copper implements, some handsome works in wrought iron, interesting wall plates, fine textiles and a ceiling of cheerful tiles set off by very dark old beams.

There are other fine hotels in Granada, notably the *Alhambra Palace Hotel,* on the edge of the hill, the newer *Nevada Palace* and the less expensive but historic *Washington Irving.* This is well named indeed, for the American author really "exhumed" the Alhambra from neglect and utter obscurity. The palace was at its lowest ebb in 1829, when he came, fell in love with it, secured from the then *private* owners a room actually *in* the palace, above the *Patio de Daraxa,* and set his pen to work.

Washington Irving is today a sort of author-laureate of Granada. Almost single-handed he drew the Alhambra from the oblivion to which the Bourbons had condemned it and offered this treasure to the world. About a century ago the first tourist wavelet gathered, curled and broke on the hill and since then the wavelets have become waves and finally big combers. Granada has been transformed from a squalid little town, dignified by a cathedral and a curious acropolis, to an attractive modern city. Fine new boulevards, lined with good shops, have been driven through noisome slums, and first-class hotels have replaced dirty inns. No wonder his *Tales of the Alhambra* and *Conquest of Granada* are on sale in every post card and curio shop, and not in English only but in Spanish, French and German. Seldom has any American left his impress on any foreign city so strongly as has Irving on Granada.

Granada has a unique attraction in its *Sacromonte Caves,* where tireless gypsy girls and men entertain tourists every night with excellent flamenco singing, guitar playing and dancing. Flamenco entertainment, in case you don't know, is so tensely dramatic that it makes most other forms of dance entertainment seem pallid by comparison. The frenetic rhythms, the crackle of stamping feet, clapping hands, snapping fingers and castanets, like a thousand educated firecrackers, and the sad but stirring songs combine to lift the beholder to outer space, all other thoughts being left behind somewhere on earth.

Alicante (*Hotel Carlton,* on the seaside Paseo) is often tagged, with due banality, "the Nice of Spain." Like Málaga it is a very pleasant seaport city and like Málaga it dominates a holiday coast, in this case the *Costa Blanca*, which runs for seventy miles northeast and seventy southwest of this key city. This White Coast is, to Americans, one of the least known parts of Spain's Mediterranean coast, yet it is one of the most delightful for its scenery and its beaches. *Benidorm*, which seems to mean Sleepwell, is one of its north-of-Alicante centers and chief attractions, a resort that is quite as eagerly sought by German tourists as it is neglected by American. Benidorm's beach is called by enthusiasts the best in Spain and I would hardly quarrel with that judgment, for it is smooth and wide, and a rocky headland adds drama by breaking it into a north beach and a south. There are many small hotels and pensions in Benidorm and all along the Costa Blanca.

Valencia del Cid officially incorporates in its title the name of Spain's half-real, half-mythical hero, El Cid Campeador, and this serves as a reminder to the visitor that Valencia is "as old as it is new." One of the realest things about the much-debated Cid is that he was Lord of Valencia for the last six years of his life and that he died there in the year 1099. The ancient and medieval sights of this city, such as the *Silk Exchange*, finest secular Gothic building in Spain, the *Palacio de Generalidad*, with its magnificent *Sala Dorada*, and *El Miguelete*, bell tower of the cathedral, are more than locally famous, but it is the modern city that first catches the eye. Valencia is modern indeed in many parts, with tall, impressive buildings, and since the turn of the decade it has had a luxury hotel, the *Astoria Palace*, worthy of its importance.

No American who has not visited Spain can imagine the percussive power of a major Spanish fiesta, and of all the fiestas that I know, none matches in violence and emotional impact *Las Fallas de San José*, occurring in Valencia in mid-March, the culminating night being the 19th. Even the famous carnival orgies of Rio de Janeiro, which I once watched from start to finish, hardly match those of Las Fallas.

The word Fallas seems to have no clear translation, though a tourist folder, blandly ignoring the dictionary, interprets it as Bonfires. In ordinary Valencian parlance the Fallas are the *competitive statue groups*, of wax and cardboard, often very comical in nature and often cleverly satirical, that are set up in many squares of the city and finally burned to the ground on the festival's final night. Each year there are about a hundred and fifty of them, the one in *Plaza del Caudillo*, heart-square of the city, being always among the largest and most intricate.

In 1957, Valencia suffered a catastrophic flood, perhaps the worst disaster of the kind ever to hit a Spanish city. Hundreds of downtown blocks were inundated by the raging waters of the River Turin, normally a mere trickle. Vast wreckage amid foot-deep mud was left by the receding flood, but Valencia is an exceptionally spirited city and its rapid recovery was but another example of its traditional vitality.

Barcelona, the Catalan capital, is a *big* city, rivaling Madrid in size and surpassing it in industrial importance. The city's de luxe and first-class hotels have undergone, and are still undergoing, a development that is hardly less noteworthy than that of Madrid, for at least *eight* have rather recently opened and another major one is under construction. Some of the older and less-new hotels, however, are still as good as the best and I would say of *Hotel Ritz*, the dean of them all, that it has one important advantage over every hotel of the new crop, namely *spaciousness* in its entrance lobby, its lounges, its reading and writing rooms, its dining rooms and bar and, emphatically, in its bedrooms and baths. The late Georges Marquet, long the president of the chain that includes this Ritz, saw fit to spend many millions of pesetas in a most drastic modernizing of the whole establishment, with due stress on bedrooms and baths, equipping them with every up-to-date convenience while keeping the *size* of them quite undiminished and leaving the high ceilings, quite naturally, to provide that extra airiness that today's low-ceiling rooms lack. There is character in a fine old hotel determinedly kept young, and the Ritz is one of that select group that commands downright affection from thousands of repeaters.

Among the many other luxury hotel of new or renewed construction the *Avenida Palace* stands out, but it is hard to pick and choose among so many. The *Arycasa*, in a central but relatively quiet location, is excellent. The *Majestic* is a gracious hostelry on the gracious Paseo (de Gracia). The *Manila* is a lively place fronting on that river of strollers and traffic called the Ramblas. The *Colón* is handsomely placed on the cathedral plaza, and in the same luxury class the *Fénix*, of the Iberia-wide HUSA chain, is the newest comer. Hotel Colón has recently opened a delightful *Residencia* in a large structure immediately behind the main hotel. This is tasteful and comfortable, with its own artistic restaurant but with lower tariffs than the chief, de luxe Colón. *Residencia La*

Rotonda and the *Astoria* are other good residential establishments for lodging and breakfast only, the first-named being de luxe, the other first-class. The centrally located *Cristina*, formerly residential, now has a good dining room. The *Emperatriz*, the *Roma* and the *Park* (this near the railway station) are three new first-class hotels with dining rooms. *Hotel Urbis*, Paseo de Gracia 23, a remodeled mansion of an 18th-century marquis, is a recommendable second-class hotel. From the crowded Ramblas to the quiet residential sections and even the background hills Barcelona has a wealth of good lodging places of every category for every budget.

The *restaurants* of the Catalan metropolis are widely varied in type and full of interest as well as palate appeal.

The *Parellada*, on the Diagonal (Avenida Generalísimo Franco) is among the veteran leaders in good food and smart atmosphere. It has also a superlative pastry shop and a smart tearoom. *Sacha*, a newer de luxe restaurant, is on the Diagonal. The *Hostal del Sol* (Calle Mallorca) and the *Sandor* (Plaza Calvo Sotelo; see below) are two other places of de luxe standing. The "most selective club restaurant," by its own admission, is the *Restaurante del Círculo Ecuestre*, perhaps comparing in social elevation to the Jockey Clubs of certain Latin-American capitals, but aristocrats such as yourself are quite welcome to lunch or dine here. The food is good, though neither lavish nor expensive.

The *Finisterre*, at 469 on the Diagonal, is shaped like the poop deck of a galleon. The steering wheel, the port and starboard lights and other features give it a marine atmosphere in keeping with its good sea food. *Restaurant Reno* is known for its tender roast chicken and for quick and pleasant service. *Restaurante El Ast* (The Spit) has a spectacular site on Montjuich Hill. It is equally popular for its roast chicken and for its view.

Typical Catalan restaurants are numerous, one of the attractive ones being on Calle Lauria, directly opposite the main entrance to Hotel Ritz. It is called *El Canario de la Garriga* and is perhaps self-consciously "atmospheric," its entrance being a replica of the first train in Spain, an amusing little yellow wagon that used to toil on tracks from Barcelona to Mataró, a distance of eighteen miles, in the middle of the nineteenth century. Another "tipico" restaurant that I have tried is the popular *Los Caracoles* (The Snails), located on Calle de Escudillers, a not-too-savory lane just off the Ramblas.

Among typical *waterfront* restaurants, specializing in sea food, the *Solé*, at 7 Paseo do Colón, is prominent.

Among *cafeterias*, of which there are many, the *Milan*, on Paseo de Gracia, is outstanding.

Smart tearooms seem to be "three to the block" in some sections of the city. Those of the *Windsor* (Diagonal) and the above-mentioned *Parellada* call for thought, as does *Salon Rosa*, on Paseo de Gracia near the *Kansas* quick lunch, as does fashionable *Sacha*, at 538 on the Diagonal. A very large and not at all exclusive bar-tearoom on the Diagonal (Number 488) is named *Granjas La Catalana*.

Cafés are several times as numerous as even tearooms, and if you like sidewalk sitting as well as I do, you will find them very relaxing, though they have by no means the appealing atmosphere of Paris cafés. Four that have at least lively locations are: *Rigat* and *La Luna*, both on Plaza Cataluña, *Navarra*, at 4 Paseo de Gracia, and *Oro del Rhin* (Rheingold), on the corner of Avenida José Antonio and Rambla de Cataluña.

Horchaterías, so distinctive of Spain's Mediterranean cities, are especially inviting in Barcelona, but one may buy a cool *horchata* in any café.

Outdoor summer restaurants of quality include *El Cortijo*, on the big circle called Plaza Calvo Sotelo that "interrupts" the Diagonal at the edge of the city, and *La Rosaleda*, on Carretera de Sarrió. These places put on floor shows at night and should perhaps be considered nighspots, but they are summer daytime restaurants as well. At the first-named place, meaning "The Farmhouse," I enjoyed dallying with a meal till 3 A.M., entertained at intervals by dainty dancers (doing the *jota*, the *paso doble*, etc.) who called their offerings *Ballet Miniaturas Españolas*, and by a lovely ballerina billed as *Muñequita Linda* (Beautiful Doll). You may have equal luck if you spend an early-morn "evening" at the Farmhouse.

Brief study of a map, procurable from your hall porter or from the official Tourist Office (DGT) on Avenida José Antonio near Hotel Ritz, will readily orient the visitor. Note that the chain of Ramblas, including that elegant shopping street called *Rambla de Cataluña* (in Catalan spelling Catalunya), runs from the inner-port square called

Puerta de la Paz, dominated by a statue of Columbus on a 200-foot column, to and far beyond the huge, central *Plaza de Cataluña*, heart of the city. Note that the old city, divided by the Ramblas into the *Gothic Quarter* (northeast) and the so-called *Chinese Quarter* (south-west), a crowded haunt of vice, is surrounded by an irregular hexagon of streets, most of which bear the title Ronda. The above features, coupled with attention to the two broad avenidas, José Antonio and the Diagonal, and Paseo de Gracia, go far to set the pattern of the city. If you add to this an awareness of the park-and-museum hill called *Montjuich* (pronounced more or less like Mont-hwee), entered from the circular Plaza de España, and of the famous background hill of *Tibidabo*, you will have scraped acquaintance with this Mediterranean metropolis. Plaza de España is of immediate and special interest, since the city terminal for air travelers coming from *Muntadas Airport*, eight miles distant, fronts on it.

Some cities instantly give the transient visitor a feeling of brightness, good cheer and intimacy, while others take a lot of knowing before one can sense a "response." Barcelona's cheerfulness is self-evident, being sparked by its lovely broad avenidas and, above all, by its *Ramblas*, which form a chain-of-life to be seen, strolled upon and savored at leisure, rather than described. This unique chain-street of many links is just about the most animated thoroughfare in all Europe. The central shaft of it, from Plaza Cataluña to the port, is a wide, tree-shaded promenade, lined on both sides with chairs that are rentable for next to nothing. On either side of this central promenade is a street thronged with traffic, one side bound toward the port, the other toward the great plaza. One portion, the *Rambla de las Flores*, is made brilliant with a flower market in the forenoon. Another portion, the *Rambla de los Estudios*, is a market of singing birds. Here and there are news kiosks and subway entrances and exits, and in every part of it are *people*. From six to nine in Barcelona's "afternoon" the whole pavement is so packed with strollers, from curb to curb, that one can hardly move faster than a creep.

The *Barrio Gótico* (Gothic Quarter) is a medieval sector that never fails to fascinate. To enter it from the Ramblas, try to find the little street called *Calle del Cardenal Casañas* and walk along it to *Plaza del Pino*, where the fifteenth-century *Church of Santa María del Pino* seems like a fort blocking further advance. Make your way around this church, named for an image of the Virgin found in a pine tree, and you'll be in another little back eddy of time, *Plaza del Beato Oriol*, whence you walk through the *Calle de la Paja* (Straw Street) to *Plaza Nueva* (New Square), a venerable square that was *once* new. From there it is but a step to the *Cathedral*, the nucleus of the whole sector. In spite of its old works of art, some fine stained glass and a cheerful cloister, the cathedral probably won't hold you long, because it is so gloomy-dark, this being accentuated by the obstructing choir in the center of the nave, as is usual in Spain, but the streets about it *will* hold you, especially the wriggling "Straw Street" by which you approached. On both sides it is lined with little shops where artistic things in various materials are being fashioned by hand about as they were fashioned when the Gothic Quarter was "modern."

From the cathedral you'll wish to find your way through the maze by *Calle Piedad* to *Plaza del Rey*, a "lost plaza" where the old *Palace of the Kings of Aragon* (and Barcelona) stands, and where also the *Barcelona Museum* is located; and from there you may thread your way portward to "emerge" on *Calle Jaime I*, a relatively broad street of heavy traffic that changes its name to *Calle de Fernando* as it proceeds back to the Ramblas. Calle de Fernando is one of the liveliest streets of *popular shopping* in the city. (In connection with shopping I should mention that in this city, as in Lisbon and Madrid, the American Visitors Bureau, Avenida José Antonio 591, 2nd floor, is an invaluable helper in wrapping and mailing gift parcels.)

One very pleasing item of the Gothic Quarter seems to have strayed beyond Calle de Fernando, on the sea side. This is the arcaded *Plaza Real*, reachable directly from the Rambla del Centro. This Royal Square is like an oasis of green in the desert of congested masonry, for it is even decorated by handsome palms. You will enjoy strolling around its long-ago-elegant arcades, reminding you a bit of the arcades around the Jardin du Palais Royal in Paris, and if it is meal time you may wish to conclude your strolling by dropping into the *Restaurant Glaciar*, which opens upon this square as well as upon the above-named Rambla del Centro.

The near and less-near environs of Barcelona, leaving aside the Balearics, which will be covered below, warrant days or weeks of exploration. Along the coast northeast of the city, stretching all the way to the French border, is the famous holiday littoral called the *Costa Brava* (Wild Coast), with a score of lovely and inviting resorts. A delightful novelty of this coast is service by *water busses*, as they are called, supplementing the traditional tours by motor coach. In these marine busses one may port-hop for forty miles from *Blanes*, some forty miles northeast of Barcelona, to *Tamariu*, or vice versa. To the southwest of Barcelona is sophisticated *Sitges*, with its big *Hotel Terramar*, goal of golfers, bathers and plain holiday loafers; and in the mountains back of Barcelona but easily reachable by car or train-and-cableway, is *Montserrat*, legendary home of the Holy Grail, one of the most celebrated pilgrim shrines in Europe. It was before this shrine that the wounded warrior Ignatius Loyola, founder of the Jesuit Order (The Society of Jesus), laid down his sword to devote his life to religious service. The setting of this lofty shrine and the monastery church has the almost frightening immensity of a towering scene in the Dolomites, coupled with the sky, the earth and the whole inimitable stamp of Spain.

Majorca Magic

Majorca (spelled hereinafter in the Spanish way only when used in the name of its capital, Palma de *Mallorca*) has a perennial lure for all travelers with a spark of romance in them. That was what drew Chopin and George Sand there more than a century ago, though I do not imply that the island's lure is illicit. It simply has everything that the romanticist could want, and nowadays, one must admit, it has a plethora of smart international hotels for the merely gregarious as well, though it shines with particular brightness as the honeymoon island of islands. On two spring visits I have sometimes thought myself the only person present not on a *luna de miel*.

Air and steamer services are frequent and excellent. Iberia and Aviación y Comercio, operating as a sort of air-duo, offer numerous flights every day from Barcelona. Others are offered from Valencia, from Madrid and, with change of planes at Valencia, from Seville and Málaga. There is also a two or three times daily service between Barcelona and Ibiza, plus inter-island connections between Ibiza and

Minorca. The *Compañía Transmediterránea* serves Majorca several times a week, with sailings from Barcelona and Valencia. These ships are good, matching our better coastwise steamers, and it works out very well to make the Majorca visit a *triangle trip*, flying one way from one of these ports and returning by the night ship to the other.

Much more ambitious triangles and other geometric patterns than the simple one above can, of course, be worked out, especially in connection with *Air France*, which operates direct Caravelle jets from Paris to Majorca in two hours, and with *Aviación y Comercio*, which has, though this may need checking, a Marseille-Palma-Algiers service. Palma as a city rather than merely a holiday resort, has some remarkable sights. First of all, its huge golden-tawny cathedral, with an immense and lovely rose window, fairly dominates everything, looming up conspicuously as seen from the tourist hotels that fringe the bay. A visit to the cathedral, magnificently located on a terrace above the harbor, is the one "must" of every visitor. Jaime I of Aragon conquered this island from the Moors in 1229 and founded the cathedral the following year, after which it grew, under various architects, for the next four centuries. Its interior is simple, gray and graceful in its immensity. Over the high altar an enormous crown of thorns is suspended, and this is significant of the cathedral, since its treasury displays, with deep, undoubting reverence, four thorns believed by the faithful of Majorca to be from the original crown, and with them a part of the sponge that was filled with vinegar and given to the Savior to drink. Other important sights of the city are the Gothic *Lonja* (Exchange), a medieval jewel situated on the bay front, and the thirteenth-century hilltop castle called *Bellver*, with a wide panoramic view. The central Paseo Generalísimo Franco, conveniently known by its old Majorcan name of Paseo Born, is a sight in itself, an animated Rambla day and evening, rimmed by sidewalk cafés and with innumerable small restaurants, bars and night dancings on the narrow side streets opening from it.

The Majorcan capital, now with 160,000 inhabitants, has had a recent tourist development that invites, even requires, high-pressure adjectives. It is, in short, fabulous, fantastic, incredible. I will list, with a few words for each, some of the more significant of the city's present three hundred hotels, residencias and pensions, murmuring also that about *one hundred more* are right now under construction in Palma, in other parts of Majorca and on the lesser isles of the Balearic group. We may commence the list with one in Palma that is rated by the DGT "above classification."

The *Son Vida*, on high ground a little way out of town, is *the* club-like superhostelry of wealthy and even royal clients. It is the newest and brightest (and most expensive) star in the Palma constellation. Its site is that of a castle given by King Jaime I to the Marquis de la Torre.

The *Bahía Palace*, a 240-room show place on the bay front near the city's center, is conspicuous and it is pleasant too, if you don't mind having its modernistic glories and art works strike you between the eyes. Its public rooms, especially its patio-pool and café, are brightly attractive and of course it has its own nightclub, *El Pirata*. A commendable and popular feature is its separate hotel annex (across the street) called *El Chico*, a more folksy establishment, but very comfortable, fronting on a well-kept garden and the harbor.

The *Fénix*, a new 100-room hotel on the sea front, is perhaps my personal favorite, for it is the very essence of comfort and artistic charm, with a glorious garden in which flamingos stalk about in dignity. It shares with the neighboring *Hotel Victoria* (both under the same management) a large, always gay, swimming pool. The Fénix cuisine is one of the best in Palma.

The *Mediterráneo Gran Hotel* has a de luxe rating and on a stay there some years ago I enjoyed its luxuries. It now boasts a *Tauromaquia* (bullfight) *Museum* and a lively nightclub featuring flamenco entertainment.

The *Nixe Palace* (100 rooms and baths), opened in 1957 at Cala-mayor, has many "talking points," a sea front location, with its own beach and pool, an appealing breakfast terrace and snack bar, modern luxuries *and* the name of a local siren. If Nixe lures you here I think she'll do right by you.

La Cala (50 rooms and baths) is a small but rather smart place adjacent to the Nixe. It, too, fronts directly on a beach, and beaches of real sand are rare in the immediate vicinity of Palma.

The new *Gran Hotel Augusta* (50 rooms and baths) and the adjacent *Rigel* (50 rooms, most with bath), both on the front, are good (as is the *Principe Alfonso*, which is pleasantly situated in a pine grove close to the sea.)

A beach section called *El Arenal* is the newest spawning ground of holiday hotels, a dozen or more new ones having appeared on or near the community's Maravillas Beach. The *Cristina* and the *Acapulco* are the present leaders of this group.

Of 1-B hotels, the quiet little *Virginia* (16 rooms and baths) and the big businesslike *Jaime I* (135 rooms, 40 baths) deserve thrift consideration, as do the *Oasis*, at Playa C'an Pastilla and the new *Panoramic* at Calamayor. *La Almudaina* is an excellent new downtown hotel.

Of a score or more *residencias* (without restaurant), half of them with de luxe rating, one of the best-liked of all, though only rated 1-A, is *Casa Martín*, at 254 Calvo Sotelo. American guests seem always to feel thoroughly at home here.

Needless to say nightclubs abound in this super-tourist town. I should say that the best one, of international type with dependably good floor show, is *Titos*, located on an upper level just back of Hotel Mediterráneo, runners-up being *Jack el Negro* and *Cuevas del Molino*. Small boîtes and bars and assorted dives are beyond counting. In two blocks of just one lane (Calle Apuntadores) opening off the Paseo downtown I jotted down the following names: Calypso Bar, Bermudas Bar, Hostal Tirol, Escandinavia Bar, Whisky Club, Los Troncos, Zaca, Bodega 23, 7 Mares Bar, Music Bar La Reja, El Tunel and Meson de Carlos I. There were more, but jotter's cramp was setting in. Along the upper street called Calvo Sotelo, behind the bay-front hotels, there are as many more such places, with names of similar type.

Hostelries in the seaside environs of Palma have grown in spread and variety quite as much as in number and you will find first-class inns, generally with lower tariffs, as you progress farther from the center, all along the rugged coastline and promontory southwest and west of the city. These include, at Bendinat, *Hotel Bendinat;* at Palma Nova, *Residencia Palma Nova* (de luxe) and *Residencia Pinos Mar;* at Paguera, the *Villamil* and the *Bahía Club;* and at *Camp de Mar*, some 17 miles out, the like-named inn, *Camp de Mar*.

If the multiplicity of Palma's hotels and inns, bars and nightclubs tends to discourage you remember that the local DGT office, at Paseo Generalísimo Franco 34, exists to give you impartial help. It publishes various leaflets on the island, including one called *Majorca, General*

Information, with all sorts of needed helps and listings, and a weekly, partly in English, called *La Semana Mallorquina* that tells you what to do and when and how if you would get the most out of your island holidays.

Motor excursions with Palma as hub are numerous and varied, featuring the famous ones to the Dragon Caves and to Valldemosa, which will be described below. Some are still "almost virginal" even in this tourist-saturated part of Majorca. These unsung goals, to take them up first, may be divided roughly into seaside and mountaintop "finds." Let's consider three seaside goals first, each of them having the word *cala,* meaning inlet or indentation, as a part of its name.

1. *Cala Santa Ponsa,* only 12 or 13 miles from Palma as one motors westward, is the most accessible of them and therefore not hard to discover, but it is of exceptional interest for its historical associations, since a headland on the cala is the very spot where King Jaime I landed 700 years ago in his conquest of Majorca. An old chapel (restored) on the headland is where this conquering monarch celebrated his first Majorcan mass.

2. *Cala Figuera,* on the island's southeast coast, is a glorious retreat where the sea has cut a deep Y into the rocky shoreline, its waters being an aqueous melody in blues and greens. This cala is an artist-writer-musician's haven, little touched as yet by foreign tourism.

3. *Cala d'Or* (Golden Inlet) is on the same coast, a bit to the northeast, and here there are several simple inns, *Hotel Cala d'Or* being one of the pleasantest, followed by *Hotel Cala Gran* and *Pensión Los Arios.* In "inlet inns" such as the above, which have been little touched by American tourists, though exploratory Germans and some British have found them, you may live well and eat well for a song, or even a ditty. The Cala d'Or, with a lovely outdoor dining terrace, rises from a wooded slope above a cove with perfect soft sand.

Four mountaintop goals, at heights of 1500 to 3000 feet, all of them with monkish sanctuaries, will be even more to the escapist's taste, for they're the summits nobody knows. In any of the monasteries on the respective crests you may lodge (a bit crudely) for 30 to 50 cents and pay another half dollar for a day's meals.

1. *Monte Cura* is a double star of discovery, with the sanctuary of *Nuestra Señora de Gracia* at a high level and *Nuestra Señora de Cura*

still higher. The first-named sanctuary sits on a lofty ledge above a broad, green plain and directly below a fantastic ledge of rock which extends perhaps thirty feet over the conventual buildings like a natural stone room.

2. *San Salvador* is a crest surmounted by a huge and too-showy monument of Jesus, more in the attitude of a Roman emperor than a humble Nazarene, but here, too, there is a monastery where simple accommodations are offered for "what you like." There is no fixed tariff for its cubicles.

3. *Galilea*, at about the same height as San Salvador (2000 feet), has actually a good third-class pension, by name *Golo*.

4. *Lluch* is the highest of our four sanctuaries and lodging there is the most expensive. The best rooms in this mountain monastery (3000 feet) may cost you up to 70 cents a night!

You'll obviously need help from the DGT or some *imaginative* travel agent to find these interesting retreats-up-aloft, each with its stupendous view, but if you do find them you'll readily admit that Majorca is not yet quite submerged in tourism.

The standard, three-star specials of Majorcan motor touring are the *Dragon Caves* and *Valldemosa*, which we may take up in turn.

"The Dragon Caves are a shadowy, mute world, where the silent forces of nature, working without rest for thousands of centuries, have built marvels which confound human intelligence." So wrote a French author in 1893, although the best portions of them had not then been discovered. Now nature has worked silently for a few more decades, undisturbed by the increasing babble of tourist talk. I am not normally a cave enthusiast but by *these* caves I was enthralled. Their millions of fantastic stalactites and stalagmites, illuminated tastefully and never garishly by concealed electric lights, form one of the most wonderful natural spectacles I have even seen. Of course the caves contain the usual features such a calcareous temple, a sinking ship, a medieval castle, a Buddha, a Chinese pagoda, but these are only the beginning of the start of the caverned wonders.

The days for the Drach trip vary with the seasons (almost daily in summer, four times a week in spring, twice in winter) and this should be checked at the time of your visit, for on those special days music goes underground, quite literally, inside the caves. Your trip can be arranged by the DGT or by any of Palma's numerous travel agencies. The distance from Palma is about forty-five miles by road and is covered by private car or by tourist bus, the busses being naturally packed to the gunwales on music days. The highway, a good one, leads to *Manacor* (stress last syllable) through the windmill region, where many mills serve to irrigate this level portion of the island, and through the almond-tree region, glorious in blossomtime (late winter and early spring) and furnishing nuts almost as good as chufa nuts for that favorite drink, *horchata;* and so to *Porto Cristo* (the Catalan spelling for Puerto Cristo), a tiny picture port close to the Dragon Caves. You will enter the caves with a numbered card, the lower numbers going consecutively to the earlier comers, and this is important, for it establishes the order by which you are ultimately ferried over a considerable lake to the *exit,* at a distant point of the underground world.

The concerts are the grand climax of a half-hour's stroll along the twisting path that threads the caves' most elaborate scenes, arriving finally at the subterranean *Lake Martel,* upon whose banks rises a shadowy amphitheater that can seat at least five hundred spectators. When all are seated a director of ceremonies calls for total silence and then every vestige of light is turned off. Expectations are built up and the actuality fulfills them. At the far end of the lake faint music is heard and presently two barges, outlined in electric lights, appear. On the barges are the musicians, their instruments consisting of violins, a cello or two and a harmonium. Slowly the barges are rowed toward the spectators and the music grows louder. A quarter-hour concert I heard was devoted to the most popular and melodious of light classics, Grieg's *Solvejg's Song,* the Barcarolle from *Les Contes d'Hoffmann,* and, of course, a few familiar Chopin gems. There was nothing in the least pretentious about such offerings, but who, in such a setting, would demand Mahler, Shostakovitch or the twelve-tone moderns? It was all as soft and silencing as the harmonies of Aeolian harps. There was no Stygian gloom, for the lighted barges traveled doubly, once in fact and once in reflection, and a million stalactites glistened in the advancing lights, while hundreds of people in the amphitheater watched and listened.

When the orchestra barges finally withdrew across the lake, others, more of gondola design, came to serve as ferries for the crowd. The director began calling out numbers, and as each visitor heard his number he entered one of the barges for the trip to the exit. The event concluded, in my case, with a mass luncheon on the open terrace of the modest little *Hotel Perelló* of Porto Cristo.

On the way back to Palma the busses and most of the cars stop at Manacor, where tourist shops specialize in costume jewelry and "Manacor pearls," works of local craftsmanship that are of real appeal despite their incredibly low cost in terms of dollar-bought pesetas.

Valldemosa, a former Carthusian convent, with a church where services are still held, has become a shrine of music lovers hardly equaled in popularity by any other in Europe. Up to one hundred thousand visitors a year, the French predominating, make their way to this hillside building, eleven miles from Palma, to pay their respects to a beloved composer and his literary light-o'-love who defied convention more than a century ago by living here together for a couple of months.

The *Cellule Musé*, or Museum Cell, is the great attraction, and a plaque at its entrance gives a self-translating tribute to *Frédéric Chopin et George Sand, à l'impérissable mémoire des deux grands artistes qui habitèrent ici 1838-1839*. The plaque was erected by a society called "Les Amis de George Sand" and by that lady's granddaughter, Aurore Sand (who took over the *pen* name), but there is no doubt that the average American tourist, a bit shadowy in his knowledge of the novelist (whose real name was Amantine Lucile Aurore, Baroness Dudevant) is far more interested in Chopin and the misguided romance that brought the couple here. There are many relics of absorbing interest, and to understand them fully—if you read French—you may purchase on the spot a book entitled *Chopin et George Sand à Marjorque*, translated from the Spanish original of Bartolomeu Merra.

Without a printed guide one may comprehend the essentials by merely looking, and perhaps asking a few questions of the pleasant attendant in charge of the museum. The whole venture of the lovers was dogged by ill luck and it proved a monumental flop. They had thought to escape the cold winter rains and winds of Paris but cold rains and winds came with painful frequency even to Valldemosa, which can be heavenly beautiful in sunshine, and there was much fog too.

Sand had brought her sixteen-year-old son Maurice (an artistic youth who designed Valldemosa's much-admired garden) and her daughter and servants, but such an "invasion" from sophisticated Paris grated on the simple islanders and they were anything but cordial. Sand retaliated with some bitter invectives about them in her writings.

Chopin ordered a piano (for 1200 francs!) from Pleyel in Paris but it everlastingly failed to arrive and he had to make do with a pitiable little piano made in Palma. A letter of Chopin's to Pleyel, penned on stationery with the monogram G.S., is seen in the museum. Finally the piano arrived, but the Spanish customs officials held it at Palma, and George Sand, the "businessman," and Maurice went to the Aduana to get it through the snarl of red tape. A dismal, cold rainstorm came up and the disconsolate composer wrote his fifteenth prelude, the "Raindrop Prelude," while he waited. When finally the Pleyel reached Valldemosa the lovebirds were so utterly discouraged with the weather and the hostility of the islanders that within three weeks they packed up and started their journey back to Paris. The weather had been as cruelly "unusual" as it could ever conceivably be, and the balminess which they had had a right to expect simply failed them. Chopin's already delicate lungs had suffered sharp deterioration.

Chopin's accomplishment during a stay that totaled just under sixty days in the monastery, seems fantastic. He wrote here not only the bulk of his celebrated Twenty-four Preludes but also the second Ballade in F major, opus 38, the third Scherzo in C minor, opus 39, the two Polonaises in A major and C minor, opus 40, the Mazurka in E minor, opus 41, Number 2 and "probably" the Sonata in B flat minor and the two Nocturnes, opus 37. I list these for the interest of piano students who may like to know which of the lovely pieces were composed in Majorca, in a frenzy of work intended to blot out disappointments.

Some decades after the Chopin-Sand interlude, Rubén Darío, the Nicaraguan poet who won for himself a world name, stayed for a time in the Cartuja at Valldemosa, as did also, in his turn, the revered Spanish scholar of Salamanca University, Miguel de Unamuno. The place has a "patina of genius" about it and will attract visitors as long as people admire special achievement. There is a touristic touch about Valldemosa, as evidenced by the Majorcan folk dances given there twice weekly during the spring season, but it is not much commercialized and the whole place has been kept up with devotion and good taste.

For an island so small, about sixty miles by forty, Majorca has a remarkable number of special spots to visit and the scenery in the northwestern third is both romantic and monumental, with many lovely villages and crescent ports and with mountains that rise to almost 5000 feet. The Majorcan *people*, the plain, friendly (to us if not to Chopin-Sand), *un*venal folk of the villages, speaking their own language, a cross between Spanish and Italian understood only with difficulty by Spaniards *or* Italians, add much to any trip.

The details of travel by bus, train or private car should be arranged by a local agency or the DGT, according to individual taste and pocketbook, but I will list here four specials, with their chief associations.

1. The often-neglected scenic *Western Peninsula* is to be visited by road only. *Camp de Mar*, with its delightful shore hotel is first seen, and then *Andraitx*, after which the road doubles back (this stretch now very poor) along the northern shore to *Bañalbufar*, whence a direct return is made to Palma by way of *Esporlas*.

2. *Valldemosa, Miramar, Deya, Sóller,* lying north of Palma, may be visited in a one-day road circuit on a highway of scenery, the *Grande Corniche of Majorca*, that is quite the equal in beauty of the Costa Brava road and vastly better in quality.

Miramar, a few miles beyond Valldemosa, is the lordly and tastefully gardened estate of a former Austrian archduke, by name Ludwig Salvator, or, in Spanish, Luis Salvator. It has a château, a Majorcan oratory, a country-by-the-sea house of the archduke and miles of landscaped walks.

Deya is merely a Majorcan village but that is saying a lot, for it is actually a painter's delight. Orange and lemon groves half hide it from the highway.

Sóller, the far point of the circuit, is a large town (12,000 inhabitants) but is chiefly attractive for its lovely crescent port, three miles distant, and for the hiker's and mountain-climber's goals that surround it. There is a separate electric rail line from Palma to Sóller town (55 minutes) and a tram or bus from town to port. This glamorous port is not what it used to be, since nowadays it serves as a submarine base and picture taking is forbidden.

3. *Petra*, a village in the interior of the island, has special interest for Californians, since it is the birthplace of Friar Junípero Serra, the devoted Franciscan missionary who built up the chain of missions in California and lies buried in the Carmel Mission of that state. He was born (in 1713) Miguel José Serra but later took the clerical name of "Juniper." His home village is proud of its native son and erected a monument to him in 1913. Californian tourists, especially those from the Carmel-Monterey region, often make their way to this little community, which is decidedly off the beaten track, though not far in miles from Manacor.

4. The *Cross-Island Tour* through *Inca* to *Pollensa* and *Cap Formentor* is a climactic one that should include a stop of at least one night, if possible, at *Hotel Formentor*, though the out-and-back trip (85 miles in all) is not difficult to put through in a day.

Inca has a rather startling "Andean" name but it is merely a large and venerable town, now chiefly devoted to making shoes for export, there being about twenty-five shoes factories in the town. In various European lands, notably France and Italy, the words "Made in Mallorca" are considered a symbol of good workmanship.

Pollensa, guarded by an interesting calvary, is known for its religious and civil festivals, the former occurring on January 16 and 17 and during Holy Week, the latter, with open-air folk dances and "fights" between "Christians and Moors," coming on the first three days of August, but if your trip doesn't touch these dates you will want to roll right along to the pretty *Port of Pollensa*, which is a beach resort as much as a port.

Formentor is a long and lovely cape with a special resort inn that is known in all tourist quarters. Hotel Formentor is, in fact, the dean of Spain's fine resort hotels, though some newer ones have now surpassed it in luxury. None has or can surpass it in setting. It has its own beach, its own golf course and tennis courts and about five thousand acres of beautiful pine woods.

The lesser Balearics consist primarily of *Ibiza* and *Minorca*. Ibiza, with its direct and frequent air service from Barcelona, has blossomed rather too much to suit lovers of things-as-they-were. They bemoan the "tourist damage" to this lovely island, but "what can't be cured must be endured," and one may as well love Ibiza anyway. You will discover that there is really no need for alarm if you read the illustrated *Ibiza* booklet in the series published by the *Islands in the Sun Club* (673 Fifth Avenue, New York). The reportage by Shirley-Elizabeth Warren, a dedicated permanent resident, is bright, warm, beguiling. She asserts that in spite of recent inflation you can "live mighty well" on the island for $66 a month, as she is doing. For short stayers there are two second-class hotels, the *Montesol* and the *Noray*, and four pensions, the two best being *El Corsario* and the *Marigua*. Bigger and better hotels will inevitably rise.

Even Minorca, though linked by plane only with Ibiza, is coming into its own, helped by a new and good hotel, the *Delfin*.

REVISION SUPPLEMENT TO CHAPTER 8

GOOD news for visitors to France is a recent government decree abolishing cover charges. Originally intended to defray cost of linens, flatware, china, and such, the cover charge had become an annoyance to many. All that is now gone, and the only extra charge allowed is for service.

As mentioned in the text, France and her shoreline are amply covered in *"All the Best in France,"* another book in this series and one that has just been brought completely up to date. I would refer you once again to that companion book and will only list here, for easy reference, some of the new developments, particularly in Corsica, which has lately begun to come into its own as an important holiday goal.

French Line has increased its passenger-car ferry service with the addition of the *Fred Scammaroni*, a ship named in honor of a Corsican *Résistance* hero. French Line also sells seven-day package tours that include fares and a motorcoach tour of Corsica. In line with its obvious interest in Corsican tourism, the Line is also building a large luxury hotel on the island to be opened in 1967. More and more hotels of this high quality are rising, along with lesser ones, and those who contemplate touring the island (or the Riviera) would do well to secure the official list from the French Government Tourist Office, 610 Fifth Avenue, New York City. (Regrettably, the Island in the Sun Club, mentioned on page 152, is no longer a source of information, having gone out of business.)

Road travel, whether by your own car, by ordinary bus or by touring coach, must face up to the fact that curves and more curves, mostly sharp ones, are of the essence. The automobile road race of 1300 kilometers (800 miles), held annually in November, is nicknamed by the Corsicans *Le Rallye des 10,000 Virages* (curves). If you are motoring on your own go at a moderate pace and don't make it a long day, for 100 miles on roads like these can seem like 300 on a good pike. If you go on a guided tour the driver will doubtless have mercy on his customers, but if you go by ordinary bus just hang on. You'll think you're on a roller coaster. Main tourist centers of the island, in addition to *Ajaccio*, its capital, are *Calvi*, an ancient-but-modern town on the northwest coast; *Bonifacio*, a truly spectacular cliff town at the extreme southern point; and *Bastia*, the largest city, with the scenic drive north of it, along the shore of Cap Corse. Adding to its growing renown as a goal during mild months, Corsica has recently entered the rapidly growing field of ski resorts! On New Year's Eve of 1965 the island inaugurated its first winter sports resort at *Asco*, in the northern mountains, with a chalet to accommodate 130 guests and a *remonte-pente* (slope-climber) machine for transportation to the top.

Little mention is made in the text of car rental in France. As in other places, renting a car is one of the best ways to see the country, and in France particularly, the Riviera. The 2000-mile shoreline of France is self-consciously prismatic in nomenclature, every little segment has its own tinted name. One can run through the whole rainbow. If you supply yourself with a full set of *dépliants* (folders), you will discover the alluring possibilities of the Emerald Coast, the Jade Coast, the Nacre (Mother-of-Pearl) Coast, the Silver Coast, the Vermilion Coast and finally the Azure Coast (all traveling under their French names, of course).

The going is superb all the way from Marseille to Menton and beyond (in Italy), whether by train or car. The train swings inland at the beginning, and again from Hyères, near Toulon, returning to the coast at Saint-Raphaël, but the scenery is always grand. The main coastal road swings inland at Toulon, back of Chaîne des Maures, along with the railway, thereby missing lovely Saint-Tropez, which you should certainly follow the signs to see.

At Saint-Raphaël begins the popular, crowded French Riviera of fashion. Probably more smart perfections of villa residences and of tourism pepper the next sixty miles to Nice and Menton than any consecutive 60 miles on earth, yet even those who have no use for fashion cannot help loving this coast.

The *Esterel Massif*, between Saint-Raphaël and Cannes, is one of the superlative stretches and should be taken, if possible, by road, but there is a choice between the old Route Nationale 7 (N7), with its countless scenic curves, and the new *autoroute*, a splendid, though somewhat less scenic, toll road. A third choice is the coastal road, which literally never quits the sea. The hills of porphyry and sandstone seen from either of the inner roads are a treat to the eye. So to Cannes, with its sophisticated elegance, the social center of the whole Riviera. Always geared toward the water, with beaches and sailing, Cannes now is a terminal point for a ferry running to San Remo. The hundred-minute trip sometimes stops at Nice, Monaco and Menton en route. Further boat adventures are offered by the trip to Sainte-Marguerite, a small island in the harbor at Cannes, for *Son et Lumière* (Sound and Light) performances in the fortress during July, August and the first two weeks in September. The boat departs from Cannes at 9:00 P.M., the two-hour round trip, show included, costing only 6 francs ($1.20).

To return to our tour of the coastline, we stop next at *Juan-les-Pins*, a resort of crowds and trippers, and continue on to *Antibes*, with its old town and its ultrasmart Cap; big *Nice; Monaco*, with its Monte Carlo; and *Menton*, almost at the French-Italian frontier. In Nice there are no less than 15 different car rental companies, including *Hertz* and *Avis*, so car renting is no problem. During the heavy summer months advance arrangements should be made.

Monaco, that tiny principality that seems a magical name to many Americans, has made numerous improvements during the past few years. Here are some of them: Two railway tunnels totaling almost two and a half miles, that have put the rails out of sight under the principality; some 50 acres of land, now being rapidly developed, that have been reclaimed from the sea; a splendid new Avenue Princesse Grace that has been built on land similarly reclaimed; two new beach areas that have been made; and other developments, such as an Olympic-sized swimming pool, a heliport, new hotels and high-rise apartments galore and plenty more. The driving power behind this surge is universally credited to Prince Rainier, perhaps nudged or steered now and then by Her Serene Highness, Princess Grace.

Hotels along the Riviera are so incredibly numerous that I make no attempt even to list the leaders, which would number in the dozens, but I must make some brief allusion to Monaco's famous *Hotel de Paris* in Monte Carlo, overlooking the Casino and its park as well as the crowded harbor and the blue sea, for this is the nucleus of five Monaco hotels owned (51 per cent) by Aristotle Socrates Onassis. It has recently added three new floors of air-conditioned luxury, an eighth-floor grillroom, like an elegant way-up crow's nest, being the showpiece of this magnificent hostelry.

Possibly the most newsworthy item along the French Mediterranean coast these days is the development (really, creation) of a *new* Riviera along the long-neglected southwestern end of the coast. This is the *Languedoc coast*, with over 100 miles of windswept beaches, many of which are separated from the mainland by lagoons. Some of the lagoons are perfect harbors and will be turned into havens for pleasure craft. For years, the only tourists who could reach the area were large flocks of mosquitoes(!) but pest control has all but cleared the coast of these visitors. New roads have been built, thousands of trees (which were previously almost nonexistent) have been planted, and an elaborate ten-year development program has been inaugurated, making the Languedoc littoral a place to watch.

Finally, a note about air travel to and within France. *Air France* has added more frequent service from Paris to Marseille and to Nice and the Riviera and even, without change of plane, from New York to Paris to Nice. Marseille, by the way, has a magnificent new airport and a motor speedway from it to the city, reducing the transit time from a tedious one hour to 17 minutes! *Pan American*, somewhat neglected in the text, has two highly popular services to Nice, one from New York via Lisbon and Barcelona, the other from Miami via San Juan, Puerto Rico, the Azores, Lisbon and Barcelona. *Sabena* flies from Brussels to Nice, KLM from Amsterdam and BEA from London.

CHAPTER 8

COASTAL FRANCE AND CORSICA

Skimming the Cream

THIS book, to interject an explanatory word, is touching very lightly on coastal France and Italy, to conserve its space for portions of the Mediterranean that are less widely publicized and known. In the case of southern France, covered in this same travel series (*All the Best in France*), I shall do hardly more than list the places that seem to me the cream of the crop, with occasional practicalia and current notes.

France's *Côte d'Azur* (Azure Coast) has been the playground of the world almost since man began to play and its popularity has never waned. Today, it is more sought by general travelers than ever before and is no longer dominated by the wealthy playboy set. Taxes have decimated this lush segment of humanity, opening the whole coast to a wider patronage.

Air France planes tie the Blue Coast to Paris and to North Africa in veritable skeins of flights, Marseille and Nice being the points of knotting. *In 1963 one-stop jet service, New York-Paris-Nice, was opened!* Fast railway expresses tie the whole Riviera to Lyon and Paris. Passenger ships, through the port of Marseille, and cruise ships, through the port of Cannes, tie it to all oceans and the countries on them. We will have a look at "what to see and what to do," but first some basic tourist facts.

French Money, Folding and Ringing

One of the most beneficent developments that came to France with the Fifth Republic under President de Gaulle was the reform of the franc. Two useless ciphers were erased from the currency, transforming 100 old francs into 1 new franc, 1000 old francs into 10 new francs.

After the initiation of that reform the new franc was called just that, *Nouveau Franc*, represented on the paper money by the initials NF, but now that temporary title has been dropped, the changeover to plain, old-style francs dating from January, 1963. The *centime*, which had not been in evidence since before World War II, is finally back and in good standing, though the older coins (brassy) below 1 franc may also continue for some time to clutter the currency. The new coins of 10, 20 and 50 centimes are of cupro-aluminum, those of 1, 2 and 5 centimes of stainless steel.

Since the rate of exchange had firmed at approximately 490 old francs to the dollar, with very slight and negligible fluctuations, this meant that 4 new francs and 90 centimes (the *word* new now deleted) became, and are now, worth one dollar. To state it in another way, the present franc is worth just a trifle over 20 cents. To myself I said, "This is where I came in," for I confess that I was a youthful tourist way back in the days before World War I, when also the franc was worth 20 cents.

Glances North and West

Marseille is the take-off point for everything in southern France except the Riviera and the Maritime Alps, for which Cannes and Nice are the natural centers. Marseille itself is a very big port city, with a reputation for rowdiness because of the considerable Communist element among the dock workers. Its chief thoroughfare, la Canebière, is as lively as its counterpart in Spanish cities, and its chief high spot, the *Basilica of Notre Dame de la Garde*, offers a wonderful prospect of the Vieux Port and the sea. The Old Port lost its celebrated garishness, with accent on vice, when the German occupation authorities razed its most lurid quarters during World War II to clean out a supposed nest of saboteurs, but the quays are still aglow with life and they are flanked by as many fishy restaurants as ever.

Due north of Marseille, some twenty miles, is *Aix-en-Provence*, a small town, sleepy and beautiful, that is dear to artists and escapists. A little distance up the Rhone, by the trunk rail line to Paris, lie *Arles*, of Greek background, whose women—well, *some* of them— certainly are as pretty as tradition paints them; *Avignon*, a city of the popes during their "Babylonish captivity"; and *Orange*, of Roman background, with its Roman theater in a remarkable state of preservation. To the west, along the coast toward Spain, lie many wonders, the nearest being the *Camargue*, or Rhone delta, a weird region of cattle and cowboys, with two curious, moribund ports of stirring story, *Aigues Mortes* (Dead Waters) and *Les Saintes-Maries-de-la-Mer*. The Marys were three in number: Mary the wife of Cleophas; Mary, mother of James and John; and Mary Magdalene. According to tradition they were here cast up by the sea after fleeing in a small boat from persecution in Judea. Their swarthy servant Sara, who was cast up with them, became and still remains the patron saint of gypsies, who flock to this curious village in thousands to do her honor. She is supposed to be buried in the crypt of the local church, while the first two Marys above named lie in the main portion of the church. Mary Magdalene's bones made their way to Vézelay, in central France. The Camargue, almost never visited by tourists, is a worthy goal of exploration (easily reached from Arles), attracting those with a desire for the unusual.

Beyond the Camargue lie *Nîmes*, almost as Roman as it is French; erudite *Montpellier*, an attractive university city; *Cette*, a lively but unvisited port; and finally *Carcassonne*. In Carcassonne the one top place to stay is the luxurious *Hotel de la Cité*, within the ramparts of the old city, but if that is full the tourist who takes a room in the *Ville Basse* (Lower City) may comfort himself by feeling that at least he can look at Carcassonne in its entirety, which a dweller within it cannot do.

The vogue of this town is not accidental. The moving lines of Gustav Nadaud about the unfortunate old peasant who never had seen Carcassonne may have done their bit to publicize it, but it has always been its own best press agent. There are other well-walled towns in France, but generations of tourists have visited the eastern Pyrenees solely to see this one unforgettable sight. Classic plays have often been produced here in an open-air theater for the delectation of the summer throngs. Hamlet has trod the boards murmuring *"Etre ou n'être pas, telle est la question,"* and the ghost of his father has put in its appearance on the very walls of the old city. Pictures have been filmed here and tons of enthusiastic post cards mailed to all parts of the tourist world. If you come to Carcassonne yourself you will sense its unique glamor without, perhaps, being able to define it satisfactorily.

The Riviera and Its Alps

Cannes is the Riviera's smart-set center, but *Nice* is its metropolitan excursion center. With the single exception of *Grasse*, where four thousand tons of roses and orange blossoms alone are converted each year into bottled fragrance, the other places of major tourist interest, both along the shore and in the Maritime Alps, are easily visited from Nice. There are swarms of excursion busses, ranging from the big Europabus chariots to the small and smaller busses of several private purveyors of trips. Rails and roads skirt the shore in both directions and good roads climb many a steep valley to points of Alpine majesty.

To the west of Nice lie, in this order, castled *Cagnes*, a hilltop village that has special lure for artists; ancient *Antibes* and its smart peninsula of the *haut monde, Cap d'Antibes; Juan-les-Pins*, with one of the Riviera's few good sandy beaches; and farther to the west *Saint-Raphaël* and *Saint-Tropez*. To the east of Nice lie *Villefranche*, its bay often a place of anchorage for American naval craft; scenic *Cap Ferrat;* quiet *Beaulieu; Eze*, a stone-dead village of the Saracens high above the sea; the *Principality of Monaco*, with *Monte Carlo;* and finally *Menton*, a favored resort of the British very close to the frontier of Italy.

Mountain excursions are offered almost by the dozen. I once lived for six months in Nice and I think I took them all. Of the multitude, I strongly recommend the following four.

1. *Les Gorges du Loup*, and up the gorge to the stunning *Saut du Loup* (Wolf's Leap).

2. *Sospel*, on the edge of Italy, in a valley of gnarled olive trees.

3. *Peira Cava*, high in the mountains, where you can sit on a mossy ledge and listen to the monotonous chant of cuckoos two thousand feet below.

4. *Saint-Martin-Vésubie*, gorgeously situated at the head of an Alpine valley in *La Suisse Niçoise*.

Three-Fold Monaco, Principality of Luck

The Principality of Monaco has been one of the luckiest eight square miles, financially speaking, in all the world. Because two gambler-brothers named Blanc were driven out of Homburg in 1861 and chose to set up their roulette tables here, on a rocky headland known as Monte Carlo (Mount Charles), it has become wealthy, glittering, world-renowned, instead of just another pretty place on the Riviera. Despite its separate character as an independent miniature state it has never set up any customs or immigration formalities at its borders, these being absorbed in the general formalities of entering France, and except for small coins it has no Monegasque currency. French francs, whether ringing or folding, are in general use. The principality has three distinct sections: *Monte Carlo*, with its sumptuous casino and luxurious hotel life; *La Condamine*, a low-lying section with a curious church, deep in a ravine, dedicated to Sainte-Dévote, the "national" patron saint; and finally the *Rock of Monaco* itself, where Prince Rainier, present scion of the Grimaldi dynasty, lives with his lovely American Princess Grace and their children in a stage-set palace, decorated with gaily uniformed guards.

The Rock of Monaco is by far the most striking thing in this minature state yet many a visitor never deserts the green tables of the casino long enough to visit it. Not only are the walks along the steep cliff of wonderful beauty, but there exists here one of the world's very few comprehensive museums of oceanography, a scientific institution built up by Prince Albert I, himself a distinguished oceanographer, who died in 1922. In the same building is an aquarium, with as many incredible fishes, fantastic in their "design," their colors, their queer equipment of clown masks, pig snouts, glowing lamps and so forth, as even the aquariums of Naples, San Francisco and Honolulu. *Don't miss the Rock*—is my plea to all who visit Monte Carlo.

Information about the principality may be had by addressing the *Monaco Information Center*, 610 Fifth Avenue, New York 20, N.Y., or the *Commissariat Général au Tourisme*, Monte Carlo, Principality of Monaco. For information on the French Riviera and all of Mediterranean France, including Corsica, one may contact the *French Government Tourist Office* at 610 Fifth Avenue, New York.

I must conclude this brief coverage with the regretful comment that French francs have a distressing tendency to melt away, especially in tourist areas such as the Riviera, like snowballs in a sauna, for France, at least in its urban and resort areas, is now undoubtedly one of the most expensive countries in Europe. Costs can be brought down to modest levels if the visitor is content to stay in the small, un-touristy resorts, but in the leading hotels of such centers as Cannes, Nice and Monte Carlo they often seem staggering. Hotels add big service charges, which one is supposed to supplement with tips of 5 to 10 per cent, and the better restaurants and hotel dining rooms can demolish a 10-dollar bill for a meal-plus-wine without even trying. However—and this is a three-syllable "but"—no holiday region on earth surpasses the French Riviera in sustained, unflagging popularity, the costs be hanged. There must be a reason, and there is, as the tourist world confirms year after surging year. If you are a first-timer you may as well succumb and join the crowd, soothing your budget as best you can.

The French cuisine, as I need hardly say, or repeat, is the pace-setter for the whole epicurean world and in countless Riviera restaurants it lives up to its reputation. A world-famous specialty of Marseille, featured in many a restaurant of quality not only along the Riviera but in Paris and other cities, is *bouillabaisse*, that amazing brew of "Mediterranean bisque," a rich fishy and lobstery soup that is a passion of French gourmets. It is at its best in its natal town and even the hurried visitor should relax and enjoy it in some sidewalk eating place on the old port quays, the Cannebière (main street) or the Cours Belzunce, which is devoted almost exclusively to marine restaurants.

The Tourist Tide to Corsica

Ever since Napoleon's day Corsica has been something of a traveler's goal, but only since the coming of fast plane service, especially that of France's Caravelle jets, has this French island, a political *département* of the republic, been subjected to a waxing tide of tourism. Air France now maintains pure-jet Caravelle flights from Paris to two major cities of Corsica, Ajaccio, the capital, and Bastia, the flight time to either city being a mere hundred minutes. Piston-engine planes of various types fly also from Marseille and Nice to the above two cities and also to Calvi in times varying from 50 minutes to about an hour and a quarter. Super-Constellations are the fastest ones now used, but Breguet 763 Deux-Ponts the most novel. These are double-decker planes, the top deck (Pont Supérieur) being the more desirable for vision. The round-trip economy fare from Nice to any of the Corsican airports is at present well under $25.

Sea crossings to Corsica are handled by the French Line, which term is short for Compagnie Générale Transatlantique. The company's ships sail from Marseille and from Nice to Ajaccio, Bastia, Ile Rousse and/or Calvi. Most passages involve overnight journeys but from Nice there is a day service in summer, the distance from Nice being much shorter than that from Marseille. The two newest ships in service are the *Sampiero* and the *Napoléon Bonaparte*, the latter a new 4500-ton ship with a capacity for over 1200 passengers and 100 cars. The *Napoléon* is the motorists' choice not only for its car capacity but because one can drive onto the ship by means of a ramp. For the other ships one's car must be hoisted aboard by a crane. Car reservations should be made far ahead, for the favored ship is always booked solid in summer.

The French Line sells seven-day package tours that include the steamer fares and a motorcoach tour of the island. *Europabus*, the giant all-Europe coach network operated by the associated national railway systems of Europe, and in the case of Corsica by the French National Railroads, offers a seven-day tour of the island, starting in Calvi (at present on Monday) and concluding in Ile Rousse (on Sunday). The lucky ones with time to linger in Corsica will find a dozen or more new small government hotels, typical of which is the one named *De La Pietra* in Ile Rousse. That small town, by the way, boasts the island's only hotel of official de luxe rating, named, as you would expect, the *Napoléon Bonaparte*. The leading hotel in Ajaccio, a most attractive and well-managed one, is *Hôtel des Etrangers*, two lesser ones being the *Continental* and the *Highland*. In Calvi, the best hotel, though nothing to write home about, is the *Palace*. Bastia has not had any good hotels, but the new *Imperial*, a large one, is nearing completion. Finally, if you halt at Vizzavona, high in the mountains but directly on the little railway line and the transisland highway, take thought of the chalet-type inn called *Du Monte d'Oro*, which could have been lifted bodily from, say, Grindelwald.

Now let's go, using, if time permits, the daytime ship from Nice. Ships bound for Ajaccio follow a course parallel to Corsica's west coast, and if visibility is good, you welcome the ship's deliberate pace, for the views of the island's mountain range, snow-capped even in June, are magnificent and they improve with each mile as the afternoon sun aims its rays from a lower angle and then turns its magical color effects on the peaks.

Ajaccio, port and capital, concentrates, so far as tourism is concerned, on its famous son, the "little Corsican," who was born French rather than Italian by a margin of only fifteen months, the island having been sold to France by Genoa the year before. There are two statues of him, one an equestrian affairs with the rider clad as a Roman emperor. The chief quay and the main corso of the city both bear the name Napoléon, and a lesser street is called Rue Bonaparte. Another is named for his unfortunate son, Rue du Roi de Rome, and a small old-world square is named Place Letizia for his mother, Letizia Ramolino. A bust of "Madame Mère" graces it. In the near-by Rue Saint-Charles one may see and visit the *maison natale,* identified by a marble plaque inscribed with the words: NAPOLÉON EST NÉ DANS CETTE MAISON. Inside the house, visitors are shown the "carrying chair" in which Mother Letizia was hastily brought home from church when the Napoleonic labor pains suddenly beset her.

It is possible to weary of Napoleon in Ajaccio, but it would be very difficult to weary of the city's setting. The finest feature is a superbly scenic coastal road along the northern shore of the Gulf of Ajaccio. It is called *La Parata* and culminates in a cape of the same name, beyond which are seen the ruddy *Isles Sanguinaires.* One may drive to the cape in an old-style calèche, which is infinitely more fun than going by taxi.

More ambitious journeys "up and down Corsica" are now made by the modern Europabus motor coaches and also by autorail trains. Up and up one goes by coach, train or private car to Vizzavona (see above), at the 3000-foot level. From there the road and rail line wriggle down to *Corte* and the junction point of *Ponte Leccia,* whence one may continue to Bastia on the northeast coast or Ile Rousse and Calvi on the northwest coast, Bastia and Calvi being the respective terminal points of the up-and-over rail line. Both port towns tug at tourist interest, so if you are on your own rather than a fixed tour there is no easy way of determining which branch of the Y to take. The only safe way is to take first one and then the other. Whichever one is saved for the last may be used as take-off point for an Air France flight back to Marseille or Nice, thus avoiding a return to Ajaccio.

Calvi, a double town like so many in France, has its *Ville Basse* along the bay, its *Ville Haute* up aloft on a spectacular rock that is reached by a single twisting road. Calvi is "one of the places" where Columbus was born. In fact, a plaque on a ruined house makes it quite clear that this was *the* place, a claim which the *Guide Bleu* courteously calls "*très discutable.*" Most scholars agree that the explorer's real birthplace was Genoa, but we like Calvi no less for making the old college try.

Bastia is by far the largest city of Corsica and was once its capital, but, as a local resident explained the matter to me, "Napoleon transferred the capital to Ajaccio out of respect for himself." The name Bastia is a shortened form of *Bastiglia*, referring to a lofty fortified castle built by the Genoese in 1380 and replaced later by the sixteenth-century citadel that now watches over the community.

This is a very Italianate city, climbing the hillside from the old port in colorful if untidy tiers, but even here you cannot escape Napoleon. In the conspicuous Place Saint-Nicolas is the inevitable statue of him, inevitably clad in the gear of a Roman Caesar; and as a further touch one may see, from the hills above the city, the outlines of Elba, his island of exile.

The Europabus octopus is capable of enclosing within its far-reaching tentacles virtually the whole of Corsica. One tour carries you from Ajaccio down to *Bonifacio*, that incredible two-story town whose cliff portion, at a height of 200 feet, literally overhangs the surf-beaten shore. Another circles *Cap Corse* from Bastia to Ile Rousse.

Cap Corse is that exciting "thumb" of Corsica that points to France, its adopted motherland. It is a region of vineyards producing a rough red wine that peasants like. The vines also produce, with the aid of quinquina bark and sugar and human skills, a widely appreciated apéritif that bears the region's name, Cap Corse. It is the drink one orders, in nostalgic mood, after returning to the supercivilized cafés of the French Riviera.

As a final note on Corsica I would recommend the *Report on Corsica* available to members of Islands in the Sun Club, whose address, 673 Fifth Avenue, New York 22, N.Y., is worth repeating here. This report, written by Geoffrey Wagner, is as lively as a cricket *not* dozing on the hearth, and the author follows it with an "Island Guide," of five big pages, that tells all essentials. For total coverage Mr. Wagner has authored an out-and-out handbook, *Your Guide to Corsica.*

A Ribbon from France to Italy

Express rail lines and highways edge the Ligurian Sea all the way from Nice to Genoa and far beyond, to Viareggio and Pisa. Both means of travel offer glorious views that are almost continuous, but the rails have one necessary defect. Whenever they come to a too-precipitous mountain—and this is often—they bore through it instead of climbing over it or clinging to its side as does the road.

The ribbons of Italy, to be explained below, have made news since World War II and public interest in them has been steadily sustained. They have, in fact, revolutionized tourist travel in the long peninsula and in Sicily by pioneering luxurious Pullman-coach motor service, with a multilingual hostess-lecturer on every bus, to all important points. To explain the ribbons: CIAT, which stands for *Compagnia Italiana Auto-servizi Turistici,* is the motorized portion of CIT, which stands for *Compagnia Italiana Turismo* and is the broadly ramifying semiofficial travel agency for Italy. This "tandem" of modern travel has been sparked and brought to its present efficiency by Comm. Enrico Linzi, the general manager of the senior company, and by Giovanni Galleni, who handles the foreign department and is known to hundreds of Americans as "John."

CIAT, which has been tied in with the Europabus network, designates all its various major routes and circuits by the word *nastro,* meaning ribbon, and the ribbon which is the international stretch from Nice to Genoa it designates as the *Nastro dei Fiori,* or Ribbon of Flowers. In eight hours, with a brief halt at San Remo and a two-hour halt at a later point for lunch, it makes this coastwise trip to the big Italian port. It takes you through the customs and other border formalities painlessly *en masse.* It maintains a refrigerator with soft drinks in the forward part of many busses. Its hostesses are girls of high education who speak real English. Finally, upon arrival at your destination, CIAT delivers you to the door of your hotel (*Colombia-Excelsior, Savoy-Majestic,* etc.); and if you are continuing through Italy next day, or some other day, it picks you up at your hotel and delivers you at your chosen hotel in the next city where you elect to make a stay. CIAT is an organization to know, and if you wish to get acquainted in Nice you will find its booking office at 16 Avenue de Verdun, near the luxury hotels of the Promenade des Anglais. The New York office is at 11 West 42nd Street and may be entered also from 500 Fifth Avenue.

REVISION SUPPLEMENT TO CHAPTER 9

THE Italian State Tourist Office, located in the Palazzo d'Italia at 626 Fifth Avenue in New York City, is the most accessible source of information on traveling to and around Italy. News in transatlantic steamship service to Italy has been made by the *Atlantic Cruise Line*'s operation of summer service from Port Everglades, Florida, to Naples. Eastbound ports of call include Funchal, Barcelona, Cannes and Genoa. Transportation is aboard the *Federico C*. The Florida service is a welcome addition to the services already provided from New York and discussed earlier in the Supplement and on text pages 24–26.

Alitalia, the national airline of Italy, offers special tours that warrant checking, the company's main office in the U.S. being at 666 Fifth Avenue, New York City. The tours are planned with standard passenger comfort in mind, plus a few extra incentives.

Italy has made great progress of late in programs for highways, sports, new facilities in key towns and in the burgeoning resort areas of Elba, Sardinia and Sicily, to name a few. Even Santo Stéfano, an island that was a former penitentiary near Ischia in the Bay of Naples, has its chance to make good as a tourist resort.

On pages 156 and 157 I have protested the plus, plus, plus policy of Italian hôteliers and restaurateurs in making out their bills. All that, however, seems now to be behind us, since the Italian government stepped in to abolish that nuisance. Since the summer of 1965 all-inclusive hotel rates have been in effect. The rates include room, service and all taxes. Firmly proclaimed by Tourism Minister Achille Corona as being "designed to help tourists budget their stay in Italy," the long-awaited step seems to have been effective in reducing the confusion and subsequent ill will created by the baffling accumulation of figures.

Going "the extra mile," the tourism officials also sanctioned a fixed-price meal program. Sponsored by the Hotel and Restaurant Owners Association, the fixed-price meal is offered in addition to the regular à la carte meals on the menu, providing the visitor with a full meal, service included, at a price he can see in advance. Often, the exact meal and its price are displayed in the window or on a sidewalk sign. The program is not obligatory and therefore is not in effect in all restaurants, as it is, for instance, in Spain.

Transportation in and around Italy has been greatly expedited by the ever-advancing network of superhighways crossing the country. The *Autostrada del Sole* (Superhighway of the Sun), completed in October, 1964, runs from Naples to Milan. There are no speed limits, but if your conscience and nerves don't slow you, the wayside warning signals may. Tire conditions are checked by road patrols, but the rest of the checking is left to you. The *Autostrada dei Fiori* (Superhighway of the Flowers), is the resplendent name for the route from Savona, a seaport town that lies some miles west of Genoa, to the French border, just short of Menton. Planned for completion in 1967, tunnels will dot the route, easing traffic all along the *Riviera di Ponente*, the western part of Genoa's "tandem riviera." (The name means Riviera of the Setting Sun.) The shoreline stretching to the east and southeast of Genoa is called the *Riviera di Levante* (of the Rising Sun), providing lovely scenery and coastal resorts as far as Spezia and even Viareggio, whose 80-room *Palace Hotel*, with terraced bedrooms, solarium and splendid sea view, can make a good halting point. At nearby Torre del Lago, the birthplace of Puccini, the composer's operas are performed for the pleasure of visitors. Another advance for Genoese traffic is the 76-mile Genoa-Piacenza *autostrada* now under construction as an urgently needed replacement for Highway 45.

Turning our attention to southern Italy, we find that interest is newly focusing on the area around Bari, on the Adriatic coast. A new highway is in the works between Naples and Bari, providing a sort of ankle strap for Italian traffic, as a glance at a map reveals. Bari is the jumping-off point for Adriatic Sea trips, as well as a newly discovered tourist area for cathedrals, castles, beaches, caves and villages of quaint peasant dwellings of beehive shape called "trulli," the classic example being Alberobello. From Bari, incidentally, you may visit Dubrovnik, the fabulous Dalmatian city of Yugoslavia, by a comfortable 150-passenger ferry of the *Linee Marittime dell'Adriatico*, the passage taking only ten hours. A still bigger and faster ferry is planned.

The current tourist advance of three islands of Italy, namely, Elba, Sardinia and Sicily, should be briefly examined here, working from north to south. Each of the three is a newsmaker.

Elba, once Napoleon's forced retreat, can be your voluntary one either during the festive summer months or the less tourist-laden winter months. Summer visitors take special delight in the luxurious beaches and ideal facilities for water sports at various points on this island, relatively new to the tourist world, located six miles off the Tuscany (northwest) coast of Italy.

Elba is easily reached by car ferry from mainland Piombino, the trip to Portoferraio, the main town of the island, taking about an hour and 20 minutes. There is also a hydrofoil service from Livorno (Leghorn) to Elba and on to Corsica, making the trip between Leghorn and Elba in less than an hour. Planes touch down at the Marina di Campo airfield, where the nearby *Iselva Hotel,* on the beach, offers about 70 rooms during the summer months. It closes for the winter.

In the island's scattered communities, including a few small towns, key hotels include the beachfront *Del Golfo* (about half an hour from the port of Procchio), where you can get an excellent meal; and in Portoferraio, the *Darsena* and *Massimo,* which vie for honors. This town, whose houses rise in tiers up the rocky slopes around the horseshoe-shaped harbor, is more than a mere ferry terminal point. It is a place to visit for its own sake.

There are tours of the island by bus, in case you haven't rented a car on the mainland and brought it across on the ferry. Napoleon's dwelling place in Portoferraio, the "Villa of the Mills," contains his personal library as well as memorabilia. For a superb view, there is now a cableway linking Marciana with Monte Cappane.

Sardinia is well off for transportation. In air service there are more than 120 flights a week, mostly by Alitalia. BEA also provides flights during summer months from London; Air France serves Sardinia by way of Corsica. Italian coastal ships ply regularly from Genoa, Civitavecchio and Naples to the island ports of Olbia and Cágliari; American Export-Isbrandtsen Lines ships stop at Sardinia on some cruises; and other major lines also make occasional halts. Small ferries link Sardinia with its outlying islands of Carloforte, Calasetta, La Maddalena and Palau.

As for island hotels, the Jolly chain, mentioned on page 168, dominates the scene, but there are other developments, some of them spectacular in the extreme. Sardinia's Costa Smerlada (Emerald Coast) is the site of a $176-million, ten-year development plan of the Aga Khan and the Sardinian government. The program will establish 11 hotels, enhanced by golf courses and tennis courts, in tourist villages, with schools, good roads, water and electric facilities, plus a museum, a marina and an aquarium. In short, out of beautiful, rugged scenery and temperate weather, a living area comprising about 8000 buildings for about 25,000 people is being carved. The area covers much of the land from Arzachena to Olbia, on the northern coast, and several luxury hotels are already in operation, including *Hotel Cala di Volpe* and *Hotel La Pitrizza*, at Liscia di Vacca, and *Hotel Abi d'Oru*, at the Golfo della Marinella. The Rank Organization of England has built a 100-room hotel, called *Hotel Romazzino*, near Porto Cervo, the yachting center on the Costa Smeralda. It already has a private beach, with facilities for water-skiing and sailing, and has plans for a pool and a golf course. A Belgian corporation is planning a development called *Piras* on La Maddalena Island, off the northern shore of Sardinia. It will have villas for 400 visitors and a golf course, tennis courts, water skiing facilities and a market. Development of a seaside resort near Cágliari is being planned by a Milan firm. The plans include construction of 30 hotels to accommodate 5000 guests, plus a golf course, tennis courts, a marina and markets. The resort will have minibus service. Finally, there is Santa Margherita di Pula, a budding seaside resort in the island's south, linked by a funicular to surrounding heights.

Sicily is served by frequent flights of ATI, an Alitalia subsidiary, from Naples, and by various shipping lines from mainland Italy. These include the *Salvatore Lauro Line*, making the trip from Reggio di Calabria across the strait to Messina in 30 minutes, and, as an alternate choice, the *Caronte Line*, with its ferries from Reggio di Calabria and Villa San Giovanni to Messina. But Sicily may not always be so concerned with ferries and planes for transportation. Preliminary studies have been undertaken of the feasibility of a bridge over the Strait of Messina. Famed underwater expert Jacques-Yves Cousteau led the preliminary submarine explorations to see where and how pilings could be placed to support such a bridge. The venture has the backing of Fiat, Falck, Pirelli and the Italian government, in addition to United States Steel. If the bridge is completed, the new Sicilian road network could tie in with it. Another interesting project is ferry service to cover the 86 miles between Sicily and Tunis, making a link from the toe of the Italy boot to Tunisia.

An offshore trip available from Palermo may have special appeal to those who like out-of-the-ordinary travel; namely, a jaunt by a 150-passenger hydrofoil of the *Società Aliscafi Sud Line* to Ustica, a small, remote island north of Palermo. On the southern shore of Sicily, across the island from Palermo, lies a goal of a quite different nature, the spa of Sciacca, whose curative thermal waters have been known for nearly 3000 years. Sciacca's *Grand Hotel delle Terme* is an integral part of the spa, offering 70 rooms to those who might like to "try the waters."

CHAPTER 9

COASTAL AND ISLAND ITALY

Some Notes on Money, Lodging, Food

AT THE official rate of exchange prevailing now—approximately 620 lire to the dollar—Italy is *by no means* one of the cheap countries of Europe, like Spain and Portugal, nor is it, to be fair in comparisons, expensive by American standards. Tourist Italy, the peninsula and the Sicily of the beaten track, can cost plenty if you stay only in the luxury and first-class hotels and eat only in top restaurants, but it costs "more than plenty" as we know too well, if travelers live and eat in hotels and restaurants of similar quality in our own country.

I will submit here a brief primer on Italian money, with apologies to those who know all these elemental facts. The *lira* is the basic unit, pluralized as *lire*. Paper notes, I am more than happy to say, have now disappeared in the denominations below 500 lire and even the 500-lire note seems doomed to early extinction. *Coins* are in universal use now for small purchases, replacing the ghastly mess of paper notes that long included those of 5 and 10 lire ($4/5$ of a cent and $1\frac{3}{5}$ cents). Metal coins are now issued in denominations of 5, 10, 20, 50, 100 and 500 lire, this last a big silver coin worth 80 cents. The 1000-lire notes, worth \$1.60, are the standard workhorse notes of day-to-day sightseeing and above that are the 5000-lire and 10,000-lire notes, formidable blankets that usually need to be folded twice to fit into wallet or pocketbook. It is a downright blessing to Italians and foreigners alike that coins have finally appeared in worth-while denominations, for in former times tourist tempers used to get as frayed as the pocketful of dirty bills that bought so little.

The lira is now recognized as a "hard" money, exchangeable anywhere, so it is no great matter if you have some left when you depart. It is decidedly advisable to buy a stock of at least 20,000 lire before coming to Italy for use on the first day or two. There is now virtually no spread at all between the free-market rate and the official government rate and there seems to be no black market whatever. Ten-dollar bills are wonderful things to have in Italy, supplementing your regular supply of travelers checks. The cambio dens, which is to say exchange offices, conspicuous in every city, welcome them as warm friends. Five-dollar bills are somewhat less desired than tens, and one-dollar bills are rather dimly viewed by the cambio men, who usually give slightly fewer lire for them than the regular rate. Travelers checks seem also to be exchanged at a slightly less favorable rate than "tenners."

Italy displays a notably pleasant tolerance toward American tourists, who are desirable visitors (and spenders) and who have all contributed tax money to aid Europe's recovery, our favored status being amply evident at border crossings.

Lodging, especially of tourist visitors, is very big business in Italy. The *Annual of Hotels of Italy*, published by ENIT, the Italian State Tourist Office, tells in four languages practically everything except the color of the walls in each room and the name of the chambermaid about Italy's 12,000 or more hotels. It comes out now in two volumes totaling 1332 crowed pages. Italian hotels are sorted by law into fixed categories; Luxury, first, second, third, fourth, with a residue of *locande*, translatable as humble "inns," hardly ever patronized by tourists. *Pensions* are officially considered—for tourist tax purposes—to be one class lower, all along the line, than hotels, a first-class pension, for instance, being taxed the same as a second-class hotel. In many hotels reduced pension prices, for room and three meals are granted for stays of three days, but it is a wide-open secret that in periods of lean trade many *albergatori* are quite willing to bargain about this and establish reduced pension rates for a stay of one or two days.

The whole story of Italian hotel charges is an involved one that often causes a sharp pain in the middle of one's budget *if* the traveler has not informed himself in advance about them. The *total* charge would not seem to Americans too high if all the minor charges were absorbed in it. The following paragraphs propose to ease this pain by careful explanation.

Here is a typical bill I recently encountered and paid in a provincial

city. It was for a single room for one night and breakfast in a hotel of
luxury category.

Appartamento, 4500. The appartamento was my room.

Riscaldamento, 300. This is for heating, not applicable in the mild
months.

3% I.G.E., for *Imposta Generale sull'Entrata*, 135. This was the 3 per
cent General Tax on Entering levied on all bills of so-called luxury
hotels. On hotels of lesser category it is now 1 per cent.

Imposta di Soggiorno, 200. This was the Sojourn Tax, applicable in
most cities and all resorts of Italy. It is a fixed *daily* charge, not
a percentage, and varies in amount from 200 in luxury hotels to 20
in those of the lowest class.

15% *Servizio*, 675. The service charge is 15 per cent in most places,
but 18 per cent in Rome, 20 per cent in Palermo and Catania.

Bollo di quietanza, 10. This was the "quittance stamp."

Totale da Pagare, 5810.

The total came to a little under $10 without the *Prima Colazione*, or
Continental breakfast, which was 500 plus tax. The room had a beautiful
balcony and a small but adequate bathroom. The breakfast was the very
simple one customary in Europe. Certainly the bill was plenty high by
European standards, yet by no means exorbitant, except, perhaps, for
the 80-cent-plus-tax breakfast of coffee, rolls and jam. My point in presenting the above analysis is to forewarn the reader about *extras* and
more extras. In the list I have set forth there are five of them, totaling
$2.17. Personally I think it would be smart practice for Italy to work
out a system whereby the three annoying *taxes* could be absorbed and
hidden in the main bill, leaving only the basic tariff and the service
charge, but that is Italy's business. This being the case, the traveler may
as well do the next best thing and understand his bill before he gets it.

The *food of Italy* scarcely needs any introduction, for at its best it
rivals in gourmetry that of France. In a booklet called *Roman Gastronomy* published by the Tourist Office (*Ente Provinciale per il Turismo*)
of Rome you may read the details of scores of Italian dishes that are
enough to excite the most sophisticated epicure. Here I will merely offer
the warning that you need to like *pasta* in all its forms to get full enjoyment of Italian food. I love it, so I am always happy in Italy, and one

may absolutely count on pasta being well cooked and *al dente* (toothy; i.e. firm, not sloppy in the American style), whether it takes the form of spaghetti, macaroni, ravioli, tagliatelli, fettucini, pappardelli, cappelletti—I could go on, but you know what I mean. No discussion of *antipasto*, the hors d'oeuvres of Italy, nor of *pizza*, deliciously served in many a special *pizzeria*, is needed here, for these delicacies have long been familiar to Americans. *Minestrone*, a soup with vermicelli or rice and a variety of diced vegetables, is equally well known, as is *risotto alla milanese*, a well-seasoned rice dish. *Fritto misto*, a delicious "fried mixed," is a favorite meat dish, and another is *vitello cotoletto*, veal cutlet in the Milanese style. *Fegato* (pronounced fégato) *alla veneziana* is fried liver and onions, and *polpo* is octopus, a viand that can be, when properly cooked, as wonderful as it may *not* sound. Every Italian meal concludes with cheese, often *Bel Paese* or *Gorgonzola*, and of course *frutta* in the land of fruit.

The wines of Italy are very numerous and very good. *Chianti* is the wine that American tourists have taken unto themselves, and *Frascati* is also well known, but there are many specialties that surpass both, for example white *Orvieto*, a dry variety and a sweet one, and the delectable, dry rosy wine of the Verona region called *Valpolicella*.

A Look at Genoa and Naples—with Capri

Genoa and *Naples*, especially the latter with its bay and islands, are of paramount concern to the Mediterranean traveler reaching Italy by ship, so I will offer a brief run-down of their respective sights, with mention also of certain hotels and restaurants.

The crescent of central Genoa has a character quite as distinctive, in a setting quite as beautiful, as its perennial maritime rival, Naples. Naples gets the big play in tourist publicity because it has Pompeii, Vesuvius, Capri, Sorrento, Amalfi, but *as a city* Genoa matches Naples point for point in beauty and in charm, while its background far surpasses in splendor and power that of Naples. Genoa is the city of Simon Boccanegra, the vigorous "lifetime doge" (1339–63) who first raised it to a level of distinction. It is also the true birthplace of Columbus, though several other places, in other countries, maintain feeble claims to this honor. It is the city of the Dorias, a family that helped to win the city's medieval sobriquet *Genova Superba*. Its vessels roamed the Mediterranean and added conquest to conquest, though finally internal conflicts brought it low and its glory was eclipsed by the newer power and glory of Venice, its Adriatic opponent.

Genoa declined sadly, but gradually it recovered and became once more a city of wealth and prestige. During the Second World War it suffered enormous damage, especially in its port works (320 ships were at the bottom of its harbor by 1944), but recovery was remarkably rapid and today it is certainly the leading port city of Italy, with an immense maritime trade. A further stimulus was provided by the opening, late in 1962, of its fine new airport, named, one might say "of course," the *Cristoforo Colombo*. As an attraction to tourists, at least to those who give it a chance and do not hustle right away to Florence or Milan, the city has a charm all its own, for it is strongly individual. It is built all up and down against a ring of hills, with a whole battery of funiculars ascending and descending like the angels in Jacob's dream. Its tiny *vicoli*, some of them so narrow that one has to flatten oneself against a wall to let the other fellow pass, are weird and fascinating. Its *Circonvallazione a Monte*, a lofty winding highway that ties the Genoese hills with a band of scenery (take trolleybus #83 from in front of Hotel Savoy-Majestic), is a miracle of lovely tortuosity. Its Via Garibaldi is a chain of late Renaissance palaces, red, white and silver-gray. Its harbor is churned into foam with shipping whose burden, in good years, totals seven or eight million tons. Its two Rivieras, named respectively for the rising and setting sun, stretch on and on to bright horizons.

The waterfront of Genoa is the city's great magnet for many, and with good reason. If we grant that it is unkempt, disreputable, a seething sector of blatant dance halls catering to sailor sins, we must grant too that it rims a harbor of myriad activities, and we must at least take mental note of one relieving fact. The world's first bank took form here, in the 1400's, in the *Palazzo San Giorgio* on Piazza Caricamento, a building constructed at Boccanegra's order in the year 1260. The building is now used by the Port Authority, but its dignified old *Hall of the Buyers* and its magnificent *Hall of the Captains*, dating from its civic use before establishment of the bank, may be visited by special request.

Don't be dainty in viewing Genoa's water front. If you venture there at all, accept it, smells and all. In reaching it, find, if you can, the Vico dell'Amor Perfetto (Lane of Perfect Love) and stroll through it to the ancient Street of the Jewelers and the Square of the Banks. Then, on the water front itself, make your way along the frenetic Sottoripa ("Under-bank"), through the hordes of assorted market vendors, dodging the tipsy seafaring folk and the knots of dance-hall girls, greedy for cus-tomers. You'll see enough queer sights in half an hour to stock your memory cells for life.

The essentials of Genoa's orientation are easy to grasp, for one need only view it as a city of layers. The lowest layer is the bawdy and con-gested half circle of the port. The middle layer is tourist Genoa, with the big hotels, the bright shops and the places of entertainment. The upper layer is the coronet of hills, reached by zigzag streets, funiculars and outright elevators. For most of the amenities of the metropolis, which now concern us, we look, of course, to the middle layer.

This central level is, in turn, easy to understand, since it is clearly tied to two main squares, about a mile apart as the roads go, and these squares are tied together by a fast and frequent service (line 30) of trolley-busses. The northwestern anchor-square is *Piazza Acquaverde*, where the main railway station (*Porta Principe*) and the chief hotels are lo-cated (American Express, Cook and CIT are here too); the southeastern anchor-squire is *Piazza De Ferrari*, where the opera house, the fine shops, the cinemas and the big restaurants are found. One of the streets through which the trolleybusses race from the former square to the latter is *Via Garibaldi*, which I would stress again as the finest street of late Renais-sance palaces in Italy. Notable among these is the magnificent *Palazzo Rosso*, expensively and tastefully restored and reopened to the public in 1961.

The hotels on and near Piazza Acquaverde are an important and in-teresting group. The *Colombia-Excelsior* is a CIGA link, therefore axiomatically de luxe; the first-class *Savoy-Majestic*, across the way, has a wonderful welcoming warmth that is rarely matched; the second-class *Londra e Continentale* adjoins it; and nearby, on Via Balbi, are the first-class *Hotel de Gênes et des Princes* and the second-class *Britannia & Suisse*. Hotel Savoy-Majestic, whose Italian name, Albergo Savoia-Maestoso, has such an impressively musical sound, is one of my personal favorites in Italy.

Restaurants of Genoa are as distinctive as the city itself. On Piazza Dante, near Piazza De Ferrari, one may enter a *grattacielo* (skyscraper) and ascend by elevator thirty-one stories to a famous restaurant and café on the top floor, with open terraces on all sides. This establishment, known to a generation of travelers as the *Capurro* but now, under different management, named the *Olimpo*, is first class, and in the evening hours its good orchestra makes it something of a cabaret. There are, of course, other restaurants of interest in Genoa, for example *Gino*, on Via XX Settembre, *Olivo*, on Piazza Raibetta, and *Mario*, on a narrow lane in the Via Garibaldi area called Conservatori del Mare; and there are some delightful haunts for sea food in the fishy quarter called Boccadasse (Monkeymouth), especially that of *Vittorio*, but the mid-air location of the Olimpo, under whatever name, continues to "pack 'em in" more than its rivals. Seated at an airside table beside the outer railing of the terrace, you feel that you are floating on a space raft high above the bustle of downtown Genoa, which is, in turn, high above the crescent harbor. By day, by dusk, by evening lights, this place is a tourist's dream.

On the perimeter of the city restaurants are especially numerous along the seaside *corso* (with names that change from point to point) that stretches out toward Nervi and the Riviera di Levante. One of outstanding interest and merit is the *Tre Pini* (Three Pines), which extends over the surf-smitten rocks. A front table here gives you a "moving picture" of Genoa's sea traffic, heading in and out. A specialty of the house called *trenette* consists of small pieces of pasta formed in a sort of flattened elliptical shape that I can only call lens-like, and the sauce for it has very special allure. It is strongly spiced with finely chopped basil leaves, to which is added a flavoring of pine cone seeds, salt and garlic, but no onions. My taste buds found trenette different and thrilling.

In another part of town, near the Brignole Station, a restaurant of unusual interest opened in 1961 with the name *Il Cucciolo da Alfredo*. Cucciolo means "Pet Puppy" and Alfredo is the maestro who owns and runs the place. He is a connoisseur of Chianti and takes a dim view of ordinary "tourist Chianti" in wicker-covered bottles, as ordered by most Americans. His specialties are *Chianti del Vivo*, poured from a huge bottle, and *Chianti Piandaccoli*, a superior Florentine type with a bit of sparkle to it.

Naples is one of the place names that spreads "travel fever" through-out the touring world. It is unique and does not disappoint. Resembling Rome about as much as a gazelle resembles a lion, it is yet like the capital in one respect, that it is several cities in one. It is the Naples of Santa Lucia, insouciant, always rather down at heel, gay as a song sparrow. It is the Naples of the funicular-reached heights. It is the Naples of Vesuvius and Pompeii. And above all it is the Naples of its peerless bay, rich with such fabulous "accessories" as Capri, Sorrento, Amalfi, Ra-vello, Pozzuoli, Ischia.

The city is rich in special things to see. The *National Museum* con-tains many of the most important antique sculptures in the world, dug up for the most part from the volcanic material that buried Hercu-laneum and Pompeii, among the most famous being the *Farnese Bull*, the *Dancing Faun*, the *Narcissus*, the reposing *Mercury*, the *Drunken Silenus* and half a dozen "Veni," of whom the most widely applauded is the *Venus Callipyge* of Praxiteles, meaning Venus-of-the-Beautiful-Behind. She is so placed that that portion of her anatomy is what the visitor chiefly sees. The museum's bronzes and marbles are equally well known; and its Pompeiian frescoes, done largely in a red that subsequent artists have never been able to reproduce, are perhaps the most famous of all, though they seem greately unsuited to the sixteenth-century bar-racks in which the museum is housed. The *Gabinetto Pornographico* at the end of the mezzanine corridor is exhibited only to those with a spe-cial permit, but a museum attendant manages to make a good thing out of tourist curiosity. Actually, the phallic lamps and ornaments shown openly are almost as bold as anything the guard displays in his porno-graphic cubbyhole.

The *Aquarium of Naples* is a wonderful attraction, offering a weird, and in some features an almost unique, display of life in "the sea around us." The collections of the aquarium were world-famous long before Vicente Blasco Ibáñez saw and described them in *Mare Nostrum*, but the Spanish novelist added fresh luster.

The park in which the aquarium stands is wonderfully placed, for the peerless bay is directly before it, the waves slap the sea wall, and across the bay lies Vesuvius. No other mountain in the world, not even the Matterhorn or Fujiyama, has quite the universal appeal of Vesuvius. It was in 79 A.D. that the volcano burst forth from apparent dormancy in pent-up rage so terrible, so unutterably violent, that it has become a symbol of destruction throughout the ages. Some seventy times since then it has scorched with hot ashes or drowned in boiling lava the villages that dare to climb its flanks and it gives no sign of improving in temper. Its unpredictability is proverbial.

A third sight of Naples, quite lacking in fame and very often ignored even by eager repeater-tourists, is to me among the most exciting of all. I refer to the *National Museum of San Martino* in a Carthusian monastery of the fourteenth century perched high on the side of the Vómero Hill beside the Castel Sant'Elmo above central Naples. The museum itself houses countless souvenirs of the city and of the old Kingdom of Naples, but I do not urge its collections upon you, interesting though they are. Rather, I urge the vast rambling building that contains them. From several rooms and corridors, and more especially from the little room called the Belvedere, you find yourself hanging in midair, unbelievably *straight over* Naples, as if in a helicopter.

Santa Lucia is more than a song of Naples. A small-boat harbor, lined with gay "singing restaurants" and backed by the soaring, cliff-like fort called Castel dell'Ovo and the fishermen's quarter called Borgo Marinaro, it is a captivating and romantic spot, and by good fortune or good planning many of the city's leading hotels, a whole row of them, directly overlook it. Indeed they form an almost unbroken line on Via Parténope, the sea front boulevard bearing the ancient name of the city. From hundreds of hotel windows guests may view the gay doings immediately below, and then lift their gaze to the fort, to the whole great bay and to the mountain for which one of the best of them is named, *Hotel Vesuvio*. I have several times made this hotel my Naples home and have loved its luxurious amenities, its good service and its electrifying prospect. Other de luxe or first-class hotels on "Partenope Row" are the *Excelsior*, an excellent link of the famous CIGA chain, the *Santa Lucia*, the *Continental* and the new *Royal*, a 10-story, 300-room glass-front hotel with triple swimming pool, but the Vesuvio is the closest of them all to Santa Lucia.

In very recent years the hotels of Naples have advanced astonishingly, some say alarmingly. The above-mentioned Royal, with its gleaming modernity, dramatized by the startling blue and gold décor of its public rooms, is but one example. Far more spectacular is skyscraping *Hotel*

Ambassador's Palace, with 280 rooms, all facing out for the exciting city-and-harbor view. It occupies the top dozen floors or so in a 32-story building on Via Medina in the heart of the city. The ground floor lobby (with bar) and the mezzanine are lavish in tone, with much marble, thick carpets and fine furniture. The sumptuous dining room is on the 30th floor and there is a café-bar above that. This hotel would be an eye-catcher anywhere and is doubly so in this ancient city of Parthenope.

The *Mediterraneo*, a 214-room hotel occupying the upper floors (seven) of a medium-tall building downtown, is another newcomer, and adjacent to the newly built central railway station, of bold, modernistic design, is the latest of Naples' skyscrapers, a hotel and garage now nearing completion. Pensions have also developed in number and quality, a first-class one being the *Caracciolo* on a harbor-front street of the same name beyond Via Partenope.

The Bay of Naples, with its famed islands, is a big and engrossing subject which this swift coverage can only skim over, but some notes on what has recently happened and what is happening right now may be useful.

Pompeii is more easily reached than formerly, since a double-width superhighway from Naples (15 miles) has been opened. Three special things to note are the following: 1) *Free lantern lectures* are offered at frequent intervals from 9 to 4 in an auditorium built for the purpose; 2) the *Great Theater*, dating from ancient times, is the setting for classic Greek plays and dances for a limited period in August; 3) on Saturday evenings (8 to 11) from June to September Pompeii is floodlighted and the effect is one that no beholder ever forgets.

The funicular railway up *Mt. Vesuvius*, destroyed for the second time in 1944, has not been rebuilt, but it has been replaced by a chairlift which ascends to the crater's very rim, the charge for using it being about a dollar per person with guide service included. There is, of course, a tremendous panoramic view from the crest.

Cápri, as emphasized in Chapter 3, is properly pronounced CApri, though most Americans continue tediously to mispronounce it CaPRI in deference to the old song about the Isle of Caprí.

One may now reach the island by several different means, as follows: Slow steamers with a halt en route at Sorrento; *rapidi*, being fast, direct steamers; hydrofoils (in 27 minutes), these surface-skimming speed craft being manufactured in Messina, Sicily, or, hourly in summer, helicopter from a raised platform heliport on Naples' Beverello Mole to a heliport at Anacapri.

The island, small as it is in area, now has *seventy* listed hotels and pensions but despite the tourist hordes (of which you and I are a part) it can still provide a delightful holiday stay. Of the seventy lodging places I will list a few that seem to me specially worthy of mention.

The *Quisisana*, centrally located, is still the only hotel of luxury rating. It is open all year except for about a month from mid-November. The first-class *Regina Cristina*, open the year round, was built in 1959 and has the modernities that are lacking in the better known *Morgano e Tiberio*. It is Capri's only fully air-conditioned hotel. It has two dining rooms and an open terrace, also a lovely garden. Its 50 rooms, each with balcony, have a gorgeous view of the Faraglioni Rocks and the charming old Carthusian Monastery. *La Residenza*, with a good terrace dining room and garden, is of second-class rating but definitely recommendable. The small *Gatto Blanco* (White Cat) is a second-class place with a first-class restaurant. The three best pensions, I should say, are the *Villa Certosa*, the *Tragara* and *Villa delle Sirene*.

At *Anacapri* there are three first-class hotels, the *Caesar Augustus*, hanging in midsky on a cliff-edge high above the sea, the *Eden Paradiso* (no view) and the new 75-room *Europa Palace* (with swimming pool). This last seems to me too much on the commercial side, with a huge gift shop filling the ground floor. It has, however, the advantage of being adjacent to the lower station of a new *chairlift (seggiovia) to the summit of Monte Solaro*, which is 2000 feet above sea level. In connection with the upper station there is a pizzeria, with an adjacent bar. A place of second-class rating (and prices), with first-class comforts, *Hotel San Michele di Anacapri*, has, for me, an appeal not matched by any of the others mentioned. Its view, especially from the balconied front rooms, is stupendous, its cuisine exceptional and its atmosphere, fostered by the father and daughter (named Scoppi) who run it, warm and family-friendly. King Gustaf V of Sweden (Mister G.) used to stay here when he came to visit Axel Munthe, and so, many times, did his Queen Victoria. There is, in fact, a private road from the hotel to Munthe's *Villa San Michele*, which is now owned by the Swedish government and may be visited by the public.

Some things to know about today's Capri follow: Gracie Fields' *Canzone del Mare*, open from April 1 to about mid-October, is more popular than ever, but many come here just for a drink and a bathe. Lockers cost about $1, a cabin for 1 to 4, with shower, about $10. Meals are very expensive, but there are at least three modest restaurants very close by, *Ciro, Maria, Pietro*, all of which are good and *in*expensive. New roads are a Capri feature. One of them now leads from Anacapri down to the sea at the Blue Grotto, enabling visitors to board boats for the Grotto right there instead of taking the often rough sea trip from the Grande Marina. Other roads are, or very soon will be, under construction to the lighthouse and to the lofty villa of Emperor Tiberius.

"*Forgotten Ischia*" is now by no means forgotten by tourism. Morning and early afternoon steamers cover the passage from Naples to Ischia in two hours. Ischia has *forty* listed hotels and pensions, the *Grande Albergo e dei Pini* and the *Excelsior* being two of the best. The *Delle Terme* is a new thermal hostelry, a link of the popular chain of Jolly hotels. *Lacco Ameno*, a spa center of some importance, has a considerable quota of thermal hotels, the de luxe *Regina Isabella*, large and modern, with its own private beach, being outstanding. Adjoining it is the *Sporting Hotel* (an absurd name to American eyes and ears), with a fine swimming pool. The two hotels have a total of 118 rooms and baths. *La Reginella* is a first-class place in the center of the same community.

I am happy to mention that the Islands in the Sun Club (see earlier mentions of this club in connection with the Balearics and Corsica) devotes one of its sprightly booklets to Ischia.

The Port of Ischia is a sight in itself for it circles the shore of a perfectly round lake that once filled an ancient volcanic crater but was cut through to the sea about a hundred years ago to form this ship haven. The whole island is called by guidebooks, "the debris of a submarine volcano," to which one adds in admiration, "and *what* debris!" Just off the Porto d'Ischia rises the striking islet called simply *Castello*, now a complete ruin, where once lived the chaste beauty Vittoria Colonna, serious friend and inspirer of Michelangelo.

A tangent trip from Naples to Rome can be quickly and easily made, but this book can obviously not include the Eternal City in a few brisk sentences. It can tell you of a delightful way to get there, namely by the

Nastro Rosa, or Pink Ribbon, of CIAT. The company's motor coaches make the Naples-Rome and Rome-Naples journey by two routes, one the coastal highway, with a halt for lunch or dinner at *Fórmia* in the lovely *Grand Hotel Miramare,* once a royal residence, the other a more inland route with a luncheon halt at *Cassino,* preceded or followed by the ascent, on a good asphalt road, to the celebrated *Abbey of Monte Cassino.* Both roads and both halts are richly rewarding. In the dreadful spring of 1944 the abbey took an air-and-artillery pounding such as perhaps no other great monument has ever suffered in all history. Cloisters, church and convent went up in smoking rubble and splinters, the prolonged assault being made by the Allies in an attempt to dislodge the Germans who were using the lofty abbey as an observation post. It has been fully and lavishly rebuilt. Over the front portal of the great basilica, which is rich in marbles, mosaics and gilding, appears one carven word in huge letters: PAX. In the separate Chapel of St. Benedict is a bronze statue of the saint, upheld by two figures, this work being a gift of General Eisenhower.

Sardinia Opens Up

One reads even in current guidebooks that Italy's island of Sardinia is almost unknown and that it is seldom if ever visited by travelers. However true this may have been a few years ago it is not true now, for Sardinia is being discovered by more and more travelers. This is due partly to innate curiosity to see what this big, rugged island is like and partly to energetic promotion by the island's local tourist office in Cágliari and even more by a special tourist agency called ESIT, for *Ente Sardo Industrie Turistiche,* whose address, in case you wish to make inquiries, is Via Maddalena 52, Cágliari. As evidence of ESIT's eager pursuit of *turismo* as a new industry the organization offers to motorists bringing their cars a reduction of 10,000 lire on the round-trip crossing, from Naples, Rome (its port of Civitavecchia) or Palermo, which figures out as a saving of 50 to 60 per cent on cars weighing not over 2200 pounds. The *Tirrenia Navigation Company* is the chief carrier and its services are numerous, being daily from Civitavecchia, semiweekly from Naples and Genoa and weekly from Palermo. Air service, by Alitalia, is maintained on a four-times-daily basis between Rome and Cágliari.

Sardinia, next to Sicily in size of all the Mediterranean islands, has an area of 10,000 square miles but a sparse population of only 1,400,000 inhabitants. The island capital, Cágliari, is a port city of about 150,000 on a southern bay. Hotel accommodations throughout the island are not as yet difficult to come by, but if Sardinia's popularity continues on the up grade things may soon get tighter. Happily, the ubiquitous *Jolly* hotel chain has established at least six links in Sardinia. The most important one, with swimming pool and its own garage, is in Cágliari (on Viale Regina Margherita), the others being in *Sássari*, a provincial capital in the northwest and Sardinia's second city; *Olbia*, a port on the northeast coast with daily Tirrenia steamship service from Civitavecchia in an eight-hour crossing, as against fourteen to Cágliari; *Núoro*, a central provincial capital, perhaps the most typical town of older times; *Oristano*, a western "town with a past"; and *Iglésias*, a small town near the southwest coast.

Most parts of the island can be reached by railway or motor coach service. The coach tours, one of them a circular tour offered by CIT/CIAT, are very numerous. The standard motor tour of the island, starting either at Cágliari or Olbia, roughly circles the perimeter, the clockwise direction being proposed by Michelin's *Green Guide to Italy*, a wonderfully valuable tome, in an English edition, for the motorist.

Cágliari has some interesting sights, chief among then the *National Museum*, featuring prehistoric bronze sculptures; the thirteenth-century Roman-Gothic *Cathedral;* and, on high ground, a splendid *view terrace* built on the site of a sixteenth-century Spanish bastion. Few tourists, however, come to Sardinia for city sights. They come to explore the countryside and to see the people. Historically, the Sardinians are a rugged lot, given to vendettas, Hatfield-McCoy style, but outstandingly hospitable to strangers. On Sundays and festival days the country folk don their traditional costumes in a natural, not-for-tourists way that delights all visitors who mingle with the crowds, trying not to stare or be *too* obvious as shutterbugs. Sardinian women customarily wear long pleated skirts of designs varying greatly from one locality to another and adorn their heads, in the Spanish manner, with lace mantillas. The men wear overalls and old-fashioned gaiters and adorn their masculine heads with berettas, this type of headgear being a curiously horned cap, not at all Satanic. Sheep raising and cheese making are staple industries of the interior, the men often riding very small Arabian horses, while fishing (especially tuna) and lobster trapping occupy many coastal dwellers. In the southwestern part the mining of coal, zinc and iron is being increasingly developed, and at Cágliari the gleaming salt-pans are important.

Throughout the island, but especially in the regions around Múoro and Sássari, the visitor may examine some of the peculiar *nuraghi*, which were the typical fortress-homes of a pre-Christian era. It was in the nuraghi, as well as in ancient tombs, that the bronzes seen in Cágliari's museum were found. Sardinia offers few lures to the playboy or playgirl, but many to the escapist from the crowded trails of mainland tourism.

Sicily, the Trinacrian Siren; Access and Lodging

The ancients called Sicily Trinacria, which is a beautiful, melodious word suggesting three-sidedness. Handicrafters of Sicily have by no means forgotten the old name, for we see it everywhere on souvenirs and on tourist folders. Often it is symbolized by three racing legs that emerge from a smiling face, though this seems like a grand mélange of metaphors. Anyway, Sicily is a siren of the first order, a magnet that draws and halts nearly every cruise ship, the halting point for transatlantic liners being usually Palermo, but sometimes Syracuse.

Access to Sicily from Italy is convenient by air, sea or train-ferry. *Alitalia*, of course, rules the air lanes, with good daily services between Rome and Palermo (1 hour 45 minutes) and between Rome and Catania (1 hour, 40 minutes).

The *Sitramar* company has instituted a car-ferry service between Naples and Messina that is comparable to the services of the big State ferries of Scandinavia. The company dubs it *L'Autostrada Attraversa il Mare* (The Auto-Highway Across the Sea). The big ferry, named *Il Ponte* (The Bridge), sails thrice weekly in both directions, departing at 1 P.M. and arriving at 8 the following morning. A similar car-ferry service is maintained by the *Tirrenia* company between Naples and Palermo (11-hour overnight runs) and there is a thrice-monthly Tirrenia sailing from Naples through the Strait of Messina to Syracuse.

The *State Railways*, not to be left behind in the race for Sicily, operate several very fast expresses to Sicilian cities from Rome and Naples, and even from north-Italian cities. They bear such interesting names as *Freccia del Sud* (Southern Arrow), *Treno del Sole* (Sun Train) and *Conca d'Oro* (Golden Shell), this a nickname for the setting of Palermo.

Motorcoach services within Sicily and around the whole perimeter of the island are handsomely maintained during the whole year by the Europabus coaches, operated by CIAT from December through June and by SAIA, another company within the Europabus network, from July through November. The complete excursion, called *Il Nastro d'Oro* (The Ribbon of Gold), moves counterclockwise, west-southeast-northwest, starting and concluding at Palermo. It takes five days, but this includes two nights spent at Taormina. The sightseeing in Palermo itself is not included, but must be done in city tours, quite apart from the round-island journey. Subject to space being available, any part of the Ribbon Tour may be made separately. (Many travelers devote but three days to it, starting at Palermo Monday morning and terminating the trip at Taormina Wednesday evening.) The tour halts in that wonderful Etna-side resort, as I have said, for two nights, the intervening day being given over to the ascent of Mt. Etna by coach and cableway. On the final day it continues in a long ten-hour run along the island's north coast, back to Palermo. The first three days thus provide most of the varied colors of the circuit. The first one brings the coach to templed *Agrigento*. The second offers Agrigento itself in the morning and then continues to *Syracuse* for the night. The third day offers Syracuse in the morning, a double city, old and new, on a small islet and the main island, while the afternoon run carries northward to *Catánia*, a large, modern city of limited tourist interest, and then to peerless *Taormina*.

Another CIAT offering called *Nastro della Sicilia Classica* (Ribbon of Classical Sicily) concentrates solely on the southeast coast of the island, featuring Taormina, Etna, Catánia and Syracuse. This takes but two nights and three days.

Motorists touring coastal Italy and Sicily would be well advised to join the *Italian Touring Club*, if only for the wealth of tour literature available to members. The Club publishes an automotive guidebook in six volumes called *L'Italia in Automobile*, any volume of which may be purchased separately (by members) for about $1.25. The latest volume to appear is on Sicily. More and more, Italy is catering to motorists, partly by a $160 million superhighway program and partly by the erection of convenient motels. The AGIP (oil) company alone has built twenty-five of them, one of the newest being in Palermo.

Hotels of Sicily have advanced at a pace more or less commensurate with the island's increasing tourist popularity, though this is chiefly to be noted in the category of good, medium-priced hotels that are officially rated as first class but without pretensions to luxury. The *Jolly* corporation alone has added a full dozen Sicilian links to its shiny chain, including such tourist goals as Palermo, Agrigento, Syracuse, Catánia and Messina. Jolly hotels are dependably modern and comfortable though the rooms are often small. Palermo and Taormina, especially the latter, have world-famous holiday inns, which, with others of unusual appeal, merit special comment.

Palermo: The *Villa Igea* is one of the two famous inns to which I have alluded. It is of Victorian appearance and presumably of Victorian construction, though it must be said that the interior has had a much needed face-lifting, at least so far as décor is concerned. The plumbing in many of its private bathrooms has the pioneer quality of olden times —*but* don't let such considerations bar you from enjoying a luxury hotel with one of the most delightful seaside gardens in many-seasided Italy. The *Grand Hôtel et Des Palmes* (or *Delle Palme*), in the heart of the city, is of almost equal quality and far more modern. The *Mondello Palace*, on Mondello Beach a short distance from the city, is a luxury resort, lively during the high spring season.

Agrigento: The *Jolly* is the newest and perhaps the best, but give thought to the *Gran Bretagne e Gallia* and to *Hotel dei Templi*. This is officially rated second category but surely it is "on the edge of first," with a fragrant orchard-garden from which, as from many of the bedrooms, one has a perfect panoramic view of the fine old Greek temples on the slope-to-the-sea below.

Siracusa (Syracuse): *Grand Hotel Villa Politi*, in a suburban garden setting, complete with antique statuary, is a delightful first-class place, convenient to the city by bus service; *Hotel degli Stranieri* (Hôtel des Etrangers) formerly also bearing the name Politi, is on the sea front of the island portion of the city, directly overlooking the famous Fountain of Arethusa.

Catánia: This metropolis now has a de luxe establishment, the *Grand*

Hotel Excelsior, of fairly recent construction. A well-known hotel rated first-class is the *Centrale-Corona*, located on Via Etnea, within a block of the Bellini Gardens, named for a native son, the composer Vincenzo Bellini.

Taormina: The *San Domenico Palace* is a palace indeed, as is evidenced by the fact that no less a palace denizen than Farouk of Egypt, when he was king, considered it worthy of his patronage while on his honeymoon with Queen Nariman. Press reports stated that he "made do" with a mere sixty rooms here, for himself, his bride and the royal entourage.

The structure of the hotel is an old Dominican monastery, hence the name. Its comfortable "cells," with modern furnishings and decoration, all bear *names*, that of mine, which made me feel unnaturally holy, being *Amor Sanctus*. Those on either side bore the names *Agnus Dei* and *Stella Matutina*. The public rooms of the San Domenico Palace are a treat to the senses, being veritable museums of fine furniture and objets d'art, and many of the corridors are real galleries of painting. The view from the hotel's garden, one of the loveliest carefully casual gardens of flowers and flowering shrubs I have ever seen, covers the whole majestic sweep of Etna and the curving Ionian Sea. It is one of the world's very great views, in the class of Rio's views from the summit of Sugar Loaf or Corcovado.

Several first-class hotels supplement the luxurious San Domenico Palace. Of these, the vine-bowered *Timeo* adjacent to the Greek Theater especially caught my eye. Others are the *Excelsior*, the *Imperial Palace* and the *Miramare*. Among second-class places are the *Diodoro* and the *Metropol*, both with sea view equaling that of the San Domenico.

Palermo, Starting Point for the Sicily Circuit

Our circuit of the island, holding chiefly to its perimeter, calls for a brief lexicon of sights in the various cities and for this we may well start at Palermo, as does CIAT's Nastro d'Oro, following the golden ribbon course, whether actually by one of the Europabus coaches or by private car.

Palermo, the capital of Sicily, is a large city, the sixth in size in Italy, with over half a million inhabitants. In the number of racial strands that have formed it and left their rich legacy of culture to the citizens—and tourists—of today it probably ranks first, and this despite the fact that it almost wholly lacks the legacy of Greek culture, so important on the southern and eastern coasts of Sicily. The Phoenicians founded it, the Carthaginians conquered it, and then the Romans, the Goths and the Byzantines, in their turn, did likewise. Continuing the kaleidoscopic process, the Saracens seized it in the ninth century and the Normans in the eleventh. It was, in fact, just five years before William conquered England that his fellow countryman, Roger de Hauteville, conquered this Sicilian city and it was held by the Normans until 1282, when the historic massacre known as the Sicilian Vespers liquidated them. It passed to the House of Savoy, then to the Kingdom of Naples and finally, through the campaigns of Garibaldi, became a part of modern Italy. It was from the union of the Saracen and Norman elements, as different in culture as one can possibly imagine, that most of the great works of Palermitan art and architecture were born. We find mosaics that have never been surpassed, except, possibly in Ravenna, and we find queer domed churches, some of which were Moslem mosques until the Normans came. Few cities of the Mediterranean have so checkered and thrilling a past as has Palermo. For those who have the time to read its story the remarkable buildings and mosaics take on vivid meaning.

To be specific about the attractions of the Sicilian capital, the following things, all shown, if hastily, by the local CIT tours, call for much more than a casual glance.

1. The *Cappella Palatina* in the old royal palace (small fee to the monk who shows it). Does it seem extravagant to call this "the most beautiful chapel in the world"? It is often called just that. Its mosaics, scintillating rather than subdued, are on a color base of lustrous gold; the floor is of varied marbles; the ceiling is artesonado, meaning that some portions are sunk and other raised, which was a Moorish idea. Painted arabesques and strange figures of all sorts run riot on this extraordinary ceiling, which the monk illumines by flashing on concealed lights. The Palatine Chapel is indescribable. Do not by any means allow yourself to miss it. The *Palazzo dei Normanni* (Palace of the Normans), of which the chapel is a part, is now the meeting place of the Sicilian Parliament.

2. The *Cathedral*, a very imposing structure, though not to be com-

pared with many others in Italy. The interior is as bare as a barn, most of its splendid porphyry, jasper, lapis lazuli and other ornamentation having been stripped off and sold more than a century and a half ago. But do not overlook the sepulchers of the Norman kings and queens, found in two of the chapels. These give an idea of what the cathedral must once have been.

3. Churches, *San Cataldo*, a Norman church with three Saracen domes; the *Martorana*, another Norman church, with a campanile you won't forget, and *San Giovanni degli Eremiti* (Saint John of the Hermits), with an exceptionally lovely flowered cloister. The last-named curious church, like so many other old structures of Palermo, shows clearly the union of Saracen and Norman ideas of architecture. King Roger II, a Norman of the Normans, built it in 1132 but he obviously liked the bulging domes of the Moslem mosques and he employed the subjected Saracens to design and build them.

4. *Monte Pellegrino*, towering in majesty two thousand feet above the city. Its views are striking and its *Sanctuary of Santa Rosalia*, the patron saint of Palermo, is a curious feature.

5. Above everything, the visitor to Palermo should not miss its celebrated suburb, *Monreale*. The cathedral of this once-royal retreat is incomparable for the combined richness of its mosaics and its settling. The mosaics are more lustrous than those in Galla Placidia's chapel in Ravenna and very nearly as perfect, and in amount they are twenty times as extensive. The setting rivals in beauty anything in Sicily, including Taormina. Enter the Benedictine cloister, a sight in itself, and a monk (rewarded by a tip) unlocks a door and lets you through to the cloister garden, which commands a view so "sudden" in its beauty, that it would sober Bacchus. You are not in his league, but you will, at any rate, be startled into a feeling of awe. There are other views as fine, but hardly ever does one smite you so suddenly and unexpectedly. The village and the cathedral itself have shut away every bit of it *except from this garden*. Below, and a very long way below, lies the verdant valley of the Orcto, oranged and lemoned to its limits, this being the famous Conca d'Oro, or Shell of Gold. In the distance lies Palermo. All about are lofty brown hills and above is a sky as blue as any twelfth-century mosaicist could have colored it. It must have been this view that induced the Norman kings to erect here their Royal House of God.

The Big Three of Hellenic Sicily
(AGRIGENTO; SYRACUSE; TAORMINA)

The first Greek settlement in Sicily, in 735 B.C., was on a promontory below Taormina, the second, founded one year later, was, and still is, Syracuse, whereas Agrigento, called Akragas by the Hellenes, was founded as "recently" as 581 B.C. Sicily rapidly became a sort of New Hellas, some cities, notably Syracuse, rivaling even Athens in glory and culture. The Romans, efficient and warlike, finally conquered the island and cast their blight upon it about five centuries after the beginning of Greek colonization, but the blight was far from complete, for two-thirds of the entire coastal belt, from Segesta around to Taormina, is saturated with Greek remains.

Agrigento is *the* Temple Town above all others on the island. There are temples to Heracles (Hercules), Concord, Jupiter Olympus, Castor and Pollux, Demeter and Persephone, and Vulcan. The town of today sits on a steep hill with arbored promenades, whence the stroller may look down upon the array of many-columned ruins, some of which are so well preserved that they hardly deserve that word at all. *The Temple of Concord* ranks, indeed, with the Temple of Neptune, at Paestum, as one of the two best preserved temples in all Italy. Marble statues and items of ancient pottery, vases, lamps, little earthen gods, are so abundant that almost any property owner may dig them up at will. I have an Italian friend residing in the town who sent me, clear to Massachusetts, a box of small pottery finds from his garden and they all arrived unbroken. A new *National Museum* stressing the Greek antiquities of the region has been recently opened.

A Temple Tour is provided as one of the features of the Golden Ribbon Tour and even ruin-shy businessmen confess to finding it interesting. I will mention just two features among many that make it so. In the Temple of Concord the columns and the roof are so designed that one of the aisles, as we look through it, outlines a perfect amphora, or two-handled Greek vase, that is, a vase of pure Sicilian *sky*. It is an amphora of cobalt blue, so perfectly formed that you feel you could pick it up, if you had the strength to hold so large a thing. The other feature that I have in mind is sheer luxuriance of flowers, shrubs, almond orchards, like carpets of snow in spring, and citrus groves. In one of the hotels I was shown a phenomenal lemon, locally grown, that weighed exactly *one kilo*, which is two pounds and two tenths. It was about the size of a child's football.

Syracuse is like a double star that astronomy reveals. The new city is on the small island called by the Greeks Ortygia. The ancient city, with some modern residential sections, is on Sicily itself—one can hardly call it mainland—and stretches far and wide, for in its heyday this was a Hellenic metropolis of great proportions, with a million inhabitants.

On Ortygia Island the so-called *Fountain of Arethusa* is the chief sight, being a large basin of fresh water at the sea's edge filled with reeds and marine plants. It seems that way off in the Peloponnesus the river-god Alpheus was annoying the nymph Arethusa. He chased her so persistently that Diana came to the aid of the fleeing girl, turning her into a spring and causing her to come up for air in distant Ortygia.

In old Syracuse the sightseer's sights include the *Roman Amphitheater*, where classical comedies (Plautus, Aristophanes, etc.) are given in the summer, and the *Greek Amphitheater*, where classical tragedies (Aeschylus, Euripides, etc.) are given in the spring. A third sight of importance is the *Caves of the Latomie*, being ancient quarries that gave up the stone for so many large structures. The most famous of these caves is called the *Ear of Dionysius*, an enormous twisting grotto carved out of the solid rock, narrowing in its upper (roof) section to a hole that emerges, or formerly emerged, to the surface of the earth. The acoustics of this cavern are amazing. The guide strikes a match and it sounds like a rocket going off. He tears a sheet of paper sharply and it sounds like a cannon shot. The tradition is that at the orifice of the great ear Dionysius, a tyrant of Syracuse, eavesdropped on the talk of his political enemies imprisoned in the cavern below.

Taormina is the darling of tourism and will be so as long as tourists like "atmosphere" that is genuine, scenery that is enchanting, shops that are full of good things to buy and a climate so balmy that sea bathing (from the beaches of Giardini and Mazzarò far below) is possible, and even probable, in January and February. A recently polished facet of Taormina's atmosphere, this one contrived by man but no less genuine for that, is a *Sound-and-Light Spectacle* (see "Mediterranean Evenings and Nights" in Chapter 3), one of those spirited evening shows with no live actors but only recorded voices and cleverly designed lighting effects which originated in France but have become popular tourist features in several Italian cities and indeed in other Mediterranean cities, such as Athens, Cairo and Baalbek (Lebanon).

The Greek Theater, wonderfully placed on a lofty ledge on the town's very shoulder, is the only sight of importance, but the entire town, a mountain village really, is its own best sight. In saying that Taormina deserves all the gushing encomiums that have been heaped upon it one says the bare, minimum truth. It would hardly be possible for words to exaggerate its beauty, its quaint, "unrehearsed" graces and glamors and its outlook, as broad as the world, one would say. And Taormina shops, those tempters of the unwary and conquerors of the wary, are enough in themselves to draw visitors to this flank of Etna. Blouses and lingerie, daintily embroidered, handkerchiefs, scarves, napery, textile novelties, angora wool sweaters—but I won't go on. You know what I mean better than I do. It takes the average woman about twenty-five minutes a block merely to walk along the town's main street, allowing nothing for the time spent *in* the shops.

High above Taormina, soaring from a base that is nearly a hundred miles in circumference to an altitude of 10,784 feet, Etna, the highest volcano in Europe and one of the two or three largest in the world, keeps its threatening watch over the scores of communities that cling to its sides and cluster around its base. The tours take passengers to the *Sapienza Refuge*, at 6260 feet altitude, for lunch, allowing ample time, in connection with the luncheon break, to ascend by cableway to the observatory on the mountain's crest, at 9650 feet. Skiing on Etna's upper slopes is practical and popular during several winter months. The cableway from the Refuge is Italy's longest. The ascent takes 25 minutes. Persons wishing to make the ascent on their own, say from Catania, may drive from that city to the Refuge, a distance of 42 miles. For individual trips the favored hours are those of sunrise and sunset, when the magnificent panorama is at its best.

On the day when I made the Etna trip a brand-new smoke hole appeared near the halting point on the side of the mountain! Its sudden appearance gave ample evidence that this smithy of Vulcan, whose eruptions, about 140 of them, have been recorded by man for at least twenty-five centuries, is still by no means too old to smoke nor too old to have fits of fiery temper that frighten villagers out of their wits but can never quite drive them from their ancestral homes.

REVISION SUPPLEMENT TO CHAPTER 10

REGARDLESS of new construction, the *Phoenicia* in Malta's capital, Valletta, seems likely to reign supreme as the *grande dame* of the island's hotels. A Hilton hotel is under construction at St. Julian's, outside Valletta; and a large development is planned for Manoel Island. Among the smaller places not mentioned in the text are two that can properly be called character hotels. One is *The Palms*, a 17th-century shooting lodge that has been converted into an exclusive hotel proclaimed to be "for the aristocracy," one feature being a swimming pool in the center of its garden. As a special flourish of aristocracy, you will be met at the airport, if you're lucky enough to get a reservation, by the owner's own Rolls-Royce. The *Selmun Palace Hotel*, overlooking St. Paul's Bay (see page 184) on the way to Mellieha, is an 18th-century castle that has been converted (but not *too* converted) for guests. A first-class restaurant at St. Paul's Bay is *The Harbour*, specializing in seafood.

At what used to be known as Military Bay, a short drive from St. Paul's Bay, there's a resort called *Golden Bay*, comprised of the *Golden Sands Hotel*, a 214-bed hotel on a bluff overlooking the sea, and the *Côte D'Or*, on its private beach below the Golden Sands and connected to its sister resort by elevator. At Mellieha, you may visit the *Tunny Net Restaurant*, whose bar is made from a Maltese fishing boat. The atmosphere is as nautical as you might suspect and its food is delicious.

The hotel mentioned in the text as being built on the small island of Comino between Malta and Gozo has been named the *Comino Hotel*. The unoriginality of the name is compensated for by the original and rustic surroundings. This 200-room hotel offers shops and a movie as well as a swimming pool and a vast area for sunning. The total native population of Comino is listed as 37, these island folk being greatly outnumbered by the hotel employees and guests!

The Island of Malta, now a full-fledged nation and a member of the U.N., fairly turns itself inside out in celebration of carnival. This pre-Lent "Fiesta of Fun," beginning on a Saturday and ending on Tuesday, the eve of Ash Wednesday, dates back to 1535 and is made up of dancing (formal competitions or just bouncing around in the streets in time to the bands that play on every corner), costuming and gala parades, with elaborate floats.

During the summer months, there are water-sports festivals and yacht races. Water-skiing has become so popular in and around Malta that it now has a formal part in the Independence Day Celebration on September 21. Independence Day, celebrating independence from Great Britain, is like our Fourth of July, complete with fireworks and parades. Religious "festas" are celebrated throughout the summer months in small towns and villages in honor of their patron saints. They can last two or even three days and are indigenous, with local variations, to the towns in which they take place.

Malta is the prime beneficiary, and you will be too if you're Malta-bound, of the additional service by the *Tirrenia Line* from Sicily. The *Città di Alessandria*, a car-ferry, has been added to the service of the *Città di Tunisi* and the *Città di Livorno*, sailing from Syracuse, Sicily, to Malta on Wednesday, Friday and Sunday. The overnight trip makes its return voyage on Monday, Thursday and Saturday.

If you plan to drive in Malta, and this has its rewards in hidden coves and spectacular views, you do not need any special license. Your home-state one will do. But do get a *good* road map. Even the government folders admit that "the island is not yet fully signposted."

On the cultural side, the government has restored the historic *Manoel Theater*, reputed to be one of the oldest in Europe, and performances of ballet, opera, concerts and recitals, in addition to plays in English, Italian and Maltese, are given from October to May.

One last but by no means least bit of information concerns sources, in the U.S., of information about Malta. Although the Malta Government Tourist Board offices listed on page 182 are still the only ones available, the Malta Mission to the United Nations, 155 East 44th Street, New York 10017, can supply you with basic facts.

CHAPTER 10

DROPPING IN ON MALTA

The Strands that Wove Valletta

BRITISH European Airways and Malta Airways work in union, providing, frequent flights between Rome and Valletta, the island capital. The flight takes about two hours, so nothing could be easier for travelers who are in Rome than to drop in on Malta, a world away in background and ways of life. Sea passage may be booked on Tirrenia vessels that make frequent sailings from Naples to North Africa with a halt at Malta. These ships accept a limited number of cars. A far shorter sea voyage, actually only five hours and costing only about $6, may be made on the motor vessel *Città di Tunisi*, from Syracuse to Valletta. These sailings are scheduled three times a week and thus make an easy tangent trip available to travelers touring Sicily.

Malta, with a population of 350,000 and a total area of 1225 square miles, is less than twice as large as Nantucket, yet it has had history enough for an island the size of Sicily. Since the Stone Age men have inhabited it and for three thousand years or more they have striven for possession of it, for it lies squarely in the path of traffic, and conquest, between East and West. The usual Mediterranean races to which one grows accustomed, Phoenicians, Greeks, Carthaginians, Romans, Saracens, Normans, owned it in turn, and finally came a "race" of military-religious knights, the *Knights of the Order of St. John of Jerusalem*, called also Knights Hospitalers and Knights of Malta, to whom Emperor Charles V, head of the Holy Roman Empire, assigned the island in 1530, after the Order had been forced out of Rhodes. They held it, sometimes against terrific odds, until Napoleon conquered it in 1798, taking up his temporary residence in the Palazzo Parisio, now the post office of Valletta.

Upon Napoleon's downfall it passed into the hands of Great Britain *at the will of the Maltese people.* The italicized words tell an honest and interesting story, for few portions of any European colonial empire have been incorporated without some show of force. Malta was the exception to the rule. The tides of nationalism finally reached it in full strength in 1958, when the Malta government "took a walk," leaving Britain to govern by decree. In 1962, a new constitution, granting the island self-government, became operative and the political situation is now completely stable. Perhaps, in a few more years, the island will attain full independence as a "nation," as the island of Cyprus has done. Its people, to this day, speak Phoenician Maltese, which is a lingual legacy from the earliest settlers, overcast with Italian and plentifully interlarded with words from nearly all the Mediterranean tongues, especially Arabic.

In World War II, Valletta and its naval harbor took a terrible pounding from Italian and German bomber planes, but the island never surrendered. Its people were as stout of heart as the garrison and displayed the utmost heroism in supporting the Allied cause. Upon the war's successful conclusion they received letters of high praise from King George VI and President Roosevelt, both of which letters are reproduced and placed in plaques on the front wall of the Palace of the Grand Masters, now the Governor's Palace. In the armory of the capital is one of the three pathetic little Gloster Gladiator planes that helped defend Valletta. The three were named Faith, Hope and Charity, and the one we see on display is Faith.

The most heroic chapter in the island's story, perhaps excepting that which recounts its heroism in World War II, is the tale of the Knights' defense of Valletta during the Great Siege of 1565 by a powerful force of Turks sent by Sultan Suleiman the Magnificent. In five months of increasing suffering, including, as an incident of the siege, the complete wiping out of the garrison of St. Elmo, though the Turks lost six soldiers to one in achieving this, the Knights never faltered. Finally, the Turks gave up and the Knights became the idols of all Europe. The pope and various monarchs gave great sums of money for the rebuilding of Valletta and the development of it into a bulwark of Christendom, a fortified port hardly rivaled anywhere. Today's visitor may gain some impression of its strength, and a wonderful view thrown in, by finding the *Upper Barracca Gardens,* which fairly hang over the Grand Harbor.

They lie only a short stroll from the King's Gate, past the Church of Our Lady of Victory and the clearing called Castile Place.

The hero of the Great Siege was the Grand Master of the Knights, Jean Parisot de la Valette, for whom the capital is now named. (The accepted spelling adds another *l* for the town.) He had previously taken part in the defense of Rhodes. On another occasion he had been captured by the Turks and forced to row as a galley slave for many months until he was ransomed. At the peak of his glory, he was offered a cardinal's hat, but he had the restraint to remain what he was, a "knight's knight."

Malta used to be a bit casual in seeking its share of the tourist trade, but since the establishment, in 1958, of the *Malta Government Tourist Board*, with an outstandingly vigorous and effective promotional program, it has gained rapidly as a choice all-year goal of sun-and-sea worshippers. No visa or currency difficulties exist to deter the visitor. Malta issues its own paper currency, exactly equivalent to sterling, and for small transactions British coins are in use.

The capital, Valletta, with the town called Sliema across a small indentation of the sea, has a population of about 45,000. The leading hotel of Valletta is, and has long been, the excellent *Phoenicia*, appropriately named for the maritime race that was an early settler on the island. It is a place of moderate luxury and real charm, an established center of Maltese life, both tourist and social, but newer places are now threatening its supremacy. In nearby Sliema, which is a very good residential town facing the sea, there are two modern hotels of good quality, the *Tigne Court* and the *Modern Imperial*, and a new quality hotel of about 175 beds is nearing completion. This will be enhanced by a pool and by facilities for beach bathing. As a further important fillip for tourism the Malta government has signed a contract with an Anglo-German syndicate for the construction of a casino and a first-class 200-room hotel. On the island of Gozo there are good hotels, named the *Duke of Edinburgh* and the *Starboard;* and on little Comino, lying between Malta and Gozo, a high-grade hotel "starting with 200 beds" is soon to open. The customary service charge in Malta hotels is 10 per cent.

More and more tourists, especially those who take time for an adequate visit to Sicily, are devoting two or three extra days or more to a corollary trip by the short sea journey to the Island of the Knights. If you feel the yen to do likewise you may secure information and folders by addressing the *Malta Government Tourist Board, Valletta, Malta,* or the *Tourist Information Center, Malta House, 24 Haymarket, London, S.W.1.* A new brochure in color has recently been issued by the Board and can be had, together with other materials, upon application at either of the above offices.

Exploring Capital and Island

Valletta is an extremely compact town, huddling within its immense ramparts, though it spreads outside into extensive port-suburbs and the seaside community, mentioned above, called Sliema. From the Hotel Phoenicia, just outside the walls, you enter central Valletta by King's Gate and walk through Kingsway, which cleanly bisects the town, terminating in Fort St. Elmo, of heroic memory. At the point where Kingsway opens on the right into Queen's Square and then on the left into Palace Square, the buildings of chief interest are found together in a group.

There are only three that really demand seeing, the *Palace of the Grand Masters,* the adjoining *Royal Malta Library,* with the Archives of the Order of St. John, a mine of fascinating documents of medieval Europe, and the *Cathedral of St. John,* former conventual church of the Order, deceptively dull and dumpy on the outside but extremely rich inside, made so by the Knights during their three brilliant centuries. The Knights were organized into seven (later eight) "*langues,*" or languages, meaning roughly races of Europe. Seven of the chapels in the cathedral are those of the seven langues, and in Valletta we find that several of the great buildings were formerly *auberges,* a word translatable more or less as headquarters, of the respective langues. With the aid of a town plan—a clear one is to be had from the Government Tourist Board— we may easily run down most of them, the *Auberge de Castile et Léon,* the *Auberge d'Italie,* the *Auberge de Provence,* the *Auberge d'Aragon* and the *Auberge d'Angleterre et de Bavière* (Bavaria), though this last was added to the others as late as 1782.

The *Armory* of the Knights, housed in the Palace of the Grand Masters, is so replete with interesting specimens of ancient armor that it should on no account be missed. There are more than five thousand pieces, including some captured Saracen helmets and Turkish battle-axes, but when knighthood was in flower in Malta the storehouses had full armor for twenty-five thousand Knights. The weight of individual pieces would seen to have been quite intolerable in the Mediterranean's warm climate. One of the iron helmets on display weighs forty-six pounds and a single full suit of armor can weigh up to two hundred pounds! The steps of the main staircase of the Palace are wide and very low, as otherwise the armored Knights could have found it difficult to hoist themselves up, step by step.

Before leaving the Palace every visitor sees the *Tapestry Room*, and marvels at it, for tapestries of great value cover the walls *entirely*, to the very ceiling. This is where the legislative body met until the walkout of 1958, and may likely be the early future meeting place of a new legislative assembly.

The people of Valletta are quite as interesting as its buildings, and two odd items of "Maltana" are always noticed, the old women in black mantles and enormous black hoods and the native boatmen plying their gondola-like craft. The mantles and hoods are worn by relatively few women nowadays and in time this curious style will die out completely, but it is a tribute to Maltese spirit, and memory, that it has lasted this long, for it dates from 1565, when the Great Siege was laid by the Turks and raised by the valor of the Knights. The women of Valletta swore a sacred oath that if God would grant the defenders victory over the Turks they and their descendants would wear this black garb for two hundred years. It has now been four hundred, so perhaps, after all, the habit will never die out. One rather hopes that it will not, for it adds a delightful touch to street scenes. The hoods are enormous beyond anything you can picture. You will swear that each one could hold two pecks of garden produce instead of an old and wrinkled feminine face.

The boatmen of Valletta harbor, whose task it is to carry passengers to and from the ships, are nautical descendants, so to speak, of the Phoenicians, and their boats, called in Maltese *dghajsas*, terminate at both bow and stern in a Phoenician staff two or three feet high. The ferrymen are almost a race by themselves, and they have their own full quota of superstitions. The most important of these is that the boat must *never*, under any conditions, touch land, even to the slightest scraping against a stone jetty. They invariably make their customers jump over a gap of a foot or so, between boat rim and wharf, lest some unfortunate lurch cause the boat to touch "earth" and bring disaster to the owner.

Things to be seen in Malta outside of its congested capital attract visitors of several different interests. Those who are interested in man at his very earliest period, when he was hardly man at all, may find various megalithic monuments, not only on the soil of Malta itself but on its 26-square-mile satellite Gozo and even on tiny 1-square-mile Comino. The greatest single find from this dawn-of-time era is Malta's *hypogeum* (rock cellar) of *Hal Saflieni*, thought by scholars to have been a resting place for the dead. This, however, is no more than a paltry 5000 years old. For traces of the Neanderthal Age, wherein men lived and loved, and certainly fought, 200,000 years ago, *Ghar Dalam* may be hunted up. The Tourist Board will be happy to arrange a paleolithic and neolithic excursion.

Those interested in architectural curiosities will find an important one in the village of *Mosta*, for its huge church has an unsupported dome 118 feet in diameter. There are only two or three larger ones in Europe. It is said that this remarkable dome, which would seem to pose problems to builders anywhere, was constructed over a century ago by local volunteer labor.

For those who trace the journeys of Paul in the Mediterranean, and not a few do since he was an interesting and tireless traveler, there is a special goal in St. Paul's Bay, near the northern tip of the island. This is where, in the year 58, Paul was shipwrecked while traveling to Rome as a prisoner of the Roman procurator Festus and under the immediate surveillance of a centurion named Julius. For a narrative of sustained excitement about Paul's imprisonment and journey, together with the shipwreck interlude, see the last three chapters of the Acts of the Apostles. Perhaps you have not read this since Sunday School days, if ever. In any case I guarantee that you "can't lay the book down" till you have finished the tale. Paul, who was appealing his case directly to Caesar, was taken by a later ship to Syracuse, and so to Naples (specifically Puteoli, the present Pozzuoli) and Rome. Islanders of Malta show visitors—I believe this is authenticated fact, not fiction— a small islet in the bay where Paul first touched Maltese soil. It is mentioned in Acts 27:41 as the place "where two seas met."

There is an inn on the edge of St. Paul's Bay and this is, indeed, a delightful vacation spot. Aquaplaning is popular, as is snorkel fishing, with glass mask and a spring gun. At night Phoenician-style fishing boats equipped with bright lights carry fishermen in scores over the shallow waters looking for octopi, which they catch by spearing the writhing hulks. Octopus is, of course, a fish delicacy (often known to menu cards as *polpo*) throughout the Mediterranean lands.

The bright lights of the octopus fishers are outshone on Malta by one of the most garish streets in the whole Mediterranean, a steeply descending lane that runs parallel to Kingsway and next to it, on the northwest side. I do not know its name, but local residents call it "The Gut." For several blocks it is a double, unbroken row of dives, honky-tonks, beer parlors, dancings, cabarets and dubious-looking hotels. The Gut is a sailor's paradise and it is something to see—and hear. Blatant and more blatant dance bands and canned jazz fill the helpless air with rich cacophanies. Before almost every door stands a girl, or several girls, stridently inviting passers-by to come in. I entered one of the "joints," bought a beer at three times the normal price and another for a hostess. In a tone of wonderful ungraciousness she demanded that I buy a beer also for her "aunt," a dreadful, shambling creature whose face proclaimed that she knew every seam in life. I fled after a stay of no more than three minutes. Yes, Valletta's Gut is something to experience, raw life in a sailor's town. If you walk its gantlet at all consider the street merely a foil to the pleasant social life in your hotel.

THE four countries covered in this chapter have all seen great advances in recent years as the independence struggles and political upheavals give way to stable government and general improvement in living conditions. Morocco and Tunisia, particularly, have taken great strides along the paths of an orderly tourism development, largely thanks to efforts of the Agency for International Development, a branch of the hydra-headed U.S. international activities. Both countries have entered into ten-year programs for development in which tourism, handicrafts and diversification of industry figure prominently. Algeria and Libya, while somewhat behind their Moslem sister-countries in tourist development, have been blessed with important oil deposits developed by the large oil companies. The tourist industry inevitably follows this success.

As is the case with most of the Middle Eastern countries, you may not take local currency in or out of the country. U.S. money or your travelers checks may be exchanged at more than 250 places in Morocco and at an equally convenient number of booths and authorized offices throughout Tunisia, Algeria and Libya. *Be sure* to record all currency transactions and have your declaration form, which you receive on entry and must relinquish upon leaving, stamped with official notification of transactions. In Tunisia, the *dinar* is the unit of local currency and, since September, 1964, one dinar has equaled $1.92. In Morocco the *dirham* is now largely used; one dirham is made up of 100 francs and is worth about 20 cents.

MOROCCO benefits from direct *Pan American* flights from the U.S., which, although making several stops, including the Azores and Lisbon, provide one plane service to Rabat. Moroccans who make the trip frequently seem to favor the faster *TWA* service nonstop from New York to Lisbon connecting with *Sabena* for the Lisbon to Casablanca portion. From the continent, *Air France* flies frequently from Paris to

Tangier, Casablanca and Rabat. *Sabena* offers flights from Brussels, Lisbon and other cities to Casablanca and *Royal Air Maroc* offers flights between major European cities and Rabat, Tangier and Casablanca.

Tangier is a popular Mediterranean cruise port. In addition to major cruise lines, *American Export-Isbrandtsen Lines' Atlantic, Spanish Lines' Guadalupe* and *Covadonga*, and occasionally *Italian Lines'* ships stop at Morocco. From Spain, there is daily ferry service from Málaga to Tangier via *Compañía Trasmediterránea* and the *Bland Line*. From Italy, trips are made from Genoa and Naples to Casablanca on the *Grimaldi-Siosa Line*.

The Moroccan National Tourist Office (MNTO), at 341 Madison Avenue in New York City, provides information on currency restrictions, hotels, transportation and so on, sweetening the humdrum factual part with a helpful and interesting monthly magazine called simply *Morocco Tourism*.

The MNTO in Morocco operates nine hotels, all but three in the southern part of the country. One of the newer MNTO hotels is the *Hotel Ez Zalagh* in Fez, which the tourist office has operated for about five years. In addition to the chain operated by the MNTO, the Moroccan National Railways also operates hotels, among them *La Mamounia* in Marrakech (page 191), the *Transatlantique* in Casablanca and a like-named hotel in Meknès (pages 187 and 193), *Des Iles* at Essaouira and the *Palais Jamaï* in Fez (page 194). Thus the government is in the "hotel business" both through her Ministry of Tourism and her Ministry of Public Works. All government-owned hotels are constantly being improved, with emphasis on a fully coordinated resort atmosphere aimed at luring the American tourist.

Casablanca's newer hotels include the 15-story *Hotel Marhaba*, part of a chain of like-named hotels throughout Morocco, and the 250-room *Hotel Mansour*, in the heart of the city. Intercontinental Hotels Corporation, a Pan Am subsidiary, plans a 200-room deluxe hotel with full facilities.

News in *Marrakech* centers on the casino, where the owners are deeply involved in the *Hotel du Casino*, an 80-room luxury hotel where you can comfortably collapse if gambling goes against you. The *Menara*, with 100 rooms and balconies, has a swimming pool and a typical

Moroccan center garden, but *La Mamounia* is still the easy leader. In the Palm Grove outside Marrakech, *Majorel's Garden* is open for your viewing and well worth a visit. Majorel was a French painter who lived in Morocco for many years and concentrated on southern scenes and people in his paintings. Many of his choicest paintings were on display at a hotel in Agadir when the earthquake struck in 1960 and, sadly, were lost in the rubble. The garden, now opened to the public by Majorel's widow, is adorned with exotic flowers from all over the world and is truly a sight to see.

Somewhat farther south, outside Marrakech but in the Atlas Mountains, is the improbable sight of a *ski resort* in the desert! Recent developments at *Ouka*, called Oukaïmeden on most maps, include a chair lift for reaching the upper slopes and the improvement of roads from Marrakech, making the trip possible even in bad weather. The ski lift operates during the summer months for sightseeing.

In *Rabat*, the big news is the opening of the *Rabat Hilton* in August, 1966 (page 193). This member of the Hilton family offers the usual luxury accommodations, with coffee shop and snack bars in addition to the lavish dining room that is fast becoming *the* entertainment spot in Rabat.

Although the ostrich farm (page 193) has gone from the outskirts of *Meknès*, there is a new attraction in the *Vallée Heureuse* (Happy Valley). A Frenchman with large agricultural properties in Morocco created his happy valley, complete with fountains, stairways, pagodas, gazebos and all sorts of exotic plants, on 20 acres, six miles outside Meknès on the road to Rabat. Don't miss Happy Valley!

In Meknès, the *Dar Jamaï Palace,* a Moroccan *Riad* (estate) built during the reign of Moulay Hassan (1873–1894), the namesake of the present King of Morocco, and enhanced by beautiful gardens, has become, in recent years, a museum of handicrafts and folklore. It has separate rooms for displays of jewelry, clothing, home furnishings and other items of interest concerning the Moroccan way of life. The *Hotel Transatlantique*, while suggested as the best in Meknès, is a short distance from town.

In *Fez*, the *Palais Jamaï*, barely mentioned on page 194, is at the edge of the Medina and is a former 19th-century home with 45 rooms. A restaurant in its own separate wing serves delicious food, both Moroccan and European. The MNTO-run *Hotel Ez Zalagh*, with 70 rooms, many with balcony, has a swimming pool particularly welcome during summer months.

Two new areas for tourist expansion are at *Restinga* on the Mediterranean and along the Atlantic shore at *Agadir*, a town that was devastated by earthquakes on February 26, 1960, and is being entirely rebuilt, with earthquake-proof buildings for the most part, and three new hotels, as yet unnamed, under construction. At Restinga, between Tetuan and Ceuta, there is a 120-room resort. Modestly called the *Bungalow Village*, the accommodations provide beachfront luxury for the sun-worshiping vacationer.

ALGERIA's constitution, adopted in September 1963, states that Algeria is an "integral part of the Arab world, and of Africa" and that "Arabic is the national and official language of the state." It was later decided, however, that French could also be used, which makes sense in a country that spoke *only* French (officially) in the lifetime of many of its young citizens. Most of Algeria's energies have been taken up during the years since the coming of independence with improvements in education, hospitalization and living conditions, first under the leadership of Ben Bella and then under Boumedienne. Tourism has not yet flourished but so interesting a land will not long be denied.

One unusual tourist place, of a sort, is an oasis town in the Sahara 500 miles from the Mediterranean shores, called *Bouda*, reached as of now only by an 820-mile road from Oran, the last 80 miles being dirt surface. It is a pilgrimage town, the reason for its existence as such being the allegedly miraculous springs in the area, luring the lame, the halt and the blind from many miles around to come and be cured. In a way this seems to be Moslem Africa's answer to France's Lourdes and Portugal's Fatima. Although accommodations are primitive today, the government expects to build up the area with hotels, restaurants and other proper tourist amenities *if* the springs continue to cure. Already, merchants and tourist opportunists have flocked to the area.

To come closer to the interests of European and overseas tourism, *Blida*, on the Mediterranean close to Algiers, is the town André Gide called "a little rose." Its gardens and orange trees give rise to its being called the "mythological site of the Garden of the Hesperides and the treasure-trove of the golden apples." You too could easily believe this if you were to visit Blida during spring-flowering time when the fragrance of the orange trees permeates the air.

TUNISIA'S *Trade and Information Office*, at 65 East 56th Street in New York City, is a veritable gold mine of information where little was previously to be had. Many folders are now published in English and the "Tunisia—ABC of the Tourist," mentioned on page 200 simply as "Tunisia," is still the prime booklet for visitors. It contains information on entry formalities, foods, how to get to and around Tunisia and even the depth of Tunisian harbors should you want to check them against the draft of your private yacht! The hotel folders will help you to zero-in on specific questions. Incidentally, all artifacts on display in the office were made in Tunisia and are for sale.

The new El Aouina Airport at Tunis can, and does, accommodate Caravelles and Boeings without so much as a blink of an eyelash. The airport immediately sets the tone for you to absorb the great strides made by the new Tunisia. In addition to the regular flights of *Tunis Air* from major European and Middle-Eastern capitals, Tunisia is now served by *Lufthansa*, *Sabena* and BEA, in addition to KLM, *Air France*, *Alitalia* and *United Arab Airlines*, which have long served the country.

Tunis is a stop of most Mediterranean cruises that touch the southern Mediterranean coast. *Compagnie Générale Transatlantique* and *Compagnie de Navigation Mixte* make regular trips from Marseille to Tunis; *Compagnie Tirrenia* connects Tunis with Naples and Palermo.

As part of the government interest in encouraging tourism, a "Committee of Salvation," a sort of parallel to our local historical societies, is hurrying around Tunis and other ancient areas of Tunisia, marking for restoration as many of the 16th- and 17th-century dwellings as warrant the outlay. Some of the houses in the Medina in Tunis, fortunately for us, are being restored as tourist houses. Even the *Café de la Kasbah* is now a tourist office providing much-needed assistance for touring the area.

The *Direction des Antiquités et Arts*, to call it (as on page 201) by its pre-independence name, is being moved to a new library now being built on the same street. The newer, larger library will have ample room to display many of the valuable items pertaining to the history of the area.

Tunisia's tourism story is still essentially Tunis, the country's capital, with its environs, but there are stars on the horizon, such as the Island of Djerba and the coastal town of Hammamet, that merit watching. Tunisian pride and love of country have set this nation, independent since 1956, on a well-charted course of development.

The *Tunis Hilton*, with 250 rooms and all the luxuries expected in a hotel of this chain, including a swimming pool, is the country's leader in the hotel field. Zoomed to completion late in 1965, it stands proudly on a hilltop in Belvedere Park, about five minutes drive from the center of town. The hilltop, incidentally, has been planted with 150,000 trees that will, in time, enhance the surroundings. The design of the hotel makes use of Tunisian arches in its main floor and one enters, majestically, through the arches into the open-air lobby. This hotel is the major venture in the government's program for encouraging foreign investment.

In the center of Tunis, on Avenue Mohamed V, the *Société Hôtelière et Touristique de Tunisie* (SHTT) is building a 160-room hotel with restaurant, bar, swimming pool and full air-conditioning to be completed in mid-1967. On Avenue Habib Bourguiba, the *Hotel Africa* occupies the top 16 stories of a 22-story building. Guests in the 150-room hotel will have a restaurant, nightclub, swimming pool, post office, movie theater and window shopping from several display cases in the lobby.

Outside the capital there are several good hotels, all the offspring of SHTT and geared to the wishes of most American travelers. Among this organization's hotels, all operated jointly by the government and private enterprise, are the 300-room *Grand Hôtel du Lac*, on the shore of Lake Tunis; at Hammamet the *Miramar;* at Monastir the *Ribat* and the *Esplanade;* at Sousse the *Hadrumet;* at Skanes *Les Palmiers;* at Sfax the *Mabrouk Palace;* and at Tozeur, bordering the desert, the *Grand Hôtel de l'Oasis.*

Sailing enthusiasts will be interested in Tunisia's program for promotion of a home industry. At Monastir, on the eastern coast, there is a firm that builds small boats. Arrangements are made to ship the boats to *Zembra,* an island in the Bay of Tunis, where the entire focal point of promotion is water sports. Boats may be chartered by the day or for longer periods and there are bungalows on the island in case you wish to confine your water sports to swimming, snorkeling and water-skiing. The island is easily reached from Tunis by boat. Other developments in the Tunis area include *Sidi bou Saïd,* also on the Bay of Tunis, about 10 miles from the city, where there is a group of 12 villas, each with two to six rooms; Sidi's shore neighbor is *Gammarth,* where 75 chalets, with a restaurant, lounge, swimming pool and other facilities, are under construction. Another neighbor is a resort called *Soliman Beach,* called by boosters the Saint-Tropez of Tunis, with good Tunisian-modern accommodations.

At Hammamet, to mention again that coastal town south of Tunis, a private firm operates the *Village du Golfe* (which is *not* golf, but gulf), with its Tunisian-style bungalows of two or four rooms each, right on the beach where another company takes care of evening activities with a gambling casino, bar and terrace restaurant. A first-class hotel is to be built in the municipal gardens of Hammamet, an inspiring setting, where there is already an open-air restaurant. Another hotel, the *Kasbah,* occupies a transformed fortress of old. The guests in its 47 rooms go to the Medina, where the *Maison des Pêcheurs* provides their meals. At Hammamet, too, there is the *International Cultural Center,* which likes to describe itself as the Lincoln Center of the Middle East and although that may be overambitious, it is indeed the scene of concerts given by internationally known artists. Since the Center is only about an hour from Tunis you may go out only for a concert or some other feature in the theater and get back without delay. Bus tours are operated by several agencies and your Tunis hotel can give you full information on what's playing when. Tickets for the Arabic plays, which are fascinating visual productions even though you understand not a word, cost from 20 to 80 cents. The French plays cost about $3. The festival operates through the entire summer, the program including plays by Shakespeare and Camus in addition to ballet and concerts. At the end of May and in early June there are art displays by prominent Tunisian and international artists.

This brings to mind the emphasis given to handicrafts in Tunisia today. In keeping with the government interest in development of home industries, Tunisia has established 13 centers throughout the country where artisans can ply their crafts under government auspices for pay. The artifacts created are displayed for sale in shops throughout the country. If you can spare the time, and it is worth the try, visit the *Office National des Artisans* on the outskirts of Tunis, near Le Bardo (page 202). Items made in this artists' "city" are shown in Tunis in a shop at the intersection of Avenue de Carthage and Avenue Habib Bourguiba.

Djerba, which some students of Homer feel sure was the *Odyssey's* "land of the lotus eaters," is Tunisia's Cinderella island. From modest beginnings, with only a picturesque mosque and a good climate to recommend it, the island is fast becoming a new hideaway vacation spot for European and American visitors. Paper plans for development of Djerba as a *Cité Touristique* have called for seven hotels, with a total of 1146 rooms, six of them to be grouped together "in an atmosphere of canals and green plantings," the seventh to be built out over the water and known as a *botel*, where guests may step out of their rooms and into a boat! Currently, there are four hotels in operation, the *Ulysée Palace* (78 rooms), built and operated by the government, being the most attractive. The *Hotel Al-Djazira*, renovated within the past year and now with 65 rooms, is perhaps the next best.

LIBYA's recent boom has been spurred by the discovery of oil and the subsequent investment in the oil industry by U.S. and European firms. From the Zelten field, the first producing field that was discovered in 1959, a pipeline connects with Port Brega, *created* for the oil industry from concrete units prefabricated in Venice, an oil-loading device shipped from Louisiana, a power plant from Spain and a refinery built in Belgium—all floated to the scene!

TWA flies directly from New York to Idris Airport outside Tripoli, and although the *Libya Palace*, mentioned on page 207, is still the top hotel, negotiations are under way to bring major foreign hotel companies to Tripoli to help alleviate the acute room shortage.

CHAPTER 11

MOSLEM NORTH AFRICA: MOROCCO; ALGERIA; TUNISIA; LIBYA

A Nettle to Grasp

THE whole of North Africa bordering the Mediterranean, including Egypt, is, of course, Moslem territory, but the people are by no means all of Arab stock. Millions of the inhabitants of Morocco, Algeria, Tunisia and Libya are Berbers, in fact well over half of the total in many areas. Their origin puzzles ethnologists. They are, at any rate, an indigenous people, sometimes called of Libyan race, and they have never been fully amalgamated with the Arab conquerors who swarmed over North Africa and across to Spain and southern France in the seventh and eighth centuries. The Arabs were able to convert the Berbers, at least nominally, to Islam, and they established their language everywhere as the official one, though the Berbers have their own Hamitic tongue, but never were they able fully to absorb them. Nationalism, however, has proved a potent force in bringing political cohesiveness. In Morocco both Berbers and Arabs are Moroccans, subjects of their king, Moulay Hassan II. In Algeria they are Algerians, and since the conclusion of the dreadful seven years of war with France and its aftermath of violence and crime by the Secret Army Organization, they have been recognized by the world as an independent nation. In Tunisia, similarly, Arabs and Berbers are independent Tunisians, and in Libya Libyans. This chapter shall step along briskly from the Atlantic shores of Africa to the border of Egypt, attempting to present the facts of tourism and the main attractions which each of the four nations offers. Tangier has been covered in connection with Spain and Gibraltar, so that city shall be omitted here. No attempt shall be made to assess the chances of calm or political strife in any country, but it seems a fair guess that all four countries will be, in the main, open to tourism and that each will extend a welcoming hand.

The Medley of Morocco

Before delving into the many-colored medley that is Morocco let us have a quick look at the Arabic language of all North Africa, which is that of Egypt, Syria, Jordan and Lebanon as well.

An Arabic vocabulary of a mere dozen words can enhance travel pleasure substantially, and while you may know these words anyway and would certainly pick them up as you go, I shall venture to list my own chosen twelve for your possible convenience.

1. Bab, gate
2. Bled, countryside.
3. Caïd, native chief.
4. Chott, lake or salt marsh.
5. Fellah, native peasant; plural Fellaheen.
6. Hammam, bath.
7. Kasbah, citadel or fort.
8. Medersa, native school of higher education.
9. Medina, Arab quarter.
10. Ouadi, or Wadi, valley.
11. Sidi, master, lord.
12. Souk, native bazaar, or lane of open stalls.

As a further language note I may mention a useful tip offered, as I recall it, by Kermit Roosevelt. "Every Arab word," he said, "has four meanings. The first is direct; the second is the opposite of the first; the third has to do with camels; and the fourth is unprintable."

Casablanca is the first port of call of many cruise ships to the Mediterranean, especially the Sunlane Cruises of *American Export Lines*, and it is a second or third port of call, after Madeira and/or the Canaries, of other Mediterranean cruises. Similarly, most air travelers coming from Europe leap straight to Casablanca—Air France offers Caravelle flights from Paris, Nice and Marseille—as their starting point for their Moroccan tour. This report shall do likewise after offering a few general tourist notes.

Morocco's currency unit is the Moroccan franc, slightly over 500 equaling one dollar, but the fiscal authorities of the kingdom have devised also a larger unit called the Dirham, represented in price quotations as DH, which is 100 francs. This move has thus eliminated two ciphers as France has done. Both units are widely used in quoting hotel tariffs but there is no great confusion in this, as the following will show. In a current publication Casablanca's *Hotel El Mansour,* a leader in the city, advertises its charge for a double room with bath as 46 DH, whereas a competitor, the 15-story *Marhaba*, advertises double room and bath at 4600 francs, which is to say 46 DH. Further information on hotels and other facets of tourist travel may be had from the *Moroccan Embassy*, Washington, D. C., or by addressing the *Moroccan National Tourist Office*, Box 19, Rabat, Morocco. In New York, the *Moroccan Consulate General*, 342 Madison Avenue, is equipped to give out certain tourist information and folders; and the *Hamilton Wright Organization*, at 30 Rockefeller Plaza, serves as United States Publicity Representative of the National Tourist Office.

"Mysterious Morocco" used to be a name dear to travel folders and posters, but "Modern Morocco" might fit today's scene better. Coming under French protection (except for the small Spanish portion) as late as 1912, it made a most remarkable advance, in the European sense, yet managed to retain its rich legacy of indigenous life in a way that challenges neat analysis. For both of these happy results the celebrated Marshal Lyautey, who died in 1934, was in large measure responsible. As a colonial administrator his record is one of the most brilliant in history, yet he was by no means a ruthless destroyer of the older civilization which that of Europe replaced. He had a profound appreciation of the mysterious lure of this mixed and curious heritage (Arab, Berber, Moor, Negro, Jew) and sought to preserve it so far as it could possibly be made to conform with requirements of sanitation. He even went so far as to forbid the building of any European structures in the native medinas.

In 1956, Morocco became a fully independent nation, including what had been the colonial portion under both French and Spanish control, as well as that incongruous anomaly Tangier. With independence there was a further and sustained advance, which goes right on today and is perhaps best exemplified by Casablanca.

In the past fifty to sixty years Casablanca has grown from nearly nothing to a great metropolis of almost a million souls. In 1907, it was a squalid little place of about 25,000 enclosed in a wall which today marks the boundaries of the Old Medina. Its population is given today by the Moroccan government as just under a million and the appearance of its new portions, both business and residential, seems almost miraculously modern. It has blocks of buildings eighteen stories high. It has a remarkable central square named for the United Nations and a very lovely park named for Lyautey. One of its beaches has what is claimed to be the "largest swimming pool in the world," fed daily by tidal sea water. The city's impressive residential quarter named Anfa was the setting for the famous and fateful tête-à-tête in January, 1943, between Franklin Roosevelt and Winston Churchill. The *Anfa Hotel*, in which they met, is still a going concern, open to tourists. Yet with all Casablanca's modernity there is the sharp contrast of the Old Medina, the bazaars and crowded market squares, also the mad medley of *Place de France*, where the old town rubs shoulders, and fenders, with the new.

The city's name, the Portuguese equivalent (with a slight change in spelling) of White House, recalls the fifteenth century, when Portugal captured the city to suppress its pirates, who were almost as great a nuisance as those of Algeria. Portugal soon lost interest in the place, and Casablanca, called Dar-el-Beïda, the Arab form of White House, reverted to type. In the early years of this twentieth century the French, as I've said, took it in hand, and with the beginning of formal control in 1912 began their great and sustained effort to build up Morocco and all its cities, not merely Casablanca. The boulevards of this great commercial center are magnificent, its civic buildings, happily in Moroccan style, handsome and gleaming white, its shops smart and ultramodern, its hotels excellent, its cafés large and lively, and several of its restaurants Paris-smart.

The *Old Medina* directly adjoins the very heart of the city and a very large *New Medina* has been built on the outskirts. In the former, old smells and old dirt are still prevalent, though perhaps they have waned a bit under patient pressure from the authorities. Here, on a noisome street whose odors are as rich as any, one may watch the native water-sellers filling their goatskins with drinking water at a fountain, then rambling off to sell their precious potation at a few francs or a part of a Dirham per cup. Each rings a bell as he walks. On the boulevard near the mosque at the sea front one may watch native life in full reek, snake charmers, dancers, fakirs, and all the wondrous, perfervid rest of it. The beholder notes that many of the young boys hanging about have the head shaved except for one solitary tuft. I inquired about this and was told that the shaving is for reasons of sanitation, to discourage lice, but the tuft is left for good luck. If the boy should die, the Angel of Death can still grab him by that tuft and carry him to heaven.

The New Medina is a self-conscious but most praiseworthy effort to coax native life into more sanitary ways. The homes are small whitewashed dens, without the overcrowded, fetid character of those in old medinas. On a glorious moonlight night, as soft as silver satin, I made my way from the Route de Mediouna into this quarter and was fascinated by it. Some of the *indigènes* were living, not in the little stucco dens, but in tents in open fields, as is the nomadic custom of the Arabs (not so much the Berbers) all over Morocco. I could see the intimacies of life—mercifully mellowed by moonlight—through the open flaps of the tents. Other natives squatted over glowing braziers in the arcades of public buildings or of the near-by palace, a courtesy palace gladly authorized during the period of French control, but rarely used now by the present king, who dwells, of course, in Rabat, the capital. The hum of Arab talk filled the air but was pierced now and then by the sharp, weird wailing of a mendicant.

A native guide, speaking good French, attached himself to me, for a consideration, and showed me the *Quartier Réservé* where public women offer their persons to all comers for about a dime. Pathetic creatures they were, with "business offices" too small, it seemed, for even *one* person to recline on the dubious matting.

"But this is nothing," said my guide. "This is the *small* reserved quarter. Wait until I show you the large one." He led me for two miles or more through a maze whose turnings I could not possibly follow. After forty minutes of brisk trudging he halted before a house in which no light whatever gleamed through the shutters. Inside, he promised, I should see an Oriental dance by sable-skinned beauties while I enjoyed a cup of native coffee. He had to have the money first, to arrange matters, so I gave him the equivalent of half a dollar and he went inside. After a minute or two he emerged looking crestfallen.

"What a pity!" he exclaimed. "All the ladies are busy—*mais attendez, monsieur, une petite seconde*," and he was off like the wind, around the corner of the building.

You know the end of the story. He did not come back. To tell the truth I was considerably relieved, for it had been in my mind that the delicious native coffee of this mysterious house might possibly contain some sedative to put me to sleep until my wallet and watch could be removed. The street was very lonely and desolate and I had not the smallest idea where I was. Presently a muscular Moor came along pedaling a bicycle down the moonlit road and I asked him the way to the *Gare Centrale*. He bade me hop on his handle bars, which I did, hanging on for my life while he rode at a scorching pace down-hill, and toward the town, as it proved. Suddenly he spied a policeman under a street lamp and seemed not to wish to meet him, so he fairly dumped me off and sped away in a different direction, though not before I had given him a few francs for transportation. The policeman looked good to me if not to the Moor. I inquired my way and within a quarter of an hour I was ensconced in the comfort of my own room, none the worse for wear. Thus ended my fling at Moroccan night life.

Marrakech, an hour due south of Casablanca by plane and four by good electric train, is the most famous city of tourist interest in Morocco, if not in all North Africa, and certainly it deserves its fame. Located in the midst of a vast palm garden, it is backed by the magnificent range of the Grand Atlas Mountains, always covered with snow.

Most American visitors promptly establish themselves in the *Hôtel de la Mamounia*, whose outstanding luxury, hidden in a superb park of orange trees and subtropical plants and vines, is just what the spirit needs in the bedlam of this city. Nearby is a smart gambling casino, with dance-restaurant, the only such doubleton in Morocco, so far as I know. A Moroccan-style restaurant of great luxury and lavish native fare is the *Gharnatta*. From the Mamounia it is but a short walk to the huge open space which is called *Place Djemaa-el-F'na*, a name to conjure with if your tongue can handle it. I cannot put into words the *concussive* power of this square. Surely there can be nothing else quite like it on earth. Its concussions and percussions tear your five senses to shreds and then tear the shreds. From five o'clock in the morning it is a roaring native market for some hours. From five in the afternoon it is a colossal open-air fair or *kermesse*, bursting with all the exhibitionist life that Africa can offer. The snake charmers, native bands, dancers, and swarthy showmen of Casablanca or Fez are but small-time curtain-raisers compared to those of the Place Djemaa-el-F'na.

You cannot move anywhere in Marrakech without one or two or ten or twenty self-appointed guides, mostly young boys, tagging along with you, and it is no use at all to try to rid yourself of them. If you seem angry they gather in larger numbers as if for self-protection. If you are pleasant they think you are weakening. If you toss them money in the hope of obtaining a little relief it shows your good heart and scores of new guides gather about you to augment the original band. If you display a resolute indifference, for however long a period, it helps you not a bit. Their patience is that of Job in rags. Your best hope is to hire an official guide from your hotel or from the local tourist office and pay him an extra fee to guarantee you immunity from other guides. His Arabic vocabulary will prove far more effective than your English or French efforts.

He will have wonderful things to show you, the glorious *Koutoubia Tower;* the richly ornamented *Tomb of the Saadian Princes;* the *Bahia,* which was the palace of the Sultans; and, if your strength holds out, other private palaces, not to mention babs, medersas and a terrific sector of souks, but the bedlam of the main square will probably impress you more sharply and enduringly than all the other sights together.

If the life of Place Djemaa-el-F'na threatens to batter your mind to a pulp you may pleasantly escape it by an open carriage, or "hippo-mobile," as it is so neatly called. The tariff is low and you may roll at your leisure, behind cheerfully clattering hoofbeats, through several beautiful parks and through miles of the *palmeraie,* or palm forest.

From Marrakech many desert excursions are to be made. A notable one leads through the Souss to its port of *Agadir,* passing through *Taroudant,* whose *Hôtel Gazelle d'Or,* designed and decorated in Moorish style, is one of the most luxurious in all Moslem Africa. Another excursion, widely known, takes you on the *High Atlas Circuit,* the modern classic of Morocco, with two passes at altitudes of over 6500 feet. All-expense excursions of various lengths are offered by *Circuits Transat.*

Marrakech may tire you, exasperate you, punish your sense of

repose—though the secluded hotel and the open palmeraie are antidotes
—but it cannot possibly fail to interest you. I think you will remember
Morocco more vividly than any other part of North Africa, and
Marrakech more vividly than any other part of Morocco.

Rabat has been the administrative capital of Morocco since the
commencement of the French protectorate and it has continued in that
role since the coming of independence. Its native quarters have an
Islamic erudition and aristocracy found in no other French-African
city and its modern quarters, largely inhabited by government
functionaries, attain such genuine elegance as to win the respect of
any city on any continent. Rabat gleams white and beautiful in the
sun and is blessed with a grand location on cliffs above the open sea.
It is separted from *Salé*, its former rival, by the broad estuary of the
Bou-Regreg, whose facilities for shipping readily explain the age-long
importance of this double city's site. Rabat's chief tourist pride, visible
even from the train as it makes a great crescent to Salé, is the *Hassan
Tower*, a strange minaret that is a relic of a thirteenth-century mosque.
From this minaret the grandson of the great Sultan Youssef-el-Mansour,
facing a fanatical audience of 200,000 persons, preached a holy war
against an invader of Islam's sanctity. The invader was none other than
St. Louis of France, soon to die of the pest in Carthage. The Hassan
Tower was partly destroyed by the earthquake which wrecked Lisbon
in 1755 but enough is left to prove its blood-brotherhood to the
Giralda Tower of Seville and the Koutoubia of Marrakech.

The leading hotel (and night club) of Rabat is named the *Tour
Hassan*, and very good it is, though it will be cast far in the shade by
the new *Hotel Rabat Hilton*, now under construction. The fact that
the Moroccan government has signed an agreement with Hilton International for the building of such a hotel, a luxury one of 250 rooms
to cost $6 million, is evidence of the faith both parties to the agreement
have in the future of Moroccan tourism.

Meknès is the city of Sultan Moulay-Ismail, for whom many a street
and boulevard in Morocco is named. In 1673 he was proclaimed sultan
and made this city his capital, setting to work some sixty thousand
slaves, mostly Christian prisoners, on the building of his palace. Meknès
abounds in interesting mosques, babs and souks, and is proud also of
a large ostrich farm where these running birds have been raised for

centuries. Not far away from Meknès are *Volubilis*, a Roman city of impressive ruins, and *Moulay-Idriss*, a holy city of Moslem pilgrimage.

Fez, once the capital of all Morocco, is easily the climax of this three-link chain of color. It is the religious, scholastic and literary capital of Moslem Africa, with a small but smart European quarter. In all things native it has twice as much to offer as Meknès; and in addition to this there is the beautiful tour around Fez, to be made preferably in an open calèche, with a stop at a hillside café for a remarkable panorama of the city. Your driver will play the role of cicerone in a brand of French that you will be lucky to understand. He will not let you miss the remarkable stork colonies in the tree tops of the valley below your road, nor, surely, the troglodyte women— *femmes d'occasion* he calls them (women at a bargain)—who live in rock caves outside the city walls and bellow for masculine trade as you drive past them. For those who can linger in this walled city of unique atmosphere, the head and heart of Moslem Morocco, there is an excellent hotel, the *Palais Jamai*.

Fez is a wonderful epitome of all that makes up the mystery of indigenous Morocco. To see it properly you will need a guide, but guides are never lacking in North Africa.

Algeria—From the Valley of the Shadow

It may be some time before Algeria will again be the magnet that it long was to Mediterranean tourists, or this happy development may come sooner than anyone expects. In July, 1962, Algeria won its full independence, while still retaining business and cultural ties with France, and has since been going through the pains and illnesses of national infancy. The advance of Moslem Algeria to adolescence and maturity will be eagerly watched. For current tourist information address the Arab Information Center, 120 East 56th Street, New York.

Algeria has been a civilized region for well over a century, and the maritime world may be grateful to France that this is so, for prior to that its coast was a lair of ruthless corsairs who preyed on all the shipping that ventured through the Pillars of Hercules. It was no small task for the armies of France to subdue this tough region. Charles V (the Emperor) had attempted it, as had Louis XIV. America's Decatur and Britain's Lord Exmouth had more or less suppressed piracy but had not permanently eradicated it. Fourteen years of determined campaigning finally brought success to France in 1844 and for many decades there was no safer, more dependable, more profitable part of Greater France than this same pirate country. Algeria was drawn into a very special sort of intimacy with its colonizing power. The three administrative divisions of the northern portion, Oran, Algiers and Constantine, were represented in the French Chamber of Deputies as full-fledged *départements*, making them, in a political sense, parts of France.

The capital city of big, sprawling Algeria, with its desert hinterland, is, of course, *Algiers*, now exceeded in size by only four or five cities in France. Its population, by its own claim, is rather less than that of Casablanca, but a large majority of the inhabitants are, or until the explosive war were, Europeans, that is French, which is far from the case in the Moroccan metropolis. Algiers (*Hotel St. George; Hotel Aletti*) is truly magnificent, rising from the sea, tier on tier, like an architect's dream city designed for some great exposition. Its newer portions are monumental in plan, brilliant, imposing, artistically effective. The huge but balanced mass of the Government Building, above the War Monument and the Grande Poste, is a striking but by no means unique example of what France achieved, taking advantage of the city's hillside and harborside location. The lift and sweep of this building "massif" stays in the memory for years, after one seeing.

Algiers is quite as handsome looked down upon as looked up at, and there is no better way to spend one's time than to roam the upper lifts by car or on foot, with a good plan, such as that of the *Guide Pol*, for reference. The *Colonne Voirol*, reached from the central post office by the bus marked HYDRA, is a good starting point for ambitious hikers, since it is close to a lovely pine wood. A glorious viewpoint—but a taxi's help may be needed in finding it—is the *Parc Belvédère Saint-Raphaël*. This is, in fact, the finest viewpoint in all Algiers, if any single one can claim this absolute superlative.

In all parts of Upper Algiers villas and apartment houses cling to the hillside at the most striking angles and in fantastic poses, many of the streets and avenues in this portion of the city writhing like serpents in their efforts to climb and descend. Thrilling views are a franc a

dozen, and from many points one can see the little islets that give this
city its name, for Algiers means "The Islands." On these little specks
in the blue the earliest settlements grew up.

The traditional sights of Algiers are the Winter Palace and the
Summer Palace, the National Library, the medersa, the cathedral, in
Moorish style, with an interior as dark as Erebus, and the three chief
mosques, ordinarily closed to tourists but occasionally open to them
when large groups wish to enter. All these things are impressive, but
one sight that seems to me as worthy of a visit as anything in the
city rarely gets any play and it is not even mentioned in ordinary
printed lists of *Sites et Monuments.* I refer to *Notre Dame d'Afrique,*
a church on a cliff at the extreme northern edge of the city.

Our Lady of Africa broods over two cemeteries below, one for
Christians and one for Jews, over a football (soccer) stadium, too, and
over the restless open sea. The view from the front terrace is immense.

There is a special mariner atmosphere about the church, for three
ship models are affixed to the wall and above them are the Latin words
Ave Maris Stella (Hail, Star of the Sea). Below and all around are
hundreds of votive offerings, many from sailors whom this Virgin's
intercession is supposed to have saved from shipwreck or some other
disaster. But the thing that caught my eye especially was an inscription
that backed the high altar, above which rose the blackened Virgin
herself, Our Lady of Africa. The inscription read: *Priez Pour Nous
et Pour les Musulmans.* (Pray for us and for the Moslems.) That, I
think, is a remarkable petition, a moving example of tolerance in
religion. One hopes that Moslems in their mosques, despite the revolting
cruelties of the Secret Army Organization during the months before
and immediately after independence, may be able to offer "reciprocal
prayers" to Allah.

And what about the Kasbah? Is it really like that? Is it "like the
films"? The average visitor to Algiers is politely interested in the
city's modern buildings and its beauties, but the one thing that he, and
usually she, is fairly panting to explore is the Kasbah.

I would say that the Kasbah, in its outward appearance, is rather
more like Hollywood's conception than I, in a debunker's mood, had
originally expected to find it. Rising so steeply from the harbor that
some narrow streets, whose houses actually meet and bump each other

overhead, are resolved into sheer flights of steps, it climbs up past hammam establishments, souks, various assorted and dubious dens and Moorish cafés, past houses of harlotry too, by the dozen. I had innocently supposed the Moslem veil, covering feminine faces, to be a fixed symbol of modesty and reserve, but in the Kasbah "it ain't necessarily so." Many of the native prostitutes are Ouled Naïls, a desert tribe whose women are said to be raised from childhood for the oldest profession and to be highly regarded as practitioners. So numerous are the brothels in some streets that any house which is not a brothel puts up a protective sign reading "Maison Honnète" (Respectable House).

But this feature of the Kasbah is, after all, only a small fraction of the whole. Those who are lucky enough to enter one of its wealthy private homes, which will probably look like a hovel outside, similar to all the rest, will be transported instantly to another world quite unknown to the film industry. I induced an Arabic-speaking English resident to take me into one of the better homes and I was amazed by its tasteful beauty, surrounding a lovely patio, and by its modern comforts and even luxuries. It was an oasis of clean fragrance amid the Kasbah's assorted squalors. The Arab grandmother greeted us and showed us her treasures, then indicated that we might climb to the roof-terrace.

The Kasbah as its roofs see it is really *something*. We could look down almost perpendicularly straight into a good half-dozen homes. A goldfish bowl has nothing on the Kasbah in matters of "privacy on display." On a neighboring terrace, a lift or two lower, stood an Arab girl of about fifteen, too old and too pretty to be unveiled in public, but she was *not* technically in public. We looked down at her and she looked up at us. She *loved* it, and even preened herself. We waved, and she waved back—a little. I have no doubt that she felt deliciously wicked!

At the very top of the Kasbah, on a rude hillside above the motor highway called Boulevard de la Victoire, is Algiers' open-air Flea Market (*Marché aux Puces*), and such a wretched, pathetic travesty of trade I have never seen quite equaled. I saw tiny piles of kindling offered for sale, no more than a single handful to each pile. I saw *one* rubber glove and *one* shoe, with a doughnut in it the size of a silver dollar. I saw a pile of cast-off bread, garnered from the waste of restaurants, many pieces half eaten. These dainties, like everything else in the Flea Market, were on sale to an eager public, which looked over the merchandise, chaffering at length, and finally bought, with grudging francs. Such *total* poverty seems appalling, but it must be remembered that Arabs are by nature lighthearted. They laugh very easily, accept hard conditions as the will of Allah and do not worry themselves unduly over poverty—which isn't to say that they like it.

Beggars exist wherever poverty and tourists exist. There are myriads of them in the kasbah and they swarm like mosquitoes about each new tourist group, but I learned the phrase that is supposed to disperse them. One says, "*Allah y noub*," which means "God take my place." A faithful Moslem considers it impious to continue pestering a tourist who has appointed God as his alternate. I wish I had known this phrase in Marrakech!

Constantine is a masterpiece of drama. Ancient capital of the Numidian kings, and anciently named Cirta, later a favorite city of the Emperor Constantine, who rebuilt it and bequeathed his name to the city, it is now the capital of a prosperous province of Algeria, lying but an easy air-hop from Algiers. By rail it is a day's run or a night's run to the east, and oddly enough it is the same rail distance, to the exact kilometer, west of Tunis, though the trip to or from the latter city takes longer. A dining-car by day, sleeping-cars (from Algiers) by night, make this run civilized and comfortable. But if it were not so, if one had to go by camelback or bicycle, it would still be worth whatever it cost in travel trouble. Constantine is *wonderful*— and how flat that schoolgirl adjective sounds to characterize this Numidian stronghold. As a picture to look at, Constantine is the most exciting large city I know in the whole Mediterranean, though rivaled, in a different way, by that other city named for the same emperor, Constantinople, now Istanbul. This is strong talk and courts disagreement but I am "of the same opinion still." Other important cities have seemed to me physically tamer since the first time I crossed the bridges of Constantine and walked the circuit of the Boulevard de l'Abîme, called also Boulevard Joly de Brésillon. (Some of these French names may now have suffered change in Algerian Algeria.)

Constantine rises above the deep gorge of the River Rhummel much as Ronda, in Spain, rises above the gorge of the Guadalevín, but on a large-city scale. Everywhere, except at a small point on the south-western rim of the city, steep cliffs fall away in a vertiginous plunge, as if attempting to reach "absolute zero" of altitude before being stopped by earthly obstructions. The Rhummel gorge, which circles more than half of Constantine and is bridged at four points, is about six hundred feet deep, and on the open, westward side of the city the plunge to green meadows is quite as steep and brilliant.

Two classic walks dominate tourist planning here. One is around the cliff boulevards mentioned above, and back through the Israelite quarter or by the cliff route (Rue Nationale), passing the interesting Arab medersa, to the Place de Nemours, animated center of the modern city. The other is the weakly named but incomparable Chemin des Touristes, a hair-raising path that is, in many places, a boardwalk anchored to the rock. It passes directly through the gorge and not very high above the tumultuous yellow river. One ordinarily enters this path beneath the Pont de Sidi-Rached on the right bank and emerges far downstream, to return to the lofty Boulevard de l'Abîme by a cliffside elevator. The whole circuit needs about three hours, unless one is racing against time.

I am happy to report that civilization came to Constantine without ruinous effect. One does not—yet—feel at all overwhelmed by tourism, though one can find comfortable hotels and even a smart *Casino*, on a level just below a pleasant double park in the southwestern part of the city. In the Casino one may eat well, drink well, be well entertained by movies or by attractions that attract and lose good money at roulette or baccarat.

Other high spots than Algiers and Constantine can only be listed briefly, though some of them deserve more than a brief visit. In this directory of the lesser attractions of Algeria geographical sequence cannot be attempted.

Oran, far to the west, is the second city of the country, a flourishing port and a fine metropolis of 300,000 inhabitants.

Sidi-bel-Abbès, a little south of Oran, is known for its association with the Foreign Legion of France, which, to the regret of all romanticists and all who remember *Beau Geste*, went out of existence when Algerian Algeria was born.

Tlemcen, farther to the southwest and not much short of the Moroccan frontier, is an exceedingly interesting Arab-Berber city with some veneer of French civilization. The lure of Tlemcen's shops is considerable. I saw more things of native craftsmanship that really tempted me here than in any other small city of North Africa. The sky-line of the city, as a native writer has well said, is "prickly with minarets."

Philippeville, handsomely located on two rounded eminences called nipples in the bold vernacular of French guidebooks, serves as a port of Constantine but is a flourishing city in its own right.

Bône, another up-to-date port, more wooded than Philippeville, lies a bit farther to the east and also serves Constantine.

Biskra is a pretentious and touristical oasis town south of Constantine. Though by no means what it was a generation or two ago it is still of interest, still entertains tourist groups with staged rites of weird character.

Timgad, lying roughly half way between Constantine and Biskra, is widely known for its Roman ruins. For the desert trip to the two places named just above, Constantine is the natural take-off point, and the return to such a city is, in itself, a thing to be looked forward to.

Tunis and Nine-Lived Carthage

Tunisia suffered relatively little in her advance with the tide of independence that swept North Africa during the 50's and early 60's. Now it welcomes tourists with much more warmth and effective aid than ever it did in the days of French control. In Tunis, the capital city, there is an alert *National Tourist Office* (*Office Nacional de Tourisme*), which does a very commendable job of promotion, publishing among its many illustrated folders and brochures an unusually complete and easy-to-use compendium, called simply *Tunisia,* of everything that pertains to tourism. The address of the office is Avenue Mohammed V, Tunis, Tunisia. The currency seems stable—420 Dinars make one dollar—and there are good hotels in the capital, the *Tunis Hotel Majestic* being the leader, followed closely by the *Tunisia Palace Hotel.*

Tunis city, one must say in fairness, saw great progress during the eight decades of French control, and any visitor who comes here with a feeling of skepticism concerning the French capacity for colonization would do well to examine the case objectively. It happens that this was the first French colony I ever visited—it was between the two World Wars—and certain picturesque sentences from *Trader Horn* were then fresh in my mind, paving the way for one of the surprises of my life. I had been led by the book to suppose that France was deplorably careless, sloppy, indifferent, in the matter of colonization problems, but I came, I saw and I was conquered. My hat swept the ground in apology to Marianne. For most visitors Tunis is the country's high spot of travel interest. Its European portion is a delightful and prosperous French-looking city, with a broad, central promenade made brilliant by a flower market. Its medina, the most interesting one in North Africa, unless possibly Marrakech can challenge this claim, has a far more Oriental tinge than do its counterparts in other cities, and the souks are easily the most tempting to the eye. Whatever you do or fail to do in Tunis do not miss the souks. Wandering up the main avenue and past the old city gate, you enter the Place Lavigerie, whence the traffic, now solely foot traffic, splits into two ribbons, ascending two equally busy streets. The left-hand street, called Rue de l'Eglise, is the more colorful and to enter it is to enter a picture of native life so throbbing with vivacity that it knocks your senses into a disordered heap.

About a hundred yards up this street, on the right, under a long and heavy archway, is the inconspicuous and unlikely entrance to the headquarters of the *Direction des Antiquités et Arts*. The library of this Tunisian government bureau, aided by UNESCO funds, has assembled 200,000 books and manuscripts in many languages, more than a tenth of them being in Arabic. At any hour of any day you will probably find all desks in the research rooms occupied by Arab students.

You continue up the hill, circling the *Grand Mosque Djama-ez-Zitouna*, and climb on and on to the kasbah, passing a mélange of crowded stalls where everything under the Arab sun is made and sold in public view, the different trades being assembled in compact areas. The leather workers' souk, the tailors' souk, the perfumers' souk, the jewelers' souk, the brass workers' souk and many more vie with each other in spectacular animation and certainly in purchaser temptation.

Many of the streets are covered over with rushwork to keep out the sun's rays. The *Mosque of the Kasbah* is near the top of the hill but no non-Moslem may enter it. If you are near it at one of the times of prayer you will hear the weird call of the muezzin, who is perched high in one of the minarets, summoning the faithful to their orisons.

Aside from the souks, which are enough in themselves to reward a visit, Tunis, with its environs, offers a wide variety of unusual sights.

Le Bardo, about two miles from the center, was once the palace of a Turkish dynasty and as such it had a well-ordered harem, or seraglio. This harem, an enormous one that could accommodate a small army of wives, concubines and odalisques, was turned into a museum in 1888 and has become by far the greatest archeological museum in North Africa. More accurately, it is four museums in one, a Punic, a Roman, a Byzantine Christian and finally an Arab museum. It has many special items of rare significance and its collection of mosaics is claimed to be the most extensive in the world, but for all that it is the "museum nobody knows." Relatively few tourists visit Tunis, though the number is bound to increase now that independence and stability have come, and few of those who do come ever hunt up Le Bardo. Perhaps you will wish to be "different." The museum, officially named *Musée Alaoui*, is open every day except Monday, the traditional *jour de repos* for public buildings. If and when you visit this remarkable place you will likely be quite alone in it, as I was, but that can have its advantages. You feel that you are a trail blazer.

The Punic section contains many rather rude works of art in ceramics and glass but none in marble, for the early Carthaginians never mastered that medium, and very little in bronze. There are, however, ancient medals in carnelian and jasper. The most *gruesome* Punic relics are the numerous urns that were found in the ground of Carthage, each filled with the ashes of a child between three months and six years of age, as analysis has proved, who were sacrificed to the god Baal or the goddess Tanit. The word Moloch refers to the sacrifice itself, not to any deity. The infant was thought to attain divinity when burned and mothers were usually delighted to have their children selected for so great an honor. If they were not delighted they had to appear so—*or else*. They were required to stand beside the priest, who generally cut the child's throat and then placed the infant in the hands of Baal, whence it slid down through an aperture in the great image into the fire. These revolting details are vouched for by the Sicilian-Greek historian Diodorus.

The most interesting Roman antiquities are finds from a ship which sank in a storm off the Tunisian coast in 81 B.C. during the dictatorship of Lucius Sulla. The ship foundered in water 130 feet deep near the present port of Mahdia, south of Souss, and it still lies there, but some important things have been salvaged from it, including a few marble columns of a cargo that Sulla was having transported to Rome. A bit sea-eaten by twenty centuries of immersion, they now grace one of the halls in the Bardo; and there is also a superb young god from the wreck, brought up by a sponge fisherman. He is the "Genius of the Gymnasium," the god who gave victory to his chosen athletes in competitive games.

The mosaics of the museum seem to be measurable in *acres* and some of them are exquisite works of art. A very superior one from Roman times depicts Virgil writing the *Aeneid* while muses look on from either side. Good ones from the early Christian era show Jonah resting beneath a gourd tree before the whale swallowed him, and, in a rugged scene, Saints Perpetua and Felicitas being given to the lions in an arena in Carthage. Many well-designed animals are pictured in the mosaics and some lifelike ostriches as well.

The Arab portion of the museum specializes in lovely tilework. For some years everything in the Musée Alaoui was placed under the supervision of a widely known French archeologist named Gilbert Charles Picard, who personally unearthed many of the more important mosaics. Madame Picard made *from the mosaics* a film of "Roman Life in North Africa." Adjacent to the museum is the so-called *Palais Beylical* (Palace of the Bey), a renovated part of which is now used as the National Assembly House. The former Bey, now an old man "out of work" in a republic, lives peacefully in one of the suburbs. The dazzling salons of his palace are open to tourists.

Restituenda Est Carthago. Reversing the reiterated cry of Cato the Elder, "Delenda est Carthago" (Carthage must be destroyed), the Public Works Authorities of Tunisia, through the Service des Antiquités, have been vigorously *reviving* Carthage, one of the most famous of forgotten cities, aided substantially by the U.S. Carthage is an exciting discovery for those Americans who find it. All we remember from school days is the struggle to learn the sequence and battles of the three Punic Wars, culminating in Rome's final victory. What we now learn is the drama of a city that *must* exist, throughout the ages, at precisely this favored spot, the gateway to all the eastern Mediterranean, where the sea narrows to a trifling hundred miles between Africa and Sicily.

Carthage has had almost as many lives as a cat. Traders from Sidon founded it under the name of Cambē at least as long ago as 1400 B.C. Dido, whose real name was Elissar, daughter of King Mathan of Tyre, refounded it about 800 B.C. Rome eventually destroyed it, but *not* utterly, as bulldozers and excavating implements are clearly proving, and later built a Roman city. This became, in time, a seat of Christian culture second only to Rome. A Vandal, a Berber and several Arab cities followed on the same site. As a Moslem center it was attacked by the crusading St. Louis (King Louis IX of France), who died during the siege. Moslems claim that the king was converted and died a "good Moslem." Part of Old Carthage bears his name, in Arabic guise, Sidi Bou Saïd. Another part, in fact the hill that is popularly supposed to be Dido's citadel, bears his name in its French and Christian form, Saint-Louis de Carthage. An "Arabic Byzantine" cathedral, of poor architecture, named in his honor, now surmounts the hill and in a *châsse* within it, built in the form of his own Sainte-Chapelle in Paris, lie fragments of the royal saint's mortal remains, forming an object of highest veneration by the faithful.

In modern times Carthage has twice more experienced a new "life." Once was when this *Cathédrale de Saint-Louis* became the primatial cathedral of *all* Africa. Cardinal Lavigerie, who consecrated the structure in 1890, was the first primate. A statue of him is to be seen in Tunis's Place Lavigerie. A dramatic new life was granted to Carthage, and to Tunis, when the Allied armies, under Eisenhower and Alexander, liberated Tunisia from the Nazis in the spring of 1943. On May 7, Alexander's troops entered the capital, to the boundless enthusiasm of its citizens.

Modern Carthage is a cheerful suburb of Tunis, as attractive to the eye as its name is significant in history. One reaches it in half an hour by an electric train whose home terminus is on the main street of Tunis. The line, running for miles along a dike through the briny lake of Tunis, reaches the seashore at La Bouletter and continues in a direction parallel to the beach, stopping at several villa suburbs, one of which is interestingly named Amilcar, and another Salammbô. From Carthage Station one mounts the famous hill past a humble café named *A la Reine Didon* (which is to say Queen Dido) and past a hotel named for St. Louis.

The view from Carthage hill is superb, whether toward the charming seaside suburb of Sidi Bou Saïd, toward the metropolis of Tunis or toward the distant range of hills. Evidences of the city of Dido, Hannibal and Hamilcar are on every side and one may even descry, near the coast, the vestiges of the ancient port of Carthage.

Having visited Carthage twice on my own, I once plucked up the nerve to call on Monsieur Picard and ask if he could arrange to have a guide of his choosing give me an authoritative showing. He responded by dropping everything and coming with me himself. He took me to see various wonders which he was preparing to open to the tourist public. One was the vast *Baths of Emperor Antoninus*, completed by his adopted son, Marcus Aurelius. From this "quarry" of fashioned stone, some say, certain columns that support St. Paul's in London were taken, but I could not ascertain whether this was fact or fiction. Monsieur Picard showed me a little Christian basilica built in early Christian times on a Roman house built on Punic tombs; and near by, a very ancient Punic pottery furnace full of pots that were hastily abandoned when the Romans destroyed Carthage 2100 years ago.

The most absorbing, if ghoulish, sight in the whole region was the *Punic Sanctuary*, being the very spot where the priests burned infants, in appalling numbers to appease Baal and Tanit. The Sanctuary was discovered by accident. An Arab happened to find and dig up an ancient stela. He tried to sell it, but since antiquities are state property he was arrested for selling something he didn't legally own. His arrest led to the discovery of the Sanctuary. It has been partly uncovered by the Services des Antiquités but scores of the urns containing the ashes of cremated children have been deliberately left protruding from a mound.

It brings a cruel period of the past into our very presence and perhaps persuades us that the world has, in spite of all, advanced a little in the practice of "common humanity."

Tripoli and New-Old Libya

Libya, with its thousand miles of Mediterranean coast and the endless sands of its interior, relieved here and there by oasis towns, is as old as time. In school textbooks on U.S. history it is as old as 1800 and the years just before and after, for the capital, Tripoli, was a pirate stronghold of the Barbary Coast, destined to witness a war with the infant U.S. Navy, brilliantly conducted for our side by Stephen Decatur. In tourist thought, which now concerns us, it is just about the newest thing in the whole Mediterranean. Not until recent years, when *UAT French Airlines* (*Union Aéromaritime de Transport*) made it accessible did travelers begin to notice Libya at all, though oil companies, aware of its rich wells, had had their eyes and drills on it for some time. UAT has a tremendous network fanning out from Paris, Marseille and Nice that serves most of the newly independent countries of Africa and pushes on clear to Rhodesia and South Africa. Its line from Paris to Tripoli flies by way of Nice, with a halt at that Riviera center and another at Bastia, on Corsica, making it easy for the Mediterranean tourist to effect a tangent round trip without upsetting the main pattern of his travels. An associated company called NAA/Libiavia, based in Tripoli, operates regular service between Athens and Libya, providing another convenient take-off point. Libiavia's agent in Athens is Olympic Airways, conspicuous on Constitution Square. I should add some mention here of still another service, namely that of Alitalia, which makes semiweekly flights between Naples and Tripoli. UAT, which is a sort of mother company to Libiavia, has a New York office at 2 Broadway and from this office you may secure the latest news on schedules and tariffs of both companies and a steer on how to secure further information. Your Libyan visa, valid for a month's stay, is to be secured from the Embassy of Libya, 2127 Bancroft Place, N.W., Washington, D.C. In Paris, in case you fly from there, the visa may be secured by a visit to the Libyan Consulate General, on Rue Keppler (a short street near

Avenue Marceau), and similarly, if you fly from Athens you may secure the visa there.

I have confessed, in Chapter 3, that although I booked for a round-trip ticket from Athens to Tripoli I was unable to go because an Israeli visa was stamped, through error, in my passport and Libya will not admit even a friend and well-wisher if his passport is thus politically "smirched." I have heard good things of Libiavia's service and I know from personal investigation that the services of big UAT are topflight, graced, of course, by the same Gallic flair and French cuisine that Air France has long made familiar.

To give some basic facts, the currency of Libya is the Libyan pound, now purchasable at the same rate as sterling, namely $2.80 to the pound. The notes are printed in English on one side, with the words United Kingdom of Libya in bold capitals, and in mysterious Arabic script on the reverse. The pound is divided into 100 piasters, worth 2.8 cents apiece, and the piaster into 10 millièmes. Tripoli is a modern European-type city of over 100,000 inhabitants, largely built, in a fine frenzy of colonialism, by Fascist Italy. It has broad avenues and subtropical parks, impressive banks and public buildings, the beautiful palace of King Idris I, several impressive mosques, headed by the *Caramanli*, or *Jama Ahmed Pacha*, and some excellent hotels. The *Libya Palace*, opened in 1962, is the leading hotel, followed by the *Vaddan*, which name means "Big Goat," that being a sort of national symbol. Benghazi, the capital of the province of Cyrenaica and a famous name in World War II, also has good hotels, the leaders being the big *Berenice*, on the sea promenade, and the *Continental*.

Tripoli was of more than casual interest to the young United States as early as our second decade of existence, for it was one of the main strongholds of the Barbary pirates, who were a constant scourge to Mediterranean shipping, having the insolence to demand tribute for "protection," quite in the manner of modern racketeers. Failing the tribute, many a ship had to submit to looting and to the capture and imprisonment of its crew. The pirates were, in fact, the immediate cause of the birth of the U.S. Navy, which may be dated from 1798. By the early years of the nineteenth century American warships set out in earnest to wipe out this scourge, at least so far as U.S. ships were concerned. This came to a climax in a veritable war with the pirates, led by Stephen Decatur during 1804 and 1805. His most memorable exploit, a bright mark in U.S. naval history, was his bold burning of the American frigate *Philadelphia*, which had fallen into the clutches of the Tripoli pirates and was moored in the harbor. He achieved his purpose and escaped the fire of the shore batteries virtually unscathed. Other battles followed, with such good success that the pirates were taught a much needed lesson on "the shores of Tripo-li," to invoke the Marines' song, and molested American ships no more.

Modern Tripoli was founded by imperial Italy in 1911 and was pushed ahead with almost fanatical determination by Mussolini. Not only were the coastal cities built up from jumbled disorder to gleaming modernity but new desert communities were developed by the opening of wells for water supply, and a paved road was built along the coast all the way from the border of Tunisia to that of Egypt. The Italians also undertook extensive archeological works, chiefly in the excavation of the Leptis Magna and Sabratha ruins, of which there will be further mention below.

After the conclusion of World War II Libya became a fledgling nation, a monarchy, with King Idris I on the throne. Libya is lucky in having vast oil deposits, now being developed by foreign companies, including American, Standard of New Jersey, for one, already producing 200,000 barrels a day. One concession alone has been found to have a vast lake of the "black gold" 40 feet in depth 700 yards beneath the desert sand. Prosperity is sure to come to this new-born nation and with it, we may hope, political stability and steady advancement.

Tripoli got its name from a "triple" city founded on the Libyan shores by Phoenicians some three thousand years ago. Actually, there were three rather widely separated coastal cities, *Leptis Magna* (as it was called when under Roman sway), which is the easternmost of them, *Sabratha*, the westernmost, and *Oëa*, half way between them. Oëa, as the nucleus of the trio, became the Tripoli of history and of today. The Greeks followed the Phoenicians, and then, of course, the all-embracing Roman empire. Both Leptis Magna and Sabratha were vigorously excavated by the Italian fascist state and the work has gone on under the Administration of Tripolitania. Both places are easily reached from Tripoli, Sabratha lying 50 miles to the west, Leptis

(Upper) These "fruit peddlers" of Madeira wear the traditional costume of the island, topped by the oddly spiked toque hat known as a *carapuça. (Madeira Tourist Office)*

(Lower) The bay of Palma de Mallorca is lined, literally for miles, with new and newer resort hotels. *(Air France)*

(*Left*) Barcelona's unfinished Expiatory Temple of the Holy Family, designed by a Catalonian architect named Gaudi, is one of the world's weirdest ecclesiastical structures. It is an example of the madly exuberant style seen also in some of the city's apartment houses.

(*Right*) A "street" of the Kasbah of Old Algiers

The Principality of Monaco, with the palace of Prince Rainier and Princess Grace on the Rock (center of picture). Monte Carlo and its Casino fill the curving slope beyond.

The Promenade des Anglais, in Nice, is the heart of holiday on the French Riviera. Catering to mass travel, Nice still maintains its perennial elegance in hotels like the Negresco (electric sign).

Naples' Santa Lucia, famous in song, is backed by frowning Castel del'Ovo.

Amalfi, on many levels, lies on the open coast just southeast of Naples Bay. No village of the Mediterranean is more widely known and loved.

(Upper) The carts of Sicily are rolling picture galleries. *(British Overseas Airways Corporation)*

(Lower) Taormina, backed by vast, snow-crowned Etna, is by far the most popular tourist village of Sicily. It has everything, from glorious gardens to beaches-far-below and from a splendid Greek theater on a shoulder of rock to—shops. *(Vera Fotografia)*

The Parthenon has excited the wonder of architects for twenty-four centuries, not only for its beauty but for the "science of irregularity," which increases that beauty. Phidias made many deliberate deviations from straight and even lines to correct the mistakes of human vision.

The Evzone Guards of Greece are a never-failing delight to tourists and their cameras. The parade and changing of the guard (Sunday at 11) in front of the Parliament Building is a colorful event of Athens' weekly calendar.

The Palace of the Knights of St. John of Jerusalem on the Island of Rhodes. Their name was changed to Knights of Rhodes and later (on Malta) to Knights of Malta.

(Upper) The cloisters of Bellapais Abbey in Cyprus, famous in legend and literature. Built by the Norbertine Order of Laos (France), its name is a corruption of Abbaye de la Paix (Peace Abbey).

(Lower) The Rock of Romios, near Paphos. Cyprus, the legendary birthplace of Aphrodite, who here rose from the foam. A tourist strolls the surf-beaten beach.

The most famous scene of the African Continent needs no caption. These wondrous monuments are but eight miles from Cairo.

(Upper) A holiday facet of Cairo, the Nilseide Fontana Casino.

(Lower) View taken from the top of the new 615-foot Gezireh Tower shows modern Cairo, with the pyramids in the dim distance.

Israel Government Tourist Office

(Upper) A part of the Hebrew University of Jerusalem. "The Shrine of the Book," a new building on the campus, houses priceless manuscripts and the Dead Sea Scrolls.

(Lower) Haifa, Israel's great and growing port, is backed by lovely Mt. Carmel, on whose crest are fine modern hotels.

These columns of the Temple of Jupiter in Baalbek, Lebanon, are part of the largest temple ever erected by the Romans to their god of gods.

Air France

(*Left*) The fifteenth-century Fortress of Rumelihisar, looming above the Bosporus, has recently been restored, and its ground landscaped, as a major tourist attraction. An elevator hoists visitors to its lofty parapet.

(*Right*) The so-called Blue Mosque of Istanbul (from the blue faïence of the interior) is famous for its six minarets, one

Magna 95 miles to the east. The Administration distributes free folders in English on both places, with full information and clear diagrams. Leptis Magna certainly warrants the adjective in its name, for it was indeed Great Leptis, and even in its ruins it inspires awe. It long inspired greed in the imperial governments of various European countries and was ruthlessly pillaged for a century or more until the Italian occupation halted the plunder in 1911. Louis XIV appropriated no less than six hundred marble and granite columns, along with much statuary, for the building of his palace in Versailles, and George IV of England appropriated large amounts for the construction of false ruins at Virginia Water, near Windsor. This latter depredation, stealing real ruins to create sham ones, seems the ultimate in royal folly.

The "triple city" constitutes most of the tourist attraction of Libya, most but not quite all, for the easternmost province of *Cyrenaica* is making a strong bid for attention. Its *Tourist Department*, from which information may be had by addressing it simply at *Benghazi*, Cyrenaica, Libya, publishes, so far in French and Italian only, a lavishly illustrated *Guide Touristique de la Cyrénaïca* which far surpasses in quality and completeness anything that the *Tourist Department of Tripolitania*, in Tripoli, has brought out. The intending visitor to Libya, whatever he plans to do and see, would be well advised to write to both offices for current information and literature. The Cyrenaica brochure reveals that that province, too, has ruined cities of old to contrast with its large, modern capital. Benghazi, like Tripoli, has fine boulevards and palmy plazas, plus an inviting harbor-side promenade.

REVISION SUPPLEMENT TO CHAPTERS 12, 13 AND 14

THE Greek National Tourist Organization, with head office in Athens, has opened a branch in New York City at 601 Fifth Avenue, replacing the former "tentative" office on East 79th Street (page 215), and this handy location, with an energetic manager and staff, has lent dignity, as well as drive to tourist promotion. Here the intending traveler may stock up on travel folders and personal counsel.

The chief means of reaching Greece have been covered in the text, but I should here emphasize two points: (1) *Olympic Airways* now makes it possible to "fly Greek" from New York to Athens; and (2) *Greek Line* now offers sea transit from New York by its proud 26,000-ton flagship, the *Queen Anna Maria*. In addition to these standard services, persons coming to Greece from Italy might like to consider one of the ferry services. The car ferry *Carina*, with a capacity for 66 passengers and 60 cars, operates thrice weekly from Brindisi to the Piraeus port of Athens and a new line will ply from Italy to Greece with ferryboats being built in Italy as of this writing. The two ships have been named the *Eros* and *Aphrodite*, which has given rise to obviously suggested, not to say sugges*tive*, names for the shipping line, the most obvious nickname being the Sex Line!

Travel within Greece can be by various means, some of them merely getting you there, some delightful in their own right. Olympic Airways, mentioned above for its transatlantic flights, is the Pegasus of domestic travel and of late it has stepped up its service in frequency, spread and quality. The Hellenikon Airport in Athens is its home base, displaying the Olympic name and symbol far more conspicuously than those of the also-flying international lines! Hellenikon has had its face lifted with considerable grandeur but it isn't the only one of the 9 Greek airports to have had a face-lifting. The takeoff strip at Mytilene Airport (Lesbos), for instance, has been extended 2,000 yards so that four-engine craft can land on the island, providing direct contact with Europan capitals. In Kavala, the work being done to extend the runway should be completed by late 1967. This is a temporary move, I am told, until a new airport at Chryssoupolis can be built to serve the entire northeast region of Greece. Limnos Airport is also being improved and the extension of the airport of Heraklion, the chief city of Crete, has been completed, enabling it to handle more than double the previous traffic. The airport is expected to be used as a stopover point for international flights to the Near East. Rhodes Airport is also being improved so that increased air service will help that rapidly expanding tourism colony.

Cruising the Greek Islands, the nicest way to see them if you have the time, has been covered earlier in the section on cruise lines. Full details on the ever-changing itineraries can best be obtained directly from the offices given.

In overland domestic travel busses are the second-best means of touring Greece after private car. Bus routes are direct and travel is in large Pullman coaches over good roads, the only hazard being one's attempt to read Greek signs along the way, and at the stopovers. All bus destinations are shown in Greek lettering with Latin lettering below. It's best to have the concierge at your hotel write out the names of towns you plan to visit in both their Greek form and their European-and-overseas form, using Latin letters in both cases. Let me briefly explain. When the Venetians occupied Greece, they Europeanized all the names. Thus it happened that today most Greek towns have "domestic" names straight out of ancient Greece, these being still used by modern Greeks, *and* a more familiar-to-us name bestowed during the Venetian occupation and used by most Europeans and Americans. A case in point is Corfu, which is Kerkyra in Greek. Another is Rhodes, which is Rodos in Greek.

Travel by rented car is easy insofar as driving is concerned. Watch out for one hazard, however, the fact that many country Greeks are not used to the fast speed of travel by cars. You may whip around a corner only to be confronted by a leisurely herd of sheep behind whom you will have to travel until they or you turn off. Major car rental firms have offices in Greece, *Avis* and *Hertz*, being conspicuous, as also the Greek-owned *Hellascars*, which is an equally excellent firm. There are gas stations everywhere, and, as a further note of comfort, if you run into trouble with your car, just wait a while. Since they constantly patrol all main roads, you may be sure that a Greek Touring Club jeep will be along and its driver will gladly fix your car, unless it is a serious breakdown, at no charge. New roads are crisscrossing Greece at a rapid rate. A major four- to six-lane highway now goes from Athens to Corinth and one from Salonika (otherwise known as Thessaloniki) to Athens is under way, with many stretches now open.

If the language barrier threatens you, take a driver and guide for your tours. This is not inexpensive, however. A typical 4-day classical tour for four people costs about $100 per person, or $400 total. This includes everything such as accommodations, meals, entry fees for museums and so forth. A typical Athens sightseeing tour will cost you $25.50 for yourself alone, or $9.60 if you are one of a group of four.

Hotel building throughout mainland Greece and the islands continues at a seemingly frenetic pace. *Xenia Hotels*, mentioned on page 262 and throughout the text on Greece, are always a safe bet. Built by the Greek government to meet the need for accommodations in some of the more remote spots, these hotels are all standard, although of varying sizes, in offering good clean rooms and good food. They are designed by the same architectural team and have the same interior motif, although exteriors blend with locations. At the present time there are almost more Xenia Hotels than one can count, and new ones are cropping up all the time. The government has announced plans, for example, to build 23 hotels throughout Greece in conjunction with private investors. The hotels will each have from 70 to 100 rooms and will be built with from 20 per cent to 49 per cent of the capital coming from the private investor, the remaining amount being supplied by the government. This joint arrangement will last for seven years, after which the private investor may buy out the government if he so chooses. In addition to new government-sponsored hotels on Crete, at Heraklion and Canea, there are others on Mytilene (Lesbos), Patmos, Kalymnos and Skiathos in the Aegean; at Parga on the Ionian coast south of Corfu; at Thassos, Xanthi, Zagora, Edessa and Kozani in northern Greece; at Nafpakton in the center of Greece; at Olympia in the Peloponnesus; and at Mt. Parnes, outside Athens.

Noteworthy among the newer nongovernment accommodations are the *Electra Hotel*, with its 120 rooms, on Constitution Square in

Athens, and the 100-room *King Othon,* also on Constitution Square, which is planned for completion in 1967. In Delphi, the air-conditioned *Amalia Hotel,* with 90 rooms, consists of four two-story connected buildings. It has a full complement of public rooms and a view of the Amphissa olive grove and the Corinthian gulf. Twenty-five miles from Athens, along the southern coast, is the *Lagonissi Hotel,* with 280 acres of grounds. In addition to the 400 rooms, the hotel has a marina and an open-air movie theater seating 500 people.

The larger islands of Greece match the pace of the mainland, Rhodes being the most active. Two of the newer hostelries in Rhodes are the *Oceanis* and the *Park.* The Oceanis, as you might suspect, has its 175 rooms right on the beach, about two miles from the center of the town of Rhodes. For the non-beach sitter, miniature golf and tennis are available. The Park Hotel, with about 100 rooms, is in a residential part of the city with a rooftop view of the city and sea. Its greatest asset is its location, which is both convenient and picturesque. The *Grand Hotel,* mentioned on page 278, has added 32 rooms facing the pool, bowling lanes, a shopping arcade and a Greek taverna featuring guitar music, and now hyphenates its name as the Grand Hotel–Summer Palace.

A word about travel to the smaller, less sophisticated Greek Islands. You will undoubtedly want to travel by convenient boat service from Piraeus to some of these islands. It is usually not necessary to have advance accommodations on the islands though you *should* reserve your boat space (a cabin if you plan on one of the longer trips). When you arrive at a chosen island, and disembark, you will likely be greeted by a flock of residents tugging at your arm and asking you to stay at their homes. This can be a charming experience, and since most small islands have the majority of their tourist accommodations in private homes, you will be seeing Greece in Greek style. The island of Mykonos, for example, offers 300 rooms in hotels and over 3000 in private homes. If you find yourself standing alone on the dock with not only no one tugging, but no one in sight, seek out the Tourist Police, who will find you accommodations—perhaps in the home of one of the policemen. Only if you feel that you must, in every case, have good *hotel* accommodations is advance reservation advisable.

If you're so taken with Greece that you must take it with you, bid on one of the Greek Islands up for sale and it may be yours! Aristotle

Onassis bought Skorpios and is turning it into a thing of splendor, whereas the first purchaser of the islands when they were put up for sale by the Greek government was Stavros Niarchos, Onassis' fellow-magnate of shipping, who bought Spetsopoula for his private vacation paradise. Application for buying an island, and really, you need not be a billionaire, may be made to the Ministry of Finance in Athens. Lest you think that you *can* take it with you, you "buy" only a 99-year lease.

The Greek National Tourist Organization has been purchasing large pieces of land throughout the country with an eye to developing them as tourist attractions, two of the five areas so far acquired being near Athens. But of course the government does not neglect going attractions in favor of future ones. In addition to the memorable *Sound and Light* performances featuring the Acropolis, it has arranged for the regular floodlighting of many familiar monuments, among them the Parliament Building, the National Museum and the buildings of Athens University as well as the columns of the Temple of Zeus and the nearby Hadrian's Arch. To insure more "breathing room" in Athens, the government has added five new public squares to Athens by proclaiming that the areas shall be free from building and improved for leisure with the addition of benches and paths.

Some of the Greek festivals, notably the Athens Festival and the Epidaurus Festival, have been discussed on page 228. These are unmatched for cultural excellence and either one is worth considering as the nucleus of a vacation plan. However, for the sheer fun of it, try to visit Daphni, a short trip from Athens, in September at the time of the Wine Festival. Wine producers from all over Greece bring their wine kegs and set up shop in Daphni. For 50 cents you may drink all the wine you can and may join in the dancing-in-the-streets that literally fills the town. Many Greeks wear native costumes to add to the merriment.

If, of soberer nature, discoveries of ancient civilizations intrigue you, you may become part of an excavation group. Perhaps the easiest way is to address yourself and your qualifications to the American School of Classical Studies in Athens, mentioned in Chapter 13 in reference to Corinth, with request to take part in an excavation project. This is easier if you are affiliated with one of the many universities now undertaking such projects throughout Greece. If you discover some extremely valuable item you will be requested to leave it in Greece, but less important discoveries, which can be just as important to you, the discoverer, can come home with you. Secure a paper authenticating their probable date of origin, however, since antiques (defined by customs as items made prior to 1830, which these most certainly will be) can be imported to the United States duty-free.

Two further points, quite unrelated, conclude this report: (1) The funicular ascending Mt. Lycabettus, mentioned on page 230 as a hope, is now a going thing. The cable cars carry 30 passengers for the 1000-foot climb, at a round-trip fare of only 12 cents. (2) At Glyfada (page 234), on the shore boulevard south of Athens, there is a new 18-hole golf course that is said to be one of the finest in Europe.

CHAPTER 12

GREECE, KEYSTONE OF THE MEDITERRANEAN EAST

Ageless Athens, Mother of the West

I WENT to school and college in the days when Greek, as well as Latin, was still a standard struggling ground for the young and youthful. I had five years of Greek and was a chorus man in a college version of *Oedipus Tyrannus*, small fragments of which I can still sing and say. I have by heart a few gems also from Xenophon's *Anabasis* and I can recite the principle parts of basileuo, to rule. It might seem that very little has stayed with me from that five-year plan of classical Greek but I would not be without that little for a great deal. The miracle of Athens sank into my system the hard way, not merely by some lecturer telling me that Athens was a miracle. I studied the story of Greek battles and buildings, Greek sculptors and architects, Greek philosophers, poets and dramatists. It was tough going, but the image of the reflection of its glory got planted in my mind.

When I had been twenty years out of college I found myself in Athens on a magazine article commission and being in need of a haircut I bought one in a barber shop on Stadium Street. As I looked in the wall mirror, *there*, by the chisel of Phidias, was my college Greek professor, "Charlie D.," sitting behind me awaiting his turn for a trim. I couldn't believe it, but it was true enough and I leaped from my chair to greet him. He greeted me with equal astonishment, and for the next ten days we were two men together in Athens, he with all the knowledge of a devoted Greek scholar, I with all the unsullied admiration of a layman for the miracle that I but partially understood. We spent uncounted hours on the Acropolis, he explaining, I listening and asking.

We climbed the steep hill of Lycabettus to look down on Athens. At other times we made our way up to the Bema on the Pnyx Hill, not far from the rock where Socrates is supposed to have languished in prison.

Perhaps the location of Socrates' jail is apocryphal but there is no doubt that from the Bema, or orators' stage, the early Athenian assemblies were harangued by any and all who had something to get off their chests. This is the stage where democratic free speech was born. As many as eighteen thousand listeners sometimes gathered to hear the oratory. On the adjacent Areopagus, or Mars Hill, my teacher-companion located the spot, undoubtedly within a few feet, where Paul addressed "Ye men of Athens" with such eloquent exegesis that the "unknown God" was no longer unknown to the Athenians. In earlier centuries, when the Supreme Court of Athens had made this hill its meeting place, Demosthenes had been judged here, and also Phryne, the lovely courtesan, who was charged with impiety but was enthusiastically acquitted when counsel for the defense drew aside her robe to let the court view her charms. It was here, too, that Orestes was publicly absolved from the charge of having murdered his mother Clytemnestra. The Three Erinyes (Furies) were so upset at this verdict of acquittal that they fled into a cave on this hill.

From all the various heights we looked out upon the bay where, near Salamis Island, the Greek fleet, under Themistocles, knocked out three hundred Persian triremes by strategy as brilliant as that of Nelson at Aboukir. We saw, and I learned, much, much more in Athens, and not once did Charlie D. question me about the uses of the aorist tense or the forgotten mysteries of the iota subscript.

That experience, though long after my college days, was long ago and Greece has since been through the Valley of the Shadow of Death in World War II, first managing a *modern* miracle by pushing back Mussolini's Roman legions through the mountains, but then suffering at the ruthless hands of Hitler, who never tired of proclaiming his love for Greek culture! Later, Greece was again edged toward the abyss by Red "liberators" from neighboring countries, but fought off that danger also, with nick-of-timely support from the United States. The valor of Greek troops on every recent occasion when it has been put to the test has matched that of their ancestors at Marathon and Thermopylae. Of that there is no question.

The West was born in Greece and specifically in Athens. When Rome later occupied Athens and overrode all Hellas, in 146 B.C., naming the newly acquired province Achaia, Greek culture captured the conqueror. Alexandria, in Egypt, was already a center of Greek learning. Sicily and southern Italy, as we have seen, were saturated with the life and art and skills of Greece. In 328 A.D. the city on the Bosporus that Greeks had founded a thousand years earlier took on its new life and new name, Constantinople, and its Christian Byzantine (i.e. Greek) civilization gradually eclipsed that of the pagan Greeks, but this caused a further advance rather than a decline of Hellenic culture. For more than a thousand years after this refounding of the city, as capital of the Eastern Empire, the world continued to be so impregnated with Greek thought, philosophy, science, art and law that every center and monastic cell of learning continued to carry the torch of Hellas.

The civilization developed by the people of a small peninsula of Europe, chopped up by many mountain ranges, lived on, in various forms and places, even through the Dark Ages, and it is still viewed with wondering admiration by the poets, artists and scholars of all nations. Lord Byron was so stirred by it that he gave his life in a romantic attempt to be a soldier and to help set up the modern state of Greece. He died of exposure at Missolonghi and his heart is buried there. Shelley, writing in the wordy prose of his day, asserted that "the period which intervened between the birth of Pericles and the death of Aristotle is undoubtedly, whether considered in itself or with reference to the effect which it has produced upon the subsequent destinies of civilized man, the most memorable in the history of the world." An exhaustive but easy-to-read modern work, though published years ago, is Will Durant's remarkable volume *The Life of Greece*. It is an encyclopedic tome written in a direct, engaging style. A more recent work of scholarly nature but written in personal vein and salted with anecdotes of the author's travels, is *Greek Horizons* by Helen Hill Miller.

Athens was the incubator and nursery of the Hellenic spirit, and with few exceptions everybody who was anybody was born in this city, or elected to live here. It was almost solely for the aura of its great name that it was chosen, in 1834, as the capital of the modern Kingdom of Greece, replacing Nauplia, which had served as such during the first few years of the kingdom. At the time of this choice it was a bedraggled village. It had no commerce or industry worth mentioning. The region it centers, Attica, is largely barren. But this was ATHENS, city of Pallas Athena, scene of the miracle of the birth of Western civilization.

I think it is entirely true to say that no one city, even of twenty times its then modest population, ever produced in a short period so many men of brilliance in so many fields as did Athens in the Golden Age of Pericles.

The Athens you will see is a bright, modern metropolis of almost a million and a half inhabitants surrounding its treasured ruins. The Greeks are a clean race, outstandingly clean. Enter any humble home that is "unrehearsed" for your visit in some small hamlet of the mainland or any of the islands and be amazed at the meticulous cleanliness of the place. Perhaps you think I have my countries mixed and am talking about Holland or Switzerland, but no, I am talking about Greece, in the eastern Mediterranean.

The Hellenic Hub of Touring

At about the beginning of the present decade Greece fairly leaped into the tourist limelight as the trickle of holiday visitors grew into a stream and then a torrent, the number doubling in a few short years to a present annual tally of a hundred thousand or more. New hotels, several hundred of them, intelligently designed to give comfort to the spirit, and usually to the budget as well, sprang up at key points everywhere, not only on the mainland but on the far-flung islands of Greece. In the city of Athens a dozen new hotels, some of them large ones, burst into bloom, but still most of them, the central ones at any rate, were jam-packed. This tight situation, eased by the 1963 opening of the luxurious 480-room *Athens Hilton*, will continue to improve as more new hotels, already planned, take shape.

Air, sea, road and rail connections to and beyond Athens have multiplied rapidly and have improved in quality, making the Greek capital the unchallenged hub of travel, not only throughout Greece itself, including the islands, but to all the Near East countries bordering the Mediterranean and to the country of Cyprus *in* the sea.

This surge of travel, one must say frankly, is not based primarily on any general tourist passion for the "glory that was Greece," though that plays its glamorous part, but on the urge to enjoy the glory that *is* Greece, meaning scenic beauty in infinite variety, blue seas and bright islands with white towns and villages climbing the heights, all made joyously available by an average three hundred almost cloudless days a year, including the winter solstice when the "halcyon days" of Greek mythology precede and follow the shortest day.

To emerge from generalities to specifics let's take a panoramic look at the transportation picture as it involves *reaching Athens*. Later we shall consider traveling within Greece and continuing to other lands of the eastern Mediterranean.

The approach to Greece by air and sea, including the really remarkable new car-ferry service from Brindisi to Corfu and Patras, has been substantially covered in Chapter 2, but I should add here a point for motorist consideration, namely the completion of a long trans-Balkan highway from Belgrade, Yugoslavia, to Athens. More importantly, a further word is needed about *Olympic Airways*, Greece's own air system, both national and international.

This company's growth has been little short of phenomenal, for it was only founded in 1957, when an exclusive twenty-year contract was signed with the Greek government. Its fleet of about thirty planes provides Comet jets, some named for Greek queens, on its international flights, and I have found the service efficient and courteous. The meticulous thoroughness of its training of flying and technical personnel in England (for jets) and Switzerland (for piston aircraft) is a matter of national as well as company pride and the same thoroughness attends the training of its stewards and hostesses, each of whom *must* speak good English and one other non-Greek language.

The *Hellenikon Airport* of Athens is at present fearfully crowded and hectic, the terminal building outmoded and inadequate, but the skies brighten, for the Civil Aviation Department of the Greek government is vigorously at work on plans for a modern building, the design having been prepared by the famous Finnish architect Eero Saarinen. Despite the discomforts of the present building Hellenikon is among the most exciting airports in Europe. To it and from it most of the international air lines you've heard of and some you probably haven't wing their way from and to all points of the compass, including, most emphatically, the Near East, Middle East and Far East. The lines I have chiefly used are Air France and Olympic, but others that may concern you, to name a few, are Pan American, BOAC, TWA, KLM, SABENA, Alitalia, Lufthansa and such eastern specialists as MEA (Middle East Airlines), Cyprus Airways and UAA (United Arab Airlines). So important is

Olympic at the Hellenikon that a considerable part of the congested building is set aside for its exclusive use.

All this activity is reflected in the central offices of the air lines downtown. Often, Olympic's quarters, on Constitution Square, are so jampacked with customers coming and going that you almost need some husky football guard to run interference for you in reaching the counters, whether in the domestic section or the international. Air France, on the other hand, seems to have gone far in solving the problem of congestion, setting an example which other air lines and travel agencies might well follow. Behind a long, wide counter sits a row of ticket clerks, each with a full kit of information ready to hand. In front of the counter sits a row of earnest customers, calm or nervous according to disposition, each in his own armchair, absorbing the service given. Others, seated on upholstered benches nearby await their turn for the armchairs, the information service and the tickets. In another part of the room new arrivals are at the Welcome Service counter making inquiries about Athens. There is comfort in such thoughtfulness and I have no doubt that Olympic, still suffering from its growing pains, will work out some similar solution.

Information; Money; Language; Hotels; Food; Night Life

Greece is becoming ever more accessible to comfort-loving travelers, and the *National Tourist Organization of Greece* (NTO), centered at 4 Stadium Street, Athens, continues to develop its smart and pervasive promotional campaign so that we may all know the variety and comforts that this cradle of western civilization now offers to the tourist. Supplementing this head administrative office, the organization maintains two Information Offices where folders and all kinds of tourist advice are readily available. One is in the underground concourse (of which more later) in Omonia Square, the other at Number 8 Venizelos Avenue, close to the central cluster of big hotels. In New York a branch office of the National Tourist Organization has been established at 69 East 79th Street. The NTO has also a U.S. publicity representative, Bennett Associates, 6 East 45th Street, New York.

Returning to Athens, the building that houses the NTO in the very heart of the city is substantially a tourist center, with the offices of several air lines, transportation companies and prominent tourist agencies. Two of the latter are *Hermes en Grèce* and *Hellenic Express*, both of which I have used with satisfaction. *Olympos*, another active agency, is just around the corner at 4 Jan Smuts Street, mention of which leads me to a personal comment. For years a Greek lady named Mrs. Alice Coromilas, whose husband is a leading figure in the NTO, sparked Olympos with a truly remarkable know-how and personality, but in 1962 she associated herself, on a pool basis, with *Horizon Travel, Tourist and Transport Agents*, at 14 Nikis Street, just off Constitution Square, which is the city's tourist nucleus. Olympos' loss was Horizon's gain and with more freedom to work on her own Mrs. Coromilas has proved herself, in my opinion, the smartest individual in the business in Athens. Her English is as good as yours or mine and her travel contacts in the Mediterranean world are as wide as its—horizon.

The big, world organizations of travel are, of course, in the same tourist area. *American Express* is conspicuous on Constitution Square and *Cook* is close by at 6 Filellinon Street, which leads from the square parallel to Nikis Street. Olympic Airways is on the square and so is Air France. Pan American Airways is on Venizelos Avenue, no more than a stone's throw or at most two throws, from everything I have just listed. Virtually *all* the other air lines are in this same immediate neighborhood, for in tourist services Athens is one of the most concentrated of large cities. Everything one really needs is just a few steps from everything else and half a dozen of the leading hotels are also right in this nucleus.

For *printed information* the intending visitor may secure from the NTO a wealth of beautifully illustrated folders, including an excellent map of Athens and Attica packed with condensed items of practical value, but for comprehensive factual information on *everything* that concerns the tourist there is a mouth-watering annual called *Tourism in Greece*, an almanac published by *Hellenews*, whose address is 18 Voulis Street, Athens. This 160-page, lavishly illustrated book may be secured by sending a check for $3.65, or if transmission by air mail is desired, for $5.90 (but the figures may, I suppose, mount a bit). This annual is a "solid gold mine" of well-arranged factual reporting on all features and facets of Hellenic travel.

Among free publications look for a monthly tourist magazine, chock full of practical information and addresses, called *Holidays in Greece*, distributed, at least in theory, "to all tourists entering Greece." If this doesn't work out in your case the magazine is worth inquiring for from your hotel porter or travel agent. Its publication office address is 9 Stoa Pappou, Athens. Other publications are *This Week in Athens* and *Tourist Week*, the first distributed gratis by the NTO, the second sold in kiosks for 8 drachmas (24 cents). Still another publication is *Shopping Guide*, distributed by the Union of Manufacturers and Merchants of the Tourist Zone of Athens. Each of these publications includes a city plan.

Greek money has been greatly simplified since I first knew it. After World War I, and continuing to and through World War II, the drachma sank dismally from a prewar value of 20 cents to *thirty thousand* to the dollar. By exchanging $33.33 any visitor holding dollars became a Greek millionaire. Finally, the government steadied the currency and then knocked off three ciphers, making the rate thirty to the dollar. It is now a strong, respected currency and prices have settled at what I should call a medial level as compared with other European prices. Folding money is in denominations of 50, 100 and 1000 drachmas; ringing money starts, for all practical tourist purposes, at 50 lepta, which is half a drachma, which is worth about a cent and a half, though copper coins of 10 and 20 lepta do exist. Lepta is the plural of lepton, which means literally "small." There are nickel or silverish coins of 1, 2, 5 and 10 drachmas and an important silver coin of 20 drachmas, worth 66⅔ cents. A caution to be noted here is that the silver 20 is almost exactly the same size as the silver*ish* 5 and can be easily confused with it.

The *language* of Greece, which has been one of history's great media for spreading culture, is fascinating to any tourist with a bit of etymology in his system, for very many of our common words are based on Greek roots or are taken over bodily from the Greek of Pericles. It is still more fascinating to tourists like myself who studied Greek, however casually, in high school or university. Modern spoken Greek is a far cry, in idiom, vocabulary and pronunciation, from classical, but thank goodness, the letters of the alphabet, twenty-four in number, are formed exactly as they were in ancient times. Capitals are much more important for the tourist to know and recognize than are small letters, for you see them on street signs, business signs, tram and bus signs and so forth. Here, then is the "capital alphabet."

Alpha	A	Iota	I	Rho	P
Beta	B	Kappa	K	Sigma	Σ
Gamma	Γ	Lambda	Λ	Tau	T
Delta	Δ	Mu	M	Upsilon	Υ
Epsilon	E	Nu	N	Phi	Φ
Zeta	Z	Xi	Ξ	Chi	X
Eta	H	Omicron	O	Psi	Ψ
Theta	Θ	Pi	Π	Omega	Ω

Here are some specific things to note: the fifth letter, Epsilon, is sounded like *e* in let. The seventh, Eta, looks like *H* but is a long *e*, sounded like the *a* of late. The look of Theta has to be learned, as do the looks of Pi, Upsilon, Psi and Omega. The *R*, Rho, is formed exactly like our capital *P*. All other letters are easy to grasp and read. There is no *c* in Greek, the hard sound of that letter being taken over by *k* (Kappa). The letter that looks exactly like our capital *X* is a throaty, Prussian-esque *ch*, the actual *x* sound being taken over by *xi*, with its three horizontal bars in the capital form.

The oddest quirk is this: Beta is pronounced like our *v*, which leaves the Greek language with no *b* sound at all, yet the sound is absolutely necessary in coping with tourism. Hence it has been manufactured by combining the *m* and *p* sounds of Mu and Pi. Thus the important word *bar* becomes ΜΠΑΡ and Alpha Beer becomes ΜΠΥΡΑ ΑΛΦΑ. Travel posters reveal such strange places as ΜΠΕΡΛΙΝ (Berlin) and cinema posters such odd names as ΜΠΑΡΔΩ (Bardot). There's a lot of fun in sleuthing Greek signs and you will be surprised at how many you manage to pick up as your proficiency improves.

If you are ambitious to go beyond "sign language" you will do well to purchase a booklet that is a little smaller in length and width than a government postcard and that weighs only two ounces, though it has 130 pages. I refer to *Say It in Greek*, by George Pappageotes, a Columbia professor, published, in a series of "Say It" booklets, by Dover Publications, 180 Varick Street, New York City 10. This is only a phrase book, with the usual clumsy looking phonetic pronunciations of every word, but it is well arranged and has an index that serves as a sort of junior dictionary.

Hotels are a mighy subject in Athens, and only a bit less so throughout Greece. Let's take Athens first, with a condensed listing, mentioning by way of preamble that practically all the good hotels of Athens are fully air-conditioned, a feature made necessary by the city's hot summer climate. A surprising number of them, as I have said earlier, have been built in the 60's. For details of the equipment of all hotels one may consult the NTO's authorized *List of Hotels*, published annually. They are graded by letters AA, A, B and C, the first being, of course, de luxe.

Leaving aside for the moment the Athens Hilton, we find no less than half a dozen hotels of major importance clustering close together in the nucleus area, so perhaps an orientation note is needed to clarify the central city's plan.

The main stem of shopping is busy Stadium Street. It ties together Constitution Square (with the Parliament Building at the upper end) and Concord Square, the former being the tourist center of Athens, the latter the traffic center (and flower market), with busses and trams fanning out to everywhere. The underground terminal of the electric railway to the Piraeus (trains every 10 minutes), now a part of the municipality, is also located there. Just *three* Greek words of orientation are worth mastering, and being able to speak: *Stadiou* (for Stadium), *Syntagma* (for Constitution) and *Omonia* (for Concord). I once had a dreadful time on a bus because I could not think of the word Syntagma. To help fix it for you I shall henceforth call the big square by its Greek name, simply Syntagma, leaving off the word for square, which is Plateia.

Venizelos Street and Academy Street are two important thoroughfares parallel to Stadium Street. Venizelos is almost as important for shopping as the main stem, and upon it front numerous massive buildings, including the Academy, the University and the Library, all showy modern structures in the neo-Greek style.

Leading from Syntagma past the Parliament Building to the inland suburban area is Queen Sofia Avenue, a broad thoroughfare with many embassies, including the very handsome new one of the United States. The Athens Hilton is a bit farther along on this aristocratic boulevard. Leading from Syntagma toward the Gulf and the many good beaches on it is Amalia Avenue, skirting the National Gardens on the left and then passing the Acropolis. Other important streets, making a total of nine, branch off from Syntagma, but perhaps the above selections are enough to give you your bearings. The NTO publishes an excellent map called simply *Athens Greece*, with numerals spotted on it and a key to show the location of all public buildings, churches, museums, monuments, important squares and even the subway stations of the Athens-Piraeus electric railway.

Hotel Grande Bretagne, at the corner of Syntagma and Venizelos, with its main entrance directly on the square, has long been the dignified *doyen* of Athenian luxury hotels, spending vast sums to enlarge its capacity and to keep its public rooms and bedrooms abreast of the times. It offers all the amenities of a truly grand hotel that keeps service at high levels. Its huge marble lobby-lounge, its shops and travel offices, including a tour desk directly in the lounge, its modern balconied rooms, facing either Syntagma or Venizelos and Queen Sofia Avenues, combine to give it an aura of assured sophistication, but there is more than mere sophistication for this is one of those hotels, not uncommon in Europe, that has been managed for decades by a *family*, in this case Petracopoulos, père et fils, the younger Petracopoulos being now the more active. It is axiomatic that any hotel managed for a long time by father and son builds up a special pride of maintenance.

Hotel King's Palace, on Venizelos close to the corner of Queen Sofia Avenue, within a pebble's toss of Syntagma, is a relative newcomer of high quality, the central and leading unit of a group of hotels in Athens and elsewhere in Greece being developed and expanded by one of the country's most dynamic hôteliers, Takis P. Karadontis, who heads a corporation called Tourist Hotels, S.A. The King's Palace, opened late in 1959, is a first-class hotel of 240 rooms, mostly doubles, each with bath and all front rooms with balcony overlooking Venizelos Avenue. It borders on the luxury class, though it is not as yet given a de luxe rating on the NTO list. It has such expected features as a large and sumptuous dining room, three cocktail lounges, various ceremonial rooms for public receptions, a popular tearoom-card room, a streetside café and, below ground, an international cabaret, the *Coronet*. This last has long been Athens' best, but now it is, of course, faced with Hilton competition. An *un*expected feature is an active, easy-to-contact public relations office graciously directed by a Greek couple named Alec and Kaity Pomonis. In the summer months the hotel utilizes its plant-bowered roof garden as a restaurant, grillroom and sundeck, and seldom does the traveler find a rooftop retreat so inviting. By daylight or electric light the view from it is fascinating, with the Parliament House and Syntagma close at hand, the Acropolis in the middle distance and the Saronic Gulf in the background. Immediately below, the incessant traffic flows down Venizelos Street and at night the tail lights make a river of red, for the street is one-way at this point. The Tourist Hotels Corporation owning the King's Palace has acquired the adjacent building at the corner of Venizelos and Queen Sophia Avenue and will raze it to give room for the construction of a very large new part of the hotel. When this work is completed the King's Palace will rise to official luxury rating.

The corporation owns other Athens hotels that bring the present total to about a thousand beds. One is the first-class *Esperia Palace Hotel*, on Stadium Street, an air-conditioned 350-bed hotel completed in 1962–1963, another is the *Alfa*, near Omonia Square. A fourth hotel, this a new one not far from Omonia Square, is the *Marmara Palace*. This is not owned by the corporation but personally by Mr. Karadontis, who also has various hotel properties outside Athens, to be mentioned later with other extensive chains.

King George Hotel, adjacent to the Grande Bretagne on Syntagma, is a hotel of luxury rating. Special features are its very large French-style lounge on the ground floor and its delightful Tudor Hall, the main dining room, on the seventh floor. This room, with Tudor furnishings and décor, opens to a terrace high above Syntagma, on which meals may be enjoyed in the mild months.

The *Athénée Palace*, on Kolokotroni Square barely fifty steps from Stadium Street, is still another hotel of luxury class. Its lobby is a bit small, but it has a pleasant lounge on the mezzanine. This hotel has a radio in every room.

The *Amalia*, a new first-class hotel on Amalia Avenue, leading from the other side of Syntagma, has a large and devoted following. The main dining room is on the ground floor, the lounge and tearoom one floor above, and a most delightful roof garden up aloft, with a close-up view of what guests like to call their "private park," this being the lovely *National Gardens*.

The *Olympic Palace*, first class, on Philellinon Street a bit beyond the Amalia, is directly opposite the *Russian Church*, with its separate bell tower, which is one of the tourist sights of Athens. Every room has a private balcony.

The *National Hotel*, on Venizelos Avenue, several blocks from Syntagma, but still more or less in its orbit, has a luxury rating in the official listing but this seems too high. It does not have, for me at least, the appeal of those mentioned above.

Near Omonia Square there are several good hotels in addition to those of the Karadontis group mentioned above. The largest is the first-class *Ambassadeurs*, with 200 rooms, a big, bustling hostelry, more a business than a tourist hotel, though plenty of tourists patronize it. Among the good B-grade hotels are the *Atlantic*, opened in 1961, and *El Greco*, opened in 1958. Among C hotels the *Ilion* seems to have an especially good name.

The *Athens Hilton Hotel* is, one could say "of course," in a special category above the de luxe A, what Paris lists call "*hors classe*." Its acres of luxury match those of other hotels of Hilton International, now found in increasing numbers in the large cities of Europe and the Near East. Its only "out" for me is that it is located well out from the heart of the city on Queen Sofia Avenue, perhaps half a mile or more. I like to be *in* the center, but tastes in hotels, as in everything else, vary considerably and this less central location may be just what you're looking for. In any case you are sure to enjoy its superlative qualities.

Athens' suburbs may be divided into "landward" and seaside communities. Those of the first type have many good hotels in quiet locations. Kephissia, cooler because it is on higher ground, is one such suburb and of its score or so of hotels the de luxe-rated *Pentelikon* is the leader, followed by the *Cecil*.

Athens' *resort hotel* par excellence is the mountain-top *Hotel Mont-Parnes*, the justified pride of the NTO, perhaps the most noteworthy hostelry of its special type in Europe or the Mediterranean. Rising from a spur of Mt. Parnes, and seeming a part of it, the hotel soars aloft from a foundation height of 3600 feet, offering a view of Athens in its entirety, the gulf beyond it and a wide sweep of the Attic plain. Guests have a strange sense as of being quite literally out of this world, yet they are surrounded by all the luxuries of the world they "used to know." To list some of these luxuries, the Mont-Parnes has a marble lounge, of individual design, a part of which, overlooking a mirror pool with lotus flowers, serves as writing room; a swimming pool on a clifftop shelf of rock; a very large dining room so arranged as to provide a view of the world-left-below; a private cinema with regular programs; a lavish night club; a constellation of specialties such as a sky-terrace café, an outdoor dance floor that strongly resembles a flying saucer about to take off, a pool with loafing terrace at the edge of the cliff, a minigolf course, a well-equipped play room for youngsters of all ages and—much more. The hotel is managed by a Swiss hôtelier named Walter Hassler. It has accommodations for nearly three hundred guests, and the dining room can serve far more than that.

"And how do you get to this paragon hotel?" you are asking. At present you go by a paved winding highway in about forty minutes from Athens' center, but a cable railway is promised for the unspecified future. The distance from the heart of the city is 19 miles. The hotel maintains daily motorcoach service to and from a bathing beach at Voula-Cavouri.

Beach hotels, facing that string of pleasant Saronic Gulf bathing beaches that starts with the Phalerons, Old and New, and concludes with Glyfada, Voula and Vouliagmeni are numerous and of all grades, including de luxe.

The Phalerons, in the immediate outskirts of the city, consist of New Phaleron, which is actually the older, and Old Phaleron, which is the newer. New Phaleron is a station on the Piraeus Railway, hence very accessible, but both are easily reached by means of the broad motor highway called Syngrou Avenue and Old Phaleron is much more of a summer resort, with popular hotels, cafés and restaurants. In 1962–63, the Phalerons as a team were greatly enhanced by the opening of a half-million-dollar *Reception Pavilion and Tourist Salon* financed by the Piraeus Port Authority. As a reception pavilion its role is to welcome distinguished foreign visitors, including royalty, four rooms of charm and simple elegance being set aside for this purpose. Boats will bring the celebrities from their anchored ships directly to a special landing pier in front of the pavilion. As a tourist project the building and its appurtenances serve a much wider purpose. There is a large public dining room one flight up and on the ground floor a bar and snack bar partly in the open air. There is also a seaside promenade that is much enjoyed by evening strollers. A small harbor provides moorings for launches and motorboats and there is parking space for 300 cars. A swimming pool and an aquarium are contemplated, though these features are not yet assured. Certainly the ensemble of this ambitious project has given a much-needed boost to the Phalerons, which have lately been rather eclipsed by newer resorts along the gulf coast.

As one drives along the shore boulevard the better hotels seem to develop a sort of crescendo of excellence. The new, first-class *Hotel Saronis* at Kalamaki is well thought of, and the still newer *Congo Palace* at Glyfada is luxurious. Its owner, Theodore Chalicakis, spent twenty-five years in the Congo, made a lot of money and returned to Athens to spend much of it on this gleaming hostelry. It is a marble palace of moderate size not quite on the sea but on the highway close to it. Its restaurant, with open terrace, and its lounge bar are adorned with murals of Congo life done by a Congolese artist. It has three floors, with 18 doubles and 6 singles on each, and above this a roof garden. Open-air dancing is a summer feature of this Congo-in-Europe. Adjacent to it, but not owned by it, is the *Romantica* night club.

Two places of beach-bungalow type, both built and owned by *Astir*, which is the insurance company of the National Bank of Greece, are of such outstanding quality as to constitute headline news of today's Greek tourism. Both bear the general name Astir-Bungalows and both are also called *Asteria Beach*, identification being made by attaching to it the name of the community. The first one encountered as one drives along the coast is thus *Asteria Beach Glyfada*. The still newer and more impressive one is the *Asteria Beach Vouliagmeni*. The first has 100 twin-bed bungalows, the other about 70, with more building. I cannot exaggerate the sheer excellence of these remarkable beach communities, each entered by the motorist or taxi-borne guest through guarded portals. The Vouliagmeni resort has a restaurant building strikingly placed on a seaside knoll, but meals may also be had, at no extra charge, in one's own cabin if desired. An additional 120-room hotel is being built by Astir on this same Vouliagmeni "enclave," but the demand is so great, as also for the bungalows in both Astir resorts, that all accommodations are booked solid in summer, from June through September. If you wish to give yourself a memorable treat be very forehanded and book early, either through your travel agent or by writing to Astir at 38 Stadium Street, Athens.

Greek food challenges conservative taste buds and usually wins out in the end. The "experimentalist" delights in it, as does the gourmet who isn't too tightly tethered to established habits. Greek beverages, on the other hand, may need a lot of learning, some of them anyway.

I shall try to present a few of the enticing specialties of the cuisine, naming them in our Latin letters and not worrying overly about spellings. *Dolmas* is a richly seasoned rice, wrapped in grape leaves and cooked with oil. *Dolmadakia*, including minced meat and eggs with the rice, is similarly wrapped and cooked. I have found it marvelous. *Barbouni* is a Mediterranean red mullet, greatly favored by Greek epicures. *Kopanisti* is roe with sharp cheese, a bold but excellent item. To top off your meal you might try *kataifi*, a noodle affair, looking like shredded wheat, filled with a nutty stuffing and drowned in syrup. It is one of the sweetest of desserts, almost cloying.

A Hymettus-type wine, white and dry, popular with Athenians, is produced in quantity by a company named *Kampa*. *Demestica* is another company whose white, dry wine is frequently encountered, and enjoyed. A good red wine is *Samos*, a good rosé *Kokkineli*. A word on the famous (some palates say infamous) retsina wines of Greece will be given below. Greek beers are not, in my opinion, up to the European average, but they are at least fair to middling and if served *cold* can be pleasurable, especially when imbibed in a sidewalk or seaside terrace café. The Greek climate lends itself to such pleasures. A brand called *Alpha*, mentioned above in connection with our language run-down, is conspicuous, as is FIX, which has a big modern brewery, pointed out as a tourist sight, on Syngrou Avenue, the main Athens–Piraeus highway. *Metaxa* brandy is definitely recommendable, but a far more typical Hellenic beverage, usually taken as an apéritif, is *ouzo*, an anise drink that turns cloudy white when mixed with water and has a kick like a hydrogen bomb. Many Greeks sip ouzo, well watered, as a standard table beverage to lubricate lunch or dinner, and by persistent effort I have learned to do likewise, and like it.

The *taberna*, which we may spell taverna since beta is pronounced like *v*, is a basic institution of Greece, an intrinsic feature of tourism. One finds these typical little restaurants, casual and unpretentious, everywhere in and around Athens. They abound in the central Plaka section of the city near the base of the Acropolis, in the Tourkolimano Harbor section of the Piraeus and on the Castella Peninsula above it, and along the beaches south of Athens, while other good ones are to be found in such suburbs as Kephissia and Ekali. Of late years some of the central Athenian tavernas have become actual night clubs, with lavish floor shows, thus losing the simple character of the original taverna, which is highly atmospheric and is usually made gay by the music of strolling guitarist-singers. In places of this type spontaneous singing by Greek patrons, and even tourists, is common, this feature having been given quite a boost by the comic film of 1960, *Never on Sundays*, which was chock full of taverna scenes. Spoofing the efforts of a tourist visitor to reform a Piraeus prostitute, this hilarious film's theme song became, and has remained, almost as important a "prop" of Greek tavernas as the theme song of the long-past thriller film *The Third Man* has of Vienna Keller restaurants.

My comment on tavernas is offered partly by way of introducing certain items of sea food and the wine that goes with them. At a humble beachside taverna named *Kalliopi's* I first scraped acquaintance with a dish called *kalamarakia*, being fried baby squid, and I found it wonderful. The traditional thing to drink with it is *retsina* wine, so named because it contains resin. It takes a lot of conscientious learning by an American palate, but once learned it is liked. I know because I forced my reluctant palate to learn. However, if you do not wish to impose this task on yours you need only say to your waiter, when ordering wine at any taverna, *"Aresinato,"* which means without resin. Another marine dish popular at tavernas is *marides* (whitebait), and the above-mentioned barbouni is always in demand.

To name a few good tavernas of the simple type I would call attention to three in the Plaka area of Athens, namely the *Xynou* (without music); the *Vakhos* (Bacchus), with a splendid city view from the terrace; and the *Epta Adelfia* (Seven Brothers). Among places outside of central Athens I might mention the *Soupies*, at Kalamaki on the sea boulevard to Athens' airport; the *Samaltanis*, in Kefissia; and the *Aura*, in Tourkolimano, though this last is now swamped with bus-tour tourists every evening. A very special place of lavish fare in Piraeus is the *Taverna Basilainas*, where a meal may prove a formidable affair. You don't order anything. The waiter just brings it—unendingly —and you wash down as many of its courses as you can manage with equally unending retsina. The final course turns out to be fish and soup.

A particular variety of taverna is called *bouzoukia*, a term covering the whole genus. In the bouzoukia the only musical instrument used is a sort of outsized Oriental mandolin that was introduced to Athens some forty years ago by Greeks fleeing from Asia Minor. These places, unlike many of the tavernas, are not tourist-conscious. Three worth considering bear the glamorous names *Triana*, *Pindos* and *Rossignol* (Nightingale).

Conventional restaurants are fairly numerous in Athens but I should say that few of them are outstandingly good and there is no doubt that tourists tend to patronize either their own hotel dining rooms *or* the tavernas. A few separate restaurants, however, deserve honorable mention. *Averoff*, on Apollo Street just off Syntagma, is a leader; *Kosti's*, on Korai Street, is another. Venizelos Street abounds in eating places, led in popularity by *Zonar's* and *Floca*, both close to the hotel sector and both doubling as afternoon tearooms, with broad sidewalk terraces. Farther along the same street are *Tsitas*, *Palladion* and *Pantheon*, all good. The *Corfu*, on central Jan Smuts Street, is less expensive, and in the YMCA, on Amerikis Street, there is a budget-conscious cafeteria.

The *night life* of Athens is of various types and falls into several brackets, from elegant to seamy, but except for the tavernas there is little about it to lure the overseas visitor. For elegance the hotel cabarets, especially in the Hilton and the King's Palace (Coronet) are at the top, but in summer they yield their popularity to such chic places as the *Asteria*, in the Astir Bungalow Colony at Glyfada Beach, and the *Country Tavern* at Ekali.

Of the fashionable *taverna-night clubs* the present leaders, all in Athens, seem to be *Vrachos* (meaning Rock), *Kastro* (Castle) and *Palia Athena* (Old Athens). Another called *Folia Tis Alepous* (Fox Hole) has also won attention. I recently witnessed a floor show in the Palia Athena that would have done credit to a metropolitan nightery in Paris or New York, but the orchestra could hardly wait to strike up the hackneyed "Never on Sundays" theme. "Tourists expect it," said a waiter to me.

Entertainment of real Hellenic nature is far more worth seeking and this exists in plenty, especially during the warm months. For one thing there is the many-featured *Athens Festival*, running from August 1 to September 15, this being preceded by the *Epidaurus Festival*, from mid-June to mid-July. A major attraction of the Athens Festival is the open-air *Odeon of Herodes Atticus*, an ancient theater at the base of the Acropolis, where classical Greek plays and symphony concerts are presented. Restored for modern use, the Odeon seats 3500 persons. Among the plays staged are the great tragedies of Aeschylus, Sophocles and Euripides and the racy comedies of Aristophanes. In the field of music, audiences are privileged to hear the greatest orchestras in the world, led by the greatest maestros. Celebrated soloists and ballet companies add variety to the symphony concerts.

A newer and even more glamorous evening attraction, offered three times a week (except on nights of full moon or nearly full) for a five month period from the first of May to the end of September, is the Sound and Light Pageant called *The Acropolis of Athens*. Spectators make their way by bus, taxi or footwork to the Pnyx Hill, directly across a valley from the Acropolis, and are seated on folding chairs at a cost of only a dollar apiece (but a comforting cushion is 65 cents extra!), whence they may see and hear the spectacle in Greek at 8:30, English at 9:30 or French at 10:30.

It is stirring drama about the great days of ancient Hellas. While watching the lights play in changing patterns and colors on the peerless Acropolis, now picking out the Parthenon, now the Erectheum, now the Propylaea, and now that diminutive gem, the Temple of Niké Apteros, we are brought into the very presence of the classical Athenians by listening to the people as they worry, for example, about their war with the Persians. The talking and the sound effects, as in all the Sound and Light shows, are transmitted by cleverly concealed loud-speakers planted, in this case, at various points on and near the Pnyx. We hear the distant footsteps of a runner. Can it be? Yes, it is— the courier from the field of Marathon. The sound of the footfalls grows louder, nearer, and then we hear the panting message of the runner, who gasps out the great news of *victory at Marathon* and then falls in death, his mission accomplished. In another scene we hear the oracle warning the Athenians to seek safety within the "wooden walls," meaning the fleet, and so we are led to the bay and to the naval victory of Salamis, won by Themistocles. Still another scene has us listening, and in imagination watching, as priests decorate the statue of Athena Parthenos at the conclusion of the Panathenean Day. (For more on this see the description of the Parthenon in Chapter 13.) There are *never* any live actors or actresses, only voices, sounds and clever lighting, but the effect is all the more eerie for that. The French association that dreamed up the whole idea of *Son et Lumière* (Sound and Light) stages it here, as in many other countries, in co-operation with local authorities.

Would you like a good anticlimax? You may find it in the low dives that call themselves night clubs. I have a fair collection of cards, given me by touts in central Athens, each inviting me to patronize one of these boîtes, but I have never managed to find just the right evening to accept the invitation. The *Miami-Bar*, on Venizelos Avenue, promises "Low Prices, The Best Drinks, HOT Music, Full and Complete Satisfaction, 20 GIRLS." The *Copacabana*, on Korai Street, is 50 per cent more ambitious, promising "Strip Tease Show With 30 Beautiful Girls, Low Prices. The Best Place To Amuse Your Self." Well—this last claim might be debatable. It's a safe bet, in any case, that your *budget* will not be amused in any of these dives.

CHAPTER 13

OLD ATHENS AND SOME TETHERED TOURS

Twelve Steps to the Acropolis

THE *Acropolis of Athens* is a world in itself. No other Mediterranean city has so compact a nucleus of sights. Not only is the rock itself covered with great temples but the history-laden Pnyx and Areopagus are close by. At the base of the Acropolis are the stone theaters of ancient times, the Odeon of Herodes Atticus and the Theater of Dionysus, and a quarter mile to the southeast rise Hadrian's Arch and the Temple of Zeus. Just across the Ilissus River, a dry one much of the year, is the great marble Stadium.

A few things may need special finding, for example the wonderfully preserved Temple of Hephaestus, sometimes called the Theseum; the Tower of the Winds, where a water-clock and sundial kept the time for Athens; the best of the old Byzantine churches; two remarkable museums, the National Archeological and the Benaki; and even the chapel-crowned hill of Lycabettus, which soars from the heart of the city. This has as yet only a single, elusive path of approach to the summit, though a funicular is under (intermittent) construction. In general, it is fair to say, Athens is one of the easiest large capitals of Europe for the stranger to understand, as it is one of the hardest for the stranger to resist.

Every Greek city had an acropolis, a citadel on lofty ground, but Athens alone had *The Acropolis*, spelled by dictionaries as well as by tourists with a capital *A*. The standard tours of the city build up, in a natural crescendo, from great sights to greater and greatest, with the Parthenon and Erectheum on the Acropolis as the resonant notes of climax. For the sake of tourist convenience, and because it makes sense, the ensuing report, or syllabus, shall do likewise, numbering the "steps" to the uppermost goal. Daily guided tours, starting by bus

230

from Venizelos Avenue close to Syntagma, are conspicuously offered, even trumpeted, and able cicerones are securable through the National Tourist Organization or any travel agency. Printed guidebooklets are purchasable at any news kiosk.

1. As an opener, the tour-taker under the wing of a professional guide is usually shown the *Tomb of the Unknown Soldier*, in front of the Parliament Building, that barrack-like mass (on Syntagma) which was the old royal palace. The memorial is an interesting relief of a soldier of ancient times. *Evzone* guards pace solemnly back and forth in front of it. In a special ceremony the guards are changed every Sunday morning at 11:15. Evzones are the most picturesquely clad soldiers in the world, surpassing in color even the Scotch "kilties." With tasseled cap, embroidered white tunic, short flaring skirt, "long-handled drawers," white but gartered in black, and with shoes graced by gay pompons at the toes, they seem like something from the chorus of an operetta, but they are, in fact, muscular men of battle, and during the conflicts in the years from 1912 to 1921 Evzones were among the best fighting troops in any war theater. Nowadays, the Evzones are used exclusively as guards for the royal palace and for such national monuments as the above. The regular infantry wears khaki. Athens' Royal Palace is no sight in itself but its guards, these skirted élite of Greek soldiery, certainly are.

2. The *Stadium* was first built under Lycurgus, statesman and orator, about 330 B.C., filling a natural hollow. It was used for the Panathenean Games, not to be confused with the earlier Olympic Games. The quadrennial Olympic Games, to clarify this point, were started in 776 B.C. in Olympia, Peloponnesus, site of the forty-foot gold and ivory statue of Zeus by Phidias, one of the Seven Wonders of the World. The four-year periods between the games were called Olympiads and were used by the Greeks as their calendar, which began with the first holding of the games. In 393 A.D. this pagan calendar was finally abolished by Christian Emperor Theodosius and for good measure he abolished also all pagan games.

At the Panathenean Games in Athens the stadium spectators stood, or sprawled on the banking, for there were no seats. About two centuries after Lycurgus (above) the Athenian plutocrat Herodes Atticus rebuilt it all in white marble from Mount Pentelicus, using for this munificence virtually all the remaining stone of the quarries then open. The Stadium could seat, at that time, about fifty thousand spectators. Some four centuries later, under Theodosius (above), these games were discontinued and the Stadium fell into disrepair. In the period of their blighting ascendancy the Turks used it as a ready-made quarry and removed all the marble, but in 1896 a modern Greek millionaire named Averoff, a resident of Alexandria, restored it once more in marble, providing seats for seventy thousand, and the quadrennial Olympic Games were revived, this time in Athens. The first holding of them was in this Stadium in the year named above, and special Olympic Games, not in the four-year cycle were held here also in 1906. To open the games a flaming torch was brought by runners all the way from Olympia, a distance of over two hundred miles, the flame, produced from the sun's rays, being from the Temple of Olympian Zeus in that distant city.

3. The *Temple of Zeus*, lying directly between the Stadium and the Acropolis, was once the largest in Greece and nearly all of it was of marble, but the Turks used this, too, as a quarry and only some bits are left. The temple was started by Pisistratus a century before the time of Pericles, but it was in the reign of Emperor Hadrian, during the era of Roman occupation, that it was completed. Its base was about 120 yards in length by 45 in breadth. Sixteen of its 104 marble Corinthian columns now remain. On top of one of the columns a medieval monk lived in a tiny hut for twelve years, some 56 feet above ground. He was, however, a comparatively recent "pillar sitter," for Simeon Stylites of Syria started the custom in the fourth century A.D. and his pillar was 72 feet high. *Hadrian's Arch*, marking the boundary line of the old wall between Greek Athens and the newer Roman quarter, is at the western edge of the temple enclosure. The Greek side is inscribed: "This is the Athens of Theseus, the former city." The Roman side is inscribed: "This is the Town of Hadrian, not Theseus."

4. Two blocks distant from Hadrian's Arch is a structure as beautiful as it is hidden and small. It is the *Choragic Monument of Lysicrates*, meaning that it was set up to exhibit the prize won by Lysicrates for the excellent singing of his boys choir in the Dionysiac Games in 335 B.C. Such monuments, resembling minuscule temples, were customary for choral winners and in ancient times there was a long row of them,

beginning at the exit of the Theater of Dionysus. This is the only survivor. It is well preserved because it became the library of a convent of French Capuchins that existed here until the founding of the modern Kingdom of Greece.

5. The *Theater of Dionysus*, Greek equivalent of Bacchus, is one of those at the base of the Acropolis. Originally there was a small wooden building for the actors, an "orchestra," meaning a central stage where they stood reciting their lines, and a hillside where the spectators sat as best they could. Later, wooden seats were provided, and finally substantial stone ones, the front row, made of Pentelic marble, being for high dignitaries. Here the plays of Aeschylus, Sophocles, Euripides, Aristophanes and others (what a roster of "local playwrights"!) were first presented. I once sat in the throne-like marble seat of the high priest of Hephaestus (Vulcan) and listened to my Greek professor, "Charlie D.," as he recited, and translated and explained, some lines from "The Frogs," by Aristophanes. This was one of the dramatist's pointed comedies, full of subtle digs and local hits. Those who were not the victims of the digs and hits must have been in stitches. Perhaps even the high priest of Hephaestus may have indulged in some good belly laughs at the expense of rival priests of rival gods.

6. The *Odeon of Herodes Atticus* is the other theater at the base of the Acropolis. The same generous citizen who first marbled the Stadium built this, as a place for concerts and lyric plays, in memory of his wife, Appia Annia Regilla. The lofty façade of the actors' building, once four stories high and roofed with cedar, still stands in part. The theater seats 3500 spectators and is now used, as I have said, for summer concerts, classic dramas, dance festivals and other performances.

7. The *Hill of Philópappos*, to the southwest of the Odeon, offers from its summit a superlative view of the ensemble of Athens and its classic hills. On the crest is a forty-foot marble statue, from the second century A.D., of Philópappos himself, an Asia Minor kinglet who became a naturalized Athenian. In January, 1951, a lightning bolt struck the statue and demolished the top portion. Philópappos lost his head, and other needed parts of his person, but all has long since been restored.

8 and 9. The *Pnyx* and the *Areopagus*, flanking the motor road that

skirts the Acropolis, have been already mentioned. The Areopagus, peopled in our imaginations with many dramatic figures of the past, is especially interesting as a reverie hill.

10. *Propylaea* is the plural of the Greek word meaning Before-Gate and it signifies an entrance too grand or grandiose to be a mere Gate. The Propylaea of the Acropolis, built under Pericles' direction, is a Golden-Age approach to the hill of the Golden Age. It is a central portico building, with two smaller porticoes at right and left. The imposing columns that face us from three sides are of the Doric order, meaning that they have no base at all and their capitals are severely simple. Within the central part of the Propylaea, on either side of the stone roadway, we find a double row of Ionic columns, always recognizable by the spiral volutes (curlycues to us laymen) of their capitals. (There are no Corinthian columns on the Acropolis, but since we are on the subject of the famous three orders of Greek architecture, Corinthian columns are recognized by their capitals in the shape of inverted bells surrounded by acanthus leaves. The fifteen columns of the Temple of Zeus, one of the steps of this basic tour, are Corinthian.)

11. The superb little *Temple of Athena Niké,* called also *Wingless Victory (Niké Apteros)*, the name signifying that victory was robbed of wings so that she could not take flight, is on the north side of the Propylaea. The Turks, when they used the Acropolis as an arsenal, destroyed this wonderful structure to make room for a battery, but nineteenth-century German archeologists found most of the fragments in sufficiently good shape so that the temple could be, and was, faithfully rebuilt.

12. *The Acropolis itself* needs here a word of review, since it is the heart of the Athens we are seeing. This conspicuous rock, rising 230 feet above the city and 520 above the sea, was a mythical stronghold of the gods and then the actual stronghold and council chamber of the earliest Athenian kings. Pisistratus embellished it with fine buildings, but in the year 480 B.C., when the Athenians, at the bidding of the oracle, retired to their "wooden walls," oracle talk for ships, and Themistocles then won the naval battle of Salamis, the Persians, having temporarily overwhelmed Athens itself, "wiped off" the Acropolis as clean as a washed slate. The Persians had to quit Greece because of

their disastrous naval defeat and then Themistocles and Cimon built
the encircling walls of the Acropolis. At this time also the whole city
set to work with a will and built the Long Walls, tying Athens to the
Piraeus and to Phaleron. Shortly thereafter came Pericles and the
Golden Age. The Acropolis we know dates largely from that era and
is definitely a hill consecrated to gods and heroes.

Two thousand years later it was the turn of the Turks to take over.
They captured Athens in 1456 and made it a down-at-heel provincial
town, which it remained until Greek independence restored it in the
last century. The Venetians were enemies of Turkey and twice attacked Athens, in 1464 and 1687. The defenders hesitated not at all
to make the Acropolis their arsenal and fortress. They stored much
powder in the Parthenon, which was then serving partly as a mosque,
complete with soaring minaret, and some also in the Propylaea and, as
stated above, they tore down the lovely Niké temple. About the middle
of the seventeenth century a bolt of lightning struck the Propylaea
powder magazine and wrecked that structure. In 1687, a "lucky"
bomb hurled by the Venetians hit the Parthenon powder magazine
squarely, and the terrible resulting explosion wrought damage beyond
any appraiser's power to compute. In 1801, Lord Elgin "hit the
Parthenon when it was down" by taking much of the best sculpture
to London, where it still reposes in the British Museum. Modern
restoration, bit by patient bit, some of it, alas, poorly done, has brought
the Parthenon perhaps "half way back" to what it was when seventeenth-century war precipitated ruin. It should be mentioned that this
century's Nazis did *not* bomb the Acropolis, as the Allies, in taking
Rome did *not* bomb the sacred monuments of that city.

The *Parthenon*, even in its present imperfect state, is a masterpiece
of masterpieces, indescribable in words. It must be seen, and in all
lights, including moonlight, a thing which is quite practicable, for the
public is allowed on the Acropolis on nights when the moon is full,
or nearly so. One may state that there are forty-six Doric columns,
some in restoration, that there was, just below the cornice, a continuous
frieze, made by Phidias and his pupils, the greatest work of its kind
ever achieved in any land in any age, running 524 feet around the
building. I have an ancient Baedeker and thirty-seven words of it
demand quoting. "On the W. front the frieze is still in its place, and

there are also a few fragments on the S. side; twenty-two slabs are preserved in the Acropolis Museum, and the rest are in London." The five concluding words seem, somehow, the saddest—"the rest are in London." Lord Elgin, the envoy extraordinary to Turkey, wangled from the sultan a royal decree permitting him to remove from the Acropolis "a few blocks of stone with inscriptions and figures." A hundred laborers were employed by him to take away the "few blocks of stone" as the few grew to most of the frieze, many of the metopes and also the very celebrated sculpture of the east and west pediments, these being the triangular spaces formed by the gables. He took from the Erectheum, of which more presently, a caryatid (one of six), a column and some other desirable bits. The British government bought the whole lot for £36,000, said to be about two-thirds of what it had cost Lord Elgin to get them to London. Vindicators of the Englishman are earnest in claiming that he "probably saved them from destruction." Perhaps this is quite true, but it sounds rather grimly reminiscent of many other takers of spoils in all ages who have removed treasures "for safe keeping."

Before wandering quite away from the Parthenon I must call attention to some tricks of the trade which the Pericleans mastered as no others before or since have ever done. The columns all have a slight swelling in the middle and this makes them *look* straight. Architects call it entasis. Also, the columns all taper toward the top and lean very slightly inward. The corner columns are a bit thicker than the others, to prevent them from looking thinner. All these devices, in the field of mathematical-optical science, serve to correct mistakes which human vision would otherwise make. The whole line of columns also bends slightly, again to make it look straight. No line in the Parthenon is quite straight and not one of the loftily placed, square metopes is actually quite square, but all lines and metopes *look* magnificently straight and square when seen from the gazer's perspective. If this sounds fantastic just let your own eyes compare the Parthenon with, for instance, Napoleon's "Temple of Glory," now the Church of the Madeleine, in Paris. The lines of the Madeleine *are* straight—absolutely—and so are all the columns, but how flat and dull they look beside the beauty of the lifelike Parthenon, yielding to the faults of human vision.

Another Periclean trick was to make the flutes, of which there are twenty to each column, grow *narrower*, though no less deep, as they mount toward the capital. This gives a fascinating effect of "extra shadow." In Centennial Park, in Nashville, Tennessee, is an exact reproduction of the Parthenon, built of closely similar marbles and in the same exact dimensions, decorated and colored identically, though some missing parts required scholarly guesswork. This Parthenon, too, goes in for entasis and for curves to correct the incorrect vision of man. Since one cannot see the original Parthenon as Athenians saw it, fresh from the plans of Pericles and Phidias and Ictinus and Callicrates, it is decidedly worth while to view this painstaking copy in Nashville.

The Parthenon's reason for being, unless beauty was its own reason, was to house a magnificent gold and ivory statue of Athena Parthenos, or Athena Virgin, another masterpiece of Phidias. This was about forty feet high. The eyes were of onyx and their pupils were precious stones. At the conclusion of the Panathenean Games of 438 B.C., the populace first gained admittance to the newly finished Parthenon and first saw the city's patron goddess, as conceived by Phidias. The virgins of Athens had woven a huge saffron-colored *peplos,* or robe, for her and at this ceremony it was placed upon her towering form. Those were surely great days when the West was being born.

The *Erectheum* may seem, when compared with the Parthenon, like an anticlimax of the Acropolis, but this is not fair to the smaller temple, for it, too, is an architectural treasure of the first importance. It was dedicated to Athena Polias, meaning Athena of the City, in her capacity as guardian of Athens. Its feature of widest fame is its Portico of the Maidens, or Caryatides, where six larger-than-life maidens, each with a basket of fruit on her head, support very easily and gracefully the heavy stone entablature. The maiden next to the end on the west is a *copy* of the original, now with the Elgin Marbles in London. The word Caryatides, by the way, is a modern one deriving from the beautiful dancers, or maybe priestesses, of the ancient town of Caryae, near Sparta. Parthenon guides like to assert that Caryae produces, to this day, the loveliest women of Greece.

Of the separate monuments of Athens that do not fall clearly into the pattern of steps to the Acropolis, the most important is the *Temple of Hephaestus,* so often called, or miscalled, the *Theseum.* It is now thought to have been erected to Hephaestus, the Vulcan of the Greeks, and perhaps also to Athena as co-deity. The marvel of it is its almost perfect preservation. It was probably completed about 421 B.C., a date which has been found in one of its inscriptions, and it became a Christian church in medieval times. Doubtless its relatively sheltered position in the lee of the Areopagus helped to save it, but sheer luck must have played a large part. The Greek Temple of Neptune at Paestum, near Naples, and the Temple of Concord at Agrigento, in Sicily, are rivals for the title of "best preserved," but neither quite matches this "Hephaesteum" of Athens and neither has the golden patina of Pentelic marble that illumines this as if with an inner glow.

Among the churches of Athens two stand out and neither one of them is the large *Metropolitan Church*, or Cathedral of Saint Mary, despite the glitter of that church's interior. This structure was built from the materials of seventy smaller churches and chapels that were demolished. One of the artistically important ones is the tiny church of *Panaghia Gorgo-epikoös*, meaning "Our Lady of Quick Hearing," actually a sort of Metropolitan Chapel adjacent to the cathedral and dedicated to St. Eleftherios. It is a fascinating bit of "church jewelry" dating from the ninth century. Its chief treasure is a block of gray marble inscribed: "This is the stone from Cana of Galilee, where Jesus Christ our Lord turned the water into wine." Scholarship considers that this probably *was* a stone bench, that its source may be traceable to Cana, and that Jesus therefore may have sat on it.

The other Byzantine church worth finding, and it is near those just mentioned, is the *Church of Kapnikarea*, another ninth-century one that stands squarely in the middle of Hermes Street, a thoroughfare leading directly to Syntagma. Each of these little masterpieces is built in the Byzantine style of a cross surmounted by a dome, but the one named Kapnikarea is complicated by an amazing array of tiled gables. Certainly it is the Church of Seven Gables—and then some.

This book, contrary to those of Baedeker inspiration, has not often stressed museums. It feels that few pleasure travelers develop a sufficient sense of leisure to enjoy them in a way that gives them meaning. But there are two in Athens that are able to overcome "museum inertia," the *National Archeologial Museum* and the *Benaki Museum*.

The first-named is one of the world's richest in ancient Greek sculpture. I would offer eight samples of perfection for you to look for, though your guide, if you have one, will not let you miss them anyway.

1. A large bronze *Poseidon* (Neptune), done by the school of Phidias, is called by some students the greatest of Greek bronzes. It was "caught," in five or six pieces, by fishermen off Cape Artemision, in Boeotia. The sea god presumably held a trident in his right hand, but the trident has not been found.

2. The bronze *Jockey Boy*, done in the Hellenistic period (specifically, the second century B.C.), was found, also at or near Cape Artemision, as recently as 1928. This magnificent action piece makes you lean with the jockey and tell his (missing) steed to GO!

3. Two "*Zeuses*," one of them a small and very ancient god hurling a thunderbolt, the other large and lusty.

4. A *Soldier of Marathon*, of the army of Miltiades.

5. A splendidly fashioned bronze *Charioteer*, found near Delphi.

6. A smiling small boy, labeled *Janiskos*, whose left hand is fondling a goose. His smile is so infectious that most visitors smile as soon as they catch sight of him.

7. A "*Paris*"—maybe, who once held an apple—maybe. This handsome man, whoever he was, was fished out of the sea by a lucky fisherman.

8. A *kouros*, found in 1959 by workmen digging a subway in Piraeus and first exhibited in Athens in 1962. A kouros was a young athlete *always* sculptured standing ramrod straight. This find, one of three bronzes unearthed at the same time in Piraeus, is considered one of the great finds of our time.

The *Mycenean Room* of this same museum is so rich in treasures, many of them in gold, that it has been called the special glory of the museum. Important things to note are the *Death Masks of Agamemnon* and a pair of magnificent *Gold Cups of Vaphio*. Most of the finds in this room are from Mycenae, in Argolis, and were unearthed in the nineteenth century by the German archeologist Dr. Heinrich Schliemann.

Of intimate interest, as relating to Hellenic symbols and customs, be aware that any sculptured woman holding an *apple* in her hand is a virgin; any woman holding a *pomegranate* is a matron. And if you are wondering what the very earliest Greek women, concerned with personal beauty treatment, did for *mirrors*, note that the museum contains many terra cotta plates, each with the inner part painted jet black. These plates, when filled with water, made, and still make, very serviceable mirrors. If you doubt it, try the experiment sometime.

The *Benaki Museum*, on Queen Sofia Avenue, was a private one of a rich Athenian, but he gave it, both building and contents, to the Greek government. It was built up as one of the great *personal* museums of the world, "personally arrived at" by a skilled connoisseur, an establishment fit to be compared with the former Liechtenstein Gallery of Vienna or the Kröller-Müller Museum near Apeldoorn in Holland. Its collections cover a wide range of subjects, from archaic art to that of modern Greece and from exquisite Chinese porcelains to equally exquisite embroideries and rare books. While the National Archeological Museum is for the specialist in Hellenic sculpture the Benaki is for glimpses of what many races of the earth have done in many periods of civilization.

When emerging from the Benaki Museum the explorer of Athens may cross the avenue, enter Herodes Atticus Street and walk two or three blocks, with the *National Garden* on his right, to reach the modest *Royal Palace*, on his left. He will identify it by the guards at the entrance, these being, of course, *Evzones*.

Around the Dial of Attica

The Athens map distributed by the NTO includes a clear map of the province of Attica, with mountain elevations and sights of tourist interest indicated. This present listing of things to see shall swing around the Attic map clockwise, starting at the north. To see Attica involves careful choosing of a few things that are of primary interest, since the most satisfactory way of touring, except for those rare visitors who speak Greek, is by private car, preferably with guide, and the hire of a car will cost about twenty cents a mile, if kept for the whole circuit, and much more if used for one way only. If several travelers can team together and split up the cost it becomes less formidable. Any travel agency can arrange everything.

The *Convent of Daphni* lies northwest of Athens on the "Sacred Way" to Eleusis. Both of these historic spots may be easily included as halts on the much longer trip to Delphi (far beyond Attica's borders) *or* the one to Corinth, Mycenae and Nauplia, but being neighbors to Athens they shall be treated here as points on the dial of Attica. A feature of the ride to Daphni is an ancient and much gnarled olive tree, still bearing olives, which is said by guides to be twenty-five hundred years old and to have provided shade for Plato's outdoor academy. Knowing how much a guide's good story enlivens a trip we are perhaps entitled to apply a generous pinch of salt to this one.

Daphni (or Daphne) means laurel, or bay tree, and has reference to the nymph of that name who changed herself into a laurel to escape the pursuing Apollo. As a place name it here refers to a village nine miles northwest of Athens where there is an appealing Byzantine church, with convent, standing where a temple to Apollo once stood. A single ancient Ionic column is still embedded in one of the walls. Within the church are some exceedingly quaint mosaics about eight hundred years old, the oddest one being a representation of short-statured Zaccheus climbing a sycamore tree to see his Lord. In the dome is a large mosaic of the head of Christ. His ear is missing and it is said that Chritian Crusader soldiers, shooting at the eyes just for fun, missed them but got the Lord's ear instead. It seems an odd sport for soldiers of the cross. The church still has a sarcophagus of one of the crusading leaders, a Frankish duke named de la Roche.

Eleusis, fifteen miles from Athens, was the terminus of the Sacred Way, the place of the Great Mysteries, whose ritual secrets, on a very high spiritual plane, were so well guarded, under penalty of death for the slightest revelation, that they have never, to this day, been discovered. Freemasonry is said to be a heritage of these Mysteries. Extensive excavations of the Temple of the Mysteries are to be seen, but the scattered fragments give up none of their secerts. The Mysteries were dedicated to Demeter, the equivalent of the Roman goddess Ceres, patroness of abundant crops, whose name is incorporated in our word cereal.

Kephissia, nine miles northeast of Athens, is an attractive resort, or garden suburb, on a spur of Mount Pentelicus. It has such a cluster of hotels and so many hundreds of attractive villas that it serves both for tourists and residents as a pleasant dormitory handy to Athens.

Marathon village is twenty-eight miles northeast of Athens, but the burial mound (*soros*) marking the spot where "the Athenians, fighting for the Greeks, defeated the golden-dressed Persians" must be 26 miles and 385 yards away from the Athenian Stadium, for that is the exact official distance of today's Marathon races, including the most famous of them, from Ashland, Massachusetts, to Boston. The quoted words above are from the poet Simonides but we owe to the historian Herodotus the first account of the battle. He says that 192 Athenians were slain and their bodies lain away and then covered with the big memorial mound that we may still see rising from the Plain of Marathon, half a mile from the gulf.

The *Marathon Dam* and the resulting lake that helps to supply Athens with water may be visited a few miles to the west of the village and battlefield. The dam is tremendously impressive, and beautifully landscaped as well. In a very lovely glen at the base of the dam, *far* below the beholder on its top, a little white temple-like affair is seen. This is a replica of the *Treasury of the Athenians,* a building in ancient Delphi.

In stating that the dam, built in 1933, helps to supply Athens with water I refer by implication to the tremendous problem that long beset this fast growing metropolis. For decades there was never enough water, but heroic efforts in tapping another lake and opening many wells have finally brought relief. Leaving such problems to those whom they may concern, you will find, at the far end of the roadway across the dam, a very pleasant refreshment pavilion maintained by the NTO.

Cape Sounion, 38 miles from Athens, is the extreme southern tip of Attica, and a more dramatic beginning, or ending, of a land it would be hard to imagine. Walls of rock descend two hundred feet to the sea on every side and they are as sheer as the walls of a skyscraper. On this "prow" of Attica rise the ruins of a white temple to Poseidon, white because marble of Agresila was used instead of the marble of Pentelicus, which tends to take on that soft yellow patina so notable in the Temple of Hephaestus. This all-white marble is of coarser grain, and the strong winds of more than twenty centuries have somewhat filed the eleven columns that still stand, but the artistic effect is perhaps even heightened. The visitor will note that the Doric columns on the front row do not have the "optical corrections" of the Parthenon's columns. They are straight (without entasis) and they do not lean inward; therefore they *seem* to lean strongly outward. It is supposed to have been at Cape Sounion that Byron wrote

> "Maid of Athens, ere we part,
>   Give, oh give me back my heart!"

The poet's light o' love, at that moment, is said to have been named Therisia. His name (but not hers) is scratched into one of the pillars.

Here at Cape Sounion, as at the Marathon Dam, there is a nice refreshment house, in fact a full-fledged restaurant, with good cuisine, built and owned by the NTO but now under lease to a concessionaire. In it I enjoyed a delectable "marine platter." Persons wishing to remain for a bit at Cape Sounion will find two A-class inns, the *Aigaion* and the *Belvedere Park Motel*, both providing bath or shower with every room.

If the return to Athens is made by the coastal road along the Saronic Gulf a surprise awaits you in the area of Vouliagmeni, mentioned in Chapter 12 as the climax of the beach hotel chain south of the city. I refer to a spa called *Limne Vouliagmeni*, which has an unforgettable setting on a small sunken lake backed by a high, rugged cliff, which is penetrated by fjord-like arms of the lake. The lake water is warmed by earth's fires, and within the spa hot mineral baths used in the treatment of rheumatic troubles are available. The "cure" is supposed to take three weeks, but in three minutes you may drink in the drama of the amazing scene, perhaps from the grounds of a new hotel named *Greek Beauty* on a knoll above the spa. Vouliagmeni, by the way, means Fallen Mountain, and the cliff does indeed look as though it had fallen from the sky with such force that it cracked at several points allowing the entrance of the fjords.

The Piraeus is a big peninsular port-city and much of it is congested and uninviting, though the main water front is always a pleasant madhouse of activity, its quays lined solidly with ships of every size and type, every mission and every flag. The southeastern shore, across the peninsula which the port fills so tightly, has some very delightful stretches. *The Old Harbor* is packed with fishing boats, the *Tourkolimano Harbor* is lively with trim sailboats, and the shore avenue between them has expensive villas, some good cafés and, on a dramatic shoulder of rock, the handsome *Royal Yachting Club*. Along the Tourkolimano crescent are many sea-food restaurants with life galore. The Piraeus completes the clockwise dial of Attica and may warrant much more strolling time than the above words have suggested. At 72 Aitolikou Street is the *Taverna Basilaina*, mentioned in the food review early in this book. It is "all food and no style."

A Day for Delphi

Delphi, the ancient sanctuary of Apollo, the home of the Pythian oracle, the seat of what has been called the "first League of Nations," lies on the northern shore of the Gulf of Corinth, a little over a hundred miles from Athens. It may be reached by private car, at a cost of about seventy dollars, the trip being possible in one long day, and if the costs are shared by several persons this is moderate enough. The rugged traveler may achieve the trip individually for a tenth the outlay by ordinary bus, the plan calling for two days with an overnight halt at one of the hotels of Delphi. The leaders are the A-class *Delphi*, followed by the *Vouzas* and the simpler B-class *Appollon* and *Kastalia*. Guided tours are, of course, standard offerings of all the tour agencies. American Express prices the two-day tour at $17 to $22, inclusive of lodging and meals. It also offers a one-day tour at $10, including lunch. Two Greek firms that make a specialty of bus touring are CHAT and KEY. The busses start from Victor Hugo Street 54, where also information and tickets are procured, but the traveler who speaks no Greek will need help from an agency in planning this challenging journey.

The ride to Delphi is a delight in itself and would be so even without so supreme a goal. The road passes through Daphni and Eleusis and then, with many changes of scenery, to the plain and town of *Thebes*, which city, under the brilliant Epaminondas, had its glorious decade of supremacy over all Greece in the fourth century B.C. The town is unimportant now but its region is one of the most fertile in the country. *Aráchova*, not far short of Delphi, is a small hill town as striking in appearance as any in Italy or southern France. That is strong talk but true. It clings to the side of a very steep hill, and on a separate knoll a towered schoolhouse looms up into the blue in a way actually to suggest the pinnacle shrines of le Puy in Auvergne. The people of Aráchova make tempting hand-woven textiles which may be bought in some of the home workshops.

Delphi itself is quite as striking, in its big, awesome way, as is Ará-chova in its village way. At a height of nearly two thousand feet it clings to a slope beneath threatening cliffs of *Mount Parnassus*, and indeed Parnassus' threat has not been a vain one. Several times in the distant past grim rock slides, perhaps set in motion by earthquakes, damaged or even destroyed the Temple of Apollo, but always it was rebuilt here, for the place had a sacred quality all its own. It was the center of the Apollo cult, the place where the Earth Mother spoke in narcotic vapors to the oracle and through her to all Hellenes, and to barbarians as well. It was the religious meeting place of the city-states of Greece and the scene of the quadrennial *Pythian Games*.

The first thing the approaching visitor sees of Delphi is the Kastalia Spring, where pilgrims washed hands and feet and also drank of the spring water ever flowing through stone gargoyles. A quarter of a mile farther on is the entrance to the *Sacred Precincts*, and once inside this entrance the visitor is carried back to classical Hellas.

The *Sacred Street* winds up the steep hillside past votive offerings and then past the *Treasuries* of many state-members, the handsomest one being that of Athens, which we have seen in replica below the Marathon Dam. It is a marvelous little structure of Parian marble. Higher up, in the exact center of the Sacred Precinct, is the *Temple of Apollo*, or what remains of it. The most intriguing thing about this temple, and about Delphi itself, is the question of the exact location of the *Oracle*, the spot where the prophetic virgin (in later times a married woman) called *Pythia* sat on a golden tripod chewing laurel leaves, fell into delirium and then uttered the garbled noises which the priests alone understood and translated into hexameter verse for the inquirer. The *Adyton*, a small room within the temple, has been theoretically located and identified as the spot where she operated, above the mysterious chasm, but so thorough was the Christian obliteration that nothing is certain about its position.

The power of the Delphic Oracle was one of the strangest phenomena of all time. Even as early as the era of Homer, roughly a thousand years before Christ, she was of great importance, and for some fourteen centuries her hazy utterances, reported by the priests, guided statecraft, started or prevented wars, caused the building or the destruction of cities. Her celebrated ambiguity let her out, and the priests too, if things did not turn out as seemingly prophesied. To Croesus, king of Lydia, she said, "If you cross the Tigris you will destroy a great empire," but she forgot to say which empire and it turned out to be that of Croesus himself. Still she was right. To Alexander the Great she once said, "Go Arrive Not Die," but she neglected to place any stop periods in this telegraphic answer to his query. It could read, "Go. Arrive. Not die," or it could as well read, "Go. Arrive not. Die." Of course a system such as this lent itself to corruption, and sometimes, as asserted by Herodotus, it became an outright racket, bribery of the priests being not uncommon, but in general it maintained its strange power over the minds and will and plans of men. Even the Romans sent messages to inquire of Pythia on important matters of state.

Above the Temple of Apollo, but still within the Sacred Precinct, is the impressive hillside *theater*, dedicated to Dionysus. In its weed-grown stones I watched a peasant woman gathering wild celery, which must have seemed tame stuff to the ghost of the god of wine!

A short climb above the Sacred Precinct is Delphi's greatest surprise, a level *stadium* of considerable size clinging to the slope by its eyelashes. The visitor knows in advance that there must have been a stadium, else how could the Pythian Games have been held at all? But he cannot picture where or how it could have existed on such a slippery slope, until, upon rounding a wooded curve, one suddenly comes upon it. It is one *stadion* in length, the Delphic stadion being 631 feet. Its breadth is nearly 90 feet and the lower side was laboriously banked up to make the course level. This structure could seat six thousand spectators yet its bulk is so hidden from immediately below that it is completely invisible until one is practically in it. The monumental scenery is decidedly *not* hidden from the stadium, for the prospect is magnificent. One wonders how the watchers of the games could have kept their eyes on track and field.

On the way from the ensemble of ancient ruins to the modern village of Delphi all visitors stop at the local *museum*, which has many masterpieces found in the Sacred Precinct, the most famous being a bronze charioteer. And so to lunch or dinner at one of the hotels. A feature of this is usually Parnassus *feta*, a snow-white cheese from goat's milk, perhaps accompanied by a dry white wine called St. Helena. If the humbler

Hotel Kastilia is selected, the chief feature of the meal will be its unob-
structed view down, and still down, to Delphi's tiny port of *Itea* on an
indentation of the Gulf of Corinth. This view is even more overwhelming than that from Delphi's stadium.

Four Goals of the Peloponnesus
(CORINTH; MYCENAE; NAUPLIA; EPIDAURUS)

In one full day the four places named above can be visited from
Athens by means of a private car, at a cost of about sixty dollars, but the
agencies offer one-day tours and two-day tours, priced exactly the same
as their corresponding tours to Delphi. If Epidaurus alone is one's goal
it is entirely practical to take the Diesel train to Nauplia, the first capital
of modern Greece, and hire a car there for the relatively short run to
Epidaurus and back.

It is a bit on the awful side to rush these famous towns and sites,
though for many a tourist it must be thus or not at all. The lucky leisured ones may find many things along the day to delight their spirits,
nor is the inner man or woman forgotten. To the comfort of travelers
in the provinces of Korinthia and Argolis much is contributed by an
organization called TEAK (Tourist Enterprises for Argolis and Korinthia). TEAK has in its kit of comforts four tourist pavilions in convenient locations along the route of this tour where information and
light meals may be had. They are: *Canal*, at the Corinth Canal; *Lais*, in
ancient Corinth near the museum and the ascent to Corinth's acropolis;
Atreus, at Mycenae near the famous ruins of that ancient city; and
Thymeli, at Epidaurus near the sanctuary of Asclepius and the great
theater, now the center of an early-summer festival. In Epidaurus
TEAK is not alone in such services, for the government's *Xenia* chain
maintains an excellent guest house.

The TEAK company owns and operates the modern A-class *Hotel
Amfitryon* at Nauplia and this seems to me a goal of goals, for each of
its fifty bedrooms, all with private bath, faces the Bay of Nauplia and
is provided with a comfortable balcony. The hotel has excellent indoor
and outdoor restaurants, a swimming pool and a private garden, but it
is the close-up harbor view that especially calls me, for there are few to
match it even in the wealth of views from Greek hoteldom on mainland

and islands.

One of the very good links of the *Xenia* hotel chain is also to be found in Nauplia, and though it has only a B rating in the official list as do most of the Xenias, being government owned, you will find it of thoroughly good quality. Still another Nauplia hotel, plainly seen from the Amfitryon's balconies, is the A-class *Hotel Bourdzi,* a curiosity of the first magnitude, for it is an old Venetian fort out in the bay (reached by small boat), and until well on into this century it was a Greek Alcatraz and more, being a prison for criminals under sentence of death and also a jail for the public executioners. By an old Greek custom all executions are effected by convicts who have themselves been sentenced to death but "excused" to perform this gruesome task. Executioners have been subject to popular abhorrence and drastic ostracism, Bourdzi Island being forced to share all this. Nowadays, however, those travelers who stay on the executioners' island find themselves in a hotel of great charm, though the architectural lines of the fort have not been changed. There are pleasant terraces for sunbathing and a roof-garden café-restaurant for refreshment. The accommodations are limited to a mere twelve rooms, of which only four have private bath (shower), but for all that the place is rated in the quality bracket.

Corinth, gateway to the Peloponnesus, which area was long called the Morea but is now restored to its classical name, is about fifty-two miles west of Athens. It lies at the point where the tenuous Isthmus of Corinth, cut by a ship canal in 1893, attaches that great, mountainous peninsula to the rest of the country. The ruins of ancient Corinth, whose period of glory was ancient indeed, antedating that of Athens, lie about four miles west of the modern town, which was moved to its present location after an earthquake had wiped out the older community in 1858. The move did it no good, earthquakewise, for in 1928 another terrific temblor destroyed the new Corinth. It was rebuilt, on a larger scale, chiefly through gifts from America, the campaigns for which some of us well remember.

The excavations of *Old Corinth* have been carried on chiefly by the American School of Classical Studies in Athens, which still continues the work. There are the remains of a Temple of Apollo, a market place, a theater and an Odeon, but the most different thing about these ruins is *water*, for here was the *Fountain of Peirene*, most famous in Greece, and the most amazing thing about the water is that it came, and still comes—you may listen to its gurgling beneath the masonry—not from local springs but from high up on *Acro-Corinth*, the mighty acropolis of the city soaring not 230 feet, like that of Athens, but 1900 feet above the plain. It takes a hard hour's climb to reach the summit, for one of the grandest panoramas in Greece. It is said that there are three hundred springs on or near the top of that mountain citadel and one of them, the largest, started gushing when a hoof of Pegasus happened to strike the hill in flight!

Mycenae, in Argolis, about half way between Corinth and Nauplia, is the site of a city so ancient that its name is used for a whole period of civilization, the Mycenaean Age. The structures and tombs we see there were largely excavated in the nineteenth century by Dr. Heinrich Schliemann, whose removable finds, as mentioned in the previous chapter, fill a large room in the National Archeological Museum at Athens. They date from at least 1400 B.C., half a millennium before Homer. More recent discoveries made in 1950 tend to place the date of Mycenae's Golden Age much earlier, perhaps about 2000 B.C.

The most photographed item in the ancient city is the familiar *Gate of the Lions*, and the most eerie is the misnamed *Tomb of Agamemnon*, equally misnamed the Treasury of Athens, an underground beehive-shaped chamber fifty feet in diameter at its base and fifty feet in height. It was undoubtedly built as a tomb, though not that of King Agamemnon, the Mycenaean monarch who sailed with his forces to Troy to recover Queen Helen, his brother's wife. To round out this famous tale, Agamemnon, upon his return to Mycenae with the prophetess Cassandra, was murdered by his wife Clytemnestra (her alleged tomb is seen near by) and her paramour Aegisthus. The king's children, Orestes and Electra, avenged him by murdering their mother, and the whole bloody sequence has been a favorite subject of tragic drama, from Aeschylus to Eugene O'Neill. The interior of the big beehive is shown in a novel way by local guides. They light sprays of dried thyme and hold them aloft as torches.

Tiryns, a neighboring city dating from the Mycenaean Age, has other ruins that may be visited, but one curiosity that catches the eye of even the passing motorist is a venerable stone bridge over a brooklet near the highway. It is an authenic Mycenaean bridge and may fairly be dated from 1500 B.C., making it, beyond reasonable doubt, *the oldest bridge in Europe*.

Nauplia has been mentioned as the first capital of the modern Kingdom of Greece and as the possessor of unusual hostelries, but it has more than history and hotels to recommend it for it is a wonderfully pleasant little port, dominated jointly by a castle hill, which was its old acropolis, and a lofty Venetian fortress of former times. The latter, reached by climbing exactly 999 steps, rises as an almost perpendicular backdrop. This town, with its healthy situation, pellucid atmosphere and striking scenery, may serve as a pleasant headquarters for trips to many Peloponnesian points.

Epidaurus was the center of the widespread cult of Asclepius (Roman Aesculapius), the god of healing, and as such it strikes a different note in the world of Hellenic ruins. Two things in this rich center of archeology attract every visitor, be his brow high, low or medium, namely the hillside *Theater* and the temple *Tholos*. The theater, dating from the fourth century B.C., is the largest in the Hellenic world and also the best preserved, far surpassing that of Delphi and those of Greek Sicily. The acoustics are wonderful beyond belief. From the loftiest seats of the 18,000-seat crescent you can plainly hear every syllable as the guide, or one of your friends, speaks from the orchestra circle where the actors stood. Even if the speaker's voice is reduced to a low monotone you still hear it as if he were seated beside you. So perfect is this theater, so fraught with tradition and "ready" as it stands, that the Greek government, as I have indicated, uses it for festival purposes, principally for presenting classical plays, a perennial favorite being the trilogy by Aeschylus dealing with the tragic figures mentioned above.

The Tholos of Polyclitus is a circular place of sacrifice sunk in the floor of the vast temple of Asclepius, which sprawls over acres of the plain, some distance down from the theater. It is 8 feet deep and 107 feet in diameter and was formerly beautified by two concentric rings of columns, the outer one of the Doric order, the inner one of Ionic columns with capitals of the Corinthian order. It is hardly more than a round pit today, yet its design, if one pictures it as it was, proves so original that it is of never-failing interest.

Olympic to Salonica

Olympic Airways provides tethered tours from Athens to many interesting points of the Greek mainland as well as to the islands. Specifically, it has lines to *Kalámata* in the western Peloponnesus; *Agrínion* in west central Greece; *Ioánnina* in Epirus; *Larissa* in Thessaly; *Salonica* (and Kozani and Kavala) in Macedonia; and *Alexandropolis* in Thrace, near the border of Turkey. I have taken several of Olympic's domestic flights, out and back, and have enjoyed the simplicity and ease of them, the lack of fuss and formality. It is perhaps not *quite* as simple as a boy hopping on his bike to pedal to school, but it reminded me of that. Most of the flights are made in about an hour.

One of the company's most valuable lines, and certainly its busiest, is to Salonica, with no less than four round-trip flights every day, the transit time, as usual, being about an hour.

Salonica, with a population of nearly half a million, is the second city of modern Greece, as it was, in earlier times, the second city of the Byzantine Empire. It has a lot to offer, as tourism is just beginning to discover, and in addition to its own attractions it is the take-off point for many interesting points in Macedonia, notably the Holy Mountain, or Monastic Republic of Mt. Athos, of which more later. The city rims the upper end of the Gulf of Salonica and has a fascinating shore boulevard, extended in 1959, that runs for three miles close to the sea and then, as an ordinary highway, twelve miles farther, terminating finally in a new and well-installed beach development called *Akti Thermaïkon*, under the supervision of the NTO. The shore boulevard, named King Constantine Avenue, calls for a couple of sound clichés, for it is as bright as a button and as lively as a cricket, with countless sidewalk cafés on the inner side and plenty of "sea life" on the outer side. I should add here that on August 6, 1917, a terrible conflagration destroyed a great part of the city, the net result being that we now have a twentieth-century Salonica, and new structures of importance are still continually rising. Another reason for the city's newness is that it has been a dyed-in-the-wool Greek city only since 1912, the year Greece took it over from the Turks, who had controlled it since the year 1430! Greek national feeling and ambition have had a salutary effect. A splendid new *civic theater* and a new *museum* were opened late in 1962 in connection with the twenty-seventh International Fair, this annual event being a very big and important one. There is also a new *stadium*, seating 65,000, and many of the buildings of the university are gleaming new.

A lack of good hotels has played a major part in holding back the tourist tide but this deficiency is now being corrected in an impressive way. One very large sea-front hotel, supported by fifteen hundred reinforced concrete piles sixty feet long, is nearly ready to open. This will have five hundred beds. A second large hotel, with two hundred beds, is being built in a central location near the front. Of the older crop of hotels the *Olympic*, not on the front, is perhaps the most presentable, and in second place, on the sea front, the venerable *Mediterranean*, which has the advantage of being directly adjacent to the Olympic Airways city terminal and just around the corner from the office of the Macedonian NTO. This office, I may say, is very much on the ball, one of the most alert and well run of all those which I have encountered in Greece.

There are some attractive restaurants in Salonica, especially along the coast between the city and the new NTO beach. One, of special charm, in Nea Krini some eight miles from the center, is happily named *Remvi*, a word which can be translated only as "Relaxed Feeling." Here I have enjoyed barbouni (red mullet), a specialty of the house, prepared in a way which local enthusiasts declare to be the best in Greece. In the city's center, on the sea front near the Olympic terminal, is a humble looking but excellent restaurant named *Olympos Naoussa* where Greek dishes such as dolmadakia (previously described) are dependably good. Fruit desserts can be a pleasant feature, for Macedonia's fertile lands produce abundant peaches, pears, apricots, apples, melons, grapes and strawberries.

On Alexander Street, some two or three blocks in from the sea, *Floca* has an outstandingly fine tearoom, and in other locations a good, self-service restaurant and a snack bar. All this is natural, since Floca, so conspicuous now in Athens, originated in Salonica (as a chocolate factory, still in operation) and still keeps its headquarters there. Near the Floca tearoom is one of Greece's leading wine and liquor shops, by name *Boutaris*, whose locally manufactured ouzo is considered by connoisseurs the absolute best. In case you wish to try it out on your palate you'll find it available, through various representatives, in the U.S. One representative that I happen to know about is C. Pappas and Company, 540 E Street, South Boston, Mass.

The sightseer in this metropolis of Macedonia and its environs may follow a trail of historical treasures perhaps second only to the twelve-step trail outlined previously in Athens. Certainly eight points of special interest are musts and these should be seen under the guidance of a local cicerone provided by the NTO. I will present my eight nuggets from Salonica's wealth, but first a word about the city's past.

Salonica, a shortened and altered form of Thessaloniki, the Greek name for it, was founded in 315 B.C. by Cassander, one of the generals of Alexander the Great. He gave it the exact name of his wife, who was also Alexander's sister. Alexander's own birthplace was Pella, only a few miles to the west of the city. The Romans conquered Macedonia and built the Adriatic-to-Constantinople highway called Via Egnatia, which passes straight through Salonica and is one of the city's main streets. Bible students will recall the urgent plea of the early Macedonian Christians to Paul, "Come over into Macedonia and help us." He answered the call. In later centuries, Salonica, always a rich commercial city, was attacked, and often sacked, by Goths, Avars, Slavs, Saracens and Normans. In 1430, the city was captured by the Turks and became an outpost of the Byzantine Empire, remaining in Turkish hands clear up to our own time (1912).

Most of the historic monuments were at least partially spared by the Great Fire and some of them came through entirely unscathed. Here, then, are our eight specials. To see them all, without much wearying footwork, a taxi is necessary.

1. The *White Tower*, now centering a small park on the sea front, is an imposing fortification of the old sea wall built in the fifteenth century. Round and strong and tall, with a crenelated top, it is a gracious ornament on the city's seaside promenade.

2. The *Arch of Galerius*, erected about 300 A.D. by the general of that name to commemorate a victory in Asia Minor, is Salonica's Arc de Triomphe. It has interesting relief carvings.

3. The *Rotunda*, a massive circular building constructed about 300 A.D. by the Romans as a mausoleum for Galerius, was converted into a Christian shrine in 410 by Emperor Theodosius, and into a Moslem

mosque, with minaret, by the Turks in the fifteenth century. Now called the Church of St. George, its minaret has vanished. Its marvelous mosaics, mostly gold in color, are of Hellenistic legacy, with oriental overtones. They were made to the order of Theodosius. In World War II Bulgarian soldiers damaged many of the mosaics and destroyed some of them, but much of their glory still survives.

4. The *Citadel*, or Acropolis, rises 1400 feet above the sea, providing a fine broad view. From here also one may clearly see the exact limits of the 1917 fire, new Salonica versus old. The old wall of the city, nearly four miles in length, was never wholly destroyed. Nearly half of it is still in good condition.

5. The *Church of St. Demetrius*, a large basilica with no less than five naves and four rows of marble columns, was built in the fifth century. In it is the sepulcher of the saint, who is the city's patron, with his bones in it. Demetrius was a Greek Christian officer of the Roman legion, imprisoned and martyred by Galerius. The mosaics of this church, mostly gold and white and depicting, in one scene, the saint between the bishop and the governor, are considered by some scholars the finest made anywhere during its period, which was the seventh century. An oddity of the church is that traces of a Roman road are seen running straight through the crypt.

6. The *Church of the Twelve Apostles*, built in the early 1300's in pure Byzantine style by Patriarch Niphon, is remarkable for the brickwork patterns of its outside walls, done in mellow red and buff. The mosaics and frescoes have some rather startling features. For example, Jesus, being baptized by John, is represented stark naked, an immodesty said to be unique in the world's churches. Another oddity is Salome, dancing in abandoned fashion for Herod's pleasure.

7. The Church of *Panaghia ton Chalkeon* (Our Lady of the Coppersmiths) is an old and especially graceful brick Byzantine structure dating from the eleventh century.

8. The *Church of St. Sophia*, a very old edifice dating from the early eighth century, "looks like new" inside, for its huge golden dome, ellipsoid in shape, was thoroughly and expensively cleaned in 1962. The ikons of this church are especially interesting, ranged as they are on a gold and olive *ikonostasis*, which is a sort of rood screen separating the sanctuary from the rest of the church.

Have you had enough? I think the answer is yes, though guides have plenty more to show, churches galore, a famous monastery (*Moni Vladaton*, with superb view), museums of archeology and folk art, modern civic buildings. "Some other time," let's say.

Pella is a recent discovery of utmost importance, lying only twenty-five miles west of Salonica. Pella is known to have been the capital of Macedonia under King Philip at the time when his son Alexander the Great was born. Not many years ago the whole area was a dismal marsh-land, but it was reclaimed and made into healthy, serviceable ground for the cultivation of tobacco and grain. In 1959, some children dwelling in a rude home here unearthed a stone dog of ancient times, causing excitement in archeological circles. Then a peasant, digging his cellar, found part of a capital of a marble column.

The *Hellenic Service of Antiquities* then got very busy, some money was raised and excavations were started, with results that astonished even the most sanguine archeologists. Some superbly preserved mosaics were uncovered and are on display. As a layman I would venture to say that they are the most perfect I have seen, at least in the open air, in the whole Mediterranean area. One portrays two naked warriors, possibly Krateros, a friend of Alexander, and Alexander himself, in process of spearing a lion. Another shows a Dionysiac procession, including a chariot drawn by three horses abreast. Other treasures in mosaic work and sculpture are being brought to light every week, almost every day, and hopes are high that the foundations and flooring of the probable palace of King Philip will sooner or later be revealed, the very place where Alexander was born.

Pella bids fair to become a major tourist attraction in the early future and as a start the authorities have already built a small motel and restaurant directly opposite the entrance to the excavations.

I have called Salonica the take-off point for Macedonian tours and it is just that, but I have to confess that the most exciting place of all has so far eluded me, for I have never visited the *Monastic Republic of Mt. Athos*, an independent entity under Greek protection. This amazing Holy Mountain or Holy Community—it goes under both titles—consists of some twenty monasteries, many dating from the tenth century, and they are said to be fabulously rich in art works and manuscripts.

The republic rises amid spectacular scenery, the *Monastery of St. Gregory* being one of the most photogenic, on the easternmost prong of the three-pronged *Peninsula of Chalcidice,* which stretches south from Macedonia into the Aegean Sea. At its peak of prosperity centuries ago there were some twenty thousand inhabitants, all monks, but Mt. Athos has fallen on hard times and now there are hardly three thousand.

To reach the community one may take the daily bus from Salonica to the village of Ierissos and a bit beyond to a miniature port named Tripiti at the inner end of the bay between the middle and eastern prongs, proceeding thence by motorboat to Daphne, the port of Mt. Athos, and then by bus to *Karyes,* the seat of government. I understand that there is an inn with twenty or so double rooms within the Mt. Athos area but this should be checked with the NTO, which is actively developing the tourist industry throughout Chalcidice.

From Karyes several monasteries are within walking distance. Non-Greeks wishing to visit the place must secure a letter of introduction from their consulate and present it to some authority, the handiest one empowered to give permission being the NTO office in Salonica—but that's not all. You must be over twenty-one years of age and you must be a male, for Mt. Athos is strictly and positively an all-male community, this rule applying, believe it or not, even to animals. Cows, sows, mares, nannygoats and—excuse me—bitches are strictly barred. The problem of keeping out female birds and queen bees must give the monks many a sleepless night! The Holy Virgin Mary is the only feminine personage welcomed, and she reigns supreme.

This monkish community is a living anachronism. Although it associates with Greece to the extent of having a Greek representative resident in Karyes it lives quite by itself and unto itself. It clings to the old Julian calendar, which is thirteen days behind our normal one. Its timepieces are set four and a half hours in advance of Greek time. The monks rise at 6 o'clock and pray until 7:30. At noon they take a three-hour siesta and the whole community goes stone dead until 3 o'clock.

Well—I'll hope to join a stag party some day and set out for the Holy Mountain. As we board the bus at Salonica we'll sing "Farewell ladies, we're going to leave you now."

CHAPTER 14

THE HELLENIC ISLES BY PLANE AND CRUISE SHIP

Sifting for Selection

THE islands of Greece, numbering well over five hundred, are among its greatest fascinations, even as seen on a map. As seen from the air, the sea or in actual visits literally scores of them are of great beauty. Leaving out Euboea, which runs for a hundred miles closely parallel to the mainland's east coast and is reckoned almost a part of it, let us do some rapid scouting and sorting.

The chief islands of the *Saronic Gulf,* immediately to the west and south of Athens, are *Salamis; Aegina;* and *Poros;* with two more, *Hydra* and *Spetsai,* in the open Aegean Sea just south of the Peninsula of Argolis.

The *Ionian Islands,* in the Ionian Sea west of Greece proper, are, to mention the chief ones only, *Corfu; Ithaca,* home of Odysseus (Ulysses), whence he started his adventurous odyssey; *Cephalonia* and *Zanta.* These were ceded to Greece by Great Britain in 1864.

Cythera, just south of the Peloponnesus, was the center of the Aphrodite (Venus) cult, hence her alias Cytherea. This island is a geological stepping-stone to fabled Crete, by far the largest of all Greek islands. Crete will be discussed later.

The *Aegean Islands,* comprising nine-tenths of the grand total, fall into several groups. The *Cyclades* lie southeast of Attica and include such strongholds of charm as *Andros; Tenos; Syra,* capital of the group, with a white city that climbs two hills; *Delos,* the birthplace of Apollo, with extensive excavations of its former wealth of buildings and sculpture, including the much-photographed Terrace of the Lions; *Mykonos,* a popular holiday isle and a transfer point of local sea traffic; *Paros,* rich in snow-white marble; *Naxos,* largest of the Cyclades; *Milos,* where the Venus de Milo, now in the Louvre, was found in 1820; and *Santorin,* a double star of loveliness, with its chief town, Thira, clinging to a mountain spur high above its bustling port.

The *Sporades* is a term that needs explanation. In its broadest sense it denominates, or used to, all the islands of the Aegean not in the Cyclades group. The word means "Scattered," and from it we have our word sporadic. At present it applies especially to a small group, the *Northern Sporades*, lying east of Euboea. Its largest island is *Skyros*, where Rupert Brooke lies buried. (Have you ever eaten in that vast palace of low-cost food, the Lyons Corner House on Oxford Street, in London, and have you noticed in its five hundred tons of decorative marble a wall picture with some blood-red marble in it? If so, be advised that these scarlet touches came from Skyros, the only place in the world where marble of that hue has been quarried.) The "Scattered" Islands formerly included the Southern Sporades, a group along the Asia Minor coast from Samos to Rhodes inclusive, but most of these lie in the "Dozen" group that came to be called the Dodecanese, so the name Sporades has lost its old significance.

The *Dodecanese*, as its name tells us, consists of twelve islands. The group was long held by Turkey but was acquired by Italy in the Tripolitan War (1911–1912) and held by her until the conclusion of World War II, when it went to Greece, of which it is a part by every consideration of background and race. *Rhodes*, the largest island, the capital and by far the most interesting of them all to travelers, will be covered later in this chapter. The only other of the twelve having special significance is *Patmos*, also to be covered below, where John wrote the Apocalypse (*The Revelation*), a work that has given theologians more headaches than any other in the Scriptures. At the conclusion of the first millennium it had the entire Christian world in a state of panic, waiting for the end of the world. The Revelator records in these words the impetus that set him to writing: "I John, . . . was in the isle that is called Patmos . . . and heard behind me a great voice, as of a trumpet, saying, 'I am Alpha and Omega . . . and, What thou seest, write in a book.'" Patmos today is an exceedingly pleasant retreat, reached by steamer only, including some excursion steamers, and guests are accommodated, for a maximum of three days, at the big *Monastery of St. John*.

Of the Greek islands that rim the Asia Minor coast from the Dodecanese to and beyond the Hellespont, five need mention. *Samos*, the birthplace of Pythagoras the philosopher, was a maritime power in its own right in the fifth century B.C. *Chios* is claimed as the birthplace of Homer and it long maintained a school of Homeric poetry. *Lesbos* is famous as the home of Sappho, the supreme poetess of Greece, whose name is always associated, whether fairly or not, with Lesbian love. *Lemnos* was considered, in ancient times, to have a magic quality. Its earth was exported in blocks as medicine. But to husbands the place once proved unhealthy. Legend says that when the Argonauts of Jason put in at this island they found only women, for each woman had proudly asserted her superiority by murdering her husband. *Samothrace*, a little north of the Hellespont, was an island of special sanctity. It is known to all travelers for one statue that was found here and is now on a landing of a main stairway of the Louvre, the stirring "Victory of Samothrace," its sculptured figure standing on a ship's prow. The victory it celebrated was the brilliant performance of a Samothracian ship in the Battle of Salamis (480 B.C.).

Olympic's Island Flights

Olympic Airways services fan out from Athens not only to several islands of the Aegean Sea but also to lovely Corfu in the Ionian Sea, so far to the north that it is actually nearer to Albania than to Greece. The Corfu Airport, only a mile and a half from town, is being enlarged to enable even Comet and Caravelle jets to use it. The four ribs of Olympic that fan to Aegean points reach the following islands: *Crete*, with two terminal points, Heraklion, the capital, and Chania, far to the west; *Rhodes*, lying very far to the east, close to Turkish Anatolia; *Lesbos*, with airport at Mytilene, which name is sometimes applied to the whole island; and *Lemnos*, which lies only 40 miles southeast of the Mt. Athos Republic.

Travelers vary radically in their views on group travel, by cruise ship for instance, and rugged individual travel, which is lucky both for shipping lines and air lines. It is simple to lie back in a deck chair while at sea and trot meekly after a tour guide at every port of call, and there's a lot to be siad for such nonworry about the details of touring, but there is stimulus also in plotting one's own course, thus earning one's pleasure. Olympic can handle group travel all right but its clientele is composed primarily of individual travelers and it can be a friend in need to the impulsive traveler. "Let's visit Rhodes," he says, "*today*," and he has three choices. Flying in the morning, the early afternoon or the early evening, he will touch down in eighty minutes at the City of the Knights.

Corfu and Its Palace-Casino

Corfu's past is as checkered as one comes to expect in Mediterranean isles. Here are the high lights.

1. In the Peloponnesian War, 431–404 B.C., a strong Corfiot navy won glory by wiping out the fleet of Corinth.

2. Byzantine era 377–1204 A.D.

3. First Venetian era 1204–1214.

4. Ruled by the Despots of Epirus 1214–1267.

5. Ruled by Angevins 1267–1386.

6. Second Venetian era 1386–1797.

7. After several Turkish failures to capture the island it fell under the power of the French Republic and then the Napoleonic empire 1799–1814; called by Napoleon the "Ionian State."

8. The British ruled Corfu, very well and wisely, 1814–1864, Lord Guildford, an esteemed figure in history, founding on the island the first Greek university, called the Ionian Academy.

9. A Corfiot named John Capodistria, whose statue is conspicuous on Corfu's Esplanade, became the first "governor" of modern Greece. This was in 1828, preceding the founding of the Kingdom of Greece the following year.

10. Corfu joined Greece, 1864.

11. World War I. The Allies occupied Corfu 1916–1919. In 1918, in Corfu's Municipal Theater, the Republic of Yugoslavia was proclaimed.

12. Prince Philip of Britain, a son of Greek Prince Andrew and grandson of Greek King George I, born in Mon Repos Palace, Corfu in 1921.

13. Italians, goaded by Mussolini, bombarded and took Corfu, August 23, 1923.

14. In World War II Corfu was repeatedly bombed by both sides in turn. It suffered severely, but most of the damaged buildings have been

repaired or replaced by new ones.

In Corfu we come into touch with three interesting hotel chains, so important in provincial travels that they call for mention.

Gauer Hotels are operated by a Swiss corporation of Bern, headed by Jack Gauer, one of the most experienced and dynamic hotel men of that land of tourist hotels. Mr. Gauer has two hotels on Corfu, both de luxe, and one, similarly de luxe, on Rhodes. The Corfu hotels are the *Corfu Palace*, on the short-front boulevard in town, and the *Miramare*, a beachside bungalow development at Moraïtika a few miles outside of town. The Corfu Palace has view-giving balconies, and of course private baths, with all rooms. In every way it is a quality hotel, with good cuisine and good service. There is a well-stocked gift shop in the lobby. I like the waiters' costumes, which are neat dark trousers, white soft shirt, gaily colored cummerbund and string tie to match. In the majority of fashionable hotels abroad, even of resort type, the waiters must still suffer in traditional dress suit, hard-boiled shirt and black or white tie, so it is a real relief to the guest's spirit when he occasionally sees them comfortably and sensibly garbed. Foreigners, by the way, may not own *border* property in Greece— Corfu is considered on the border of Albania—but in the case of Mr. Gauer, a Swiss, a special royal decree waived the law. The Corfu Palace is his property. The Miramare, a beautiful twelve-acre property, is under lease to his company. Each of the hotels has a Swiss resident manager. Guests may hire a "Miramarette," which is a low-slung sport model of the Fiat 600 with special straw seats, on a basis of $11.50 a day with full gas tank and insurance covering four occupants. A sea-water swimming pool is about to be built on the Palace grounds, with a landscaped pool area and a bar surrounding it. The Miramare has six hundred yards of private beach available to guests. Bathing is pleasant for nearly six months of the year, and two speed boats are available for water-skiing. The gardens and olive grove are illuminated nightly by colored lights.

Astir Hotels, mentioned in connection with the superlative beach bungalow developments near Athens (at Glyfada and Vouliagmeni), constitute a substantial chain, island links being on Corfu and, several of them, in Rhodes. The Astirs are all A or AA, the chief one in Corfu, which is located on the town's harbor front near the car-ferry, being of the lesser rating. It has a pleasant roof garden used in summer as an open-air restaurant. A convenience of the Astir is that it is only a few steps distant from the source of all local information, the Corfu office of the NTO.

Xenia Hotels, mentioned in connection with Epidaurus and Nauplia, are mostly of B class but some are rated A, or at least with an A restaurant. This is a large group, numbering over thirty already and continually growing. All are modern hotels built by the government and operated by the NTO. They are admirable holiday inns invariably placed in beautiful surroundings. Xenia means hospitality, and the word fits well. The *Corfu Xenia*, about two miles from town, rises from a wooded knoll above the sea and is cleverly designed to fit the sloping terrain. It has purposely been held to a B rating, to give it B prices, but the lovely dining room is officially and rightly of A rating. In many an island and on many a lovely shore you will find a "Hospitality Hotel" and always, I think, you will feel that you are indeed a personal guest of the government.

In addition to the above, Corfu has at least one other hotel worth noting, namely the *Castelo*, at Ypsos, a beach village eight miles north of town. This was a mansion built about 1900 by an Italian nobleman, who named it Castello Mimbelli. In the years before World War II it served as the summer residence of King George II.

Corfu city "sees itself," to use the European reflexive, without the necessity of a guide. In the heart of town, only an easy stroll's distance from the Palace Hotel, up a short rise and through a spacious esplanade, is the actual former royal palace, now a *Museum of Archeology*, built by the British early in the nineteenth century. It is a fine Georgian structure of Maltese limestone revealing its "authorship." The *Old Fortress*, rising on a rocky peninsula adjacent to the esplanade, fairly dominates the town, and just below it, by way of ornament, stands the Church of St. George, with its six Doric columns, close beside the sea. The Old Fortress was the Byzantine acropolis, fortified later by the Venetians, who built also a *New Fortress*, now several centuries old, on the Hill of San Marco west of the palace-now-museum.

There are churches galore in the town and its outskirts, the most venerated one being the *Church of St. Spiridion* in the heart of town.

Spiridion is the patron of Corfu and his embalmed body lies in a gilded reliquary in an inner chapel of the church. Joining an eager throng of the faithful one afternoon, I edged into this sanctuary and found it rich in religious ornament, with a solid mass of gold lamps suspended from the ceiling. Everyone, including this foreigner, was invited by an officiating priest to show reverence to the saint by kissing his foot, which was encased in a very fancy jeweled slipper, and this I did. The following day happened to be one of the saint's special days—there are four each year—and his relics were carried through the town and around the esplanade in solemn procession. The cannon on the Old Fortress barked a powerful salute. I *thought* I counted twenty-one blasts, but Spiridion was not a king or president, so I must have been wrong. After the procession the watching crowds melted away, many taking seats in the sidewalk cafés to enjoy beer, Turkish coffee, or perhaps a tart local liqueur called koum kouat. The cafés of Corfu, quite filling the arcades on the west side of the esplanade, are a delight to Corfiot and visitor alike.

The island's countryside varies from the lush loveliness of rolling hills and meadows, interspersed with groves of old olive trees and sentinel cypresses, to mountain and cliff scenery and some strikingly beautiful islets along the coast and in various bays. The favorite tour leads north-westward across the island to the resort-hamlet of *Paleokastritsa*, some sixteen miles distant by a paved road. This main road ends at a small sandy cove, hemmed in on both sides by towering headlands, where the NTO maintains a pavilion for refreshments and a few simple rooms (running water). You may lunch here on lobster so undeniably fresh that you may select your own "lob" from the pavilion's pens. There is also a very humble hotel, the *Zefiros* (Zephyr), and in the same area an unpretentious but good restaurant called *Lucciola* (Firefly). Ulysses' Cave is at Paleokastritsa and a French scholar has claimed that this is the exact site of the city of King Alcinoüs, described by Homer, and that the shipwrecked Odysseus (Ulysses) encountered Nausicaä, the king's daughter, at another small beach nearby.

The tall, straight cypresses of the neighborhood, piercing the sky like minarets, contrast sharply with the gnarled olive trees, and in the background all about are soaring hills, solid with verdure, or rugged **sea** cliffs. Local folk say the cypresses that stand so straight and tall are all males and that the type with the "middle-aged spread," seen here and there, indicates females, but to me that explanation sounds suspiciously like the fabrication of a "gynephobe." Be that as it may, every visitor should take a steeply ascending side road, paved, to the twelfth-century *Monastery of Paleokastritsa* on the summit of the western headland, where ancient monks live out their placid lives blessed with one of the broadest and loveliest views that even Corfu can offer.

And now the big news of Corfu, which proves already to be old: The *Achilleion,* or Palace of Achilles, has been drastically and expensively converted into a gambling casino by the German entrepreneur who operates the famous casino at Baden Baden. I watched the work going on in its initial phases and one of the representatives offered to bet me a thousand drachmas that his principals would finish the formidable job and open the casino before I could write and publish this book. I didn't take the bet, for I felt sure he would win. He did. Its opening, attended by six hundred of the elite, was an international event.

What is the Achilleion? It is an imposing palace, built in 1890 to the order of Empress Elizabeth of Austria on the crest of a hill above the inland village of Gastouri. In 1907, Kaiser Wilhelm II of Germany took it over and lived in it each spring until World War I interrupted his holiday program. The palace is of three stories and is constructed on and against a steep slope in such a way that the third floor debouches onto a formal garden on the slope's crest. The name was chosen by Empress Elizabeth because of her admiration for Achilles, and on the wall of the upper level there is a grandiose and striking mural of Achilles standing in his chariot dragging the body of Hector around the walls of Troy, while Priam, in distress, surveys the gruesome scene from the city's walls.

The palace is, or was, dull and Victorian, with a lot of ornate statuary, but its location and view are superb. I am eager to see what the casino folk have done to it. No doubt it glitters nicely and no doubt it brings a lot of much-needed money to Corfu's coffers. The representative I have mentioned told me quite frankly that casinos expect, as an average, to win 85 per cent of the money wagered, leaving 15 per cent for the lucky few. I think my own gambling in the Achilleion will be largely mental!

The Ships That Cruise

Ship travel from Athens to the Greek islands is big business in these days. Ships by the dozen, it seems, scurry constantly from the busy quays of Piraeus in one-day trips to the islands of the Saronic Gulf, and in tours of varying length to the islands of the Aegean Sea, especially the Cyclades and the Dodecanese, the latter group led by lovely Rhodes. Crete, too, gets full and deserved attention from the cruise ships.

The high points of these cruises will be covered below, but here I shall attempt to sort out the various companies that purvey island tours, with a swift run-down of what they offer the customer.

The one-day tours in the *Saronic Gulf*, continuing to *Hydra* and in some cases to *Spetsai* in the open sea off the coast of Argolis, are made daily by a veritable covey of small ships. One on which I booked was the *Mario*, but any travel agency can supply lists of them, with details. They start from Piraeus rather early in the morning and return at dusk, or even after dark, making a twelve-hour day of it. A faster cruise, touching at Hydra and Spetsai only, may be made by the hydrofoil ship *Express*, of Greek Coast Lines (10 Othos Street, Athens). This type of vessel, originating in Messina, Sicily and mentioned too casually in the chapter (10) on Italy, is something of an "unmissing link" between sea and air travel. To attain their impressive cruising speed of 38 knots (43 miles) they rise up, as it were, on their "forelegs" and skim the water as though half airborne, yet they are comfortable craft with 125 pullman seats and a pleasant lounge and bar. Hydrofoils are becoming increasingly popular in sheltered European waters (Norway, Italy, etc.) but are not practical in very rough seas.

Tours in the *Aegean Sea* generally last five or seven days, some only three, following, in the main, this pattern: *Heraklion* (the Cretan capital); *Rhodes; Cos; Patmos; Delos; Mykonos;* and return to Piraeus. Some cruises alter the order of the above, and some omit Cos and Patmos, substituting *Santorin*. Further variants of the above are also offered by certain lines. To clarify the picture I shall list here some of the companies that provide regular cruises.

Epirotiki Lines (2 Bouloulinas Street, Piraeus), using a ship named

the *Semiramis*, offers the cruise outlined first above. I have taken and
enjoyed it and will describe it in later pages.

Nomikos Lines (Tanpy Building, Piraeus), provides two three-day
cruises a week, from mid-June to late October, one a week from mid-
April to mid-June, this, however, being supplemented during those two
spring months by special trips to Patmos, Kusadasi, in Asia Minor, for a
visit to Ephesus, and two islands of the Sporades, Chios and Skiathos.
Either of these two special spring offerings may be combined with a
regular cruise to make a seven-day tour. The regular cruise is squeezed,
as I've said, into three days, thus omitting Cos and Patmos but including
Santorin. Its ship is the *Delos*.

Greek Islands Cruise Lines entered the field in the spring of 1963
with the 2500-ton, 20-knot *New Hellas*, making three-day, four-day
and week-long cruises. Bookings on ships of the above three lines may
be made through *Greek Line*, 10 Bridge Street, New York City.

Typaldos Lines, with a handsome street-floor office at 500 Fifth
Avenue, New York, offers a wide variety of two-day, five-day and
seven-day cruises, depending on the season, in two vessels named the
Kriti and the *Aegaeon*, sailing from Piraeus *and* Istanbul. Two other
ships, the *Mt. Athinai* and the *Mt. Acropolis* make cruises from Venice
to mainland Greece, Rhodes, Cyprus and Israel. The Aegaeon was the
former *Princess Alice* in Canadian Pacific service from the West Coast
to Alaska. The "Mt." ships were the Grace Line's earlier *Santa Rosa*
and *Santa Paula*, later replaced by Grace with like-named new ships.

Olympic Cruises, with a New York office at 655 Madison Avenue,
combined with that of Olympic Airways, has been mentioned earlier.
Its fine, yacht-like ship the *Agamemnon* provides spring cruises start-
ing alternately from Venice and Genoa to Dubrovnik (Dalmatia),
Athens, certain of the Greek isles, then Istanbul and, rather amazingly,
some Black Sea points behind the Iron Curtain, namely Constanta, a
Romanian port, and two famous points of the USSR itself, Odessa and
Yalta. The company's *regular* year-round services in the *Agamemnon*
and the *Achilleus*, from France and Italy to Greece, continuing to Egypt,
Cyprus and Lebanon, have been included in the listings in Chapter 2.

Sun Line (North American general agent Home Lines, 42 Broadway,
New York) has two fine "Stella" ships, the *Stella Maris* and the
splendid 3000-ton *Stella Solaris* (not to be confused with the famous

Stella Polaris), which was the former German ship *Bunte Kuh*. This "Piebald Cow," which was built in Hamburg in 1960 and which I have known in connection with service from that city to Helgoland, has air conditioning, stabilizers and an outdoor pool. With the older *Stella* it provides weekly cruises from Piraeus to Crete, Rhodes, Ephesus, Istanbul, Delos and Mykonos, though this route may be altered from time to time, a caution which applies also to the other lines mentioned.

International Cruises, a company formerly calling itself Flair Cruises, offers summer-long 13-day cruises and an October 20-day cruise, starting from Venice, in the 3700-ton passenger steamer *Romantic*, a good Italian ship with pool, Lido Bar and ample deck room for sports and sun worshipping. Both cruises feature the Greek isles, including Corfu, and the longer one adds Egypt, Cyprus and Lebanon. In 1963 this company put into service the *Carina*, providing a passenger and car ferry service from Brindisi (Italy) to Athens, with a halt at Corfu, the one-way passage taking only 21 hours.

National Hellenic America Line's *Queen Frederica* has been mentioned in Chapter 2, as has *Greek Line*'s *Olympia*, but as regards the latter I should state that the *Olympia* offers an exceptionally comprehensive 50-day tour from New York, usually starting in February, that includes not only the usual Mediterranean halts but four halts in the Black Sea, at Romanian, Bulgarian and Russian ports.

It should be kept in mind that *regular* Greek steamer services are very numerous in the Aegean, leaving Piraeus on frequencies ranging from once or twice weekly to daily, to all important islands, including many of the smaller ones such as Mykonos (for Delos), Paros, Naxos and Santorin in the Cyclades, Cos in the Dodecanese and Skyros in the Sporades.

Among vessels more of yachting character several need mention.

The *Dolphin Line*, 3 Karageorgi Servias Street, Athens, offers regular twelve-day cruises to the Aegean Islands by schooner. Some fifteen islands are included.

The *Kyknos*, a fast motor yacht (contact Alkyon Tourist Organization, 98 Academy Street, Athens) offers circular cruises in the Northern Sporades and the Gulf of Euboea. They start from Chalkis, north of Athens, which is reached by Pullman coach or by Diesel railcar.

The *Marilena* is a new, fast, Diesel-powered ship with 230 berths frankly calling itself a "tourist vessel." Its tours, covering a dozen or more islands, are under the operation of the Kriti Tourist Agency in Piraeus.

And finally about *private yachting*. The chief office for this increasingly popular sport is the *B. Koutsoukellis Yachting Agency*, 3 Stadium Street, Athens. This agency has at least fifty craft of greatly varying type, from the 112-foot motor yacht *North Wind* and the two-masted schooner *Toscana* to such modest craft as the motor caïque *Aghia Varvara* and the auxiliary sloop *Varres*.

A Day (or Two) for the Saronic Gulf

The one-day cruise from Piraeus down the Saronic Gulf to the historic island of Aegina, the dramatic Straits of Poros and the shippy-arty island of Hydra, perhaps pushing on to the sailors' island of Spetsai, is a hardy perennial. Most tourists, as I've said, achieve it in a single long day, leaving their Athens hotel at 7 o'clock in the morning and getting back about 8:30 in the evening. This is obviously a bit tiring and those who can take time to relax over night, say in Hydra, will be well advised to do so.

Under "The Ships that Cruise," just above, I have outlined the course of one typical cruise and also that of the hydrofoil lightning ship that barrels along to Hydra and Spetsai only, but regularly scheduled steamer services are numerous and any travel agency can work out whatever combination may be desired.

Aegina lies squarely in the middle of the gulf about sixteen sea miles from Piraeus. Some ships moor to the quay of the island's capital on the western shore, while others tie up to a rude wharf on Aghia Marina Bay on the eastern shore, permitting passengers to climb by bus or on donkeyback to the *Temple of Aphaia*, who was a sort of island version of Artemis, the Greek Diana. In the early classical Greek period Aegina was a considerable naval power. It carried on various private wars of piratical nature but contributed also very strongly to the victory of Salamis. Before the Persian wars the island was a formidable rival of Athens itself but was finally crushed by that city-state in 455 B.C. and suffered the humiliation of having all its inhabitants expelled. In short, Athens "liberated" Aegina in the manner of currently warring nations, replacing its people with trusted Athenian colonists. In modern times, in the year 1828, Aegina became the first (temporary) capital of Greece under the governorship of John Capodistria, who was, as we have seen, a native of Corfu. This was a sort of temporary tryout and in a matter of months the *kingdom* was founded and the capital was shifted to Nauplia.

Poros is a white town climbing the like-named island steeply from the harbor. It is on the sheltered western side separated from mainland Argolis by the narrowest of straits. The bay of the town seems like a salt-water lake. The *Mario* pushes on right through the strait heading for Hydra, but stops on the return journey. Many of the *regular* gulf services, but not the cruises, halt also at Methana, on the mainland near by, a sulphur springs spa of some importance. Poros is a camera's delight for it rises in gleaming whiteness amid groves of olive trees and orchards of lemon.

Hydra is the high point of the Saronic cruise. Its whiteness of appearance is relieved by many individual houses of blue. In the eighteenth and early nineteenth centuries Hydra became an incredibly wealthy community of ship owners able to fit out whole fleets to fight victorious engagements with the Turkish and Egyptian fleets. Famous families such as Coundouriotis and Mioulis became, for their day, as fabulous in fortune as the Greek shipping tycoons of our day. During the period of contraband trade that lasted for two decades during the Napoleonic wars their wealth waxed to Croesus levels, and in 1821 they owned well over a hundred ships. In the War of Independence Hydra had 37,000 inhabitants but now it has less than a tenth that number. After the era of sailing ships subsided some Hydra seamen went to Tarpon Springs, Florida, to become sponge divers. Many more settled on the Greek mainland, especially in Piraeus, but happily, and remarkably, the island port of an earlier way of life came through all its wars, great and small, virtually unscathed, which is our good luck. The mansions of the eighteenth-century shipping plutocrats are still right there and some of them we may visit, or at least gawk at from the outside. The *Tombazi* house has been converted into a *Hostel for Artists* of all nationalities and this mansion, certainly, may be visited by us tourists, whether artists or not. Nearby are the *Voulgaris* house and two great houses of the

Coundouriotis family.

Even the ordinary "shore excursion" in Hydra town, though tantalizing for its brevity, is worth taking. It starts with the quayside Town Hall and an adjacent church, both of which were once parts of the *Monastery of the Dormition of the Virgin.* A characteristic touch in the church is a cluster of ship models hanging from a chandelier. Another is the veneration of St. Nicholas, who, we are soberly told, was "the Christian Poseidon (Neptune)." Leaving this church and civic complex, the guided tour follows the quays for a short distance and then climbs by an easy path to higher parts of town for a series of lovely views.

On the return, by a different path, one sees, in big letters, the word ΞΕΝΟΔΟΧΕΙΟΝ, which means hotel, and there are indeed two or three small B-class inns where one may put up for a night or two in reasonable comfort. Perhaps the best of these places is the *Leoussi*, with twenty-five rooms, most of which have private bath or shower. There is also a small *Xenia*, with only eight rooms and no private baths, but it is quite all right or it wouldn't be a link in the Xenia chain.

Hydra has become very arty, in fact almost a colony of artists and we see studios here and there as well as arty-looking young men and women. It's a do-as-you-please island much loved by the nonconformist. You, too, will love its atmosphere, but your chief thought will probably be of the old shipping masters, part pirate, part patriot, but wholly he-man.

The Aegean Cruise, Island Climax

I have visited various Aegean islands at different times by different means, air and sea, so the comment hereinafter shall be in some degree a composite coverage, but in the main it shall be a report on my most recent visit, a five-day, six-island tour by the ship *Sermiramis* of the Epirotiki Lines. This five-day standard, leaves Piraeus at 6 P.M. on Monday and gets back to Piraeus at 7 A.M. on Saturday, having visited, in turn, Crete, Rhodes, Cos, Patmos, Delos and Rhodes.

Crete, the Grandfather of the West

Crete's vast age makes it an island of legend, but it is no myth that at the dawn of time, as Europe reckons time, it developed a flourishing civilization at Cnossus. This is usually dated from 3000 down to 1200 B.C., a period far preceding the Mycenaean Age, and it is called, from its semimythical King Minos (Minos was actually the generic word for king), the *Minoan Age*. This Cretan civilization was already hoary with the centuries, though still in full flower, when the temples of Luxor and Karnak were built and when Tutankhamen was laid to rest amid his golden furnishings. If Mycenae is the father of the West we know, certainly Cnossus, which begot Mycenaean life and then merged into it, was its grandfather.

Zeus himself, or, as some say, a local Zeus, was born on Crete and was suckled by nymphs on Mount Ida. King Minos was his son, by Europa. Queen Pasiphaë, Minos' wife, fell madly in love with a white bull which Poseidon had sent to Minos for sacrifice and the offspring of this match was the horrible monster known as the Minotaur, with a bull's head and a human body. Later the Athenians murdered a son of King Minos because they resented the many victories the prince had won in their athletic contests. In revenge Minos required that seven youths and seven maidens of Athens be sent to Crete every nine years as morsels to be devoured by the Minotaur, dwelling in his noisome labyrinth. That is the story in outline. Mika Waltari, in *The Egyptian*, offered many grim and fanciful details in the chapter called "The Dark House," and he brought to his readers a vivid picture of the wealth and sybaritic civilization of the people of the island. "Their houses," reports the physician Sinuhe with amazement, "contain many bathrooms where both hot and cold water runs from silver pipes into silver baths at the mere turn of a tap. In the privies, running water sluices out the pans with a rushing sound, and nowhere else have I seen such a refinement of luxury." Assuming the author's research to be correct, one is forced to the conclusion that Crete had more bathrooms in 1350 B.C. than it does now, for tourists at least. It is considerably less developed, in hotel accommodations than is Rhodes, but one visits Crete for its wonders of the past rather than for its comforts of the present.

This does *not* mean, however, that reasonable comfort is lacking. *Heráklion*, the leading city, is becoming more tourist-conscious. The A-class *Astir*, for example, lives up to the promise of its name by offering normal amenities and some forty rooms with private bath. It does not have a restaurant but several good ones are to be found near by.

The B-class *Candia Palace*, though a bit ambitious in its name, is pleasant in a modest way, as is the comparable *Cosmopolite*. The little *Restaurant Caprice*, on a square centered by a romantic old Venetian fountain, offers all one could ask in good food and unpretentious charm. Several of its tables are placed on the sidewalk and even on the open street. A much newer and showier restaurant, built actually on the massive sea wall is called in Greek *Peripteron* and in tourist English *Glass House*. Here, one afternoon, I found a feminine pink tea going on, with music from a three-piece orchestra. The scene could have been duplicated in any U.S. city from Maine to California.

Heráklion (often called Candia) is not the capital of the island—that honor goes to Canea, in the west—but it is by far the largest and most important city, the fifth in population in all Greece, and it happens also to be the chief tourist goal because of its close proximity to the famous ruins of Cnossus. From May, 1941, till the end of the Second World War Heráklion was occupied by the hated Nazis, and the battering of the city was terrible. Most of the public buildings and more than half of the homes were bombed to rubble, but within a decade local and national efforts, stoutly aided by Marshall Plan funds, achieved wonders of restoration. Before leaving the subject of the war a local Nazi note may be set down here. It seems that after Max Schmeling landed by parachute on Crete he was killed by Cretan patriots in the village of Kandanos. The Nazis, one learns, then gave one of their customary "lessons" to conquered folk who were so rash as to liquidate a Teuton celebrity. They made of Kandanos a Cretan Lidice! For a note of pleasanter character I am happy to record that Eleutherios Venizelos, perhaps the greatest leader in statecraft that modern Greece has produced, was a native of Crete.

Cnossus, the chief center of Minoan remains, lies but three or four miles east of Heráklion. It is one of the most stirring sights in the world of archeology, for it reveals that a high state of civilization existed here five thousand years ago when Europe's people lived in caves at a level of culture hardly above that of wild beasts and when even Egypt's Pharaonic era had not begun to develop. The impressive ruins of three Minoan palaces, representing the three Minoan periods of culture, are clearly to be traced with the help of an English-speaking guide whom the cruise tour automatically includes or whom the local NTO office will provide. Guides are also available through a local travel bureau named *Creta*. The ruins cover about thirty thousand square yards and are a splendid monument to Sir Arthur Evans, who undertook the excavations in 1900. For those making a real study of them the classic guidebook is J. D. S. Pendlebury's *A Guide to the Palace of Cnossus*. (The later palaces were superimposed upon the earlier one, hence the use of the singular in his title.)

Even the most casual visitors always find their interest caught and held by certain special features of the construction and decoration, a few of which I shall set down here, more or less at random.

1. Much of the stone used was gypsum, which at first exposure "melted like sugar in warm rain," to quote one of my guides, leaving to the ages a curiously scarred or corrugated appearance. Much limestone, too, was used.

2. The pillars were always *smaller* at the base than in their upper portions.

3. The third and latest palace, dating from about 1300 B.C., was a four-story skyscraper rising from the remains of the earlier palaces.

4. Running drinking water was guided by a system of stone troughs to each of the chief rooms of the palace.

5. Enormous earthen jars, used for the storage of wine, olive oil and grain, are much in evidence.

6. In the mural decorations the skin of men was invariably painted in a ruddy hue, that of women in chalky white.

7. The women in the frescoes are always represented as having excessively slender waists. In one of the pictures a procession of such damsels marches past the eye, the background being a blue-flowering vine which the guide calls Arabic jasmine. Cretans state with assurance that their women are still remarkably slender-waisted. You are invited to take a look and form your own judgment.

8. The motif most typical of the Minoan palaces is a *labrys*, or two-headed ax, symbol of authority of the Minoan kings. The word labyrinth is derived from the same root as labrys and the construction of labyrinths, which also were symbolical of authority, was held by the kings to be their sole and royal prerogative. The mythical labyrinth that housed the grisly Minotaur was supposed to have been near Cnossus.

The work of excavation, and particularly the deciphering of the pre-

Phoenician inscriptions of the Minoans, a discovery and special passion of Sir Arthur Evans, still goes on at a steady pace, having been given great impetus by American aid. The importance of it to man's knowledge of the world's earliest real civilization is very great, for without the Minoan developments there would have been no Mycenaean Age and no Golden Age of Athens, to which we are eternally indebted. The most important finds of Cnossus, Phaestos and other archeological sites of Crete are assembled in the splendid *Museum of Heráklion*, which is an essential supplement to the ruins themselves. It should not be missed by even the hastiest tourist.

A famous son of Crete, born in the village of Phodele in the immediate vicinity of Heráklion and Cnossus, was Domenicos Theotocopoulos, known to the world as *El Greco*. Unfortunately none of El Greco's paintings are to be seen in his native island, but in the *Metropolitan Cathedral* of Heráklion there are five paintings, including a good "Last Supper" done on wood, by Michel Damaskinos, who was his able, though relatively obscure, contemporary. This cathedral brightened like other Greek Orthodox churches by gilded ikons, should surely be visited, and with it the appealing little church adjacent to it. This latter is now a museum of lovely little works of art, mostly on wood like the paintings of Damaskinos, and always with much "Greek gold" in the composition.

Heráklion's five-to-eight life when all the world sits in outdoor cafés or parades tirelessly in the streets in front of the cafés, is wonderfully lively, but its evenings are as quiet as one would expect. There is, however, one character restaurant, on an open upper terrace, that is worth finding by means of a taxi. It is called *Voyadzis* and its extreme simplicity is deceptive, for its chef is capable of serving as good (if inelegant) a meal as you will have anywhere in the islands. With Cretan hosts I dined one balmy evening on the Voyadzis terrace and it was indeed an experience. The *pièce de résistance* was a memorable mixed grill which included lamb chops, kidneys, sweetbreads, brains and tiny meat pies in the shape of cigars. The meal was preceded by the familiar ouzo, that aniseed firewater of Greece, and was accompanied by island wines, including local Malmsey, ancestor of Madeira's Malmsey, and, for those who could take it, the sharply resinous retsina, mentioned earlier. All in all, the Voyadzis meal, under lanterns and a Cretan moon, constituted one of the high lights of my own Mediterranean wanderings.

The classic tourist trip on Crete outside the Heráklion-Cnossus area is the cross-island tour to Gortys, Aghia Triada and the climactic Phaestos, where the night may be spent, if any of the ten beds are available in the government tourist house, which is well run and makes up in hospitality what it may lack in pretentious installations.

The road, an interesting one regardless of the historic sites to which it leads, runs through miles of vineyard and olive land (the export of raisins is a major source of island income) and other miles of Malvasia (Malmsey) vineyards, to reach a pass about half a mile above sea level, from which point it gradually descends to the plain surrounding Phaestos. The most dramatic sights passed on this portion of the journey are a rugged profile of Zeus, seen on the summit of a mountain range, and the chapel-crowned mountain on which stood the ancient town of *Rizinia*.

Gortys, which the road directly passes, once had a hundred thousand inhabitants and now has none. Its Temple of Pythias Apollo, its small but elegant Odeon and its early Christian basilica of St. Titus are of major interest, but its Doric inscriptions, on the temple wall, are what chiefly excite archeologists and attract visitors. In this primitive form of the Greek language the Laws of Gortys are lengthily chiseled by a system called *voustrophithon*, meaning "ox-turn." That is to say, the inscription runs several yards in one direction, then turns, like a furrow plowed by oxen, and runs *backward*, only to turn again when it reaches its starting point—and so on and on. The reader walked slowly forth and back, reading as he walked, until he had read the whole thing, from top to bottom, turn and *return*! The characters of the script are substantially larger at the top of the wall, for easy deciphering, than they are at eye level and below.

Aghia Triada, close to the southern shore of Crete, is far older than Gortys, for its two royal villas date from the Middle and Late Minoan period, or, more specifically, from about 1600 and 1300 B.C. Here, as in Cnossus and Phaestos, intricate arrangements for channeling water to the various rooms proclaim the Minoans' amazing know-how in "plumbing."

Phaestos is a really wonderful climax to one's Cretan jauntings. To reach it one drives to a mountain ledge on which the tourist house is built, on ground a little above the ruins of more Minoan palaces. The visitor is greeted—our party was anyway—by Alexander and Despina, a Cretan brother and sister who have run the place for the NTO for many years. For me this remarkable pair, each diminutive in body, each with a heart "as big as a whale," *make* that travelers' retreat. Kindness and eagerness—not of the tip-thirsty variety—radiate from both. When I first visited the tourist house it did not provide running water—now it does, cold only—but I didn't mind. Rain water was stored in a cistern and in handy barrels. Despina gave me a piece of soap, then dipped an earthen jar into one of the barrels and poured the water over my hands. With the aid of her personal service, offered with infectious smile and a torrent of Greek which I couldn't understand, I achieved a fairly good wash. Then she and Alexander consulted me about my wishes for dinner. Being again unable to converse, I simply left it to them and amid much laughter and two-language banter things proceeded toward a dinner that was ultimately laid on the table on the open porch. In such a setting the fare that Alexander and Despina managed to provide tasted like a banquet. The Minoan palaces were just below, the wide green valley *far* below and the purple mountains of Crete in ranges all about. The brother and sister have now learned some English so you will not have to resort to the sign language. Indeed, Alexander has advanced to a point where he has been put in charge of all the Phaestos antiquities.

The inspection of the ruins, presumably by early morning light so as to get a good start for the return journey to Heráklion before the sun is too high, reveals much the same sort of gypsum and limestone construction as at Cnossus, the same elaborate thought for royal comfort, the same colossal jars for the storage of wine, olive oil and grain, some of them quite intact and unbroken after the passage of thousands of years.

The Phaestos ruins, though impressive, are less extensive and important than those of Cnossus, but the setting here is beyond compare. The lofty ledge on which Phaestos stands would be worth a visit if there were nothing here but nature. Add the interesting ruins as a special goal, then add Alexander and Despina as a special dividend, and you will probably vote Phaestos your Cretan climax.

Rhodes in Blue and White

It seems that when Apollo, the son of Zeus, grew to manhood there was no wife for him. The supreme god, under pressure to do many things at once, had quite forgotten to provide for this contingency, so he racked his Olympian brain and brought forth a perfect solution to the problem. He made Rhodes as a spouse for his son. Apollo was instantly infatuated, but he wanted to give his bride a present worthy of her beauty so he devised—color. From that day to this Rhodes has been decked with color unsurpassed in the Mediterranean world. The colors of the Greek flag are blue and white, which also are the colors of Rhodes, plentifully backgrounded with forest green.

The cruise ships touching at Rhodes, usually in the morning to remain moored until midnight, do not find any Colossus straddling the harbor, as of old tradition, but they do find a fascinating walled city named Rhodes like the island. Air travelers approaching the landing field a few miles west of the city are thrilled by the dazzling whiteness of the villages, contrasting with the mat of purest blue which is the sea fringing the island with white surf. As you ride to the city you notice that most of the houses have touches of Greek blue on the white plaster. This is no accident. It is a definite way of expressing the joy of the householder that as Greek in race they are Greek also in allegiance. It is a way of draping the flag about the house and there is obvious elation in it, as a symbol of release from the Italian yoke that weighed on them from 1912 to 1945. During the unhappy years when the island was subject to Mussolini's whims the blue and white color scheme was forbidden by law. Houses so painted had to be scraped and left in an unsightly state or else painted yellow. You still see an occasional yellow house, perhaps because the owners cannot muster the money for repainting, but blue and white houses now outnumber yellow fifty to one. Memories of near-starvation days of 1942 and 1943 are sharp and bitter. Some Rhodians then went so far as to try to escape to Anatolia, across the nine-mile strait, paddling along even in washtubs!

Rhodes is a flawless tourist town and island. It has an exciting background, from the era when its bronze Colossus guarded the harbor until the official reversion to its mother Greece on March 7, 1947. It has, in marked degree, a *pleasure present*, with touches of luxury.

The many tourist hotels of this island, both in the capital and in the countryside and mountains, reveal its character as a vacation goal and this is corroborated by the ample facilities for swimming, boating, shopping and dancing, which could be called the Big Four of Holiday. In the town of Rhodes and its environs the dean of the luxury hotels is the long-established *Hotel des Roses*, a big, resort-type seaside inn with private beach that has been deservedly popular for a long time. It is a prideful link of the Astir group, which, in itself, is enough to recommend it. Near it looms the ultramodern 200-room de luxe *Grand Hotel*, which opened its doors in the spring of 1963, contrasting sharply with the mellow old "Roses." A bit farther along the coast and almost as new, but of entirely different type, is the *Miramare*, a Gauer bungalow hotel like the Miramare of Corfu, and even more sumptuous. It has 180 bungalows, many of which are separate little villas while some are of apartment style in two-story groups. The whole development is centered by a large pool which is surrounded by quite an array of dining rooms, open or glassed in, bars, shops and a taverna. Minigolf, tennis and various other sports vie with bathing, sailing and water skiing, for this is a fine and full-fledged resort in its own right. Miramarette Fiats are available at about the same rental rates as those in the Gauer hotels of Corfu, namely $11.50 a day, with insurance and a tankful of gas.

Astir goes all out in Rhodes in providing tourist facilities of several categories. The Roses is its "flagship hotel"; the *Thermai*, near the walled city, is a central A-class place; the *Pindos* is B-class; and the *Lindos* is C-class. *Kallithea* is a seaside spa seven miles from the town, with important curative mineral waters. And finally, *Elafos* and *Elafina*, of which more later, are A-class inns in the mountains. For full information and for guidance in making individual tours the visitor should consult the NTO office on Kountouri Square between the Government House and Hôtel des Roses. An English-language folder, with clear key maps of the town and the island, is available there.

Shoppers attention! Rhodes is a free port and the various goods available in the city and hotel shops seem to average about 30 per cent cheaper than similar goods on the mainland. I inquired about customs difficulties in introducing such purchases into mainland Greece and was told that tourists encounter no troubles at all (which proved true) but that Greek residents may be challenged.

The town of Rhodes, capital not only of its own island but of the whole Dodecanese, is quite enough in itself to warrant a visit. The new town, with pleasant residential streets and parks and with solid public buildings in Venetian Gothic style, encloses in its encircling arms the old town of the Knights Hospitalers of St. John of Jerusalem, who were called at one time the Knights of Rhodes, and at a later period the Knights of Malta. This is the best preserved medieval town of the whole Mediterranean, clearly surpassing in glamorous appearance that other stronghold of the Knights, Valletta. It is completely surrounded by deep moats and a crenelated wall with eight gates, and shows evidences of Byzantine and Turkish occupations before and after the period of the Knights. The Turkish period is represented by several mosques with their lofty pencil-shaped minarets.

At the town's highest point, reached by walking up the superlative *Street of the Knights*, is the *Palace of the Grand Master*. The palace is a tremendous spectacle though made a little "queer" by Mussolini's heavy-handed ministrations. In 1939, he had its interior rebuilt to serve as a summer palace for himself and for the king and royal family of Italy. Its modern splendors, its absurdly grandiose tiled bathrooms, its modern plumbing and heating, seem a bit grotesque for the residence of the Grand Master of the Knights of Rhodes. Since 1947 the Greeks have done what they could to tame down the grotesqueries, but a complete rebuilding, to restore the structure to its pristine knightliness, would cost many millions of drachmas. The Palace is glamorized nightly by a stirring "Sound and Light" show.

Two other things within the old city need special seeing, though it seems almost discriminatory to mention anything as special when everything in such a scene is special. The *municipal flower garden* is one feature, a floral treat to the eyes, where flowers are grown for public sale. You may walk in, pick out the blooms you want and have them snipped for you from the stalks or branches. The *Museum of Rhodes* is the other specialty, located in the old hospital of the Hospitalers. Among its many items from Rhodes' many pasts is the world-known *Aphrodite* (Venus) *of Rhodes*, as lovely a goddess as was ever fashioned even by the Greeks. She dates from the Hellenistic period, which flourished after the death of Alexander (323 B.C.). During the Italian Fascist occupation this was transferred to the Naples Museum, but upon the restoration of Rhodes to Greece it had to be returned.

The shore front of the city, just outside the old walls, is lined with imposing public buildings erected mostly by the Italians, who were undeniably energetic colonizers. In the office of the Governor of the Dodecanese, in the large *Government Building,* I was interested to see two standing bronze deer, one on either side of his desk. Outside the building, on two columns at the edge of the sea, stand two more, these being respectively a large bronze buck and doe. Live deer may be seen in the moat between the Old City and the New City, all of which is appropriate enough since the deer is the symbol of Rhodes. It seems that a certain Grand Master of the Knights introduced deer to this island to eat snakes. The campign has been called a full success, though one notices that all peasant women, without exception, still wear stout, high boots for protection against snakes when they work in the fields. Town folk assert that this is no more than an oddly surviving tradition.

"And what about the Colossus of Rhodes?" you are surely asking. This bronze statue of Phoebus Apollo, the sun god, who was the patron deity of the Rhodians, is supposed to have been made by a sculptor of Lindos and set up in 280 B.C. in the harbor of Rhodes. It was more than a hundred feet high and was universally considered one of the Seven Wonders of the World. Tradition has it that the statue straddled the entrance to the main harbor, providing a gateway for ships, but this is considered impossible, because when the sun god fell, being rocked by a terrible earthquake in 227 B.C., he fell *in* toward the land, in a way he could not have managed had he been straddling. There is not a trace of the statue today. A Jewish trader bought it as junk several centuries after its fall, broke it up and sold it to the Turks. It was shipped across the strait to the Asiatic mainland and carried off on the backs of nearly a thousand camels. The probable site of the statue is the point directly across the smaller harbor from the Government House. Or the god *may* have been leaning on a gigantic staff on the nearer side of the harbor.

Perhaps this is as suitable a point as any to name the Seven Wonders of the World, since two of them were on Greek soil. Here they are: 1) The *Statue of Zeus* by Phidias in Olympia; 2) the *Colossus of*

Rhodes; 3) the *Pyramids at Giza* (Cairo); 4) the *Pharos* (Lighthouse) at Alexandria; 5) the *Temple of Diana* at Ephesus; 6) the *Mausoleum of Halicarnassus* (in Asia Minor); and 7) the *Hanging Gardens of Babylon.* The first two have been covered in this book and Numbers 3, 4, 5 and 6 will have mention as we reach Egypt and then Asia Minor. Babylon is far beyond the Mediterranean shores.

Tourists, whether coming by cruise ship or otherwise, are first shown the sights of the town and then taken to the acropolis of the ancient city, on which there are extensive remains, including three columns of a 600 B.C. Temple of Apollo. From this hill there is a broad panoramic view of town and sea, but the big surprise is the hill's name, Mt. Smith! This name, believe it or not, is an absolutely *Greek* name, not English, a shortened form of Hermes*smith*eos.

Three Rhodian Cities of the Golden Age

The Golden Age of the island was between the Mycenaean and Periclean Ages, reaching its peak at or before 600 B.C. Its three great cities, each formerly larger than Rhodes is today, were Ialyssos, Lindos and Kámiros. These cities, according to the fanciful legend, were the three sons of Apollo and his wife Rhodes and each is interesting in its individual way.

Ialyssos, whose acropolis was the thousand-foot *Mount Philerimos,* less than ten miles southwest of Rhodes, has been almost obliterated by time, but the summit of this hill, reached by a good highway, offers a magnificent view *and* the lovely *Monastery of Panaghia,* a most unusual affair, built originally by the Knights, but rebuilt, still with fine old lines, in 1931. Each monk on Mount Philerimos bore the name of a flower, and one of them was Rose! About all that is left of ancient Ialyssos is a fragment of the Temple of Minerva. On a spur of the mountain the Italians erected an eighty-foot statue of Christ, but during the war it proved such a landmark for enemy bombers, heading in to attack the near-by Maritsa Airport, that they took it down.

A corollary of the Mount Philerimos visit, if you are in Rhodes in summer, should be the *Valley of the Butterflies (Petaloudes).* I was there in the winter and in midspring, so I did not see the butterflies, but I am assured that if disturbed by a thrown stone or stick they will rise from this jungle-filled valley in veritable clouds. Their color is variously given as ranging from rose-gray to gold-red, which is quite a spread on the spectrum. Perhaps you can catch one and study his color scheme for yourself.

Old *Lindos*, once a city of Dorian Greeks, is gloriously placed on a lofty coastal promontory some thirty-five miles south of Rhodes and at its base, almost burrowing under it, is Greek-clean new Lindos, striving to make a living from agriculture. In its great days it was probably a city of more than a hundred thousand inhabitants and indeed it was the head of an empire. The important city of Gela, in Sicily, was one of its colonies.

The acropolis of this 3000-year-old city looms above a double harbor, into one part of which, a handsome crescent, Paul is thought to have sailed on one of his missionary journeys. The hill was adorned with a primitive temple of 1500 B.C., whose foundations are still traceable, and later with a splendid temple to Athena Lindos, important portions of which remain. Athena liked, whenever possible, to have her temples surrounded on three sides by the sea, as is the case here. Many dignitaries, throughout the ages, brought rich gifts to the Lindos temples and one of the bringers, we are solemnly assured, was Helen of Troy, who donated a golden cup molded to the exact form of one of her beautiful breasts. The cup has disappeared into the mists of mythology, which is sad indeed. What would not an enterprising American manufacturer of foundation garments give for it as a model for his "Queen Helen bra"! We presume this golden gift was a B cup, but in any case it was perfect.

An early Byzantine church and town hall on the Lindos crest are surrounded by the Knights' massive crenelated wall, and adjacent to the church one may visit the impressive three-story *Palace of the Grand Masters*. All the civilizations of Rhodes, including that of modern Greece, are represented in this double town. The homes in the lower village and on the flank of the hill are marvelous to see. I plucked up nerve to enter two of them and was cordially received both times. Black and white pebbled floors were typical of their décor, and scrupulous cleanliness was their keynote.

On the opposite side of the island from Lindos lie the ruins of *Kámiros*, the third of the ancient Rhodian cities, "sons" of Apollo and

Rhodes. To reach it one may ride across the island over a forested mountain named Profiti Ilias, which is to say, Prophet Elijah. On a spur of this height, with an extensive view over the slopes below and the blue Aegean Sea, are two modern resort hotels (mentioned above) of Astir ownership by name *Elafos* and *Elafina*, meaning Buck and Doe. These names, so typical of Rhodes, hint of the fact that fairly numerous deer do exist in the vicinity. The two hotels are close together and provide, between them, for all forms of holiday pleasure in a cool mountain setting.

Kámiros is, I think, more understandable *as a city* of very ancient times than is any other excavated town in the whole of Greece. It is even comparable, in its early Greek way, to the later Roman Pompeii. On a shelf of a foothill of a mountain, and on a broad plateau just above this shelf, the visitor may see, with a little imagination, exactly how the Kamirots lived. He may walk down Main Street and enter its homes and shops. He may see where the people bathed, with water piped into their homes as in the Cretan towns of that day. On the plateau above he may see the big market of the city, with its exceedingly long row of columns, six of which still stand. He may see the big reservoirs, fed by pipes that came from higher mountains five miles distant. As a revelation of life in the early dawn of Western time Kámiros is rarely matched anywhere.

Greek internecine wars brought to an end the Golden Age of the Three Cities and in 407 B.C. they merged together politically to form a single state. With their combined resources they built the town of Rhodes, which has had several lustrous eras of is own, including the present golden age of holiday.

Tourists on some of the cruise ships, including the *Semiramis,* may avail themselves of a Rhodes-by-Night tour which is offered every Wednesday evening starting at 8:30 from the office of the *Caryanides Travel Service* at Macarios Street 16, or the company will pick up stay-over guests at their hotels. The tour first goes by coach to Mt. Smith for the night view and then continues to the village of *Kallithies,* where a folk dance show in costume is offered, along with what is ambitiously called a wine festival. This attraction seems likely to be eclipsed in the immediate future by a lavish casino operated by the same German interests that operate the Achilleion Casino in Corfu.

Cos of Hippocrates and Patmos of John

Cos and Patmos are seen by *Semiramis* guests in one day, the former in the morning, the latter in the late afternoon, with a four-hour sail between the two.

Cos, shaped like a dolphin, is second in size to Rhodes of the twelve Dodecanese islands, second, too, in historical importance, for its like-named capital had two periods of real magnificence. One was in the fourth, third and second centuries B.C., the other, after destruction by an earthquake in 182 A.D. and a remarkable job of rebuilding, was in the second, third and fourth centuries A.D. after which it was again laid low by an earthquake. In our own time, on April 23, 1933, it was once again destroyed by a terrible-tempered temblor and has again been rebuilt, for it seems that you can't keep a good city down. The old walled quarter of the Knights of Rhodes, however, was left open for archeological excavation.

The greatest days of Cos were in the fourth century B.C., when its fame almost overshadowed that of Athens, whose Periclean Age had dimmed. It was then that a native islander, Hippocrates, the Father of Medicine as he is always called, founded his famous clinic and seminar under a plane tree that is still pointed out to tourists as *the* tree. Actually, this is fictional, since a plane tree's life is only about five or six hundred years at the most, yet certainly the Coan doctor did practice and teach under *a* plane tree. This one, with a trunk forty feet in circumference, plays its part effectively. The Hippocratic Oath, formulated by Hippocrates, is still taken by students receiving their degree in medicine. It governs a doctor's ethics as it did in the days of the great pioneer. An excellent statue of Hippocrates is to be seen in the Cos Museum.

The Greco-Egyptian dynasty of the Ptolemies showed great devotion to Cos, and Ptolemy II Philadelphus was born here. This word Philadelphus, which means, as in the case of Pennsylvania's capital, Brotherly Love, was given by him to his deceased wife, Arsinoë II, who was also his full sister. In other words she practiced brotherly love in the most literal sense, greatly shocking the couple's Greek subjects, though not the Egyptian. The surname Philadelphus was later applied to the king himself.

Other celebrated Coans were Theocritus, the pastoral poet of the fourth century B.C., a resident though not a native, and Apelles, the most noteworthy painter of that same period. And across the five-mile strait in Asia Minor, clearly visible from Cos, is Halicarnassus (now the Turkish city of Bodrum), which was the birthplace of the pioneer historian Herodotus. Halicarnassus, known in history as the capital of ancient Caria, boasted one of the Seven Wonders of the World, the gigantic *Mausoleum of King Mausolus* and his wife Artemisia, so this king's tomb, as a common noun, has been a fixture in dictionaries for more than two thousand years.

The chief sights of Cos, aside from the plane tree, are the ancient Odeum, a third-century concert hall well preserved; a Roman villa with fine mosaics; the Museum, rich in Hellenistic statuary; and, two miles from town, the Asklepeion, a sanctuary dedicated to Asclepius, the god of healing and medicine, who was a son of Apollo. Here the town guide, or guidess invites his or her flock to be seated on the temple steps and give attention to a lecture. In the case of my *Semiramis* tour the guide was a pretty young girl, but her lecture was as bold and spicy—and charming—as anyone could wish.

Stayers-over find a pleasant new *Xenia Hotel,* in fact two Xenias, one of them on the beach, and another shore hotel called the *Zephyros,* all three of Class B. Today's town and island are placidly pleasant, made colorful in spring by orchards of bitter almond trees displaying a glory of purplish blossoms.

Patmos, less than forty square miles in area, is the smallest island of the Dodecanese, and also the most northerly. To many visitors it is also the most appealing, quite aside from its association with John the Revelator. The chief settlement is a dramatic double town consisting of Scala, which is the port, and six hundred feet higher up a striking pyramid of white houses constituting the village of *Chora,* dominated by the *Monastery of St. John.* One mounts to this crest, a distance of about a mile and a half by pilgrim path, longer by road on donkeyback or by means of one of the town's two taxis. Those who choose the donkey find plenty of mounts available, each under the guidance of a boy who doesn't care how many times he trudges up the steep slope if a few drachmas are bestowed each time.

Half way up is the celebrated *Grotto of the Apocalypse*, where John wrote the cryptic book called *The Revelation of John*. A great accretion of legend has, of course, grown up around this grotto. We are shown a triple crack in the rock through which God spoke to John. We are shown his stone bed and stone pillow, a grip by which he raised himself from bed, a stone desk on which his secretary-disciple Prochorus took down the details of the apocalyptic vision as John dictated. This sort of build-up is inevitable in the case of any great religious shrine but we may take refuge in the certainty that John did write the book in Patmos, for he says so himself in the first chapter. "I John, . . . was in the isle that is called Patmos . . . and heard behind me a great voice, as of a trumpet, saying, . . . 'What thou seest, write in a book and send it to the seven churches.'" He did so and the strange vision has puzzled theologians ever since. Its four horsemen served as a theme for Ibáñez' novel *The Four Horsemen of the Apocalypse*, made into a famous early film with Rudolph Valentino.

Continuing up to the summit and finally winding one's way on foot through ascending streets of the seventeenth century village of Chora, one reaches the eleventh-century monastery. It is rich in this world's property, which includes, in theory at least, the whole island of Patmos, and in actual fact valuable lands in Crete, Santorin and Cyprus. Its library is especially rich, with enormously valuable Byzantine and Frankish and even Turkish manuscripts. Over the centuries, many of these treasures have been "acquired" by the Vatican, by the ever-acquisitive British Museum and by other museums all over Europe, but much of the best, over seven hundred items in all, still remains. The most valuable item of all is a fifth-century Gospel of St. Mark (over thirty leaves of it anyway) called the *Codex Porphyrius*, done in intricate gold and silver lettering on purple vellum.

Patmos is by no means a stay-over center like Cos, but a *very* simple hotel is available, as also some few lesser accommodations in small inns and private homes. Cruise-takers content themselves with the donkey-back tour and a bit of relaxation down in Scala, but those who come by the semiweekly steamer from Piraeus may enjoy several days on the island if they prepare their minds and bodies to rough it for the sake of an unusual experience. In any such venture the basic cleanliness of almost every Greek inn or home, however humble, can be counted on.

Delos of Apollo and Mykonos of Pleasure

Delos, in the Cyclades, is one of the strangest phenomena to be found in all the five hundred islands of Greece. Perhaps no other island of them all is so ill-favored by nature, yet it is a major tourist goal. *Mykonos*, a delightful and well-favored island, though only one of many, owes its prosperity largely to its nearness to Delos. As in the case of Cos and Patmos, these two islands are covered by most cruise steamers, including the *Semiramis*, in one day, Delos in the morning, Mykonos in the afternoon. They are only an hour apart either by steamer or by motorboat and many visitors elect to stay on Mykonos for a few days making several visits to Delos. There is also a public caïque that makes its way under sail from Mykonos to Delos every morning.

Delos owes its tourist importance solely to the philandering of Zeus, the supreme deity of the Greeks. Like their other gods he was subject to normal human temptations of every sort and certainly he had an eye for the girls. He also had a wife, by name Hera, and she was given to normal jealousies. One of Zeus's many affairs was with Leto. He "got her into trouble" and very serious trouble it was, for Hera was lynx-eyed and knew all about it. She threatened with her displeasure any community which should grant asylum to the expectant mother. All refused to receive her, but there was a wretched island called Delos which drifted about aimlessly in the middle of the Aegean Sea. Poseidon, moved by the plight of Leto, decided to anchor it and make it available to Leto. This he did, and thus, finally, Delos, which was such a miserable place anyway that it couldn't lose much from Hera's spleen, did let her come in and bear her baby. He proved to be Apollo the Huntsman, who was god of many other things, including music, poetry, prophecy and later the sun itself. As early as the eighth century B.C. a tremendous Apollo cult sprang up. In the seventh century the people of Naxos Island took over Delos and from their era of domination dates the famous row of guardian lions, five of which have survived the attacks of the elements and the pilfering powers of Europe. From the same era dates the 23-foot statue of Apollo, two huge fragments of which are still seen.

After the Naxians came the Athenians, who formed, to their own special advantage, the powerful Confederacy of Delos, called also the Delian League. By a clever application of power politics in the guise of religion Athens built up the League to formidable proportions in commerce and in naval power, and the island sanctuary received also many ex-votos of great value proffered by the Greek city-states. In 454 B.C., Athens highandedly removed the treasury of the Confederacy to home ground. She then ruled with increasingly heavy hand and in 426 she promulgated the theory that on this special holy island no human being might die or be born. Pregnant mothers and all persons appearing to be at death's door were removed to a small neighboring island, now pointed out to tourists, called Rheneia. All bodies were exhumed from Delian burying grounds and thrown into a ditch dug on the perimeter of Rheneia. This campaign was called purification.

I have mentioned that Delos is ill-favored and certainly this is true, for it is rocky, treeless and terribly arid, with only one puny stream that flows solely during the period of winter rains. It has not even any good harbor or anchorage and the sea winds, especially the violent summer gales called *meltémi*, lash the ruins with relentless force. It is an insignificant island in size, only three miles long by about a thousand yards wide, and today it is virtually uninhabited except for the handful of guardians and other persons catering to tourism. Yet here there grew up what is commonly called the most important island of classical times and a chief focus of interest to present-day travelers.

I read in various accounts that it is impossible to tire of Delos, to which claim I beg to demur, just a bit, for I am sure that thousands of tourists every year find the endless acres of ruins, mostly flat on the ground, quite capable of creating at least physical weariness. The dedicated student or archeological buff, on the other hand, can indeed spend excited hours, days, weeks in eager examination.

The standard tour is long and fatiguing. On many a day the winds and/or rains make sightseeing difficult, as the plodding tourist seeks vainly for shelter, of which there is none. But I must not go too far in such comment lest I establish myself as a debunker. Beyond a doubt Delos is wonderfully important, intriguing and above all wildly improbable in having reached the zenith of fame despite a total lack of natural advantages. It shows what man, spurred at first by religious zeal, and then by the desire for gain can achieve. *Ad astra per aspera!*

Among the most interesting features of the tour are the remains of the sumptuous private homes built during the commercial Hellenistic period, after the yoke of Athens and then the yoke of the Ptolemies had been thrown off. Huge cisterns storing the winter rains gave water enough to do with and many of the "name houses," for instance, the House of Masks, the House of the Dolphins, the House of the Trident and the House of Dionysus, must have been magnificent. The finest and most elaborate mosaic scenes covered the floors and several of these are shown to tourists. In the House of Dionysus, who was the Greek equivalent of the Roman Bacchus, there is a superlative floor depicting the wine god riding a tiger, and not a "blind tiger" at that. Actually the beast seems more panther than tiger. Dionysus holds a staff in one hand, a plate, or maybe a cymbal, in the other, and his head is crowned with ivy. As a note of comic relief the guides point out a note scribbled on the wall by a small boy some twenty-three hundred years ago. With many mistakes in grammar and spelling it reads: "We were playing dice, but one boy was a little blind, so the other cheated." If this were of today the viewers-with-alarm would bemoan it. "What are we coming to? The youth of today has lost all sense of morality."

Mykonos, quite regardless of its famous neighbor, is a flourishing goal of tourism, appealing especially to the pleasure-bound. It is a lovely white town, its extremely broad quays are lined with numberless cafés where drinks of all sorts—*tourkiko*, being Turkish coffee, is standard— may be ordered, perhaps with an almond cake of local fame called *amygdaloto*. Relaxation rules, and there are tourist shops galore, led in feminine acclaim by "Maroulina's Little Shop," where exquisite gifts, ornaments and women's accessories are on sale. Many artists set their sights for Mykonos, as do Greek and foreign celebrities and, to some extent, even playboys and playgirls of the international set.

The life of the quays is fascinating. It ranges from the bustle of loading and unloading along the front, interspersed with donkey traffic and the constant passing of sailors, fishermen, tourists and any other types that make a motley, to such pleasant trivia as a pair of trained pelicans tossing toy balloons about in the manner of kittens with balls of yarn. It is all great fun and from the quay lead cool, narrow lanes amid the whitewashed houses.

Hotels are fairly abundant. The *Leto,* named for the unmarried mother of Apollo, is at the far end of the quays, a delightful A-class hotel with many refinements, including private balconies facing the town and its life. Then there is the *Xenia,* of the government NTO chain, located to the west of the center squarely on the sea front. The *Delos* is a recommendable C-class place and the *Apollo* D-class, but a special feature of this island is rooms offered to visitors in private homes. It is said, in fact, that Mykonos initiated the system in Greece of householders inviting tourists to rent private accommodations. It is axiomatic that all such homes are immaculate.

On a part of the Mykonos shore front there is a most striking section called *Venetia,* a considerable row of mellow old houses that rise on rock shelves straight from the sea's edge, their jutting balconies overhanging the churning water. Back of Venetia rises the Hill of Windmills, with many of the cylindrical white windmills, roofed with thatch, that are so typical of this island.

Mykonos is altogether charming. The dazzling whiteness of the houses is relieved by touches of color on doors and shutters and on the domes of the town's many churches. The colors are often blue, sometimes pink. There is plenty of pink in the oleanders, too, and blazing red in the hibiscus blossoms. It works out that historic Delos and lovely, light-hearted Mykonos make a natural team, each complementing the other.

REVISION SUPPLEMENT TO CHAPTERS 15, 16 AND 17

EGYPT's noteworthy advances in tourism continue at a rapid rate. Hotels are sprouting up in Cairo and in other tourist meccas throughout Egypt. *United Arab Airlines* (UAA), mentioned on page 292 as planning service from the United States to Cairo, is *still* planning for that service, which officials hope will commence early in 1967. Even without direct service, however, UAA has cooperative arrangements with several transatlantic carriers, which help them to offer a 21-day $535 round-trip fare to Cairo. In order to qualify, you must spend 12 days in the Middle East; your remaining nine days may be spent anywhere you choose en route. The airline currently flies from major European capitals to Cairo. UAA has an office not only in New York City (720 Fifth Avenue), but now also on the West Coast, at 510 West 6th Street, Los Angeles.

Visas are still required for entry into Egypt. If you are coming directly from the United States to Egypt a smallpox vaccination (which you need anyway for reentry to the U.S.) is all that's required in addition to your passport and visa. The UAR Consulate in New York City, mentioned on page 291 with a Park Avenue address, has now moved to 655 Madison Avenue. Be sure to check with a UAR office on whatever else is needed if you plan to come to Egypt from India or various other Eastern locales, since regulations in such cases differ from those applicable for U.S. or European points of departure. Your visa now costs $2.30, of which $2.00 goes to the fund to save Abu Simbel. That seemingly impossible task is already well under way with the moving of sections higher up the riverbank to ground safe from the rising water level caused by the new Aswan Dam. Egypt has pledged $12 million of the $36 million needed to save the monuments from being covered by 120 feet of water. UNESCO, which made a sizable financial contribution to the project, has approved plans submitted by the Egyptian government to cut up the statues and move them to safety, so the race is on to complete this gigantic job before the new dam and the subsequent flooding can interfere with it, the dam's expected completion date being sometime in 1967. In gratitude for the U.S. contribution of $16 million to save the Nubian monuments, the UAR has given the 2000-year-old Temple of Dendur to the U.S. and the 633-ton monument will be reassembled in the U.S., the exact location still undecided as of this writing.

A report on Abu Simbel as of now, with its prospects for the future, will be given below, but first a rundown of the newer hotels of Cairo and other localities, for hotel building in Egypt is flourishing as never before.

El Borg, meaning the Tower and often called the Tower Hotel, is on Gezira Island directly across the Nile from the Hilton; *El Nil Hotel*, next door to El Borg on Gezira Island, has 272 luxury rooms. On Liberation Square, near the Hilton and the Egyptian Museum, referred to on pages 300–302, is the *Sheherazade*. Parenthetically, the central-city *Cleopatra Palace Hotel*, barely mentioned on page 298, is a 14-story affair, though not of special quality, with a panoramic dining room on the top floor.

Two newcomers with similar names, differentiated only by their locales in Cairo, are the *Omar Khayyam Zamalek* and the *Omar Khayyam Manial*. The former is located in the northern part of Gezira Island; the latter in the northern part of Roda Island, noted for its sumptuous gardens. Both 200-room hotels are of luxury class and well run. The *Kasr El Haram's* 96 rooms are also on Roda Island. This hotel is the former *Manial Palace* (page 304), an ex-prince's palace.

Another newcomer to the city is the *Cairo Intercontinental Hotel* (PAA subsidiary) now being built on the southern tip of Gezira Island and including part of the Horia Gardens. The fully air-conditioned hotel fronts on the Nile and will offer about 600 rooms with full luxury facilities, including a rooftop restaurant.

The *Nile Hilton*, still dean of today's crop of topflight hotels, has an annex in the form of the M. S. *Isis*, a 270-foot cruising ship eventually destined to fly the Hilton flag on cruises down the Nile. The ship now provides extra rooms for the Nile Hilton, at whose front door she is moored, while her sister ship, the M. S. *Osiris*, cruises from her mooring at Luxor, near the site of the future *Luxor Hilton*, to Aswan. Both ships were recently purchased by Hilton International to cruise the Nile for the winter months and to remain moored at the Nile Hilton and the Luxor Hilton, respectively, during the summer. The four-day trip from Luxor to Aswan, with sightseeing en route, costs under $250 for single occupancy and less than $300 for two persons.

Using Cairo as a nucleus, we may "look around" to see what other localities have made important advances in hotel building. One place, lying a few miles to the south of the capital, is Helwan, a spa that I have missed on previous visits. Now enjoying a rebirth, due to the interest of visitors, especially Europeans, Helwan's most fascinating sight for me was not the curative springs, but one of the former residences of ex-king Farouk, which is now open to the public. Finished in antiques and Egyptian modern style, the small palace must have offered its onetime owner a reprieve from the wild life he was so famed for living. Most of the ex-king's former homes, in fact, have now become either museums or hotels and each is worth at least a quick visit, since the playboy king really lived it up and his many homes show it. As for Helwan, there is not much doing there, but it's a delightful place for a retreat. The *Excelsior Hotel*, where tourists can relax in complete comfort, offers 45 rooms and the chance to take advantage of the sulphur springs and those of pure mineral water as well.

The historic former *Heliopolis Palace Hotel* of Heliopolis (pages 297, 298), a residential suburb of Cairo, has *not*, even yet, joined the boom of hotel expansion, for it is still a government office building, as it has been for many years, though previous to that it was the pride of Egypt in its original capacity as a hotel.

About 140 miles north of Cairo by road or rail—but there is frequent plane service, too, via UAA—lies Alexandria, Egypt's second city and chief port. Two noteworthy newcomers to its hotel roster are the *Alamein Sidi Abdel Rahman*, with 64 rooms, and the luxurious *Palestine*, with 117 rooms. The improbable name of the latter hotel deserves explanation, which is readily given by most Egyptians. It was named to honor the *Jordanian* part of Palestine, which includes many sacred parts of Jerusalem and also the town of Bethlehem. The decision to give it this name was taken in remembrance of the 1964 summit conference of the Arab States, which was held in Alexandria.

Four hours' drive from Alexandria on the desert, but also right on the

Mediterranean shore, is the new summer resort of *Marsa Matrouh*. With 75 hotel units and 50 bungalows right on the sea, the resort is a lovely summer destination, complete with white sand beach. It can be reached by train or plane during the summer months only. It is not open in winter.

To promote travel to Luxor, the government recently introduced a Combined Railway Ticket (CRT) covering transportation and hotel accommodations for two-day visits. CRT rates start at $26.91 per person for double occupancy with half-fare charge for children between the ages of 3 and 10.

Reverting to Nile trips, it seems incredible, but at present count there are eight 150-passenger floating hotels cruising the Nile. All offer air-conditioned rooms, private baths, swimming pools (often not larger than a postage stamp), shops, and a moving panorama of life along the Nile.

At Luxor, the docking base of the M. S. *Osiris* and the site of the Luxor Hilton, as mentioned earlier, other news is now being made by Intercontinental Hotels Corporation, for this company is building a hotel there and, as is the case in IHC's Cairo venture, it is a joint enterprise in combination with the Egyptian government, which put up 80 per cent of the building cost as against the company's 20 per cent. IHC will design, build and operate the hotel.

Aswan, for those who knew it when, has undergone a metamorphosis. In little more than five years, old Aswan has become a new and thriving city, with modern buildings and a substantial year-round population that was started by the many persons working on the dam but now counts many others as well. Elaborate plans have been drawn up for the progress of Aswan following completion of the dam, which will create what is called by Egyptians the largest man-made lake in the world, 350 miles as compared to our Lake Mead of 115 miles. Plans to make the area a great winter resort include building many new hotels and tourist areas as well as lavish gardens and outdoor restaurants. Two luxury hotels in the works as of this writing are the *Nefertiti*, with 100 rooms, and the *Aswan Hilton*, still another in the Hilton International chain, this one with 75 rooms already available. Three other Aswan hotels are the 66-room *Abu Simbel*, the 120-room *Kalabsha*, both almost as new as the trio just named above and the *Amoun*, bungalows located on Amoun Island.

Abu Simbel has come far more prominently into the public eye than when the brief report on page 338 was written, but it is still a prime newsmaker all over the world. Why save *this* monument, some ask, when so many others are flooded anyway? First discovered in 1812, the temple, built by Ramses II for himself and his wife Nefertari about 3000 years earlier, makes remarkable use of the natural cliff formed by the flowing of the Nile. This, of course, will be lost when the monuments are moved up the river bank, but efforts are being made to reconstruct, insofar as is possible, the site, so that at least the impressive lighting of the monuments under the first rays of the morning sun will not be lost. It seems ironic that the man Ramses II should be a "household word" throughout the world when history shows us that he was an extreme egotist who put his name to any and all accomplishments of his time, whether or not he had played a part in their construction, and who claimed all works of art as his—regardless of who was the actual creator. However, Ramses II will live to tell his story, and an impressive one it is, for years to come thanks to UNESCO and the efforts of England, the United States and Egypt in cooperation with many other countries.

You may be interested, as I was, in the fact that with the exception of one type all statues in Egypt stand or sit. The only type of statue with any kind of action is an occasional one of a woman kneading bread! For a treat for your eye and for some idea of what used to be, examine the photographic artistry of William MacQuitty in his book *Abu Simbel*.

Boat trips from El-Shellal, a port about 7 miles from the Aswan airport, to Abu Simbel are frequent, either on the *Star of Abu Simbel*, which makes the three-day trip, spending half a day at Abu Simbel and the temples, or on the larger *Memphis* or *Lotus*, which also depart from and return to El-Shellal. A shorter trip can be made by the hydrofoil of the *Cataract Hotel* (Upper Egypt Hotels Company) leaving El-Shellal at the early hour of 5:00 A.M. and returning after dark the same day.

One further comment on resorts may creep in here. Along the Gulf of Suez and northern portion of the Red Sea, ambitiously called the Egyptian Riviera, two of the newer hotels deserve mention. The Upper

Egypt Hotels Company, responsible also for the Winter Palace Hotels and the Cataract Hotels, has built *El Ein El Sokhna*, with 97 rooms, near a spa just outside of Suez at the southern terminus of the Canal, and the *Hurghada*, with 106 rooms, at Hurghada, where the Gulf joins the Red Sea. Both facilities are luxurious, typifying Egypt's hopes for this newly developing shoreline.

CHAPTER 15

METROPOLITAN EGYPT; CAIRO AND ALEXANDRIA

First Things to Know

OLYMPIC Airways maintains a convenient thrice-weekly service from Athens to Cairo, leaving Athens just before 7 P.M. and reaching the Egyptian capital by Comet jet in less than two hours. Other lines operating this same route include BOAC, KLM and, of course, United Arab Airlines. All International flights from Hellenikon are subject to an exit tax of 30 drachmas, which is one dollar.

The arrival in Cairo used to be something of a nightmare, but it has greatly improved since the 1962 opening of the new *International Airport*, which marked the tenth year since the Revolution that threw out King Farouk and established Egypt as the fully independent republic that it now is. At the airport and in the leading hotels one finds uniformed *tourist police*, whose courteous aid is a big asset to the tourist industry of the country, especially upon arrival and departure. They stand for no nonsense from touts and other unsavory characters who would like to batten upon the tourist trade, and, believe it or not, airport porters are paid regular wages and are strictly forbidden by law to accept tips, though some of them still do it if they think the tourist police won't catch them. Egypt has not yet reached a point where the government feels it practicable to abolish visa and currency declaration requirements, as has been done in all of Western Europe, but she has made other moves that indicate her strong interest in promoting tourism. Here are five of them:

1. Visas may now be obtained not only from any UAR consulate (the one in New York is at 902 Park Avenue), but even, in case of need, from passport central offices "on the spot," when you arrive. A transit visa is valid for seven days, a regular tourist visa for three months.

2. Early in 1962, Egypt announced a 20 per cent premium on the

dollar when exchanged for Egyptian pounds at an authorized bank or representative in Egypt. Later in the year it tacked on another 5 per cent inducement, making the premium 25 per cent, so that dollar tourists may now buy pounds for $2.16 each instead of the official nontourist rate of $2.87. The pound is divided into 100 piasters, and each piaster into 10 millièmes, or mills. To give the tourist exchange rate in a different way, 46.3 piasters equal one dollar. Paper notes range from 5 piasters up and coins from 10 piasters down, the chief ones encountered being 1-piaster coins of three different types and vintages. In general, the coins, except for the 10-piaster one, which may be thought of as a quarter, are hardly more than souvenirs of one's visit. Some coins have *only* Arabic inscriptions and figures, which last are only distantly related to our so-called Arabic numerals. The Arabs themselves know their figures as "Indian numerals." The 1 is more or less like ours, but the 2 is like a 1 with a small hook attached to the top, and the 5 is a small circle. Zero is a dot. The 10 works out as a 1 followed by a dot or period. The numerals of present-day Arabic are rather important even for the short-time tourist, and here they are:

1 – ١	6 – ٦
2 – ٢	7 – ٧
3 – ٣	8 – ٨
4 – ٤	9 – ٩
5 – ٥	10 – ١٠

Numbers containing more than one digit, be it known, read from left to right, as with us, but Arabic script reads from right to left.

3. In 1962, Egypt set in motion a progressive "Add Egypt" campaign to induce overseas tourists to tack a week-in-Egypt onto their European vacations, estimating the cost at $250 "including air fares (if the approach is made from Athens), lodging and meals at a first-class Cairo hotel, sightseeing, night life, camel rides and souvenir purchases." Reports indicate that the campaign has met with substantial success.

4. *United Arab Airlines* has opened a New York office at 720 Fifth Avenue and plans a service by Boeing jets between New York and Cairo. It is gradually becoming a system of considerable international

range, especially in Asia and Africa.

5. In Cairo an active and very courteously run tourist promotional office has been established under the name *UAR Tourist Administration*. Its address is 5 Adly Street, in the heart of the city. Its New York branch, the *UAR Tourist Office*, at 630 Fifth Avenue, has been mentioned, with applause, in Chapter 3.

The currency control, as it operates upon arrival in Egypt and upon departure, is something of a nuisance, but I may say frankly that its bark is worse than its bite. Upon entering the country you have to fill in, in duplicate, a ponderous form declaring all currencies in your possession and also all amounts in travelers checks and letters of credit and even, in theory at least, all jewelry and gold articles. By present law you may not legally bring in or take out any Egyptian currency at all. Upon leaving you may take out what funds you brought in, minus what you have spent, and this, too, you must declare. Egyptians pounds that you may have left may not be taken out but may be exchanged for a foreign currency. At the airport this is done with reasonable dispatch. The regulations sound awful, but in practice one's task is merely a time-consuming bore. Your word is unlikely to be questioned, though you should certainly play safe by saving all evidences of your exchange transactions, and unless you're a mighty suspicious looking person you will not be subjected to any search whatever. Let's hope that Egypt will soon relax her currency declaration rules.

The ride from the new airport into the hotel sector of big Cairo takes the better part of an hour but passes for several miles through beautiful residential sections, including Heliopolis, and much of the highway itself is a landscaped parkway of distinguished nature, with lovely flowers and thousands of topiary trees, made gay nightly with colored lights. The business and shopping center is by no means beautiful except in some of its squares and parks, but merely big, busy and utilitarian. The three main shopping streets, since we're on the ubject, are 26th of July Street (which date marked the conclusion of the 1952 revolution), Kasr el Nil Street and Talaat Harb Street, formerly named Soleiman Pasha, with widely known Opera Square as a sort of nucleus. If you come to town by motorcoach of the air line you used you will be deposited at the company's downtown office and make your way to your hotel by taxi.

Explanation of Misr and UAR

Misr means Egypt in the Arabic language, and to Egyptians it means also an empire of banking, industry, trade and transportation that has played a leading role in lifting the country up to its present position as one of the important modern nations of the Mediterranean basin. The Egyptian air network, United Arab Airlines, was founded by this business empire under the name of Misr Airways and continues to play its very important role in the national economy. Within Egypt it maintains a vital network of lines, some of them vital also to tourism. One may fly from Cairo to Alexandria by UAA in forty minutes, from Cairo to Luxor in an hour and a half, and from Luxor to Aswan in forty-five minutes. These services, similar in caliber to those of European systems, are worth knowing about not only for their saving of time but because Egypt's state trains, traveling *through* deserts instead of over them, have to cope, on windy days, with sand and dust. Cairo's new International Airport—a second one, named Almaza, is now used only by the military—is one of the busiest centers of plane traffic in the Mediterranean world. The role played in the nineteenth century by the Suez Canal in knotting East and West together by sea is now being played in "aviation counterpart" by this airport.

The Misr business empire, founded by an Egyptian genius of the first magnitude named Talaat Harb Pasha, is an epic of enterprise and of enlightened capitalism, seeming as American, in general and in detail, as any parallel empire of business in the States. The powerful Bank Misr in Cairo is its financial heart, and the giant Misr Spinning and Weaving Company at Mehalla-el-Koubra, some eighty miles north of Cairo, is its largest single enterprise. This cotton mill is called the biggest in the world and certainly only one or two others anywhere could challenge the claim. It employs 20,000 men and a few hundred girls, but the figure can quickly be raised to 30,000 or more in times of emergency. Its care for its workers in matters of health, hospitalization, living quarters and social amenities is as meticulous as that of the most paternalistic corporation in the States and its efforts at adult education are a special feature suited to a country where illiteracy is still high. The Misr empire, including almost every enterprise the mind can imagine, from tanneries to fisheries and from insurance to Egypt's largest movie studio and a chain of theaters, is of outstanding interest to visiting businessmen if not to pleasure-bent tourists. It is the Egypt of today and tomorrow as against the Egypt of the Pharaohs.

The term United Arab Republic, represented by the letters UAR, puzzles many a visiting tourist, and with good cause. The chronology of the name is briefly as follows. On February 22, 1958, Egypt and Syria united as a two-part nation under the leadership of Egypt's president, Gamal Abdel Nasser, the capital being Cairo. The kingdom of Yemen was also associated with it as a member of the United Arab States. It was hoped by Egypt that various other states would join in a great Moslem nation of Arabs but this did not happen and the awkward republic, composed of three widely separated states, broke up. In 1961, Syria broke away and re-established itself as a republic, with Damascus the capital, and soon afterwards Yemen also dissolved its association with Egypt. In 1963, however, came another turn of the political wheel. A bloodless revolution in Syria paved the way for that country's return to close affiliation with Egypt, though not as an integral part of a single UAR nation. Egypt, Syria and Iraq then formed a new *federation*, with Egypt's President Nasser, as its titular leader, and so things stand today.

Egypt has made noteworthy advances in recent years. Important developments in housing, in road building, in civic improvement, in education and certainly in tourism, have taken place. As a sample and symbol of this, since we live in an age of youth, take a look at the University of Cairo as it is now. Take a look and be amazed— but I shall discuss this later.

The Facts of Tourist Life in Egypt

I have mentioned the basic facts of Egyptian money, but now I must say, with due emphasis, that *tourist life in Egypt is very inexpensive.* Your dollars, converted to Egyptian pounds and piasters at the present special tourist exchange rate, go far indeed. I would say that Egypt vies with Spain as the most inexpensive Mediterranean country and it may even be true, as Egypt claims, that Cairo is the tourist world's most inexpensive large capital. There is support for this in statistics gathered by the U.N. As just *one* statistic I may state that luxurious double rooms in the Hotel Nile Hilton, with last-word private bath and a broad balcony hanging over the Nile and its riverside corniche, with the 615-foot Tower of Cairo just across the river and the pyramids to the left in the distance, are now priced at 6 L E for two (the letters stand for Egyptian pound), which sum, figured at $2.16 to the pound, means $13, perhaps a half to a third of what such palatial accommodations would cost in New York—or Paris.

Cairo, with its more than three million inhabitants, is located at what has been called the *throat* of Egypt, but in shape at least, the part of Egypt that is made viable by the Nile is more like an inverted funnel, with Cairo at the base of the flair. The flair is, of course, the Nile's great delta, the largest single stream of it reaching the Mediterranean at Rashid (Rosetta), while the narrow part of the funnel stretches 650 miles south from Cairo up to Wadi Halfa at the Sudan frontier.

Since Alexandria is but forty minutes distant from Cairo by plane and less than three hours by Diesel rail express or motor coach or car, nine tourists out of ten make their headquarters for all Lower Egypt in the capital, visiting Alexandria on an out-and-back sortie. Cairo has recognized this fact of tourism and has gone far to meet it, with a group of fine, modern hotels and no less than eight more, of varying types, now or soon reaching completion. Since dollar rates are so low at the favorable exchange few tourists look for quarters in hotels of less than first class, and many budget watchers consider that the very best is for them.

The very best is, of course, the *Nile Hilton*. This great steel-and-glass temple of tourism, opened only a few years ago, is one of the shiniest links in the Hilton International chain, vying for supremacy in the eastern Mediterranean with its sister hotels in Athens, Istanbul and Tel Aviv. With 400 air-conditioned rooms and baths and a vast array of lounges, restaurants, bars, shops and service offices, it is verily a city unto itself. It has its own post office, just off the main lobby, a galaxy of attractive shops, another of (eight) air line offices and travel agencies, including American Express, a Turkish bath and Finnish *sauna*, a full set of repair shops in the basement, including sections for carpentry, upholstery, machinery repair and electrical equipment, and a staff of 640 persons, including the cutest and pertest elevator girls in Egypt. In 1962, a large swimming pool and Cabaña Club were opened on a lot adjoining the main building. Among the hotel's restaurants are the ground-floor coffee shop called the Ibis Room, which never closes, the main dining room, Gawharat El Nil (Jewel of the Nile) on the second floor, the Pyramid Roof restaurant and bar, the Belvedere supper club, with open summer terrace, also up aloft, and Safari Bar, a group of private restaurants called Aida, Yasmina, Amira, and—but maybe that's enough to list. I may add that in a country where you cannot talk with the man-on-the-street and cannot even read the big neon signs done in Arabic script there is solid comfort, begetting a sense of confidence, in the atmosphere of this Hilton "city," yet you still know you are in Egypt, as witness a large panel on a wall of the main lounge. It is an exact and very interesting re-production of a panel "from the Hypostyle of the Temple of Karnak (1298–1235 B.C.) representing the Ceremony of the Sacred Boat of Amon Ra and Ramses II offering incense."

Following the Nile Hilton we find a row of large and good hotels lining the Rue Corniche du Nil, as the central part of the forty-mile Nile-side boulevard calls itself. Three of these are: The *Guezireh Palace*, old but recently renewed and inexpensive; the *Semiramis*, an important but slightly aging place; and the glittering new 500-bed *Shepheard's*, for which, along with the famous former Shepheard's see comment below. On this same Corniche another large hotel, not yet named but aiming at the luxury trade, is being built by German interests. The pace of hotel construction is a dizzy one, calling almost for monthly report-ing. To name just three of the newest ones, there's the 1962 *Cleopatra* on Kasr el Nil Street, the *Mokattam*, on high ground outside of the center, and the *Cairo Airport Hotel* at the International Airport. Among older hotels, in the heart of the city, are the spacious, old-fashioned *Hotel Continental-Savoy*, on Opera Square, given a modern touch by the Pan American Airways office, and the *Cosmopolitan*, en-tered from Kasr el Nil Street. A very inexpensive but really good hotel is the *Lotus*, on Talaat Harb Street. Two suburban hotels call for special mention, the *Heliopolis Palace Hotel* in Heliopolis and the mellow and ever-popular *Mena House* in the pyramids-and-Sphinx sector. The Heliopolis Palace, constructed with three hundred rooms and baths and fifty suites, has been in government use, not as a hotel, for a decade or so, but I understand that there is a fair possibility (only) that it will soon be restored as a hotel, with necessary reconstruction. As I knew it in former years its colossal, marble, mosque-like central salon had a famous Oriental rug eighty-three feet long by thirty-seven wide, requiring the labors of thirty-two men to lift and carry it. The ballrooms and night clubs could cater to three thousand guests at once. It had its own private golf course and its own riding school. The whole community of Heliopolis and the hotel were founded by a Belgian promoter named General Baron Empain, the hotel being opened with great ceremony in 1910. Perhaps I may as well date myself by mentioning that the first travel article I ever wrote was about Heliopolis. It was published in 1913 in *Suburban Life* and I was paid ten dollars for it. I almost died of joy.

Mena House, in contrast to the Palace, is a family hotel of old-fashioned but delightful type, with every amenity dear to tourists, including a pool. It rises from an extensive garden area with tennis courts. Like other *resort* hotels of Egypt, as against city hotels, it has a high season, from November 1 to April 30, and a low season, May 1 to October 31, the rates being then 20 or 25 per cent lower.

Cairo interests publish and distribute a useful *Cairo This Week* pamphlet of the what-to-see-and-do type, but the city does not lend itself to unguided wanderings as many European capitals do, for one may easily get lost in the downtown labyrinth, especially in the sprawling bazaar section, and the utter incomprehensibility of the Arabic language, both spoken and written, hampers even the experienced traveler. Fortunately, licensed, English-speaking guides (called dragomans) are numerous and can be easily secured either through one's hotel or through the Tourist Administration, by which they are trained and through which they must secure their licenses. Steps are now being taken to require that every intending guide bone up on Egyptian history until he earns an official *degree* in the subject. Otherwise he may not practice and may not even call himself a guide.

A further tourist fact of importance is that whereas department stores and shops, including the bazaars, close on the Christian *Sunday*, business offices and banks close on *Friday*, the holy day of Islam.

The Shepheard Saga, Old and New

Until early in 1952, when one of history's most senseless outbreaks of xenophobic rioting, allegedly instigated by Communists, burned it to the ground, the original Shepheard's Hotel of Cairo had been a cynosure of millions of travelers from West to East and vice versa. They had been dropping in since 1841, when Samuel Shepheard started his first primitive inn in a then quiet spot near Lake Ezbek, later to be filled in and become the Ezbekiyeh Gardens, heart of the present city, adjacent to Opera Square. He named his place The New British Hotel and intended it as a sort of halfway house for British travelers between Great Britain and India, who then moved in tortoise-slow fashion overland between Alexandria and the Red Sea, en route to or from the East. The Suez Canal was not destined to be built for nearly thirty years. With quickly developing trade Samuel Shepheard soon moved to a large mansion near by that had been the palace of a princess whose father was Mohammed Ali, father also of Modern Egypt. This mansion was directly on the site of what became the Shepheard's of tradition. It grew with the times and probably figured by name in more tales of travel and adventure than has any other hotel in the world.

I first visited Cairo long ago, I being then a youth fresh from college roaming with my parents, and of course we "dropped in at Shepheard's," as everybody did, whether or not as guests. More than thirty years later, only a few months before the fire, I made a fortnight's stay there, and what an extraordinary impression it made on me, as on all guests. Every room was to some extent a museum of period furniture and bibelots, with genuine Persian and Turkish rugs that were worth, in the aggregate, an Egyptian, or American, fortune. Even some of the small bedroom rugs were individually valued at over $500, and a staff of rugmenders was continually at work keeping them cleaned and in repair.

The Shepheard Saga, which ran through eleven decades and more, was starred with world figures, whose names were to be seen in its Golden Book. Henry M. Stanley lived there in 1890, writing his book *The Relief of Emin Pasha.* A decade or so later Lord Kitchener of Khartoum was given a gala dinner there. In 1910, Theodore Roosevelt addressed a garden party of Americans at Shepheard's. Crowned heads and heads that had once been crowned were a piaster a dozen, so to speak, on the pages of Shepheard's register.

This great caravansary was a milestone of tourism until Cairo had its self-inflicted Ordeal by Fire in 1952. On that occasion all hell broke loose—for one day and night—and before sanity returned a number of foreigners had been killed and several hundred foreign-owned buildings and businesses had been burned to the ground, one of them being the famous Turf Club, in whose destruction some of its British members were done to death. Total property losses ranged up to two hundred million dollars.

Now we find the *New Shepheard's* on the Nile Corniche, a ten-story hostelry of modern grandeurs opened to the public in 1957. It has a huge Oriental lounge and cocktail room on the ground floor, a plushy night club below ground and on the tenth floor a dining room, opening to a terrace in summer. The ninth floor is given over entirely to split level suites, some of them actually bridging over the corridor from which they are entered, with rooms on both sides of the hotel. Of all Cairo's hotels I would rate Shepheard's second only to the Nile Hilton, but new and newer hotels may soon warrant a change in any such rating.

The Luster of the Pharaohs

To discuss Cairo in detail is to discuss an Egyptian Rome or an Arab Paris. It cannot be done within the confines of a part of a book, but some hints on what to see and how to see it can be offered. A map is essential and a good one is to be had, gratis, from the Tourist Administration. Another, more condensed but still very serviceable, is included in the pamphlet which Hilton guests receive upon registering, and still another is included in *Cairo This Week*, distributed in the hotels. A local, paper-covered, pocket-sized guide called *Visit Pharaonic Egypt*, by A. Hamada, curator of the *Egyptian Museum*, gives, in compact form, the essentials about this museum and about Giza, Sakkara, Luxor and Aswan. For the Egyptian Museum alone an 80-page paperback published by the Tourist Administration will prove more than adequate.

I suppose that the one thing to which every visitor gives high place on his agenda of things to see in Cairo is still the treasure taken from the tomb of "King Tut" upon its discovery, on November 4, 1922, by Dr. Howard Carter and Lord Carnarvon, for there has surely been no archeological find in modern times that has aroused such universal excitement. The entire treasure that was in this tomb, including, it is said, two tons of gold objects, is now to be seen in an upstairs gallery of the Egyptian Museum and in a large room opening from the gallery, all, that is, except the king himself, who still lies, in mummified splendor, in a large gilded coffin within a huge stone sarcophagus in his own tomb in the Valley of the Kings at Thebes. When found, the mummy lay within a gold coffin, within a larger one of gilded wood, within a still larger one, also of gilded wood, all three, in their graded sizes, lying within the stone sarcophagus, but the smaller and smallest coffins are now on display in the museum at Cairo and the one that contains the mummy in Thebes is the *outer* one of the three. Being on the subject, I may state here that the innermost coffin, of pure and solid gold, weighs 242 pounds and is one of the most splendid works of ancient art, perhaps *the* most splendid in its glitter and glory, ever found in or on this earth. It depicts the king, decked in a false beard and holding his whip and scepter of authority, surrounded by the gods and goddesses of Egypt, who shelter him with their wings.

This coffin of gold is but one of many treasures in that part of the museum that concern TUTANKHAMÛN, as he is labeled. (I shall use hereinafter the usual spelling Tutankhamen.) The aureate array dazzles the eyes and overwhelms the mind, giving some idea of the immense wealth and artistic development of ancient Egypt, for this particular king was not one of the great ones, in the long succession of them in many dynasties. I asked where all the gold came from and was told that most, or much, of it was from mountains in the desert near the Red Sea, where at least one gold mine is still worked, in a small way, near the present town of Koser.

The largest items in the Tutankhamen collection are the four *shrines*, which are in graded sizes like the king's coffins, each of the smaller ones fitting neatly inside the next larger one, while the smallest of all, still as large as a very big trunk, contains the Canopic chest of alabaster. This chest, with four compartments, holds four small coffins of gold in which lie the mummified heart and other internal organs of the king. The largest of the graded shrines, looming up in the museum's gallery like a small house, is covered with sheet gold and has a door of two leaves held fast by bolts of ebony. In the adjacent room is a large gold mask that formerly covered the mummy's head. It is a striking work of art, showing infinite detail of artisanship, such as eyebrows and eyelids of lapis lazuli. The "head cloth," hanging down on both sides below the shoulders, is enlivened with inlaid stripes of blue glass that contrast sharply with all the gold.

The king's state chariot is another "Tut" item of outstanding appeal, as is also the royal throne of carved wood, coated with gold. The carving on the back of this throne pictures the king in a most lifelike pose together with his very pretty queen, Ankhesenamon, who lays a tender hand upon his left shoulder. Other items of this king's furniture, jewelry, games, ship models, implements of war and the chase, are enough to fill a separate building, yet the things pertaining to Tutankhamen are but a tithe of the riches of the vast Egyptian Museum, which is, in turn, but one of eleven museums in Cairo.

I confess to a fellow-feeling for the struggling author of the *Guide Bleu*, an archeologist by the name of Marcelle Baud. He devoted ten of his seven hundred pages to the Egyptian Museum, putting them in his finest possible print, yet he *does not touch Tutankhamen*. He tells what rooms and galleries the collection occupies and then bows out with a confession of defeat.

Mosques and Citadel

There are at least thirty mosques in Cairo that are considered by connoisseurs to be worth visiting, but we may boil this number down to four of the best and thus see a cross section of mosque architecture and get a sense of the mosques' life and atmosphere. A dragoman will certainly be necessary. On entering any mosque one's shoes must be exchanged for scuffing slippers, for the use of which a small tip is given to the attendant. Beyond this there is no charge.

Four that are surely in the top bracket of interest shall be listed here, the first three being important for their beauty of architecture, the fourth for its location.

1. *El Azhar*, called "The Splendid" and the "The Most Flourishing," is at the point where the Mousky (Street) approaches the covered bazaars of Khan Khalil. It is the very ancient mosque of the like-named university, which for a thousand years has been the most important center of Islamic and Arabic study for all the Arab world. This university, not to be confused with the modern co-ed university, has some twenty thousand students, instructed by two thousand professors, who lecture under the porticoes as the students sit grouped about them on the floor. The total area of the mosque (the word is interchangeable here with university) is close to ten thousand square yards, and surrounding the usual central court are such extensive porticoes, along with a huge "*liwan*," or hall, that it takes more than three hundred marble columns, row on endless row, to support the roof. Each *mihrab* (prayer niche; there are two in this mosque) faces, of course, toward Mecca, as is the invariable rule.

2. The *Mosque of Sultan Hassan* is magnificent. Dating from 1362, it is considered a masterpiece of Arab architecture. It has one immensely high minaret (284 feet), the highest, in fact, of all Cairo's forest of them, and a smaller, later, less impressive one as foil.

3. The *Mosque of Ibn Tulûn*, dating from 876 and built, it is said, somewhat in imitation of Mecca, is Cairo's oldest Arab monument. Among its many curious features is the old and ancient minaret, which is spiral with outside stairs, a feature unique in such construction.

4. The *Mosque of Mohammed Ali*, on Cairo's Citadel, is almost modern, having been built in the first half of the nineteenth century by the remarkable viceroy for whom it is named, great-great-grandfather of Egypt's ex-King Farouk. It is called the Alabaster Mosque because of the walls and columns of that luminous stone. Red carpeting covers the whole vast area of the floor. No less than fifteen hundred electric light bulbs illuminate the edifice. Mohammed Ali's body is entombed in a separate room. A feature of the courtyard is a big clock given to Mohammed Ali by King Louis-Philippe of France.

There are two other, smaller mosques also upon and within the Citadel, giving this conspicuous hill the appearance, from a little distance, of a mountain of domes and minarets, two of the latter, on the Mohammed Ali Mosque, soaring high up into the sky, their crests aimed at heaven. The call to prayer by the muezzin is still given five times a day from minarets all over the Moslem world, but it has lost some of its spiritual glow in modern, mechanical times. I believe the muezzin now often remains on the ground and calls the faithful through a microphone connected with loudspeakers up aloft! This at least saves many an arduous climb. And I am told that some of the calls to prayer are even given over a radio network. It is a case of *autres temps autres moeurs,* or perhaps one could say, without undue flippancy, "Prayer marches on."

The *Citadel* was first built (starting in 1176) by none other than the great Saladin, enemy extraordinary of the Christian Crusaders. It later became the seat of government of the Mameluke sultans and still later of the Ottomans, but it was Mohammed Ali, father of modern Egypt, who gave the hill its present contours.

The view from the parapet of the Citadel is a breath-taker. All of Cairo, rimmed by the Nile, is spread out below as if in a model of papier-mâché. In the river is the extensive and smartly residential island called Gezira, with a fashionable *Sporting Club* that is said to be the largest in the world, since the decline of the one in Singapore. Beyond the Nile is the broad green ribbon of luxuriance that is the annually renewed gift of the river, and beyond that ribbon the illimitable desert, from which the pyramids of Giza conspicuously protrude. The scene is one to cross oceans for, or, to be more geographical in this case, to cross an ocean and an inland sea for.

Ex-Royal Palaces and a Co-ed University

Both Cairo and Alexandria are "well palaced," each city having two ex-royal palaces, all now museums, of prime interest. We shall take a look here at the Cairo pair.

Manial Palace, on an island in the Nile south of the central city, was built by Mohammed Ali, a grandson of the great Mohammed Ali. Its chief interest, to me at least, lies in its magnificent gardens, its huge, England-smooth lawns, its beautiful trees, illuminated nightly, including banyans of colossal spread. The palace ensemble consists of a main hall, replete with gold and red-plush grandeurs, a private building of the founder, a small but very lovely gold and blue mosque with much coffee-colored woodwork and with excerpts from the Koran done in calligraphic writing, and, to complete the ensemble, a separate building housing various treasures and remembrances of the founder. In the private palace are many signed photographs, including those of Queen Victoria, Queen Mary, Queen Mother Elizabeth, Sir Winston Churchill and one inscribed "For H.R.H. Prince Mohammed Ali from his friend Franklin D. Roosevelt."

The *Abdin Palace*, near the heart of the city, was the usual home of the Khedives, the Sultans and then the Kings of Egypt, including Farouk. The building is famous chiefly for its luxuriously decorated and furnished Byzantine Hall, said to have cost a khedivial fortune, but the guides show many other rooms, including the Festival Hall, the Suez Canal Room and the Throne Room, and in one of the wings, need I say, the Harem, called in Arabic Haramlek. This palace, like the Manial, is open daily to the public from 9 to 6 and tips to the attendants, be it known, are forbidden.

Egypt is making notable progress on the long, hard road to popular education and the road is *modern* and *secular*, in contrast to the traditional Islamic and Arabic atmosphere of El Azhar Mosque-University. Statisticians say that a new school is opened in Egypt on an average of every three days. Cairo has an important university of Western style, while lesser ones flourish in Alexandria and Assiout. I was frankly amazed at the spectacle of Cairo University, for it could have been in Cairo, Illinois, if that were a city of three million instead of fifteen thousand. Young men and girls, dressed much like American campus youths, were roaming from building to building, meeting in little knots, studious or social, calling wisecracks to each other, dropping in casually at the snack bar-café. The university has eight faculties and an enrollment given as 33,000. These young people, though Arabic and Islamic to the core, give every evidence that they are "of the West Western." I was thrilled to see it. While on this subject I must mention that there is, in the heart of Cairo, only two blocks from the Nile Hilton, a flourishing *American University*. This does not have the influence on Egypt that the American University in Beirut has on the life of Lebanon but it plays its worthy role in the pattern of Egypt's educational program. Many of its faculty members live in the garden suburb of Maadi, whose community life has a most interesting multinational flavor.

Cairo University is only one witness ot the forward surge of today's

Egypt. Another is the 33-story, circular-front TV building, opened in 1963. Another is Egypt's first homemade automobile, the small Ramses, launched in 1962, and still another is the *Cairo Tower*, located on Gezira Island directly across the river from the Nile Hilton. This is a 615-foot shaft whose surface is covered with 120 million pieces of colored mosaic. It was opened to the public in 1961. To enter the tower one pays 25 piasters (about 50 cents) and ascends by elevator in 35 seconds to the two-level summit, where a circular café and revolving restaurant and view terrace greet the visitor. There is nothing de luxe about either the café or the restaurant, but the ascent to them is an experience and the view is as close, and quite as interesting in its way, as is that from the Eiffel Tower. In one feature it outdoes all such views from all such towers in the world, for off there to the southwest, very clearly outlined, are the three mighty pyramids of Giza.

All around the tower are sporting clubs galore, the chief of them being the *Gezira Sporting Club*, 90 per cent of whose six thousand members are Egyptians. It has an eighteen-hole golf course, thirty-four tennis courts, nine squash courts, a bowling green, three swimming pools and facilities for almost every other sport one can think of.

The Pyramids and the Sphinx—with Moses

Moses was my camel on the occasion of one of my visits to Giza and he was a most reluctant one at that, balking continually, lifting his haughty chin even higher than nature required and groaning most ungraciously every time his driver bade him squat, so I could mount or dismount. I hired my humped conveyance and his man from in front of the Mena House, the attractive desert inn mentioned above, and so to the *Great Pyramid of Cheops*.

What a thing it is, this mountain of masonry erected by the sweat of men forty-five centuries ago! I saw it by moonlight on my first youthful visit many years ago, and by full sunlight and then at gloaming on my second and third visits. It is too familiar to the world of travel to need much comment here, but a few statistics are always impressive, however often repeated. The Great Pyramid, although stripped by builder thieves of its top and its outer coating, is still 446 feet high and the length of each side is 740 feet. It covers twelve acres and contains two and a half million blocks of stone averaging two and a half tons each. King Cheops' tomb, in the very center of it, some two hundred feet above the foundation sand, is solidly walled and roofed with granite slabs, certain single slabs in the roof weighing over fifty tons each. All this granite, and indeed all the granite used by the Pharaohs everywhere in Egypt, was quarried by primitive but effective methods in and near Aswan, to be floated down the Nile (550 miles to Cairo) and dragged into position by manpower and beastpower, using long ramps where it was necessary to raise it to high points. Rough limestone was also used, this material coming from the nearby Mokattam Hills. It took one hundred thousand men twenty years to build this pyramid. Grave robbers, over many centuries, have painstakingly worked at their trade and stolen everything of value from it, but the huge granite sarcophagus of the king is still in place in its mortuary chamber.

Everyone climbs up inside the Great Pyramid, and those of exceptional heart, lungs and ambition ascend on the outside to the very top, a strenuous and "perspirational" job, as I know from experience, but of course rewarded by a splendid view.

There are two other pyramids at Giza, the larger of them built as a tomb for Khephren, son and successor of Cheops, and the lesser one for his son and successor, Mycerinus, but the *Great Sphinx*, most widely known monument in the world, is near by and captures all the attention. I climbed aboard Moses for the short jaunt and was one in a procession of at least fifty camels and persons, for on every winter afternoon Giza draws visitors in endless files.

The Sphinx is, of course, a lion with a human head, but although the head is thought to have been modeled from that of Khephren, the whole figure represents the god Harmakhis. Presumably it was built in Khephren's reign as a further glorification of him. Desert winds have fought endlessly to shroud the Sphinx in sand, while men and monarchs have fought as endlessly to remove the shrouds. A granite stela between the Sphinx's paws records that Thotmes IV had the job done—this would have been about 1425 B.C., when the Sphinx was roughly a thousand years old—because he was commanded in a dream to do so. It has been done again and again from his day to ours and will be done as long as mankind marvels at this most curious monument.

Memphis, Sakkara and the Holy Cats

The traveler who has time even to dabble in examination of the wonders of Sakkara, a great area of pyramids and tombs only twenty miles from Cairo, finds that ancient Egypt clutches him and holds his fascinated interest, but on the way to that desert of the buried past he will surely find time to halt at Memphis.

Memphis, despite its immense importance as the earliest capital of Egypt, founded, some say, by Menes, the very first king of the First Dynasty, is now little more than a vestige of its once brilliant self. Few things remain today to indicate its former status. It reached its peak of glory during the Third and Fourth Dynasties, but the chief relics, two colossal statues of Ramses II, date obviously from very much later, for that king was of the Nineteenth Dynasty. Memphis is now a sort of sunken city, that is, an extensive area of almost swampy land in a handsome palm grove. The center of it all, the Temple of Ptah, who was the special god of Memphis, can be traced more or less in outline. The reasons why Memphis is presumably lost forever are that Egypt's soil has risen, through accretions, to grow up and over it and that man's irrigation projects have put the actual city, or whatever may be left of it, below the water level, making excavations fruitless. Egypt rises, it is said, at the rate of one centimeter every ten years, which would not seem express speed, but arithmetic shows what has happened. If the land rises one centimeter per decade, hence 10 centimeters per century, it rises one full meter every millennium. There have been four to five millennia since the city flourished, which means that it would be covered by four to five meters of now marshy soil. A meter is 10 per cent more than a yard, so our "example" works out as a covering of at least fifteen feet for Memphis—in soggy terrain.

A feature of the place is a pair of recumbent *Colossi*, the larger of which is now housed in a shed. Around this visitors may walk, at a convenient level, to see it all. It is carved from very high-grade limestone, as against pink granite for the smaller Colossus, but it has withstood thirty-two centuries of wear and tear. Part of the crown is missing and the statue is a double amputee, so far as legs go, but even so it is wonderfully impressive, being considered one of the finest works of

Egyptian sculpture ever fashioned. It must once have been about forty-three feet high. The king's nipples, as I found by measuring them, are three inches in diameter, which vital statistic gives an idea of the statue's size. The cartouche of Ramses II is plainly visible in three places, on the figure's right shoulder, on the chest and on the buckle of the girdle. Something else of great interest was visible to me at the time of my inspection. In the left of the king's head was a cavity carved by time and in it a swallow had built her nest, laid her eggs and hatched her young. I saw the mother bird, with splendid indifference to royalty, flying into the king's head from time to time with choice tidbits for her babies, and then out again to forage for more.

About *Sakkara* I can set down only some random notes, hoping that they will serve to stimulate your own research. The discoveries here go on and on. Archeologists estimate that no more than 20 per cent of this amazing necropolis has been uncovered and they talk longingly of new methods of finding buried tombs and temples by the same means geophysicists use to discover likely areas of oil. The idea seems not so farfetched as it may sound, for conservative scientists concede that "something of the sort *might* prove effective."

Meanwhile, what is now to be seen, even in swift glances and by much hurrying along, is enough to fill a full day to its utmost gunwales. The so-called *Stepped Pyramid* was built as a tomb for the first King Zoser, founder of the Third Dynasty, who is supposed to have begun his reign in 2778 B.C., while some of the tombs, and also the *Serapeum*, or *Tomb of the Sacred Bulls*, are thought to date from the Eighteenth Dynasty, 1200 to 1400 years later, and still others from the Nineteenth and Twentieth Dynasties, thus covering seventeen centuries of the Old, Middle and New Empires. With such a great spread of time it is obvious that there is also a great spread of archeological treasures.

Parenthetically, it adds interest to the Sakkara visit to bear in mind that the latter part of the Eighteenth Dynasty, from about 1400 B.C. on, is that covered in 1950's best-selling novel by Mika Waltari, *The Egyptian*. The "autobiography" of the Egyptian physician and skull surgeon Sinuhe covers the period from his birth, "in the reign of the great King Amenhotep III," through the reign of "that one who desired to live by truth and whose name may no longer be named because it is accursed," revealed as Akhnaton, whose lovely queen was Nefertiti, and so, through several more short reigns, including that of Tutankhamen, to the accession of the warrior Hotemheb, last monarch of that Dynasty. How, by the way, do we know that Nefertiti was lovely? Because her head mask is the one most often seen on brochures and leaflets to proclaim Egyptian queenly beauty. This mask was found about half a century ago by German archeological explorers, who covered it, according to a Cairo version of the story, with dirty plaster and managed to smuggle it out of Egypt and so to Berlin. At the close of World War II it was found by the American Army in one of the salt mine depositories in Germany and was installed by the Monuments Commission at Wiesbaden. Later it was restored to Berlin, fortunately *West* Berlin, and now reposes in the Dahlem Museum there. Egypt claims the queen and, conceivably, may sometime recover her.

There are about seventy pyramids in Sakkara besides the famous Stepped Pyramid of King Zoser, and of course there are many *mastabas*, or tombs. The Pyramid of Zoser is not only a masterpiece of its era but it is the first large structure of stone ever built on earth, now some 4600 years old. Pyramids grew, layer on layer, casing on casing, like a crystal of salt, and this one is a marvelous example, whose growth can even be traced, like the growth of a giant redwood, by its rings. Napoleon's artillery used the pyramid as a shooting range, firing at it happily with their cannon for hours at a time, and this chipped off many chunks. A rock slip on one side damaged it further, all this making its construction more visible, but the net effect of the great mass is still extremely striking. The entrance to all pyramids was on the north side and in Zoser's pyramid there is a hole through which the royal "tenant" could peep directly at the North Star. In general, a king's pyramid in Egypt was built during his lifetime and if he died ahead of schedule the pyramid was never properly finished, as his successor would always choose a different site and start over again, but Zoser seems obviously to have lived long enough.

This tomb mountain is actually more a "growing sarcophagus" than a true pyramid, for its "steps" are really six large mastabas, one above the other, the original plan having been altered again and again. The whole mass stands in an enclosure wall which was once over thirty feet high. The visitor makes his way into the enclosure through the entrance of ancient times, marveling at a colonnade of magnificent columns, in a double row, that leads into a hypostyle hall some of whose pillars have been painstakingly restored by Egypt's Department of Antiquities. By a stroke of luck I here teamed up with some American Embassy people who were being shown Sakkara by the chief architect then in charge of excavations, Hilmy Bey Pasha, and I wish it were possible even to *list* the wonders and curiosities he pointed out to us that day.

The *pyramid-tomb of King Unas,* last of the Fifth Dynasty, is second in importance to that of King Zoser, not at all for its size, which is insignificant, but for the hieroglyphics on the inner walls, these being the world's earliest religious writings. The so-called Pyramid Texts have enthralled scholars since their discovery in 1881, for they constitute "the Chaucer of ancient Egyptian," helping to form the language as it took shape about 2000 B.C. Robbers long ago violated Unas' tomb with great persistence and engineering skill and picked it clean of treasures, but they did not deface the writings.

Unas "buried two wives" in tombs that were exact twins—no favoritism there—and left quite a clan of princesses, each destined later to have her own tomb. On the walls of one of them is a frieze showing a female hippopotamus bearing her young—*under water.* A crocodile, mouth wide open, waits eagerly to devour the baby hippo.

The scenes inscribed on the walls of Sakkhara's tombs are, in actual fact, scholarship's chief source book of all that went on in the social, domestic, agricultural and religious life of the very early days. One such scene shows a veterinary examining the tongue of a cow. Another shows young people dancing cheek to cheek. Another gives recipes for various table delicacies. Many of the carvings, often touched up with pigments whose colors have lasted four thousand years, show the Egyptian symbol of life, claimed by some to have been the prototype of the Christian cross.

The *Serapeum,* or Tomb of the Sacred Bulls, taking its name from Serapis, a god who united in himself Osiris and Apis, is perhaps the most curious single item in all the wealth of Sakkara. The Apis bull, begotten by a flash of lightning and conceived by a sacred cow, was the emblem of Ptah, the mighty god of Memphis. Each king, from the Eighteenth Dynasty onward, insisted that a bull grown from an Apis calf to maturity and finally reaching old age and death, should be embalmed in the Serapeum. The "Bull Catacombs," now excavated and shown to tourists, were those of the Twenty-sixth Dynasty, made as recently as the sixth century B.C. In the gallery through which visitors walk, numerous chambers cut in the walls reveal the sarcophagi that formerly held the sacred mummified Apis bulls. These giant bovine "coffins"—twenty are still left—are hewn, in each case, from a solid block of granite, red or black, weighing, on the average, over sixty tons, some weighing seventy tons or more. The largest of all these sarcophagi is so utterly monstrous, even for a sacred monster, that the mind will hardly believe what the eyes report. *How*, with the aid of Ptah himself, did men ever manage to get it in here—yet here it is, beautifully made and polished to the hue of a black mirror.

"And what became of the mummified bulls?" I queried.

"All the sarcophagi were rifled ages ago," said our guide, "all except *one*, that is. One was left. The French wanted that, after these catacombs were discovered, about a hundred years ago. They wanted it so much that they dynamited the tomb and freighted the bull to Paris!"

In the afternoon of my Sakkara day Hilmy Bey Pasha took us to his modest Sakkara bungalow and in the course of refreshments mentioned that there were at least a million *sacred cats* buried in catacombs directly under where we then ate and drank. We expressed a desire to see them and he admitted that it could be done, so several of us slid and slithered into a steep, sandy cave near his porch and walked the underground corridors, to the illumination of fitful flashlights. It was a weird half hour, but the cats were there all right, in the ramifying corridors, thousands of them mummified, others in ossuary piles. There were bones of dogs, too, and even some "late" human skeletons, of persons who had merely been laid here by surviving relatives to repose in comfort. The public never hears much about Sakkara's Holy Cats. They are simply there—further witnesses to the ceremonial life of a nation that led the world at the dawn of civilized time and managed to remain great for more than two thousand years.

Lighter Cairo—Day and Night

Shopping is a lighter facet of Cairo's tourist life, though not for the pocketbook. There are many shops and stores of standard type on the streets I have mentioned earlier, including department stores such as the big four-story *Cicurel* on 26th of July Street, but virtually all tourist shopping is done either in the hotel shops or in the world-famous *Khan Khalil Bazaars*, reached from Opera Square by Mousky Street. This incredible complex was founded by Prince Jarkassy el Khalili in the fourteenth century and has grown by many accretions through the centuries since then. A jewelers' section called al-Saghah adjoins it. In these combined bazaars one may purchase Oriental goods and gifts and items of jewelry almost beyond imagining. You will find, in a vast, mad jumble of shops and stalls, exquisite items in brass, copper, ivory inlay, silks, perfumes, spices and so forth ad infinitum. In one small hole of a shop, I believe it was the Tiger Bazaar, I bought an alexandrite ring and found the stone fascinating. Alexandrite is a type of chrysoberyl that changes color according to the light. By day it is normally a sparkling blue and by electric light a deep red-purple, but it turns to other variant hues and tints like a mineral chameleon. In a den called Abd-el-Aziz Aly Lotus Palace of Oriental Perfumes I was constrained to buy two tiny bottles of attar of lotus, "one for winter use, one for summer use," and was informed that it takes five hundred lotus blossoms to make one fluid ounce. I was invited by Mr. Abd-el-Aziz Aly, but managed to decline, to try some Turkish "amber cigarettes," made with a tincture of ambergris to eliminate nicotine. These, I was assured, are the finest cigarettes in the world.

In wandering through the working areas of the bazaars, led by a guide, I was surprised at the number of extremely youthful artisans toiling on intricate inlay and metal work and on rug-making, often in very dim light. Many of them were subteen-age children, boys and girls. "What about schooling?" I asked. "Oh, they go to school mornings," was the easy reply. I asked about their wages and learned that their wages are usually 20 piasters, about 45 cents, for three hours' work. The kiddies seemed cheerful enough. A radio was blasting away in almost every workroom.

The *restaurants* of Cairo, except for those in the tourist hotels, are not very numerous or outstanding, but some are interesting. Of more or less international type, serving Continental fare, are the *Kursaal*, with an open summer terrace, the *St. James*, a dull-looking but quality place opposite the Kursaal, the *Parisiana*, the *Regent* and the *Ermitage*. Far more typical of the East is the *Khomias*, where guests seat themselves on great hassocks and eat Oriental fare from outsized brass trays. *Abou Chakra*, a gentleman running a restaurant that bears his name at 69 Kasr el Aini Street, parallel to the Nile, serves only shish kebab, and *very* good. He is a dedicated Moslem who thinks nothing of breaking off a sprightly conversation to spread his prayer rug toward Mecca and devote five minutes to his orisons. He never defies the Koran by serving beer or wine—bottled lemonade is the beverage—but these are minor matters. His shish kebab is probably the best in Cairo. He is about to open a smart new shish kebab restaurant on the Nile, near Shepheard's Hotel, but the old one will continue in service.

Pastries and sugary concoctions are popular with Egyptians, and at least one of them, called *halawa*, a paste made of sesame seeds and sugar, has proved popular with tourists. For such sweets, of every conceivable kind and most of them as rich as Croesus, try any one of the three establishments of *Grappi*, an internationally famous restaurateur-pâtissier.

Of special type, keyed to Egypt's live-giving stream, is a row of restaurants on Gezira Island opposite the Nile Hilton, some on the river's bank, others on ships moored to the quay.

Floating restaurants, some perhaps more properly called night clubs, include three that need special mention.

1. The big *Kassed Kheir* was the yacht of King Farouk. His royal emblem, with crown, is seen on the side. From December through March it is in tourist service, leased from the Tourist Administration by the Eastmar Company, making regular tours from Cairo to Luxor and Aswan. In the other months it is a restaurant, and in summer, from June through September, a supper club operates on the upper deck, including a floor show, or deck show, of Oriental dancers.

2. The *Omar-al-Khayyam*, another good-sized floater, is open from noon on, guests eating from tables topped each with an enormous copper tray. This ship turns into a night club as the zero hour approaches.

3. The *Laïla*, a much smaller ship, serves lunch and also turns into a night club.

On the shore, the big place is the *Kasr el Nil Casino*, serving lunch and dinner the year round and providing floor shows in summer. It has a long, three-level terrace from whose tables the show is seen on the deck of a small ship moored below. *El Nahr* is a riverside café close by, an evening place made gay with colored lights that look carnival-bright as seen from the Hilton's balconies.

Cairo's night is by no means the blatant, bawdy thing it once was. I recall from my youthful visit that in those days, or nights, a vast red-light area, as wide open and garish, not to say dangerous to life and limb, as any then existing in Europe or the Mediterranean—and there were other tough cities—filled many streets just north of the Ezbekiyeh Gardens surging almost to the terrace of Shepheard's. Soon after World War II the authorities decided that this quarter flouted Moslem law (and gave Egypt a bad name), so they closed it up as tight as a kettledrum, and it has stayed closed. I suppose there is hardly another city of its size in the world where ladies of the night are so rarely seen on the streets or in doorways. The police have instructions to crack down, and not sort of, upon any evidences of a rebuilding of the traffic.

This does not mean that Cairo's night has lost its gaiety, for there are many European-style night clubs and some of them are luxurious and with first-rate entertainers. It does mean, however, that the belly-dance places, supposed by Americans to exceed the most sexy efforts of American burlesque, are relatively tame today. The girls do certainly writhe like serpents of sex but they do not undress—much—and they perform their undulations with an almost ceremonial exactness of technique. There is no crescendo about it. Their first writhings are just about like their last ones and the act is always *long*, to the point of monotony. The dancing must have more meaning to Arabs than to Anglo-Saxons, as otherwise this endless just-the-same *danse du ventre* would grow very boring. Actually it never does. The Arabs go plumb crazy. They yell with delight and all but clamber up on the stage.

The handiest places to see a show of this type today are the *Abdin Palace Casino* in the Abdin Palace Gardens, with European and Oriental show, and the *Granada* in Opera Square, but the suburban places are far more popular. A few warrant special mention.

1. *Mokattam Casino* is a spectacularly located gambling casino, with floor show, on the Mokattam Hills. The gambling, on the upper level of the building, is for foreigners only, Egyptians being denied admittance to this floor. The minimum play at the roulette tables is 20 piasters (43 cents), the maximum L E 105 ($227). On this same hill, nearby, is

another nightspot called the *Monte Bella*. Both buildings provide a superb prospect of Cairo-under-lights.

2. *Sahara City*, a tent night club out beyond the pyramids, offering an Oriental floor show, enjoys a large and enthusiastic patronage.

3. *Auberge des Pyramides*, on the Pyramids Highway, is perhaps the plushiest of the lot, rivaled to some extent by its neighbor the *Arizona*. With its lovely garden setting, its big but not garish dance floor and its tremendous floor show, the Auberge packs 'em in night after night, year after year. A climactic number by a black Nubian folklore dance troupe of men and girls which I witnessed here was the most exciting thing of its kind that I have seen in years. A "battle for the males," in which a foreign white girl exercised her charms on one Nubian male dancer after another but was always outcharmed by a girl of his own race, was the violent superclimax. It was also, I will candidly report, plenty sexy.

A night spectacle of vastly different type, and to many visitors far more exciting than any floor show could possibly be, is the *Sound and Light* performance staged at Giza, guests being seated on chairs placed in the sand in front of the Sphinx. I have seen quite a number of the Sound and Light shows and am inclined to vote this desert spectacle the most stirring of them all, as it tells, through recorded voices coming from the Sphinx and other points, the amazing story of pharaonic Egypt. Written, prepared and staged by the same French organization that made the Athens *Son et Lumière* show and has made others all over Europe and the Near East, it talks English three times a week in summer, twice a week in winter. At other performances it talks Arabic, French and German. Costing only 25 piasters and reachable from Cairo in half an hour by bus or taxi, it is one of the greatest of bargains in after-dark entertainment. So successful did it prove, in fact, that a second Sound and Light show, this on Cairo's dramatic Citadel, was opened in July, 1962, on the tenth anniversary of the Revolution.

Alexandria, Once Great, Now Great Again

Alexandria, as everyone knows, was founded by Alexander the Great (in 332 B.C.) and named for him. A mile-long mole tied the mainland to the island of Pharos, on which Ptolemy Philadelphus later built the most powerful lighthouse in the then world, the island's name creeping into many languages of the world, including French and Spanish, as a common noun. This lighthouse site is now being enhanced by a *Wax Museum* of Alexandrian history, personalities and costumes, abetted by a good tourist restaurant.

The population came to number 300,000 free citizens, mostly Egyptians, Greeks and Jews, in addition to myriads of slaves. It quickly developed an aura of great learning and "in a sense which no future city ever shared Alexandria was the center of world scholarship." These quoted words are from the book *Alexandria in Western Culture* by J. J. Auchmuty, and the author goes on to explain that this city far surpassed contemporary Athens in scientific scholarship because of the unparalleled opportunity for research afforded to rich Greeks—and they had a natural bent for study—by the presence of abundant native labor. For five hundred years Alexandria was the "university of the Western world," its culture fueled chiefly by its museum and its marvelous library. This library was tragically burned to the ground as an incident of the siege made against Julius Caesar, who had intruded in 48 B.C. and had set himself up in the palace quarters. The fire resulted in the greatest single loss to scholarship in all history, far surpassing such modern tragedies as the burning of the Louvain Library by the Germans. Antony, in his time, reconstituted it in a temple and had many works brought from Pergamum, but it was "never the same." It was, of course, in Alexandria that Queen Cleopatra became the mistress first of Julius Caesar and later of Marc Antony and it was here that she met her dramatic death. On the site now occupied by the central Ar-Raml Square she built, in Antony's honor a temple called the Caesarium. At its entrance she had two ancient obelisks placed, but they were destined, many centuries later, to travel abroad, each under the name of Cleopatra's Needle. One now stands on the Thames Embankment of London, the other in Central Park, New York.

After Cleopatra flashed upon the screen of history the city fell to Rome (30 A.D.) under Augustus and remained for a time a commercial metropolis, its population probably reaching half a million, but then it gradually declined and the decline was speeded by the founding of Constantinople in 328 A.D. The descent to nothingness was one of the strangest civic reverses in the world's story, for by the time Napoleon came, in 1798, it had sunk to the status of a wretched Turkish-Arab village numbering no more than six thousand inhabitants. Other ports, such as Rashid (Rosetta) and Damietta, took away what little trade it had enjoyed, but a new canal, commenced in 1819, brought irrigation to the whole region and, more importantly for Alexandria, united that moribund community with the Nile.

This connection was like wine to the spirit and body of an all but dead port. It sprang into life again and its population, especially under Khedive Ismail, grandson of Mohammed Ali, jumped phenomenally, reaching nearly a quarter of a million. Ismail's extravagance led, however, to new difficulties and ultimately to the occupation of Egypt by the Powers—which turned out to mean England. (This occupation ceased when Egypt became sovereign and independent in 1922.) As a dismal incident of the occupation, the European quarter of Alexandria was demolished by a naval bombardment in 1882, but the result was a brand-new Alexandria, the one we see now.

Today it is a splendid metropolis, numbering nearly a million and a half inhabitants, including 150,000 Europeans, especially Greeks and Italians, and is therefore three times as great in size as it ever was in its first incarnation. It has "gone to sea" by occupying a made peninsula that absorbs the ancient mole and pushes out to the Pharos. A broad seashore boulevard, commonly called the Corniche, rims the resulting East Port with a two-mile crescent of impressive parkway and fine buildings, continuing on and on beside the open sea for twelve or fifteen miles. It is here, along this Corniche, that the tourist hotels stand, the *Cecil* and *Windsor*, centrally located, the gardened *Beau Rivage* and the swanky *Salaamlek* far out from town. The Alexandria office of the Tourist Administration, well staffed and maintained, is centrally located on Saad Zagloul Square. From it you may obtain a bimonthly pamphlet called "Two Weeks in Alexandria," which is equivalent in its listing of practical tourist information to Cairo's pamphlet "Cairo This Week."

The two ex-royal palaces, now museums, of Alexandria are in some ways more interesting than their opposite numbers in Cairo, especially for their connection with the life and the hasty flight of King Farouk. *Ras el Tin*, spelled also Ras at Tin, was the official palace where state functions were held and where business was transacted, the other, *Montazah Palace*, was the private royal residence in a park far out at the end of the Corniche. We may take a look at them in turn.

Ras el Tin, on a peninisula between the inner harbor and the open sea, dominates the port. Visitors are shown the Gothic Hall, its walls plated with pure 24-carat gold; the Throne Room, with its incredibly lavish Arabic décor and its elaborate chandelier; the marble Ball Room, facing the sea; the Chandelier Hall; the great Dining Room; the Royal Bath; the Royal Business Office, with a large oil portrait of King Farouk and Queen Nariman; the Royal Railway Station; and much more, to the point of weariness-of-splendor. Farouk's Document of Abdication, referring to him as "King of Egypt and Sudan" (but Sudan is now independent), is conspicuously displayed. It was from this palace that Farouk fled in 1952. Also conspicuous in various parts of the palace is the capital letter *F*, standing for all the recent ex-royalty, King Fuad and his Queen Farida, parents of Farouk, whose first wife was Queen Fawzia and whose daughter was Ferial. In divorcing Fawzia and marrying Nariman (who is now married to a commoner) Farouk broke the *F* chain and with it, perhaps, his royal fortunes.

One special and quite unexpected feature of Ras el Tin is a *permanent* exhibition of dolls from all over the world, some thirty or forty countries having sent entries. This was originally a contest, instituted by the Tourist Administration. Japan won it hands down. The United States of America also ran, with Baby Twinkie, Shirley Temple and Raggedy Ann.

Montazah Palace, some fifteen miles from town, was a retreat far more private and personal in nature than Ras el Tin and it was here that Farouk kept his famous collections. His philately collection was sold after his flight for a reputed half million dollars. The pornography collection is still there, but is kept under lock and key and is rarely or never shown to tourists, even of the male sex. His *alleged* instruments of sadism and/or masochism, leg irons of different sizes, whips and so forth, are indeed shown in a large glass case by the guides, and with great relish, for Egyptians have no love for their ex-king, but a legend, whether of saintliness or sin, tends to grow with the years and tourists should not be too ready to believe all they hear from leering guides. The ground floor of Montazah has been converted into a gambling casino, as usual for foreigners only, the floors above being the museum. The gardens, extending to the edge of the sea, are wonderfully beautiful, and within the palace area is the new, de luxe *Hotel Salaamlek*, with its private beach. Just beyond the palace grounds is *Montazah Beach*, with its hundreds of bathing cabins, perhaps the largest and best equipped of Alexandria's long string of public beaches. A soothing note to shiverers may be injected here, namely, that the water bordering Egypt's beaches is claimed to be the warmest in the entire Mediterranean.

I have a heretical but persistent feeling that the visitor to Alexandria is entitled to neglect all the ancient sights and merely enjoy this wonderful modern city, relaxing for hours on its superb Corniche and perhaps its beaches. Excursion busses take their customers to Pompey's Pillar, the Catacombs, the Necropolis and the *Museum of Greco-Roman Antiquities*. The last-named houses important and highly interesting collections, one item of many being an exact reproduction of the Rosetta Stone, the original of which is in the British Museum. I will confess, *sotto voce*, that I thought the much-vaunted and misnamed Pompey's Pillar, which I first hunted up on my own—my taxi man simply could not locate it—a column not worth the effort of finding or describing in a land where ancient works of instant interest are like the sands of its deserts for number. (Perhaps I am unfair to Alexandria's "sights." An unusual prewar guidebook by an able novelist is *Alexandria, a History and a Guide*, by E. M. Forster, and it makes out a strong case for the city's sights. The book was published by Whitehead, Morris Ltd., of Alexandria.)

Two trips from Alexandria that are of sure historic interest are those to El Alamein, a full day excursion by tourist bus, and to Aboukir.

El Alamein, sixty-five miles west of Alexandria, is, of course, one of the lustrous names in history, for here, at long last, Rommel, the Desert Fox, was turned back and driven half across Africa by Montgomery's Eighth Army. The war had reached about its lowest ebb for the Allies (September, 1942) and this turning point enabled the world to breathe again. In very special particular it enabled Egypt and its threatened seaport to breathe again and one hopes that the Egyptian-in-the-street occasionally takes time out to remember this!

The visit to *Aboukir*, not much featured by the travel agencies, can be made personally and easily by train or bus, an hour each way, and *in* Aboukir by unformidable footwork. The trip involves a pleasant coastal ride of fifteen or twenty miles.

Aboukir is more or less of an Alexandrian summer resort but its chief appeal to the Anglo-Saxon traveler is the bay where Nelson so daringly sailed his fleet on both sides of the French fleet, raking it with cross fire and destroying it. Napoleon later defeated a large Turkish land army at Aboukir, but in the end the Egyptian campaign proved an utter failure. Some of his abandoned troops remained permanently in Egypt, and the town of Abnoob, on the east bank of the Nile, opposite Assiout, is one of several communities largely composed of descendants of the DPs of a former war.

On my Aboukir excursion I fell in with some American residents of Alexandria and picked up some items of Arab lore that I found interesting. Here are a few of them.

Primitive Arabs have always counted, and still do, by means of the three portions of the four fingers of one hand, hence the duodecimal system of English money, twelve pennies to a shilling, of measure, twelve inches to the foot, of a dozen dozen to form a gross, and so on.

Egyptian newspapers print the date in three forms, Moslem, Coptic and Western Christian, each quite different from the other two.

In Egypt, the ancient land of embalming, all funerals must take place within twenty-four hours of death, since embalming is never done!

Censer-swingers enter shops in Egyptian cities swinging their censers to perfume the air for the benefit of trade, the charge for this service being half a piaster, about a cent.

One further item has point in connection with Alexandria. In the wonderful stained glass of the Cathedral of Bourges, in central France, are twelve panes portraying the life of St. Mary the Egyptian, who was, in her younger days, a prostitute of Alexandria. One of the panes shows her standing at the door of her Alexandria brothel soliciting trade from passing men. She apparently did very well, for she earned enough money to provide for a pleasure trip to Jerusalem. There she was converted and thoroughly abased. She returned to Egypt and lived for forty years in the desert as a lady hermit, with the companionship of friendly, purring lions. For clothing she used the tresses that had so beguiled her clients in the big city. Finally, a pious abbot found her— Mary the Penitent—lying dead on the sand. One of her lion friends, with tears streaming from his eyes, told of her death and then helped the abbot to dig a grave for her body. All this is in the glass of Bourges, and St. Mary the Egyptian is also in the sculpture of at least one French cathedral, that of Rouen. In Paris, in the market sector, there is a tiny street, Rue de la Jussienne, which honors her name, for la Jussienne is a corruption of the words l'Egyptienne!

CHAPTER 16

THE EGYPT OF LUXOR, KARNAK AND THEBES

Notes on the Nile

THE Nile is an epic in riverhood. It has always been a favored theme of poets, novelists and even biographers, for Emil Ludwig's *The Nile; The Life-Story of a River* was a biography of this stream, "from birth to death," and H. E. Hurst's more recent *The Nile* is a current handling of the river's life story. The Nile is four thousand miles long and drains an area of more than a million square miles. It is the maker of Egypt and to the ancients its was sacred on that account. Sometimes its floods *un*made great parts of Egypt, but since man has learned to control it, by an elaborate system of barrages, or dams, it no longer causes much damage, though it floods great areas every year, including even parts of Old Cairo, especially in the area of the Coptic churches. The seasonal flood, always coming at a period exactly known in advance, is never a cause for alarm, since it is regulated by "river engineers." People know not only when it will come, but when it will recede. It is as regular in its behavior as the swallows of San Juan Capistrano, and plans are carefully laid each year for coping with the waters.

The Nile leads a double life until it gets clear down to Khartoum, in the Sudan. The *Blue Nile*, bringing the rich silt that annually refreshes Egypt's soil, comes from the melting snows of Ethiopia and specifically from the Lake of Tana. The *White Nile* comes from Lakes Victoria and Albert, the former situated mostly below the equator, and even from feeders of these lakes much farther south in the Tanganyika mountains. In an enormous swamp called the *Sudd* it gets bogged down and disappears so utterly that its actual original source was not known till about a century ago. At Khartoum the Blue and the White unite in a mighty flow that is gradually merged to the color of coffee, and so to Wadi Halfa and the border of Egypt, then, wriggling ever northward, to the Temple of Abu Simbel, now much in the news, Aswan, Luxor, Assiout, Cairo, the Delta and sudden death in the Mediterranean Sea.

Up-Nile transportation may be effected by various means. United Arab Airlines, as we've seen, flies to Luxor in ninety minutes and from there to Aswan in forty-five more; air-conditioned trains with dining and sleeping cars roll to Luxor in about twelve hours; and steamer transport, in winter and early spring only, is arranged by travel agencies in three stages: Cairo-Luxor; Luxor-Aswan; and Aswan-Abu Simbel. All-river services are special and occasional, the more customary plan being for the visitor to go by fast train from Cairo to Assiout, continuing upstream from that point by ship, or to fly directly to Luxor and later contiuue upstream by ship. The Eastmar Company has a regular seasonal schedule, using the *Sudan* and the *Memphis* for the Assiout-Luxor-Aswan journey, the *Memphis* and the *Kassed Kheir* for the shorter Luxor-Aswan stretch. The *Kassed Kheir*, you will remember, was King Farouk's yacht, now used in the warm months (see Chapter 15) as a river restaurant of Cairo. From Assiout southward up to Abu Simbel the steamer *Star of Abu Simbel*, of the Karnak Tourist & Transport Company is available, and in 1963 the same company put into service a fast "water pullman," with 84 slumberette chairs, making the trip from Aswan to Abu Simbel in 6½ hours, returning after dinner. A detailed *map*, more than any number of words, aids the intending visitor to understand what the Double Nile, White and Blue, is and what it does for Egypt.

Moonlight over Luxor

The geography of the Luxor-Karnak-Thebes complex is a master muddle in the minds of most first-coming visitors to Upper Egypt and a few words of clarification here may be justified. In ancient times the *entire* complex was called Thebai, or Thebes, at least by the later Greeks, this being their approximation of one of the city's Egyptian names, Apit. The far-spreading *City of the Living* was on the east (right) bank of the Nile and included the area covered by the modern villages of Luxor and Karnak and all that lay between. The *City of the Dead* (part of ancient Greater Thebes) was what we know as the

Necropolis, on the west (left) bank.

Luxor is a modern community whose smart-sounding name is only a corruption of the Arabic El-Qasr, from a Roman *castra* (camp) once located there. Built on a ridge on the bank of the river, it is the center of tourism for all Upper Egypt. Here are the various hotels and pensions, the *Winter Palace*, with 150 rooms, many air-conditioned, being the traditional leader. A new air-conditioned building immediately back of the Winter Palace and a part of it, has lately opened. It has a smart restaurant-night club and a swimming pool. Much simpler hotels of the resort are the *Luxor* and the *Savoy*.

Karnak, a group of temples formerly connected with Luxor by the famous two-mile Avenue of the Sphinxes, this being slowly uncovered by patient excavation, is usually reached by slow-moving horse-drawn carriage.

The *Necropolis of Thebes* is reached by a cross-Nile ferry, now with adequate landing facilities on both sides. The Necropolis of the ancients is a very great area of tombs of kings, queens and nobles. Egyptians invariably "went west" for burial and that is asserted to be the origin of our war phrase "going west."

I happened to arrive in Luxor for the first time by the light of a full moon, and in Upper Egypt's night that means a celestial floodlight, saturating everything it touches and casting sharp shadows on everything it cannot touch. I shall never forget the strange, magical effect of the *Temple of Luxor* as it smote me, eye and mind. The temple lies directly in the hotel sector, directly on the river's bank, and is therefore inescapable. One cannot quite believe that right here, in the very lap of tourism, lies a thing so remote from the world we live in.

The temple was built under the Eighteenth and Nineteenth Dynasties to the glory of the god Ammon-Ra. Amenhotep III erected it in the first place; Akhnaton turned against Ammon, set up a new capital for himself farther down the Nile and had all the Theban temples closed; Tutankhamen returned to Ammon worship and continued the construction of the Luxor Temple, adding also some decorations which Horemheb later altered; then finally Ramses II added enormously to the whole thing with a magnificent new court whose massive pylon is guarded by six colossal statues of that king and *was* guarded also by two pink granite obelisks. Only one of these obelisks is left. The other is the one that millions of tourists have admired in the center of the Place de la Concorde in Paris. I have mentioned the preceding names, except that of Ramses, chiefly as a reminder that the Eighteenth Dynasty Pharaohs are the ones figuring so vividly in Mika Waltari's *The Egyptian*. That book is a victim of our American reading habits. It had its enormous and prolonged popularity in 1950 and then slid down into oblivion, yet it is not in any way "dated" and would read quite as stirringly in 1970 as in 1950. For those who have not read it or who have forgotten its rich detail it is to be recommended as a considerable enhancement of a visit to Luxor-Karnak-Thebes.

The temple of Luxor should be understood for what it was. Ammon and his wife Mut and their son Khonsu, the Triad of Thebes, lived in the temples of Karnak but were brought once a year by Nile boats up to Luxor (about two miles) and carried into the temple here, in connection with a glittering festival that occurred at the time of the September inundation. So Luxor's temple, large as it seems, is but the Chapel of the New Year of the *Grand Temple of Ammon* in Karnak, which is Egypt's and the world's largest house of worship. Between the two, to provide for the elaborate processions on foot, while the gods were being brought in boats, was the aforementioned Avenue of the Sphinxes. Built by Amenhotep III about 1500 B.C., this was the frequent parade route for processions to honor the gods or the monarchs of Egypt even as late as Cleopatra's time. It must have been an overwhelming paradeway, for the ramheaded sphinxes were erected in a double line, at intervals of a few yards, for the whole great distance. In 1949, archeologists working under the authority of Egypt's Department of Antiquities, uncovered eight of these sphinxes, four on either side, at the Luxor end of the avenue, directly in front of the temple's northern entrance. There is earnest talk of uncovering the entire avenue in a ten-year campaign of excavation involving the removal of a million tons of earth, but the job would call also for the removal of part of Luxor itself, whose encrusted growth rises a hundred feet above the avenue. It seems an impossible task, but of course it would actually be far less Herculean than the digging of the Suez Canal, which de Lesseps achieved over a century ago. In this case, as in the earlier one, foreign capital would presumably be needed.

I have wandered from the Luxor Temple, but before abandoning it

I must mention a few of its features. Inside the great court of Ramses II a gleaming white mosque to the Arab saint Abu-el-Haggag has grown up and it leans cozily against the temple's Pharaonic portico. It looked to me wonderfully romantic by moonlight, and almost as much so next day by sunlight, but it is the archeologists' master headache. Its demolition is obviously and absolutely essential, they say, but this would severely wound Arab sensibilities. A few archeologists are even against its removal on artistic grounds, and so, if a layman dares whisper it, am I. I think it gives us a cross section of time, Islam nestling on the bosom of Ammon.

The temple guide or dragoman will point out the Chapel of the Sacred Boats; the granite colossi of Ramses within the court as well as without; the huge-pillared colonnade of Amenhotep III, leading to that king's columned court; the interesting Birth Room, in which Amenhotep proved, by an elaborate series of reliefs, that he was descended not from the previous Pharaoh but from Ammon-Ra himself. This is quite a tender story. Amenhotep's mother, actually Queen Mountemouia, meets the god secretly and she becomes pregnant. Ammon-Ra has already shaped his child on a potter's wheel and Isis has given life to it. The child is born. He is passed around from god to god, in admiration, and is given the breast by goddess after goddess. It is all seen right there in the everlasting stone, so how could any faithful subject have doubted the story? Beyond the Birth Room is a chapel where Ammon's private boat was once stored. Alexander the Great rebuilt this chapel and it took his name. The ensemble of the temple also includes a Christian basilica and some chapels of the Roman gods, all parts of the cross section of time which this construction surely is.

On one of my visits to the temple I was accompanied by Hassan Bey Fathy, one of Egypt's leading architects, who was building a model village called Gourna across the river so that the ten thousand or so Arabs then living *on* the Necropolis, hampering or preventing needed excavations, might be evacuated to new quarters. He regaled me with feasts of architectural lore, including the theories of the "new school." This school holds that everything the ancients built had a *meaning* more than would meet the casual eye. The shape of the Luxor temple, for a single instance, is considered to be a recumbent figure and any competent new-schooler can show where the head, shoulders, thighs, knees and feet are. Hassan Bey himself adhered firmly to the theory that the ancients possessed a strange "direct knowledge," akin to instinct and quite atrophied in moderns. He compared it to the direct knowledge of local lizards, which, if attacked and poisoned by a scorpion, will scurry off at top speed to find and pluck a certain herb, make a poultice of it with good lizard saliva and apply it to the wound, thus effecting a sure cure. Well—for a mere tourist it is very stimulating to knock about amid such robust theories.

A Carriage to Karnak

The carriage ride to Karnak, along the bank of the Nile, is a delightful thing in itself. About half way to Karnak the rider passes a building of special interest to Americans, for it is called *Chicago House* and is the headquarters of the Egyptian Division of the Oriental Institute of the University of Chicago. Supported by the university, it exists purely for research, and specializes in the photographing and scholarly study of inscriptions found in Greater Thebes. The *French Institute*, since we are on the subject, is very active in excavation work in the Necropolis, and Italian archeological interests formerly contributed much work, especially in the Valley of the Queens, but of course Egypt's own Department of Antiquities is more concerned than all others with the diggings that go on in Egyptian soil and the unceasing train of discoveries resulting from them.

Karnak's temples forbid all but the most elementary comment here. They cover four hundred acres in all. The *Temple of Ammon-Ra* is by far the largest. Others are consecrated to his colleagues of the Theban Triad. A fourth is to Ptah, the god of Memphis, and there are several more, of smaller scope and importance, to smaller gods.

There is something Texan or Californian about ancient Egypt, for one is constantly being informed that this or that is the "biggest in the world." The *Hypostyle Hall* of Ammon's temple, built by several Pharaohs of the Eighteenth and Nineteenth Dynasties, was perhaps the greatest pride of royal Egypt for centuries. Covering about 50,000 square feet, it is certainly the largest single hall of any temple in the world and its gigantic size is dramatized by the enormous columns, all of which find plenty of room for their elephantine yet graceful bulk.

The twelve that form the central nave are the largest, having a height of 70 feet and a circumference of 33 feet. The architraves upon them weigh 63 tons and they support tremendous roof blocks that seem quite at ease 80 feet above the ground. The periphery of each column's capital, taking the form of opened papyrus, could hold fifty persons. The 124 lesser columns, having closed papyriform capitals, are 43 feet in height and any single one of them would seem gigantic in an ordinary setting. All in all, this Hypostyle Hall reminded me of nothing I have ever seen quite so much as of Bull Creek Flat in California, where a forest of giant redwoods crushes your ego into nothing. Each tree is so big that a Greyhound bus, if hung on one of its branches, would seem rather like a Christmas toy, and so it is with Ammon's columns, terminating not in verdure but in papyriform or flowered capitals.

Another thing that stands out in bigness, even at Karnak, is the *Obelisk of Queen Hatshepsut*, who lived about 1500 B.C. A monolith of pink granite, it soars almost to 100 feet and weighs 320 tons. Once it was one of twin obelisks, but its twin was toppled and broken and we see a great piece of it near by, close to the edge of the so-called *Sacred Lake*. At the instance of my guide I slapped this piece with my open palm and it gave forth a clear, ringing, musical tone. Close to this prone section of obelisk is a mammoth *Granite Scarab* that was dedicated to the sun god. On the base of the obelisk that still stands is a lengthy inscription telling how the twin shafts were quarried in Aswan, floated down the river, polished, inscribed and set up within a period totaling seven months. Modern engineering and artistic skill would find it very hard to duplicate that feat. It makes one say of the direct knowledge theory that "there must be something in it."

"Going West" to Thebes' Necropolis

To "go west" on the trail of the ancient kings and nobles, but with much less finality, is a remarkable experience even in this rich region of remarkable things. Six great things are featured in Dead Thebes and we shall list them, with a glance at each. The canned tours seem often to be badly organized, bringing the tourists to the Ramesseum, say, at hot high noon, but perhaps this can hardly be avoided if only one day is available for all. Of course the early hours of the morning and the late ones of the afternoon are the best.

It should be understood at the outset that the body *and* the spirit of the Pharaoh had to be looked after separately. The body was embalmed for preservation and sealed deep within its tomb. The spirit was kept nourished by food and drink offered in an adjacent funerary temple. In the earliest times a pyramid was the chosen tomb, but by the time of Thebes' ascendancy the practice of robbing graves had caused such concern that the kings went to any length to conceal the location of their intended tombs. Sometimes they had their stonecutters construct two or three "blinds," just as towns of camouflage have been built in modern wars to fool bombers. The funerary temple for the spirit was no longer adjacent to the tomb, as it had been earlier, but was located far away, again as a sort of decoy for robbers. The Necropolis of Thebes was that of the Eighteenth, Nineteenth and Twentieth Dynasties, comprising the same kings, in general, who built the temples across the river. And now the Big Six.

1. The *Valley of the Kings* is at the base of a mountain shaped remarkably like a pyramid, and beyond a doubt that was the reason for the choice of this site. Fifty-eight royal tombs (according to most authorities) are known and marked on maps, that of *Tutankhamen*, the most recently found, being naturally Number 58, but it is believed that several more await discovery. The wonders found in Number 58 have been mentioned in connection with the Egyptian Museum in Cairo. The king's mummy, as has been said, rests here in this Theban valley in a huge stone sarcophagus deep in the base of the mountain. Visitors descend into the electric-lighted tomb, see the sarcophagus and learn that it is bigger than the tomb's entrance, which adds another mystery to the many surrounding ancient life. Did direct knowledge give the mortuary engineers some magic power to shrink and expand an enormous box of rock? After answering, "No," we ask, "Well, *how*, then did it get here?"

The story of the finding of this tomb gives us a glimpse of the curious instinct that many assert to be instilled in the Egyptian spirit. Howard Carter, we are told, instructed his chief excavator to "start here." The man disobeyed and started operations at quite another point. Carter was furious about it, but the man stuck to his opinion—and found the tomb.

The Tomb of Amenhotep III, Number 22, is one of the camouflaged ones, with a false tomb to decoy and mislead robbers, while that of Seti I, Number 17, has two such decoys. The actual tomb of Seti I has a Last Judgment scene, with Ammon-Ra as judge, that is strikingly reminiscent of the Last Judgment scenes on the portals of many French cathedrals. If the king is adjudged worthy he walks on a bed of vipers unharmed; if found unworthy he falls into a burning pit. Four beds are pictured, to provide repose for the king on his way to his final reward, a blessed one, we may be sure, for of course the story has a happy ending.

2. The *Funerary Temple of Queen Hatshepsut*, the queen whose obelisk one sees in the Karnak Temple, is a masterpiece of construction and a marvel in setting, against a lofty red cirque as striking as any cirque in the Pyrenees. The temple is enclosed, along with another minor one of Menuthotpe, in the precincts of a Christian monastery (Deir-el-Bahari) of the seventh century, which simply "moved in," nobody saying nay. An interesting thing in the decorations is that the queen's face was deleted from every representation of her. This was done by her brother, Thotmes III, who considered that he had been wronged in some way by her. It was a sort of revenge, and also it prevented her soul from haunting him. Pharaoh Akhnaton did much damage to this beautiful temple, as he did also to those of Ammon, whom he deserted and hated, in Karnak and Luxor. The visitor learns gradually to feel a strong personal wrath toward this well-meaning, idealistic king, even if he did "desire to live by truth." As an image-breaker he was the Oliver Cromwell of his time.

3. The *Ramesseum* is the funerary temple of Ramses II. The most striking thing in it, even in ruin, is a colossus of the king, seated, that is estimated to weigh one thousand tons! It was hewn from Aswan granite and when undamaged was about 56 feet high. The king's chest is 23 feet across; his forefinger 39 inches long. There is much else in the Ramesseum but this statue is quite enough to warrant a visit. It is another "largest in the world."

4. *Medinet Habou*, taking its name from a Coptic Christian village that once flourished here (to this day Copts, of Christian faith, are very numerous in Upper Egypt), is a double temple, that of Ramses III being by far the greater and more interesting. The reliefs on its extensive walls

are intimately reportorial about life as it was lived, and are of such artistry and sharpness, after thirty-one centuries of exposure, that they are a photographer's dream. Fairly late afternoon gives the best light for professionals or amateurs.

5. The *Tombs of the Nobles* number in their hundreds and offer a virtually inexhaustible field of archeological research for centuries to come. Several selected ones are shown to visitors. The scenes, domestic, political and religious, in the decorations of these tombs never fail to surprise and delight the visitor. They are shown by means of mirrors, or boards covered with tinfoil, so adjusted as to reflect the sun's light inside, giving a clear, soft illumination. In *Tomb 69* I saw two gleaner girls (in the reliefs) engaged in a fine hair-pulling scuffle, perhaps over some man they both wanted, and in another scene a girl was carefully removing a thorn from the foot of a fellow-gleaner. A scene of the hunt showed sportsmen attempting to knock birds out of the sky with boomerangs! In *Tomb 100* I was shown the text, in hieroglyphics, of the law concerning a minister's duties to his king and to his people. Rude peasant families lived, in successive generations, inside this tomb, and others too, for centuries, until modern interest in research caused their eviction. Of course they had no reverence for the priceless report-age on the walls of their humble homes and much damage was done. In *Tomb 51* I saw the god Horus carefully weighing the heart of a de-ceased person to see if it warranted his entrance into heaven. These are but the barest samples of the underground wealth of art and chronicles in the nobles' Necropolis. It makes one doubly glad that the fellaheen who live in primitive squalor all over this area are being so firmly but gently removed to vastly better quarters such as those in the nearby model village of Gourna.

6. The *Valley of the Queens* is not to be compared in interest with the Valley of the Kings but there are a few tombs here, two especially, with decorations that have human interest to a marked degree. One, *Number 66*, is that of Queen Nefertari, the wife of Ramses II. She was a stylish lady even if we allow for flattery by the artist, and we see her here, in several scenes, offering gifts to various gods. *Tomb 55* is that of Amen-her-khoshef, a young prince who was the son of Ramses III and who died at the age of twelve. There is genuine sentiment in the pictures here, for the boy's father is introducing him to the various

gods, Thot, Ptah and so forth, and one of the gods chucks the worried boy under the chin in friendliest fashion. We can almost hear him saying, "Buck up, son. You'll like it here with us."

Oh, to have been a tourist in the time of the Ptolemies, who flourished in Egypt in the centuries just prior to the Christian era, culminating with Queen Cleopatra. Regular conducted parties, with guides, viewed the Theban Necropolis then, when relatively little damage had been done. Even now it is not the elements but *people*, greedy, thieving, fighting, ruthless people, who have done the harm, and some of it not too long ago. A French archeologist said to me dourly, "The French and British consuls of the nineteenth century were rival bandits, plundering this place at will. More was taken away then than in all the previous years since 1000 B.C." Government and industry both put their hands to plunder too. He showed me where the roof of one of the courts in the Ramses III Temple at Medinet Habou had been removed in 1840, with government approval, to be used in the construction of a sugar refinery!

Gourna, the model village mentioned above, grows at a brisk pace only four or five miles from the City of the Dead. It is more than a refuge for persons displaced by archeology. It is a novel experiment in teaching the fellaheen to live in sanitary homes and like it. The architecture is so natural and native that it doesn't shock them, yet many improvements have been slyly introduced. In the various new homes the cattle stall is right within the home, for an Egyptian peasant will not and cannot sleep if separated from his animals, which are his "estate." *But* the archway between this stall and the court where the family lives is just a little too narrow to permit a cow to stroll through it, spreading contamination among the children. Gourna has two general schools and a craft school, a market, a mosque, an outdoor cinema, but above all it has families, more than a thousand of them, ushered into modern living as graciously as Ramses III ushered his son into the dwelling-place of the gods.

CHAPTER 17

ASWAN, THE ROCK OF EGYPT

How Granite Was Cut with Wood

EVERYWHERE in Egypt the open-mouthed beholder asks, "*How* did they do it?" In no field is this query more universal than in that of rock quarrying and cutting. *How* were vast masses of granite hewn from their mother rock? *How* were they handled, transported, cut to shape, set up in place, sometimes a hundred feet aloft on roof or cornice? The how of quarrying was answered for me in some detail by an expert of Aswan, from whose general area, as we have seen, all of Egypt's granite came and comes. The very word Aswan means granite in the ancient tongue of this region.

The quarriers, he told me, had two principal ways of cutting granite from its bed, both by means of wood. Where a natural "grain" or "fault" existed, meaning that a layer of granite had been superimposed by nature upon or against another layer, a row of holes, along the line of the grain, was cut, and in each hole a wedge of sycamore or acacia was placed. The wedges were soaked with water and kept constantly wet until they swelled, perhaps in a week or so, to such a degree that they cracked the granite cleanly. But when there was no grain this process would not develop force enough, even in a year. In such quarrying, pieces of wood in each of the holes were set on fire and when at their hottest were doused with cold water. This, he stated, created enough force to crack the solidest granite.

Dr. Hamada mentions a third quarrying process, not exclusively involving wood. Wooden ramming instruments, each tipped with a ball of very hard stone called dolerite, were used to pound and "stun" the granite along a given line. It could then be cut with bronze cutting tools. Hundreds of the dolerite balls were found in the quarries near a mammoth obelisk that was partly cut and then abandoned. But this method involves new "hows." How could bronze be tempered to a hardness that would cut the tough dolerite into balls and would cut and inscribe granite with such beautiful precision? There seems to be no answer to this tempering problem. It is a mystery, the mystery of the unknown process.

The quarries of Aswan are exciting to see. Rows of holes, cut for the wedges, are pointed out, and some of the holes show traces of charring. The *Unfinished Obelisk* gets and deserves the most attention. Had it been fully cut and removed and set up it would have been—the biggest hewn stone in the world! It would have stood 135 feet in height and would have weighed about 1170 tons! It was abandoned not because it was too big to handle but because flaws were revealed that would have spoiled it. On the wall of granite that rises above the bed where this half-hewn obelisk lies, guides point out a "time sheet" carved into the stone. It indicates the individuals who worked from day to day and how long they worked.

Elephantine Charm

Elephantine Island, important in the past of Egypt, lies directly opposite the *Cataract Hotel*, one of the most livable, attractive and well-placed hotels in Egypt, recently improved by the addition of a fine new section of 80 air-conditioned rooms and baths. From the hotel's wharf feluccas take visitors to and around the island, and certainly one should circumnavigate it, not only for the holiday pleasure of it, but to see the cartouches—that is to say the names, within their oblong "cartridges"—of various Pharaohs carved on open boulders. A felucca, typical of Nile transportation, is a long narrow type of craft, with lateen sails, that can be effectively propelled by oars on windless days.

The most famous thing on Elephantine Island is the *Nilometer*, an ancient gauge of the river's height at various dates and seasons. It is a rock ladder of ninety steps leading from a cliff down into the water and on the walls the water levels were marked, including the levels of some disastrous floods. The markings are in Greek and Demotic, which latter was a simplified picture writing. The Egyptian government still uses the Nilometer, the scale being now on marble tablets fastened to the rock.

There is on interesting little *museum* near the Nilometer and it includes an ancient skull that was cracked open by a surgeon (page Sinuhe, the skull-opener), and then sewed up. The holes of the elaborate stitching are plainly to be seen.

As an offset for a sight so gruesome we may step out into the *King's Garden*, formerly named Kitchener's Garden, for this is the chief charm of Elephantine Island. A perfect rose-arbor path leads straight through the center of it to the southern tip of the island and many small paths cut patterns in it. In places bougainvillea, strident in its beauty, riots in big eye-searing patches of purple. Exotic trees capture the attention of all. We see teak and tamarind, rosewood, papaya, mahogany, with strangely light bark, ebony, with the blackest of all barks, and we see what the gardener calls a tomtom tree. Now this is a strange member of the tropical forest family and I think there must be a sermon in it if only I could think what the sermon is. The male tomtom is covered with thorns, sharp, strong stilettos protruding straight from the trunk, while the female tomtom has no thorns at all. Her bark is as smooth as a beautician's claims. Perhaps Lewis Carroll's hero, who slew the Jabberwock, was also puzzled about this,

> "So rested he by the Tumtum tree,
> And stood awhile in thought."

The Great Big Dams

The dam, or barrage, four miles upstream from Aswan is a very big thing by any standards, including those of American engineering, yet it is destined to be dwarfed by a far bigger and higher dam now under construction some four miles farther upstream. The first dam is a mile and a quarter in length, 137 feet high and over 100 feet in breadth at its base. Its 180 sluices (or as many of them as may be open at any given time) roar like watery thunder and the spray bounces up to form a continuous rainbow which the visitor may admire from his stance on the dam. A hydro-electric power plant has been built to produce 400,000 kilowatts of electricity, but it is chiefly as a master dam for the irrigation of Egypt that this is so important. Other dams are at Esna, Assiout and several more points, with a huge one just north of Cairo at the beginning of the Delta.

From a wharf at El-Shellal, a short distance upstream from the dam, the tourist steamers mentioned above take off, in winter, for *Abu Simbel*, whose giant statuary is in such danger of early "drowning." From the same wharf *Sudan Government Express* steamers take off twice a week for *Wadi Halfa*, just within the Sudan frontier, whence Upper Nubia trains run to Khartoum. With the completion of the new dam, estimated for 1965 or 1966, the take-off wharf will, of course, have to be moved a few miles farther upstream.

The Engulfed Temple of Philae

Debussy presumably wasn't thinking of Philae when he composed "La Cathédrale Engloutie," but he might have been, for since the completion of the first big dam this famous island and its temples have been completely swallowed up every autumn in the silt-laden water that backs up from the closed dam. When the sluices are opened, progressively, in the late spring and early summer, to let the beneficent Nile inundate Egypt—always under strict control—the pylons and pillars emerge from their mud bath, and finally, for two or three months of late summer and early fall, all the old temples to Isis, Khnum and other deities, are fully visible, the island, actually a great granite rock, being bone dry. By November, as the sluices close again, the waters begin to pile up, re-swallowing Philae and all its works.

Since the "visible" months are unbearably hot in this latitude and the hotels are closed, very few pleasure travelers ever see the temples now. Only the twin tops of the massive first pylon of the *Temple of Isis* are visible in winter, two reefs of solid masonry rising a few feet above the surface. It is possible to hire a boat and circle this pylon, but it is quite as satisfying to see it from the middle distance of the dam itself, which is the culprit in the annual calamity. If we are tempted to bemoan the dunking in muddy water of an island so richly templed we may cheer ourselves by reversing an adage and admitting that there's no small loss without some great gain. The big dam, aided by lesser ones downstream, has taught the Nile to be a kindly mother instead of a destructive one to the land of Egypt which she brought into this world so many centuries ago.

Saving Abu Simbel, a Job for Giants

Ever since the inception of the plan for the newer and still bigger dam Egyptologists, archeologists and many common or garden laymen have mourned over the impending doom of the huge *Temple of Abu Simbel*, destined to be swallowed up by the waters of the great lake which the dam will create. It was built by Ramses II and is estimated to weigh four hundred thousand tons, which is the equivalent of New York's Empire State Building. To lift it from the water it will have to be raised nearly two hundred feet up the side of a sheer cliff yet this feat is actually being considered by the UAR, which *hopes* ardently for financial aid from UNESCO, though this has so far been denied, and other sources. An Italian construction firm has agreed to undertake the giant job if the money can be raised, and the project will be watched, metaphorically, by millions of eyes throughout the world. It is estimated to cost $70 million and another $30 million has been earmarked for the rescue of the Philae temples and others. Surely never in history has so much money been devoted to salvaging treasures that have only esthetic or artistic value.

In Cairo I recently met an amateur lecturer from Chicago who was on his way to Abu Simbel to do research on the temple and to take photographs of it. His aim was not to make a personal profit but only to stir up public interest and to earn what little his lectures might bring in for the sole benefit of what is called "The Nubian Project." It seemed, on the surface, as futile as to attempt to build another pyramid with a pickax and a wheelbarrow and yet, as we all know, great oaks from little acorns grow. Perhaps, if the engineering project comes to seem too hopelessly grandiose and costly, bringing on dark counsels of abandonment, such efforts as his, multiplied in many circles in many lands, could turn the tide.

REVISION SUPPLEMENT TO CHAPTER 18

THE Tourist Department of Cyprus' Mission to the United Nations, 165 East 72nd Street, New York 10021, can be very helpful in supplying not only information, but also current facts on traveling in Cyprus insofar as currency and visa restrictions may be effected.

Generally, Cyprus has joined other Middle Eastern countries in the attempt to make tourism the number-one industry. Key lures for Cyprus investment are the loans offered by the government of up to 100 per cent of the fixed cost at low interest rates for new hotels or for extensive renovation of existing properties for hotel purposes. Cyprus has a hotel school and all hotels are rated according to accepted standards. This assures the guest good, clean rooms.

The highway network has notably improved, as have also the lesser mountain roads, which are getting better each year. As one example, the *Forest Park Hotel*, once an isolated mountain retreat, is now at the welcoming end of a much improved mountain route. The pool there, incidentally, makes you feel as though you were swimming in the clouds! The new Paphos-Limassol road, to mention another specific improvement, should be finished in late 1966.

There are several good car rental firms and if you rent a car, which you may easily do with only an international driver's license or a Cyprus driving permit obtained upon showing your home-state license, remember that you will drive on the *left* in good English fashion. Try your driving on the straight stretches before you head for the narrower mountain routes. There are busses connecting all the towns and villages if you'd prefer to leave the driving to an expert.

Partially due to the government's liberal financing plans mentioned above and to the desperate need for top tourist hotels, facilities are growing at a rapid rate. Leader among the seven comfortable facilities recently opened or about to open is the *Nicosía Hilton* (called the Cyprus Hilton on page 343 in early reference), which is about to open its doors. Located about one mile from downtown Nicosía and the

Ledra Street shopping area, the hotel is to have 150 rooms and a swimming pool. As the third largest hotel in Cyprus, the Nicosía Hilton will be a natural takeoff point for historic tours of the area. Other new Nicosía hotels are the *Catsellis Hill Hotel*, a venture of the same family that owns the Dome Hotel in Kyrenía (see page 349), with 42 rooms; the *Excelsior*, with 37 rooms; and the *Europa*, a large, modern hotel between the city and the airport. With all the new Nicosía hotels, there's still none better than the *Ledra Palace*, to which the text gives ample praise. Like so many of the older hotels in cities where new facilities are cropping up, the Ledra Palace has an air of elegance that would be hard for a new place to match.

The enlarged *Dome Hotel* at Kyrenía, to refer to it again, now has 156 air-conditioned rooms. At Limassol, the new *Miramare Hotel* offers 62 rooms right on the beach. Up the coast at Famagusta there are at least two new hotels. The *Grecian Hotel*, on the beach, has 75 rooms, and the *Hesperus* also has clean and comfortable accommodations.

The government has outlined 12 tourist zones along the coast. Development will be controlled in these areas—both for the residents and the tourists. No overdeveloped tourist meccas these! Programs call for a limited number of hotels and guest houses and improvement of restaurant, touring and entertainment facilities as well.

Don't miss Cyprus festivals if you can include even one in your plans! The *Kyrenía Festival*, mentioned briefly on page 350, has become a three-month affair, from June through August, with a variety of performances at the Bellapais Abbey. This is a cultural festival in a spectacular setting, not to be missed if you can possibly attend.

The *Salamis Festival* (page 355) is also held all during the summer. From its modest beginnings in 1963, the Festival has now taken shape as one of the top events in the area, offering Greek and Shakespearean dramas at the ancient theater.

Except for the brief mention of these two festivals, the text neglects Cyprus' rapidly increasing festival roster. In addition to gaiety for gaiety's sake, the festivals give you an opportunity to see the Cypriot—Greek or Turkish (and he refers to himself as a Greek Cypriot or a Turkish Cypriot)—relaxed and enjoying himself. Other festivals than those named above, some of local origin and therefore enchanting because they are *not* primarily for the tourist, may be listed here, one being the *Limassol Wine Festival,* held in late September and early October. This takes a page from the famous Oktoberfest of Munich, Germany. Free distribution of local wines leads to frantic folk dancing and singing and a gay carnival spirit. Somewhat more sedate but none-theless interesting is the *Lefkara Lace Festival,* which takes place in early July. Primarily for the purpose of allowing local lace makers to show their craft, the festival provides an ideal forum for folk dancing in costume.

Kataklysmos, the celebration of Pentecost, is truly a Cypriot cele-bration, with sea games, dancing and singing. This festival is celebrated locally in most seaside towns such as Paphos and Limassol and many smaller places. The festival is a sort of country fair, with displays by local residents of their jams, jellies, fruits and baked goods. Games in-clude swimming races, diving exhibitions and a greasy-pole contest for those who *think* they are sure on their feet. This is truly a test of the contestant's ability to walk the straight and narrow, since he must walk along a well-greased pole that floats in the water! He inevitably gets a dunking, to everyone's great glee.

Two final mentions in this festival roster are the *Orange Festival,* held in Famagusta for a week in February, an affair only recently organ-ized with floats and plays; and the *Flower Festival,* held at the Limassol Public Garden in May's first week.

CHAPTER 18

CYPRUS, A WORLD ON AN ISLAND

The Story of Ledra

LEDRA was the earliest name of Nicosía, the present capital of Cyprus. In 280 B.C., when the town was already venerable, its name was changed by a ruler named Leucos to Leucosía, as it is still called by Greeks. Other Europeans know it as Nicosía, but its pristine name, simplest and most glamorous of all, will not die. The main shopping thoroughfare is Ledra Street and a chief hotel is the *Ledra Palace*. The life of Ledra fairly throbs along the city's central street, especially during the promenade hour late Sunday afternoon, when you can hardly make your way through the strolling hordes; and it throbs several evenings a week in the Ledra Palace, where important banquets, fiestas and social gatherings of Cyprus often take place.

The name Cyprus is said by some authorities to derive from the Greek *kupros*, meaning copper, an ore in which it was abundant for many centuries during Phoenician and Roman times. Cupreous pyrite mines are still important in island industry as are mines of asbestos, chromium and gypsum. Forests of *cypress* from this island rivaled in trade the famous cedars of Lebanon, but by a strange turn of arboreal fate Lebanon now has only a few hundred of her noble cedars left, whereas Cyprus is estimated by local foresters to have twenty-five thousand of them in the western hills.

This island has been a going concern since the late Stone Age, say 3500 B.C., with some monuments thought to date even from as early as 5800 B.C., but it never developed as intricate a culture as that of Crete. In the *Cyprus Museum* of Nicosía, considered of great importance by students of the remote past, *ten* separate "Ages" are set forth, from the Neolithic to the Hellenistic and Greco-Roman, this last carrying from 250 B.C. to 250 A.D. In the Christian era it ran through the usual gamut of occupations, Roman, Byzantine, Saracen, Turkish, but inserted a few colorful specialties of its own. In 1191, Richard the Lion-Hearted, while on his way to the Holy Land, stopped to seize Cyprus and then celebrate the victory by marrying Berengaria of Navarre in the town of Amathus, now practically obliterated, near Limassol. He even had her crowned on the spot Queen of England.

The next year Richard, after a brief business with the Knights Templars involving ownership of Cyprus for a matter of months, transferred the entire island to Guy de Lusignan, who had been the crusader king of Jerusalem. The Lusignan Dynasty held it for three centuries and gave it, late in life, its Golden Age, from 1192 to 1489. Today's visitor comes frequently upon buildings and various relics of the Lusignans.

The Genoese and Venetians in turn, bitter enemies each of the other, held Cyprus, especially the fortress port of Famagusta, for some decades and it was in a tower of that city that Othello, the Moor of Venice, murdered Desdemona. In our thought we may transfer historical drama to historical fact as local Cypriots easily do, pointing out "Othello's Tower" to tourists. The Turks followed the Venetians and held the island until 1878, when Great Britain acquired from Turkey the right to occupy it. When Turkey picked the wrong horse in World War I, siding with imperial Germany, she lost what shadowy sovereignty she may still have had. In 1925, Cyprus became a British crown colony, but the urge to throw off the shackles of colonialism waxed strong, culminating in prolonged guerilla warfare. In 1961, Britain granted the island independence, reserving important military bases and firm guarantees for the Turkish minority. The move worked out well and Cyprus is now an independent nation voluntarily within the British Commonwealth of Nations. Instead of the Union Jack we see on flagpoles the flag of the Republic of Cyprus, with two olive branches and an outline map of the island.

The Tourist Welcome

The *Cyprus Government Tourist Office*, which is a part of the Ministry of Commerce and Industry, issues to all comers a leaflet called *Cyprus Tourist Information* bearing these words in large letters: "The moment a visitor sets his foot on Cyprus soil he is considered a sacred person. Hospitality, which started four thousand years ago as a divine command, still flourishes strongly today." Perhaps we shrink from admitting a sacred status, but being human we "welcome the welcome," which is indeed warm, genuine and island-wide. Those who have read Lawrence Durrell's moving account of his Cypriot contacts in *Bitter Lemons* have found in his pages ample confirmation of the veritable passion of hospitality which inheres in every Cypriot. This is fully evident on the tourist level, so often subject to the inroads of commercialism. Upon my recent arrival at the Cyprus Airport after an absence of ten years, I signalled a taxi for the ride into town and asked the man what his charge would be.

"Nine shillings, sir."

"Is that the standard fare?" I asked, in somewhat doubting mood.

"Sir," was his reply, "you are in *Cyprus* now," and that was all he said, or needed to say. I recognized myself right off as a sacred person!

The *currency of Cyprus* has some odd quirks. The country is in the sterling area and its pound is the exact equivalent of the British pound sterling, namely $2.80 to the pound, *but* the Cyprus pound is divided into one thousand mils. Thus 50 mils equals 1 shilling and is invariably so called by Cypriots. One hundred mils is 2 shillings, 500 is 10 shillings and so forth, but in a single minor matter Cyprus coinage departs drastically from the British norm, for it takes *ten*, not twelve, of the 5-mil copper pennies of the island republic to make a shilling (50 mils). Above the penny we find cupro-nickel coins of 25, 50 and 100 mils and notes of 250 and 500 mils, followed by £1 and £5 notes. A portrait of Queen Elizabeth is engraved on all paper money and stamped on all coins. Her portrait appears also on all postage stamps. A further evidence of British background is seen in motor traffic, which keeps to the left! This does not, however, argue any strong *devotion* to England. The English language is rather widely spoken, or at least understood, yet throughout Nicosía *all* street names appearing on signs in English have been clumsily blotted out with daubs of black paint.

Entering Cyprus is a simple matter, for no visa on one's passport is required and if there is any currency control it is so mild that you are hardly aware of it.

The headquarters of the Government Tourist Office, together with its *Tourist Information Bureau*, is at 26 Evagoras Street, Nicosía and there is a branch Information Bureau at the airport. Other branches are in Famagusta and Limassol.

Taxis charge 4 shillings (200 mils) for a ride anywhere within Nicosía's limits. In other cities the fare is 3 shillings.

The climate of the island makes it a goal of travelers from all directions and latitudes. Those from northern lands revel in the warm sun of the beaches, where continuous rainless weather can be counted on for half the year, from May through October. Those from hot southern climes, especially Egypt and the Middle East, revel in the lofty resorts among the piney mountains. In the winter months skiing at 5500-foot Troödos—Mt. Olympus rises above to 6400 feet—and bathing from the beaches below are simultaneously enjoyed by devotees of the two sports. The beaches are only an hour's distance by car from the winter sports areas.

Expansion projects are now under way that might daunt a considerably larger country, for example the new £800,000 terminal being constructed at the Nicosía airport, with the announced ambition to make this "the best in the Near East"; £11,000,000 allocated for new and improved harbors; £5,500,000 for highway development; and, of special impact upon tourism, a Five-Year Plan of tourist promotion costing £3,000,000.

The hotels of the island are striving valiantly to keep abreast of the demand. Over a hundred, in all categories, now exist and others are popping up all over. To keep up the pace the government now contemplates establishing a chain of high-grade but inexpensive hotels similar to the Greek government's Xenia chain. Four specific locations are already spotted on the map.

In Nicosía the delightful Ledra Palace has long held sway. Although placed within broad gardens and having about it the air of a comfortable resort inn, it is no more than eight or ten minutes' stroll from the heart of the city. The public rooms and garden terrace are pleasant, and all bedrooms and baths are being, or have already been, air-conditioned. A swimming pool is planned for immediate construction. But best of all, the Ledra Palace has a "personality" that the guest instantly senses and enjoys.

Its only competitor in the luxury class, and that not too serious, is the *Regina Palace*, but Hilton International has announced an agreement with the government of the republic whereby a 150-room hotel will be erected, to be known as the *Cyprus Hilton*. It will, of course, be de luxe, with all the features customary in the Hilton chain. Two lesser but good A-class hotels of Nicosía are the *Acropole* and the *Crown*.

The *restaurants* of the city are not especially noteworthy, but one should consider, at least for its design, the *Ship Kebab*, shaped like a ship, on Homer Street. *Angelo* is a recommendable Greek restaurant, and a good country place near the airport is *Makedonitissa*. *Charley's Bar*, in town just off Ledra Street, is in part a snack bar patronized by tourists. Ten shillings buys a pretty good meal.

Naturally, the food of a Greek nation with a considerable Turkish minority and a European "frosting" offers various specialties, though the Greek dishes mentioned in Chapter 12 certainly predominate. Among distinctively Cypriot dishes you will likely encounter *shamishi*, whose ingredients sound dubious. I haven't tried it but it is, if I understand its composition, a thin flour cake filled with semolina and fried in cottonseed oil and it is usually eaten with a companion concoction called *loukoumades*. The most characteristic food oddity of Cyprus, however, is nuts strung on a string and dipped over and over again into liquid sugar until each little nut has attained the size, and more or less the appearance, of a grape. Everywhere you see the ropes of "grape nuts" —if I may be forgiven.

Two local table wines that cost only about fifty cents for a half bottle even in hotels like the Ledra Palace have remarkably interesting names. The white wine is called *Aphrodite*, the dark red wine *Othello*. This is appropriate enough since Aphrodite (Venus) was born in Cyprus foam (at Paphos) and Othello is said to have died in "Othello's Tower" in Famagusta. An aristocrat of Cyprus wines is *Commandaria*, a sort of heavy Madeira, "as originally made for the Knights Templars, 1096–1291." When you read the label and then drink the bottle's smooth contents you will readily admit that the good knights knew good wine.

The anise liqueur called ouzo that is so familiar in Greece is equally popular in Cyprus, where also it seems to flourish under the alias *ziviv*. Another drink, quite as potent, is *zivania*, made from the residue of pressed-out grapes. If you can down more than one of these at a sitting you're an able drinker.

Life-at-night in Nicosía has more gaiety than one would expect. There are half a dozen cabarets, led by the pretentious *Chanteclair* and the *Asty*. The floor shows in both these places are astonishingly good for night clubs in so small a capital. A tourist publicity release of Cyprus Airways mentions, with the wisdom of experience, "If artistes are invited to the table, remember they prefer expensive drinks, usually priced at 10 shillings, champagne approximately £5 a large bottle." Expensive tastes are natural to artistes and hostesses in all the night clubs of the world, so there is nothing unique about those of Nicosía. Possibly you will prefer the more general gaieties of the Ledra Palace, where, even on off nights, there is likely to be dancing to good music in the Grill Room, and before very long the Cyprus Hilton will be offering night club attractions.

Sightseeing is perhaps not a major tourist sport in Nicosía, but there are a few things of importance to see in this capital. Among them are the former *Cathedral* (Gothic) *of St. Sophia,* for several centuries and even now a mosque; the *Bedestan,* a church-museum adjacent to it, with good Lusignan relics; the so-called *Sultan's Library;* the *Women's Market,* on Fridays; the *Greek Orthodox Church* of the Archbishop of Cyprus, with Byzantine paintings; the *Church of the Armenian Prelature* of Cyprus, with a beautiful old-world courtyard; the important *Cyprus Museum,* mentioned earlier; and the six-domed *Tekké,* or *Church of the Turning Dervishes,* whose strange rituals are performed, and may, with luck, be seen, once every six weeks. But strolling the narrow streets is, after all, the main thing. Nicosía, more than any other Cyprus town, is a racial whirlpool and its life is unendingly awash with Mediterranean colors. Geographically, the town sits in a broad plain enclosed on every side by mountains, some of which are of dramatic profile against the sky. The most striking of them is the *Pentadactylon,* a gigantic fist of four knuckles and a thumb, hence the name, meaning Five Fingers, punching the northern sky.

Boxing the Compass of Cyprus

Cyprus has four chief seaports of mellow age and color, like spokes of the Cyprus wheel centered by Nicosía, the inland hub. They are *Kyrenía,* on the north coast, *Famagusta* on the east, *Lárnaca* and *Limassol* on the south. The big cruise steamers, when they touch at Cyprus, often stop at Lárnaca, but the Greek Line's *Olympia,* the

Anchor Line's "C" ships from Liverpool and various other shipping companies use as anchorage the roadstead of Limassol. In planning motor trips to these ports or anywhere else by the island's eight hundred miles of paved highway the visitor will wish to consult the Tourist Information Bureau or one of the numerous travel agencies. In addition to aiding in the various arrangements, the Information Bureau distributes leaflets, maps and town plans. A comprehensive local guidebook, with maps and photographic illustrations, is Kevork K. Keshishian's *Romantic Cyprus*, procurable for 12 shillings (600 mils). A monthly tourist guide pamphlet called *Discover Cyprus* is distributed free. For superb photography of Cyprus scenes and persons I would strongly recommend the books of Reno Wideson, whom Lawrence Durrell called "a poet of the camera." Wideson's latest such book, titled *Portrait of Cyprus*, seems to me his best yet.

For trips to points outside Nicosía taxis now charge a little less than ten cents a mile on a straight mileage basis, but fixed prices, on a lower scale, are officially listed by the Tourist Office for various trips to places of tourist interest. There is much comfort in this, since haggling, the bane of car travel in many Eastern lands, is eliminated. In addition to taxi and car hire services there is a truly amazing network of jitney services which the traveler should certainly consider. These jitneys travel at frequent intervals and the visitor may engage a single seat, or as many as he likes, at the following rates, one way, from Nicosía: To Kyrenía 3 shillings; to Lárnaca also 3; to Famagusta 5; to Limassol 8; and to distant Paphos 15. The jitney will pick you up at your hotel and will deliver you at any reasonable point in the town of your destination. One need not be in the least timid about using these public jitneys, for one's fellow-travelers, mostly native Cypriots, recognize foreigners, you remember, as "sacred persons" and treat them with due courtesy despite the language barrier. I have taken several such trips and have loved them. So has my budget.

As a practical matter it should be understood that Cyprus touring falls into four convenient divisions based on the four points of the compass. The north includes the Greek monastery of St. Chrysostom, on the Nicosía side of the mountain range, and the fantastic St. Hilarion Castle and lovely Bellapais Abbey, both near Kyrenía, which key town serves as a sort of North Star for this division. The east means chiefly

Famagusta, a marvelous medieval town, and its ancient neighbor Salamis of the Romans, with a look at the newly revealed ruins of *very* ancient Engomi. The south has the mountaintop monastery called Stavrovouni, reachable by car despite its great height; Lárnaca and the near-by mosque called Hala Sultan Tekké, a shrine where Mohammed's aunt is buried; modern Limassol, with ancient ruins on either side; and the special lace-making hill village of Léfkara. The west is an area of high mountains, with resort hotels, cedar forests and, in the "far west," mythical-historical Paphos. The above, trimmed of what is merely good to leave only the best, represents the highest of the tourist high lights.

Zigzag to Kyrenía

The *Monastery of St. Chrysostom* is not too easy to reach, since this involves considerable travel by a secondary road in a direction well to the east of the Kyrenía highway, but it is richly worth finding. St. John Chrysostom, considered a founding father of the early church, was born at Antioch in the fourth century. He became not the silver-tongued orator but the golden-tongued, or golden-mouthed, which is the literal meaning of his name. This monastery in Cyprus is a branch of the Greek Orthodox Patriarchate of Jerusalem, lying within that old portion of Jerusalem administered by Hashemite Jordan, and is, I believe, the only such establishment outside the paternal home.

The physical appearance of the place makes it an idyl of bucolic-religious peace, an unsurpassable artist's bit, and this includes, or did when I visited it some years ago, the venerable archimandrite, Panaretos Vomvaris himself, one of whose titles was Exarch of the Holy Sepulcher. With his long hair done up in a pug he worked like any strenuous farmer except at times when his religious duties called him. A flock of ducks in the white courtyard raises an infernal hullabaloo at times, drowning out the cooing of monastery doves, but this racket serves only as foil for the rustic tranquility of St. Chrysostom's. The courtyard is centered by a giant cypress tree ninety feet high, and there are luxuriant rose gardens too. Whenever a girl of the vicinity is married she receives a bouquet of roses from the archimandrite.

The monastery church has a remarkable door, fitted with many sepa-

rate pieces of carved wood so effectively and handsomely harmonized
that a replica of it has been made to serve as a door in the *Government
House* at Nicosía. Beside this church is another very primitive one dating from the year 1090, when it was dedicated. Its walls are scribbled
with the names and dates of visitors who have come during its many
centuries. One date that I noticed at random was April 15, 1508!

The Exarch insists that the visitor partake of his hospitality, for like
any Greek, and particularly any Cypriot, lay or of the cloth, he would
just about die of shame if he were deprived of this gracious privilege.
In extending his hospitality to me, he had hot coffee, cakes, a curious
black walnut jam and hawthorn jelly brought to his modest reception
room, but his personality was the best spice. He showed me his Golden
Book, with the names of many celebrities, including that of Haile
Selassie, in Abyssinian script. He showed me, too, a votive picture of
a queen of Buffavento, which is indicated by a conspicuous skyline
castle of the neighborhood, accessible by a road of sorts. The picture
showed the queen bringing her leprous son down to the church to be
cured by holy water. Presto, the cure was effected, queen and prince
climbed back to their castle and "lived happily ever after."

The *Castle of St. Hilarion*, on the north side of the pass leading to
Kyrenía, is one of the most incredible operetta-stage castles in existence,
quite equaling in fantastic profile any of the castles of the mad King
Ludwig of Bavaria. Even in ruin it is a thing to make you believe
you've eaten unwisely and are having a dizzy spell. It was the royal
castle of the Lusignan kings and queens who ruled Cyprus for the
centuries of its Golden Age, and its checkered story would give challenge to any writer of massive historical novels. Its walls and battle-
ments climb a double pinnacle of such height and steepness that the
more timid queens of the Lusignan house must have viewed with
alarm every ascent to it, but you are not timid and your heart and
lungs and legs are good, so you will not hesitate to climb its tortuous
paths and endless stone steps to the very summit, or perhaps to both
summits. Below you, yet still far above the sea, you will view the level
field, clinging to a cleft in the mountain, where knights jousted while
the royal family and court looked on from the various balconies and
parapets. Local folk insist that St. Hilarion served as the model for
Walt Disney's castle in "Snow-White and the Seven Dwarfs." Be this

as it may, the ensemble of crags and soaring masonry will serve as the fulfillment of your dream of what a medieval castle should be. A leaflet with a historical account of the castle and a "ground plan," from the barbican to the lofty royal apartments, may be procured at the lower gate.

Bellapais Abbey, on a hillside near Kyrenía, dates from the fourteenth century, though its actual founding dates back to 1120, when it was established in primitive form by the Norbertines of Laon, France. The name is a corruption of Abbaye de la Paix, which title it certainly deserves in its lovely somnolence. Sometimes, and more properly, it is spelled Bellapaix, as in Durrell's *Bitter Lemons*. The *village* of Bellapaix, near the abbey, was the very community in which the author settled. The church and the refectory are in a good state of preservation, the latter having a curious pulpit from which a monk used to read preprandial Scriptures, not too lengthily one hopes, to the other monks assembled for the important business of eating. At the entrance to the refectory the custodian points out on the lintel the carved Lusignan arms, and inside he shows various individual marks of medieval masons. The marks were in effect bills to the Order: "I Richard (or John or Henry) did set this stone. Kindly remember to pay." The view from the refectory windows of the lemon groves, the sloping meadows, the woods and the surf-smitten north coast is one of unsurpassed loveliness.

A modern belfry of Bellapais is a source of considerable controversy. It is striking, as seen from a distance, but in its airy slenderness it has not even a speaking acquaintance with the solid old style of the church and refectory.

The peaceful courtyard of the abbey is unforgettable. It is a quadrilateral of flawless green lawn surrounded by a rosemary hedge of almost overpowering fragrance and dramatized by four dark green "minaret-cypresses" of great height. Adjacent to it is a well-tended flower garden, and in the entrance court is a curious tree that bears, through grafting, four different kinds of fruit, oranges, bitter oranges, tangerines and lemons.

"What?" I asked. "No bitter lemons?" The guide, who recognized the point of my query, shook his head regretfully.

Kyrenía, final goal of the northward trip, has a beautiful horseshoe harbor, with a dramatic castle of the early Lusignans at one end and a modern, first-class hotel at the other. This *Dome Hotel*, run by a hotel dynasty named Catsellis, is a place of some distinction. It is a favorite of honeymooners, as you may see by glancing about you in the seaside dining room or at the pool, and also of elderly English folk, who "see Kyrenía and then die," though not right off. The place is wonderfully appealing to any traveler, young or old, in love or not, who wants a good meal in a good setting as reward to his body for the pleasant but arduous labors of sightseeing. The Catsellis family maintains its own farm and is proud of its "farm-fresh" produce.

Kyrenía's tourist popularity is growing fast and to meet it new and newer hotels are springing up. One central, harborside place of good quality is appropriately named the *Coeur de Lion*. Another, small but first-class, bears the odd but easy-to-remember name *Hotel Ruby Rock*. It is built on rocks at the edge of the open sea and a swimming pool has been carved out of the rocks so extremely close to the surf that on breezy days salt spray bounces actually into the pool. The dining room, upstairs, has a terrace directly overlooking the pool and the sea. Another hotel, less new and of lesser stature, but now in process of major reconstruction, is the *Hesperides*.

Kyrenía's Lusignan Castle, mentioned casually above, is a thing that should not be casually viewed, for it is a sight of major interest. Among its features are four ancient towers, three of them altered to permit the firing of cannon, the other still with mere slits for bowmen's use. The fort played a valiant part for the British in World War II and was used by the British Army until 1959 in the guerilla war with the Cypriot Freedom Fighters, as the patriots styled themselves. Sixteen of them were at one time imprisoned in the bowmen's tower but escaped through a narrow aperture by a rope of knotted bedding. One of them, affectionately dubbed by his compatriots Houdini because of his many escapes, is now an honored cabinet minister of His Beatitude Archbishop Makarios III, President of the Republic of Cyprus.

There are other things in Kyrenía's castle to catch the eye. One is a tiny, cavelike eleventh-century Byzantine chapel built literally *in* the wall, a most striking curiosity. Another is the great courtyard, used by the Lusignans as a Tournament Field. A third is the oubliettes, or dank dungeons, where prisoners languished. We are shown gratings above, through which the jolly hosts and guests, enjoying sumptuous

dinners, liked to drop leftover tidbits from their plates, as if to dogs. If
they forgot, or finally tired of the sport, the prisoners died. It was that
simple in the good old times.

More cheerful is the thought of drama festivals given annually in
the castle. The Greek Theater has played here and so has the Hallé
Orchestra and the Old Vic. When I was last there this famous company had been engaged to play *Romeo and Juliet*. I have not witnessed
a performance in the castle, but the setting is marvelous and I am told
that the acoustics are wonderful, rivaling those of the Epidaurus
amphitheater.

The High Forest Road to Kantára Castle

Some years ago a new road of importance to tourism was opened
along the high ridge of the Kyrenía Range to Kantára Castle. It was
built primarily to further the government's forestry program, seeking
to redevelop the great forests of this range which were wiped out by
disastrous fires some forty years ago. As a secondary purpose, the road
was foreseen as a major tourist attraction, for it runs, at an average
altitude of half a mile, directly along the sharp ridge that is the north-
south watershed of eastern Cyprus.

Kantára Castle, present terminus of the road, is a mere tumbled heap
of masonry, dating from the Lusignan period, but its commanding position on a high spur of the range makes it one of the finest viewpoints
in the island, rivaling even that of the better known Stavrovouni Monastery. Kantára Village, a tiny mountain resort on the forest road a
mile or so west of the castle, has two or three simple inns. One of them,
the *Regaena* (so spelled), has a café terrace that seems to hang in the
upper air high above the broad plain that extends to the southern
beaches and Famagusta.

A sensible circuit for the motorist, one that avoids retracing the same
highway to Nicosía, is to *approach* the high forest road from the
northern coastal highway that runs many miles east from Kyrenía, and
to *descend* from the ridge to the south at Lefkóniko, perhaps pushing
on to the seaside village of Boghaz for a swim on the southern beach and
lunch at the clean little hotel of the village. From there one may drive

along the coast to Famagusta, returning to the capital by a main trunk road.

Before reaching Famagusta the motorist will "stop by" at two nearby points to see *Salamis* (see later section), some five or six miles short of Famagusta, and the important new excavations at *Engomi*, where a city of the Mycenaean Age, meaning, in this case, about 1600 B.C., is being gradually brought to light by the French Archeological Mission and the Cyprus Department of Antiquities. Old Engomi is a city that arouses curiosity in the archeological breast. It seems to have been a Bronze Age city of Phoenician, or maybe early Greek, origin, or a mixture of both, destroyed by corsairs about 1200 B.C., but its great extent and the strength of its walls both proclaim that it was a metropolis of the first rank. When more is known of it new light may be thrown on the whole era that preceded the dawn of Greek civilization.

Famagusta, Bastion of Venice

Famagusta, reached in forty miles by a direct highway from Nicosía is a town of considerable tourist development. It has two hotels in the central area, the A-class *Savoy* and the B-class *Famagusta Palace;* two on the beautiful sandy beach called *Glossa*, the *Florida*, A-class, directly on and over the sand (water skiing here), and the *King George*, B-class. The good but declining *Hotel Constantia* is located on a shore point of its own, with a seaside dance-restaurant and with a private beach and small harbor. This name recalls nearby Salamis, later renamed Constantia, the commercial center of the Levant during the era of Rome's control of Cyprus and now being vigorously excavated. Famagusta, enhanced by Salamis, is the most interesting old port of Cyprus and could use a major hotel. No doubt it will soon get one.

The port is marked with the indelible symbol of Venice. Everywhere on its ancient walls and fortifications one sees the lion of St. Mark, but the Queen of the Adriatic was not the power that made this Mediterranean city great. That honor fell to the refugees who flocked here in 1291, escaping from Saracen oppression in Palestine, and it fell later to Genoa, which got control of the city in 1327 and held it for a century. The turn of Venice came in 1489 and Venice made Famagusta merely a military bastion of tremendous strength, building the powerful walls that still enclose it. Othello, in Shakespeare's imagination, was a Venetian general in charge of the defense of Cyprus, and if such a swarthy man actually held this post he must certainly have made the fortified castle, or citadel, of Famagusta and the *Palazzo del Provvidatore* (now called the Venetian Palace) in the center of the city his base of operations. On the wall of the castle, a huge square fortress that tourist booklets call, in its ensemble, *Othello's Tower*, are some marble plaques adorned with the winged lion of the Venetians, and one of these plaques is conspicuous over the main gate. Shakespeare has as the setting for Act II "A Seaport in Cyprus, An open place near the Quay," and all the scenes of Acts II and IV are laid "Before the Castle" or in its rooms and garden. Perhaps the bard's Cyprus research was on the sketchy side but like any well-informed Englishman of his time he would know that only a few decades earlier, before the Turks had finally captured and blighted it, Famagusta had been the richest emporium of trade in all the Mediterranean, with many millionaire families and with a life of general luxury scarcely matched in Europe. It was an interesting setting for his play, which may indeed have been based partly on historical fact. A highly educated Cypriot told me that a swarthy commander of the fort—I believe his name was Cristóforo—did kill his wife, in the year 1506 in the bedroom of Othello's Tower. In 1571, a gruesome incident occurred. The last governor, one Marcantonio Brogadino, was captured by the Turks and flayed alive as part of a general massacre. Good old times again.

To return to the present, I happened to see an unrehearsed drama in the very setting chosen by Shakespeare "before the castle wall." A strong wind was blowing and by a cruel trick it snatched a small yellow balloon from the hand of a ragged Turkish child of six and bowled it along playfully toward the deep moat of Othello's Tower. The child came tearing after it at top speed, twice almost caught it, almost but not quite. The pathetic toy, half deflated, blew into the moat and my heart almost stopped as I thought the child was going to jump in after it, which would have meant a fall of thirty feet or more. Instead he lay on the edge and cried his heart out, a tempest of sobs shaking his whole body. I gave him several piasters, enough to buy two or three such balloons, but it was no use. He wanted *that* balloon, *his* balloon. After a quarter of an hour he was enough comforted so that he trudged off, the money in his grubby hand. I have no doubt the balloon is still there. It would take a fire department's hook and ladder to rescue it.

The traveler visiting Famagusta enters through the Land Gate piercing the southern wall and finds the local Antiquities Office in a former army mosque actually *in* the city wall beside the gate. He is allowed to mount to the top and survey the moving scene inside the ramparts. Famagusta is reputed to have once had 365 churches but only fifty of them still stand. A great many of them were torn down by the conquering Turks for their sturdy materials. The three outstanding sights of the city, in addition to Othello's Tower, are the *Venetian Palace*, originally built as a royal residence for the Lusignan Dynasty; the *Church of St. Peter and St. Paul*, lavishly built by a rich merchant of the fourteenth century from the proceeds of a single business venture; and finally the *Cathedral of St. Nicholas*, where each successive Lusignan monarch was crowned "King of Jerusalem." This so-called "Reims of Cyprus" really does have some modest resemblance, especially in its façade, to Reims Cathedral, where French kings were crowned. After the Turks captured Famagusta in 1571 it became a Moslem mosque and thanks to the present islanders' religious tolerance is still a mosque, the only *Gothic* mosque in the world. It has a funny, ill-fitting little minaret that is quite unworthy to be superimposed upon so noble an edifice.

The people who live within the old city walls, only two or three thousand nowadays, are almost all of Turkish descent, and therefore Moslems. The street names are signed in Turkish, *not* in Greek as they are in Nicosia and other towns. Modern Famagusta, called *Varosha*, lies a mile to the south of the walls and is virtually an all-Greek community, looking very prosperous amid its wide-spreading orchards of fragrant orange trees. The Greek town market is a model, as clean as are most other things Greek, whether an independent country such as Cyprus, or under Greek rule, as in Rhodes.

The Turks of today, in their own land, seem almost a new race, a race of Westerners, but the Ottoman Turks of old were wreckers whenever they conquered alien territory. They cast upon Famagusta a terrible pall of negligence and from 1571 history recorded almost nothing about this once famous city. Earthquakes aided the Turks in destruction and in the nineteenth century the builders of the Suez Canal aided the earthquakes by carting off great amounts of stone from buildings, churches and city walls for their purposes of construction, especially for the building of the quays of Port Said. Still there is an immense amount left. Mr. Keshishian's guidebook quotes from H. V. Morton's *In the Steps of St. Paul* a sentence which I had noticed and liked in the original text: "Medieval Famagusta is one of the most remarkable ruins in the world, and it could be made one of the wonders of the world by one millionaire in search of immortality." No such plutocrat has yet come forward, so this is your chance!

Emerging Salamis and Its Festival

When I first saw Salamis, in 1952, only a few sparse relics such as broken pillars, were to be seen, but the excavations achieved in the years since then are little short of startling. I will try to tell, in syllabus form, what is now visible, with a hint or two about the future.

Salamis was founded in the twelfth century B.C. by Teucer, a hero of the Trojan War, who was the son of King Telamon of the Greek island of Salamis. Hence the name. The city enjoyed its Golden Age of Greek Cypriot power and culture under King Evagoras, who ruled from 410 to 374 B.C., at which period it is thought to have had 200,000 inhabitants, making it an enormous city for those days. It flourished again under the Romans, as it did, indeed, under each successive power, for it had a strategic location, a good harbor, good rulers and steady trade with all the eastern Mediterranean lands. I will list some of its wonders so far unearthed, and of course there are many more to be found.

1. A *marble gymnasium* of Roman times has "changing rooms" all around it. Here, also, was the stoa, a covered portico with wall on one side and pillars on the other, where teachers conducted their classes by means of open seminars. Included in the ensemble were four cold water pools and a sudatorium, or steam bath. An aqueduct 37 miles in length was built by Emperor Septimius Severus. Surrounding the gym we see many statues of pagan deities, but in every case their heads were

knocked off in later times by the outraged Christians. One statue only, that of Demeter (the Roman Ceres), goddess of agriculture and fruitfulness, is of black marble. Why? Because she was in mourning for her daughter Persephone, whom Pluto had abducted, married and taken down to Hades. Recent excavations have determined that a Greek gymnasium lies beneath this Roman one, but it cannot, of course, be revealed without destroying the Roman one.

2. There were four Roman forums, or markets, in Salamis and one of them, the *Stone Forum*, was the largest in the whole Roman Empire. It was at its busiest from the first century B.C. to the first century A.D. Just beyond it are the remains of the Temple of Salaminian Zeus.

3. The *Church of St. Epiphany*, who was the first acknowledged Bishop of Salamis, was built by the saint himself and was, in its early time, the biggest Christian church in the Levant. (Salamis begins to sound like Texas!) It was utterly destroyed by Arab invaders in the seventh century but some good mosaics are still seen.

4. A *Roman amphitheater* that is estimated to have seated 17,000 spectators was first discovered as recently as 1959–1960 and since then strenuous efforts have been made to excavate and restore it. It has sixty rows of seats and is ninety feet in diameter. So strong an impact did the amphitheater's discovery make on the Cypriot authorities that it was decided to establish an annual *Salamis Festival*, the first one being announced for 1963. For current information address the Government Tourist Office.

There is much more to see in Salamis but if the mind tires of ruins and relics the *Monastery of St. Barnabas*, a few miles away, will provide relief and special interest, for its presiding personalities are three white-bearded brothers, both religiously and actually, who have been here for something like fifty years. Their names, in order of descending age, are Khariton, Stephanos and Barnabas and all of them are skilled ikon painters, from the sale of which works they make their living. As early as the fifth century a church named for St. Barnabas existed here, and the body of Barnabas himself, reputedly a native of Salamis and known to have been a cousin of John Mark the Evangelist, lies in a tomb here. When Paul and Barnabas, with the younger John Mark, set out from Antioch on what is now called Paul's first missionary journey their first port of call, a fact of history and Scripture, was Salamis.

The Southern Coast to Lárnaca and Limassol

Lárnaca, though purely a city of today, is actually as old as the *Old Testament*, for it is mentioned, under the name of Kittim, even in the book of Genesis, and there are many subsequent references to it in the books of the major and minor prophets. Despite this very importance it is not a city of much historical interest but it is decidedly pleasant and it has a first-class hotel, the *Four Lanterns*, on the shore, offering something to its guests that I have rarely, if ever, seen offered elsewhere. Living as a guest on the regular pension arrangement, at about six dollars a day for room and private bath and three meals, plus early tea or coffee in the morning and tea with cakes in the late afternoon, you may order *anything* from the ample *à la carte* list without extra charge. The hotel's dining room is enlivened by an orchestra and in summer there is a pleasant roof-garden café.

Lárnaca boasts two former celebrities, Zeno, the Stoic philosopher, born here in 326 B.C., and Sir Basil Zaharoff, modern munitions king and mysterious man of money, whose shadowy career intrigued the world for many decades. He was born of Greek parents in Anatolia but made his start in life in Lárnaca. The building where he first went into trade is a curious one that juts out into the shore-front roadway near the Four Lanterns.

One thing of major interest close to Lárnaca, on the west, is the *Hala Sultan Tekké*, mentioned earlier. It seems that Umm Haram, Mohammed's aunt (higher critics say it was his wet nurse), fell from her mule hereabouts in 646 A.D. and broke her neck. She was buried where the present mosque of the Tekké rises and her bones lie beneath a curious dolmen that is always covered with a curtain. Many faithful Moslems believe that the enormous upper stone flew miraculously from Mecca and remained stationary in the air above the relics, serving as roof, for hundreds of years. I believe they generally admit that two upright stones now support it, though these are considered quite unnecessary. Cold-hearted archeologists assert that the dolmen dates from some three thousand years before Umm Haram fell and died.

Today's Lárnaca is an important port and has also considerable industry. One of its industries—you would never guess—is the manufacture of false teeth! These dentures, be assured, are expertly made and are exported in quantity.

The *Monastery of Stavrovouni*, some twenty miles west of Lárnaca, is a goal to reach at any reasonable cost of tourist time and it can be reached in comfort by an ordinary taxi. It crowns the crest of a mountain 2260 feet above the sea, half of Cyprus being spread out below its terraces. St. Helena, mother of Constantine, is alleged to have founded it and to have given it a splinter of the true cross, now embedded in a modern cross of considerable size that is reverently shown to visitors. That sacred splinter gave the name to the establishment, for Stavrovouni means Mountain of the Cross. Those who find the claim too nebulous are stirred by another cross in the monastery made of olive wood and silver by one George Laskaris in 1473. It is a fine piece of intricately fashioned cabinetry.

To many visitors the monks themselves are the most interesting feature of Stavrovouni. They keep honeybees to help support the place, and in addition to this industry each monk works at a definite craft. They are as gay a company as can be imagined and will laugh as easily as so many schoolgirls. Greek priests and monks *never* shave their whiskers or cut their hair, so each monk has abundant facial foliage and a formidable pug of hair under his tall, black cylinder hat. The monks love to take visitors to their roof and show them "the four corners of the earth." It is an awe-inspiring sight and the eeriness of it is heightened by the extraordinary clarity of the atmosphere. Not only can one see for miles upon miles, but the smallest sounds, the cry of a baby, the yapping of a puppy, the household sounds of a distant farm, come soaring up from the plain as though they originated just below. In Stavrovouni, as in all Cypriot monasteries, a visitor is treated as a guest, welcome to lodge there and partake of monastery fare without charge. When he leaves he may, if he likes, leave a small gift, but this is by no means compulsory.

A few miles to the west of the monastery mountain and at nearly as high an elevation, is *Léfkara*, a hill village of remarkable individuality. Many of its stone-built houses are painted blue all over and the rest are pure white, giving the "Greek flag" effect so noticeable in Rhodian villages. Virtually every woman of this community devotes much of her time, as a business or a hobby, to the making of delicate lace called

Lefkaritika, which many of the menfolk peddle in Europe and even in the States, but it is purchasable also fresh from the hands of those who make it. In dozens of doorways, at almost any hour, you will see women industriously at work on Lefkaritika. Another industry of the place, though less important, is the making of *lokoum*, a Cypriot version of Turkish delight, but regardless of any special industries Léfkara is a treat to the eyes of all who see it.

Limassol is a lively and large town concerned chiefly with exporting such items as wine, the production of which is a major industry, carob pods, asbestos and chromium. The leading hotel is the de luxe-rated *Curium Palace*, but it is not on the harbor front. Lesser hotels on the front are the *Continental* and the not-so-palatial *Palace*. Amathus, the port that Richard Coeur-de-Lion knew so romantically, is now no more than a rubble-strewn area not worth hunting up, but another ancient neighbor of Limassol is very much worth finding. That is *Kolossi*, about five miles to the west. Here is the massive stone tower, square and three stories high, which was once the headquarters of the Grand Commandery of the Knights of St. John of Jerusalem. The delectable Cyprus wine called Commandaria, mentioned earlier as a type of heavy Madeira much admired by connoisseurs, takes its name from this town.

The Mountains and the Far West Shore—with Aphrodite

Cyprus is lucky in having a large area of well-forested mountains only about thirty miles west of Nicosía. Several resorts ranging in altitude from 3600 to 5500 feet provide cool and bracing retreats in summer, skiing and other sports in winter. So copious is the snow, though it varies considerably from year to year, that the branches of the Aleppo pines sag perpetually from the weight that they are obliged to bear for some two or three winter months. The mountains are becoming well known to tourists and they are always popular with town Cypriots. *Troödos*, with many camp hostels and several A-class hotels (*Hotel Troödos* best), is the highest resort (5500 feet), but *Platres* (3600 feet) is by far the largest and most developed community. *Forest Park Hotel* here is a quality establishment, its only real rival being the newer *Splendid*. In the same general mountain area are *Hotel Berengaria*, at Prodhromos (4600 feet), and *Hotel Pinewood Valley*, at Pedhoulas

(4000 feet).

Trippers who come to the mountains just for the day may enjoy fine meals in wonderful settings at these smart hotels or they may regale themselves with suckling pig and baked macaroni at such garden restaurants of rustic charm as *Psilo Dendron* (Tall Tree) or *Valley of the Graces*, both at Platres. The Tall Tree has the advantage of a burbling stream and a small cascade in its garden, a brilliant one with hundreds of dahlias.

The *Far West of Cyprus* refers to that broad crescent from Limassol on the south to Karavostassi on the north, with the best and seldomest seen natural scenery on the whole island. There is a good road all the way.

Curium, just west of the Kolossi Commandery, was a center of Apollo worship and about ninety years ago an American consul to Cyprus, by name General di Cesnola, secured from the then Turkish authorities permission to excavate. He was lucky and unearthed marvelous items of gold and silver and jewelry, which now, together with some marble statues from the temple, are treasured in the Metropolitan Museum of New York. Curium is magnificently located on a verdant plateau above an indented sea cliff. It has the usual Roman features, including elaborate baths and a theater that is now in process of restoration.

Episcopi, west of Curium, is one of the two military bases retained by Britain in the treaty arrangements of 1959, the other being Dhekelia. Episcopi, even seen from the road in passing, is as British as roast beef and Yorkshire pudding. We see meticulously kept polo, cricket and soccer fields, as also a golf course. The whole community looks smartly kept up, and for the benefit of the men and their families a tunnel has been cut through a hill to the beach.

Kouklia, a coastal village farther west, was Old Paphos, once the chief center of the cult of Aphrodite, who rose in her beauty from the very surf of Paphos and has been "caught in the act" by countless sculptors and painters, from the earliest chiselers in marble to such Renaissance masters as Botticelli and many a more modern artist. She was caught, well almost, also by me, for at my guide's instructions I left the car and walked to the edge of the road high above the striking rock formation called Romios and gazed down at the dark beach in the lee of it, with powerful breakers continuously rolling in. They kick up a lot of spray and it was from one such comber's spray that the goddess of love sprang forth, fully and divinely formed. The Rock of Romios, reached two or three miles before Kouklia as you roll west, is unmissable.

New Paphos, like everything else, was *once* new. Today it is the small port of a large village called Ktima that stands on higher ground about two miles in from the shore. It is at Ktima that visitors spend the night, or perhaps two or three nights, for there's a lot to see in the neighborhood. *Hotel New Olympus*, A-class, has by far the best accommodations and I may mention that the proprietor, by name Mr. Barnabas, lived for many years in Boston, Massachusetts, and speaks Boston-Greek English. It is advisable to see New Paphos, meaning the port region, first, and after that the Paphos Museum, which is at Ktima.

New Paphos was the Roman capital of Cyprus and of the whole Near East, where the governor, Sergius Paulus, was converted to Christianity by the preaching of Paul. Cyprus has always enjoyed, and still does, a very special place in Christian ecclesiasticism, for the Church of Cyprus, though Greek in ritual and doctrine, is completely separate and independent of the Orthodox Eastern Church. Its Archbishop Makarios became the first head of state of the newly independent country. Entitled "His Beatitude The Archbishop of Nova Justiniana and of all Cyprus," he retains the old right to wear imperial purple and sign his name in purple ink. His Beatitude of today was crowned in a gorgeous Byzantine ceremony in Nicosía's Cathedral of St. John in 1947. The distinction between the Church of Cyprus and the Orthodox Church is based on the very early conversion of many Cypriots to Christianity by Paul, Barnabas and John Mark. The above-named trio of missionaries preached for a time in Salamis and traveled overland to New Paphos, where the exciting debate occurred, in the governor's presence, between Paul and Elymas the sorcerer, as recorded in Acts 13:1–12. Paul easily outshone the wicked Elymas, and Governor Sergius Paulus was won for the Christian fold.

Before this happy event Paul suffered harsh treatment and one of the sights of the port is *St. Paul's Pillar*, to which he is supposed to have been tied to receive "forty stripes save one," this being one of five such scourges he endured. The pillar was once twenty feet high but has been cut down by centuries of souvenir hunters. Close to the pillar are the remains of the Roman Palace, and here, too, is a thirteenth-century Gothic-Byzantine *Church of Chrysopolitissa*. A far more venerable meeting place, dating from the first century and considered one of the world's very earliest houses of Christian worship, is the underground *Church of St. Solomoni*, who was a feminine saint. Sprouting directly from one of its walls grows a husky terebinth tree.

In 1962, some extremely well-preserved mosaics were discovered, and *un*covered, one of them showing Dionysus in a chariot being smartly pulled by a pair of panthers, another portraying the grand-operatic tragedy of Pyramus and Thisbe. I happened to be present at the first "unveiling" and I should say that they almost, but not quite, rival the newly discovered mosaics of Pella, Philip of Macedon's capital. (See Chapter 13.)

The *Paphos Museum* is small but of considerable interest. Three of its special items are an Aphrodite statue found in New Paphos in 1956 by a British soldier; a bust of Governor Sergius Paulus; and a giant phallus, three feet high. The original of this indecent monument, indecent by our modern standards but not so in the view of the ancients, is in the museum at Nicosía. In the same National Museum is *the* Aphrodite of Cyprus, pictured so frequently almost as to be the cognizance of the island, a work of the Hellenistic period found at Soli, on the north coast.

A few miles in from Ktima is the interesting and superbly placed *Monastery of St. Neophytos*, he having been a holy hermit who lived his life there in a cave, but something tells me that enough antiquities, mosaics, museums and holy buildings are quite as good as too many. I will spare you.

The scenic ride around the Far West continues to *Polis*, with a tangent to the romance-rousing *Fontana Amorosa*, the Spring of Love, called also the Baths of Aphrodite, and then along the northern coast to Karavostassi. A perfect climax to far western wanderings may be made by striking off south into the mountains from Karavostassi to the *Monastery of Kykko*, the largest and most famous of Cyprus' monastic establishments. It is on a hilltop 3800 feet in altitude not far from the high pleasure resorts. It was for centuries a pilgrim shrine of major importance, partly because of a Madonna ikon supposed to have been painted by Luke the Evangelist. Time and again the monastery was destroyed by fire and then rebuilt, but never could the flames even singe the sacred ikon.

From this holy high spot the traveler may return to Nicosía by way of the mountain resorts and the central highway or by way of the northern coastal road to Kyrenía. He has seen a lot, but if he had the temerity to visit, unintroduced, some country homes in unsung villages he will perhaps consider such visits the most memorable moments of his whole Cyprus sojourn. Country Cypriots, to repeat somewhat from my earlier comment, will literally fight for the privilege of extending hospitality to any stranger in their midst. If their "total net worth" is next to nothing it makes no difference at all. They will somehow serve coffee and bread and walnut jam, for this passion of kindness to the stranger is ingrained and absolutely *honest*. There is not the smallest ulterior motive or hope of reward in what they offer.

REVISION SUPPLEMENT TO CHAPTERS 19, 20 AND 21

ISRAEL continues her astounding development and the mature adult that is emerging makes her presence felt worldwide, not only with her products and her cleverness in the performing arts but even in the fashion world. The sheer will of the local tourism planners has created a record $65-million tourist income for the most recent year for which statistics are available, all this not counting the revenues of Zim Lines' steamship service and El Al's air service to Israel and elsewhere. There is now a Ministry of Tourism in Israel's government, its director elevated to cabinet level, thus giving tourism a potential voice in all national policies. The visa problems at the Mandelbaum Gate separating Jordan and Israel in Jerusalem unfortunately continue, but in spite of this a former Director-General of the Ministry of Tourism has stated that at least 40 per cent of the visitors to Israel last year did actually come *through* the Mandelbaum Gate. I would remind you again, however, to ask for your Israel visa *on a separate paper*, since most of the Middle Eastern countries of Moslem faith still do not honor a passport indicating a visit to Israel. Not too many months ago, an American steamship company was refused passage through the Suez Canal by the UAR if the ship kept to her advertised world-cruise schedule, which included a stop in Haifa. United States government officials intervened, but the problem was sticky until sailing date, when things were finally cleared up.

Spreading her sources of tourist information in the U.S., Israel has added offices in Atlanta, Georgia (Peachtree Street); Montreal (1117 Sainte-Catherine Street, West); and has changed the address in Los Angeles to 615 South Flower Street. These offices are in addition to those given on page 372. Israel currency exchange can be effected at both the *Bank Leumi Le-Israel*, mentioned on page 387, and at the newer *Israel Discount Bank*'s office at 511 Fifth Avenue, New York City. Lest you hurry off to get your money at a discount, let me explain that the word *Discount* is a literal translation of the Israeli bank's name and, unfortunately, no such discount applies at the bank! Exchange brokers, including the firms mentioned on page 39, can also handle Israeli currency matters.

Tel Aviv, with its surrounding area, has new hotels galore, some small and strictly kosher, some larger, many of them, but not all, kosher. Two of vastly different backgrounds are the *Tel-Aviv Hilton*, mentioned on page 380 but not actually opened until rather recently, and the *Deborah*, with 68 rooms and a strictly Orthodox life. The *Park Hotel*, referred to on page 380, has been closed for four years while it is being completely done over. The new hotel will have 150 completely modern rooms. The *Sheraton*'s new wing (page 379) is completed and gives the hotel a total of 220 rooms for visitors. The Sheraton's *Magic Carpet* nightclub presents a sparkling array of international talent, including a not-so-international belly dancer. The *Appalonia*, newly built by England's Rank Organization, is at Herzliya-on-Sea, near Accadia.

To get back briefly to the Hilton, since it, as one of the brightest stars in Tel Aviv's tourist firmament, is a prime goal of many U.S. visitors to Israel: The hotel stands on the grounds of Israel's Independence Park, right on the Mediterranean, yet is also in the heart of the city's business and shopping district. It is enhanced by typically Hilton restaurants, these with an Israeli fillip, and gay nightclubs, and each of its 428 rooms has a view of both the sea and the city. For sports enthusiasts, the hotel has excellent tennis courts.

At *Caesarea*, the hotel referred to on page 400 grew up to be the *Caesarea Golf and Beach Hotel* and is a luxury resort from which many visitors tour the rest of Israel. In this same community the *International Music Festival*, also discussed on page 400, is now a regular annual event in August, with international artists participating.

Tiberias (page 405) is in vogue these days as both a summer and winter resort. Air-conditioning has made the summer heat bearable and the emphasis on water sports makes the beaches appealing the year round. The 72-room *Grand Guberman*, built on a hill overlooking the town, has recently opened its doors. The *Galei Kinneret*, mentioned on page 405, has redecorated many rooms and has added a 250-seat indoor meeting hall as well as a 300-seat amphitheater to accommodate convention groups.

At *Ashdod*, a new port is in operation to alleviate pressure on Haifa. The new area, 60 miles south of Haifa and 25 miles south of Tel Aviv, will help develop the area of Ashkelon and other southern resorts. Already at Ashkelon, the new *Hotel Semadar*, supplementing the long-established Dagon (page 410), offers 24 nice, though unpretentious rooms on the route to Eilat.

Eilat (page 413), Israel's port with access to the Red Sea, is coming into its own, with emphasis on skin diving and underwater sports. Largely through the efforts of Denise Osterlund, an enterprising Swede, the *International School of Aquasport* has come to Israel, with headquarters at Eilat. By 1968, the government hopes to hold an International Skin Diving meet, with Israel and Greece as co-hosts, inviting competitors from all over the world. The Hertz Corporation has opened its own office in Eilat, in addition to three offices in Tel Aviv (one at the airport) and one each in Jerusalem, Haifa and Caesarea. You may rent a car at any one of the towns and drive to another town to leave the car there and proceed by plane. Incidentally, roads are excellent and road signs are well placed and easy to follow. If you are driving, be sure to obtain *Carta's Israel Road Guide*, an invaluable booklet with pages and pages of area maps clearly showing all routes and places of interest. Touring busses in Israel are good too, as mentioned in the text, if you want to leave the driving to them.

And now *Jerusalem*, not only the capital of Israel but a city dear to the religious world, Jewish, Christian and Moslem: Jerusalem's newest hotel in the Israeli sector is the *Ganei Yehuda* (Judea Gardens), with 140 rooms and a swimming pool, located in a residential area of the city. More rooms are being built and, as mentioned on page 388, *all* the best *Jerusalem* hotels are kosher.

The new *Israel Museum* in Jerusalem, which was only just beginning to take form on my last visit, is truly a sight to behold and is just one more monument to the awe-inspiring creativity of the youthful State of Israel. Started with a grant of $850,000 from U.S. funds and matching funds from Israel, the museum has benefited from many private contributions. In acknowledgment of the cultural needs of the country, the government set aside 22 acres on a hilltop, which, more than incidentally, provides a spectacular view of sculpture framed by the sky as you look uphill. The Museum is made up of a complex of buildings, including the *Shrine of the Book*, where the Dead Sea Scrolls now "live," having moved from the Hebrew University, mentioned on page 397;

the *Bezalel Museum of Fine Arts;* and the *Bronfman Biblical and Archeological Museum,* all of this being given a gracious and exciting touch
by the *Rose Art Garden.* Perhaps you remember the photographs in
U.S. papers in 1964 of the late Billy Rose standing in the street before
his Manhattan home surrounded by some works from his valuable
sculpture collection, which was destined for Israel and display in the
sculpture garden that bears his name.

The Shrine of the Book, designed by Messrs. Kiesler and Bartos, cannot help but move you with its stark black wall and bright white dome.
In a booklet published by the Cultural Relations Department of the
Ministry for Foreign Affairs, the following comment about the Shrine
of the Book sums up succinctly the meaning of the structure and the
significance of the Scrolls to modern Israel:

> The Dead Sea Scrolls were brought to light after their millennia
> of obscurity almost the same week as the United Nations voted
> Israel's independence, and this extraordinary coincidence of rebirth
> pointed the way—irresistibly—to the design of the sanctuary that
> would house them. . . . It is symbolic of the ancient manuscripts
> enshrined in the sanctuary that this is possibly the only public build-
> ing in the world planned in such a way as to be essentially sub-
> terranean, thereby, in its functional entirety, conveying the story of
> the Scrolls, which were so long hidden from the eye of man.

Further news was made recently by the Hebrew University when
plans were announced to commemorate former President Truman's
crucial decision to recognize the new State of Israel in 1948 with a $3.6-
million library to be known as the *Harry S. Truman Center for the
Advancement of Peace.* The structure will serve as a center for international studies and will house the library and papers of the philosopher
Martin Buber, who died in 1965.

And now for three closing, noteworthy but unrelated comments on
present-day Israel:

(1) Even with a minimum visit, I would urge you to spend at least
one night in the guest house of a kibbutz (see pages 367–68) to expose
yourself to the true flavor of Israel today. All food in kibbutzim is, of
course, kosher and accommodations, while comfortable, are by no
means luxurious. A guided stroll around a kibbutz will help you to see
the effects of communal living.

(2) For students, there are a number of programs for organized tours to and within Israel. One particularly worthy of mention is arranged by ISSTA, the *Israel Students Tourist Association*, with head office at 2 Pinsker Street in Tel Aviv. The tour originates in major European cities and can include stops in Italy and Greece. You may visit a kibbutz or may work in one. To quote from the Association's folder about the work camp in a kibbutz, "The camps consist of 15 to 20 students from different nationalities working mainly in agriculture and receiving free accommodations, meals, laundry and cigarettes in exchange for their work." The registration fee for work in kibbutzim is $8. This portion of the trip is in addition to a week in Tel Aviv and whatever other stops you may choose to make en route.

(3) In a precedent-setting announcement in early 1966, the United States and Israeli governments announced, tentatively, a joint project for building a large nuclear-powered desalting plant that would tap the Mediterranean as a source of fresh water for Israel. Although plans are still on the drawing boards and final implementation depends on how much money the U.S. is willing to put into the project, such a desalting plant *could* be a key to answering the political differences that have grown out of the Middle East's competition for water. If the plan proceeds as hoped, a desalting plant could be in operation by late 1972!

CHAPTER 19

ISRAEL, A TEEN-AGE PRODIGY

A Synopsis of Birth and Growth

"How on earth did it happen?" asks many an amazed foreign visitor to Israel, realizing that he is beholding a teen-age nation that has already emerged from its period of growing pains and looks very much like a mature adult. Granting such basic elements as the Jewish faith, on which I, as a gentile, feel inadequate to comment, and granting also the spur of perfervid nationalism in a new-born nation, it still seems impossible that so much could have been achieved in so short a time, hated, heckled and fought as was this infant, child and youth by its ring of Arab neighbors.

"World Jewry did it," runs the superficial comment, "and U.S. aid, with an assist from West Germany's conscience fund drawn from remorse at memories of Hitler." These outside aids have, of course, been big factors, but the biggest, surely, is the indomitable spirit of the Israelis themselves, supplying boundless drive and sustained energy.

Mind you, *I am not taking sides* in the international political quarrel that goes on and on, for this is a travel book, aiming to reveal what "mine eyes have seen and mine ears heard." And so, without further preamble, I propose to set forth, merely as a calendar of happenings, the events that brought forth Israel and led it up the ladder of growth.

1948, May 14. The British completed their evacuation of Israel and the State of Israel was proclaimed in Tel Aviv by a Legislative Assembly. David Ben Gurion was chosen to head a provisional government.

1949, Spring and Summer. Armistice agreements with Egypt, Jordan, Lebanon and Syria finally brought an uneasy peace. Meanwhile, domestic political events were happening in Israel.

1948, November, to 1949, March. The first population census was taken; the first elections to the Knesset (Parliament) were held; the opening session resulted in the election of Dr. Chaim Weizmann as the first President of Israel; and on March 10, 1949, the first constitutional government received its vote of confidence from the Knesset. Israel was not only born but weaned.

1949, March 10. In conclusion of a year of confused fighting with Arab armies Israeli troops marched, almost unopposed, to Eilat, on the Red Sea, securing the big Negev "arrowhead" for Israel, with Eilat as a future Red Sea port. This venture came to its successful end on the very day of the Knesset's acceptance of the constitutional government.

1949.   The *Law of the Return*, unique in world politics, was one of the first laws passed. This gave the right to every Jew in the world to migrate to Israel, settle there and become a citizen. Mass immigration immediately ensued, doubling the population in three years from about 600,000 to well over a million. (It is now over two and a quarter million.) The absorption of this ill-assorted throng, many thousands destitute, literally from all over the world, created enormous problems, but as time goes on the many elements are creating a remarkable amalgam.

1956, October 29 to November 3. This was the period of Israel's Sinai Campaign and the attack on Egypt by England and France, quickly thwarted by the UN, spurred thereto by U.S. opposition to the attack. Again, this, as a travel book, shall offer no comment, but just a fact or two. Israel, sensing an imminent extermination campaign by the united Arab forces of Egypt, Syria, Jordan and Saudi Arabia, jumped the gun and took the whole Sinai Peninsula, but at UN insistence, withdrew from all of it by March, 1957. The occupied area, including the grim Gaza Strip, was restored to Egypt, but the Strip was, and still is, guarded by a UN Emergency Force.

Israel still maintains a strong military force. Every Israeli boy must devote two and a half years to military training and *every girl two years*, but since 1947 the country, by and large, has enjoyed sufficient peace, and certainly sufficient stability, to permit of very notable advances on all fronts.

As to the amalgam mentioned above, it breaks down about like this: Jews number two million or more, some 65 per cent of whom are foreign-born; Moslems number about 165,000 including 20,000 Bedouins living in the Negev; 50,000 Christians and 23,000 Druses, these being members of a strange semisecret sect, basically Islamic but with Christian overtones, which originated in Egypt a thousand years ago. There are also a few hundred members of the Bahai sect, whose world headquarters and "mother temple" are in Haifa. Most of Israel's Christians, surprisingly enough, are Arabs, at least in language, Nazareth being their largest center. Many are Greek Catholics, some of the Greek Orthodox, Roman Catholic and Maronite faiths, plus a variety of Oriental sects and a few Protestants maintaining missions.

"Shalom"

The universal word of greeting and of farewell in Israel, even when the meeting is casual or the parting very temporary, is "Shalom," and it means—just in case you haven't heard—"Peace," as does the Arabic word Salaam. It is even more a fixed part of speech and of life, and of travel in Israel, than is the pleasant word Aloha in Hawaii.

The fascinating story of Israel's "borning" was very well and fully told in 1950, soon after the event, by Thomas Sugrue in his book *Watch for the Morning*, with the explanatory subtitle "The Story of Palestine's Jewish Pioneers and Their Battle for the Birth of Israel," and since Mr. Sugrue was a Roman Catholic, his vivid, factual account cannot be classified as propaganda. It has been called "a report on a new chapter of the Old Testament."

Many visitors are interested in Israel chiefly as the Holy Land of Scripture, though some of the most sacred spots, including Bethlehem and vital portions of Old Jerusalem, are in Arab hands, administered by Jordan. For those who wish to follow, step by step, the Bible narratives, of both the Old and the New Testament, the books by H. V. Morton, though written before the birth of Israel, are still, I think, the most enthralling. I refer to *In the Steps of the Master, In the Steps of St. Paul* and *Through Bible Lands*, the St. Paul book covering not only Palestine but many Mediterranean points that are touched upon in this present volume.

Of fledgling Israel it is enough to say here that the sheer *confidence* exuded by this hard-beset young nation is something for any visitor to behold with wonder. It still has problems enough to swamp in Bunyan's Slough of Despond a nation of fifty times its size and fifty times its modest span of experience, yet I, at least, have never encountered a single Israeli in official or private life who found it possible even to conceive of failure. Partly, this confidence is built on a passionate consecration, felt and plainly shown by thousands of the homeland Jews. I should say that the racket complex has scarcely dared to show its ugly nose as yet in any part of Israel or any field of its activities, and there is no doubt that many persons, young and old, are giving everything they have, for meager pay or none, to the development of housing, scientific farming, refugee relief and public health. Of course there is a glow about it all, the glow of novelty and the glow of infinite satisfaction at having acquired, at interminable last, a national home that is their acknowledged own. It may have waned slightly with the years, but not much.

Another basic reason for the self-assurance of Israel is, I think, the fact that women and girls have a position of absolute equality with men and boys in life, in business and the professions, even in the Army. Every girl, as I have said, must do her two-year stretch of Army service (unless she marries) and she gets the same pay as men. (After this service, *men* serve one month a year to age 45, *girls* to 28.) Upon reaching maturity she votes and is eligible for election to Parliament or any of the state councils. She may become, as one woman has, an ambassador, and then a government minister. You see the pride of equality in the whole bearing of feminine Israel, the free but not bold ways of the girls in public, somewhat startling in the Near East, their addiction to wearing slacks or shorts and sweaters, their zeal to get on in life and not remain the subservient distaff part of a union heavily weighted in the males' favor, as is the standard situation in most neighboring lands.

I shall not soon forget a young girl law student, a niece of friends of mine, whom I met in Tel Aviv a few years ago and specifically at one of the tea dances at the Sharon Hotel. She was as breezy as any American college girl. Though her knowledge of English was halting, she talked and laughed and danced as unconcernedly as if we had been of the same age and had known each other for years. She had been a frontline soldier in the war and told me, but not with heroics, about her experiences. She was enrolled in the Law School of the Hebrew University of Jerusalem, and was in earnest about her studies. She considered that she had just as good a chance to get on as did any of her masculine schoolmates. This girl was no freak of nature. She was just a typical Jewish student bent on making a go of her chosen profession.

A problem that causes annoyance to many Israelis and astonishment to many visitors, is the strength of the Orthodox Jews in imposing their narrow and archaic views upon a vigorous, modern nation. This text, avoiding the political questions involved, shall present a verbal snapshot of the ultra-Orthodox (Hassidim) Jews, as strange a people as the earth contains, when it reaches their quarter in Jerusalem. It need only be said here that they and their far more liberal, yet still Orthodox, associates have been able, so far, to maintain a tightly-closed Sabbath, that is Saturday, throughout the land. Theaters, movies and cafés are closed. Trains do not run and for years no busses ran, but now they are permitted to operate in Haifa and Nazareth and between those two cities. You may hire a taxi, if you can secure one, but there have been extreme instances in Jerusalem, Safed and a few fanatical villages where Sabbath taxis have been stoned or set on fire by religious fanatics. The Jewish Sabbath runs from sundown Friday to sundown Saturday. "When you can see three stars on Saturday evening," they say, "the Sabbath is over." Presumably on cloudy evenings the meteorologists know when you *would* see three stars.

One more item under the head of religion, a small matter, which I do not mention in any vein of mockery but only as an interesting point of view, is this: Jewish law forbids the official public display of any statue of a man. Why? Because the Second Commandment forbids the making of "any graven image." God made man in his image, therefore the making of a statue of a national hero would be, in effect, the making of an image of God himself. In the president's garden in Jerusalem I have seen one "more-or-less" statue of what *seems* to be a woman, but the object has no real head.

The *refugee problem* continues to be so huge and overwhelming that it tends to overshadow all others, including those begotten of religion. Israel has quadrupled her population in the period since the establishment of the armistice in 1948 and new refugees are still pouring in at the rate of three to seven thousand a month. The Arab language is an official one in the country, along with Hebrew, and several Arabs are members of Parliament. (No Arab forgets, however, that 800,000 of his people fled Israel, many of whom still live in camps in utter wretchedness!)

The influx of refugees into Israel in the early years was as if 2,500,000 immigrants a month, or 30,000,000 a year, were to pour into the United States, most of them destitute and some from such primitive regions of the earth that the newcomers had never seen a bed, never heard of a knife and fork. Early in the nation's life I watched one of the government immigration planes deposit some fifty incoming Yemenites on the airfield of Tel Aviv and the appearance of those backward people was fantastic. In one or two cloth bundles each carried his or her entire stock of possessions. Israel welcomed, and still welcomes, them all—*all*. It is a point of democratic pride that none shall be refused. Many have come from Morocco and other regions of North Africa, many from the Balkans, many in the past—and they are an extremely valuable element, strengthening the nation immeasurably—from Central Europe, especially Hitler's Germany. The Führer did a very great favor to the Zionist movement by forcing into exile so many thousands of skilled and intelligent European Jews. One is reminded of the Huguenot persecutions in the France of an earlier age and their beneficent results for neighboring lands which welcomed the exiles, but in this case such high-level refugees are far fewer in number than the hordes that have come, and still come, from undeveloped regions such as the Imamate of Yemen, in the baked area near Aden. David Ben Gurion has called Israel, "not a melting pot but a pressure cooker."

Israel's complete lack of coal and iron, her modest production of oil, some 15 per cent of her own needs, and her initial lack of forests, though much afforestation has now been achieved, proved a frightful handicap. There is now eager hope of finding ample oil in the Negev, that big wedge of southern Palestinian desert, left by the UN settlement to Israel. The Negev is looked upon, in any case, as a major hope of the nation in agriculture and in space to spread out.

A few Hebrew words and organizational names encountered by every visitor need clarification, for the benefit of those who are as uninitiated as I was upon my first arrival.

A *kibbutz* is a collective settlement where housing, food, clothing, medical attention and everything else, even to pocket money and funds for an annual vacation trip, comes from a communal treasury. Education, entertainment and recreation are fully met by the community; there is therefore no need for any money to circulate within the kibbutz. This sort of living is pure communism, not political Communism, with a Red capital C, and it has worked extraordinarily well in Israel, for one sees *kibbutzim* (the plural of the word) in virtually every part of the country. About 225 of them have so far been established and more will be. The principle of the kibbutz, as officially stated, is that "every member gives to the community according to the best of his abilities and receives from it according to his needs." Anyone may apply for membership and there is then a trial period of a year to determine whether or not he likes the life and whether or not the kibbutz finds him worthy. If accepted, as he usually is, he pays no membership fee, but on the other hand he is required to turn in whatever property he may possess. He may leave if he likes, whenever he likes, and is, of course, entitled to no compensation. All members over eighteen "own" the community and govern it through a General Assembly, which elects an executive body, or management committee, headed by an elected secretary. The assembly also elects special committees to run such departments as farming and various services. Every member must accept and perform, over and above his regular job, such extra tasks as the assembly may specify. A nightly work sheet is prepared, setting forth just what every member shall do the next day. Annual vacations are provided, and financed rather well by the community treasury. Children live in houses specially built for them, sleeping, eating, receiving their education, over a period of twelve years, together. Age groups, each numbering about twenty youngsters, are organized and they must take care of their rooms and beds and do their share of KP. After hours they visit their parents, who live as conjugal pairs like couples anywhere.

Personal spending money allowances vary. In one kibbutz where I made inquiries I learned that each individual, whatever his position or work, received clothing money of about $28 a year, plus enough for shoes, a general shopping allowance of $23 and pocket money amounting to $20 a year.

Whether the kibbutzim will continue indefinitely as pure, unsullied and successful as they are now is a much debated question. To sink everything in a common cause calls for understanding, mutual trust and selflessness of a high order. The human desire for individual advancement is as natural as breathing and some Jews and outside observers believe these collectives will not be able permanently to buck the tide. In any case they *are* successful now, and what's more, they continue steadily to increase in number. So far there seems to be no weakening of morale and no lessening of zeal.

I asked the director of a very successful kibbutz what made his collective tick. "It never would tick," he said, "if economic considerations were its sole basis. Idealism, Zionism, the desire to make the desert bloom, these things make it tick. Also the fact that it is completely voluntary. Pressure is never exerted to make a person join it, or remain in it. He may quit whenever he likes, and some do. Take the phrase 'one big happy family.' The phrase is a cliché, a joke. Here, though, it is an absolute fact."

In Robert St. John's book *Shalom Means Peace* the spirit and working of Israel's kibbutzim are well and readably covered. Books of more detailed coverage are Moshe Pearlman's *Adventure in the Sun* and its enlargement, *Collective Adventure*.

"But why all this discourse on a social curiosity?" someone may ask. A very practical answer is that ten or a dozen of the kibbutzim maintain first-class guest houses, usually equipped with all modern comforts and conveniences, where we tourists may stay. I have stayed in three of them and have found them all meticulously clean and well run, cheerful too, and serving good meals. There is no work sheet for us guests!

The *Histadrut* is the General Confederation of Jewish Labor in Israel. Its Sick Fund is of incalculable importance to the nation. Every member pays into it about 4 per cent of his salary and employers pay a similar sum, the government also contributing a smaller amount. The Fund now gives medical treatment to more than half the population; and to *all* immigrants, regardless of membership in the organization, it gives free treatment for the first few months after arrival. In its thousand-odd dispensaries it takes care of the medical and hospitalization needs of more than 800,000 persons. Such nation-saving work did not just happen of itself. In the days of Turkish control, and negligence, the "hospitals"—one must use quotes—were found to be hardly better than death traps. Many Jewish intellectuals and doctors and surgeons who had fled to Palestine from the Russian pogroms were eager to devote themselves to farming, being convinced that in the good earth, however poor in actual fact, lay the only solution of the Jewish problem, but health conditions were so appalling that they had reluctantly to give up their desired work and tackle the Herculean labor of building a healthy race. The Histadrut Sick Fund has been a major factor in meeting that need. In the *Municipal Hospital* and the *Zamenhoff Polyclinic* in Tel Aviv an incredible number of persons, perhaps 6000 daily as an average, are examined. The *Beilinson Hospital* has completed buildings with 800 beds, making this the largest hospital in the Near East. It is stated that Israel has one physician to every 400 inhabitants, as against one to every 750 in the States.

Hadassah is the American Zionist Women's Organization, operating Hadassah Hospitals and Health Institutes in various parts of Israel and also schools for special, advanced training. In Jerusalem I saw the workings of one of these schools and was impressed by the practical nature of the instruction, which in no sense duplicates that of the regular educational system. The Boys' Vocational School, which was dedicated to Rabbi Stephen Wise on his seventy-fifth birthday, specializes in printing and in the making of precision instruments. Many an Israeli gun would not have functioned properly in the war without the precision instruments made by boys of this school. The girls are trained to be executives and forewomen in industry, department heads in offices, teachers and leaders in occupational therapy, domestic economy, hotel management, fashion designing. Only the outstanding few, of both sexes, are accepted, for this is specifically a school of leaders, not followers. In Tel Aviv, Haifa and Jerusalem, Hadassah has *Clubs for Overseas Visitors*, where travelers are welcomed and given counsel on where to stay, eat and shop and how to plan local tours. The roots of Hadassah, even in its local organizations, were and are in America.

WIZO, the Women's International Zionist Organization, is a world organization and was so from its inception. It enlisted many thousands of women in more than fifty countries to promote the Zionist cause, and its good works in health, education, immigrant training, handicrafts and so on are too numerous even to list. As mentioned in this book's preview

372 ALL THE BEST IN THE MEDITERRANEAN

of shopping, the tourist will find personal interest in the WIZO gift shops, conspicuous in all the cities, where handmade textiles and artistic items in metal and wood attract the window-shopper.

The *Jewish Agency* derived its authority in the beginning (1922) from the Mandate for Palestine. The *Zionist Organization* was its core but it now includes representatives of non-Zionist Jewish bodies in many countries, and for all practical purposes Agency and Organization are fused into one. The Jewish Agency is called the "Father of Israel" and it now exists to raise money abroad, which the government obviously cannot do, and to keep in contact with Jewry all over the world.

The *Knesset*, as we have seen, is the Parliament of Israel, meeting in Jerusalem.

The *Haganah was* the Jewish defense organization in Palestine before the Israeli Army came into being.

The *Israel Government Tourist Information Office*, to reach matters that more directly concern us, is the tourist-contact department of the *Israel Government Tourist Corporation*, which plays an important part in the nation's economy, tourism being Israel's second industry, following citrus. The Corporation's offices are in Building Number 3, Hakirya, Jerusalem, a part of the new university development, but the Information Office is at 60 King George V Avenue, with branches in Tel Aviv (and its airport), Haifa (and its port), Nazareth, Tiberias and half a dozen other tourist centers. Its U.S. offices are: New York, 574 Fifth Avenue; Chicago, 5 South Wabash Avenue; Los Angeles, 9350 Wilshire Boulevard, Beverly Hills. I have found the TIO, as I shall initial it, one of the most efficient and thoroughly organized such offices in the Mediterranean area and perhaps this can be called a matter of heritage. On the word of a scholar named Rabbi S. F. G. Nathan, with the Tourist Corporation, the very word tour is of Hebrew origin. In the Bible (Numbers 13:16) representatives of the twelve tribes are sent by Moses to the Land of Canaan (Palestine) not to "spy out" the country, which Rabbi Nathan says is a mistranslation, but to "*tour*" the country, bringing back to Moses a detailed report of it. These, then, were the first tourists to Palestine (Israel), antedating you and me by three or four thousand years.

The TIO publishes and distributes a wealth of tourist booklets, leaflets and maps. Its pocket-sized compendium *A Visitor's Companion to Israel* covers the essential ground in 75 small but packed pages. A pocket-size ($1.00) *Israel Tourist Guide* was rather recently brought out in New York by an organization called Tourism International Association. A general, hard cover guidebook, published in Israel and recommended by the TIO, is Efraim Orni's *This Is Israel*, and a pocket-sized paperback published by the Council of Women's Organizations is Alice Campbell Klein's *The Stranger Within Thy Gates*. Published in New York, by Doubleday, is Joan Cornay's *Everyone's Guide to Israel*. Supplementing all these handbooks is *This Week in Israel*, published by "Bazak" and giving the usual information of such publications on "What to do, to see, to buy; Where to go, to eat, to stay."

The Tourist Information Office has instituted a weekly "Tourist Forum," held in varying hotels in each of the three main cities, the visitor being invited to "Ask Your Question." This is a question-and-answer evening, presided over by a panel of experts, and for sugar coating short films on Israel travel are shown. The TIO also sponsors a "Meet the Israeli" system similar to that prevailing in Scandinavian and other European lands. If you'd like to meet an Israeli personally "over the coffee pot" or otherwise, of an afternoon or evening, the TIO will quickly arrange it.

Tourist Fact Sheet: Money, Lodging, Food

A reminder: *Don't get an Israel visa before your arrival in that country, and when you arrive ask the immigration officer to give you the visa on a separate paper.* If you are going from Israel *only* to Turkey, this caution is needless, for Turkey, though a Moslem land, is not an Arab land. Relations between Israel and Turkey are, in fact, so very cordial that Israel's Tourist Corporation maintains an outright working agreement with the Turkish Department for the promotion of travel.

The way to a tourist's heart is through his budget and this fact Israel seems clearly to have recognized, for it has kept tourist prices low in Israel pounds and in 1962 it devalued its currency, putting into effect a far more favorable foreign exchange rate. This made the Israel pound, called in Israel the Lira and written IL, exactly three to the dollar instead of 2.16 to the dollar plus a tourist premium that brought it up to 2.51 to the dollar. With the coming of the better rate the old premium was, of course, canceled, and as a *very* slight offsetting move, the airport tax, payable upon arrival, was raised to IL 5 ($1.66). The pound, in notes of IL ½, 1, 5 and up, is composed of 100 agorot (plural of agora), with brassy coins of 5, 10, 25 and 50 agorot and a scalloped, tinny coin of 1 agora. There are also some remaining coins of an old type called prutot, ten of which equal 1 agora, 100 ten agorot, etc. Confusing? Yes it is, but in time the prutot will disappear from circulation. On arrival in Israel the visitor receives a "Foreign Currency Exchange Card," which is clipped to his passport and must be presented at any bank, exchange office or authorized store when dollars are to be exchanged for pounds. The agency making the exchange notes it on the card and the card is to be held for presentation when leaving Israel. Unused Israeli money may then be reconverted to foreign currency.

Hotels, finally to reach this basic tourist topic, are springing up all over Israel as if by waves of a magic wand. The *Israel Hotel Association* publishes an annual list of them, securable through the TIO, containing all possible information, including the facts of category (A, B or C), on and off season rates, air-conditioning, pool or not and kosher cuisine or not. Some of the leaders and thrift hotels will be mentioned as this book reaches the various communities but I may say here that, at the current exchange, hotel rates are very moderate. Just about the most expensive tariff the book reveals in the most luxurious hotels is $10 per person American Plan (with meals) for double occupancy. There is a standard service charge of 10 per cent and this is supposed to take care of tipping in this labor-minded state, but most tourists, especially Americans, give small tips anyway. Service seems very little influenced by the thought of tips. It is impartially given.

Most tourists eat in their hotel dining rooms, maybe varying this by taking some meals in other hotels, for Israel has not built up a name for fine separate restaurants. Many of the leading hotels offer only the European Plan, meals to be brought separately, and many others offer a choice of either plan. Where meals are bought separately Continental breakfast seldom runs over IL 2 or the full Israeli breakfast over IL 3. Major meals have a present maximum of IL 8 or 9. In many good hotels they may be had for IL 5 or 6.

Kosher food and *Sabbath rules* are two problems peculiar to travel in Israel. Almost every good hotel in the country is kosher, or kasher as it is usually spelled in Israel, and thereby hangs a problem for gentiles. I am no expert on the dietary rules laid down by Moses in the Book of Leviticus (Chapter 11), but like any tourist I note what happens in dining rooms. It is my understanding that the Mosaic laws of the Pentateuch forbade the eating of the flesh of any except cloven-hoofed animals (hence no pork, ham, bacon) and any sea food except of fishes with scales and fins (hence no shell fish), all others being "unclean." Also "a kid may not be cooked in its mother's milk," and there are elaborate rules for the killing of food animals and for squeezing out every possible drop of blood, but transferring our thought from Leviticus to present-day tourism let's see how things actually work out in Israel's luxurious kosher hotels.

Basically, if you have meat or fowl for your meal you may not, for a period of several hours, partake of milk or any dairy product, including coffee with milk or cream in it, and conversely, if you have any dairy product you may not have meat or fowl, though in this case the abstention is required for 30 minutes only. In dining rooms separate table cloths, plates, cups and cutlery indicate whether the food consists of meat or dairy products.

In kosher dining rooms you may not smoke on the Sabbath, meaning from sundown Friday to sundown on Saturday. *No cooking* is done on the Sabbath in kosher kitchens. It is prepared on Friday in accordance with the Sabbath Laws laid down in the Pentateuch, and if it is necessary to serve food warm the gas or electricity is turned on low Friday afternoon and left simmering till after sundown on Saturday, for it would be "cooking" to light the stove. In ultrareligious villages, when cows are milked on the Sabbath to relieve the animal's suffering the milk is thrown away. While the Sabbath begins technically at sundown Friday it starts in practice about 3 or 4 P.M. Banks and businesses are closed and so are the post offices. Business resumes with considerable flair Saturday evening and goes full blast, as does everything else, on Sunday. In this connection I remember seeing a large bulletin in the lobby of a leading Jerusalem hotel with this notice: SHABBAT (the Hebrew spelling) begins at 5:38 Friday and ends at 6:55 Saturday. On Saturday morning at 10 there will be Praying in the Banquet Hall.

Saturday evening Dancing and Orchestra Music."

I would urge visiting gentiles neither to scoff at the Sabbath rules nor be irked by them, remembering that we, too, have our Sunday blue laws and curfews. The Jewish Sabbath can be an interesting experience, and the impact of kosher regulations another *if* you take them both in stride.

Shopping, Touring—and Other Things

Shopping in Israel is facilitated by the Government Tourist Corporation, which publishes a very comprehensive and easy-to-use indexed booklet called Shopping in Israel and which authorizes certain shops to place in their windows the sign "Recommended for Tourists." These are not only dependable in their goods and prices but they have the special right to accept foreign currency. Goods now available in the city shops have a broad range, from smart clothing, knitwear being especially prominent, and furs to Jewish religious articles, and from Iranian rugs to Yemenite embroidery and costume jewelry. As a matter of fact, refugee-made handicrafts form an exceedingly interesting part of Israel's offerings to shoppers and so do art works of all types, for Israel has become an important art country. More than three hundred artists of some importance make it their home, old Jaffa being one stronghold and Safed another.

Nota bene: Tel Aviv is now one of the world's centers for duty-free, tax-free shopping, along with many European airport terminals such as those of Shannon, Paris, Amsterdam, Copenhagen and Rome. One such shop, providing savings of 10 to 50 per cent, is in the Exit Hall of Tel Aviv's *Lod Airport* (now undergoing a major reconstruction), another is in the *Sheraton Tel Aviv Hotel.* Goods so purchased are, of course, to be delivered at departure gates of international airports or at steamer wharves.

Touring in Israel is as well organized as if the country had been in the business for many decades. If you tour in your own car your home license is subject to endorsement by the Licensing Authority, which has offices in the three chief cities. Self-drive cars are available everywhere from Hertz, Avis or a firm called Sightseeing, Ltd. If you plan to tour under the aegis of some agency you will find many of them eager for your patronage. *Egged Tours* (called Egged Dan in Tel Aviv) is very active everywhere. *Holyland Tours* and a firm called I.T.S. have their main offices in Tel Aviv. *Travex, United Tours* and *Kopel* are three others of prominence, but these are almost random selections, for there are *many* more. In making your program you may, of course, either join one of the canned tours—over one hundred special tourist busses go everywhere, from Tiberias in the north to Sodom on the Dead Sea and Eilat on the Red Sea—or you may figure out your own tour itinerary, with or without driver-guide as convoy. Israel has about eight hundred qualified guides.

If you are such an individualist as to enjoy do-it-yourself touring by public conveyance, be advised that urban and interurban busses cover the whole country (except on the Sabbath), as do jitneys, selling single seats like those in Cyprus described in the previous chapter. In Israel the word for this type of transport is *Sherut*, meaning service. Seats for interurban travel may be reserved in advance through central taxi companies which operate them. (Consult your hotel porter.) Ordinary city taxis, "cruising" as with us, have illuminated roof signs. Railway service extends from the coastal resort of Nahariya (north) to Beersheba in the south. Those who do-it-themselves find a mixture of thrills and troubles, but with experience the troubles grow fewer while the thrills remain. Finally on the subject of touring, there is an air taxi service, operated by Levinson Brothers, 33 Hashmal Street, Tel Aviv, that flies Cessnas anywhere to order and also arranges regular air tours. They fly from Tel Aviv to Haifa in 25 minutes, to Jerusalem in 20 minutes, to Galilee in 30, Eilat in 70, and so on.

Night life exists in the cities, even, I'm told, to the extent of some stripper shows in Tel Aviv, but most of the tourist night life, chiefly dancing, with some entertainment features, is concentrated in the big hotels. Jaffa's small arty-exotic night clubs are exceptions, as are the Theater Club and the exclusive Key Club. Distinctive of Israel are the musical and cultural events to be enjoyed, especially in Tel Aviv, where the modern, 3000-seat *Fredric Mann Concert Auditorium* is the frequent scene of great musical events, headed by concerts of the Israel Philharmonic Orchestra. Other high-grade orchestras of this notably musical country are the Kol Israel Orchestra and the Municipal Orchestra of Haifa. Additional evening goals of Tel Aviv are the *Opera House*, which was reopened in 1958–1959 serving as the home of the Israel National Opera, and the *Amphitheater* in the Exhibition Grounds, where music, song and stage dancing by various groups furnishes nightly entertainment. English language performances called "Faces of Israel" are also regularly offered at the *Israel Playhouse*. Revues of comedy, song and dance are further enlivened by a 9:30 Fashion Show, presented during the intermission as a sort of extra dividend. Good plays of varying types are given in the *Little English Theater* in the ZOA House (Zionist Organization of America). On my most recent visit Aldous Huxley's *The Gioconda Smile* was the play. Come to think of it, there *is* a very considerable night life in Israel, at least in the Jewish-Parisian atmosphere of Tel Aviv, which is a municipality, including Jaffa, with a present population nearing the half million mark.

CHAPTER 20

THE BIG THREE CITIES:
TEL AVIV; HAIFA; JERUSALEM

Tel Aviv, Metropolis in the Sea Breeze

I have referred to Tel Aviv as a municipality that includes Jaffa, but for all practical *tourist* purposes it includes also Ramat Gan and Herzlia, this latter resort-suburb being seven or eight miles north on the coast. All along this sea-breeze coast good hotels and even superior ones are springing up like troops for review by King Neptune. It is impossible even to list here all those worthy of mention, but I shall attempt to select a very few, first in Tel Aviv, then north to Herzliya. You'll find the whole directory of them, with the category of each, in the free booklet, *A Visitor's Companion to Israel. All hotels listed below are kosher* unless otherwise noted.

Tel Aviv. The *Sheraton Tel Aviv*, directly on the sea at the northern edge of town, is an exceedingly plushy tourist palace, with air-conditioning, lovely public rooms, pool, night club, luxury shops. So prosperous is the hotel that it is now adding a 200-room wing.

The *Dan*, with entrance from Hayarkon Street but public rooms, especially the dining room-grill, facing the beach esplanade, is another place of tourist luxury, with a huge and handsome lounge.

The *Ramat-Aviv*, on the Haifa Road just north of the city, is not on the sea but it has a fine pool and its bungalow accommodations, surrounded by greenery, are of very high quality. Across the Haifa Road from the hotel is a most unusual sight, the *Haarets Museum*, whose main attraction is a tracing of the history of *glass* from the earliest making of it. Jewish legend asserts that glass was invented in the historic coastal town of Acre. The museum building is circular and to see its contents you walk around and around like slaves in a treadmill, only different. Many of the ancient glass items are exquisitely made.

379

Two more Tel Aviv hotels of good quality, both on the front, are the *Astor* and the *Samuel*.

To make us dizzy, we learn that a 9-story hotel is under construction on Ben Yehuda Street and that a big *Hilton-Tel Aviv*, due for opening sometime in 1964, is going up on the shore front only a few blocks from the Sheraton.

Recommendable hotels of lesser stature and price include the *Yarden*, on Ben Yehuda Street, the *Gat Rimon* and the *Park* on Hayarkon. The first two are non-kosher. I once stayed in the Gat Rimon, close to the beach, and liked it.

Ramat-Gan. In this suburb, just north of Tel Aviv, an interesting 110-room hotel with very low rates called *Maccabiah Village* was opened in 1962. Rates, believe it or not, range from $1.20 per person in dormitory-type rooms to a maximum of about $4.00 (double occupancy) in a pleasant room without private bath. All rates include Continental breakfast.

Perhaps I may interpolate here a mention of *Bar Ilan University* in Ramat Gan. It is an *American* university in Israel, now with 750 students from all over the world, concerned with higher learning combined with Jewish culture. Its campus and 14 modern buildings are distributed over a 45-acre site.

Herzliya-on-Sea. (Herzliya town is a mile or two in from the shore.) *Hotel Sharon* is the dean of Israel's luxury resort hotels, an exceedingly well maintained and well groomed dean. I stayed here in 1951, but it was in its infancy then and is now a far finer and more luxurious place, with air-conditioning, pool, shops and all the rest of the panoply. A feature of the Sharon is a delightful Smörgåsbord Room where you eat all you can for IL 7.50 ($2.50), plus 10 per cent service charge. There is also, in such hotels, a 10 per cent welfare tax, but *tourists are exempted from this*. Guests are invited in a graceful notice *not* to take picnic fare with them.

Accadia Grand Hotel is grand indeed. It has a double pool *and* a mirror pool, an amazing seaside rock garden, an open sun-patio, with a bonfire-on-the-side for cool days, a grand dining room and a self-service dairy restaurant. This big place (200 double rooms with bath) somehow manages to seem homelike despite its size and luxury.

The *Tadmor* and the *Hod* are two very good hotels of lesser standing, not on the front. The Tadmor has, in the same building, a respected hotel school.

Tel Aviv needs little sightseeing in the conventional sense of that word. It needs only to be enjoyed and this is a very easy thing to do. The play of the sea breeze enhances all daylight activities. The steady roar of surf lulls you to sleep at night. One of the main thoroughfares of the city, Ben Yehuda Street, continuing into Allenby Road (important streets all over Israel are named for that general) is alive with crowds and bright with shops, cafés and cinemas. This street, and a more or less parallel one named Dizengoff Street, could be "anywhere in the West." Both exhibit a perpetual and cheerful liveliness. The Tourist Information Office is at 7 Mendele Street, close to the above. Dizengoff Street, even more than Ben Yehuda, seems to have won a special rating. It has been called the Champs Elysées, the Boulevard des Capucines, the Rue de la Paix, of Israel, all of which tags are plenty fanciful, but it *is* bright, smart, full of luxury shops and inviting sidewalk cafés. On Allenby Road there is a conspicuous item of Jewish significance, the *Great Synagogue*, topped by a huge eight-branched candlestick called *Hanukia*, not to be confused with the traditional seven-branched candlestick that was the symbol of ancient Israel as it is now of new Israel. A Tel Aviv savant explained Hanukia to me in these words: "Hanukia, the eight-branched candlestick, is lit during the Holiday of Hanuka, which lasts for eight days, one branch for each day. According to Jewish history, in the year 168 B.C. a hero by the name of Jehuda Hamacabi freed Jerusalem from the Greeks and entered the Temple. He found there an oil receptacle that contained very little oil, sufficient for only one night. A miracle happened and the oil lasted for eight days. In memory of the freeing of Jerusalem and of this miracle the eight-day Holiday of Hanuka is celebrated and a candle is lighted for each of those days." Needless to say the "candles" atop the Great Synagogue are electric ones. The annual event, called also the Feast of the Lights, occurs in December.

Sea bathing is not very practical for tourists from the beaches in central Tel Aviv but a good public *pool* on the edge of the beach has been opened and a splendid beach called *Bat Yam* (Daughter of the Sea), fifteen minutes drive south of the city, has been developed. Bathing cabins and rentable bathing gear make this latter very practical for enjoyment by the transient visitor. Bathing from the Herzliya beaches is also popular and all along the coast there are many pleasant beach communities, both resorts and camps, nestling amid the dunes.

Jaffa, the ancient commercial and pilgrim port of Jerusalem, considered to be five thousand years old, is almost as old in centuries as is Tel Aviv in years, yet the younger city has civically absorbed it. Jaffa goes far back beyond history into mythology, for on the so-called *Andromeda Rocks*, near the harbor, the mythical Andromeda was fastened, to be sacrificed to a sea monster sent by Poseidon. In the nick of time the hero, Perseus, rescued her and slew the monster. Many centuries later (in 68 A.D.), in connection with one of the Roman campaigns, Emperor Vespasian destroyed the city. In the Crusader-Saracen conflict it was destroyed again (1345), and in 1947–1948, when Israel was winning its independence, much of it was once more laid waste. For a few years it was a sorry spectacle, but now the old port area has been completely razed and rebuilt, to supplement the new port of Tel Aviv, which was built in the midst of the fighting and was financed through voluntary subscriptions by almost every citizen, including school children.

How drastically times have changed! I first landed in Israel, then Palestine, in 1913, from a steamer riding the open roadstead outside Jaffa. To this day I recall the fearsome ride in an Arab-rowed boat from the steamer's ladder to the littered wharf. I recall waiting for a wave to heave the boat up so that I could leap from its rail to the stone steps. I recall that my father and mother and I were all but torn to pieces by a mob of clamoring Arabs fighting each other and us for our patronage and thrusting into our very faces undesired articles for purchase. Palestine, then under Turkish rule, was infested with bandits and before setting out on a carriage journey to Nazareth and Lake Galilee my father bought two pistols. We found an uninhabited area and practiced shooting at a target affixed to one of the trees. Today this country, need I say, is a highly civilized land of Western democracy. Landings are not subject to mob action. There are no bandits. Yes, times have changed. *Per angusta ad augusta* (Through difficulties to things worthy of honor) would be an appropriate motto for the State of Israel, though one must admit that the young nation still has *angusta* in plenty.

Jaffa is now an exciting part of the double municipality. Among its sights are the important *Archeological Museum;* the *Church of Tabitha* (Acts 9:36–42); the site of the *House of Simon the Tanner* (Acts 9:43; 10:6); and the *Mahmudiya Mosque,* a ridiculous feature of which is the upside-down columns, capitals at the bottom, that were looted by the builders (in 1810 et seq.) from Caesarea and Askelon. It is not to see old sights, however, that most tourists come to Jaffa. They come to visit the little art studios, to enjoy the arty night clubs on the steep Rock of Jaffa and to look for treasures in the local flea market. The nighteries of Jaffa bear such names as Caliph, Omar Khayyam and Hamam, this in a former Turkish bath, and are becoming increasingly popular. Of the art studios perhaps the best one to visit is that of Jean Tirache, a figure in the Jaffa colony of Jewish and international artists. I was told that current paintings purchasable in this and other Israel studios are not subject to customs duties either by Israel or the U.S., but this latter might bear checking in the Tel Aviv consulate.

Travelers interested more in what Israel is doing than in what it offers by way of tourist pleasure will find three things in the environs of Tel Aviv especially worth hunting up. One is the kibbutz called *Givat Brenner,* the largest one in all Israel, with about two thousand members. It is even quite practicable to take lodging in its guest house, (as also in that of the *Shefayim Kibbutz* near Herzliya). The grounds of Givat Brenner have an interesting pool which is an exact replica, on a tiny scale, of Lake Galilee.

A second thing to see is the government's *Agricultural Research Station,* where all the soils and waters of Israel are painstakingly studied. Since the irrigation of Israel's desert areas is a matter of the utmost concern, a matter of life or death for the nation, it is fascinating to see the laboratory work being done on this subject. This is really a big tourist attraction. And for students there is a postgraduate school in connection with it.

The third thing on this docket of personal selections is the *Weizmann Institute of Science,* named, of course, for Dr. Chaim Weizmann, first president of Israel, who was a man of great capacity in statesmanship and equally in science, for his name was widely known in chemistry and biochemistry circles before he was known as the head of the World Zionist Organization. One aim of the Institute, a private one, is to make Israel known throughout the world as a specialist nation in plastics, dyestuffs and pharmaceuticals, in the same sense that Switzerland is known for its watches and precision instruments. In another field, of immediate necessity to the country, it has been notably successful, namely the "de-brining" of the brackish water drawn from beneath the soil of Israel.

Haifa and Mount Carmel

Haifa is the chief seaport for all who come to Israel by ship. It is now a flourishing industrial city and claims also to be the biggest port in the eastern Mediterranean. Tel Aviv-Jaffa is very much nearer to Jerusalm than is Haifa, but since the latter is a tourist gateway of major importance, rivaled only by Lod Airport, it should, I think, be presented here before the national—and eternal—capital. Between Tel Aviv and Haifa there is an excellent rail service with seven daily Diesel-driven trains in each direction. The services between Tel Aviv and Jerusalem and between Haifa and Jerusalem are good, but of course less speedy, since the capital is half a mile above sea level. In all these journeys interurban busses may prove more satisfactory. Those under the name Egged, to repeat this basic point, are dependably good and they cover the whole country. There is an express service every five minutes between Tel Aviv and Haifa, every ten minutes between Tel Aviv and Jerusalem.

Haifa is, in some ways, and chiefly in *one* way, namely the possession of Mount Carmel with its many good hotels, a tourist center rivaling Tel Aviv, and to promote the industry locally there is a lively TIO at the junction of Herzl and Balfour Streets. Mount Carmel, reached either by a good highway or by a modern funicular train that climbs to it on a tunnel line blasted through the solid rock, is truly wonderful. The views from it are thrilling in all lights, including the lights of moon and stars and electricity, when the crowded areas below look as if some Edison-god had drawn luminous doodlings all over the city. By daylight the busy harbor of Haifa and the whole vast Bay of Acre, stretching to the walled town of Acre itself, are spread below, as on a relief map. To the east lies the Plain of Zebulon, backed by the Galilee Mountains, and far to the northeast, on the horizon, rises Mount Hermon, often with snow on its crest. This really imposing mountain, over 9300 feet high, is not within the frontiers of Israel, but serves as a boundary marker between Lebanon and Syria.

In downtown Haifa there is one good hotel, the *Zion*, but tourists almost always find lodgings on the hill. *Hotel Dvir*, meaning Palace, a new non-kosher place of European atmosphere, is marvelously placed, with a commanding view from its terrace and front bedroom balconies of town, harbor, coastline and mountains. I have stayed in the Dvir and found it good. Still more recently opened is a hotel of the Dan chain, the *Dan Carmel*, a luxury place of 200 rooms and baths, with pool. There is also the new *Dan Carmia Holiday Bungalow Village*, but here the minimum stay is 14 days, and its location, deep in the Carmel Range, is not really near enough to Haifa to warrant its consideration as a city hotel. In the Bungalow Village full-time supervision is provided for children. These are the newest links in the Dan chain, other links being Tel Aviv's Dan, Herzliya's Accadia and Jerusalem's famous King David. At least one more Carmel hotel of *many*, the *Ben Yehuda*, located about half way up the ascending road, is worth noting. It has air-conditioning, pool and, of course, a fine view, though I prefer the broader one from the higher levels.

Carmel means Vineyard of God and was, in ancient times, covered with grapevines. It is also of great importance in Biblical narrative, for this is the hill upon which King Ahab gathered the children of Israel and the four hundred and fifty prophets of Baal so that the prophet Elijah, in the presence of the king and the multitude, might put to the test whether Baal or Jehovah was the true God. Baal's prophets called on their god all day long to send down fire and consume their offering, a bullock. In an agony of supplication, they "cut themselves after their manner with knives and lancets, till the blood gushed out upon them," but nothing at all happened. Then Elijah doused his bullock with three barrels of water and called on *his* God to send down fire. It came with a rush, consumed the sacrifice . . . "and licked up the water that was in the trench." We need hardly bother with such tests, but stories of this sort, which millions of Jews and Christians have taken as literal fact, do give exciting touches to a hill that would be alluring even if it had no background of history or legend. There is a *Monastery of Elijah* here and under the high altar of its church is a cave pointed out as the abode of the prophet. This is a French monastery of the Carmelite Order, and is, in fact, the place where that order was born. The whole area hereabouts is called the French Carmel.

On UNO Avenue (for United Nations Organization), a highway connecting Haifa with the western portion of Mount Carmel, is the *Shrine and Central Headquarters of Bahaism*, a cult founded by the Persian, Baha Ullah, who proclaimed himself a new manifestation of God, succeeding Abraham, Moses, David, Christ, Mohammed and other religious leaders. The cult has a substantial vogue in some parts of America, especially in the Chicago area. A large Bahaist Temple was long considered to be one of the sights of that city and a newer and far more sumptuous temple, costing some three million dollars, has been built in the suburb of Wilmette. The "Mother Shrine" in Haifa, a magnificent structure of white marble topped by a lofty golden dome, rises from a superbly landscaped and maintained *Persian Garden*, a major sight in its own right. In the Shrine lie the remains of Baha Ullah. In an upper part of the garden stands the Bahai Library and high up on Carmel is the Bahai Archives Building, opened in 1961.

Jerusalem the Golden, Old and New

Jerusalem is a city apart. Despite its present unfortunate split into two cities, a Jewish and a Moslem, controlled by two sovereign nations, Israel and Hashemite Jordan, it remains, in the eyes of the world, *The Holy City*, as if it were a single unit. There is, indeed, but one Jerusalem on this afflicted planet, a city almost equally sacred to Jew, Christian and Arab, a place of glamor and of yearning, of deepest religious significance, of struggle and bloodshed time and again, of destruction and rebuilding time and again, of new hope now for a nation which has made its portion of the city a new and progressive capital.

It is as Israel's capital that the city is first and chiefly seen by today's traveler coming from Tel Aviv or Haifa, and in that role it is of instant and compelling interest to all. Good maps of Israel are easy to come by through the TIO and the travel agencies. The guidebook

This Is Israel has a good one (loose) but a larger one, and easier to use, is the *Touring Map of Israel* published by the Bank Leumi Le-Israel of Tel Aviv, which has branches in New York (60 Wall Street; representative also at 515 Park Avenue) and Los Angeles (8701 Wilshire Boulevard). I emphasize this map not only for its cartography but for the wealth of tourist information on the back. Following this or another map we shall approach Jerusalem from Tel Aviv.

Lod, the airport town—it took a terrible beating in the Palestine War—claims to be the birthplace and also the burial place of St. George, the saint who slew the dragon and who is the patron of England. His church, once a mosque but now of the Greek Orthodox faith, is a sight of the town. His tomb is shown to visitors.

The *Road of Courage*, east of the village of Hulda, was built during the war, mostly at night under fire. Colonel David Markos, a West Pointer, planned this feat of engineering heroism.

Tal-Shahar means Dew of the Morning, which also the surname Morgenthau means in German. For this sentimental reason Henry Morgenthau, Sr., became a sort of godfather to the whole village.

Latrun, clearly visible from the highway, though it is just across the frontier on Arab soil, is the Ajalon of the Bible. It was here that Joshua commanded, "Sun, stand thou still upon Gibeon; and thou, Moon, in the valley of Ajalon" until his troops "avenged themselves upon their enemies." It will be noted that from this point eastward, Israel is a "corridor," narrowing to its end, which is Jerusalem.

Chava Zeleth means Lily and the village that bears this name does so in honor of its founder, Lily Rothschild, of the British branch of that house. She married a gentile, which the *women* of that house were not supposed to do, since there was a superstition that such action would invite a dire curse. Rothschild men could marry gentiles with impunity. Lily had no children. Then Dr. Chaim Weizmann is reputed to have said to her, "Found a village and you will have all the children you want." She followed his advice.

Abu Ghosh is the Biblical Kirjath Jearim of the Old Testament, the name meaning "City of Forests." Barren hillsides, with myriads of stones, replaced the forest many centuries ago. Godfrey de Bouillon may likely have rested himself and his Crusaders here. In 1142, the Knights Templars built a church here and by some miracle it still stands. In the masonry a faint Cross of Lorraine can be seen.

Jewish Jerusalem hits the eyes with a forceful impact, for it is an *all-stone* city of very attractive appearance. By law every building must be at least faced with limestone. In this respect the city is utterly different in appearance from Tel Aviv or Haifa and, so far as I know, unique among the large cities of the world, though Bern, the Swiss capital, might challenge this claim.

Jerusalem, meaning now the Israeli part of it, presents a formidable poser, for few cities of its size (population about 175,000) have anywhere near so many things of prime interest crowded into so small an area, jumbled and complicated as it is by hilly topography and snaky streets and roads whose names seem rarely to be spelled the same, in Latin letters, on any two maps. The tourist interests of the city (hotels, tour agencies, etc.) have recently issued a *Jerusalem Municipal Tourist Guide* (with map), but the fact is clear that everyone who would see Jerusalem *understandingly* must have a two-footed guide and a four-wheeled vehicle unless he has unlimited time and strength. Since this seems axiomatic I shall make no attempt to guide you point by point, as could effectively be done even in a city the size of Paris or London, but shall present Jerusalem in two chronological "layers," namely the historic Jerusalem, meaning Biblical and early Zionist up to its establishment as capital of Israel in 1949, and modern Jerusalem, the "civic dynamo" that the Israelis have built since 1949, and are building.

First of all, however, the important hotels shall be listed, and you will keep in mind that since this is the religious center of Judaism, as well as the nation's capital, *all* hotels of importance are kosher. Only the *YMCA Hostel*, which stands opposite the King David, is a refuge for non-kosher holdouts, though a few of the third-class places are also non-kosher. The Y, I may say, is very good and well-run as a tourist hotel. It is a large and handsome building, with an auditorium, a library, a big swimming pool and much else. The plant is described, on a plaque at the entrance, as "The Fulfillment of the Inspired Vision of James Newlyn Jarvie of Montclair, New Jersey."

The *King David*, mentioned earlier as the dean of Israel's city hotels, is indeed just that. It has everything, including a duty-free shop, but it has lost something too. The view of its famous and wonderful garden from the plate glass windows of the lounge has been cut off by a wide terrace, which is nice in summer but not so nice in other seasons at Jerusalem's half-mile altitude. Nevertheless the King David still rules the tourist roost.

Other first-class places in town are the big *Kings' Hotel* (pleasant glassed-in café extending to the very sidewalk of Ramban Street); the soaring *President* (300 rooms, new part 22 stories, with roof restaurant); and the much smaller (50 rooms) *Eden*. A little outside of town, on a crest above the suburb of Beir Vegan, is the new and charming *Hotel Holyland*. Its public rooms, especially a large crescent lounge, overlook well-kept gardens and a lovely park on a wooded knoll. The Holyland has a swimming pool and a small pond for children's rowing, and on the knoll there is a little museum featuring a comprehensive collection of Israel postage stamps. There is also a private synagogue for the owner and his family, for he is a very religious man and he erected this hotel, I am told, on the very spot where his son was killed in the fighting for independence.

Certain less conspicuous hotels of central Jerusalem are worth noting, for example the *Moriah*, named for the mountain where Abraham prepared to sacrifice Isaac, and the *Reich*. There are also no less than four Christian hostels (besides the Y), three Roman Catholic, one Church of Scotland, and, situated near the Holyland, the *Lois Waterman Wise Youth Hostel*.

While on the subject of practicalities I should mention again that Jerusalem's Tourist Information Office, the central one of the country, is at the corner of King George V Street (Number 60) and Ramban Street, in the same building as Kings' Hotel. *Israel Touring Club*, with a good *public restaurant*, is a bit to the south on Pinsker and Alkalai Streets.

Some Landmarks of History and Scripture

Of Old Jerusalem, on the Israel side, two sights are of unfailing interest to visitors, *Mount Zion* and the *Quarter of the Orthodox Hassidim Jews*. Mount Zion is the most sacred spot in the Jewish world, for it is the burial place of the old kings of the House of David and according to a strong tradition the Psalmist himself lies here under a monument in a room that was formerly a Moslem mosque and is now shown to all comers as *David's Tomb*. This is a hallowed spot to Moslems as well as Jews and in the period of Turkish control Jews were not allowed to enter it. As a concession, they *were* allowed to peep through a hole in the ceiling above it. Now the Jews have reconquered their own. So sacred is the hill on which this tomb stands that pilgrims are eager to buy little bags of its earth, which practice caters, perhaps, to a spirit of commercialism. When entering the hilltop Synagogue of David's Tomb every male visitor must wear a hat out of respect for Jewish custom. I didn't have one with me but managed to get by with a handkerchief draped over my head.

In a confusing group of buildings erected on the Mount by Franciscans in the Middle Ages is a large and venerable hall that is asserted to be the *Coenaculum*, or "Upper Room," where Jesus had the Last Supper with his disciples. It is an exceedingly holy place to countless Christians, and also to the Moslems, who recognize Jesus as a great religious leader, whereas the Jews have no religious interest in it. Another sacred place, revered by Roman Catholic Christians, is a spot pointed out in the *Church of the Dormition* on this same hill, Mount Zion. It is called the spot from which the Virgin Mary ascended into heaven, as was proclaimed in the dogma promulgated by Pope Pius XII during the Holy Year of 1950.

A place of interest to all visitors, regardless of their faith, is a small museum containing relics of Hitler's atrocities. There are partially burned Torahs from synagogues of Berlin and Munich and there is a Nazi jacket contemptuously made of a Torah. Of more serious and comprehensive nature is the *Yad Vashem Memorial Institution* on the Mount of Remembrance, a center of archives and research dedicated to the memory of the six million Jews destroyed by the Nazis. Adjacent to it is the *Ash House*, containing jars of ashes of Jewish persons killed in concentration camps. It is a low, square, gray building, with black door, suggesting the black despair of the victims. The door is kept closed, for these ashes are not shown to the public. An eternal flame burns over a roster of victims of the extermination centers. The world's memory of Hitler's unparalleled outrages against humanity may be short, but it goes without saying that Jewish memories are long.

The *Quarter of the Orthodox Hassidim Jews* is an amazing spectacle of a world that refuses to change. The men in this quarter nearly all wear the long, tight-fitting caftan robe and big porkpie hat trimmed with fur, and the long side curls, dangling from in front of either ear, that are their symbols. Even the small children, clad in jackets and pants and dresses that look like fashion ads from 1850, wear the long, tight curls. The actual origin of these queer customs, however, is from Polish Jews rather than from Jews of Palestine. The women cut their hair extremely short and wear very tight head scarves to make themselves as untempting as possible to males. They like to talk Yiddish in their daily lives, saving the sacred Hebrew language for the synagogue. They learn by heart the Talmud, which, in its usual sense here, is the Gemara portion of the Talmud, a commentary on the Pentateuch. Book learning is their whole occupation and preoccupation and many of them are enormously learned in a bookish way, but they are impractical and fanatical folk, a great problem to modern Israel. It is they who might burn and overturn an automobile so rash as to invade their quarter on the Sabbath (Shabbat) and they might well stone a man so imprudent as to walk there hatless on the Sabbath. The most recalcitrant of them stubbornly refuse even to recognize the authority of the State of Israel, fiercely asserting that the Messiah alone can establish Israel. Of their attitude during the Palestine War, Thomas Sugrue said in his book, "[they were] more interested in reading the Torah and praying at the Wailing Wall than in fighting Arabs. They did not, in fact, believe in fighting; they were waiting for the Messiah, who in good time would come and by his appearance make effort of any sort unnecessary."

I shall never forget walking through the Orthodox Quarter late of a Sabbath (Saturday) afternoon with a Jewish savant. Small though it is there are many synagogues in it and as sundown drew near every man was seen scurrying to one of them for a final Sabbath service. Said my companion, "The Orthodox look upon the Shabbat as a young man looks upon his fiancée. On Friday afternoon they welcome it with deepest emotion and on Saturday evening they still cling to it passionately, even though the sun has set. The Shabbat is a day of peace and prayer, when all the world's troubles, and their own as well, are laid aside."

Three historical or biblical places in the immediate vicinity of

Jewish Jerusalem are, for various reasons, richly worth visiting: Mount Herzl, with the tomb of Theodor Herzl; the sacred village of Ein Karem; and the war bastion of Ramat Rahel (now with a nearby kibbutz) overlooking Bethlehem in the middle distance.

To Jewish visitors *Herzl's Tomb* is of supreme interest because Theodor Herzl, who was a native of Budapest, founded political Zionism and by his indefatigable zeal set in motion the forces that forged a nation. Of course there is no statue of this revered man, for that would be an "image." His remains lie in a prominent but severely simple grave on the Herzl "Mount," west of the capital, which lofty point, 2740 feet above sea level, also has the *Herzl Museum* and the *National Military Cemetery*. From the Mount the Mediterranean Sea is plainly visible about thirty-two miles to the west.

Ein Karem, meaning Fountain of the Vineyard, has several famous churches and monastic buildings. The *Church of the Visitation* is supposed to mark the spot where, according to Luke's narrative, Mary of Nazareth "went into the hill country with haste . . . and entered into the house of Zacharias, and saluted her cousin Elisabeth. And it came to pass that, when Elisabeth heard the salutation of Mary, the babe leaped in her womb." The wall of the courtyard of this church sets forth the Virgin's *Magnificat* in seventy (70) languages! The Franciscan *Monastery of St. John* encloses the Church of St. John the Baptist and a grotto within this church, which is soberly pointed out as the precise spot where John was born. It is dedicated to his father, the priest Zacharias. Perhaps even as an infant John had a lusty voice, giving promise of his future role "of one crying in the wilderness, Prepare ye the way of the Lord." The *Russian Church*, never finished, and the *Convent of the Nuns of the Rosary* are now cared for (or neglected) by some aging Russian nuns. This so-called Russian Compound, however sadly neglected, is beautiful to look at from the high road traversing Ein Karem, for it stands on a lovely slope clothed with cypress trees.

Ramat Rahel, meaning "Hill of Rachel," is the southern bastion of Israel's Jerusalem, the place where the fiercest seesaw battles took place between Israel and Arab forces for days and nights on end. For the terrible grimness of it, as still witnessed by the ruins, and for the heroism involved—objective reports indicate that there was plenty of it on both sides—it is a tourist sight in its own right, but Rachel's Hill is a thing also to be looked *from*, and a pavilion (café), with a view platform above, facilitates this. The ground falls sharply away as if from a sea cliff and then spreads endlessly to the south and west. Due south, in Jordan territory, lie *Rachel's Tomb*, so called by tradition, and, as clear as if it were next door, the "little town of *Bethlehem*." Some fifteen miles to the southeast gleams that strangest and lowest of all the world's bodies of water, the Dead Sea, 1300 feet below the level of the Mediterranean. Part of its western shore is Israeli territory. It receives the waters of the Jordan and other streams, but having no possible outlet it depends solely on evaporation to keep its level steady. Its salinity is variously given as 23 to 30 per cent, as against 3 to 4 per cent in ocean water. It is stated that consumption of a glass or two of Dead Sea water drunk by a human being could kill him. At any rate no animal life whatever can live in it. Bathers swim in it, or float *on* it, but are mighty careful not to imbibe it.

Perhaps some other facts of geography may find place here, for many visitors ask, "Why was Jerusalem built on a rocky ridge, making it difficult to approach?" Basically, it grew up here, four thousand or more years ago, for ease of protection from enemies and because it was a natural crossing point of north-south and east-west trails, and later roads. Its north-south road is the famous Patriarchs' Way, traversed by Abraham, Isaac and Jacob. Two other north-south highways of history are the Imperial Way, along the Jordan Valley, and the Via Maris, near the sea. An odd meteorological fact is that it can rain hard in Jerusalem and on the mountain range beyond the Dead Sea, but virtually never *on* the Dead Sea, this because the mountains on both sides trap and empty the clouds.

As far to the north of the city's center as Ramat Rahel is to the south, and likewise bordering the Jordan frontier, is an odd and rather gloomy sight, the *Necropolis of the Sanhedrin*, which I mention only for a bit of lore that I picked up here. In our party at the time was a young lady named Mrs. Kahan. From the guide, and from her, I learned that many (but by no means all) Cohens and Kahans, as well as others with closely related Jewish names starting with *c* or *k*, are lineal descendants of Aaron, the brother of Moses, and therefore technically members of a sort of tribe, stemming from that biblical priest. Collectively, Aaron's descendants are known as the Cohanim, which is Hebrew for Priests, and are barred by laws in the Book of Leviticus from standing near a grave. Mrs. Kahan said that her husband accepts and abides by those ancient laws, as do many others, but that the restriction does not apply to the wife of an Aaron descendant. The Cohanim, I have since learned, includes many Jews whose names by no means resemble Cohen or Kahan, and on the other hand many who do have such names are not within the Cohanim.

Eyes Across the Line

For views of old Jerusalem, tantalizing in case one cannot cross the Hashemite Jordan frontier to reach it, a good vantage point is Mount Zion, mentioned above, or, even better, the roof (accessible to tourists) of the *Hospice of Notre Dame de France*, owned by the Augustine Fathers of the Assumption. Being immediately above the Mandelbaum Gate, this building suffered terribly in the fighting in 1948, but it has been partially rebuilt. It is surprising how many things in Jordan Jerusalem *can* be see from any such lofty point, though this only increases one's sense of frustration.

1. The conspicuous *Sacred Enclosure,* supposed to have been Mount Moriah, where Abraham prepared to sacrifice Isaac, and *known* to have been the site of Solomon's Temple, is now graced by the celebrated *Dome of the Rock,* called also the *Mosque of Omar.* This is recognizable by the large, graceful dome, long of a gray-blue color but brightly gilded in 1960. It dates from 691, when the Moslem faith was young. The rock on which the Dome of the Rock stands is believed by Moslems to be the point from which Mohammed flew to heaven on his holy Pegasus named El Burak. The mosque, surpassed as an object of Moslem veneration only by the Kaaba in Mecca and the mosque in Medina, is the one which King Abdullah was entering for worship on July 20, 1951, when he was assassinated. A second mosque, *El Aksa,* is also seen within the Enclosure.

2. The *Church of the Holy Sepulcher,* a little nearer the viewer, marks the spot which Emperor Constantine and his mother Helena decided was the "new tomb" of Joseph of Arimathea, where the body of the Lord had lain. Other tombs and sites have been ardently claimed

by various students as the correct ones, but the tomb Constantine picked is generally considered as likely as any.

3. *Golgotha*, the *Hill of Calvary*, is actually no hill, but a mere rise in the rocky ground close to the Church of the Holy Sepulcher. At the time of the crucifixion it was never called "Mount Golgotha," that name being a much later invention.

4. The celebrated *Wailing Wall* of the Jews is the west wall (nearest to the beholder) of the above-mentioned Enclosure.

5. and 6. The *Garden of Gethsemane*, on the flanks of the *Mount of Olives*, is a short distance beyond and to the east of the Enclosure. On the famous hill itself, but of course not to be seen from Jewish Jerusalem, is the rock whence, by cherished tradition, Jesus ascended to heaven. I remember from my youthful visit being shown the footprint of the Lord's left foot! The portion of the rock showing the mark of the right foot was long ago removed as a sacred relic by Moslems, for display in the El Aksa Mosque. (I recollect also from my long-ago visit that in the Church of the Holy Sepulcher I was shown the sword of Godfrey de Bouillon, which had been known to fly out of its scabbard automatically to slay infidels; and in the Enclosure I was shown a pinch of the original dust from which God made Adam!)

7. Just north of the Old City but still within Jordan's part of Jerusalem one may plainly see the now pathetic *Palestine Archeological Museum*, richly endowed by Rockefeller. It is now "stagnant," for any worth-while finds made since the division of the city have been appropriated by museums definitely sponsored by Jewish or Arab authorities rather than allotted to this nobly neutral one established by American philanthropy.

8. Most pathetic of all the things seen in Jordan Jerusalem is that lost waif, *Mount Scopus*, on which loom up the splendid modern buildings of the former *Hebrew University* and *National Library* and the *Hadassah Medical Center*. All of these formerly thriving institutions are now empty shells, replaced by bigger and better buildings in Israel's portion of the city.

Persons planning to visit the Jordan side would do well to find out the latest facts from the *Jordan Tourism Information Service* recently set up in New York at 5 East 57th Street. The service is in the charge of an able and friendly Jordanian named Sami Awad. Here, it is enough to say that entrance to Jordan is normally feasible if a) you have no Israel visa in your passport (even though your very self walks or drives right through!), and b) if you do not try to return to Israel but make your way out of Jordan by some other route such as through Syria and presumably then through Beirut, Lebanon. You may also fly from Jordan Jerusalem direct to Beirut by MEA or Air Liban. There is a large, first-class hotel, the *Ambassador*, on the Jordan side of Jerusalem. Viewers from the Israel side, especially from the roof of Notre Dame de France, can plainly see it. Pan American Airways is to open a large new hotel, the *Jerusalem*, within a few months, this being a new link in its ever-lengthening chain of IHC hotels, for Intercontinental Hotels Corporation.

High Lights of Modern Jerusalem

So very much has been achieved in modern Jewish Jerusalem since the birth of Israel that I can hardly do more here than list the high lights, paying no particular regard to their geographical sequence on the map, with a few words about their significance.

1. The *Jewish National Institutions*, "nerve center of the State of Israel," cluster on King George V Avenue.

2. The *Government Center*, in the western part of the city, is a fast growing group of new buildings, including the new *Knesset* and at least seven Ministries; also a new *President's Residence and Garden*. A replica of the Liberty Bell, given by the City of Philadelphia, is in the garden.

3. The *National Museum* is taking form a bit south of the Government Center, financed partly by the U.S. under its Special Cultural Program for Israel but far more heavily by an American Jewish family named Bronfmann.

4. The new *Hadassah and University Medical Center* is an enormous building well out of town, built and equipped in the most modern way. An internationally famous art feature is a series of twelve stained glass windows in its synagogue, a masterpiece of the great Russian-French painter, Marc Chagall.

5. The *Hebrew University of Jerusalem*, on a ridge called Givat

Rim west of the Government Center, replaces the lost one on Mt. Scopus, and what a proud replacement! It has twelve faculties, a fine campus, the interesting Wise Auditorium, a huge National and University Library, a National and University Sports Stadium, a Planetarium, an amphitheater, a University Synagogue of unusual design, various lecture halls and laboratories and a tall Administration Building with a special ground-floor room housing a few of the *Dead Sea Scrolls* under glass. This last proves a tremendous tourist attraction, for all the world seems to know of these scrolls, dating from the very time of Christ, and some of them seeming to promulgate His precepts, yet discovered only in our time and first deciphered by the late Professor Eleazar Sukenik, head of the university's Department of Archeology. Among those that I noted, half charred or damaged by time, were *The Manual of Discipline*, *The Thanksgiving Scroll*, *The Scroll of the War of the Sons of Light Against the Sons of Darkness*, and some parts of the major and minor prophets (Isaiah; Habakkuk). The permanent home of the Scrolls and many other rare manuscripts is to be in a new building now under construction on the University Campus, to be called *The Shrine of the Book*.

In the University bookstore I saw an item that interested me almost as much as the Scrolls. It was a book of big format called *Chronicles: News of the Past*, compiled from "newspapers" published by the students. You will see the point of it from some of the headlines which I copied down at random:

SODOM AND GOMORRAH WIPED OUT IN WORST DISASTER SINCE THE FLOOD. (Pictures "Before" and "After.")

PRINCE MOSES ACCUSED OF SLAYING EGYPTIAN OFFICIAL. MOSES' SISTER UNDER ARREST. PHARAOH'S DAUGHTER STANDS BY HER SON.

MOSES RETURNS FROM MT. SINAI. SMASHES TABLETS OF THE LAW.

Then comes a huge set of headlines within a broad black frame:

MOSES DEAD. ENDS GLORIOUS CAREER ON THRESHOLD OF HOLY LAND. JOSHUA TAKES OVER. BURIAL PLACE A SECRET.

Under each of these headlines was a full factual account of the incident, written in today's journalese.

There are many more new public buildings in this modern city, including a very large *Jerusalem Theater*, now nearing completion but perhaps you could use a bit of light relief. On the northwest edge of the city is a *Biblical Zoo* with eighty-five species of animals that are mentioned in the Bible. The next step, one would think, would be a giant-sized Noah's Ark: Come and see the animal couples, folks!

CHAPTER 21

NORTH TO GALILEE AND DAN;
SOUTH TO BEERSHEBA AND EILAT

The Northern Loop, Point by Point

DESPITE the lacerated look of maps of Israel, resulting from the United Nations' attempt to divide the land between Jew and Arab, the State of Israel has a greater north-south length than did Hebrew territory in the Biblical days, when it stretched "from Dan to Beersheba." The Negev arrowhead, pushing to its tip on the Gulf of Akaba, an arm of the Red Sea, adds another eighty miles—of desert.

The northward loop from Tel Aviv to Dan, and so westward to the sea and back along the coast to its starting point, can be achieved in a private car in three full days, and if the circuit is only from Haifa to Haifa it can, at a pinch, be compressed into two. The points of interest along the circuit are numerous and only the chief ones can be mentioned here.

Nathanya, a very flourishing coastal town eighteen miles north of Tel Aviv, is named for the American philanthropist, Nathan Straus, in gratitude for his generosities. The place was founded only in 1925, but it now has over thirty thousand inhabitants. Jewish diamond cutters and polishers, fleeing from Antwerp when Belgium fell under Hitler's heel, have established their interesting industry here and it now flourishes mightily. America imports industrial diamonds in substantial quantity from Nathanya. It is, of course, as a resort that it chiefly interests foreign visitors and in that role it plays its part well. It is usually bathed in a pleasant sea breeze and the park-promenade that tops the cliff at the edge of the sea is superb. Here, too, is an open-air theater at the very edge of the fallaway. There are good, but not luxury, hotels almost by the dozen, some directly on the front. One front hotel, new but quite unpretentious, is the *Taleyeth*. Another is the *Ein Hayam*.

Caesarea, a historic coastal community half way between Nathanya and Haifa, began to come into its own as a tourist attraction in the early 1960's with the unearthing of spectacular remains of a Roman and Crusader port and the work goes on with speed and determination. Specifically, a company called the Caesarea Beach Resort Corporation, headed by a U.S. industrialist (Monte H. Tyson) and with a U.S. address at 1528 Walnut Street, Philadelphia, is developing a 36-acre project which will include a high-grade 110-room hotel to be known as *The Caesaria*, a restaurant, a shopping center and all the accouterments of a beach resort. It is expected to open in the very early future. Guests will be accorded the privileges of the Caesarea Golf and Country Club, only two or three miles distant, this being Israel's first golf course of high quality, opened in 1960.

The excavation of the extensive ruins is a joint venture of the Israeli government and the family of Edmond de Rothschild, founder of the Palestine Jewish Colonization Association, whose son, the late James A. Rothschild founded the golf club and is building a large luxury hotel adjacent to it. The most exciting feature of the excavations is a huge Roman Amphitheater which was christened, as it were, in 1961, when Israel's *First International Music Festival* was held here with Pablo Casals as recitalist. It is hoped that performances at Caesarea may become an integral part of a fixed annual Israel Festival to run for about three weeks from mid-August. For the 1962 Festival Igor Stravinsky was engaged to conduct the Israel Philharmonic Orchestra and John Gielgud to star in drama. Other ruins, both from Roman and Crusader times, are full of interest. Perhaps the most intriguing items are some handsome columns that are buffeted by the daily surf, and two colossal Roman statues. One of these is of porphyry, the other of white marble and both are seated, both headless. Their identity seems not to have been established.

From Caesarea our loop leaves the coast and swings in, heading northeast to the Plain of Esdraelon, which is as important in Israel's present economy as it is in Biblical history. Esdraelon is the later Greek equivalent of the name Jezreel, and dominating this plain was fortified *Megiddo*, which is thought to be none other than the *Armageddon* of the Apocalypse, traditional place of violent conflict and slaughter. It was here that Thotmes III of Egypt came as invader and ruthless conqueror in the fifteenth century B.C. It was here that the Israelite forces of Barak, goaded on by Deborah, destroyed the whole army of Sisera the Canaanite, "and all the host of Sisera fell upon the edge of the sword; and there was not a man left." Sisera himself fled to the tent of Heber's wife, Jael, who finished him off by driving a spike through his head into the ground. It was here that "the sword of the Lord and of Gideon" triumphed over the Midianites. In modern times Napoleon here administered a sharp defeat to the Turkish army. And in our own time Allenby also here defeated the Turks and from the victory acquired his official title Lord of Armageddon.

As a further item from the innumerable Bible stories about this plain, one should recall that Naboth's vineyard was on a slope above it. King Ahab and his wife Jezebel wanted the vineyard, so Jezebel, whose name is a byword for wickedness, contrived to have Naboth stoned to death. Elijah appeared and pronounced a terrible curse from the Lord. Ahab was soon slain in battle and later Jezebel met a death so gruesome that only the uninhibited Bible could report the details. These are boldly set down in I Kings 9:30–37.

Today's Esdraelon is a wonderfully cheerful place. Its malarial swamps, absolutely uninhabitable a few decades ago, have been drained by the Jewish National Fund, and this whole valley, now supporting more than forty thousand people, has become an agricultural pride of new Israel. It produces grain, honey, bananas, olives, dairy products. It breeds cattle, sheep and poultry in a big way. It has valuable fish hatcheries. In a local kibbutz I heard a wire recorder recite, in English, the valley's accomplishments, and the machine could have done the same for me in eight other languages!

Ein Harod is the kibbutz referred to above and the name means Well of Harod. This is a significant name, for the Book of Judges tells us that Gideon and his hosts "pitched beside the well of Harod," and it was from the waters of this well, actually a spring and a brooklet, that Gideon chose for his army "the three hundred men that lapped." There is no better or more cheerful place in all Israel to see a kibbutz at work than here. A special attraction is the *Shturman House*, a gallery of local art and archeology and a museum of fauna and flora. Ein Harod's guest house gladly takes in transients, including tourists, but it has very limited accommodations. Fifteen thousand visitors come here annually and of this number about one fourth are tourists eager to see the phenomenon of a successful collective whose guiding force is idealism. The ideal, in this case, was transforming a miasmic swamp into a garden and a ranch. The kibbutz folk like to boast that from the roof of the guest house you can, if your eyesight is good, "visit Gilead without a passport." Gilead, the ancient territory of the tribes of Manasseh, Gad and Reuben, lies east of the Jordan and is therefore Hashemite soil today. Only a few miles east of Ein Harod and well within Israeli territory is the community of *Beit Alfa*, with a quaint and beautifully preserved Byzantine mosaic of the Zodiac Cycle and the Four Seasons, done in the local synagogue by an unknown sixth-century artist.

Mount Tabor, due north of Ein Harod and due east of Nazareth, is the traditional "high mountain apart," where the Lord was transfigured before Peter, James and John. Matthew records that "His face did shine as the sun," and Mark that "His raiment became shining, exceeding white as snow; so as no fuller on earth can white them." A monastery and a nunnery, both of the Franciscan Order, are on the summit and can be reached by a good, though narrow, road.

Nazareth, as the home of Jesus, is of course one of the most sought places in all the Holy Land, and fortunately it lies in Israel. For a few years after the line between Israel and Jordan was drawn it was an all-Arab town, mostly of the Christian faith, giving allegiance to Israel. Since 1953, however, a large Jewish community has developed in an upper quarter of the town. Many of the Arabs are of surprisingly fair complexion, even with blue eyes and blond or red hair, this phenomenon being traceable, we are told, to the Crusader blood in their veins, for Nazareth was an important Crusader center.

The visitor usually halts in the lower part of the town to secure an Arab guide, this being virtually required by local custom, and guidance being quite necessary in any case. Nazareth's best hotel bears the almost unforgivably dull name of *Grand New Hotel*, but it is at least a *good* new hotel, its rooms having both air-conditioning and heating. Its terrace has a magnificent close-up view of the whole city, which now numbers almost 30,000 inhabitants.

The two most sacred sights of Nazareth are the *Church of the Annunciation*, now being rebuilt and enlarged by a Milanese architect to become the largest church in the Near East, and the *Church of St. Joseph*.

In the former the guides point out the exact spot, the so-called Column of Mary, where "the angel came in unto her, and said, Hail, thou that art highly favored." There have been three earlier churches on approximately this spot, covering a deep grotto that is said to be warm in winter and cool in summer. "*Mary's kitchen,*" with unmistakable marks of smoke, adjoins the grotto. St. Helena, mother of Constantine, built the first church here and she was the one who "identified" the sacred spots of Nazareth and many others all over Palestine. Her visits occurred only three centuries after the time of the Holy Family and it is not being too credulous to suppose that by following strong and fairly recent tradition she may actually have located, with some authenticity, some of the holy places in Nazareth and Jerusalem. It is certain, however, that she "pushed her luck" and identified many things, such as the crown of thorns and the sponge, by sheer wishfulness or guesswork. The Crusaders built the second church, the Franciscans the third.

The Church of St. Joseph covers a deep cave where the Holy Family is supposed to have lived after the return from Egypt. There is a splendid cistern here, similar to many now in use in Nazareth homes, and on a level above it is "*Joseph's carpentry shop.*" The water for the cistern *must* have been brought by Mary from the fountain that is now called *Mary's Well,* for its water flows from the only spring in the town, a spring that rises from beneath the Greek Orthodox *Church of Gabriel.* The women of Nazareth still come to this well, at a crossroads on the farther side of the town, and return to their homes with filled jars on their heads, or sometimes with filled gasoline tins, these being the accepted water jars in many lands of the East.

The above sights of Nazareth, together with the synagogue, built on the site of the old synagogue where Jesus taught, have attracted pilgrims, Crusaders and plain curiosity seekers literally by the million throughout all the ages. To accommodate their needs for nourishment a very large Histadrut restaurant has been built.

A Nazareth interlude to "plant a tree with your own hands" is enjoyed by many tourists, as it was by this one, the place being the Balfour Forest, a beautiful rolling area of made woods in the Nazareth hills. The afforestation of Israel has been one of the country's major needs and policies, and a most impressive start has already been made by the Jewish National Fund, which has planted more than fifty million trees so far and sets its sights for at least another hundred million within the next few years. Visitors are invited by the slogan I have quoted above to participate in the program, each one being also invited to pay IL 6 ($2) for the privilege. One is inevitably reminded of Tom Sawyer's charge to his playmates for permission to paint a part of his fence, but even so this seems to me a valid and worthy way of arousing international interest in this campaign so vital to the life of Israel. There are six plant-a-tree forests in widely scattered areas, as follows: The *Jerusalem Forest*, on the northern outskirts of the city; the *Martyrs' Forest*, near Jerusalem; the forest around the *Massua Observation Tower*, southwest of Jerusalem (this tower is worth a visit for its breathtaking view); the *Simchoni Forest* in the Negev; the *Birya Forest*, near Safed in Galilee; and the aforementioned *Balfour Forest* at Nazareth.

I have heard that visitors alone have so far "hand planted" about a quarter of a million trees and while this is but a twig-in-the-forest compared with the hundred fifty million goal it is a gesture of good will and is actually good fun besides. For your efforts the local forest guardian pins a badge on your heaving bosom and gives you a fancy receipt. If you wish to do things in a big way you may finance in your name a garden (100 trees), a grove (1000 trees) or a forest (10,000 trees).

Cana of Galilee has been identified by Bible scholars as the present Arab village of Kafr Kanna, a bit north of Nazareth, though one or two other villages make rival claims. In this setting of the first miracle of Jesus, turning water into wine at a wedding feast, local priests go all out in their zeal for detail. The Roman Catholics show the cave where the wedding took place. The Greek Catholics show the very jugs in which the water became wine!

Lake Galilee is a remarkable and vastly intriguing body of water, for it is the "low spot" of this northern loop. Its surface is 681 feet below sea level, yet, unlike the Dead Sea, which is 1300 feet below sea level, it is completely fresh, this because, unlike the Dead Sea, it is a "flowing lake," with the Jordan not only as affluent but as effluent. Dead Sea waters have nowhere to go except into the atmosphere by evaporation. The motorist's approach to the lake on a road that winds down from many hundreds of feet *above* sea level, is one of the marvels of travel. This lake has many names and they are a bit confusing. Four others than the one above are: Sea of Galilee, Lake Gennesaret, Lake Tiberias and Lake Chinnereth, or Kinnereth. A popular American steamship folder glows about the beauty of "Lake Kinnereth," a name which means nothing to most tourists. Galilee is liquid and beautiful in sound as the lake is in fact.

Tiberias, on the shores of Galilee, is a considerable resort city, taking its name from Emperor Tiberias. With at least three fine hotels, a galaxy of good but less pretentious ones, a lake-front strip lined with garden-cafés and a really important spa called *Tiberias Hot Springs*, with radioactive mineral waters beneficial in treating rheumatism and nervous disorders, the resort has an air as of long-established European sophistication. Long-established it certainly is, for it was founded by Herod Antipas in the year 19 C.E. (Christian Era), which is Israel's way of saying A.D. (Hebrew religionists can hardly be expected to say *Anno Domini!*). A stone bathhouse of the Herodian period is one of the town's sights. A defect of Tiberias, in summer, is the heat, for a resort 206 meters below sea level, as emphasized by a "Minus 206 Club" on the lake's edge, is bound to be hot. Lake breezes, however, and lake bathing do a lot to temper the heat. The leading hotels, all first-class, are the *Galei Kinnereth* (bedrooms air-conditioned), the *Ginton* and the *Yaabon*, the two latter air-conditioned throughout, and a very good place of bungalow type, with common dining room, is *Hotel Ganei Hamat*, situated in a ten-acre park near the shore and very close to the Hot Springs. This, be it noted, is *not* a kosher place. So important is Tiberias in the tourist picture that the Israel Philharmonic Orchestra and top recitalists and entertainers regularly appear here. I have even been told that Tiberias is the only place in Israel outside of Tel Aviv where strip teasers are permitted to tease. Is that a knock or a boost? You may decide.

The *Jordan*, as we know, flows into Lake Galilee in the north and out of it in the south. It is possible to "go over Jordan" and ride up the eastern shore of the lake to a kibbutz outpost of Israel called *Ein Gev* and even to lodge there in the guest house. *Deganiya*, another kibbutz, the earliest one established in Israel, is at the southern end of the lake on the Jordan's east bank and here, too, the visitor may find lodging. Deganiya was founded in 1909, the same year as Tel Aviv. Not far from this point is the very handsome *Sahne Pool and Park*, maintained jointly by the Israel Tourist Corporation and the Regional Council. Swimming

in this delightful *natural* pool, surrounded by sloping lawns, is a wonderfully pleasant experience in the below-sea-level temperature, as I
know from having done it. There is a good public bathhouse, with
showers, for changing.

Tabyha, or *Tabigha*, on the northwestern rim of Lake Galilee, is supposed to be the spot where Jesus wrought the miracle of the loaves and
fishes.

Capernaum, where Jesus "entered into the synagogue and taught," is
on the northern shore of the lake. The synagogue of Jesus' time has not
been found but Capernaum does have a most remarkable *second-century*
synagogue in an excellent state of preservation, now under the care of
Franciscan monks. Many of the designs seen on Israel coins of today,
for example the sheaf of wheat on the 1-agora coin, were modeled directly from carvings noted in the decoration of this synagogue.

The *Mount of Beatitudes*, just north of the lake, above Capernaum,
is the spot where, by tradition, Jesus preached the Sermon on the
Mount. On its crest, of modest height, stands the odd, round Franciscan
Church of the Beatitudes, adorned with a circle of outside arches. Here,
too, is a nun's hostel for tourists. This hallowed hill, perhaps deplorably,
has become a favorite picnic goal for tripper groups from the little
steamers that cruise on the lake.

Ayeleth Hashahar, meaning Morning Star, is a very pleasant kibbutz
far in the north between two little lakes near the larger Lake Hula. It
has one of the most modern tourist hostels in Israel, donated by an
American Jewess named Bessie Brasley Cohen.

Nabi Yusha is a hill fortress close to the Lebanon frontier. It cost the
Israelis many lives to take it by storm. The view from its summit is one
of the best in the north.

Dan has little to warrant a visit except its fame as the extreme northern
outpost of Hebrew lands in Bible times, and now. If you are interested
to see how very well "aggression paid" in olden times, read, in Joshua
19:47, how Dan became Dan. It was really *something*.

Alma is a tiny hamlet in the north. It *was* the hamlet of San Nicardo,
in Italy. An old woman of that Italian village had a dream in which God
commanded that the community move to the Holy Land. It listened
and complied. The village was Roman Catholic. Today it adheres to the
Jewish faith.

Safed, or Safad, an ancient Talmudic city with curious medieval synagogues and with "layers" of brightly-tinted houses seeming to clamber one upon the other, is one of the most picturesque hill towns—I believe this is the first time that adjective has slipped by my guard—in the eastern Mediterranean. It is wonderful when looked *at*, equally so when looked *from*. And if you drive to it from the direction of Acre, as I did on one visit, there's a strange phenomenon. Now you see it, now you don't, and so on *interminably*. Maybe twenty times the wonderful sight reveals itself only to be blotted out at the next curve, and just when you're ready to pronounce it a mirage or a clever hoax of the TIO there you are, coasting down to the entrance of a fine modern hotel that was opened in 1962. This mountain hostelry, by name the *Rakefet*, from whose bedroom balconies, *high* above a green slope, you can "spit a mile"—I quote from a young American tourist—seems to have been the forerunner of a tide of hotel building, for at least two others, one very large, are now under construction and more are planned. On Mt. Canaan, at the 3200-foot level above the town, there is a popular summer resort with many good hotels, each with a grand view, the *Mines House* being the leader. Of the older Safed hotels, the *Herzliya*, with delightful family atmosphere, is still deservedly popular. Safed is the home of one of Israel's largest and eagerest art colonies but many of the young artists have only hopes to live on. The lady who runs the Herzliya often gives them free meals, letting them pay later, perhaps with paintings.

You will love the atmosphere of Safed, for there's nothing else quite like it in Israel or in the whole Mediterranean. "Atmosphere" breathes from its every pore, and so does art. There are many little private studio-galleries and one public one, called the *Artists' Club*. There are four or five tiny night clubs, too, and on a street like a parapet you'll see a "Davidka" on display. This is a mortar ambitiously invented by a young Israeli named David, others of his design being on display in Jerusalem and Capernaum. There was just one trouble with the Davidka. The thing wouldn't fire.

Safed started as a Roman town, became a Crusader town and finally, in the sixteenth century, a very important Jewish town, exceedingly prosperous in this world's goods and spiritually prosperous too, a holy of holies for Jewish sages and religious authors. Of all its great men of religion the most revered was Rabbi Isaac Lurie, called the Ari (Lion).

When a nineteenth-century earthquake destroyed all of Safed it spared just one thing, the *Synagogue of the Ari*, where the holy man lived in a cramped cell working on a scroll of the Torah, When I recently visited this sacred edifice one of the most ancient men I've ever seen was serving as custodian. He shuffled about at a snail's pace croaking information about the scroll and the saint until finally, overcome by curiosity, I asked him his age. I thought he would say a hundred and twelve, but the age he gave me was seven years younger than mine—and that's all I'm going to tell you!

Nahariya, on the seacoast not far south of the Lebanon border and the city of Tyre, is an attractive beach resort populated almost wholly by refugees from Nazi Germany. One hears mostly German in its streets and cafés.

Acre is a natural grand climax to this northern circuit, which then goes south the few miles to Haifa and so to Tel Aviv, perhaps with halts to see the enormous wine cellars in *Zikhron Jaakov*, second in size only to those of Bordeaux, and then the "reviving Roman ruins" of Caesarea, already mentioned. In Zikhron Jaakov there is a handsome park and a grotto in which lie buried Baron Edmond de Rothschild, great benefactor of Israel, and his wife.

Acre is, to me, the most "different" place in Israel. Under various names, including Acco in the Old Testament, Ptolemais in the New Testament and Saint-Jean d'Acre when ruled by the Knights of St. John, it has been fought over for twenty-five centuries. In the era of the Crusaders it was twice captured by them, the second time under the command of Guy de Lusignan, succeeded by Richard Coeur de Lion, and twice recaptured by the Saracens. In 1517, the Turks took it. In 1799, Napoleon *failed* to take it after a long and famous siege, the city being immeasurably aided by the British fleet under Sir Sidney Smith. In World War I, the British captured it from Turkey and Palestine went under British mandate. And the latest on Acre? It fell to Israeli troops on May 18, 1948, partly because the effective blaring of a loud-speaker deployed outside the walls led the Arabs inside to believe that their position was hopeless. Actually the besieging forces were laughably meager but the ruse worked.

The walls of Acre are double ones dating from the Crusader wars, and have but a single entrance road. Inside the walls the visitor finds himself in an all-Arab city. He might think himself in Syria or Egypt. The narrow, twisting streets are pictures from the Moslem East, and the splendid mosque of Ahmed Jazzar Pasha accentuates the impression. The thing to do in Acre is to find, by luck or persistent inquiry, an unpretentious native café directly beside the Old Port and take a surfside table, ordering coffee, baklava and perhaps some little buff-colored balls of sweet stuff called *awami*. The outlook is one to take permanent lodging in a specially selected memory cell. In the waves close beneath your table lies a granite column that got smashed in some Crusader-Saracen battle. Across the broad bay rises teeming Haifa, crowned by Mount Carmel. Out at sea, if the time is late afternoon, the sun, finishing its day's run, is about to dunk itself in the Mediterranean, simultaneously flinging into the sky a parting trail of colors, from cradle pink to royal purple.

Down the Narrowing Southern Wedge

I have called the Negev an arrowhead, and its shape, as seen on any map, does bear this out, but perhaps wedge would be a better word, for it is just that, narrowing to a point at the head of the Gulf of Eilat (Jordanians call it Akaba), wedged tightly between Jordan and Egypt. Until rather recently Eilat was hardly accessible except by air, but now the Tel Aviv-Eilat Highway through the desert is regularly traversed by busses and taxis, making the trip in about five hours.

The approach to the Southern Wedge should certainly include a halt at *Ashkelon*, which has had a big past and has nowadays a big present, as a major seaside resort. The resort lies only 33 miles south of Tel Aviv and is reached in one hour by Egged busses that depart on a regular schedule every twenty minutes.

Ashkelon has been a going concern for at least four millennia, dominated first by Egypt, but coming into prominence in the twelfth century B.C., when it was an important harbor and stronghold of the Philistines. It was here that Samson slew thirty Philistines and stole their robes, and later slew a thousand more with the jawbone of an ass. It was here that he fell for a Philistine maiden named Delilah from Nahal Sorek up the coast a bit (see Judges 16:4), had his famous haircut (Judges 16:19) and lost his strength. But then his hair grew a bit and during a "fiesta" in honor of the Philistines' god Dagon he pulled down the temple (Judges 16:29–30) and "slew at his death more than he slew in his life." What a man!

The Israelite kingdom waxed strong but even at its height could not subdue Philistine Ashkelon, which was a thorn in its side. When Saul died King David lamented, "Tell it not in Gath, publish it not in the streets of Ashkelon lest the Philistines rejoice." The word Palestine, by the way, is said to be a corruption of Philistine, applied, in contemptuous vein, by the Arabs. The Biblical name for the land was Canaan.

Nebuchadnezzar, King of Babylon, succeeded, in his time, in conquering Ashkelon, and so did Alexander the Great in his time, transforming it into a Hellenistic city. Later it became a Roman city and "at the turn of the era" Herod the Great, who was born here, built splendid structures, including the *Hall of the Pillars*, whose ruins are one of the sights of today. Of course the Crusaders came. They built massive walls, still visible in a crescent around the city, but held the place for only 37 years. Then Saladin took it and destroyed it. The Mamelukes came along and erased even the little that Saladin had left. It lay fallow for six centuries until Egypt took over, and then, in 1948, the forces of Israel. In 1952 began its Tourist Era. A group of South African Jews made a careful advance plan and began building the resort we see, starting with a beautiful modern community which they named *Afridar*. This alone is worth coming to Ashkelon to see, for it has been planned with rare skill, its municipal center graced by the Town Hall, the Museum of Antiquities and a campanile-like Clock Tower, the whole surrounded by broad lawns.

Two new hotels in Afridar are the *Dagon* (non-kosher), and the *Ashkelon* (kosher). I have much liked the Dagon for its relaxed holiday atmosphere and for its outstanding food, appropriately lubricated by a smooth wine of Israel labeled "Askalon." The Dagon is owned and managed by a Belgian Jewish couple (if my memory serves me) named Dorot, whose presence adds a personal, family touch.

A big road sign invites travelers to visit the nearby *Delilah Beach and Restaurant*. I haven't tried the restaurant, but I must say that the beach of Ashkelon, four or five miles of flawless sand cooled by sea breezes and beaten by steady but unfrightening surf, is as fine a strand as I have seen in the whole Mediterranean and the water rivals that of Egypt's beaches as the Inland Sea's warmest. All in all the Ashkelon of today has a lot to offer the tourist. For me it was a most happy discovery.

The *Gaza Strip*, only a few miles south of Ashkelon, is still a pathetic political orphan, a waif among the nations. With two Israelis I drove to the edge of it, where I noted a "Courage Monument" in a field, and just within the barrier, the large letters UN outlined in white stones. As we approached, so, from a watch house on the other side, did three Swedish UN soldiers in a jeep. Jumping from the car and standing with fixed bayonets, they merely looked at us, seemingly not with hostility, in total silence and we looked at them. Then we drove away. The Swedish soldiers were there to guard, not to talk, and it was explained to me that silence is maintained to appease the Arabs, who fear that the soldiers might fraternize with the hated Israelis.

Beersheba, the Biblical "Well of the Oath," or "Well of Seven"—authorities agree only that Beer means Well—which was the geographical antipode of Dan, is the capital of the Negev. It is now easy to visit in connection with an overland trip to Eilat, Israel's new and fast advancing Red Sea port. A branch road runs from the main one over to *Sodom*, on the Dead Sea, where Israel has built a big potash plant to exploit the heavy mineral content of that strange, sunken body of water. Israel dreams of exploiting also for tourism her small portion of the Dead Sea, with a railway from Beersheba to Sodom and motorboats running from Sodom up to *Engedi*, or Ein Gedi, for its hot springs. Sodom is, indeed, already a tourist goal of sorts, for the tour companies offer regular one-day tours to it from Tel Aviv, making a halt both ways at Beersheba. A stone somewhat in the shape of a woman is pointed out by earnest local guides as Lot's wife!

Beersheba gives quick evidence of the tremendous drive that powers Israel's advance. In 1948 it had 3000 inhabitants, in 1962 50,000 and it still advances at a rate of several thousand a year. Its features include a Community Center, with swimming pool, public library, restaurant-grill and Tourist Information Office; a well-stocked Shopping Center, with restaurant; a Solar Energy Plant; a Negev Research Center for probing the region's mineral and agricultural resources; a 400-bed hospital with a flat roof for helicopter landings to bring in patients from every direction; and a cinema palace that is called the best in Israel. For spicy night life there is (if it continues to live) a fantastic little night club called *Last Chance* (La Dernière Chance), owned and run by a young Belgian woman. Until 1962 most visitors stopping for a night or more in Beersheba stayed at the *HIAS House, a* hostel of United Hias Service built to provide good accommodations and a homelike atmosphere for experts and technicians from many countries converging on the city to aid in the development of the Negev. Now three new hotels, the *Zohar*, the *Sharon* and the *Desert Inn* have opened. The last-named, believe it or not, is an enterprise of the Motels Development Corporation of the Bahamas!

Beersheba isn't a goal for Good-Time Charlie but it is for the man or woman who wants to see what brains, energy and dedication can do with a big, dry desert. A sort of satellite to Beersheba is the town of *Dimona*, which had *no* inhabitants in 1952 but had 14,000 a decade later. It was born as a center for phosphate workers of Sodom and Oron, but quickly built up its own industry, especially in textiles. It also has one of Israel's two atomic reactors, twin to one outside Tel Aviv.

The Negev covers 4300 square miles and its weather is about the most temperamental in the world. In some winters it may rain in buckets time after time, with the winters before and after producing not a drop. Floods, drought, dust storms, floods—you never know in the Negev, but man, the Israeli man, will not be denied. Gradually he is making the desert bloom, and he is finding some treasure under the sands.

Eilat has been dubbed the Back Door of Israel, but more and more persons and industries are using it as a normal gateway. For the tourist, the easiest way to reach it is, of course, by plane from Tel Aviv, the carrier being not El Al but *Arkia*. The transit takes less than an hour. It's a wonderful experience, this flight, enabling the passenger to look down upon the tumbled wadi-chiseled sands as he flies. The chiseling is done by tremendous torrents of rain that pour down from the mountains during the brief and unpredictable rainy spells and are largely wasted by emptying themselves into the Dead Sea, or by evaporation, but numerous reservoir projects are under study and ambitious plans have been undertaken for piping fresh water down from the Yarkov River, above Tel Aviv. Wells can already provide enough water for drinking purposes and for small farming projects. Despite nature's frowns Israeli planners look at the Negev with solid assurance as the future garden and granary of Israel.

Eilat is at present a "Port of Good Hope," though much has already been done to convert hopes into facts. The first Jewish soldiers reached the coast of the Gulf of Akaba in March, 1949, at which time there was literally nothing there except one stone house that had been occupied for years by a British recluse, a self-made geologist named Williams. He fled with the retreating Bedouins. Today there are nearly 8000 Jewish civilians resident at Eilat and a housing project and a kibbutz have been built. There is a good, first-class seaside hotel, the *Eilat*, under the same management as the Sharon in Herzliya, and also a quality motel called the *Tropicana*. The port has rapidly developed, for it gives Israel direct access to India, Australia and all the East. Tourist lures are not forgotten. At the very start an outdoor theater was built and Jascha Heifetz was one of the first artists to play in it—to the soldiers and port-builders of those pioneer days. Eilat is the only community in Israel where bathing is entirely practicable twelve months in the year and it capitalizes this advantage by promoting skin diving and various other water sports. Glass-bottom boats convey tourists over the submarine forests of white coral. There is a good *Maritime Museum*, and plans are afoot for a novel type of aquarium where viewers will descend into a chamber of glass to watch the polychrome fishes on all sides. The only thing needed for realization of this project is a good angel. Perhaps you are the one.

The political geography of the Gulf of Eilat [Akaba] is fascinating, for at its head four nations come together, Egypt, Saudi Arabia, Hashemite Jordan and Israel. In a two hours' coastal ramble one's feet could touch the soil, or sand, of all four. Akaba, the Jordan port, has attained recent importance as a gateway for much-needed heavy material, including, to mention one item, ten thousand sections of water pipe to carry water from a Hebron well to the traditional Solomon's Pools, near Bethlehem. (This move, incidentally, gave a big boost to Jerusalem's water supply.) Along the Saudi Arabia shore runs the pilgrim road to Mecca. Eilat itself has good potentialities as a deep-sea port, for the water is thirty feet deep close to shore, a priceless boon for shipping.

In these waters are some very curious fish that are caught with traps. One crustacean type, shaped like a cigar box, has a shell so hard that only with difficulty can it be broken except by hammer blows. It is fashioned into actual boxes and sold to tourists.

Among the birds, the oddest type, easily to be seen by visitors, is a sort of sagebrush hen which can run but not fly.

Among local mineral products are kaolin and mica, and among "animal products" the white branch coral mentioned above. This handsome material from the sea is eagerly bought by visitors, and the sands of the Negev, strange as it may seem, are equally in demand, for they are of many brilliant hues and are arranged in fancy designs in bottles, duplicating the color effects of the bottled sands of Alum Bay, on the Isle of Wight, so familiar to tourists visiting England.

It is stimulating to see the vigor of this distant port-in-making, a vigor compounded of enthusiasm and determination. Eilat long ago succeeded in growing some watermelons of extraordinary size, the first of these having been sent as a present to Prime Minister David Ben Gurion. He placed it proudly on a polished table of the Knesset where it was hailed by the Parliament members as a symbol of the future of Israel.

REVISION SUPPLEMENT TO CHAPTER 22

LEBANON's tourist picture is bright and promises to get brighter. The government is 100 per cent behind tourism, partially as a result of the fact that President Shihab, leader of the republic, was previously president of the National Council of Tourism. The current president of the Council is the *son* of the first president of the republic. To cap this resultant "understanding" of tourism, there seems to be a strong feeling that the early future will see the establishment of a Ministry of Tourism, thereby putting tourism on a cabinet post level.

Lebanon needs hotels. The new ones that are going up are not keeping pace with the demand and many hotels are booked to capacity the year round, particularly those frequented by American industrialists and others in the country on business. As of this writing, negotiations have been completed for two major new hotels in Beirut, a Hilton and a Sheraton, supplementing the superlative *Phoenicia* of the IHC (Pan Am) chain; and a group called Sogetour General Tourism Company has recently completed an 11-story hotel on the beach at Beirut. This has 100 rooms, each with air-conditioning and private bath. The roof restaurant has a glorious view of the Mediterranean and the city below. In addition to many shops and a post office on the basement floor, there is an authorized foreign exchange office. This same group is building a tourist area not far from Beirut that will include bungalows and a hotel with swimming pool. Sogetour has interests in Syria and Jordan as well as Lebanon, and also operates a travel agency.

Just a few miles north of Beirut, beyond the Casino du Liban and before you reach Byblos, the *Tabarja Beach* is a tourist city with 100 individual apartments and a large hotel. In addition to the usual vacation luxuries of swimming pools and a beach, the Tabarja Beach resort provides a French and a Lebanese restaurant, all water sports and convention facilities. An advertisement for the resort carries a special note to honeymooners to the effect that "a stay of seven days will get two extra days with the Compliments of the Management." Who said two can't live as cheaply as one?

The maze of roads in and around Beirut is being made less labyrinthine by the addition of wide avenues. In spite of the displacement of some familiar old buildings these avenues are a great step forward. Many avenues have already been completed and others are under way to tie in with the new countryside highways such as that connecting Beirut and Tripoli. In Tripoli, there are plans for a new large hotel to be built by local interests. As of now, however, the old *Montaza* (page 433) is still the best.

Two pertinent comments may conclude this comment on Lebanon: (1) In the festival rundown on page 425 the *Byblos Festival* is mentioned as being "on a tentative basis," but this is now very much a part of the festival scene and takes place annually; (2) the *American University*, mentioned on page 417, continues to play an integral part in the cultural life of Beirut and all Lebanon, and indeed of all the Middle East. Dr. Samuel B. Kirkwood, the new president, succeeded Dr. Burns, who resigned in 1965.

CHAPTER 22

LEBANON, LITTLE GIANT OF THE LEVANT

How Does It Get That Way?

EVERY first-time visitor to Lebanon who hasn't been duly "warned" is pleasantly shocked by what he finds. This smallest Mediterranean country, less in size than Connecticut, is in the heart of the Levant and should, it seems, look Levantine, but actually its capital, Beirut, looks Western, and in many ways it acts Western. Cliché-droppers call it the Paris of the Near East, and it is a fact that no other Eastern Mediterranean city approaches it in wide-open, uninhibited appeal to the pleasure senses. Its new Casino du Liban is Las Vegas-in-the-Levant, the biggest and most pretentious thing of its kind anywhere on Mediterranean shores, not even excepting, in my view, the Casino of Monte Carlo.

How does it get that way? There are some partial answers that do not quite satisfy, so this strange fact of geopolitics must be laid chiefly to a special spirit that specially animates the Lebanese people. It is a spirit of Americanlike urgency, of eagerness to get on, to make money, to build, to boost, to plan for bigger and better things. The words "Great Lebanon," which are occasionally encountered, are as significant as they are startling. They refer to the nation's present boundaries, achieved as a result of World War I and proclaimed by General Gouraud during the period of the French mandate. Prior to that, Small Lebanon, an autonomous region in the shadow of surrounding Turkish oppression and paying annual tribute to Turkey, had consisted only of the country's central, mountainous core. It had included none of the coastal cities, not even Beirut. After 1920, with its natural boundaries from the sea to the crests of the Anti-Lebanon range restored, it was comparatively "Great"; and on December 31, 1946, upon the withdrawal of the last of the Allied troops after World War II, it became the free and independent Republic of Lebanon, with Sheikh Bechara

El Khoury its first president.

Lebanon is as old as the East. It was the home of the Phoenicians, who set their stamp on the whole Mediterranean world and whose Queen Dido founded Carthage. Its cities of Sidon and Tyre, where Tyrian purple was made, were famous ports of commerce at the dawn of civilized time, as also were Beirut and Byblos, farther north. The grandfather of all the alphabets of the world, as distinguished from picture-writing symbols and glyphs, was definitely a Phoenician invention, as was proved beyond doubt by the finding at Byblos of the sarcophagus of King Ahiram. This treasure bears a long inscription in the first alphabet, a 22-letter affair from which our alphabet and all others have descended. Of it the French archeologist, M. R. Dussaud, has said ecstatically, "They [the Phoenicians] worked out a remarkably simple system of symbols in which every letter could, at a glance, be distinguished from all the others. Their very first effort was perfect and the changes which have since been made in it have not improved it." The Ahiram sarcophagus, with its inscription, may be seen, for the wonder it is, in the *Gallery of the Alphabet* in the *National Museum* at Beirut. It is quite as important to us in our daily lives as is the first Gutenberg Bible, ancestor of modern printing.

Lebanon was the Biblical "land of milk and honey," a phrase thought now by scholars to refer to two water springs named Milk and Honey. At any rate springs and cool rushing brooks and rivers are typical of Lebanon today, as they have always been, in contrast to the parched and barren nature of so much Near East terrain. Throughout the Greek and Macedonian and Roman eras, and later in the struggles between Saracens and Crusaders, Lebanon was always a prize of the first importance and hence a place to be fought for tooth and nail and lance and sword. It had great times and grim times, but its ghastliest trial by fire came as recently as the period of World War I, when Ottoman Turkey, siding with imperial Germany, broke her agreements that had allowed Lebanon a measure of autonomy, overran the country and then wrecked, tortured and starved it to such an extent that over a third of its remaining 600,000 inhabitants (many thousands had fled to Egypt, to the Americas and to Australia) were done to death. It was from that dreadful ordeal that Small Lebanon emerged into Great Lebanon and finally Free Lebanon.

It is stated in an official publication that "modern Lebanon was born of the alliance, centuries ago, between the Druses and the Maronites" and this calls for a word of explanation. The Druses are a branch of Islam, originally disciples of Hakim, the Fatimite Caliph, who established this new cult in the year 1000. The Maronites are a Christian sect, being numerous in Lebanon but spread also throughout the world, owing obedience to the Pope. This union of Islam and Christianity, a shotgun marriage at first, the gun being the threat of Mameluke, and then Ottoman, oppression, has worked out well, for there is a tolerance in Lebanon that is rare in the East. Christians, of Maronite and Greek Orthodox faith, greatly predominate in Beirut and the surrounding towns though they all speak Arabic, the official language of Lebanon, as a matter of course. Moslems, of standard and Druse varieties, greatly predominate in, for example, the important city of Tripoli. Each side respects the other's right to freedom of worship and nowhere is this more evident than in the compromise make-up of the government. By law the president must be a Maronite Christian, the Prime Minister a Sunnit Moslem, the Speaker of the House a Shiite Moslem. (The Sunnites accept the Sunna as a true supplement to the Koran; the Shiites reject it.)

French and American influences have both been of vast importance in the development of modern Lebanon. The era of the French mandate brought great material improvement to the country and left its strong cultural stamp. The French *University of St. Joseph* in Beirut, with an *Oriental Library* that is still a sight of the city, did much to make this capital one of the most literate and best-educated cities in the Near East. Similarly, the *American University* in Beirut, called the largest American educational unit outside the United States, has been of immeasurable value to the country, as any Lebanese will be quick to admit. Its successive presidents, Dr. Daniel Bliss, his son Dr. Howard Bliss, Dr. Dodge, Dr. Penrose and currently Dr. Norman Burns, have made an impression on the country that is like widening circles in a pond. City streets are named for them, and an extraordinary number of persons prominent in government and in professional, business and social circles are proud to say, "I was educated at the American University." Through all the country's wars, with their terrible dislocations of life, this university has kept functioning. It occupies an extensive and lovely hillside region overlooking the sea.

How does Lebanon happen? One answer, of course, is its location as gateway to a great portion of the Near and Middle East. To borrow and transfer Prince Metternich's dictum, "if it did not exist it would have to be invented."

Other answers, for what they are worth, may be seen in the brief outline above of the forces and influences that have shaped this country, especially the successful "marriage," maintained for centuries, of two great religions of the human race, religions that have often been bitterly antagonistic. But most of all, the answer is that Lebanon happened because of its own unquenchable determination to happen. It is a West-East land, a Christian-Moslem land, a polyfaith land, a pattern of tolerance; and for us travelers it is a land of rare enticements to holiday pleasures, ranging from those of warm seas to those of deep snow fields.

Tourist Life in Gay Beirut

Relaxation, compounded of sunshine and sea by day, of dining, dancing, gaiety by night, is of the essence in Lebanon's lively capital. It really takes over, for Beirut, with a present population of about 600,000, is a city that needs to be enjoyed, holiday style, rather than "done," tourist style. In addition to the National Museum, with its Alphabet Gallery and much more, there are a few things that are called sights, the Grand Mosque, the Oriental Library, the bizarre Pigeon's Grotto on the shore south of the city, but with the exception of the University, which makes the American bosom swell with pride, and the museum, none of these things seem to me musts. The Grand Mosque is in the heart of the city, easy to see, but as a spectacle it is not the smallest patch on the Grand Mosque of Damascus, which you are sure to see anyway.

It is the gay, unfettered, bathing-suit-and-terrace life of Beirut that takes all comers into camp, with attractive restaurants and a veritable multitude of assorted night clubs for late diversion. The "life of Reilly" centers chiefly about the big hotels, one group in the heart of the city, though bordering the sea, another group on the southern outskirts along the shore drive named Boulevard Jinah that stretches to the airport, but there are also some appealing surf-side establishments quite independent of the hotels. An area of growing popularity is the string of bathing restaurants—*St-Simon, St-Michel, Côte d'Azur, Acapulco*—in the suburb of Ouza'i, reached by the shore drive just mentioned. Nearer town and fronting on the boulevard are *Eden Roc*, a smart hotel-restaurant-night club, and *New Maxim's*, with a view terrace. At another point, on a cliff high above the sea, is the *Ghalaini Restaurant*, a good place for native fare patronized largely by Arabs.

The hill resorts immediately above Beirut are an integral part of the holiday city and in high summer the most important part of it, relegating the beaches to the second-fiddle section. High summer, in the most literal sense of the adjective, starts with a bang in early July when schools let out for the long vacation. From that day on, the splendid corkscrew highway (part of the international road to Damascus) that lifts the hot city dweller up to Aley, Bhamdoun, Sofar and other cool suburban resorts is absolutely packed with cars, bumper to bumper, for a couple of hours every afternoon, and similarly packed every morning with commuters driving down to work. This spectacle is *so* American that one can hardly believe oneself in a country of the East. Mercedes and Jaguars are now the snob cars, but there are tens of thousands, including taxis, of big, shiny ones of the General Motors, Chrysler, Ford families, each looking as if it hadn't yet been broken in, though the speed of them all and the whistling tires on the curves belie this. Lebanon's Westernized prosperity is evidenced by these myriads of modern cars and the country's boosters claim seriously that it has more automobiles in proportion to its population than any other country in the world except the United States and Canada. The claim is not hard to believe as one watches the endless traffic on the summer highways.

It is time to pound in a few brass tacks of the practical facts of tourism:

1. A *passport visa*, obtainable from any Lebanese consulate—the New York consulate is at 9 East 76th Street—is compulsory and the regular one costs five dollars. If, however, you are in possession of a ticket to an outside destination you may secure a transit visa at the airport free, provided your stay is to be no more than 72 hours, but subject to a fee if it is to be longer than that and no more than 15 days.

2. *Lebanese currency* is based on the Lebanese pound, written L.L., now exchangeable at about three to one dollar. The pound is composed of 100 piasters. Notes are printed in denominations of LL1, 5 and up; coins are minted in denominations of 50 piasters (silverish), 25 piasters

(brass) and down. I am happy to state that there is no currency control at the borders.

3. The *Lebanese Tourist Office*, called *Commissariat Général au Tourisme*, has an information booth at the airport, its main office being on Rue Justinien, which is a bit difficult to find on foot. The *taxi rate* within the city is LL4 per ride. The Commissariat publishes a handsomely illustrated annual *Tourist and Hotel Guide for Lebanon*, which is distributed, as the title page states, "by MEA (Middle East Airlines) in all its offices in Lebanon, Europe, America, Africa, the Middle and Far East."

4. This leads me to add a note right here about this company. Rarely have I seen such vigorous and sustained tourist promotion by an air line. It publishes its own 200-page pocket guide, starting with Lebanon and covering all its routes, with many city maps. Twice a month it publishes a tourist guide pamphlet called *Lebanon Fortnightly*, packed with the practicalia of local tourism, and once a month it publishes a general illustrated travel magazine called *Cedarwings*, for the cedar of Lebanon is its symbol. In addition to all this it publishes a spate of lavish brochures and maps in color. MEA's enthusiasm is natural, for Beirut is its home base and it has its own big maintenance plant near the airport, where it services the planes of many air lines and those also of the U.S. Air Force and the U.S. Navy. The company has several offices in Beirut, a handy one being on Rue Minet el-Hosn, near the St. George Hotel. MEA acts as handling agent for a number of international air lines.

Another group, or "team," with active Near East and Middle East services is *Air Liban* and *Lebanese International Airways*, called LIA for short, these being closely associated with *Air France*. Since, on my current visit, I flew to Beirut by Air France I went one afternoon to the office of this company, parent of Air Liban, on Rue Jouvinel at the big square called Bab Edriss to check my ticket and found it a ready source of general information. I asked one of the men about the UNESCO quarters in a southwestern part of the city and he promptly said, "I'm just going home and I don't live too far from there. I have a scooter. Hop on and I'll give you a ride." I did hop on and he gave me a ride I shall never forget, weaving in and out of Beirut's ever perilous traffic, dodging Arab vendors and Cadillacs with equal agility. He ended up by showing me far more than the UNESCO Building. Our tour, I hanging on behind my host for dear life, included the big *Cité Sportive*, with its stadium and Olympic pool, the *Turf Club*, the *Race Track* and much else. He ended up by scootering me back to my hotel, which was nowhere near his home. This was "the extra mile," and I was glowing with satisfaction. What's more, I got back in one piece.

To add a note, perhaps anticlimactic, on international air traffic that concerns tourist planning, I may mention that *both MEA and Air Liban fly from Beirut to the Arab portion of Jerusalem in one hour. Air France flies from Beirut to Damascus in a quick thirty minutes.*

5. *Tourist costs*, I would say, are in the lower medium range in Lebanon. In Beirut's super-de luxe *Hotel Phoenicia Intercontinental*, leader of them all, a room and bath is now about $10 to $13 single, $13 to $17 double. First-class hotels may run at about 60 or 65 per cent of such rates, second-class hotels at less than half. There is a service charge of 12 per cent and most tourists sweeten this with small direct tips. If, in a restaurant, no service charge is included on the bill a tip of 15 per cent should be given.

6. *Tourist shopping* is perhaps not a major sport in Beirut but tempting goods of the East are certainly to be had. These include, to amplify the mention in Chapter 3, gold and silver articles, brocades, Persian rugs, articles in leather and in brass and inlaid mosaic work. The old part of town has a nest of jampacked Eastern bazaar streets, but these are not a patch on those in Cairo, Damascus or Istanbul.

The *hotels* of Beirut are legion, the legion of tourism, and there seems to be no end to the building of new ones. The top one, as I've said, is the Phoenicia Intercontinental, the only Near East link in the 30-link chain of the Intercontinental Hotels Corporation, owned by Pan American Airways. This 14-story, 325-room luxury hotel, designed by the widely known architect Edward F. Stone and costing about $10,000,000, is more than merely luxurious. It is of distinguished and unusual style. Its main part, rising in a tall *white* block, given life by balconies with every room on all sides, is topped by a roof that extends in brooding manner over the whole thing. The two lower floors, running for a great distance along the sea front, are largely walled by plate glass and on the upper of the two is an open patio, or court of marble, with a heated swimming pool, surrounded by furnished cabañas. The extensive lobby is one flight up, reached by escalator from the main entrance on a wide

street ascending from the sea front. Leading from it are the Age d'Or
(Golden Age) Rôtisserie and Oriental Café. From another corner of it
one enters L'Amérique Coffee Shop, which is open twenty hours a day
for light, inexpensive meals. A big mural of early Americana by Roy
Little depicts Indians, Pilgrims, Washington Crossing the Delaware, a
Mississippi paddle-wheeler and Abraham Lincoln, complete with stove-
pipe hat. The top floor, with superb sea view, is given over to a sophisticated cocktail lounge called La Panache, which word means the plumes
of a Crusader's helmet. Below the lobby is a supper club, Le Paon Rouge
(The Red Peacock), and there is also a bar called Sous la Mer (Under
the Sea) which circles the glass wall of the swimming pool. Here, if the
hour is right and luck with you, you'll watch your fellow-guests, mer-
maids, mermen and mermoppets, as in an aquarium. Maybe, as you sip,
you can introduce yourself to some desirable creature by lip talk. On
the same level as the Undersea Bar is a branch of the Intra Bank, a room
of very fancy, undulating design which the bank's founder, Yusuf
Bedas, calls "the world's sexiest bank." There are luxury shops and various services on both lower floors, there's a 400-seat theater—and so on.
All in all, the Phoenicia is a tourist city in itself.

It is impossible here to discuss all of Beirut's seven other hotels of
luxury class and thirty or more recommendable ones of lesser standing,
but I must mention a few that especially catch the eye or appeal to the
budget. The *St. George* (or St-Georges) is a holiday hotel of luxury
rating located on a point that is three quarters surrounded by the sea.
Each of its hundred rooms has bath, shower and a private terrace, this
last being of supreme interest in such a location, where the distant
mountain views and the holiday fun down below vie for your attention.
Breakfast may be had on one's personal terrace, the other meals, as well
as drinks and high tea, on the large public terrace just above the lapping
waves. These terrace meals—orchestra, dancing, gaiety, sea breezes,
French food and wines—may, of course be enjoyed whether or not you
are a guest and they should prove high points in your Mediterranean
travels. The hotel's private beach and large raft are conspicuous centers
of salt-water fun.

The St. George is only a slingshot distant from the Phoenicia and
halfway between them, on the curving shore road called Rue Minet el-
Hosen, is *Hotel Alcazar*, which has a luxury rating but advertises its

policy, with considerable fairness I think, as "Luxury Without De Luxe Prices." A good meal for five, with local wine, enjoyed in its upstairs dining room closely overlooking the harbor, cost me only $17.50. *Hotel Le Beryte*, in this same neighborhood but one lift back from the shore, is a popular family-type place of low tariffs, with a pleasant streetside dining room and terrace. The *Excelsior*, luxury class, and the *Palm Beach*, first class, are other hotels of the central group, and a lodging place that you might not expect to find and use is the *American University Alumni Club*, which is open to all and keeps its rates low.

On the shore boulevard, approaching the string of beaches, are numerous front hotels, two of luxury quality being the *Carlton* and the *Riviera*. The Carlton especially, with its magnificent outlook and its full range of luxurious amenities, has impressed me most favorably, though I have never stayed there. Two of luxury standing but not on the front are the *Commodore*, with an important night club, *La Casbah*, and the *Bristol*. The latter, long famous for its cuisine, has one feature you would never expect, namely a small ice-skating rink, with snack bar, in the basement.

An oddity of most Beirut hotels, though not applicable to the Phoenicia, is that all rooms, front or back, more desirable or less, are priced the same in any given hotel. This is strange indeed, but several proprietors assured me that it is a fact, so it seems to be a case of "first come first served."

Restaurants of Beirut, as distinguished from hotel dining rooms, are not *quite* as numerous as hotels, but there are plenty of them, both European and Arabic. The *Lucullus*, at 118 Avenue des Français, serves fine French food in a humble setting. In the cluster of streets centered by Rue de Phénicie and Rue Ibn Sina near the Phoenicia Hotel there are dozens of all kinds and flavors and atmospheres, for example *Ristorante Italiano* and *Quo Vadis* (both Italian), *Rhenanie* (German), *Espagnol* (Spanish), and in case you'd like to try a meal of an Iron Curtain country the *Bucarest*, featuring Romanian food. In the coastal Raouché section overlooking Pigeon Rocks there are dozens more. The *Sindbad*, for one, serves good European food, specializing on chicken, and the *Yildizlar* serves Turkish food. Avenue des Français, near the harbor, abounds in nightclub restaurants, with dancing and show, the better ones being *Kit Kat*, *Lido* and *Ève*.

If you enjoy, as I do, eating, now and again, the food of the country you are in, try the *Ajami Restaurant*, on Rue Trablos near the harbor. Here, guided by a Lebanese resident, I started off with a jigger of *arak*, the Lebanese national drink, which is much like the Greek ouzo, a grape alcohol and anise "bomb," that looks like water but turns white when water is poured into it. Thus off to a good start, I partook of *tabouli*, a finely chopped salad based on tomatoes and tinctured with parsley, *shawarma* and *hommos*, being slices of highly seasoned lamb garnished by a paste of chick peas and some *bourghol* (a sort of wheat mash) and seasoned with mint, garlic, sesame oil and I know not what other spices. For dessert I had a very sweet cake, called, if I spell it right, *usmaliyeh*. It was a good meal from start to finish. On another occasion, eating at the seaside Ghalaini Restaurant, mentioned earlier in the beach roster, I partook of such delicacies as *kebi*, a wheat and meat concoction garnished with *hashíshit bahar* (pickled sea grass from the adjacent rocks in the surf), and *beit jain* with *tihiny* (eggplant with sesame oil), lubricated with a pleasant local wine. If the foreign words make you menu-dizzy you may regain your composure with ham and eggs in the Phoenicia's American coffee shop.

The night clubs of Beirut floor me. I am tempted to give up, for they *swarm* like flying ants, but I'll describe one, which is often called the best of its type, and then will escort you to the flashy Casino du Liban. The one I refer to is *Les Caves du Roy* (The King's Cellars), in the *Excelsior Hotel*. This is a tiny, plushy dive where you may eat and drink very well, and expensively, and be well entertained. The chief attraction, however, is its famous bartender, Aldo Mancini. He has been there a long time, and long may he remain, for he has delighted thousands of clients. Aside from a gift with liquors, a sparkling personality and a large repertoire of jokes, he is a magician. Before your eyes, as you stand at the bar, he does things that can't be done, lots of them.

The *Casino du Liban*, standing on a cliff at Maameltein above the Bay of Djounié some fourteen miles up the coast from Beirut, is unique in the Mediterranean in its grandiose proportions and splendors. Opening in 1961, it startled all comers by its spectacular nature, so unexpected at the far end of the Tourist Sea, importing as it did the best and most expensive talent, whole droves of it. A large French troupe I saw there doing a typical Parisian revue had just completed its run at Las Vegas.

In June, 1962, the ceremony of choosing Miss Europe was held at the Casino but this was only one of a long series of headline events. The gambling salons have the same look, the same tense atmosphere, that such rooms have everywhere. At most of the roulette tables the minimum stake is LL5, the maximum 500. I was content to let others lose their money, as plenty of clients were doing, and will do, for the hope of a big killing "springs eternal."

Festivals and *Shows* are making their appearance in Lebanon in increasing numbers. One, which made its bow in 1962 and has become an annual fixture, is the *International Flower Show*, held in Hotel Phoenicia early in May, flowers being brought in from all over Lebanon and flown in from many countries, far and near. Another, so far on a tentative basis, is the *Byblos Carnival*, in the coastal city of Byblos, which will be further mentioned in this chapter. A third, also on a trial or tentative basis, is in the *Grotto of Jïita*, easily reached (thirteen miles) by a side road from the coastal highway a little north of Beirut. Regardless of plans for a festival this Grotto of Jïita has become, in its own right, a major tourist attraction since its opening to the public in 1959–60. Discovered in 1836 by an American named Thomson, it was not seriously considered as a tourist possibility until 1955, when the Tourist Commissariat joined with a group of Lebanese spelunkers and set to work in earnest to undertake the development of the grotto, which had proved to be an extensive chain of underground lakes. In 1958 it was illuminated and finally revealed to the public, which now makes the tour at the rate of a hundred thousand a year or more. Visitors see the grotto's wonders from a boat on one of the subterranean lakes. If the proposed Grotto Festival becomes an annual event it will be a major seasonal attraction (July), but in any case the grotto has proved itself Lebanon's answer to Majorca's Dragon Caves. (Lebanon's major event of the festival calendar, *Baalbek International Festival of Music and Drama*, will be presented in the ensuing section.)

From Beirut to Incredible Baalbek

Baalbek is among the most improbable of all the great remnants of the past in Mediterranean lands. Founded by Phoenicians as a shrine to the

god Baal and developed by successive peoples, especially and most surprisingly, by the Romans, it is not only improbable but highly "seeable."
Even the confirmed ruin-hater is won over by its dramatic temples and
its cyclopean blocks of stone, which modern machinery could hardly
cope with. Situated fifty-two miles from Beirut, but only twenty-four
from the junction point of the main Beirut-Damascus highway it is easy
to reach and the tour-taker finds many interesting sights along the way.
We shall look at some of them.

Aley (2800 feet altitude), the first important hill resort on the main
highway, boasts some twenty hotels and a smart casino, with a gay
swimming pool for daylight fun and a night club for the late and early
hours.

Bhamdoun (3650 feet) is proud of its *Hotel Ambassador*, which looms
up like a cliff upon a cliff, very high above a verdant valley, and is a
focus of attraction, especially in summer, when it engages topflight
dance orchestras. *Shepherd's Hotel* is of the same high grade and there
are many others.

Sofar (4300 feet), which name means "Whistle," has its *Grand Hotel
Casino Sofar* and several smaller hostelries. The resort is considerably
quieter than Bhamdoun, less gay but more restful. One may pick one's
hill resort—there are many more in the Lebanon range—"according to
taste."

Beyond Sofar the main turnpike, after reaching an altitude of almost a
mile at *Dahr-el-Baidar*, a stretch often blocked with snow in winter, descends to the *Bekaa*, a long, broad valley, about three thousand feet
above the sea that separates the Lebanon and Anti-Lebanon ranges. The
junction town in the valley is *Chtaura*, which is a favorite resort of
honeymooners. You will see why when you regale yourself with a long,
cool drink in the de luxe *Chtaura Park Hotel*, or even in the park-café
of *Hotel Massabki*, which is of far humbler type but is cooled by a clear
stream, complete with ducks. This siesta may be followed by a walk in
the bosky paths near by.

Southeast from Chtaura the international pike leads through a wild
pass to the Syrian frontier (Lebanese and Syrian customs here) and so
in another twenty miles to Damascus. North from Chtaura, the direction that now concerns us, runs the Bekaa Highway to Zahlé, about four
miles distant, and Baalbek, a further twenty miles.

Zahlé, in the Berdouni Valley, is a place of sheer delight. It has a good hotel, the *Kadri*, with its pleasant and very civilized restaurant, but this we may leave to whom it may concern. The picnic restaurants that line both sides of the rushing Berdouni Stream—some streamlets run *through* restaurant booths under the tables—are the goals for all who halt in Zahlé on the way to or from Baalbek. At these restaurants, of which there are half a dozen bordering the little torrent, joy is unconfined. There's music in the air, not "when the infant morn is nigh" but at almost all other times of day and evening during the summer season. Arak is the accepted preprandial stimulant and he or she who does not quickly develop a fine tenor or soprano voice under its influence has no vocal cords at all. With the arak go various hors d'oeuvres, such delicacies as the now familiar kebi and luscious, gooey things like *labni* and *mtabal* that tease the taste buds. The meal itself, for most of these places are real restaurants rather than cafés, may be as ordered, chicken fried in oil—my mouth waters now as I set this down—being the usual central theme. A well-known valley wine called *ksara*, popular both in white and red, is the usual beverage.

The best bet for this Bekaa trip *if* it must be made in one day is to start early from Beirut, say seven o'clock, hasten right along to Baalbek in the morning, spend a couple of hours seeing its mighty ruins, with another hour added for the famous store of Papa George, and then drive back to Zahlé for lunch. If, weary from ruin-walking, you then spend three hours during the heat of the day eating, drinking and singing beside the chattering Berdouni that is as it should be.

By the above stress on Zahlé I do not wish to belittle Baalbek itself, the chief goal of all valley excursionists. The place is of sure appeal, one of the greatest aggregations of historic ruins in the world and now the setting of an annual summer festival.

Phoenicians from beyond the Anti-Lebanon were settled in this upper portion of the Bekaa as early as 1000 B.C. and built the first temple in the place they named Baalbek, meaning Lord (Baal) of the Bekaa. The Greeks and then the Romans called it Heliopolis, but during the period of Arab ascendancy, many centuries later, it reverted to its original Phoenician name. The location of Baalbek, protected as it is by two lofty mountain ranges, Lebanon and Anti-Lebanon, and watered by two rivers, the Orontes, flowing north to the Mediterranean via

Homs and Antioch, and the Leonte (now called Litani) flowing south
to the Mediterranean, its mouth near Tyre, proved ideal for a great
city and Baalbek did indeed grow great, though now it is an insignificant village. Some historians estimate that at the time of Caesar
and Augustus it may have boasted a quarter of a million inhabitants.
This fact is one of its notes of "improbability." "Why," one asks,
"should the Romans have devoted such effort and money to building
up a great city, with huge temples, in a place so far from the coast
and at that time so inaccessible, even though it was favored by nature?"

It was the emperor Nero, of all people, who first undertook, in
57 A.D., the construction of temples to the Roman gods, but it was not
until a century later that Antoninus Pius and his successors, up to and
including Caracalla, erected to Jupiter and Bacchus the magnificent
temples whose ruins we now admire. The work went on intermittently
for more than two hundred years and ironically enough was completed,
if such massive works can ever be considered completed, just about
at the end of the pagan era.

The heyday of Baalbek lasted but a few decades, when Emperor
Constantine, having embraced the new Christian faith, converted the
imposing hexagonal court into a church, ruining its architectural
symmetry in the process. Some sixty years later Theodosius converted
the central court into a basilica and about a century and a half after
that Justinian filched a number of the granite pillars of the hexagonal
court to embellish his mighty project in Constantinople, the Church
of St. Sophia. At a much later date the Arabs converted the whole
ensemble into a citadel, with a mosque adjacent to the *Temple of
Bacchus*. Recurrent earthquakes, including the terrible one of 1759,
sieges, thefts, drastic alterations, as for instance the destruction by the
Arabs of the grand stairway to provide room for a trench to bring
water to the mosque's ablutions court, robbed Baalbek of much of its
grandeur, and even as recently as 1901–5 German archeologists removed many of the temple's choicest treasures to Berlin. Some Baalbek
arches, it is said, were incorporated in the Reichstag of imperial days.
The wonder is, however, not that so much is gone but that so much
remains. Six magnificent columns of the *Temple of Jupiter* still stand
in mute testimony to the established fact that this was the largest
temple ever erected by the Romans to their god of gods.

To understand even the barest elements of the wonders of Baalbek one needs a first-rate guide who speaks real English, not guide patois. Such a man exists—I hope he will not let me down by vanishing—in the person of Lofti S. Haidar, who has been showing these ruins to visitors with unstinted devotion for more than thirty years. He is the chief *dragoman officiel touristique*, a man to secure, if you can, through advance application to the Tourist Commissariat in Beirut. To me Lofti offered many tidbits of information not too readily found in conventional guidebooks. I will report a few of them.

The pillars, of which there were once eighty-four of rose-colored granite in and around the hexagonal court and fifty-four of gray granite in the Temple of Jupiter, came, as you have guessed, from Aswan in Upper Egypt. They were floated on rafts (to accept the guide's figures) twelve hundred miles on the Nile and the sea to Tripoli and then *rolled*, on low parallel walls specially built, from Tripoli to Homs and thence to Baalbek, a hundred and fifty miles. It seems utterly incredible, physically impossible, but so do many other things about Baalbek which our own eyes may see and our senses confirm. There are, for instance, in one of the enclosure walls, three gigantic blocks of hewn limestone, each weighing eight hundred tons or more, each measuring about sixty-five feet by fourteen by twelve. They are comfortably reposing twenty feet above the ground, where they have rested for over seventeen centuries. A still larger stone, over seventy feet long and weighing almost twelve hundred tons, may be seen in a quarry outside the village. Stones weighing four hundred tons each were so common that some of them were used as a mere promenade. When built into the walls these vast monoliths were almost as perfectly fitted together as the famous blocks of Inca masonry in Peru's Cuzco.

Baalbek developed a very profitable racket, Lofti told me, in Roman times. Beautiful maidens were brought here as vestal virgins. They were converted into bacchantes and taught to do the dance of the seven veils, Rome's strip tease, for the entertainment of pilgrims. It was but a step then to convert the bacchantes into willing prostitutes, and the Temple of Bacchus into a sacred brothel. The pilgrims paid well for the intimate services of the bacchantes and most of the money went to the priests, who doubled as procurers, and to the fund for the upkeep and development of the temple.

A small but exquisite *Temple of Venus*, some two hundred yards outside the main ensemble, was shown to me by Lofti and it served as a sort of extra dividend. It is a heptagonal affair with convex sides and lovely monolithic columns adorned with Corinthian capitals. It is noteworthy that *all* the columns of Baalbek, from these dainty ones of Venus to the forty-foot ones of Jupiter, were of the Corinthian order.

In the little dust-blown park surrounding the Temple of Venus four or five tiny girls, none I judged over eight or nine years of age, treated me to a concert on improvised drums and tin-pan tambourines. Like an innocent abroad I couldn't be sure whether this was for fun or for purpose of gain, but to play safe I tossed them a few coins. With squeals of delight they pounced on them. The concert was over. The "musicians" will grow up to be poor village women, for they will have no opportunity to be anything else, but I couldn't help suspecting that if this were the era of imperial and bacchanalian Rome they would likely grow up to be vestals—and then bacchantes.

Baalbek's *International Festival of Music and Drama*, now with almost a decade of annual development, occurs in July and August, with intermittent periods of entertainment by world-famous orchestras, ballet troupes and opera and drama companies. These special groups, engaged for periods of three days to a week, are supplemented by a Sound-and-Light Show that runs for a much longer season, from April to October, English versions being presented each Saturday evening. This is Lebanon's first venture in this popular form of entertainment and the response has been good, as well it should be, for Baalbek's setting rivals, point by point, the settings of the Athens and Cairo shows. Baalbek's best hotel, but don't look for luxury, is the 30-room *Palmyra*, followed by the still smaller *Khawam*.

The Coast, the Cedars and the High Snow

Lebanon's roads, responding to the demands of the thousands of cars seen everywhere, are improving steadily. In addition to those already mentioned there is a trunk road that skirts the entire coastline, from below Tyre in the south to above Tripoli in the north, though its improvement to a fine modern highway, a work first undertaken through the Point Four Program, is far from completed. A most ambitious new mountain highway is under construction (this is bound to be a very long job) from *Jezzine*, in the mountains east of Sidon, to *Bcharré* and *the Cedars* in the northern mountains, east of Tripoli. This road, now extending in its new form only as far as Zahlé, will run at altitudes between 2700 and 6000 feet and will be of prime interest to travelers. *Beit-ed-Din*, about halfway between the two points just named, should on no account be missed. Its palace, or perhaps the word should be pluralized since it is an ensemble of building upon elaborate building, garden upon fountained garden, is something of a masterpiece of Arab art, and its location, on a peak three thousand feet above sea level dominating a deep valley, is reminiscent, though I hate to inject such a thought, of Hitler's aerie above Berchtesgaden. The palace was built about a hundred and thirty years ago by Emir Bechir, a Druse leader who was a powerful sovereign of Lebanon. The romantically decorated tomb of the emir's wife, who was said to have been a Christian, is seen in a garden below the palace.

Tyre and *Sidon*, known today as *Sour* and *Saïda*, are the chief points of tourist interest on the southern coast of Lebanon, but their interest lies more in what they were than in what they are. The vestiges of their ancient Phoenician days of greatness, when their merchant fleets roamed all the known seas, are meager now, but ruins from medieval times are impressive. In Tyre there are remains of the huge Crusader church where Frederick Barbarossa is supposed to have been entombed after his death in Cilicia in 1190, and in Sidon, on the harbor islet called *Kalat-el-Bahr*, is a strikingly interesting sea castle of the thirteenth century.

The Lebanon coast north of Beirut is a chain of exciting things to see, link upon link. Here are some of them.

1. *Nahr-el-Kelb*, a ravine close to the mouth of a river, is a place of awesome significance in history, for this narrow, dramatic valley, with an imposing cliff on its south side, has been the road of conquerors since the beginning of written history and all of the conquerors have taken pains to record their achievements by inscriptions chiseled into the rock. Here one may see, though it takes rugged scrambling to reach them all, inscriptions in Egyptian, Assyrian, Latin, Greek, Arabic,

French and English. A bilingual inscription in the two last-named languages commemorates the passage of the victorious Allies in 1918, at the conclusion of World War I, and another, in French, recalls the victory of 1920 over the cherifian troops. A special placque does honor to General Gouraud, who proclaimed Great Lebanon that same year. From World War II an inscription in English records that "In June–July, 1941, the First Australian Corps captured Damour, while British, Indian, Australian and Free French troops captured Damascus, bringing freedom to Syria and Lebanon." But the climactic inscription is the one commemorating the final departure of the last of the Allied troops on December 31, 1946. From that day Great Lebanon, completely independent and sovereign, was on her own. It is a colorful drama in many acts that the cliffs of Nahr-el-Kelb reveal.

2. *Djounié*, a port village of minor significance, is backed by a beautiful amphitheater of hills and on the crest is a huge statue to Our Lady of Lebanon, emphasizing again the hold of the Christian faith on a great portion of the people of this member country of the Arab League.

3. *Maameltein*, just north of Djounié, has already been noted as the location of the grandiose Casino du Liban.

4. *Jbail*, named by the Greeks *Byblos*, is a place of historic ruins second only to Baalbek itself. This port was the first Phoenician capital. It is the place where the previously mentioned tomb of Ahiram was discovered by French archeologists, the tomb with the world's first inscription in alphabetic letters. This find dates from the thirteenth century B.C., fifty years or so before the siege of Troy. Byblos was important at many periods of history, even from as early as the Twelfth Dynasty of Egypt (a ruined temple dates from that era), but it reached a relatively recent time of glory under the Crusaders. From that period dates the bulky castle whose roof provides a superb view to reward the climb to it. The walls of the castle are reinforced by scores of large columns which the Crusaders appropriated from Roman temples. In the village adjacent to the castle there is a Maronite church, in regular use, which the Crusaders built from the handy and abundant ruins left by earlier civilizations. There is a good possibility, as stated above, that Byblos will soon become the scene of an annual carnival, Nice-in-the-Levant.

5. *Windmills*, miles and miles of them, line the coast like sentinels from Chekka clear to the suburbs of Tripoli and the first-time beholder is puzzled by the fact that they are all on the very edge of the sea, sometimes even lapped or lashed by the surf. Their purpose is to pump salt water into hundreds of little reservoirs cut into the rocks or built upon them. The briny water evaporates to leave a residue of salt and one learns that the salt industry is of some importance to the economy of this local strip of the coast. When the Lebanese government undertook, some years ago, to suppress this industry as needless and archaic a storm of popular anger compelled the authorities to reconsider.

6. *Tripoli*, little known to the travel world, deserves a larger "audience." It is a big, clean, appealing city of definitely Moslem persuasion, with the striking *Castle of St. Gilles*, once a stronghold of the Crusaders, to give it background. For practical foreground, in case riding and ruins have roused complaints from the inner man, the visitor may drop in at one of the interesting confectionery-cafés on the main street for an exotic dish called *kenafy-khouchta*. It is a cheese and cream and syrup concoction and even though you may now be recoiling in horror I am almost prepared to guarantee that you will find it delicious. If not, or if a real meal seems to be in order, the leading hotel, by name *Hotel Montaza*, may be visited.

The mountain road that leads up and inland from Tripoli to Ehden, Bcharré and the Cedars has a lot of climbing to do, for Bcharré is about 4900 feet above sea level and the Cedars 6500 feet. The road passes through—you would hardly expect it—*apple country* of real and increasing importance. With the gradual planting of two hundred thousand new trees of American stock, the government is making apple raising big business. Through the mountain towns of Ehden and Kfar Sghab one climbs on and up to reach Bcharré, a larger community which is of special interest as the birthplace of Kahlil Gibran, the mystic whose beautiful poetry has made a deep impression on the literary world. Gibran's dictum, "Do whatever you will so long as you do it beautifully," is somewhat akin to St. Augustine's injunction to his followers, "Love God and do as you please." Gibran spent part of his youth in America and studied later in Paris. Strangely enough the English language became his chosen literary medium before he was twenty and few persons of poetic gift even born to the language have ever achieved such mastery of its metrics and sound and such beauty of expression. He died in 1931 at the age of forty-eight and his body was taken to his native Bcharré. Here it was enshrined, bringing fame to his home village.

The scenery throughout this mountain region is magnificent, yet by no means savage. One is astonished again and again, when rounding a curve in the road, to come upon a village perched precariously on a ledge half a mile above some valley, the remainder of the ledge and all its sloping hinterland a mass of waving, golden wheat. Flowing water is seen on every side, and it should be mentioned that not far short of the Cedars there is a calcareous grotto of great beauty, reached by a spectacular mountain path. It is called the *Kadiche Grotto* and its stalactites and stalagmites are the equal, on a far more limited scale, of those in the Grotto of Jiïta.

The *Cedars of Lebanon*, in a small but very lovely grove, are almost the last of their race in their name land, though many thousands of these forest aristocrats are now found on the Island of Cyprus. The branches of all the trees in this grove lie almost flat, tier on tier, because of being weighted down by snow for months every winter. There is remarkable dignity about the trees, the dignity of a serene old age, for some of them have been standing for fifteen centuries. No more than four hundred of them can now be counted, even by the most optimistic census takers, in this surviving grove.

It is pathetic, in a way, that one must now motor nearly a hundred miles from Beirut to find "the Cedars," in quotes, whereas once all the Lebanon range was covered by millions of them. In another way their destruction has meant prosperity for the country, since the broad fields of grain that all motorists admire have replaced the forests. It was during the early Arab era, in the seventh century, that the great change began and hundreds of years of toil have completed the alteration. In the earlier era of the extensive forests, Lebanon cedar wood was famous for two or three thousand years. Hiram, King of Tyre, had cedar wood cut and shipped to his fellow-king Solomon for the building of the temple in Jerusalem. The Pharaohs of several Egyptian dynasties imported cedar for beams and also for coffins, and cedar resin for embalming purposes.

In Lebanon itself cedar was used lavishly in Baalbek. The hexagonal court, for instance, was roofed with it. The cedar is still the beloved symbol of Lebanon. It appears in the design of the national flag, a symmetrical tree on a snow-white background between two bands of red. The white background itself is a further symbol, for it is said that the word Lebanon, in the language of the old Samaritans, meant *white*—for snow.

Above the Cedars is a *télésiège*, or chair lift, built in 1950 by the Tourist Commission, that hoists all comers in half an hour to a height almost ten thousand feet above sea level. The cable is a mile and two-thirds in length, mostly at a steep gradient. I took this télésiège one early July day and found deep snow in many patches near and on the summit. Winter sports, especially skiing, are becoming a more and more popular attraction of Lebanon. In the Cedars area, where the roads are kept clear by snowplows all winter long, skiing is regularly practiced from December to mid-May, sometimes even till the first days of June. The slopes of *Mount Hermon*, which is 9200 feet high, offer some very long runs to the skier, who must be of the rugged type, since there is no ski lift here to pamper him. Ski lifts *have* been built at three rather widely separated points, namely *Laklouk*, reached by a climbing road from Jbail, *Faraya*, similarly reached from Djounié, and *Baidar*, which is hardly more than twenty miles from the capital by the regular highway to Bhamdoun and Chtaura.

The summer visitor to the Cedars and its mountain lift should, if possible, get a very early start from Beirut, for the ride is a long one. If he can muzzle his appetite long enough he may lunch marvelously (arak, kebi, labni, fried chicken, wine, fruit) in an unpretentious but delightful restaurant named *Sarkis*, at Ehden. There is no style at all to this place but there is a wonderful hominess about it, with women preparing the food before one's eyes, and there is, as one comes to expect everywhere in Lebanon, *running water*. A swift stream, as cold as mountain snow, flows directly through the restaurant.

Lebanon at all levels is a country to fall in love with. For the haver of a sheer good time there are few Mediterranean lands to match it. The temples of Baalbek and Byblos and the palace of Beit-ed-Din may therefore be considered thrown in as outright extras.

CHAPTER 23

DAMASCUS, THE AGE-OLD SYRIAN CAPITAL

Damascus, the capital of Syria, competes with several other places, including Lebanon's Baalbek and Byblos, in calling itself the world's oldest city. Its claim is far better than most, since it is still, as it has been without a break since the first predawn of recorded time, a *city*. It has never shrunk to the proportions of a small town or village, and today, with 400,000 inhabitants, it remains the largest city, with the sole exception of Beirut, for hundreds of miles around. *Aleppo*, far to the north but lying also within the borders of Syria, might challenge this statement, since it, too, has close to 400,000 inhabitants.

Syria traces its ancestry to a fusion, some four or five thousand years ago, of Aramites and Canaanites, with some tincture of the still earlier Chaldean blood. The fusion produced the Phoenician race, which was later overwhelmed by Egyptian conquerors, and the mixed population of the region fell ultimately under the sway of Rome. In 638 A.D., Roman civilization was in turn overwhelmed by the Arabs, heady with their new religion of Islam, and from that day to this, except for two centuries of intermittent disturbance from the invading Crusaders, it has been a major citadel of the Moslem faith. Damascus has even called itself "Capital of the Islam and the Arab world," a claim which quickly raises Cairo's eyebrows in protest.

In relatively modern times Syria was, of course, a mere province of the Ottoman Empire. The turmoil resulting from Turkish control was followed by the confusions of World War I, the French mandate period and World War II, after which Syria, like Lebanon, finally found complete independence as recently as 1946. The exact date of the final withdrawal of Allied troops in that year was April 17, which is now a national holiday like Bastille Day in France or Independence Day in America.

The traveler who flies from Beirut to Damascus in half an hour, perhaps by the Air France semiweekly Caravelle service, or who crosses the mountains by car or bus in three hours, including halts at both the Lebanese and Syrian douanes, finds himself transported in that short space of time from one world to another, and almost, it seems, from one planet to another. The contrast is like a blow to one's sense of what is credible. My own visit to Damascus (as a youth I had visited the city during the era of withering Ottoman control) happened to bring me there in the period of Ramadan, that greatest fast-and-feast of the Moslem year, which may come at *any* season because it is geared to the *lunar* year of 354 days (12 times 29½).

Without attempting any full reportage on Ramadan I may mention briefly that during this 29-day period, from earliest dawn (when a white hair can be distinguished, at arm's length, from a black one) until sunset, the faithful Moslem may not eat *anything* and he may not drink *anything*, even a few drops of water, and in strict theory he may not swallow his saliva—a form of "drinking"—though outside control of this would seem to be as difficult as thought control. He may not smoke a single puff and he may not kiss his wife, much less have intercourse with her. The least infraction of any of the harsh rules, if detected, causes the observer of Ramadan to lose a day and he must make it up by fasting two extra days. A serious infraction, if detected, may result, in a few fanatical regions, in imprisonment.

At dusk every day during Ramadan a cannon is fired in Damascus, and you will surely hear it if you are there at that season. It indicates that the day's fast is over. The citizens then *rush* to eat and drink and smoke. An hour before dawn you are awakened by another cannon shot. It is fired to wake the faithful so that they may eat before the daylight deadline and do their early prayers and ablutions.

Obviously Ramadan creates the worst hardship when it comes in the long days of summer, as it did when I was there. Damascus is on the same parallel of latitude as Atlanta, Georgia, and the nights of June and early July are only about eight hours long. It is almost tragic to think of sixteen consecutive hours of total fasting from nourishment and drink in the hottest days of the year, while work, including outdoor labor in the sun, must go on and on. I watched the waterless construction laborers who were at work on a new hotel in Damascus and wondered how they could possibly take it. The temperature, during many hours, lurked close to the hundred-degree mark. There is no doubt at all that thousands of upper-class people in all the Moslem lands flout the rules of Ramadan in whole or in part, but tens of thousands of the laboring class strive honestly to observe them. One hopes that the celestial bookkeeper of Islam gives each of them a gold star for such Spartan devotion, for it makes the most rigorous Lenten fasting of the Christian world a mere token, by comparison.

Damascus is an outright gift of the River Barada as Cairo is a gift of the Nile. Rising in the Anti-Lebanon Mountains, it flows eastward, emerging from a gorge shortly before entering the city's limits. The Greeks called the Barada by a more romantic name, Chrysorrhoas, or Golden River, presumably because of the wealth its waters brought the region, though some historians think the river did literally yield gold, as the Pactolus of Lydia did for Croesus. Barad water is piped by channels and conduits to all parts of the city. Aided by several lesser branches, the river then proceeds to irrigate the extensive surrounding plain called the Ghouta, providing an area of luxuriant orchards, vineyards and gardens for many miles, to lose itself finally in the marshy Ateybeh, or Meadow Lakes.

Perhaps, before entering the heart of the city, I should make a halt to set down a few *tourist practicalia*.

To enter Syria (its association with Egypt as a part of the United Arab Republic was dissolved in 1961, but re-established in a *federation*, with Iraq included, in 1963) a visa must be secured. The currency of Syria is the Syrian pound, divided, as usual in the Arab countries, into 100 piasters, the exchange rate now being about 3½ pounds to the dollar. The leading hotels of Damascus are the *Cattan* and the *New Semiramis*, both close to the river, the *New Omayad*, in a quiet residential area, and the older, centrally located *Orient Palace*, which was long the cock of the roost and has had to modernize itself to compete with the newer hotels. Its rooms are very spacious, in the old manner, and the hotel is well kept up and still popular, with a very good cuisine. Among the city's separate restaurants of repute are the *Tour d'Argent*, the *Socrate* (Socrates) and *L'Oasis*, all of these with French fare to go with their French names. There is a good restaurant also at the airport. Among night spots are the *Caravan* and the *New Semiramis* cabarets and the *Orient Club*, where dancing, drinking and gaming are the sports of the night. Hotel costs are very moderate. There is a standard service charge of 10 per cent. Near the central hotels and the river there is an office of *Tourism Service*.

Shopping seems to me a far more important tourist sport in Damascus than in Beirut and for certain special possibilities of top interest I would refer the reader to the coverage of Syria in the "Shops and Souks" section of Chapter 3. It is enough to say here that the city has bequeathed its name to the world's dictionaries as noun, adjective and verb in such words as damask and damascene, which is an obvious tribute to the craftsmanship of her artisans.

The crowded metropolis huddles, as it always has, close to the Barada, nearly all of the older portions being on the right bank. In the western portion and also in an area just south of the central citadel Damascus has two considerable business sections, with impressive public buildings, office buildings, banks and shops, while the modern residential sections, on higher ground to the northwest, reveal surprising wealth and elegance, but it is for the ancient *East* that visitors come to this city and the crowded, hit-or-miss, enthralling East is very much in evidence. One enters it, as through a door, only a hundred yards or so from some of the tourist hotels, and from the central *Merjeh Square*. In the middle of that civic nucleus, by the way, is a curious bronze column that is obviously a holdover from an earlier era, the era of Turkish dominance. It was erected by order of Sultan Abdul Hamid to commemorate the establishment of a telegraph line from Damascus to the Holy Cities of Islam, Mecca and Medina. On top of the column is the oddest touch of all, a clumsy, topheavy reproduction of the Yildiz Mosque in Istanbul. The monument was cast in Germany, for Kaiser Wilhelm and Abdul Hamid were pals in the political chess games of that period.

From Merjeh Square, or, more directly, from the Orient Palace Hotel, one should make one's way by an imposing modern boulevard to the entrance to the *Souk Hamidieh*. There you are in the heart of the East and on every side you hear and feel the throb of that amazing "organ." But a special qualifying word is needed. Do not do your exploring of Damascus on a Friday, the Moslems' Holy Day, for then the heart of the bazaars beats with feeble pulse, only the Christian shops, as a rule, being open for business.

The Souk Hamidieh is a hodgepodge of shops and stalls, jammed elbow to elbow, on both sides of a covered thoroughfare fifty feet wide and two fifths of a mile long. The covering is of corrugated metal, now pierced by thousands of jagged holes, many from various bombardments, others from "natural causes," which let in plenty of sunlight—and on wet days rain drippings. The life of this bazaar is eminently Oriental but many of the goods are European. Adjacent bazaars, such as *Souk Arsouniyeh* (hardware and narghiles, which are pipes enabling the smoker to draw smoke through water), *Souk El Harir* (silks), *Souk Es Sagha* (jewelry and fine work in gold and silver) and *Souk El Bezourieh* (Turkish delight and all sorts of sweets) are even more satisfying than the vast Hamidieh. One more famous thoroughfare of bazaars cries for notice here, namely *Souk Midhat Pasha,* which is none other than the "street called Straight" of the Biblical narrative. In Arabic its popular name is Derb El Moustakim, which means Straight Street.

It will be recalled that Saul of Tarsus, "breathing out threatenings and slaughter against the disciples of the Lord" (Acts 9:1–27), had come to Damascus to arrest any followers of Jesus and bring them bound to Jerusalem. On the highway, just short of Damascus, "there shined round about him a light from heaven" by which he was blinded—and converted. His companions led him to the house of one Judas in the street called Straight, and to that house came, by heavenly command, a disciple named Ananias to cure Saul of his blindness and baptize him. So Saul the Persecutor became Paul the Apostle. A mosque now rises on the exact site—they say—of the house of Judas. Be that as it may, the street called Straight is certainly right there where it has always been and it is a very "bedlam of interest." Its multitudinous bazaars are not especially alluring but its mad maelstrom of traffic, from camels to Cadillacs, and of races, from Arabian to Scandinavian to Californian, is something not to be missed. You will be choked by dust and deafened by assorted cacophonies—and will think these afflictions well compensated by the spectacle which Straight Street offers.

To tidy up the matter of orientation, the Souk Hamidieh leads from the modern boulevard I have mentioned past the huge citadel, of minor interest, directly to the Grand Mosque, or Omayad Mosque (see below), one of the noblest and most significant structures in the Near East. The street called Straight is exactly parallel to the Souk Hamidieh but continues three times as far, veering not a hair to right or left. Between these two main bazaar streets lies a tangle of lesser (but no less crowded) souks, with the Azem Palace, of which more presently, in their center; and a bit to the west of this tangle a rather surprising sector, the *Harika Quarter*, of banks, commercial agencies and bustling business offices. With the above features in mind the unguided stroller in Damascus (but dragomans are always to be had through your hotel) may reasonably hope to avoid getting lost—permanently. There is a Green Guide booklet called *Damascus, Gate of a World*, purchasable in Damascus and Beirut, and its map and legend will be far clearer than any words of orientation.

The *Grand Mosque* is not just "one more." It is a sight of such rare beauty, matching its vast size, that it is often labeled *the* most beautiful in the Moslem world, though Istanbul would surely dispute the claim. On this site was once a pagan temple, then a synagogue, then a Christian church and finally this mosque, which has been severely burned and rebuilt no less than six times. A legacy of the church, which was dedicated to John the Baptist, is the head of that crier-in-the-wilderness enshrined in a sarcophagus surrounded by a grill of gilded bronze. This is the chief sight within the mosque, and Moslems revere the relic, entertaining no doubts whatever of its authenticity. It should be understood, as was mentioned in connection with Jerusalem, that Islam is always ready to honor the important figures of the Christian faith, especially Christ himself. One of the three tall minarets of the Grand Mosque is officially named the "Jesus Minaret," this being the point, one is soberly told, upon which Jesus shall descend on the Judgment Day to confound Antichrist.

The visitor feels that the Grand Mosque is somewhat commercialized. He pays a Syrian pound for an entrance ticket, with use of the usual *babouches*, or scuff-slippers, unless he prefers to leave his shoes at the door and enter stocking-footed, and another pound for a guide, whose bored and boring prattle, if my experience was typical, proves to be worth approximately nothing. But one's grouch is quickly dissipated by the splendor of the building. Its dimensions are 435 feet by 126 and its height is 63 feet, the roof resting on massive columns of beautiful marble. The interior was decorated with utmost lavishness by the Omayad caliphs, who ransacked the world for the finest materials and the most skilled artists, and in spite of fires and one bad earthquake some of the ancient mosaic work remains.

Adjacent to the mosque is the main court, larger than the mosque itself, and surrounding this are arcades, from which open numerous student chambers, for like many another mosque in all Moslem lands this serves as a school and a hostelry as well as a house of worship.

One may leave the mosque by the Lime Burners' Portal on the north side to visit the *Mausoleum of Saladin*. The German Kaiser visited Damascus in 1898 and curried Moslem favor by having a silver lamp hung above this tomb. Modesty did not prevent the giver from having the lamp ornamented with his own initials, intertwined with those of Sultan Abdul Hamid. He also had a crown of laurel, in gilded bronze, placed upon the tomb, but this tribute was "lifted" by the Allied troops when they entered Damascus on October 2, 1918, and has not been seen since. One wishes that they had replaced the crown with another that would not have lacerated Allied feelings, for Saladin, or Salah-ed-Din-el-Ayoubi, to state his full name, was one of the great and noble figures of all time. The accounts of his magnanimity, chivalry and tolerance, matching his genius in war against the Crusaders, are as glowing from his enemies as from his friends. A medieval French tribute, typical of many, seems worth quoting. It says of him, "*Il fut moult bon Sarazin, car il fut moult large et moult emohnier et pitous de cuer et de grant bontey.*" (He was a very good Saracen, for he was very liberal and very generous and compassionate of heart and of great kindness.)

Directly south of the Grand Mosque, as I have said, lying in the center of a warren of souks, lies the *Azem Palace*, the city's finest example of eighteenth-century secular Arab architecture. It was built by Essad Pasha-al-Azem, who was governor of Damascus and who also held the exalted post of Chief of the Pilgrims when great pilgrimages to Mecca were organized. Although considerably damaged by fire in 1925 it has been intelligently restored and it still gives the Westerner a wonderfully clear idea of the construction of a Moslem mansion. In briefest explanation, it consists of two main portions, the *salaamlek,* or outer part, for welcoming and entertaining guests, and the *haramlek*, or private, inner part, reached by a tortuous passage with a succession of three doors. This latter was strictly reserved for the wives, children and servants, and of course for their lord and master, the great pasha. There is also an annex section with an elaborate hammam and in this, as I was informed, local folk may still take their Turkish bath. Servants' halls and two kitchens complete the rambling ensemble. Bought some years ago by the government for about half a million Syrian pounds, the Azem Palace is today a very lovely and peaceful thing to see, worth far more to any visitor than the modest admission charge. Unlike the Grand Mosque, it gives one no feeling of being mulcted as a tourist.

South of the city, on the line of the ancient walls, one may find, with the aid of a taxi, for it is rather a long distance to walk, the so-called *Church of St. Paul*, where, as the hostile Jews waited at the gates to kill the apostle because of his preaching the new religion, "the disciples took him by night, and let him down by the wall in a basket." The church, or tiny chapel, is built into a portion of the ancient wall. The aperture through which Paul was supposedly lowered is not exactly a window, for an outer casing shuts out virtually all light, but it is a hole large enough for a man's body to be eased through, and Paul, we know, was rather small of stature. The escape is vividly pictured in relief on the wall. If Paul did not actually escape by this aperture it was certainly from one something like it in the very near neighborhood.

To the southwest of Damascus, about two miles distant, is the suburban *Midan Quarter*, which is almost as different from central Damascus as that is different from Beirut. Midan is the historic gathering place for pilgrims from many parts of the Moslem world intent on setting out on the arduous pilgrimage to Mecca, over nine hundred miles distant by direct geographical line. In the past, sometimes caravans of ten thousand pilgrims and twenty-thousand camels, mules and horses assembled here for the dangerous trek. There are now different ways, including air ways, of making the journey, but the Midan Quarter has not lost its old characteristics. Its people are perhaps more fanatically loyal to old Moslem traditions than are any others of the widespread family of Islam. Midanese look with reproach and even horror at the "heretical" folk of Damascus, whose women wear only thin veils, through which the face may be faintly seen. A Midan woman who appeared on the street with a veil like that, even on the hottest day, would be almost risking her life, and her husband or father would be consumed with shame. Midan veils are thick veils, proper veils, with the narrowest possible eye slit that will permit the woman to see where she is going. And we may be sure that Midan men and women observe Ramadan with utmost rigor.

used these

the

(3) the Bosporus section of the city;

REVISION SUPPLEMENT TO CHAPTERS 24 AND 25

THE Turkish Tourism and Information Office at 500 Fifth Avenue, New York City, as mentioned on page 37, dispenses excellent information about Turkey, including a booklet of Turkish recipes so that you may prepare your palate prior to the trip or entertain your friends with a post-trip Turkish meal and tales of Turkey.

Although Istanbul is a popular stop on most Mediterranean cruise itineraries, other parts of the country are becoming more accessible with the increase of Aegean sea cruises, including those operated by the *Sun Line,* the *Epirotiki Line,* the *Chandris Line* and other of the Greek Islands' cruise lines. The *Turkish Maritime Lines'* 19-knot ferry, which can carry 100 cars and 584 passengers, runs between Istanbul, Izmir, Piraeus and Brindisi, making the trip through five seas, the Adriatic, Ionian, Mediterranean, Aegean and the Sea of Marmara.

In addition to the airline service discussed earlier in the Supplement, *Pakistan Airlines* began service to Turkey on its London-Karachi run in mid-1966. Two flights a week stop at Istanbul.

The national program to welcome visitors to Turkey, which includes radio announcements to the Turkish people, has been so effective that some persons have opened their homes to visitors. For example, many townsfolk of *Emirgan,* an Istanbul suburb (see page 465), offer bed and breakfast in their homes for as little as $4 per night. All rooms made available are in homes fronting on that marvelous "sea-river," the Bosporus, and can be had by writing to Emirgan Guest Houses, Dedirmentepe #1, Emirgan, Istanbul.

A list of specific measures in the tourism program set up by the Turkish government includes having all signs written in English, French and German in addition to the native Turkish. Roadside plaques are appearing on monuments and areas of particular interest advising the visitor of its nature and history. School gardens are being used as camp sites for visitors during vacation periods and teachers of foreign languages work in government tourist offices during the summer months.

Roads are being improved, museum hours are longer, and restrictions have been put into effect at excavations to prevent the taking of artifacts from Turkey so that museums may have the benefit of them for the public.

All government departments are working together for improved tourist relations. The Ministry of Communications is setting up information offices and taking special care of cruise ships in port and of airline passengers arriving at the terminal. Telephone service is kept active 24 hours a day and duty-free shops are appearing at all ports. The Office of Religious Affairs is making every effort to open all religious buildings, whether for viewing their art and architecture or for worship. The Ministry of the Interior is responsible for improving roads. The building of camp sites and information offices in local areas is left to the municipal governments affected. Five of the newer ones are in Antalya, Izmir, Ephesus, Göreme (the Valley of the Cones) and Mersin.

Efforts are being made to simplify the customs and money declarations by making it possible for the traveler to obtain the forms (now printed in English and French, in addition to Turkish) in advance and mail them either to the Turkish Tourism and Information Office in New York City or to the head office in Ankara (see page 446) prior to taking off. The currency restrictions have been relaxed to allow taking out of Turkey some of the gold items you may wish to purchase in the souks (market stalls). You are now allowed to buy up to 5000 lire worth, which is about $500, being five times as much as you may bring back duty-free to the States!

In keeping with its policy of encouraging tourism, the government has offered tax incentives and loans to many hotel builders, with the result that hotels have been cropping up all over Turkey. In Istanbul, the newest is the *Harem*, the largest hotel erected thus far in the Asiatic (trans-Bosporus) section of the city, located near Chamlija Hill (page 448). Reached by ferry in half an hour from the European side, the Harem provides a magnificent view of the Bosporus and the Sea of Marmara. It is five stories high and all rooms have private bath. Facilities of the hotel include, in addition to restaurant, bar and full entertainment, a Turkish bath and sauna.

The 450-room *Taksim Hotel*, now under construction on Taksim Square, heart of Istanbul, is scheduled for completion in mid-1967. The restaurant, grillroom, snack bar and terrace tea garden will be topped by a rooftop nightclub overlooking the Bosporus and the Sea of Marmara. In addition to indoor parking for 100 cars, the hotel will have a swimming pool and a gymnasium. The *Tarabya Hotel*'s 250 rooms already offer luxury accommodations to visitors. Opened early in 1966 on the shores of the Bosporus, the hotel's conference halls offer simultaneous translation facilities in four languages.

In the center of Izmir, perhaps Turkey's most sought tourist goal after Istanbul and Ankara, the *Grand Hotel Ephese* (known in Turkish as the Büyük Efes Oteli) has recently opened with 326 rooms, a banquet hall for 400, a restaurant, bar and nightclub, fresh-water swimming pool served by its own bar accommodating about 200 guests, and a nearby pool for children. On the ninth (top) floor, there is a sun deck and restaurant if you choose to drink in more than the magnificent view.

From Izmir you can make a trip inland to Sardis, where Harvard and Cornell excavation teams have uncovered a bazaar from a Turkish city that was destroyed in the 7th century B.C. City planning experts are interested in the discovery of a completely walled-in area of shops and industries as well as a separate residential area. The shopping center is believed to have been planned during the reign of Gyges, who is presumably buried in the Royal Cemetery near Sardis. Preliminary excavations as of this writing have not yet yielded his chamber, but digging continues and by the time of your visit no doubt newer, or older, finds will have come to light.

Farther south, in a coastal section called Marmaris and known to many as the holiday paradise of Turkey, is the *Hotel Lidya*, which deserves mention as a modern resort, located right on the beach, with all modern appointments. Each guest has a beach cabana in addition to a gorgeous view from his room either seaward or toward the rich forests. In addition to boat and road connections with other parts of Turkey, there are daily boat services between Marmaris and the Greek island of Rhodes.

The "tourist imagination" of the government is evidenced in a novel feature: Dotted around Istanbul, there are 10 areas originally planned for employees of Turkish banks and insurance companies to use as vacation areas and now opened to allot up to 30 per cent of the occupancy to foreign visitors (such as us). These tourist centers, called camps but not in our sense of the word, provide an exciting and extremely inexpensive way to vacation in Turkey, with an opportunity to meet its people. Any group of seven visitors may apply for accommodations at one of the tourism areas by writing to the Turkish Tourism and Information Office. Facilities at the camps include tourist bungalows each sleeping two people, with room for children if you're taking them along. For a modest $4 or $5 per day all meals are provided, along with use of the beach, bar and all entertainment facilities. Although English is not spoken fluently by all guests, many will speak a fair brand of English and the director will most certainly speak it well. There will be a doctor on the premises.

In case thoughts of food should cross your mind, or tempt your palate, be aware of a gustatory delight in Istanbul. As you pass over the Gálata Bridge linger (as you're sure to do anyway) to watch the local fishermen who flock to the bridge. As you wait, you may watch "your" fish being caught, unhooked and cooked before your eyes. *Bon appetit!* Fresher fish you'll never eat. Another comment on eating is not so cheerful, for the restaurant and coffee shop referred to on page 451 as being about to open in the *Gálata Tower* have *not* yet opened and no exact prediction about the date is available. A complete revamping of the Tower, involving architectural problems, has been undertaken and this has caused great delays, but perhaps by the time of your visit the famous, historic Tower will once again be open, new restaurant, coffee shop and all. If the tower is essentially on your sightseeing list rather than your dining list don't let its present closing disturb you too much, for two other great goals are very much open and more interesting than ever. Both are palaces. *Topkapi Palace* is one of them, and what a wealth of artifacts it displays. In the Third Treasury Department of this palace items are on display that have been until recently in the Central Bank of Turkey (since 1928) for safekeeping. The collection includes a fabulous array of emeralds, diamonds, pearls and rubies that once belonged to the sultans of Turkey. Among them are the Kasikçi Diamond, one of the world's largest gems, and some gold candlesticks weighing over 105 pounds, each set with 6282 diamonds! Imagine the table that would support these candlesticks. The Apartment of the Mantle of Felicity shows Ottoman interior decoration at its best. The

Apartment was built by Sultan Mehmet as a private office and was regularly used by him and his successors. Ceremonies connected with the ascension to the throne and demonstrations of allegiance to the sultan took place here. Following the conquest of Egypt by Sultan Selim I, in 1917, objects and relics sacred to Islam, including a mantle worn by the Prophet, were collected and put in the Apartment.

The *Dolmabahce Palace* (page 461) is the second of the palaces to which I referred above. The text is gloomy about its being closed to the public, perhaps for years, but *it is again open*, its marvelous museum in full operation. That is my reason for mentioning it here, as an item of current good news. Its treasures and curiosities are described, or at least hinted at, in the text and need not be here reported.

In the southeastern part of Turkey, between Ankara and Konya, the *Sultan Han Caravanserai*, one of the world's oldest inns, has been restored. Built by the Seljuki King Alaeddin Keykubat in 1228, the inn has offered hospitality to kings, conquering heroes and paupers alike for centuries. In its first years of operation, legend has it that the first three days' lodging was "on the house," bills being presented only after the third day. The inn is divided into two parts by a small mosque, one side having been used for storage and livery stables, the other for lodging. It has a VIP room with 32 columns and the typical Seljuki pointed arches, in addition to excellent examples of Seljuki artists' stone carvings on the walls.

Theater in Turkey can be a very exciting experience. In Istanbul, the Municipal Theater, started in 1914 under the leadership of France's André Antoine, performs in the western manner. Recent seasons have included performances of Clare Boothe Luce's play *The Women* and works by Ustinov, Hugo, Molière and Shakespeare among others. Performances for children have included such plays as *The Pied Piper* and *The Magic Top*. An important part of the Municipal Theater is the conservatory where budding actors and actresses learn their art and the best ones win the chance to perform in the Municipal Theater, perhaps in Hamlet. Summer performances are held at *Rumelihisar*, a castle on the shores of the Bosporus, built in 1415 for the conquest of Byzantium. It makes a breathtaking setting for plays.

During the summer, Istanbul is the scene of an International Youth Festival where companies come from all over Europe. The Turkish

National Ballet and Opera, with headquarters in Ankara, sends its people all over the world, though reserving ample time for performances at home. The new Opera House in Istanbul is home for the City Opera, which gives regular performances and has a remarkably large following. You may obtain tickets at the box office or through your hotel and it is best to get them in advance. The National Theater, of first-rate standing, is centered in six theaters of Ankara, though it may be enjoyed in Izmir, Bursa and other cities while on tour. It has also played in European capitals, offering popular European plays as well as plays by native-born authors. Also in Ankara, two private companies, the Ankara Art Theater and the Arena Theater, give plays during the season.

In case you wish to plan your tour after your arrival in Istanbul you will find good tour agencies ready to help you. *Antur Agency*, with head office in Istanbul, provides a number of tours lasting from two to 21 days, the longer ones including Greek islands in the Aegean or a full itinerary in Anatolia. *Egetur Agency*, with head offices in Izmir, at Atatürk Caddesi 126, will provide a wide variety of full-day and half-day tours as well as longer tours of the Turkish Riviera or the Aegean. Arrangements can easily be made on arrival at either city, or by writing ahead.

If you are a hunter, be advised that a hunting tour can be arranged by *Cem Travel and Tourist Agency*, with offices in Istanbul, at Halaskâr Gazi Caddesi 68. These tours extend to every part of Turkey, enabling you—who knows?—to bag a wild boar or leopard, or perhaps a brace of partridges. Hunting guns and 500 cartridges may be brought into Turkey along with hunting dogs, but both must be registered and also checked out of the country when you leave. Fishing, especially around Antalya, is noteworthy, fresh-water trout being found in many streams.

I must not leave the subject of special tours without mentioning British Petroleum Company's *Kervansaray Chain* of accommodations for motorists, for the company has launched an ambitious project of *Mocamps*, otherwise known as Motor Camps, throughout Turkey. Arranged in conjunction with gas stations, the 16 camps now in operation provide camping areas near frontier-entry posts and beaches for those families who have succumbed to the recent "camping epidemic." A special note on the Mocamp information folder states that "all campers are welcome even during the closed season, when the staff of our Mocamps will try to make the visitors as comfortable as possible." What more could motor campers ask?

CHAPTER 24

TURKEY, ONE COUNTRY ON TWO CONTINENTS

Some Things to Know on Entering

TURKEY, straddling the Bosporus to occupy territory both in Europe and Asia, is one of America's best friends, which is the first thing to know. In any case, you sense it right off, for the generality applies in a personal way to your particular self as a part of the West. On my first day in Istanbul on my current visit I dropped into a crowded café-bar on the main street, Istaklal Caddesi (Independence Street), eager to see this facet of Turkish life and to wet my whistle with a raki. I ordered the raki, to set me afire, and a good Turkish beer to put out the fire. I gave the waiter a note for ten Turkish liras and he handed me some assorted change. Then a man standing at the bar sidled toward me diffidently and asked, in good English, how much he had given me in change.

"I don't mean to be inquisitive," he said, "but you may not understand our money and I want to be sure you got all you should. As a rule these fellows don't cheat, but a little mistake could happen, you know." I showed him the change and he said it was correct for what I had ordered. Then he stayed and talked. He proved to be a Turkish specialist who had taught ecology for some years in a U.S. university. The conversation concluded by his urging me to go with him to the apartment of a brother-in-law nearby and have a glass of wine. I went with him, and the brother-in-law, who spoke French but no English, was as urgently cordial as he. His wife joined us and presently, showing the same eager hospitality, she invited me to come to dinner with the family the following evening. My raki-and-beer had started a chain reaction, and I report this incident merely to illustrate Turkish friendliness to the U.S. and its traveling "samples," you and me.

Now for some tourist facts.

1. You need no visa.

2. The official tourist organization of the Turkish Government has this name and address: *Ministry of Press, Broadcasting and Tourism, Tourist Department, Ankara,* and if you would like to cope with its Turkish name here it is *Basin-Yayin ve Turizm Genel Müdürlügü.* So there you have it. This efficient organization has branch offices all over Turkey, with an information office in Istanbul handily located in the entrance arcade of Hotel Hilton Istanbul. The New York office, to repeat this from Chapter 3, is at the very "crossroads" of Manhattan, at 500 Fifth Avenue, corner of 42nd Street. Another active promoter of tourism is the *General Tourism Bank* (Genel Turizm Bankasi) of Istanbul, which owns important tourist installations and plays a close supporting role with the Tourist Department.

3. Turkish currency is the lira, which is Turkish for pound, and this is divided into 100 kurush. The coins are in denominations of 1, 2½, 5, 10, 25, 50 kurush and 1 lira. Bank notes are in denominations of 2½, 5, 10, 50, 100, 500 and 1000 liras. The last one I take on faith, having never seen it. The present exchange rate is 9 liras to the dollar, making the lira worth 11 cents plus. You have to declare your money, travelers checks and valuables such as gold and jewelry, and may bring in no more than 200 liras in Turkish money. When you leave you may take out only what you have brought in, minus what you have spent. You may not take out articles of gold (except charms), platinum or other precious metals (except silver) bought in Turkey, a regulation which is impossible to enforce and serves chiefly as an irritant, for the Istanbul bazaars are replete with wonderful gold and platinum articles. One wishes that Turkey would liberalize all of its currency and customs laws, as, indeed, *it now shows some clear signs of doing.* All Turks who deal with foreign tourists detest certain outmoded regulations (perhaps already is the discard) with which *they* have to cope. "The rules drive us nuts," said a Turkish hotel man to me, but the only thing you and I need remember is to *keep* our slips showing what moneys or checks we have exchanged, so that they may be shown to the currency officer on leaving. And of course we should not exchange into liras more money that we may reasonably expect to use in Turkey.

4. *Tourist costs,* such as for lodging, meals and transportation, are *very low* in Turkey.

5. The *Turkish language* is one by itself, utterly different from Arabic. The letters used (ever since the Atatürk reforms) are Latin ones like ours, so you can at least read Turkish signs and more or less pronounce them, even if you don't know what they mean. Some things to know about pronunciation are the following: The vowels have a Continental sound except the *undotted i,* which is pronounced rather like a "weak *a,*" as in sofa. The *dotted i* is like *i* in hit. Consonants are more tricky. The letter *c* is pronounced like *j* in jam, while *ç* (c with cedilla) is like *ch.* G is hard; *j* is soft; *ş* (with cedilla) is like *sh.* These chapters on Turkey may sometimes use Turkish spellings, as in cami (pronounced jami and meaning mosque), and sometimes English, as in Chamlija Hill (spelled in Turkish Çamlica). They just cannot take time out to worry about it.

6. The *hotels of Istanbul* are completely dominated by the magnificent *Hilton Istanbul,* dating from 1955 but still far and away Turkey's leading hotel, especially since the addition, in 1963, of an ultramodern new wing with 144 rooms. It is truly wonderful, both in intrinsic quality and in its setting. It has everything you would expect and more, huge and luxurious public rooms, with a broad terrace facing the Bosporus and Asia-cross-the-way, a bank, a post office, a luxury restaurant, a glassed-in night club, an inexpensive coffee shop, a late-hours rooftop supper club, a lot of tourist and air line offices, shops galore and three hundred bedrooms, baths and balconies, very many of these latter with stunning views of the Bosporus and its ever busy traffic. Among its travel offices are *Türk Ekspres,* which is the American Express correspondent, and in the entrance arcade the *Turkish Government Tourist Office.* *Cook* is very near by, on Cumhuriyet Caddesi, and at Number 8 on the same avenue is a very active agency called *Turist Seyahat,* headed by an energetic and widely traveled Turkish expert named Tevfik Sencer. *Pan American Airways* and *Turkish Airlines* (THY for Türk Hava Yollari) are in the arcade, KLM in the hotel, *Air France* a short distance away facing the big central Taksim Square. (Strictly, the last letter in Yollari above should be an undotted *i,* pronounced like a final *a.*) The Tourist Office, source of tourist information for the whole country, is a great asset to the Hilton, a great convenience to guests. It is well and courteously run.

There are other fine hotels in Istanbul, notably the first-class modern

Divan, very near the Hilton, and the *Çinar Hotel,* a luxury resort place on the beach near the airport. In 1963 a big new one, the luxurious 360-room *Hotel Tarabya,* opened at Tarabya, a suburb on the Bosporus.

Among secondary hotels are the *Park,* with close-up view of the Bosporus, and the *Plaza.* Across the Bosporus, on a beautiful belvedere height called Chamlija (Çamlica) Hill, another big hotel is *planned,* but this plan may not mature for years. By contrast, Suadiye Beach, on the Asian side, has a large resort hotel, called also the *Suadiye,* that has recently developed great popularity. This appealing place, reachable by ferry and then taxi, rims the blue Sea of Marmara and is a delightful goal, its main dining room being practically "at sea."

7. *Restaurants* and *night life* are subjects too demanding to be sandwiched in here and shall be considered at the end of this chapter.

8. *Printed information* on Istanbul's current tourist life, with various lists and useful addresses, is found in a publication called *The Week in Istanbul,* distributed free.

9. *Local transportation* is by taxi and trolleybus—the clumsy old street cars are seen no longer—and by *dolmus cabs,* which are jitneys similar to those in Israel and Cyprus. You pay nearly nothing for a single seat and get off at any point you like by signaling to the driver. They are easy to use, especially in going from the street outside the Hilton's gate to Taksim Square and down that roaring main thoroughfare that I have mentioned, Istaklal Caddesi. You flag the first one you see—they sometimes flow in a veritable stream—and merely murmur "Gálatasaráy" (the last syllable is like eye), which is their turnaround point at the far end of the main street. The dolmus system works also all along the road paralleling the Bosporus, from Taksim Square to Sariyer, beyond which suburb the Bosporus opens out to the Black Sea. Scooting minibusses also cover this route.

The ferries are reasonably easy to master. They all leave from the Gálata Bridge and all have their destinations plainly marked. Some traverse the whole length of the Bosporus; some cross to Üsküdar or to Kadiköy and the railway terminal; some serve the beautiful holiday islands in the Sea of Marmara called Princes Isles (Büjükada is the chief one), affording a pleasant day or half-day trip of picnic type. For more individual travel on the water the tourist may take delight in hiring a caïque, or Turkish skiff. Scores of these charmingly painted and gilded "Istanbul gondolas" lurk about the Gálata Bridge eager for your patronage.

One link of transportation in the modern quarter of the city may come as a surprise. There is a good, though short, subway called *The Tunnel*, which climbs from a point near the Gálata Bridge to the ridge of Beyoglu, along which, for three quarters of a mile, runs Istaklal Caddesi, extending from Tunnel Square, the upper terminus of the little subway, to Taksim.

Istanbul, Metropolis in Europe and Asia

Turkey covers 296,500 square miles, beating Texas by 10 per cent, but less than 5 per cent of its area is in Europe. The other 95 per cent fills the whole of Asia Minor, which the Turks call Anatolia. Greater Istanbul, mostly on the European side but with large suburban sections on the Asian side, links the two continents, connecting them with a veritable skein of busy ferries, though there is plenty of talk of a future bridge or tunnel. At its narrowest point the Bosporus is only about one third of a mile wide.

For all the things that unite to create glamor the Istanbul that was Constantinople, and before that Byzantium, has few rivals anywhere, and if such a statement seems born of rash enthusiasm you are invited to pause and consider.

Historical background is surely one of the components of glamor. For more than eleven centuries, from its "second founding" by Constantine the Great in 328 A.D. as capital of the Eastern Empire to its capture by the Ottoman Turks under Mohammed II the Conqueror in 1453, Constantinople was the most important city in the world, though there was a brief, unhappy interlude when it was taken by Venice, under Doge Enrico Dandolo, and held for a few decades. Despite that reverse it remained the undisputed center of Greek culture and scholarship, which carried the lamp of civilization during the Dark Ages. Its capture by the Turks dispersed Greek culture throughout Europe, giving strong impetus to the Renaissance movement, but Moslem civilization gradually gave Constantinople a new glamor, superimposed upon the old. The building of splendid mosques and imperial palaces gave the ancient city a different look and a new skyline, which has become etched on the mind of travel almost as clearly as has the skyline of New York. In 1922, Sultan Mohammed VI was deposed, and the following year Mustafa Kemal, who later took the name Atatürk (i.e. Father of the Turks), became president of the Turkish Republic. With the zeal of a prophet and the force of a whirlwind he set about to effect the Westernization of Turkey and the sweeping changes he introduced soon created a "modern background" for Constantinople to go with its new-old name Istanbul. Ankara became the capital of the republic, but Istanbul remains its great metropolis.

Ancient modes of dress were abolished. The wearing of the fez became illegal. Women were given extensive rights and were strongly encouraged to discard the veil, a suggestion with which the city folk, if not the peasants, eagerly complied. Education was nationalized, Western legal codes were introduced and Parliament adopted the Gregorian calendar, the 24-hour day, and even the Western Sunday (rather than Friday) as the day for business closing. It also adopted the Latin alphabet in place of the old Arabic script. Turkey is still a thoroughly Moslem land but it is thoroughly Western, too, and thus unique in the family of nations. It is a free country. You don't have to be cautious about what you say or what you write in letters and post cards, lest a heavy hand be laid upon your shoulder.

So much for the background of glamor. Its scenic ingredients in Istanbul speak for themselves, for in splendor of location no large city, unless possibly Rio de Janeiro, can surpass it and not more than three or four—one thinks of Naples, Sydney, San Francisco, Hong Kong—can claim to equal it.

The geography of glamor needs a brief blackboard talk to make Istanbul quite clear and understandable to the first-time visitor. Fortunately a printed "talk" of book length in *English* was prepared and published some years ago. The direct but unexciting title of this excellent volume is *Tourist's Guide to Istanbul*. Its authors are Rakim Ziyaoglu, Heyreddin Lokmanoglu and Emin Erer, its translator—into readable English—Dr. Malcolm Burr. Some such handbook for Istanbul is essential. A so-called "Tourists' Plan of Istanbul," being a clear map of the city and its two-continent environs, is also available at any of the city's bookstores. For oral information and help in seeing the sights one should visit the Tourist Office in the Hilton arcade and even before leaving the States one should contact the aforementioned Turkish Information Office in New York (500 Fifth Avenue). There the intending visitor may secure a handful of provocative folders and brochures to study en route.

The name of the metropolis needs explanation. *Istanbul* (*n* is preferred by the Turks to *m*) derives from three Greek words, *Eis tēn Polin*, meaning "Into the City," so the first syllable is actually only a preposition, and the middle syllable the definite article. *Bul* is polis (city), as in metro*polis*.

Old Istanbul rises on a rounded promontory at the very "tip of Europe," a promontory that is bounded on the north by the famous *Golden Horn*, an offshoot of the Bosporus; on the east by the Bosporus itself, a 17-mile "salt river" connecting the Sea of Marmara with the Black Sea; on the south by the Sea of Marmara; and on the west by the small remainder of Turkey-in-Europe. On the other side of the Golden Horn, crossed by the world-known *Gálata Bridge* (nowadays a modern bridge of boats, replacing the earlier wooden one) and by the newer bridge named for Atatürk, is the mercantile quarter called Gálata, rising steeply to the modern quarter of smart shops, hotels, consulates, travel and air line offices, restaurants and night clubs, the quarter that was long known as *Pera* and is now called *Beyoglu*. As seen from the Old City, this Gálata-Beyoglu complex is dominated by a round, medieval tower built originally in 597 but dating in its present form from the period when this hill was a fortified stronghold of Genoese merchants. It is variously called the *Gálata Tower*, the Genoese Tower and the Tower of Christ. Recently it has submitted to a surprising innovation, or perhaps "indignity." A coffee house and restaurant have been built on its 220-foot summit and three elevators are being installed in preparation for its early opening.

Greater Istanbul stretches along the whole Bosporus on both the European and Asiatic sides. Directly across the Bosporus from Beyoglu is the suburb of Skutari, now officially *Üsküdar*, a place that is mellow with age, and adjacent to that a newer suburb called *Haydar Pasha*, which is important to know as the terminus-near-Europe of all the railway lines that make their way through Anatolia.

Taksim, mentioned several times above, needs here a special note of its own, for this large square, or circle—it is almost an Etoile, in the Parisian sense—is the hub of Istanbul's Westernism. The name, a popular one, is taken from that of a great octagonal reservoir (now a garden-park) on the high point just above it. Its literal meaning is "Division," referring to the "windshed," where the winds divide. The square's name in little-used officialese is Cumhuriyet Maydani, meaning Republic Square, and in its official dignity it is centered by the imposing *Monument of the Republic*. Consulates by the dozen cluster about Taksim. The Air France office, as I've said, fronts on it. Park Hotel, with its magnificent views of the Bosporus, is close by, as are the city's leading nightspots, the Taksim Gazino (Casino) and the Kervansaray. The Taksim hub is a major center of bus, minibus and trolleybus transportation and a starting point for city tours.

To recapitulate and sum up tourist orientation: If you learn the main stem of Beyoglu, Istaklal Caddesi, with Taksim at the upper end and Tunnel Square at the lower, if you learn the Gálata Bridge, with its many ferries and more caïques, and if, for explorations in the labyrinth of the Old City, you frankly deliver yourself into the hands of guides and taxi men, you will feel that in all essentials you "know your way around." It is quite possible to know your way around that ancient part as well, but this means very close study of guidebook and map, a great deal of rugged footwork, for distances are great, and some knowledge, gained by trial and error, of the bus lines. If you have plenty of time it is wonderful fun to accept the challenge of the winding ways.

St. Sophia, Sanctuary of the Ages

St. Sophia, built as a Christian church, altered into a mosque and in recent times proclaimed by the Turkish Republic a museum, is one of the world's supreme structures of religious inspiration. In architectural significance it can be classed quite on a par with St. Peter's in Rome or St. Paul's in London, and though its exterior is disappointing to the eye its interior is unsurpassed for artistic beauty and originality.

The story of this church-mosque-museum has emerged with greater clarity since 1945, when a former director, a Byzantine authority and scholar named Muzaffer Ramazanoglu Bey, now succeeded by Feridun Dirimtekin Bey, undertook important excavations under the floor of the nave and elsewhere. I once secured an interview with the former director, to clear up confusions in my own mind resulting from several conflicting accounts, and this is what he told me. Aghia Sophia, or Aya Sophia, meaning Divine Wisdom and having no connotation of a feminine saint named Sophia (but everyone *calls* it St. Sophia, as this text shall do for convenience), was dedicated, in its first primitive form, in 347 A.D. by Emperor Constantius II, son of Constantine the Great. It was demolished in connection with disturbances caused by the exile of the Patriarch Chrysostom, rebuilt by Theodosius II a few years later and largely re-destroyed in another riot in 532. From that year on, Emperor Justinian undertook the construction of the building we see, but this was, in actual fact, an achievement of *re*building and extension rather than the completely new achievement that has usually been credited to him. Regardless of the exact apportionment of credit, the final result is a glorious masterpiece.

St. Sophia's construction, in the form of a vast basilica surmounted by a dome 107 feet in diameter at a height of 179 feet, is unique and has never been copied, for architects are said to feel that despite its matchless beauty the form is impractical. The present dome was built in the 1100's, replacing one that had succumbed to an earthquake. Since this one has lasted for eight hundred years, and there have been plenty of other earthquakes, some of them severe, the layman feels inclined to call the design reasonably practical. Cracks have appeared, however, after all these centuries, and concern is felt for the dome's safety. Certain areas of the floor are even fenced off as being too risky for visitors.

To explain the elements of its design, there are half domes stretching eastward and westward from the cornice of the main complete dome, and these, in turn, rest each on three *smaller* half domes. To quote the words of Dr. Alexander van Millingen, a professor of history at Robert College in the suburb of Rumelihisar, "The nave is thus covered completely by a domical canopy, which, in its ascent, swells larger and larger, mounts higher and higher, as though a miniature heaven rose overhead."

The Christian mosaics of the interior are among the building's greatest glories and from 1932 on, the work of cleaning them from Moslem incrustations and restoring them to their pristine beauty was entrusted by the Turkish government to an American scholar, Professor Thomas

Whittemore. He died in 1950, but the work has continued.

Perhaps the most striking feature of ornamentation in St. Sophia, aside from the mosaics, is the array of enormous disks of gazelle skin affixed to the lofty cornice. These disks, dyed green, are ornamented with huge Arabic inscriptions, being texts from the Koran. The calligraphy is a marvel of decorative art. Other features that arouse wonder are the great chandeliers, seeming to hang from the sky itself, so long are the chains that hold them. Each chandelier is a circle of the traditional glass oil jars, now modernized, perhaps unfortunately, to hold electric light bulbs instead of oil and wicks. These lighting fixtures, despite their vastness, are mere details in the St. Sophia ensemble, which is overwhelmingly rich in ornamentation of many kinds and materials, including much marble and porphyry, for Justinian ransacked the pagan temples of the whole Roman world, including the celebrated ones in Baalbek and Ephesus, to secure the columns and other treasures that he wanted. The saying goes that when his church was finished the emperor cried out in jubilation, "Glory to God! I have beaten you, King Solomon!"

In the excavations opened up in the nave are some splendid early mosaics, and in a lofty gallery reached by a long, dark ramp and visited only by special permission of the director, are some ninth-century mosaics that are among the most beautiful and valuable in existence. Another feature of this gallery—one wishes that it could be open to the public since it offers a satisfying view of the building's interior—is the tomb of Enrico Dandolo, the famous Venetian doge who captured Constantinople in 1204. Death, it seems, is no respecter of doges, even when they have the luster of a great leader and conqueror.

Mosques Above the Golden Horn

To the gazer at Istanbul's skyline it seems that this old city has built as many mosques in the last five hundred years as Rome has built churches in the whole Christian era. Of course this is by no means true, but the forest of domes and minarets contributes strongly to that impression. Some of the main domes are supported by as many as four semidomes and almost every mosque of importance has more than one minaret. The Blue Mosque has six. Turkish minarets are even slenderer than most, which gives them the appearance of so many rockets on their launching pads.

A mosque tour can be very confusing to the visitor whose brief time compels him to crowd one mosque upon another upon another. I shall try to construct a step-by-step path, followable with a map, and I may mention here that Mobiloil publishes a splendid one, showing with great clarity the whole city, on both sides of the Bosporus, with an inset of the Bosporus in its entire length, from the Sea of Marmara to the Black Sea. Our path-among-the-mosques shall include eight of the most important ones, and shall mention in passing certain other items of special significance that can be seen as corollaries. One preliminary item, not far from St. Sophia, is the huge covered *Cistern of Yeri Batan*, built by Constantine and rebuilt by Justinian. The city once had scores of cisterns, intended to preserve an adequate water supply in times of siege. Some fifteen or twenty of them still exist, this one of Yeri Batan being among the largest examples. It is 460 feet long by 325 feet wide and its roof is supported by 336 columns. The water is still about 4 feet deep, this supply being maintained by springs that drip steadily into it. Facilities are planned for rowing tourists about in a small boat, and the cavernous place is to be attractively illuminated. This cistern is at present open to the public every afternoon except Sunday.

And now the mosques, with a "repeat note" that the Turkish word for mosque is *cami*, pronounced, and sometimes spelled, *jami* in English.

1. The *New Mosque* (*Yeni Cami*), popularly known as the *Queen Mother Mosque* (*Validé Cami*), looms up close to the Stanbul end of the Gálata Bridge. The forceful lady whom it honors was a seventeenth-century dowager who did some temple plundering in Asia Minor to get the materials she desired. She was the mother of Mohammed IV. This building is not an outstanding masterpiece of architecture but its mounting mass of domes, in such a setting, is imposing.

On the way up the slope of Old Istanbul from here one passes the *Sublime Porte*, which we remember as the Foreign Office of Imperial Turkey in the days of the sultans. It became the seat of the provincial and city government, but Istanbul now has a large, modern City Hall on Atatürk Boulevard. The name Sublime Porte, referring to the imposing doorway with its enormous sloping roof, was a popular tag, like France's Quai d'Orsay or Britain's Number 10 Downing Street.

2. The *Sultan Ahmed Mosque* is on higher ground near the main en-

trance to the Old Seraglio (to be discussed separately in a later section). This is the one with six minarets, and because it was given six the Great Mosque of Mecca, which already had six, was given a seventh, so that it might retain its minaret supremacy. A fragment of the black stone that Gabriel gave to Abraham, the celebrated Kaaba, Mecca's holy of holies, is alleged to be in the mihrab (prayer nook) of this edifice. The interior of the mosque, its dome supported by four colossal pillars, is a brilliant blue, which accounts for its popular name, the *Blue Mosque*. Some of the blue is of a very lovely and delicate hue, on faïence. More of it is preposterously garish, being blue decorations crudely painted on the columns and vaulting, but this ugly work is gradually being replaced by tasteful blue tilework.

Immediately to the west of this huge shrine of Islam is the *Hippodrome* of the early empire. It must have been a place of earth-rocking excitement when the military triumphs and the big chariot races were held there. In the middle of the *spina,* around which the charioteers raced, Emperor Theodosius I erected an obelisk brought from Heliopolis in Egypt, and it still stands where he placed it sixteen centuries ago. Also marking the spina are two other relics, a weather-greened column of twined serpents filched by Constantine from Delphi, where it had been erected in 479 B.C. to mark the victory of the Plataeans at the Pythian Games, and a small stone pyramid built by Emperor Constantine Porphyrogenitus (Born-to-the-Purple) in the tenth century. As the grand anticlimax of the Hippodrome, visitors are shown the squatty fountain that Kaiser Wilhelm II gave to his political crony, Sultan Abdul Hamid.

3. The *Mosque of Sultan Suleiman the Magnificent,* flanked on one side by the old *University* (vast new buildings have now been constructed in a neighboring quarter) and on the other by the *Museum of Islamic Art,* befits the name of its builder, for it is the largest and most grandiose of all the city's mosques and is sentineled by four large minarets. To increase its effect still further, it rises from the crest of a cypress-gardened hill dominating the Golden Horn. In a separate structure near by are the tombs of Suleiman and his wife Sultana Roxelana. The man in charge of the mosque's construction was Sian Aga, the most celebrated of all Turkish architects. Among the many marvels of its

interior the amazing acoustics are noteworthy, matching those of the Baptistery in Pisa or the Ear of Dionysius in Syracuse. Suleiman the Magnificent, most famous of the Ottoman sultans, was a tremendous figure of history, worth brushing up on, if you have lost track of his great exploits and equally great failures. It was he who drove the Knights of St. John from Rhodes. It was he who failed to drive them from Malta. Most importantly of all, it was he who lost, in 1529, forty thousand men in the Siege of Vienna and had to retire without capturing the city. All Europe trembled in its boots while the Austrian capital stood firm against the tidal wave of Turkish power.

4. The *Mosque of Fatih*, reached by a broad street that hides in the lee of the fourth-century *Aqueduct of Valens* (still in use), is the special shrine of Mohammed the Conqueror, who captured Constantinople in 1453 and established the power of Turkey. An earthquake overthrew it in 1768 but it was rebuilt in its present, somewhat Italianate style. It is chiefly notable for its size and for the great number of buildings that surround it, the small domes of these buildings producing the effect of a sea of masonry bubbles. There are schools, hospitals, students' quarters, pilgrim lodgings, baths and I know not what else, for a mosque of Islam, as we have seen, is very much more than a place where the faithful go to wash and pray.

5. The *Sultan Selim Mosque*, near the Golden Horn, receives little attention from tour organizers, but it well repays a visit. Sultan Selim was the father of Suleiman the Magnificent.

6. The *Fetiyeh Mosque* was formerly the Greek Orthodox Pammacaristos Church and some of the Christian inscriptions may still be seen in its stonework. Moslem Turkey justly prides itself on its completely tolerant treatment of rival religions. The Orthodox Eastern (Greek) Church is strong in Istanbul, which is, as a matter of fact, one of the four recognized patriarchates, along with Alexandria, Antioch and Jerusalem.

7. The *Kariye Mosque*, another former church, is of outstanding charm because if its superb mosaics. This lovely little Byzantine structure is so appealing that it has been converted, like St. Sophia, into a public museum.

8. Finally, the *Mihri Mah Mosque* was built by Princess Mihri Mah, meaning Moon-of-the-Sun, who was a daughter of Suleiman the Mag-

nificent and Roxelana. The master architect, Sinan Aga, was its designer, and although reconstruction has been necessary as recently as 1907, its original lines and luminous cheerfulness have been faithfully retained. It seems to fit the name of its princess.

To the Café of Pierre Loti

Pierre Loti was a devoted "Constantinopliphile" and wrote two of his strange, dreamy masterpieces, half novel, half narrative, about his experiences here, namely *Aziyadé* and *Fantôme d'Orient*. Part of the second one is supposed to have been written in a humble outdoor café on high ground above the inner end of the Golden Horn and certainly he did spend many hours there, indulging his fancies and memories. In all the region he could not have found a lovelier spot, as you will agree when you treat yourself to a *kahvé* or *tchai* in the same establishment, which is quite as humble as in his day and seven or eight decades more decrepit.

Some things along the route to Loti's hillside, a little way outside the city, can enhance the journey to that goal. In the neighborhood of the last four mosques mentioned above, are some of the gigantic ancient cisterns that were so carefully made and maintained in imperial days. The *Cistern of Arcadius*, to the rear of the Selim Mosque, could contain, it is estimated, six and a half million cubic feet of water, and when you see it—for this one is uncovered and open to view—you will concur in the estimate. Another large one is the *Aspar Cistern*, between the Fetiyeh and Mihri Mah mosques.

The road goes through the *Adrianople Gate*, piercing the enormous double walls of Emperor Theodosius, and from there on you are continually passing the jolliest cemeteries in the world. They may not *look* in the least jolly, but that will be because you have not been inoculated with the cheerful Turkish philosophy about death. The gravestones tip at the craziest angles, looking all the odder because of the jaunty turbans of stone so often crowning the monuments, and many lie flat on the ground, but that is part of the idea. Turks say, in all earnestness, that life tips and falls down, so why not the monuments to those who have lived. These are never raised back to an erect position, as that would be a defiance of the facts of life and death. There is, in Turkish thought, no sadness whatever about a cemetery. There is high good cheer, and even much humor. I asked my guide to translate some of the old Arabic inscriptions and these are two that he read to me: "Here lies . . . , who used to enjoy 120 grams of opium regularly and lived 134 years. You may try it."; "Here lies . . . , who had 40 years of quarreling with his wife. He couldn't stand it and died." Most of the epitaphs, however, are more serious, though no less personal, as : "I died for this country and you must pray for me."

Above the Golden Horn one encounters another famous mosque (I have omitted mention of five or six more of almost equal importance), in fact the holiest one of them all. It is the *Mosque of Eyub*, honoring the bearer of that name, who was also the Bearer of the Standard of Mohammed. This hero lies in a separate tomb behind a gilded grille and always there are faithful Moslems praying at this grille. To give accent to their prayers each fingers his Moslem rosary, called *tesbi*, of ninety-nine beads, reciting a prayer for each bead. The mosque itself, built of white marble in a design of great elegance, was constructed at the order of Mohammed the Conqueror. It contains an item of supreme sanctity, the very sword of Mohammed, the Prophet of Allah. In Ottoman days each successive sultan girded himself with this sword in a ceremony marking his accession to the throne.

And so, by a further short ride, to Loti's café. The view from there is enough to induce romantic reveries in the most phlegmatic spirit. To the right, as one gazes out, is the inspiring ensemble of the Old City, piercing the sky with a multitude of sacred spears, the minarets of Islam. Beyond this, one sees the Sea of Marmara, dotted with the Princes Isles. Below, at the base of an exceedingly steep slope of bright green meadow grass, lies the narrowing Golden Horn, and trickling into it the brooklet which meanders down from the treeless but pretty campagna so pleasantly named "The Sweet Waters of Europe." It is no wonder that the French Huguenot author who wandered so far afield and took his pen name from the lotus of India found this lofty and peaceful retreat more to his liking than any other in the world he knew. On an inside wall of the tatterdemalion café is a picture of Loti in military uniform inscribed to the proprietor in memory of one of his visits.

Three Palaces and Their Harems

The palaces of Ottoman Turkey are an amazing heritage. There are three in Greater Istanbul, the Old Seraglio near St. Sophia, the Doma-bahçe, directly on the Bosporus, and the Yildiz Kiosk, in a wooded park above that blue ribbon of water.

The *Old Seraglio*, called also the *Topkapi Palace*, replaces the ancient imperial palaces on the Byzantine acropolis. It was abandoned by the sultans more than a century ago in favor of the palace on the Bosporus, but as long as the sultans continued to rule they came here on a cere-monial visit each year to do honor to the sacred relics of the Prophet, for example his coat and a single hair of his beard that are kept here. The Old Seraglio is a complex of buildings, surrounding three separate courts, rather than a single palace. The usual entrance is through the Bab-i-Humayum (*Bab* is Arabic for Gate), and this gives the visitor a logical chance to pause and admire a marble masterpiece of Moslem art, the *Fountain of Ahmed*, which is a separate structure in front of the gate and close to the northeast (rear) portion of St. Sophia. In the Se-raglio precincts is a larger building, of equal interest, the former Greek *Church of St. Irene*, now the *Armory* of old Turkish weapons, including among its treasures the swords of all the conquering sultans. The church-armory also contains a wealth of lovely old tiles and porcelains. Almost adjacent to it is the important *Museum of Antiquities*, whose most celebrated possession is an elaborately carved sarcophagus of Pen-telic marble, popularly called the *Sarcophagus of Alexander the Great*.

Within the Seraglio's inner gate are the Throne Room, the Treasury, the Kiosk of Bagdad and the Harem. The Treasury fills a large outer wing of the palace that had been closed to the public for many years but was reopened in 1961–1962 as a museum of Chinese and Turkish porcelain, religious calligraphy, treasures of the sultans and much else. The Chinese porcelain, including some exquisite items of various eras from the tenth to the fifteenth centuries, plates and bowls in cobalt blue, olive green, mustard yellow and other fascinating hues, is considered by connoisseurs to be without equal anywhere. In the calligraphy sec-tion one curiosity is the entire Koran written in a beautiful but minus-cule Arabic script on a parchment about one yard square. The most admired thing in this whole wing, by many a tourist anyway, is an unexpected view. The guide leads you through vestibules and rooms and corridors to emerge upon a small balcony that fairly hangs in the sky above the point where the Bosporus, the Golden Horn and the Sea of Marmara converge. If you have some undelivered "Ohs" and "Ahs" I beg you to save them for this balcony.

Offsetting the opening of the Treasury has been, alas, the closing of the harem, with the Bagdad Kiosk, for repairs, which, proceeding at the usual snail's pace, will likely take years. Luckily I was able to see it before the closing and will try to describe it, though I can hardly hope to do it justice, since splendors of palace life reached very lofty levels in the eighteenth century and the early part of the nineteenth.

Visitors to the harem were first shown (and will be again when all is reopened) the adjacent *Bagdad Kiosk*, which was once a room for masculine repose and conversation over coffee. This is a dignified chamber beautified by some of the finest tilework in the Near East. The harem was a place apart in which the sultan's wives and concubines lived in idle luxury even though prisoners of custom. Outside it there is a little pool, and on a promontory jutting into the pool the sultan used to seat himself, on balmy days, to watch his women frolic about him naked in the water and on the pool's edge. This was an important part of their "work." In the tulip gardens surrounding the pool gay fiestas went far into the night. To enliven the scene wax candles were affixed to the backs of tortoises and the wicks lighted. The tortoises lumbered about among the flowers, irked, no doubt, by the burdens they were obliged to carry, but making a fairylike pattern of moving lights.

The entire point of the peninsula on which the Old Seraglio stands has been made into a park and the views of the Bosporus not only from that special balcony but from the Bagdad Kiosk and other buildings, through cedar and cypress groves and gardens of roses and carpets of violets, are as memorable, in their different way, as is the view from Loti's café.

The *Dolmabahçe Palace* was built over a hundred years ago and its nineteenth-century immensities and splendors surpass anything that the visitor can imagine in advance, but I must state right here that for two or three years to come you may be able to see it in imagination only. It is "closed for repairs" and will be opened as a public museum—sometime.

I visited it before its doors closed and, as in the case of the Old Seraglio, I will attempt to describe its wonders as I saw them. I believe that I have strolled through practically all the former royal palaces of Europe, including those of Berlin and Vienna and those of the French and Spanish Bourbon kings, but it seems to me that I have never found such vast acreage, at least on any one floor, as here. You walk for what seems an eighth of a mile and then learn from the guide that you have nearly reached the central portion. This palace has within its marble vastness many things to marvel at. There are several of the world's largest chandeliers, one, a present from Czar Nicholas II, weighing three and a half tons. There are mementos or gifts from most of the kings and queens of nineteenth-century Europe and some from an earlier period, including certain interesting souvenirs of Napoleon. One of the emperor's gifts to one of the sultans is a table with enamel insets of all the women in his life. All? Well, some anyway. Among them are his mother, his sister Pauline Bonaparte, and his two wives, Joséphine and Marie Louise, getting along together very amicably.

A special sight of the palace is the alabaster room for the cleansing of the imperial body. It is a bath with heated floor, such as even Mussolini never achieved when he remodeled for himself the Palace of the Grand Master of the Knights of Rhodes. Another palace sight is the bed, big enough for Hercules and grand enough for Zeus, that Abdul Hamid II had built for the visit of Kaiser Wilhelm II. Still another is the death room of Atatürk, who used the palace at times and died there in 1938.

But of course the *harem* arouses our special interest, since this provides an exotic, Eastern touch. And *what* a touch! It seems to me that the sultans must have had a good acre of women in Dolmabahçe. In the women's wing one room stands apart, the red and gold and white boudoir of the head wife, being that one who was lucky enough to bear her lord his first acknowledged son. The gleaming blue reception room of this quarter of the palace is the salon where the sultan would sometimes gather together *all* his wives and children, as if in a family convention.

The *Yildiz Kiosk*, newest of the three palaces, is a delightful building, of understandable proportions, beautifully sheltered by woods yet offering good views of the Bosporus. It is a very modest place by comparison with the others, but its modesty had the usual limits. Here, as in the Old

Seraglio, there is a pool where the naked odalisques of the harem disported themselves before the doting eyes of the sultan, seated comfortably in his pavilion. The Yildiz Kiosk is now a pleasant summer café, without, alas, any lovely odalisques.

Alice in the Grand Bazaar

The *Grand Bazaar*, in the heart of Old Istanbul, a wonderland for shoppers, has been mentioned with awed enthusiasm in the "Shops and Souks" section of Chapter 3 and it is almost enough to say here again, "*Don't miss it*." The present hive of trade, completely roofed over, was constructed in 1898 after being heavily damaged by an earthquake four years previously. It has ninety-two streets, each devoted to some special type of merchandise. One type, barely mentioned in my earlier paeans, is *gold*. You haven't seen so much of the real stuff since gold was "called in" decades ago. Shops by the glittering dozen sell ornaments, chains, trinkets of every conceivable form and variety and the prices are determined by the bourse quotations on pure gold on the day of your visit. They are determined also by the weight of the item on jeweler's scales, as well as by the quality of the craftsmanship. If you are a resident of Istanbul and buy an item of pure gold in the bazaar you can sell it back whenever you want to at very little loss, or perhaps even at a gain, if the official quotations are high at the time. It has already been sadly mentioned that gold items, with the exception of small charms, may not legally be exported from Turkey.

One caution is worth trumpeting. If you want to see the Grand Bazaar at its incredible best, do not go on a Sunday, for, quite unlike the Damascus custom, the Moslem merchants here close up shop on Sunday, just as the Christian merchants do, and they keep open on Friday. Turkey is more or less unique among Moslem lands in this concession to business convenience and to the general Western custom, though one does find a somewhat similar concession operative in Cairo. Bargaining is permissible and expected in many of the bazaar's shops but tourists are not fleeced indiscriminately and the tradesmen seem to be a generally honest lot. One of them, in my experience, reached a peak of business honesty seldom attained, for he displayed in front of his shop a sign that read, in big letters: BROKEN ENGLISH SPOKEN.

The Waters of Holiday

One of the greatest delights of a visit to Istanbul is holiday fun on its many waters. This may take the form of ferry or caïque rides *on* the water, motor rides *beside* it or bathing *in* it. Most likely it will include all three.

The Bosporus is, of course, the main stem of water fun. For about fourteen miles your ferry will carry you along between Europe and Asia, stopping now at one continent, now at the other. You see the palaces and mosques and towers as the whitecaps see them. You catch many a glimpse of life as lived in villages and villas and summer resorts on both sides. Some of the main halts may be listed here.

Üsküdar (Skutari), across the way in Asia, calls for a special visit, if time can possibly permit, to see the "last refuge of local color," as a French folder somewhat inaccurately phrases it, and to view the Istanbul ensemble from the lofty vantage point of *Chamlija Hill*, mentioned earlier as the site of a future luxury hotel.

Beylerbey (on the Asian side) is the station for the sumptuous white marble palace of that name built for Empress Eugénie in 1865 by Sultan Abdul Aziz I, perhaps the most graceful and elegant of all the palaces in Greater Istanbul.

Ortaköy (Europe) is especially notable for its villas of the wealthy and for its tipsy houses of blackened wood, wonderfully appealing to the artistic eye and said also to be often extremely comfortable and even luxurious inside. One hopes they won't collapse and be replaced by modern houses that could be anywhere in Europe. Most of these old dwellings along the edge have their own caïque "garages." A popular casino-restaurant is in Ortaköy, bordering the Bosporus.

Kandilli and *Anadoluhisar* (both in Asia) are ferry halts of some importance on the south and north side respectively of two little streams that moisten the prairie here called "The Sweet Waters of Asia." Both the European and the Asiatic Sweet Waters are favorite hiking and picnic grounds on Saturdays and Sundays. Anadoluhisar has a ruined castle built by Mohammed the Conqueror. The name of the village has a special significance for me, for back in the summer of 1949 I saw, in Rotterdam's harbor, a gleaming white ferryboat fresh from the ways labeled ANADOLUHISAR—ISTANBUL. It was made by Dutch ship-builders and dispatched to the Bosporus, where, just now, I have used it for one of my holiday excursions.

Rumelihisar (Europe) has a very impressive legacy of the past, chiefly three towers connected by crenelated walls, called the *Castle of Europe*, built, as you will have come to expect, by Mohammed the Conqueror. In recent times the castle has been very expensively restored, hand-somely landscaped and opened to the public, in a special celebration that included music from what is called the world's oldest military band, by name the Mehter. The players wore their traditional red and blue uni-forms and used certain archaic instruments that are now normally seen only in museums. The three towers are named for three of the Con-queror's generals, *Habib Pasha*, *Zagamos Pasha* and *Sarica Pasha*. The first-named tower is the one entered and ascended by visitors, and yes, there's an elevator, which is lucky, for the tower is a tall one as well as big. When in military use it had nine levels, now it is a huge empty cylinder. The castle is floodlighted nightly, creating an eerie but fasci-nating spectacle.

At the point where the castle stands the Bosporus is at its narrowest point between these two "hisars" (Anadolu and Rumeli) and it is thought by historians that Darius, and later Xerxes, and finally Xeno-phon, with his Ten Thousand Greeks, here crossed the strait. For Xeno-phon it was the end of his 1500-mile anabasis, his account of which has ever since been the bane of first-year Greek students. *Robert College*, by the way, which knows all about Xenophon's *Anabasis*, looms in some grandeur on the heights just south of Rumelihisar. This famous Ameri-can college, founded in 1863, has survived all political changes and been a bulwark of sound teaching, tolerance and scholarship. A girls' school connected with it is named Constantinople College.

Emirgan (Europe) has long been known to holiday-seekers for its many restaurants and cafés, including a famous one called the *Coffee House of the Oak*, but in recent years it has taken on a new aura of bril-liance because of its hillside flower park called *Emirgan Kurusu*, as lovely a sight as any dream could create. When I last saw it the pre-dominant flowers were tulips and their predominant color scarlet. The tulip, in case you don't know this bit of lore, came to Europe (and America) from Turkey, the very word, originally *tülbend*, which means also turban, being a Turkish word. In modern times Holland has had almost a monopoly on tulip publicity but the ancestor bulbs, perhaps originating in Persia, were imported from Turkey.

Here is the amazing story, which seems worth interpolating: In 1554, Austria's ambassador to Turkey brought the first bulbs to Vienna. The new flower fascinated Europe's nobility, especially the Duke of Cleves, whose little duchy was then part of the Netherlands. From 1590 an ambitious gardener in Leiden propagated bulbs on a big scale, anchoring the industry in Holland. A tulip mania soon developed and rocked all Europe during a three-year period, from 1634 to 1637. Single bulbs of rare varieties fetched the equivalent of $1500. Rich men in many lands courted bankruptcy in their eagerness to gamble on the Amsterdam tulip bourse and not a few were ruined. Poor men often gambled away their life savings. So great was the power of this Turkish flower on men's minds that the Netherlands government was finally forced to stop the growing madness by decree.

Yeniköy (Europe) is a Greek-speaking suburb of Istanbul, fringing a narrow inlet. It was in a stretch of the Bosporus more or less opposite Yeniköy that a collision occurred in 1961 between a Greek freighter and a Yugoslav tanker. It was a spectacular accident that set the tanker afire and then gradually spread its blazing contents on the Bosporus, making it a barrier of flame that blocked all traffic. For a week the Bosporus was virtually impassable and for two months the half-sunken tanker was a beacon in the water. Tourists by the thousands came nightly from Istanbul, and even from more distant points, to view the blazing spectacle.

Tarabya (Europe) has been mentioned in connection with its big, new hotel, now making its bow, but the place is much more than a hotel. There is a sort of "Swissness" about this lovely resort, rising on its own crescent cove. Before the war Tarabya was the favorite haunt of diplomats, and it still has a considerable vogue, even though Ankara, the fast-growing capital, is the natural habitat of diplomacy. Many good marine restaurants (Fidan, Fitiz, Şale, etc.) line the shore.

Büyükdere (Europe) is the take-off point for lovely forest walks and for some well-known mineral springs where, by at least one printed account, patrons who "take the waters" in various cafés are weighed upon entering and again upon leaving, the charge for the water being based on the *increase* shown by the scales. I have not yet personally visited these springs and my curiosity about the unique system of charging is so overpowering that a new visit to Istanbul takes form on my agenda "to see if it is true."

Sariyer (Europe), where a "Sailors' Venus" statue excited passing mariners in medieval times, is now a modest and pleasant little summer resort. It is a good climax to ferry wanderings on the Bosporus, since the remaining villages on both sides are of decreasing interest. It is practical and even easy for the tourist who has wearied of the ferry and wishes to return directly to the city to find and board a yellow municipal bus, a minibus or a dolmus, marked simply TAKSIM. Before doing so, however, one should consider an extension, or tangent, trip to the *Kilyos Hotel*, located directly on a like-named beach of the *Black Sea*, some eight miles from the "mouth" of the Bosporus. This hotel is by far the easiest Black Sea resort to reach and the visitor finds it reassuring to know that it is owned and maintained by the General Tourist Bank, an aforementioned institution that is active in promoting Turkish tourism. The Kilyos has a big restaurant, an open beach café, facilities for dancing indoors and outdoors, and, for the tripper, an ample installation of bathhouses.

The *Princes Isles* are a never-disappointing attraction of the Sea of Marmara, but opposite them, on the Anatolian shore of the same sea, southeast of the populous suburbs of Haydar Pasha and Kadiköy, is a string of small mainland resorts that are too often overlooked. The first is *Moda*, whose crescent bay is alive with pleasure craft and bathers every summer day, small sailboats predominating, with chromatic sails of red, pink, yellow, brown and even sea-matching blue. The *Moda Club*, a private one to be visited with a member, has an inviting seaside refreshment terrace and there are several hotels, headed by the *New Paris*, where "membership" is as wide as the tourist world. Beyond Moda is a public beach named *Fenerbahçe*, where a lot of inexpensive saltwater fun is to be had. The fun may include the purchase of an ear of steaming hot sweet corn from a giant cauldron that is wheeled about by an itinerant peddler. Beyond Fenerbahçe is *Caddebostan*, with an open-air restaurant (dancing) filling a clean pine grove on a peninsular point, and beyond that the high-grade resort called *Suadiye*, mentioned in our hotel run-down.

The Princes Isles, to return to the subject, need very little explaining, for they are easy to see and enjoy. The first one reached by the steamer from Gálata Bridge is *Kinali;* the second, *Burgaz;* the third, *Heybeli,* identified by a Greek Orthodox seminary on high ground; the fourth, which is the Big Island, *Büyükada,* formerly known to Greek residents as Prinkipo.

There are several smaller islands in the group, the most westerly and remote of them being the pyramid-shaped islet called Oxia. This is a place of grim connotation, for in 1910 it was the "concentration camp" of thousands upon thousands of unfortunate, half-wild curs rounded up in Constantinople's streets and exiled to this rocky prison, where they were left to die of starvation. In 1907, I made a boyhood visit to Constantinople with my parents and vividly remember those pestilential, yapping dogs, so thick in the streets that they made walking a hazard. Something *had* to be done to rid the city of them, but I feel certain that enlightened, republican Turkey of today would never countenance the cruel way in which imperial Turkey put them away.

Büyükada, to come to a scene as cheerful as Oxia is grim, is a thriving center of holiday life, with several good hotels and beaches, a lot of outdoor cafés and much gay animation generally. A carriage ride around the island, between steamers, makes a charming tour, and indeed that is the only way you can ride unless you hire a bike, for this island allows no motor vehicles.

Some of the bathing resorts of the *European* shore of the Sea of Marmora are perennially popular goals. *Florya,* about twelve miles from the city and reached by frequent electric trains from the *Sirkeci Station* in the old city, has a very fine beach, and to give the place prestige, there is located here a villa, built on piles over the water, that serves as a summer residence for the president of the republic. The installations at Florya's public beach are of a quality that is surprising in this far end of the Continent. Around a modern swmming pool visitors may rent private cabins, each with its own terrace, sitting room, napping room, shower and toilet. That would be something for Florida, not Florya, to publicize. The public-locker-and-small-cabin section has plenty of quality to suit me and on a sultry summer day, which proved also to be a national holiday, I sought to avail myself of it. The crowd queuing up at the gate was tremendous and when I finally got to the ticket window I alone, as it seemed to me, was refused a ticket. Nonplussed and annoyed, I tried to argue, in English, with the harried girl, who spoke only Turkish. I made no headway at all and at that point "when a feller needs a friend" I suddenly acquired one. A soft feminine voice at my elbow explained, "She says there are no lockers left and that on holidays like this, with such big crowds, they don't rent cabins to single persons, but if you would like to share a cabin with mummy and me, we'd be delighted." I was *more* than delighted, for the problem was handsomely solved. The girl and her "mummy" had first use of the cabin and then my turn came. The three of us met on the terrace for cokes and then a long swim. "We're an English family," explained the young girl, "and I work in the British Embassy, but mummy doesn't speak any English and neither does daddy. You see, mummy was Greek and daddy was born on Malta. We always speak Greek or Turkish at home, but we are English because daddy's English."

Good Food and Good Fun

Turkey is one of the most interesting countries in the Mediterranean for native dishes. There are several character restaurants in Istanbul and Ankara which are of such rare quality that they will be discussed below and in the following chapter on Anatolia. *Borsch*, though of Russian lineage, is a very delicious soup in certain Turkish restaurants (notably in the Karpiç in Ankara), quite unrecognizable as a cousin of the dreary pink liquid avoided in New York cafeterias. And now I will sharpen my typewriter keys and struggle with some Turkish words, paving the way with easy-to-spell *pilav*.

The following items, in addition to the two above, are of culinary importance. *Lakerda* is a very tender salted fish. Turks claim that the mixture of Black Sea and Mediterranean water in the Bosporus produces the tenderest fish in the world, and after sampling several varieties I would be the last to deny it. *Lüfer* (sea perch), *kalkan* (a local turbot) and red *barbunya*, a species of mullet already mentioned in Greek fare as barbouni, are popular ichthyan favorites. *Şiş kebab*, a dish well-known in America, is a delicious specialty, being bits of lamb, with onions, tomatoes and other tidbits, all skewered and cooked on a rotating grill. *Döner kebab* is another spitted array, this one being of thin, round slices of meat. *Şiş köftesi* is, as you would hardly guess, small meat balls, quite as good as the *köttbullar* of Swedish smörgåsbord. Now take a deep breath. *Zeytinyagli yaprak dolmasi* is the rice-in-vine-leaves delicacy called dolmas in Greece. *Tulumba tatlisi* is a delectable cylinder of pastry filled with cream. *Kazandibi mahallebi* is a baked cornstarch pudding, nicely browned on top and scented, at least in some restaurants, with rose water, as you can tell from smelling it. *Tel kadayifu* is the shredded-wheat-like syrup-noodle item mentioned as karaifi in discussing Greek food. And finally *baklava* is a characteristic honey cake unlike any you have tasted elsewhere, unless you have encountered it in some Arab restaurant in another land. *Turkish delight*, more a confection than a dessert, is, of course, to be had in Istanbul, and at its freshly made best. This fabulous sweet, called *lokum* in this land of its origin, is no myth. One sees it, tastes it and (maybe) loves it. Bright confectionery shops feature it in many a show window.

A good white Turkish wine from Anatolian grapes is *kavaklidere*. The dynamite liquor called *raki* is universally popular in Turkey. It should not be *mixed* with any other beverage and should be taken after having eaten something. They say that if you have had too much you can sober up effectively on another Turkish specialty, *işkenbe çorbasi*, which is tripe soup!

And now let me tell you of Turkey's greatest restaurant delicacy of all. It is *koç yumurtasi*, which is to say broiled rams' testicles. This dish is expensive and also rare, for the very good reason that most rams are castrated when very young. Koç yumurtasi should be liquefied with raki, but with or without firewater it is an epicure's dream. In Istanbul I have enjoyed it in the *Misir Carsisi Restaurant*, and I would say that I have never tasted anything more fit for the table of Lucullus.

The Misir Carsisi, meaning Egyptian Bazaar and located in upstairs rooms *in* the Egyptian Bazaar (so named because spices of the East, brought via Egypt, were formerly sold here), is easily found because it is close to the conspicuous Queen Mother Mosque. It is one of the best restaurants in the city. Several of the delectable dishes that I have attempted to describe I first sampled here. The blue-tiled rooms of the restaurant have all the ingredients of cheer and atmosphere, and the view from their windows takes in the unceasing liveliness of the Gálata Bridge. You may visit the kitchen and look over the shoulder of your chef to see just how he cooks your şis kebab or döner kebab on his turning spit. This restaurant has been going for a long time, but a few years ago it was given an added boost when a famous Greek master-chef named Pandeli took it over. Boss Pandeli, beautifully white of "mane" and eyebrows, directs the show like the absolute monarch that he is. If things seem to him to be getting a bit dull he has been known to bawl out a waiter or two with a roaring that makes the place shake. It is part of his act and means nothing. Most of the patrons love it—and him. Nowadays, the Misir Carsisi Restaurant is often called the *Pandeli*.

The *Abdullah Efendi* is considered the best straight restaurant in the city for a quality luncheon or dinner in a quality setting. It is on Istaklal Caddesi very near Taksim. Abdullah Kordoyanis, the owner, has made his establishment a distinguished international restaurant specializing in marvelous hors d'oeuvres and sea food. His mussel soup—*which must be ordered twenty-four hours in advance*—is famous throughout the Near East.

Among other good restaurants, aside from hotel dining rooms, are the *Liman*, a harborside place on the third floor of the Maritime Building near the Gálata Bridge; the *Konyali* (no alcohol here), opposite the Sirkeci Railway Station in Old Istanbul; and two outstanding places on Bosporus shores, the *Bogaziçi* (Turkish name for Bosporus) at Yeniköy, which is more especially a gay night restaurant, and the *Canli Balik* marine restaurant, where you may pick your swimming food from a pool.

Two leading tearooms, both on Istaklal Caddesi, are *Markiz* and *Lebon*, but a tea hour there can hardly be compared with one in the lounge-and-terrace of the Hilton, enhanced by orchestra music.

Night life, in all large Turkish cities is gay and widely assorted, that of big Istanbul ranging from sophisticated international cabarets of high quality to strip tease dens and a red light street that outbrazens even Hamburg's Reeperbahn. For fine food and smart, sparkling shows the *Şadirvan Supper Club* of the Hilton, the above-mentioned *Bogaziçi* at Yeniköy and two central night clubs, the *Taksim Casino* and the *Kervansaray* stand out. The Bogaziçi is owned by the General Tourist Bank and in it I once saw a terrific folklore show, given by a troupe from Konya, a city of Anatolia. By terrific I mean just that, if not downright terrifying. In one of the scenes warriors "fought" each other, tooth, nail and saber. This wonderful but harrowing display was followed by several belly dancers who certainly "took it off," garment by garment, with a boldness to make Minsky fans nostalgic. Adjacent to this night club and owned by the same bank is the former *Palace-Kiosk of Prince Sait Halim Pasha*. The bank talks hopefully about contracting with a German firm to transform this small but luxuriously furnished palace into a gambling casino. Time will tell if talk turns into fact.

The two Taksim places mentioned above are dependably excellent, with the Kervansaray perhaps a bit the better. The Taksim Casino, a very large affair, is the dean of all the city's smarter places, its reputation having been well established for years. The Kervansaray, somewhat newer but still a veteran, is the last word in luxe and good taste. Its Corinthian-pillar design and its gleaming whiteness give it a look of grandeur that yet does not rob it of intimacy. The workmanship and décor are 100 per cent Turkish. Each of these leading luxury restaurants offers a first-rate, full-length international floor show that alternates with the music of good dance bands, and each has also a late-hours (or early-hours) cabaret on a lower floor. Park Hotel, not far from Taksim, has a less pretentious but pleasant little night club, also "downstairs."

Among specialty places outside the center one that calls for mention is *Şark Gazino ve Kahvesi*, an Oriental coffee house on the hillside above the Dolmabahçe Palace and not far from the Hilton. Its outlook, by day or night is magnificent. The view takes in not only the broad and busy Bosporus, thrilling at all hours, but the whole skyline of Istanbul, with its sea of bubble domes and its forest of slender minarets. This is a *municipal* restaurant-café, not a private one. There is dancing indoors in winter, outdoors on a terrace in summer.

Istanbul is as up-and-coming a metropolis of pleasure as one could hope to find. When its new *Opera House*, in Taksim, is added to its existing attractions it will be a serious contender for top honors as a purveyor of Mediterranean evening-into-night life.

CHAPTER 25

CITIES OF ANATOLIA

Half an Hour to Bursa

THE visitor to Istanbul who merely takes a ferry across the Bosporus to Üsküdar or Kadiköy has been to Anatolia, for the name applies technically to *all* of Turkey that lies on the Asia side, being more than nineteen twentieths of the whole, but since the far side of the Bosporus is to all intents a part of Greater Istanbul it does not properly introduce the vast area that we used to call Asia Minor. An introduction may, however, be very swiftly and smoothly had by means of Turkish Airlines, and more leisurely had by means of the numerous coastal steamers and the good Diesel express trains on the main routes.

Turkish Airlines provides frequent and efficient service to virtually every city of Anatolia. Consider some of the exotic names on the flight schedule: *Bursa; Ankara; Van* and *Erzurum,* almost at the borders of Iran and Russia; *Samsun,* exporter of caviar in quantity, and *Trabzon* (Trebizond), these two on the Black Sea; the Mediterranean ports of *Izmir* (Smyrna), neighbor to ancient Ephesus, *Antalya,* a favored coastal resort on Anatolia's southern shore, and *Iskenderun* (Alexandretta); and such inland goals as *Konya,* which was the Iconium of Bible days.

The average traveler, perhaps able to squeeze from his itinerary only three or four days to sample all this wealth, must be a wise and stern selector. Fortunately three cities stand out pre-eminently, and for quite different reasons. *Bursa* is one, because it *was* the first capital of the Ottoman Empire and *is* a center of Anatolian holidays, with much to offer, from mineral baths famous for centuries, to snow fields that lure winter athletes. *Izmir* is another, because of its alluring seaside self and its nearness to Ephesus, whose great Temple to Diana, that powerful city's patroness, was one of the Seven Wonders of the World. (Turkey has two of the seven, the other being the Mausoleum at Halicarnassus.

See under Island of Cos, Chapter 14.) *Ankara* is the third, because in our
time it has jumped from a tatterdemalion market village for farmers and
goat herders to a vigorous national capital with 650,000 inhabitants and
all the trappings that modern diplomacy demands in the game of power
politics imposed upon the world.

The leap from Istanbul's airport to that of Bursa takes exactly half
an hour over the Sea of Marmara and an Asian peninsula that juts far out
into it. Storks, skittling away from your plane as it settles to earth at
Bursa's airfield, may suggest the sleepy days of old Turkey, but modern
Bursa is anything but sleepy. With its important silk-weaving industry,
tobacco factories and a broad "Green Belt" of orchards to supplement
the wealth that its holiday facets attract, it is one of the thriving cities
of the new Turkish republic.

Nine foreigners out of ten who visit Bursa go there for its baths or its
good fun and those nine are invariably surprised, as I was, to find what
a many-chaptered past it has. Omitting the Lydian, Persian, Bithynian,
Roman and Crusader chapters, consider for a moment the impact of the
Osman (hence *Otto*man) Turks upon this ancient city. In or about 1324,
Osman I captured the place, then called Prusa, and made it the capital
of his dawning empire. His successors, Orhan and Murad I, continued
the development and all three sultans built handsome mosques, together
with the customary burial chapels. Murad I conquered Thrace and
transferred his political capital to Adrianople, but because of the sacred
ancestral traditions already clinging to Bursa he wished to be buried in
that city. His precedent was followed by all of his three sucessors until
the time of the conquest of Constantinople in 1453, so it came about that
for more than two centuries Bursa, serving as a sort of Turkish pantheon, was fairly glutted with sumptuous and often beautiful Moslem
monuments, great mosques and tombs, elaborate baths, elegant fountains.

You will very possibly have become over-mosqued before reaching
this mosque-saturated city of the early Ottomans, which is a pity, for
some of the best of the whole race are here in Bursa. If you feel you can
manage only *one* of the Bursa multitude, do, by all means, concentrate
on the so-called *Green Mosque*, built by Mohammed I near the closing
decades of Bursa's pantheon period. This mosque gets its popular name
from the marvelous green faïence work with which it abounds, the

most celebrated tiles originating in the Anatolian region of Kütahya. Some keen students of Arab architecture consider that even the choicest constructions of that mosque-building genius Sinan Aga in Istanbul do not quite match the Green Mosque in perfection of proportions and decoration. But the thing that rouses ecstasies in the connoisseur is the superior calligraphy in the inscriptions from the Koran that ornament this mosque. The intricate lettering of sacred texts is the glory of many a mosque, but nowhere does this most Arabic of all the arts reach a higher level of skill and loveliness than here.

If the Green Mosque is perfect, its separate octagonal *türbé*, the Green Tomb of Mohammed I and his family, needs some adjective of still more strength, for the tilework here is overwhelming in its beauty of tone and taste. Local enthusiasts hesitate not a moment to proclaim this chef-d'oeuvre the finest faïence in the world!

If you are not surfeited by mosques and can "take more," I suggest three more in Bursa, the earliest one of importance, the *Mosque of Murad I*, dating from about 1360, the Grand Mosque, or *Ulucami*, built by that sultan's successor, Yildirim Bayazid, and the *Bayazid Mosque*, by this same eager builder. If you cannot manage so much mosquework you can always turn to the lighter features of Bursa, the mineral baths.

The healing waters of Bursa, among the best anywhere for rheumatic complaints, descend to the city from the mountain called Uludag, one of the several mountains in several countries known to the ancients at various epochs as Olympus. As early as 525 A.D. the Byzantine Empress Theodora is reported to have come here to take the waters—with a retinue of four thousand persons—but all of the bath establishments now in existence have been built in Turkish times. The oldest and most famous one, dating largely from the fourteenth century, is called *Eski* (Old) *Kaplica* and is conspicuous in the Çekirge section of the city, near the Mosque of Murad I. The *Yeni* (New) *Kaplica* is in the Bademil section, near the big Çelik Palas Hotel. Near this also are two more from the fourteenth and fifteenth centuries, name *Kükürtlü* and *Kara Mustafa Pasha*.

Nature has been so lavish in distributing mineral waters to Bursa that virtually all the hotels have natural hot water piped directly into the plumbing systems. The *Çelik Palas Hotel*, leader of the pack, not only offers a private mineral bathroom with every bedroom but boasts also a public hamman (Turkish bath) and swimming pool of real magnificence. The temperature of the hot spring feeding this palace of tourism is 44 degrees Centigrade, which translates itself to 111 degrees Fahrenheit. A large new annex costing two million Turkish pounds has been completed, and as a note of good news to your budget I may report that a private room and bath in the Çelik Palas, with full board, costs, at present, only seven dollars a day for one person, twelve for two. Meals may be had on the open terrace overlooking the city's Green Belt.

While on the subject of hotels I should mention the smaller and humbler *Hotel Gönlü Ferah*, which also has its own complete hammam. The dining terrace of the Gönlü Ferah offers a view that alone would warrant any visitor in considering the place. This hotel's rates are about half those of the Çelik Palas.

Whether or not you have rheumatism or any other ailment you really should experience a hammam at Bursa. The bath men who scrub you (if you are a male) with a rough glove are experts at their work and without hurting you they will manage to scrape plenty of cuticle from your person. This *always* happens, no matter how meticulous the customer is about his own daily bathing, so don't let it get you down. The "full treatment," including the siesta in the steam room, is much less severe than that of a Finnish sauna, and it is also much more modest, "disappointingly so" as some male visitors express it. Bath men always attend males and bath women females. You will not find the big, blonde, blushless scrubwomen of Finland, who take on customers of both sexes.

The mountain called Uludag, great benefactor of Bursa, looms directly above the city, and Bursa's planners, alarmed by the way construction is creeping over the Green Belt and absorbing it, are now striving to make it creep the other way, climbing the mountain's gentle lower slopes. Uludag provides not only the life-giving and curative waters but rich forests, ample grazing grounds for cattle and numerous patches of luxuriant berries and mushrooms; and for the transient it provides, above all, a summer and winter playground. On hot summer days the refreshing air of Uludag is a tonic and the serried heights and milder slopes offer walks and climbs to suit all legs and lungs. On winter days its ski slopes rival in popularity those of Lebanon and Cyprus. Bursa must have sensed all these things some thousands of years ago when it first took squatter's rights at the mountain's base.

Uludag may be a good place to make acquaintance with the excellent TUSAN chain of hotels and motels that has recently developed, in Turkey, for one of the links, called *Uludag Büyük Hotel*, with accommodations for two hundred guests, is here at an altitude of 6600 feet. This chain, the property of a private corporation called Tourism Industry, Inc., tied in with BP Petrolleri (British Petroleum Company), has eight links already, and others are planned. Each establishment has bath and balcony with every room and each has a good restaurant. Each has also a BP Service Station, with full touring and information aids. TUSAN is, of course, the answer to the motorist's prayer, but it also serves effectively those who journey in Anatolia by tourist motor coach or public bus. Other links of special importance are at *Ephesus*, *Pergamum* (Bergama), *Troy* (Truva) and in the neighborhood of the fantastic troglodyte community named *Göreme*, near Kayseri, southeast of Ankara. Two that I know (at Uludag and Ephesus) have impressed me by their up-to-dateness and meticulous cleanliness. In the last decade the highways of Anatolia have been greatly improved and the work goes on, the highway spurring the motels and the motels spurring the highways. It's another case of "which came first, the chicken or the egg?"

I must emphasize the importance to Turkish tourism of British Petroleum's zealous pioneering work, supported, I may add, by American government aid. All of TUSAN's hotels and motels are units of what is called Pilot Project Number 1 and all are operated by BP, through Tourism Industry. The project has been, and is, a bold one, serving to make nationwide motoring a feasible and alluring prospect. Full information, along with a touring map and handsomely illustrated folders, may be had from travel agencies or from BP Touring Service (at any service station) or by writing to Tourism Industry, Inc., P.O. Box 96, Yenişehir, Ankara.

Izmir and Ephesus

Izmir is today an up-and-coming port city and a beautiful one for location. Next to Istanbul it is Turkey's most important port of entry, and in exports (tobacco, cotton, figs, sultana grapes, olives and olive oil) it is in first place. Its annual fair, running for a month from about August 20, is among the greats. Izmir is headquarters of the NATO command guarding the eastern Mediterranean. The NATO building, with flags of all member nations flying from separate flagpoles, is a cheering and reassuring sight.

Touristically speaking the city is most attractive to the eye, for it fringes the inner end of a sheltered gulf which thrusts its way some twenty-five miles from the Aegean into Anatolia. In the city's center is a very large *Cultural Park*, as it is rather ambitiously called. It is as lovely and as popularly sought as it is cultural, for a small lake, with restaurants and night clubs on its banks, is one of its inviting features. From a residential hill called *Kadifekale*, meaning Velvet Castle, there is a view of the city and its bay rivaling that of Haifa from Mt. Carmel.

The tourist is effectively wooed by the local branch of the Government Tourist Office (126 Atatürk Caddesi), which would like to see more and bigger hotels built to attract and lure him. The only present one of luxury rating is the *Kismet*, but this will very shortly be outshone by the 300-room Grand Hôtel Ephèse, with swimming pool and night club. Then come the first-class *Kilim*, which is not on the sea, and the *Izmir Palace*, which is. Each of these three leaders has approximately seventy rooms, all with bath.

A very pleasant restaurant on the edge of the lake in Cultural Park and with some tables under the trees at the water's edge, is the *Ada*, one of whose delicacies, a specialty of Izmir, is a fish called *trança*. The geese from the lake will likely wander to your table as self-invited guests. Other good restaurants are numerous on the quays (e.g. *Deniz*), on the hilltop (*Kale*) and in the Vali Rahmi Bey Park (*Sark Sato*). Night clubs, generally with Oriental belly dancers, also abound in Izmir and several of them are in the Cultural Park. The Ada Restaurant, doubling as a night club after dark, is one. I have been told that there is at least one "naughty" night club, a must for sailors in port. I believe its name is *Numune Pavyonu*, but—deplorable confession—I had no opportunity to check its naughtiness, nor even to assure myself of its name.

Ephesus is about fifty miles from Izmir, but the road is good all the way and it can be reached comfortably in a little over an hour. The ruins of that city of many lives (from the eleventh century B.C.) and rather sudden death (in the fifth century A.D.) are of great extent and outstanding interest, even though its chief showpiece, the Temple of Diana, was so efficiently obliterated by the Goths in 263 A.D. that it was quite lost for seventeen centuries. In 1962, slight traces of it, chiefly bits of the wall, with faint frescoes, were found and authenticated by archeologists. It was the third temple on the same spot, this one built in the third century B.C. and having a life of five hundred years before it was destroyed. It was of Ionic style, surrounded by a double row of columns, and in ground measurements it was *four times as large as the Parthenon.* "Great is Diana of the Ephesians!" So went the cry of the proud people, as vividly reported in Acts 18. Well—Diana is gone but a great deal else is left. I will try to present a few of the special sights of Ephesus, as a well-informed and dedicated guide from the Tourist Office revealed them to me.

The usual starting point of the tour is a small hill, with a Byzantine citadel, above the present Turkish hamlet of Seljuk, of interest partly for its panoramic view of the whole topography of Ephesus and partly for the *Basilica of St. John,* built in the sixth century by Emperor Justinian, which crowns its summit. Here, in an underground chamber, is the supposed tomb of St. John himself, making the Basilica a shrine of deep veneration throughout the ages. An interesting sign affixed to the Basilica states that the funds for the restoration now going forward are contributed by the American Ephesus Society of Lima, Ohio. It is widely believed that Mary, the mother of Jesus, was brought to Ephesus by "the beloved apostle," to whose care Jesus had committed her. (Said Jesus on the cross to His Mother, "Woman, behold thy son," and to John, "Son, behold thy mother.") The House of Our Lady, a stone house in which Mary is supposed to have lived and died is one of Ephesus' major sights, located on a lovely hill five miles away.

The site of the Temple of Diana, with its very meager remains, is just below the Seljuk Hill, whereas the main ruins of Ephesus are about a mile and a half distant. One could spend days studying such important ruins but I shall mention only a few things that seem worthy of special note.

1. The *Marble Street*, paved with large marble blocks, was the Main Street of Ephesus during its greatest days, which were the centuries just before and after the birth of Christ. It leads gently downgrade from the Koressos Gate, named for the keepers of the Eternal Flame, to the Stadium and on to the Great Theater and many other buildings. This famous street was lined with statues, fountains, marble benches and some shops, with dwellings above them. (The long *Acadian Way*, which led from the center to the harbor, is called the first street in the world to have had regular street lighting.)

2. The *Great Theater*, built by the Greeks and rebuilt by the Romans, seated 24,000 spectators and was sometimes the scene of "demonstrations," quite in the modern manner. One such event is excitingly recorded in Acts 19:23-41. Paul preached his faith, but the Ephesians took it as an affront to Diana, so they let go with a riot royal, shouting "with one voice about the space of two hours, 'Great is Diana of the Ephesians'." Paul managed to escape. The town clerk came to the theater and finally quieted the crowd with a soothing talk which Acts records in full (verses 35-40). I mention this partly for a personal reason. When I was a boy I visited Ephesus with my parents and was constrained by my father to mount the podium where the town clerk had stood and read his speech. I did so in a lusty voice and was awfully pleased with my performance.

3. The *Agora*, at an angle of the Marble Street, was a large colonnaded market place.

4. Other interesting features include a huge bath, with all the usual rooms such as caldarium, sudatorium and frigidarium; the *Library of Celsus*, a three-story marble building from the second century A.D.; and a structure, or part of it, labeled *Ask Evi*. The words mean Brothel, signifying that the oldest profession was already old two thousand years ago.

5. The *Last Abode of the Virgin Mary*, which some scholars believe was exactly that, is worth the five-mile extra ride to see it, for the setting, in a cool mountain grove, is flawlessly beautiful and restful. The ensemble includes a chapel and a sacred spring. To the shrubbery surrounding the spring hundreds of bits of cloth torn from shirts, blouses and neckties are affixed as ex votos. It is a frequent practice,

too, of Christians and Moslems alike to fill a bottle from the spring and take the sacred water home as an aid in curing physical afflictions of the bearer or some loved one. In this we see another example of the Moslems' concern with Christianity as a sort of "auxiliary religion."

Ankara, a Twentieth-Century Capital

Ankara is a self-made capital. In our time, since its selection by Atatürk in 1923, it has increased in population *thirty* fold, from 20,000 to well over 600,000 and the boom goes on full force. Hotels are leaping skyward, three new ones of luxury class now nearing completion to join an existing one of like rating, the *Grand Hotel Balin*. Good restaurants and sophisticated night clubs have appeared as a matter of course, but to all these evidences of growth and sophistication Ankara adds the aura of modern Turkey's great founder, who is entombed on the Citadel, and the pervasive atmosphere of a flourishing diplomatic life.

One may fly from Istanbul to Ankara in fifty minutes by the big jets or sixty-five by Convairs of Turkish Airlines, but there are other recommendable ways of making the journey, slower ways that let you see more of Anatolia. A motor road all the way, partly hardtop, partly loose-surfaced, but well kept up, covers the 283-mile stretch. Public busses operated by a company called *Jet-Mas-Mengeli*, make the run in seven to eight hours, starting from Taksim Square. As for rails, a Diesel electric train (with diner) leaves Haydar Pasha Station, on the Asian side of the Bosporus at 9:35 A.M. daily, making the run in about nine and a half hours, and there's an all-sleeper night train, the Ankara Express, that reaches Ankara late enough in the morning (9:35) to give you a good night's sleep and then two or three hours of daylight for window-watching. I once made it by this means, purchasing my ticket from *Vagonli-Kook* (Wagons-Lits/Cook) and loved it. The train, in the Continental style, proved to be quite the equal of the average sleeping-car train one would find in Continental Europe. Its first-class individual compartments have every modern facility and are kept gleamingly clean and polished. The restaurant car offers a good meal at about a dollar and a half, plus something further for wine or mineral water and service. The card outlining your meal is headed Mönü (Menu) and you may order *Alakart* or take the fixed *Tabldot!* The sensible word borrowings and phonetic spellings of "Republican Turkish" are a continual enhancement of a sojourn in Turkey and I must belatedly offer some common examples. An *Ajansi Enternasyonal,* for instance, is an International Agency, and such a word as *bagaj* translates itself, as docs *tuvalet.* In your hotel, a waiter is a *garson,* a valet a *valé,* a femme de chambre a *fam dö şambr.* Ever so many other words on travel signs and printed notices the visitor may easily interpret for himself.

In the Haydar Pasha station I saw (but it may not still be there) a large and conspicuous illuminated map marking in electric lights and lines the places where American financial aid had rebuilt and modernized the Turkish rail system. It gave me a glow to feel that the outpouring of our tax dollars is well known and appreciated in Turkey and that in all international conflicts, hot or cold, Turkey is our natural and eager ally.

After the night ride and breakfast in the restaurant car, one disembarks in the *cool* station of Ankara. It was downright cold on that particular arrival on a December morning, and on two later visits made by plane in May and in July Ankara was a good ten or twelve degrees cooler than Istanbul, which has a temperate climate.

Ankara, as I've said, has jumped in a few decades from a struggling, unkempt village to a city of over 600,000 inhabitants, a modern metropolis seething with ambition and energy, and any Turk of any political party will give the chief credit to one man, Mustafa Kemal Atatürk. Portraits and photographs and busts and equestrian statues of this father of modern Turkey are seen *everywhere,* but there is no sense of compulsion about it, as in similar displays of living leaders in authoritarian countries, for Atatürk died in 1938 and sheer veneration prompts this display. Parties and coalitions may come and go, but Atatürk's image remains fixed and secure, though perhaps it doesn't shine so brightly in the peasant breast as in that of the city dweller. The peasants in Turkey's countless small villages still tend to resent the country's drastic Westernization, with its sharp impact on their primitive way of life, but it has come to stay and village folk must learn to live with it. They are seen even in Ankara, the women always wearing a faded cotton coat over long, bright-colored cotton trousers, very baggy and tied at the ankles. On their heads they wear a shawl, which can be drawn over the face, for they still feel a bit nervous about the discarding of the veil.

Ankara is, of course, enduring growing pains. Its downtown sections are not beautiful, despite the broad boulevards lined with government and diplomatic buildings, business structures and soaring new hotels. Its pleasant *Youth Garden*, featuring fountains, a lake with a boat-shaped café beside it and a miniature train chugging around it, is a homey feature and there are other "bright intervals," but the sense of urgency, of new construction here, there and everywhere, necessarily gives it a hectic, excuse-the-obstruction atmosphere. To escape this and to have a panoramic view of the city and its whole area the visitor promptly drives, or takes a taxi, to the eminence called *Çankaya Hill*, with the Presidential Mansion and the modest house where Atatürk lived, and then, for stirring climax, to the Rasattepe Hill, crowned with the magnificent *Mausoleum of Atatürk* to which his body was taken on November 10, 1953, the fifteenth anniversary of his death.

The Mausoleum is perhaps the most spectacular modern monument in any Mediterranean country. It attracts the eye by day and by night, when it is floodlighted. To offer a statistic or two, its dimensions are 180 by 235 feet, by 70 in height. A paved promenade, which surrounds a vast open quadrangle, is 300 feet long on two sides by 855 foot on the other two, each of the long sides being adorned by twelve Hittite lions carved in stone. To the right of the Mausoleum, as one faces it, is a 120-foot steel flagpole, donated by a rich Turkish-American, with the Star and Crescent flying aloft. On a white, rectangular marble stone are carved the words: HAKIMIYET KAYITSIZ ŞARTSIZ MILLETINDER, which means "Liberty Belongs to the People." A memorable Speech to Youth made by Atatürk in 1933 is set forth in full in gold leaf on the Mausoleum's façade. Inside the structure, completed in 1953 and embellished with thirty types of Anatolian marble and travertine, lies the body of the Father of his Country in a huge marble sarcophagus of reddish hue. Not a word is carved on the smooth surface. An Atatürk Museum in a low wing of the Mausoleum houses numerous mementos of the Founder, ranging from his shoes and shaving articles and tuxedo-with-bow-tie, this last almost a symbol of the man, to his gold telephone apparatus and his shiny Lincoln car. One should stroll the promenade on all four sides, totaling nearly half a mile, to enjoy the view from every angle.

Returning to the city, the sightseer is offered various sights of some interests, such as the Temple of Augustus, with an adjacent Ethnological Museum, and a Roman bath shaped like a modern Turkish bath, but a sight that is virtually unique to Ankara is the *Hittite Museum*, located on the slope of the ancient Citadel. Anatolia was *the* Hittite country, though that early and warlike race did extend its power far to the south, tangling frequently with Joshua and other Hebrew leaders. It occupied Anatolia from 2000 B.C. to about 800 B.C., soon after which time the Assyrians annihilated the Hittite Empire. One of the most interesting items in the museum is a much carved stone rather recently found at Adana, a neighbor city to old Tarsus. The inscription on the stone is thought by scholars to be a key, the first one discovered, to the written language of the Hittites, for it records its chiseled message in the Phoenician alphabet and in the Hittite characters. Efforts to analyze the Hittite symbols have not as yet been completely successful, but much of the cuneiform writing has been decoded.

Two things to see in the environs of Ankara are the *Atatürk Model Farm* and the big *Çubuk Dam*, with a casino-restaurant for motorists. Ankara itself has some fine restaurants such as the *Bekir*, the *Vasinton* (Washington) and the much favored dining room of the *Grand Balin Hotel* but one place, mentioned in the previous chapter, stands out from the rest, namely *Karpiç*, pronounced Karpich. This is a favorite rendezvous of diplomats, government folk and tourists, a genuine stronghold of gastronomy.

It goes without saying that Ankara has an abundance of night clubs such as the smart *Süreyya*, the *Göl Gazino*, this in Youth Park, and the *Kulüp 47* (Kulüp means Club), which closes its doors when the forty-seventh person has entered. And then there is the very big *Gar Gazino*, which takes its name from the French word gare, for station. This is located in a cavernous wing of the city's railway station and is as bare as a barn, but customers flock to it in numbers. I also flocked, with Turkish friends, and was rewarded by an excellent meal and a really tremendous vaudeville show. It concluded with the usual Oriental (belly) dancer, this one being nationally famous. She did a long number on the stage and then danced, close-up, on the individual tables, including ours, after which, to my utter consternation, she seized my arm with firm grip and dragged me to the stage. I didn't have time to panic! She draped a scarf about my midriff and made me join her in a twosome contortion, to howls of laughter from the crowd. I lived through the ordeal—just barely.

How sane and reassuring Ankara seemed as I escaped with my friends from Gar Gazino into the Turkish night, and how soothing the sight of the illuminated Mausoleum up on the hill. Allah's in his heaven, all's right with the world. We drove about a bit, passing some massive buildings of United States government offices and some residences of the American colony. Rarely, I reflected, does the passing tourist sense so firm a splicing of divergent cultures as in the union-for-freedom that is so clearly noted in this Anatolian city.

INDEX

Abnoob, Egypt, 321
Aboukir, Egypt, 320-321
Abu Ghosh, Israel, 387-388
Abu Simbel, Egypte, 13, 324, 337, 338
Achilleus (ship), 29
Acre, Israel, 384, 408-409
Adriatica Line, 28
Aegean Islands, 257, 267, 270
Aegina (Greek island), 257, 268-269
Aeolian Islands, *see* Lipari Islands
Afridar, Israel, 410
Agadir, Morocco, 192
Agamemnon (ship), 29
Aghia Triada, Crete, 275
Agrigento, Sicily, 170, 171, 175-176
  hotels, 171
Agrínion, Greece, 251
Aigues Mortes, France, 146
Air France, 17, 21, 22-23, 24, 36, 38, 43,
  45-46, 133, 144, 149, 151, 187, 207,
  214, 215, 216, 420, 421, 437, 447, 452
Air India, 24
Air Liban, 17, 396, 420, 421
Air mail, 45
Air service, 21-24
  to Azores, 3, 62
  to Balearic Isles, 6, 132-133, 142, 143
  to Canary Islands, 80
  to Corfu, 24, 259
  to Corsica, 149-150
  to Egypt, 291
  to Gibraltar, 5
  to Greece, 24, 213, 214-215
  to Greek islands, 259, 277
  to Jordan, 17
  to Lebanon, 396
  to Libya, 12, 206
  to Madeira, 3-4, 70-71
  to Malta, 179
  to Morocco, 187
  to Sardinia, 8, 167
  to Sicily, 169
  to Syria, 18

Aix-en-Provence, France, 145
Ajaccio, Corsica, 149, 150, 151
Akaba, Jordan, 413
Akti Thermaïkon, Greece, 251
Alcoholic beverages, customs regula-
  tions concerning, 41
Aleppo, Syria, 436
Alexandria, Egypt, 212, 281, 296, 304,
  305, 316-322
  air service to, 294, 296
  history of, 316-318
  hotels in, 318
  sightseeing in, 318-320
Alexandropolis, Greece, 251
Aley, Lebanon, 419, 426
Algeciras, Spain, 122-123
Algeria, 11, 186, 194-200
  embassy (Washington, D.C.), 37
  history of, 194-195
  shops and shopping in, 200
Algiers, Algeria, 195-198
  hotels in, 195
  sightseeing in, 195-198
Alicante, Spain, 125-126
Alitalia, 8, 24, 37, 167, 169, 206, 214
Alma, Israel, 406
Alps, 147
American Automobile Association, 29,
  52
American Export Line, 24-25, 62, 187
American Visitors Bureau
  Portugal, 91-92
  Spain, 114, 131
American Zionist Women's Organiza-
  tion, 371
Amilcar, Tunisia, 205
Anacapri, Cápri, 165
Anadoluhisar, Turkey, 464-465
Anatolia, 19, 277, 449, 451, 473-485
  highways in, 477, 481
Anchor Line, 345
Andraitx, Majorca, 141
Andrea Doria (ship), 25

Famagusta, Cyprus, 14, 15, 342, 343, 344,
345, 346, 351-354
hotels in, 351
Faraya, Lebanon, 435
Farouk, King of Egypt, 172, 291, 314,
318-319, 324
Fenerbahçe, Turkey, 467
Fez, Morocco, 194
Flamenco entertainment, 125
Flores Island, 61
Florya, Turkey, 468
Food, 36, also *see* under countries and
cities
Fórmia, Italy, 167
France, 7, 144-154
food in, 149
highways in, 153
hotels in, 149
money in, 144-145
restaurants in, 149
shops and shopping in, 49
tourist office (New York City), 36
wine of, 22-23
France (ship), 26
Freighter Travel Guidebook, 26
French Government Tourist Office
(New York City), 36
French Line, 26, 150
French Riviera, 7, 144, 147-149
shops and shopping in, 49
weather in, 41
Funchal (ship), 62, 70, 71
Funchal, Madeira, 3, 71-75
air service to, 3-4
hotels in, 73-75
nightlife in, 75
shops and shopping in, 71
steamship service to, 26
Furnas, Lake, 68-69
Furnas River, 68
Furnas Valley, *see* Las Furnas Valley

Galda, Grand Canary Island, 82
Galilea, Majorca, 137
Galilee, Lake, 16, 404-405, 406
Galilee Mountains, 385
Gaza Strip, 364, 411
Genoa, Italy, 158-161
hotels in, 160
restaurants in, 161

Gezira, Egypt, 306, 314
Gibraltar, 5-6, 117-120
air service to, 5
steamship service to, 25, 26
Gibraltar Airways, 5, 120
Gilead, Jordan, 402
Giulio Cesare (ship), 25
Giza, Egypt, 54, 300
Glyfada, Greece, 224, 227
Golden Horn, 451
Göreme, Turkey, 477
Gortys, Crete, 275
Gourna, Egypt, 327, 333
Gozo Island, 181, 184
Grace Line, 266
Graciosa Island, 61
Granada, Spain, 123, 124-125
hotels in, 124-125
nightlife in, 125
Grand Atlas Mountains, 191, 192
Grand Canary Island, 81, 82-83, 85
Grasse, France, 49-50, 147
Greece, 12-13, 210-290
air service to, 24, 213, 214-215
food in, 225-227
highways in, 214
hotels in, 213
islands of, 13, 257-290
language of, 217-219
maps of, 240
money in, 217
National Tourist Organization, 215
restaurants in, 225-227, 252
shops and shopping in, 50
steamer service to, 25, 26, 213, 214, 266
tourist office (New York City), 37,
215
transportation in, 13, 213, 251, 259
weather in, 41
wine of, 225, 252
Greek Coast Lines, 265
Greek Islands Cruise Lines, 266
Greek Line, 25-26, 266, 267, 344
Grimaldi-Siosa Line, 26
Grotto of Jiïta (Lebanon), 425

Hadassah, 371
Haifa, Israel, 365, 367, 371, 372, 377, 378,
384-386, 399, 408, 409
hotels in, 385